T0181687

Lecture Notes in Computer Science 10253

Commenced Publication in 1973
Founding and Former Series Editors:
Gerhard Goos, Juris Hartmanis, and Jan van Leeuwen

More information about this series at http://www.springer.com/series/7409

Eric Dubois · Klaus Pohl (Eds.)

Advanced Information Systems Engineering

29th International Conference, CAiSE 2017
Essen, Germany, June 12–16, 2017
Proceedings

Editors
Eric Dubois
Luxembourg Institute of Science and Technology
Esch-sur-Alzette
Luxembourg

Klaus Pohl
University of Duisburg-Essen
Essen
Germany

ISSN 0302-9743 ISSN 1611-3349 (electronic)
Lecture Notes in Computer Science
ISBN 978-3-319-59535-1 ISBN 978-3-319-59536-8 (eBook)
DOI 10.1007/978-3-319-59536-8

Library of Congress Control Number: 2017941498

LNCS Sublibrary: SL3 – Information Systems and Applications, incl. Internet/Web, and HCI

Printed on acid-free paper

This Springer imprint is published by Springer Nature
The registered company is Springer International Publishing AG
The registered company address is: Gewerbestrasse 11, 6330 Cham, Switzerland

Preface

Welcome to the proceedings of CAiSE 2017 – the 29th International Conference on Advanced Information Systems Engineering, held in Essen, Germany, June 12–16, 2017. The goal of the CAiSE conference series is to bring together the R&D community working on models, methods, techniques, architectures, and technologies addressing the design, the engineering, the operation, and the evolution of information systems.

The conference theme of CAiSE 2017 was "Digital Connected World—Informed, Disruptive Business Transformation." Private and public organizations are entering in the digital world where real-time data are available about their processes, their operations, their operating environments, third-party services offered to increase their performance as well as chances in the demands of their customers. This data abundance offers new opportunities but also raises new challenges for information systems. The key challenge thereby is to evolve traditional information systems into "digital, smart systems." These systems have to be sufficiently agile to rapidly analyze, predict, and manage the disruptive and incremental business transformations of operations. From a center of profit, information systems are now becoming the center for innovation and sustainability of the organizations. The three invited keynotes of CAiSE 2017 addressed three important aspects of digital transformation:

- Dr. Reinhold Achatz (thyssenkrupp AG): "Digital Transformation at thyssenkrupp: Challenges, Strategies and Examples."
- Prof. Dr. Jorge Sanz (Luxembourg Institute of Science and Technology): "The Need for Modularizing Industries and Accelerating Digital Transformation in Enterprises - Could Productivity Be Significantly Improved and Innovation Revamped for Growth in the World's Economy?"
- Prof. Dr. Reinhard Schütte (University of Duisburg-Essen): "Information Systems for Retail Companies – Challenges in the Era of Digitalization."

The accepted research papers as well as the CAiSE Forum addressed facets related to the theme of the conference as well as more "traditional" topics associated with information systems design, engineering, and operation. The program included the following paper sessions:

- IS Architecture, Transformation and Evolution
- Business Process Model Readability and Notation
- User Knowledge Discovery, Process Discovery
- Business Process Performance, Adaptation and Variability Management
- Data Mining, Big Data Exploration

For CAiSE 2017, we received 178 papers, from 221 submitted abstracts. This year, a new selection process was put it place where each paper was reviewed by at least two Program Committee members. At the end of the first phase, we rejected papers with consistent negative evaluations. In the second phase of evaluation, all papers with at least one positive evaluation were reviewed by one program board member. During the online discussion, the reviewer of the paper assessed the reviews. The final decision about acceptance and rejection of the papers was made at the Program Committee Board meeting, which took place in Luxembourg during February 21–22, 2017. The evaluation process of the papers resulted in the selection of 37 high-quality papers (acceptance rate of 21%). In addition, the Program Committee Board recommended 25 papers for acceptance in the CAiSE 2017 Forum. The final program of CAiSE 2017 was complemented by five workshops, five co-located working conferences, and a PhD consortium. Separate proceedings are published for all these events. We warmly thank the workshop chairs (Andreas Metzger, Anne Persson), the forum chairs (Xavier Franch, Jolita Ralyté), the doctoral symposium chairs (Raimundas Matulevičius, Camille Salinesi, Roel Wieringa), and the publicity chair (Selmin Nurcan) for their excellent work and contributions.

CAiSE 2017 would not have been possible without the efforts and expertise of a number of people who selflessly offered their time and energy to help make this conference a success. We would like to thank everyone from the Organizing Committee, especially Christina Bellinghoven, Eric Schmieders, and Vanessa Stricker. Special thanks to Dalia Boukercha, Christophe Feltus, and Richard van de Stadt for their responsive and helpful support during the paper evaluation and selection process, as well as during the preparation of the proceedings.

As editors of this volume, we also offer our sincere thanks to the members of the Program Committee and the external reviewers for their dedication in providing fair and constructive evaluations. We would like also to thank the members of the Program Board who agreed to take additional duties in the new reviewing process and devoted their time and knowledge to reviewing and discussing the submitted papers.

We hope you enjoy the proceedings of CAiSE 2017.

April 2017

Eric Dubois
Klaus Pohl

Organization

Steering Committee

Barbara Pernici	Politecnico di Milano, Italy
Óscar Pastor	Universitat Politècnica de València, Spain
John Krogstie	Norwegian University of Science and Technology, Norway

Advisory Committee

Janis Bubenko Jr.	Royal Institute of Technology, Sweden
Arne Sølvberg	Norwegian University of Science and Technology, Norway
Colette Rolland	Université Paris 1 Panthéon Sorbonne, France

General Chair

Klaus Pohl	paluno, University of Duisburg-Essen, Germany

Program Chair

Eric Dubois	Luxembourg Institute of Science and Technology, Luxembourg

Organizing Committee Chairs

Christina Bellinghoven	paluno, University of Duisburg-Essen, Germany
Eric Schmieders	paluno, University of Duisburg-Essen, Germany

Workshop Chairs

Andreas Metzger	paluno, University of Duisburg-Essen, Germany
Anne Persson	University of Skoevde, Sweden

Forum Chairs

Xavier Franch	Universitat Politècnica de Catalunya, Spain
Jolita Ralyté	University of Geneva, Switzerland

Doctoral Consortium Chairs

Raimundas Matulevičius	University of Tartu, Estonia

Camille Salinesi	Université Paris 1 Panthéon-Sorbonne, France
Roel Wieringa	University of Twente, The Netherlands

Publicity Chair

Selmin Nurcan	Université Paris 1 Panthéon-Sorbonne, France

Publicity Team

Marcello La Rosa	Queensland University of Technology, Australia
Motoshi Saeki	Tokyo Institute of Technology, Japan
Flavia Maria Santoro	Universidade Federal do Estado do Rio de Janeiro, Brazil
Eric Yu	University of Toronto, Canada

Publication Chair

Christophe Feltus	Luxembourg Institute of Science and Technology, Luxembourg

Webmaster and Social Media

Christina Bellinghoven	paluno, University of Duisburg-Essen, Germany

Program Committee Board

Sjaak Brinkkemper, The Netherlands
Paolo Giorgini, Italy
Matthias Jarke, Germany
John Krogstie, Norway
Pericles Loucopoulos, UK
Raimundas Matulevičius, Estonia
Heinrich Mayr, Austria
John Mylopoulos, Canada
Selmin Nurcan, France
Andreas L. Opdahl, Norway
Óscar Pastor, Spain
Barbara Pernici, Italy
Günther Pernul, Germany
Anne Persson, Sweden
Yves Pigneur, Switzerland
Henderik A. Proper, Luxembourg
Hajo A. Reijers, The Netherlands
Stefanie Rinderle-Ma, Austria
Colette Rolland, France
Yannis Vassiliou, Greece
Barbara Weber, Austria
Roel J. Wieringa, The Netherlands

Program Committee

Daniel Amyot, Canada
David Aveiro, Portugal
Marko Bajec, Slovenia
Luciano Baresi, Italy
Joerg Becker, Germany
Boualem Benatallah, Australia
Albertas Caplinskas, Lithuania
Marlon Dumas, Estonia
Johann Eder, Austria
Xavier Franch, Spain
Ulrich Frank, Germany
Aditya Ghose, Australia
Claude Godart, France
Jaap Gordijn, The Netherlands
Janis Grabis, Latvia
Renata Guizzardi, Brazil
Willem-Jan van den Heuvel, The Netherlands
Mirjana Ivanović, Serbia
Paul Johannesson, Sweden
Ivan Jureta, Belgium
Dimitris Karagiannis, Austria
Marite Kirikova, Latvia
Agnes Koschmider, Germany
Marcello La Rosa, Australia
Frank Leymann, Germany
Alexander Mädche, Germany
Eva Maria Kern, Germany
Florian Matthes, Germany
Isabelle Mirbel, France
Michele Missikoff, Italy
Haris Mouratidis, UK
Anna Perini, Italy
Michaël Petit, Belgium
Naveen Prakash, India
Jolita Ralyté, Switzerland
Gil Regev, Switzerland
Manfred Reichert, Germany
David G. Rosado, Spain
Motoshi Saeki, Japan
Camille Salinesi, France
Kurt Sandkuhl, Germany
Flávia Maria Santoro, Brazil
Guttorm Sindre, Norway
Monique Snoeck, Belgium
Pnina Soffer, Israel
Hans Weigand, The Netherlands
Mathias Weske, Germany
Eric Yu, Canada
Jelena Zdravkovic, Sweden

Additional Reviewers

Okhaide Akhigbe
Pouya Aleatrati
Basmah Almoaber
Kevin Andrews
Estefania Serral Asensio
Unsw Australia
Fatma Basak Aydemir
Moshe Barukh
Malak Baslyman
Björn Benner
Manoj Bhat
Alexander Bock
Dominik Bork
Faiza Bukhsh
Andrea Burattin
Fabian Böhm
Sybren De Kinderen
Antonio De Nicola
Sergio España
Siamak Farshidi
Michael Fellmann
Andreas Freymann
Mahdi Ghasemi
Jens Gulden
Jasmin Guth
Michael Hahn
Florian Haupt
Shinpei Hayashi

Marcin Hewelt
Amin Jalali
Marko Janković
Slinger Jansen
Monika Kaczmarek-Heß
Aleatrati Khosroshahi
Fitsum Meshesha Kifetew
Martin Kleehaus
David Knuplesch
Julius Köpke
Vimal Kunnummel
Michael Kunz
Jörg Landthaler
Bénédicte Le Grand
Garm Lucassen
Florian Menges
Stefan Morana
Denisse Munante
Nicolas Mundbrod
Mario Nadj
Soroosh Nalchigar
Adriatik Nikaj
Mario Nolte
Sietse Overbeek
Benedikt Pittl
Klaus Pohl
Domenico Potena
Elaheh Pourabbas
Alexander Puchta
Luise Pufahl
Christian Richthammer
Karoline Saatkamp
Marc Schickler
Johannes Schobel
Estefanía Serral
Klym Shumaiev
Anthony Simonofski
Sebastian Steinau
Angelo Susi
Eric-Oluf Svee
Johannes Sänger
Daniel Töpel
Ömer Uludag
Karolina Vukojevic-Haupt
Michael Walch
Andreas Weiß
Jan Martijn van der Werf
Matthias Wissotzki
Alaaeddine Yousfi
Michael Zimmermann
Michael Zimoch
Slavko Žitnik

Keynotes

Digital Transformation at thyssenkrupp: Challenges, Strategies, and Examples

Reinhold Achatz

thyssenkrupp AG, Essen, Germany
Reinhold.Achatz@thyssenkrupp.com

Abstract. The digital transformation is changing the world in a continuously accelerating pace. Traditional industrial companies have a good chance to be the winner of the digital transformation. They can create additional value to their customer by optimizing and extending their current business and by creating new business models offering smart services.

This keynote describes thyssenkrupp's strategy for the digital transformation illustrated by real examples.

Information Systems for Retail Companies

Challenges in the Era of Digitization

Reinhard Schütte

Institute for Computer Science and Business Information Systems,
University of Duisburg-Essen, Universitätsstr. 9, 45141 Essen, Germany
reinhard.schuette@icb.uni-due.de

Abstract. Worldwide the retail sector is driven by a strong intra-competition of existing retailers and an inter-competition between traditional and new pure digital players. The challenges for retail companies can be differentiated into a business and an application system (architecture) perspective.

Based on a domain-oriented architecture that covers all steps of value creation through to the customer, the potential influence of digitization on the tasks of Retail Information Systems are examined from five different perspectives. The domain perspective is divided into five levels: master data, technical processes, value based processes, administrative processes and decision oriented tasks.

The technical challenges of application systems are not least characterized by the complexity of such architectures. The traditional mass data problem in retail is increasing in times of big data and several different omni-channel-scenarios. This leads towards really large enterprise systems, which require an understanding of the main challenges in the future. So, that the IT manager can gain and keep the flexibility and the software maintenance of applications (and the application architecture).

The Need for Modularizing Industries and Accelerating Digital Transformation in Enterprises - Could Productivity Be Significantly Improved and Innovation Revamped for Growth in the World's Economy?

Jorge L.C. Sanz[1,2]

[1] Luxembourg Institute of Science and Technology, Esch-sur-Alzette, Luxembourg

[2] National University of Singapore, Singapore, Singapore

jorge.sanz@list.lu

Keywords: Business Modularization • Business Componentization • Business Analytics • Digital Transformation of Enterprises

Summary. In this keynote presentation, the need and challenge to build modular models of operations in industries will be addressed. While modularization (or componentization) in enterprises has been studied and applied in the context of certain operations, the focus has been generally limited to some most-mature processes and very selected competences. If a new and significant economy of scale is to be realized, enterprises across the same segment of an industry and even some Lines of Business (LoBs) in enterprises across different industries will need to undertake a much deeper level of componentization across their organizations and thus, benefit from new and significant savings.

On the other hand, while digitization has penetrated consumer markets significantly affecting individuals' lifestyles, the speed of the transformation of organizations through digital is not happening yet at nearly comparable speeds. For innovation that matters to revenue growth and for enabling additional productivity gains from the adoption of digital, business analytics brings the most promising opportunity to accelerate transformation and deliver new or much enhanced services.

In the light of a continuous decrease of labor growth rate in the world, new forms of productivity increase need to be developed and deployed across industries and enterprises to generate badly needed economic expansion. In spite of the fact that most organizations in a given industry segment have very similar operations and their differentiation is relatively limited to certain specific capabilities, enterprises have limited their outsourced operations to a few cross-industry competences such as Information Technology (IT), selected processes in Finance and Accounting (FA), Human Resources (HR), Customer Contact Centers (CCC), etc.

In addition, while advances and adoption of digitization have significantly permeated throughout the life of individuals, fundamentally accomplished by different segments in the Information and Communication Technology Industry and new companies that were born entirely digital, the reality is that genuine new revenues from business models have not been achieved to the levels expected. For example, while most enterprises in different consumer sectors have invested huge efforts in digitalization of channels, the sought improvements in "customer experience" still remain illusory.

The author maintains that there is a fundamental opportunity and need to realize much deeper economies of scale by identifying and standardizing the widely common operations that the majority of enterprises exhibit in the same industry. The level of the said standardization has to go beyond the commonly encountered in an enterprise across different geographies for its same Lines-of-Business operating across countries and regions and definitely, beyond conventional outsourcings of IT, HR, FA, CCC, etc. In addition, the opportunity for using digitization as a vehicle for generating new revenues in all industries is huge. However, this economic opportunity has not been yet fully realized. One of the pillars of this shortfall is that organizations have struggled to share information effectively and cooperatively across their entire supply chains (internally and externally).

In this keynote, the author will share his experience across hundreds of enterprises in different industries and how business componentization and business analytics are helping unleash the above opportunities and needs. Several core applied research problems as well as the ongoing work by the author in these two domains will be briefly summarized. The experiential aspects through business practice (applied and consultative research, professional services) with a number of organizations will also be shared through different examples coming from cases the author has led or been part of in the last years in global organizations operating in Asia, Europe and North America.

Contents

User Knowledge Discovery

Business Process Performance

Big Data Exploration

Process Variability Management

Information Systems Transformation and Evolution

Business Process Modeling Readability

Business Process Adaptation

Keynotes

Digital Transformation at thyssenkrupp: Challenges, Strategies and Examples

Reinhold Achatz(✉)

thyssenkrupp AG, Essen, Germany

Abstract. The digital transformation is changing the world in a continuously accelerating pace. Traditional industrial companies have a good chance to be the winner of the digital transformation. They can create additional value to their customer by optimizing and extending their current business and by creating new business models offering smart services.

The paper describes thyssenkrupp's strategy for the digital transformation illustrated by real examples.

Keywords: Digital transformation · Industrie 4.0 · Industrial internet of things · Internet business · Big data · Predictive analytics · PLM · Agile processes · Smart services

1 Introduction

Since years, thyssenkrupp is going through a major transformation from a steel and materials company to a technology company. Since the disinvestment of the Brazilian steel plant, steel is only 25% of thyssenkrupp's business. This does not only mean a change in business, this is a major culture change as well. The digital transformation is one element of this transformation.

The success of a digital transformation is built on top line growth and bottom line effects through higher efficiency. The top line growth is created through new products and new ways how products are sold. This may as well lead to new business models.

The bottom line effects are created through a number of steps of process optimization, which are supported by digital tools.

This paper will address the following topics:

- New products: Shift from mechanical to mechatronic products, new production processes
- Internet Business
- Industrie 4.0/Industrial Internet of Things
- Big data/Predictive Analytics/Secure Data exchange
- Virtual Reality/Augmented Reality/Mixed Reality
- Artificial Intelligence
- PLM and Agile Processes
- Implementation startegy.

E. Dubois and K. Pohl (Eds.): CAiSE 2017, LNCS 10253, pp. 3–12, 2017.
DOI: 10.1007/978-3-319-59536-8_1

2 Shift from Mechanical to Mechatronic Products, New Production Processes

The way how products and solutions are built, is continuously changing since many years. In the beginning, all products were mechanical and hardware-oriented. In later steps electrical and hydraulic technology was enhancing the products. Since the invention of the computer in the last century more and more software in combination with electrical and electronic solutions is replacing hardware and hydraulic components.

A typical example is the steering system in a car. Being mechanical for many years, with higher speed and heavier weight the driver needed hydraulic support. Today there is a clear shift to electrical steering. Electrical motors controlled by software are replacing the old hydraulic technology. It is creating more customer value through better sensitivity, adaptality and higher flexibility at lower cost. What might be even more important, electrical steering is the precondition for drive by wire and future autonomous driving (Picture 1).

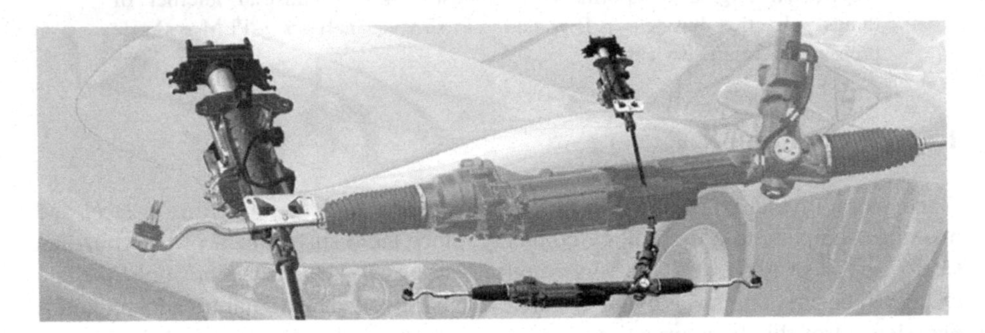

Picture 1. Electrical steering system

A second paradigm shift is happening in the elevator business. Currently thyssenkrupp is testing its new MULTI, an elevator where the mechanical component rope is replaced by magnetic forces created with electrical and electronic components and controlled by software (Picture 2).

Without ropes the system can have more than one cabin in a shaft. This allows generating a highly efficient flow of cabins instead of one cabin going up and down. For tall buildings this reduces the number of shafts needed and therefore reduces the size of space needed for services and allows more usable space per floor.

This list of examples could be extended easily.

Picture 2. MULTI, an elevator without ropes

3 Internet Business

Today more and more people are ordering all kind of products over internet. The B2C internet business is growing dramatically. Customers like it, because internet is available 24/7/365 and goods are directly shipped to their homes.

Why not do the same for industrial goods in the B2B business? Goods, which are standardized or are easily configurable by the user, are offered now on internet as well.

thyssenkrupp's internet platforms "Metals Online" in US and "materials4me" in Europe are successful examples for that trend.

4 Industrie 4.0/Industrial Internet of Things

Maybe the most recognized element of the digital transformation in industry is Industrie 4.0 or Industrial internet of things how the Americans call it.

The definition of Industrie 4.0 is the seamless vertical and horizontal integration as well as the integration over time (Picture 3).

Vertical integration is not new. Since many years we are using enterprise resource planning systems (ERP) and manufacturing execution systems (MES). What is new, is the intensity of data exchange and the new implementation structure.

Today's technology allows a seamless horizontal integration as well, the communication on all levels between sensors, machines and even factories.

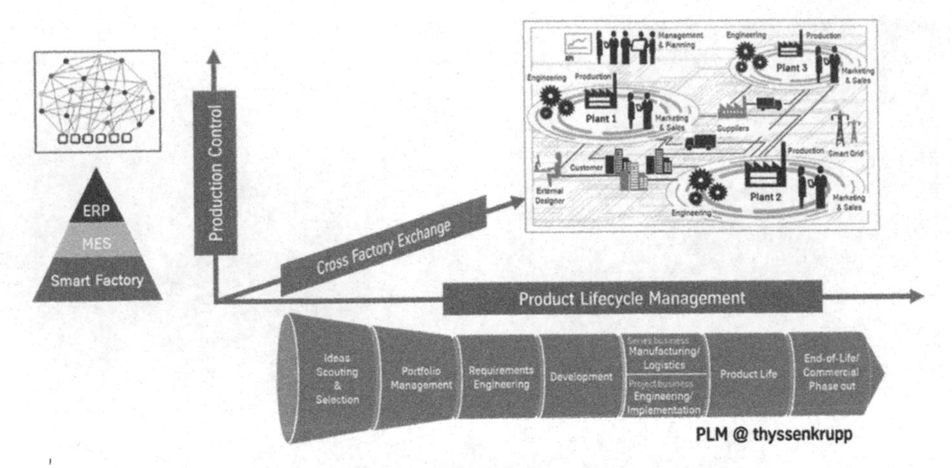

Picture 3. The three elements describing "Industrie 4.0"

I still see room for improvement in the integration over the whole life cycle which is described by Product life cycle management (PLM). There is still unused potential in the use of data created in early phases of the product in later phases.

There are numerous examples for the implementation of Industrie 4.0. For this paper I selected two.

4.1 Example: Camshaft Production in Ilsenburg

thyssenkrupp produces camshafts for the control of combustion engines for cars in Ilsenburg. This production is on one hand highly automated; on the other hand data of previous production phases are used to optimize later production steps. The production

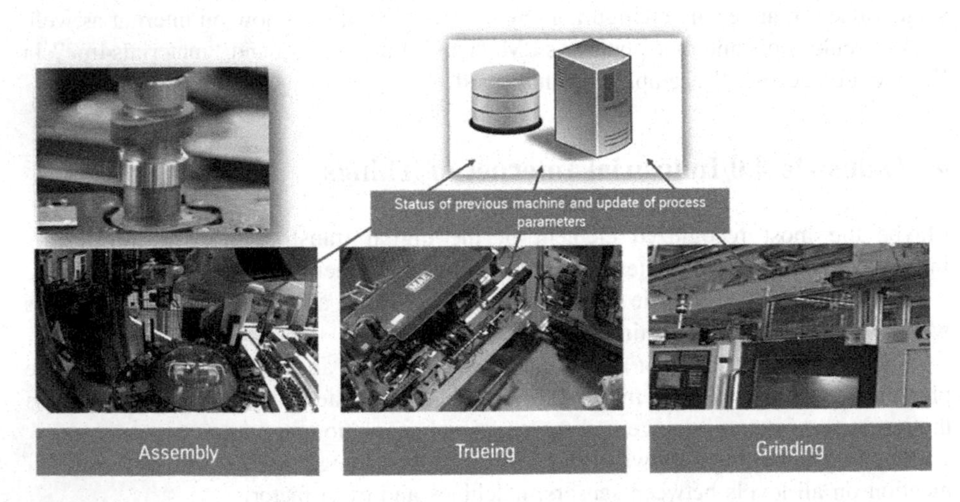

Picture 4. Camshaft production in Ilsenburg

is identifying each workpiece individually. This allows to conduct later steps in production only to the extend, which is really necessary. This optimization is only possible through 100% data transparency and tracking of each individual work piece (see Picture 4).

4.2 Example: thyssenkrupp Medium Wide Strip Production in Hohenlimburg

thyssenkrupp produces in Hohenlimburg medium wide strip coils (Picture 5). The slabs are produced by the supplier, the steel mill HKM in Duisburg, and transported by rail to Hohenlimburg. To optimize stock in Hohenlimburg, a horizontal integration between customers, the production and the suppliers was implemented. Based on framework contacts, customers order the coils in advance by specifying their need directly using the system of the producer. The producer informs the supplier of the slabs of that need. The execution order is placed only days before the customer's immediate need. This triggers the transport of the slabs from Duisburg to Hohenlimburg. The production starts, as soon as the material is available and the coil is shipped to the customer immediately after the last production step (the cooling down to transportable temperature). In addition the slabs and the coils are 100% tracked during the whole logistics and production process. This gives the customer a high flexibility in terms of production, which can be changed basically until production has started, and in delivery time.

The hot role mill in Hohenlimburg could increase its production with the available space and reduce assets on premises.

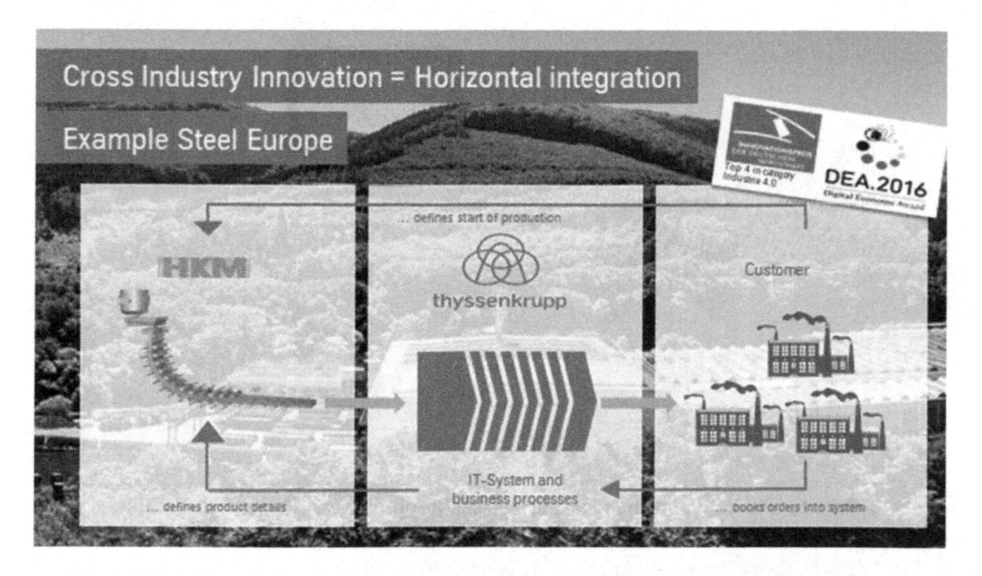

Picture 5. Order process at the hot role mill thyssenkrupp Hohenlimburg

Both examples demonstrate the optimization opportunities which seamless integration of processes through today's communication and integration technology offer.

5 Big Data/Predictive Analytics/Secure Data Exchange

Production and other devices are creating a lot of data and information. Today this data is only used to a minimal percentage or is only used locally. Modern communication and analytics technology allows utilization, which is creating more value and is much more efficient. Communication allows the transport of huge amounts of data and analytics methods, originally created to analyze behavior of users in social networks, can be used for industrial purposes as well.

5.1 Example Predictive Maintenance of Elevators

A good example is predictive maintenance of elevators. Picture 6 shows how elevator movements are collected by a so called "blue box". This box has a standardized interface to the cloud, where algorithms can identify not normal behavior of the device. Based on this information maintenance orders are created to fix a problem, even before it strikes.

The benefit for the user is higher availability of the elevator and the benefit for the service provider is the opportunity to optimize service activities.

Other examples are optimization of stock turn, optimization of utilization of loading docks for trucks or truck logistics.

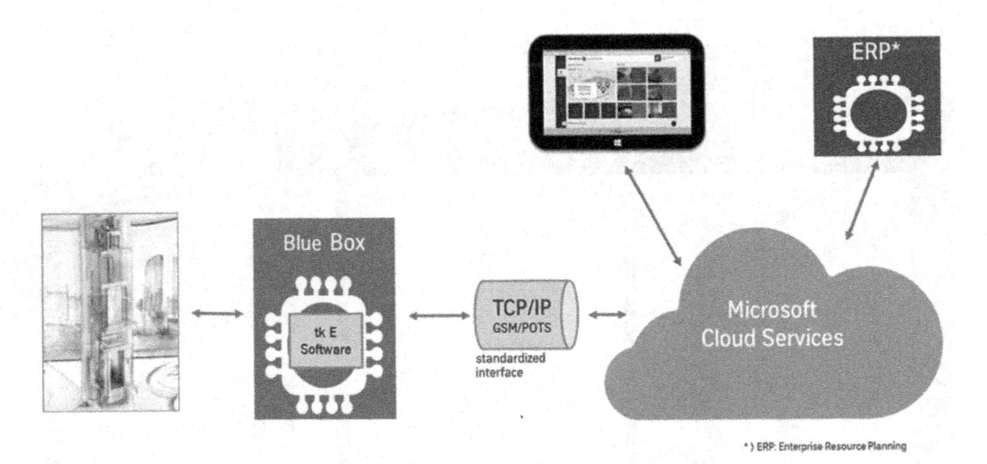

Picture 6. Predictive maintenance at thyssenkrupp elevator (Color figure online)

5.2 Secure Data Exchange

Secure data exchange is another important element in this discussion. It is obvious that the use of knowledge from data creates value; the intelligent combination of data creates even more value.

In B2C business consumers often share their data without any concern. This does definitely not work in a B2B environment. For that reason the Industrial Data Space Association was founded in January 2016 by a group of companies on basis of a technology proposal from Fraunhofer and with the support of the German government. The idea was to define an international standard, which allows the exchange of data, where the generator of the data stays the owner of the data shared. This is implemented on basis of a software readable contract attached to each piece of data. The whole eco system is shown in Picture 7.

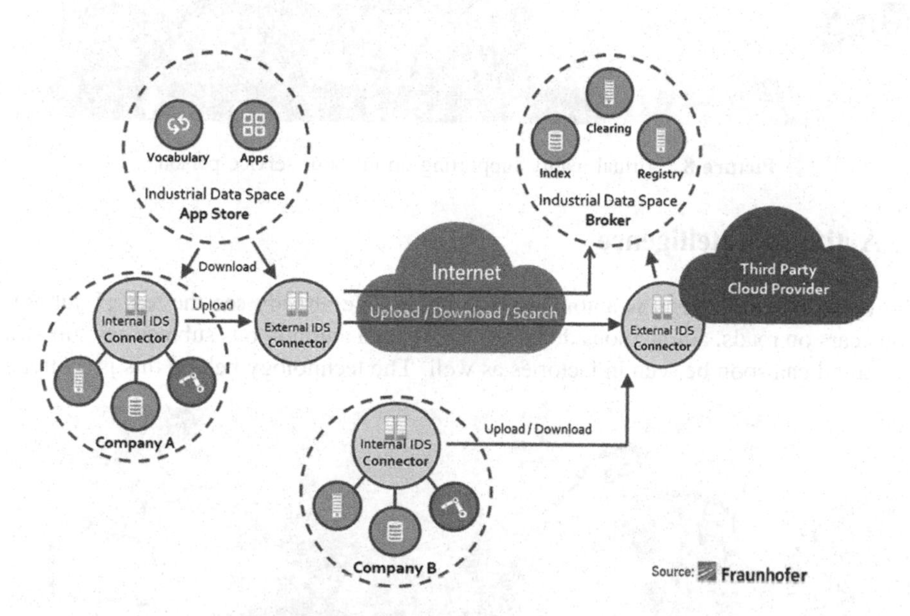

Picture 7. Industrial data space eco system

6 Virtual Reality/Augmented Reality

Virtual and augmented reality are known and demonstrated since many years. Only the development of adequate devices for reasonable cost and good performance and usability is now driving the use.

Augmented realty is implanted in examples, like maintenance support for elevators (Picture 8) or the support for a worker by showing the construction sequence during commissioning a system.

Virtual reality is widely used for training with big and expensive devices like boarding bridges in combination with airplanes or for training of complex tasks like welding.

Picture 8. Virtual reality supporting an elevator service person

7 Artificial Intelligence

The next upcoming trend is autonomous systems. We already see the test of autonomous cars on roads, autonomous drones in the air and autonomous submarines sub see. This trend can soon be seen in factories as well. The technology behind this is artificial

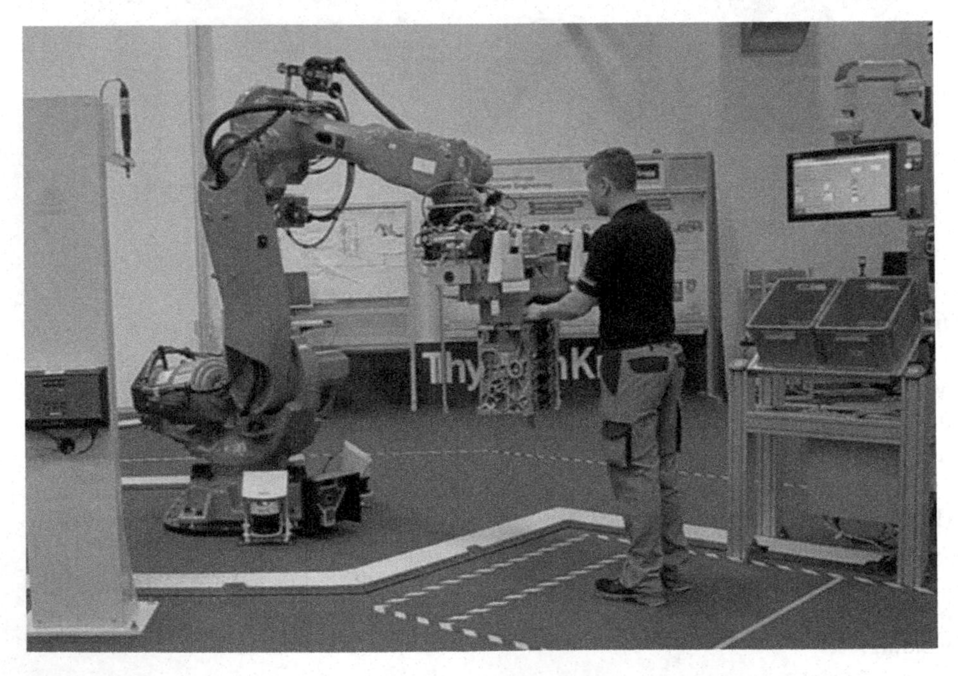

Picture 9. Human machine collaboration at thyssenkrupp system engineering

intelligence. Systems are able to see and recognize the environment, analyze the situation and define actions.

This way human beings and robots will be able to collaborate in factories (see Picture 9). Robots will take over work which is hard for people, like lifting heavy work pieces or performing highly repeatable steps in the production process.

8 PLM and Agile Processes

Adequate processes play a key role in the implementation of the digital transformation.

The implementation of the digital transformation therefore always starts with customers and the understanding of the needs of the customers. To serve those needs a company defines their business models, old ones and new business models.

The business models form the basis for the processes and the necessary data definitions.

8.1 PLM Process

One of the key processes in thyssenkrupp is the PLM process, the Product lifecycle management process (see Picture 10).

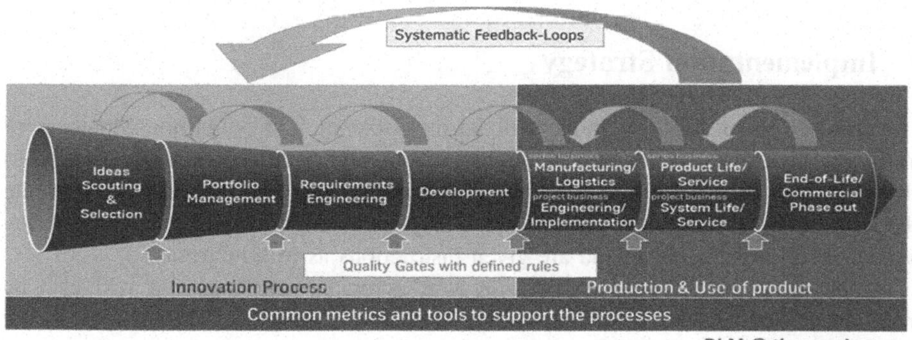

Picture 10. thyssenkrupp product lifecycle management process

This process describes the principle steps and milestones to be performed in the lifecycle of a product, a service or a system. It was designed, to make success in all phases of a product life repeatable, independent from individuals.

8.2 Agile Development Process

This process works very well in a stable environment with incremental improvement steps. It does not describe how to handle disruptive, game changing ideas.

For that reason agile extensions were defined (see Picture 11).

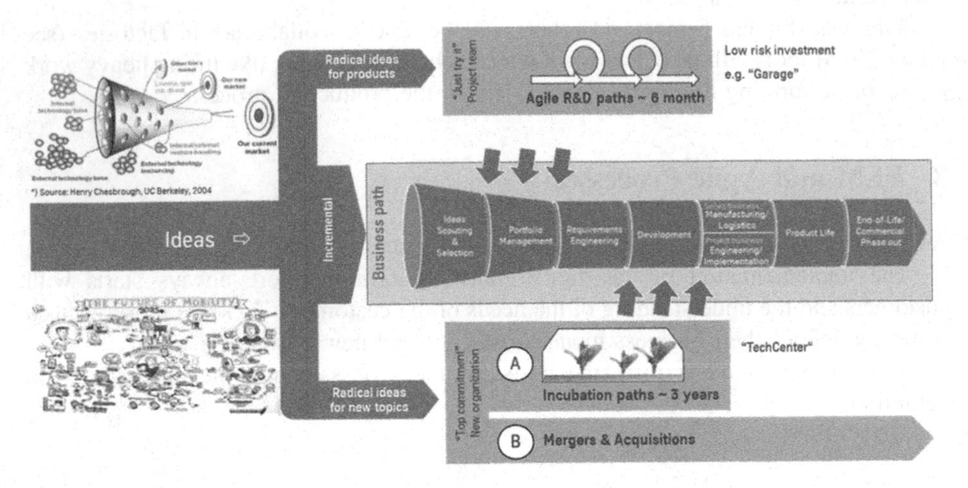

Picture 11. thyssenkrupp PLM process supporting radical innovation

This process allows flexible and lean alternative processes to implement radical ideas. In case of success of the implementation in a “Garage” or in a start-up at a defined time a reintegration in the regular PLM process is taking place.

9 Implementation Strategy

The online version of the volume will be available in LNCS Online. Members of institutes subscribing to the Lecture Notes in Computer Science series have access to all the pdfs of all the online publications. Non-subscribers can only read as far as the abstracts. If they try to go beyond this point, they are automatically asked, whether they would like to order the pdf, and are given instructions as to how to do so.

Please note that, if your email address is given in your paper, it will also be included in the meta data of the online version.

10 Conclusion

It is important for industrial companies to identify the benefits of the digital world. There are many ways for the implement the digital transformation. The tools are available today!

In the B2B arena traditional industrial companies have a good chance to be the winner of the digital transformation, if they are able to combine their classical strength like technology know-how and customer intimacy with the ability to use the new digital technologies.

It is a long journey, but even the longest journey starts with the first step.

Information Systems for Retail Companies

Challenges in the Era of Digitization

Reinhard Schütte(✉)

Institute for Computer Science and Business Information Systems,
University of Duisburg-Essen,
Universitätsstr. 9, 45141 Essen, Germany
reinhard.schuette@icb.uni-due.de

Abstract. Worldwide the retail sector is driven by a strong intra-competition of existing retailers and an inter-competition between traditional and new pure digital players. The challenges for retail companies can be differentiated into a business and an application system (architecture) perspective.

Based on a domain-oriented architecture that covers all steps of value creation through to the customer, the potential influence of digitization on the tasks of Retail Information Systems are examined from five different perspectives. The domain perspective is divided into five levels: master data, technical processes, value based processes, administrative processes and decision oriented tasks.

The technical challenges of application systems are not least characterized by the complexity of such architectures. The traditional mass data problem in retail is increasing in times of big data and several different omni-channel-scenarios. This leads towards really large enterprise systems, which require an understanding of the main challenges in the future. So, that the IT manager can gain and keep the flexibility and the software maintenance of applications (and the application architecture).

Keywords: Digitization · Retail · IS complexity · Application architecture

1 Corporations in a Globalized World

The effect of digitization is not independent of the institutional context, as, if nothing else, the investigation of North has suggested [1]. The institutional conditions are continuously shaped by decades of globalization of companies that has led to a considerable concentration on national and international markets. Trading companies have been intensively competing on particularly concentrated markets, mainly oligopolies, for a long time. Many trading businesses have reached a huge market size when revenue or number of employees serve as a rule. What is more, industrial companies have been carrying out trading functions all along, such as mineral oil traders Exxon or Shell in the Oil and Gas branch.

The existence of retail corporations (even though the term "trading company" would reflect the object of investigation more precisely since it refers to companies that

E. Dubois and K. Pohl (Eds.): CAiSE 2017, LNCS 10253, pp. 13–25, 2017.
DOI: 10.1007/978-3-319-59536-8_2

are equally active in wholesaling or retailing, for the sake of common practice we will instead only use the term "retail company" to refer to such aforementioned companies that exercise wholesale or retail functions) has been a subject of academic discussions for decades [2]. Regardless of the institutional economic discussion about retail enterprises, the tasks intended by retail functions are beyond dispute and economically necessary too. They are expressed at the levels of goods, money/capital and information in four different bridging dimensions (see Fig. 1): bridging space by classic logistical functions, transportation and handling, bridging time by the classic function of warehousing, bridging quantities by the function of handling and bridging quality by manipulating or upgrading the goods.

Bridging / Elements	Space (TU)	Time (L)	Volumes (U)	Quality (W)
Goods	Distribution of retail objects in real goods flows			
	Transport from A to B	Inventory function through keeping stocks	Merging, separating, commissioning	Sorting out, finishing, manipulating
Money	Distribution of payment objects to the flows of real goods			
	Transporting means of payment from A to B	Setting and monitoring payment deadlines	Collecting and dividing payment receipts	Determining the types of payment or payment securities
Information	Distribution of data objects to the retail and payment objects			
	Data transfer	Data storage	Collecting, processing, scanning	Consolidating, linking, interpreting data

Fig. 1. Digitization of retail corporations – analysis from a macro perspective

Against the backdrop of increasing concentration of companies within a branch and most notably the increasing extension of companies over multiple value-added steps and taking into account today's degree of digitization in organizations, it seems sensible not to structure domains too narrowly, but rather to choose a higher degree of abstraction. Thereby, application architectures can also be described by overarching value chains.

This requirement by many verticalized concerns such as H&M, Tom Tailor, Nike, Adidas, Zara, Tesco, etc. has led to the development of a domain oriented architecture for information systems that encompasses all value-added steps from the production through to the customer [3].

The development of an architecture along value-added chains takes place according to a two-dimensional structural pattern. The first dimension in line with a shell model makes a distinction between the type of task, which fundamentally starts with the master data, without which no processes are possible, and proceeds to technically dominated tasks, which are very machine-oriented, and even includes three different business management tasks (direct value-added tasks in operational terms, administrative tasks and finally decision-oriented tasks) (see Fig. 2).

The individual, business management specifications of tasks, which also together represent the form of the dispositive factor, form the second dimension. They are characterized by the relevant value-added stage, so that, taken together, they produce individual application system architectures for industry, wholesalers, retailers and customers. They take into account the potential variety of functional requirements, so that all the functional requirements can be systemized and also consolidated.

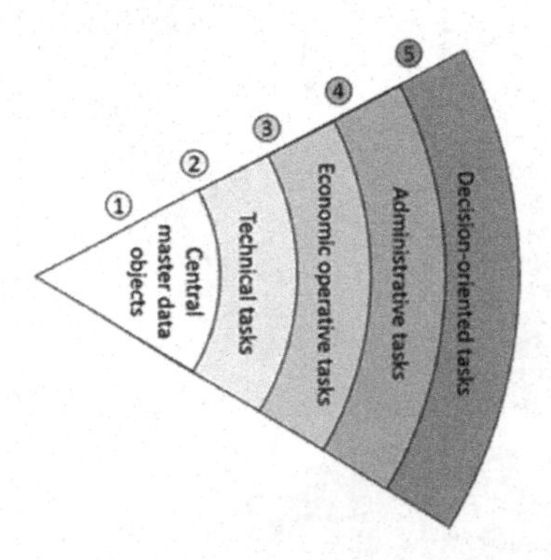

Fig. 2. The shell model underlying the domain oriented IS architectures [3]

Using the shell model, a structuring of all the functions for the retail and wholesale stage, which are necessary for completing retail tasks, has been completed for retail and wholesale corporations. This is very suitable for providing a standard framework for the different functions. The development of an architecture for information systems for tasks at a wholesale level (see the lower part for Fig. 3), is initially based on the master data, which affects the general conditions of operational business, particularly items, customers, companies and conditions (1st circle). The technical task areas are mapped based on the master data (2nd circle). The business management/operational processes (3rd level) at a retail corporation, which start with merchandise management from a tactical and operational perspective, are also based on the master data. Merchandise management covers purchase and sales considerations and forms the combination of these two tasks formerly separated in the "retail H model" [1]. The business management/administrative tasks are shown in the architecture for information systems for wholesale tasks on the fourth level and are to be viewed as a depiction of the value of the consumption of resources underlying the operational processes. The information for managing the company, which is required as part of controlling or for individual decisions about problems, is mapped in standard form in a layer known as "business intelligence" which makes available information for decision problems and ideally suggests a recommendation for a decision in algorithmic form (5th level).

The tasks for the retail stage can be structured in a similar way to the ideas for the wholesale stage (see Fig. 3 – upper part).

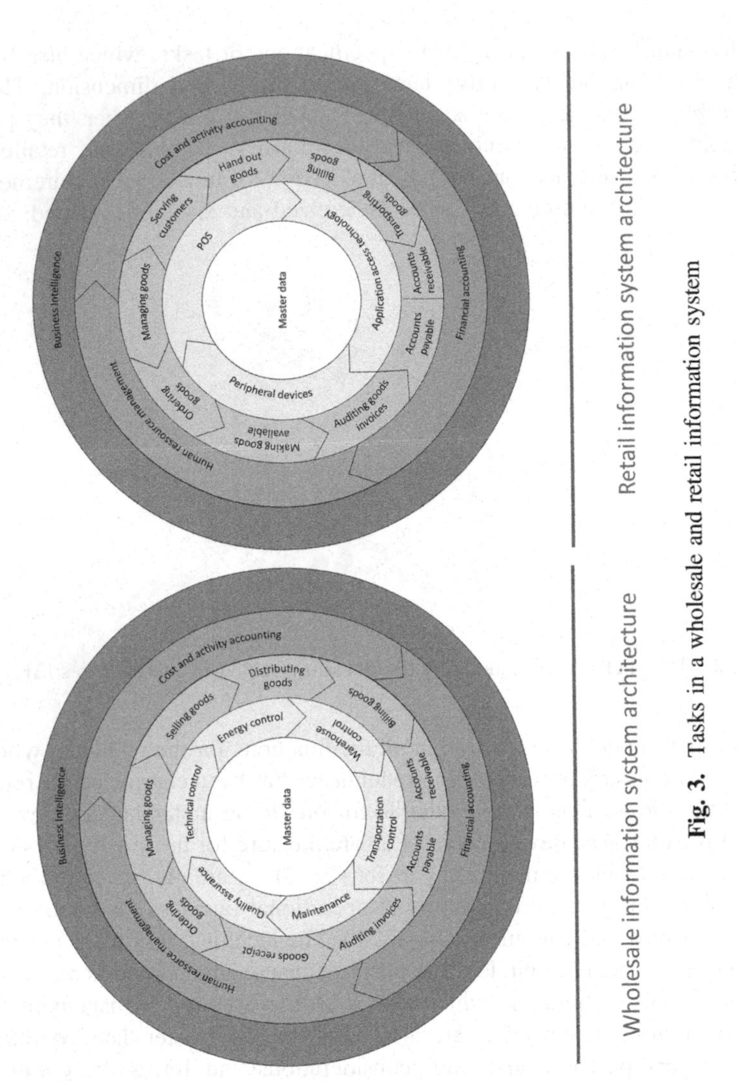

Fig. 3. Tasks in a wholesale and retail information system

2 Application Systems Challenges – Digitization Impact from a Domain Oriented Perspective

The current discussion about the "fashions" of digitization and "disruption" [4] caused by new technologies must be viewed critically from a scientific perspective. The impression is being given that there is a categorical difference between digital and "analog" corporations. Corporations or enterprises have been viewed as sociotechnical systems in business management theory for decades. This understanding of corporations still continues and there is no need to adapt this definition: No wholly digital company exists. At least the stockholders in each company are individuals or institutions. There are therefore still system elements of a technical and social nature in each corporation. It has now become normal to talk about "digital corporations" or "digital players", but it is important to state that this contradicts the facts.

The phenomenon of digitization however has to be rated as especially efficacious. By way of illustration [5], one might invoke a metaphor that is based upon the mathematical function of $2 n - 1$. For now, let n be limited to the number of squares of a chessboard, that is 64. The function yields the number of rice grains for each square, given one doubles the number of grains from square to square: On square 1, there would be 1 grain, on square 2, there would be 2 grains, on, square 3, there would be 4 grains, and so on. Then, the number of grains would grow to approx. 8 billion grains in total through square 32 and approx. 18 quintillion in total through square 64. As Brynjolfsson and McAfee [6] elucidate this constitutes the difference between a large rice field - a still conceivable magnitude - and a volume of rice exceeding that of the Mount Everest - a much less imaginable dimension that results from said power function. The phenomenon of digitization however is not only characterized by a single power function that is derived from Moore's law for the rudimentarily yearly doubling of computational power per dollar, but also from the addition (maybe even multiplication) of multiple power functions, for in other disciplines such as material science (otherwise, 3D printing would not be that relevant), genome research, robotics and kinetics similar developments can be observed. Furthermore, the power function is not limited to 64 as is the case on the chessboard. As a result, the opportunities of invention are so comprehensive, that not only the Mount Everest should serve a metaphor, but the Himalaya itself which figuratively speaking can be produced over and over again in discretionary fields and whose volume is only limited by today's scientific boundaries.

It is important to recognize that all these opportunities for invention and thus later on for innovation lie beyond our ability of prognosis and moreover that these opportunities illustrate the importance of integrating matter and information which will become a part of application development in a domain context.

The following analysis focuses on the problem of identifying potential that already exists in different areas of retail information systems and is expected by the author. It is presupposed that there is a discrepancy between the current and the possible state of digitization in a retail information system, i.e. digitization potential of more than zero exists (problem presupposition). We also assume that there are and will be technologies, which determine the degree of digitization potential (technology potential presupposition). The technologies underlying the following remarks, which have been used in our forecast of possible digitization potential for information systems, need to be outlined before discussing the digitization fields. No importance is placed on any possible classification or typification of technologies. Instead, a McKinsey study will be used as an example, which makes an important distinction in the sense of the technology potential presupposition. It was prepared between the technology's depth of impact and the medium- and long-term probability that it will occur and also for the consumer goods industry and the retail sector [7]. Figure 4 primarily focuses on 3D printing, the Internet of Things, advanced robotics, big data (and therefore also on advanced marketing shown separately in the figure), the mobile world and artificial intelligence as the enablers of new opportunities.

These developments are identified as primary trends. Trends like cloud computing, sensors and actuators, natural interfaces and the huge expansion of networks, storage capacity and processor capabilities have also become established as secondary trends.

In principle, all the trends create a situation where data formerly not accessible to information systems is subjected to processing so that the data volume to be handled and the execution capabilities of the application systems and the hardware have to increase. It has only become clear recently which development paths have to operate relatively quickly, even if the familiar concepts for designing the systems do not represent any new findings scientifically. However, because of the new opportunities and the level of digitization achieved, the solutions can be implemented. This difference is possibly most clearly evident with artificial intelligence. It is a subdiscipline of computer science, which has a long tradition and has already developed many methods and solution principles in the past and could achieve a breakthrough in many application fields in the near future.

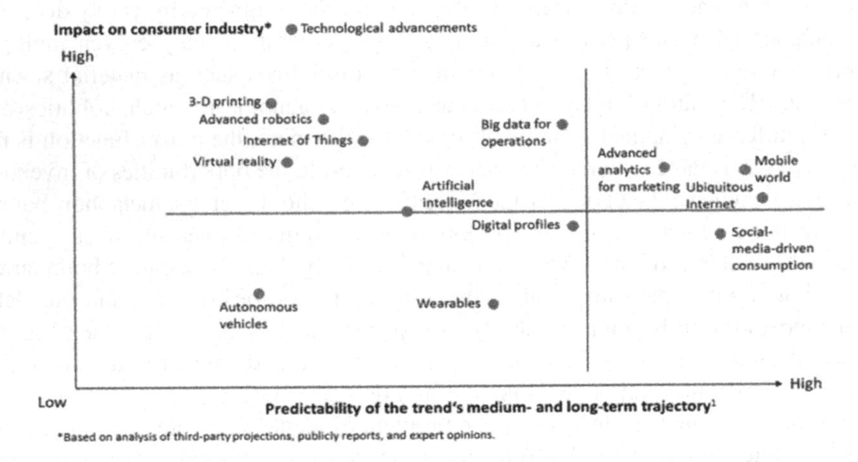

Fig. 4. Assessment of the effectiveness of technologies for customers [7]

There is a basic trend that information and objects grow together. This also triggers a need to consider all-round approaches when shaping application systems, as they find expression particularly in the integration of systems in business information technology.

2.1 Considerations on the Master Data Level with Increasing Digitization

A value-added oriented analysis of typical digitization potential is designed to initially focus on the core of all the application systems, following the shell model: i.e. the master data. Through the Internet of Things, it is possible for information and objects to become one, as it were. It is even possible to document the data on the surrounding conditions of the object and the interaction conditions of customers, which are constantly changing. This new reality will fundamentally change the master data situation in application systems. Structured and non-structured object information will grow closer. This will become more and more relevant for customers and their information requirements and there is a need to break through any thresholds between the application systems in industry and retail, which still exist, since faulty information about products, even in the form of photos of products and brands, is far too often the cause of enormous inefficiencies and sub-standard customer information in the processes nowadays. In addition to extending the master data perspective to the complete value-added chain and the increase in quality demands on the master data, the scope of master data is increasing too. Alongside ever more comprehensive information, which the law requires, there are also elements like location information, transport path information, CO2 footprints etc., which open up new information possibilities covering complete performance objects in the economy by bringing together the object and information; this is not only relevant for the corporation's system, but also for the diverse peripheral systems at an enterprise.

As a result, master data can firstly expect to grow in importance in terms of the integration perspective of the value-added chain and, secondly, as regards the scope of the information. Thirdly – and this seems to achieve a particularly long-term change in master data management in the view of the author – the question arises as to whether master data in the past was adequately mapped in terms of the character of the real objects represented in systems. Master data is that data on a real or conceivable object, which only exists in a time and space continuum. The modelling of time in conjunction with the master data, however, only has a short-lived tradition, for usually price information (purchase and sales prices) is handled in the systems related to time – but not the information on the object itself. This affects the grouping and classification logics used in systems. For example, one set of material master data in industry is embedded in standard hierarchies, but in retail information systems, groups of goods are the typical way of categorizing items and this is normally geared towards product features (e.g. food groups like yoghurt, butter, chocolate). In addition, the items are assigned to an external product classification, like the global product classification code at GS1, which also helps to conduct a comparison of sales between retail corporations.

This grouping of items creates a situation in enterprise system architectures with data warehouse systems, where, if changes are made in the assignment of groups, reclassification has to take place, which is problematic for operating the system, as millions of data sets have to be set up once again. This is based on methodically faulty modelling or non-modelling of time in master data, which was, however, necessary in the past. The individual objects are taken in their own right and depend on time in their assignment to a group. This applies all the more if the promises provided by the Internet of Things are met. The features of an object should always be available in a time-dependent manner in an information technology world without any technical restrictions in the system. The systems would create a completely different picture of master data if the demands of sensors and actuators were seriously considered, as the characteristic difference between master and transaction data – at least on the level of objects – would disappear. This fundamental modification of master data in the systems would also enable a different perspective on customers. It is also true that customers should not be mapped in a time-dependent manner, but many of their attributes can only be interpreted like this.

2.2 Digitization Potential at a Technical Task Level

The technical tasks are arranged on the second level of the IS architectures and they help integrate very machine-oriented information in applications for management and control purposes or directly in machines as embedded systems. These applications establish integration in the context of the Internet of Things, ubiquitous computing, the mobile world, etc., which was not normal in this form in the past. This newly available information allows the establishment of new kinds of processes. For example, sensible maintenance intervals or maintenance requirements can be determined at retail corporations for a large number of technical devices, ranging from freezers, fresh food areas, tills at stores to warehouse equipment and conveyor vehicles and trucks in the future (predictive maintenance), instead of planning this in advance. This enables corporations to make huge savings in maintenance, for the current practice of agreeing maintenance intervals between the investment goods manufacturers and the retail corporations in advance is very often uneconomical for retail enterprises.

In addition to the example of optimizing maintenance costs, energy controls are a second important area where considerable improvement opportunities open up through digitization and the controls available for electronic devices. This initially concerns the basic capability of controlling devices based on sensor information about temperatures, air conditions, etc. and opens up a whole new set of different control options for refrigeration units and other power-consuming devices. When retail corporations draw up contracts with energy suppliers, decisions also have to be made about the times of the day when maximum energy is consumed (or until when). These peak loads, in turn, are responsible for the costs of the contracts.

In conclusion, it is possible to state that the process innovations outlined here offer enormous potential in important resource areas at retail corporations – not only those in warehouses, but also those at retail enterprises.

2.3 Digitization Potential at an Operational Task Level

The operational tasks, by definition, involve those that are vital for the retail corporation's value added. The key task of a retail enterprise consists in ensuring that sufficient quantities of products are available in a combination of product lines at competitive prices. The key areas of competence required for a retail company involve the production or purchase of items at prices that are as low as possible (production, purchase, procurement and sales function), "designing" good items, a cheap purchase price, establishing product lines and placing them on the shelves or on websites and setting competitive or profitable sales prices. The special offer or campaign business with its independent definition of product lines, prices and positioning and the special challenges of logistics should also be mentioned.

During the last few decades, little has changed in the functions mentioned here, which are devoted to the central object of goods at retail enterprises. The fierce quality and price competition in Germany has created a situation where a personnel-oriented resource policy has largely been pursued – i.e. the oligopolists have attempted to cope with the tasks through the employees' qualifications or hiring them from rivals. Application systems have only played a secondary role, for the definition of requirements has been primarily geared to customer needs and this has only permitted automation in certain areas. This automation opportunity for operational tasks (managing prices, creating and managing listings etc.) will be increasingly linked to decision automation in the future, which is arranged on the fifth circular level of the IS architectures. The more technologies that are introduced like the approach followed by SAP for an in-memory database with the many associated optimization measures, the less potential there will be for the operational level to independently exist without the decision level. The operational tasks and the decision tasks can therefore be viewed together: Firstly, they enable an enormous leap in effectiveness, which would primarily be assigned to the decision level (automation of decision-making or thinking, so to speak). Secondly, a leap in efficiency for the operational tasks would be possible, strictly speaking, and this is primarily achieved by automating actions.

In addition to the marketing mix parameters, special focus is required for optimizing logistics processes in line with supply chain controls. The logistics costs from the supplier to the shelf at a retailer or to the customer represent the most important type of expense alongside other human resources costs and the rent. As part of increasing multi-channel offers, the significance of this cost component will continue to grow, for the delivery of the goods to customers is added as a further cost dimension (and the rent becomes less important in contrast to an in-store retail company). The logistics tasks at retail enterprises are logically differentiated between the two main processes of procurement and distribution logistics, which can also be intertwined with each other in time synchronization.

2.4 Digitization Potential at an Administrative Task Level

No radical process changes are expected for administrative tasks, which initially do not provide any value added as cross-sectional tasks. However, administrative tasks are expected to accelerate as information is available more promptly and processes are geared towards real time. The current practice of presenting accounts for certain periods does not match the need for prompt reporting about the company's economic and financial situation for managers.

The ongoing process of digitization involving efforts lasting decades to improve electronic data exchange, the increasing refinement of information from the receipt to the item level, the opportunities of exchanging data with industry and the pressure to be able to make available the latest, high-quality master data for consumer purposes will trigger enormous efficiency potential and a significantly more informative analysis basis in the areas downstream, automation in bookkeeping and make the preparation of assessments more flexible.

2.5 Digitization Potential for the Decision-Oriented Task Level

There have been some experiments with artificial intelligence tools, for example, to optimize pricing policy, but there are no all-round strategic competition models or sophisticated game theory points of contact. The aspect of forming product lines has been neglected by retail corporations in their systems too.

In the future, new digitization opportunities will particularly open up enormous potential for improvements in the value-added areas. Initially, real-time-oriented simulations will be able to reduce the acceptance barrier for using systems in the most important area at retail enterprises. Simultaneous optimization – for a retail corporation's set goal – of the different parameters in the marketing mix at retail companies will be part of the future, because the data now available enables intelligent and retail-experienced users to formulate hypotheses and falsify them by using real data in order to gain increasingly refined findings about customers and competition events through permanent checks. Based on the data available, oligopolistic assumptions about behavior (in the form of price leadership and its associated behavior) can already be confirmed. The normal trend at retail enterprises at the moment of believing that prices and product lines in the existing dimension can be controlled by people contradicts the actual situation at retail corporations. The responsibility for many thousands of items in a product line section is not economically feasible for individual managers; even the scope of responsibility at discount stores contradicts the findings about human processing capabilities. Arguments are usually presented with reference to the company's behavior in the past or references to the competition, although both argument chains do not necessarily lead to an ideal offer price. Current practice at retail corporations is not rationally justifiable and the following will be crucial in the future: There are much more effective and more efficient opportunities by involving intelligent algorithms and the application systems supporting them. Whether a simulation of the purchase prices based on the ingredients, which is linked to the development in the prices of raw materials, is used to calculate purchase and sales prices for different quantities at different sales channels or a quantity-weighted sales price analysis of rivals is used to offer industry's own sales price needs – there are many examples available. According to the author, the product line policy as the most relevant economic task is not adequately supported and there are too few experts particularly for this task.

3 Application Systems Challenges – Technological Perspective

The outlined potentials of and requirements on the tasks of trading companies will have to be modelled on the application system level, leading to even further complex application architecture, even though and because digitization progresses and actions to external demands have to be taken. The application architectures of companies are shaped by the data-driven system size, the plurality and pluralism of the systems in use and the degree of change of the single system [8] or taken together by the complexity of the system landscape (complexity as a measure for variety and dynamics of a system) [9]. Information systems in trading and retailing have to administrate and process enormous amounts of data by now and the growth is formidable. The total volume of data at Walmart, the largest trading company world-wide, amounts to about 30.000 TB [10]. Per year, 13 billion consumer baskets have to be processed [11]. Still many companies only store information on receipt level instead of item level and even more only allow access for a certain time span, e.g. two or three months.

A further restriction that has been assumed, is the dominance of standard systems in the context of Enterprise Systems and the thereby predefined number of different systems [12]. Enterprise Systems are widely understood as an advancement of ERP-II systems and consist of an ERP core, a CRM, an SCM and a BI system (with many further individual products/systems that are operated by the companies [13]. One can observe a high number at that, as an example may illustrate:

Assume the following systems in a retailing company: ERP, PIM, SRM, Financial, HR, CRM, SCM, SRM, Forecast & Replenishment, Category Management, Online Shop, Online Marketing, Middleware, POS Data Management, POS System and Peripheral Control. Then, already 16 system types have to be managed. These products are usually developed in releases, considering that the individualization of standard solutions requires professional release management. This release management however has to account for the software logistics that provides a concept for multi-stage development systems, quality assurance systems, production systems, sandbox systems, training systems, consolidation and performance test systems. As each of the above-mentioned 16 system types is instantiated for each purpose - let's just say for the 4 purposes of development, QA, production, training – one obtains the number of systems that have to be operated by multiplication, that is 64 systems in the sample concern. What is more, when as part of a template approach the systems are operated in multiple computing centers, the number of system embodiments multiplies once again. Assuming a factor of 6, the number of systems amounts to 384.

If alternative releases are in use, another multiplication supervenes. Even though, this does not necessarily mean a reduplication, possibly more than 700 systems have to be operated.

In reality, there is a plethora of additional systems, that have to be operated for reasons not to be presented here. Thus, from an Enterprise Systems perspective, more than 1000 systems may have to be considered. This complexity presents challenges to project management, requirements management, integration management, test management, development management and software logistics in an extent that greatly surpasses the problems discussed in literature. By reference to a requirement from an omni-channel scenario this complexity is illustrated in the following. When it comes to an omni-channel offer of a wholesaler or retailer, the question arises how the price calculation is to be formulated if customer price differentiation and same prices at all channels is required at the same time. Such a scenario at a traditional brick and mortars retailer with a cash system who wants to offer and sell products online will result in situation, where the price calculation logic that is implemented on the one hand in the cash system but on the other hand has to be changed in the back-end system for the online shop, so that both channels access the same functional building blocks. But then, the offline/online difficulty has to be modelled, since in today's trading companies there are no pure synchronous online connections, but always hybrid scenarios of online functionalities that involve functions that are only available offline for reasons of technical restriction.

The degree of change of the systems however is determined by especially two causes: first, by the strategy and system manifestation of the standard software producer and secondly by the strategy and system requirements of the domain company, i.e. the company that uses the software.

At first glance, one has to state that the Enterprise Systems market is dominated by few vendors: it can be characterized as a supply oligopoly. This background competition policy must always be considered at the domain companies, as there are distinct principal-agency problems that are debated insufficiently even though they can lead to significant problems because of diverse information asymmetries. But the strategy of the software producer presents a paradigmatic restriction for the domain company so that an adoption of the software producer's strategy is required for the trading company. For instance, SAP has provoked a pressure for change at the customers' sides when – with the development of the SAP HANA database and the (partially) newly designed applications such as S/4 HANA Financials, Merchandise Management etc. – they announced the end of the maintenance period for 2025. Hereof, the degree of change is at times very high, since SAP has completely change a number of functions due to new architecture principles. For example, following the strategy of abandoning aggregated data (by integrating OLAP and OLTP), new processes are created and the implementation of the system does not only change single applications, but the entire system architecture. This means, that a strategy for the comprehensive application architecture is require in order to prevent product specific responsibilities and perspective which in turn lead to a subpar solution. A further dimension of complexity is elicited by the fact that applications are being narrowed for service considerations and cloud use cases. In order to be economically advantageous in the cloud, standardization is needed which is currently not the case. Therefore, the implication is not to realize existing demands with cloud solutions. In many case, the only alternatives are "Standardization 2.0" in the cloud vs. on premise usage. If a cloud service is used, the problem of system integration emerges. There are many cases in the past, where an order in a Salesforce system could not be integrated in an SAP system. Hybrid approaches that allow for a connection of Software as a Service and self-operated application will become an integral part of the architecture and application management.

The domain company itself has also its own release strategy, that covers the integration of changes by the standard software producer – via releases and patches – and the realization of requests by the domain company itself. Ultimately, the functional and technological changes coalesce in the release management, independent from the origin of the change.

The change of complex application systems and architecture requires – as elaborated on – among others multi project management, cross-application requirements management, integration management, integrative test management. The integration of separated tasks becomes necessary and an essential success factor for the management of system landscapes in a world of applications that is subject to change.

References

1. North, D.: Institutions, Institutional Change and Economic Performance. Cambridge University Press, Cambridge (1990)
2. Becker, J., Schütte, R.: Retail Information Systems. A Domain-Oriented Introduction into the Discipline of Information Systems (in German), 2nd edn. Redline Wirtschaft, Frankfurt/M (2004)

3. Schütte, R.: Modelling of retail information systems. A cumulative habilitation thesis (in German). Westfälische Wilhelms-Universität Münster, Münster (2011)
4. Christensen, C.M.: The Innovator's Dilemma: When New Technologies Cause Great Firms to Fail. Harvard Business Review Press, Boston (1997)
5. Kurzweil, R.: The Age of Spiritual Machines. When Computers Exceed Human Intelligence. Penguin, London (2000)
6. Brynjolffson, E., McAfee, A.: The Second Machine Age. Work, Progress, and Prosperity in a Time of Brilliant Technologies. Plassen, New York (2014)
7. Benson-Armer, R., Noble, S., Thiel, A.: The consumer sector in 2030: trends and questions to consider. Consumer packaged goods and retail, December 2015. McKinsey-report (2015)
8. Dern, G.: Integration Management of Business-IT. A system theoretically oriented recommendation for shaping IT-Landscapes and IT-Organizations (in German). Vieweg +Teubner Research, Wiesbaden (2010)
9. Beetz, K.: Effect of IT Governance on IT Complexity in Companies: Influencing the IT Redundancy with Shared Responsibility Within the IT Project Portfolio Management (in German). Springer, Wiesbaden (2014)
10. Walmart: Walmart Shareholders Meeting 2014. http://news.walmart.com/executive-viewpoints/picking-up-the-pace-of-change-for-the-customer. Accessed 28 Mar 2016
11. Walmart: Annual report. http://s2.q4cdn.com/056532643/files/doc_finan-cials/2014/Annual/2014-annual-report.pdf. Accessed 28 Mar 2016
12. Böhmann, T., Krcmar, H.: Simply better? About the applicability of industrial complexity management on IT services with many variants (in German). In: Wirtschaftsinformatik Proceedings 2005, vol. 24, pp. 449–468 (2005)
13. Olson, D., Kesharwani, S.: Enterprise Information Systems: Contemporary Trends and Issues. World Scientific, New Jersey (2010)

Information Systems Architecture

Understanding the Blockchain Using Enterprise Ontology

Joost de Kruijff(✉) and Hans Weigand

Tilburg University, P.O. Box 90153, 5000 LE Tilburg, The Netherlands
{j.c.dekruijff,h.weigand}@uvt.nl

Abstract. Blockchain technology is regarded as highly disruptive, but there is a lack of formalization and standardization of terminology. Not only because there are several (sometimes propriety) implementation platforms, but also because the academic literature so far is predominantly written from either a purely technical or an economic application perspective. The result of the confusion is an offspring of blockchain solutions, types, roadmaps and interpretations. For blockchain to be accepted as a technology standard in established industries, it is pivotal that ordinary internet users and business executives have a basic yet fundamental understanding of the workings and impact of blockchain. This conceptual paper provides a theoretical contribution and guidance on what blockchain actually is by taking an ontological approach. Enterprise Ontology is used to make a clear distinction between the datalogical, infological and essential level of blockchain transactions and smart contracts.

Keywords: Enterprise ontology · Business model ontology · REA · Blockchain

1 Introduction

It has been said that blockchain is the emergent technology that everybody talks about but few actually know what it is [1]. According to [2], blockchain research arguably lacks scientific rigor due to its young age and is primarily concerned with what blockchain could become as a disruptive technology for the Internet of Things (IoT). Glaser and Bezzenberger [4] state that existing academic literature with regards to cryptocurrency and blockchain is predominantly written from either an economic- or technical perspective, like the various types of blockchains [1–3, 5], ledgers [1, 3], consensus mechanisms [3, 4], crypto-currencies [6–8] and governance mechanisms [9, 10]. To date, no paper provides a formal overview of the blockchain concept and ecosystem across the various types and implementations, thereby missing the opportunity to reduce ambiguity and formalize blockchain as a concept. This scientific reality is also evident in blockchain trials in the financial services industry, which struggle to develop an industry-wide and generic blockchain solution, as many banks developed a proprietary implementation instead of joining collective blockchain tests (e.g. R3cev). The result is an offspring of blockchain solutions, types, roadmaps and interpretations. For blockchain to be accepted as a technology standard in established industries, it is pivotal that policy makers, ordinary internet users and business executives have a basic

E. Dubois and K. Pohl (Eds.): CAiSE 2017, LNCS 10253, pp. 29–43, 2017.
DOI: 10.1007/978-3-319-59536-8_3

yet fundamental shared understanding of the workings and impact of blockchain. Against this background, this paper aims to provide a theoretical contribution and guidance on what blockchain actually is instead of what it could become by using an ontological approach. The main result of this paper is a blockchain domain ontology which so far does not exist. This ontology, once validated, could serve as a reference for blockchain research concerned with the structure, applicability and impact of blockchain.

Ontology has been recognized as a useful instrument for reducing conceptual ambiguities and inconsistencies while identifying value-creating capabilities in a certain domain [11]. Ontology is becoming an increasingly important instrument for reducing complexity by structuring domains of interests [12]. According to the popular OntoClean methodology [13], domain structuring starts with the identification of a set of classes in a taxonomy, followed by assigning metaproperties for each property. Then, it needs to be verified whether constraints are violated by these metaproperties.

In order to formalize the blockchain ecosystem, it would be insufficient to study it solely from an information systems' perspective, as it should also relate to the business operation and processes of potential enterprise adopters. Enterprise ontology provides a collection of terms and natural language definitions relevant to these enterprise adopters. Well-known examples of enterprise ontology frameworks are TOVE, EO [14] and the Enterprise Ontology ofDEMO [15]. DEMO is inspired by the language/action perspective, which has been initially developed as a philosophy of language and was built on the speech act theory [16]. It is based on explicit specified axioms characterized by a rigid modeling methodology [17], and is focused on the construction and operation of a system rather than the functional behavior. It emphasizes the importance of choosing the most effective level of abstraction during information system development in order to establish a clear separation of concerns [18]. As DEMO has been proven to be a helpful methodology to formalize systems that are ambiguous, inconsistent or incomplete [17], especially when it comes to reducing modeling complexity [19], this paper will use Enterprise Ontology to describe the blockchain ontology from a datalogical, infological and essential (business) perspective.

The structure of this paper is as follows. Section 2 provides an introduction to blockchain terminology in order to identify the key concepts. Section 3 presents a blockchain ontology using the three levels of abstraction of Enterprise Ontology. In Sect. 4, we use this ontological analysis to get a better picture of what is new in blockchain compared to existing Information Systems The research outcomes and directions for future research conclude this paper in Sect. 5.

2 Defining the Basic Terminology

Ontology design only makes sense once the designer and audience have basic yet fundamental understanding of the various blockchain structures that exist. In essence, blockchain is a distributed consensus system for parties that do not trust each other to transact. Hereby, blockchain differentiates from traditional transaction systems with respect to how it irreversibly stores transaction data in a distributed ledger. Once verified and stored, there is no way to manipulate data on the blockchain, as changes are immediately reflected in all active copies of the ledger across the network. Economic transactions (e.g. payments) are tracked and combined into blocks, each of them with a unique block header, which cryptographically commits to the contents of the block, a timestamp and the previous block header. Together with previous block headers they form a chain. Each block also contains the chain's Merkle root or 'hash of all hashes', which prevents the need to download the entire chain in order to verify the validity of the chain for each transaction (Fig. 1).

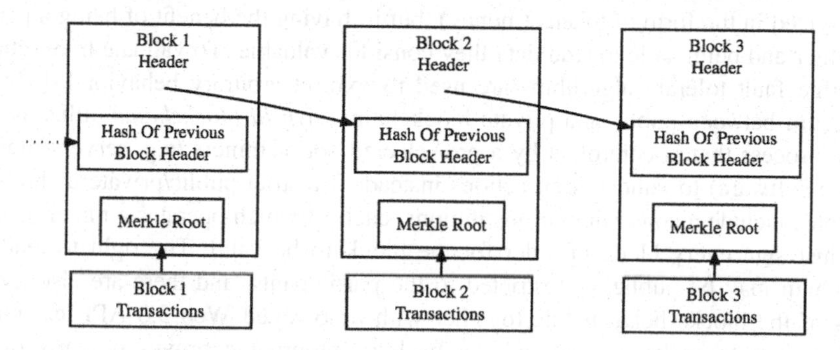

Fig. 1. Illustration of a blockchain transaction [20]

There are various ways to name this chain; most people refer to this chain as a 'blockchain', as 'blockchain technology' or as the 'blockchain concept', which could refer to either 'the Blockchain'(in the case for Bitcoin) or to an altchain like Ethereum. The Bitcoin blockchain is hereby capitalized, as it is often regarded as the original blockchain, every alternative is considered an Altchain. In this paper, the concept of a chain is decomposed and explained. As transactions come by, the chain builds a digital ledger that is distributed, sequential, digitally signed and contains validated records of ownership [21]. Like the decentralization of communication lead to the creation of the internet, the blockchain is believed to decentralize the way we manage information [10] and may refresh mindsets toward established concepts like voting, contracts and registries. A recent development accelerating the impact of blockchain is the concept of *servification*, whereby physical goods can be risk-free exploited as a service, like car rental services that remotely disable the ignition system if the event payment fails according to data available from the blockchain.

Blockchain operates in three forms; *public*, *private* or *hybrid*, each form will be briefly explained. A *public blockchain*, like Bitcoin, is an open blockchain whereby anyone can participate by reading or sending transactions or by joining the consensus process (Proof of Work, Proof of Stake, etc.) by means of an anonymous node. Public blockchains offer maximum transparency and its main goal is to prevent concentration of power. In contrast, some industries only transact with trusted peers, like the banking industry. To fit those industries, *private blockchains* have emerged that operate in a more closed environment, making the blockchain seemingly more attractive to entities that do not like the idea that users are anonymous and that the consensus process is performed by anonymous nodes. Participants prefer that write permissions are privileged to a single organization like a Government or Notary, which amount to an organizational process of Know-Your-Business and Know-Your-Customer allowing for the white listing (or blacklisting) of user identity [3]. Read permissions may be public or restricted to an arbitrary extent. Likely applications include auditing systems, concerned with evaluating data integrity, system effectiveness, or system efficiency and systems internal to a single company. Public readability may not be necessary in many cases, though in other cases public auditability may be desired. As opposed to a public blockchain network, the transaction validators in a private blockchain are not (always) incentivized in the form of tokens (money), but in having the benefit of being a part of the ledger and being able to read data they consider valuable. To validate transactions, byzantine fault tolerant algorithms are used to exhibit arbitrary behavior [3]. In the continuum between public and private blockchains, *hybrid blockchains* utilize a consensus process that is controlled by a pre-selected set of miners (e.g. servers running specific software) to validate transactions instead of a strict public/private dichotomy. Examples include a consortium of institutions, each of which operates a miner or node and must sign every block in order for the block to be valid. The right to read the blockchain may be public, or restricted to the participants, and there are also hybrid routes of the blocks being public together with a so-called Web 3.0 API that public members use to make queries and get back cryptographic proves of parts of the blockchain state [3].

As common with emerging technologies, there are multiple interpretations of blockchain technology found in whitepapers and literature and as a result, no formal blockchain model and terminology exist that can be applied for research purposes. For example, the terms blockchain versus distributed ledger are used interchangeably and often confused. Some mention 'permissioned blockchains' while others call those 'private distributed ledgers', which refer essentially to the same construct. The arbitrary usage of 'tokens' versus 'public/private keys' is confusing as well, even for those with knowledge of security concepts. Figure 2 is a collection of terminology as provided by whitepapers [1–3] and articles [4–9] and aims to clarify the various terminologies used for blockchain constructs. This paper refers to this terminology going forward.

Consensus	Type	Governance	Trust	Scalability	Use
Decentralized, based on proof	Public, Not permissioned	Anonymous nodes	Low	Limited	e.g. Virtual currency
Hybrid, based on validation	Consortium, Private, Permissioned	Pre-selected set of nodes	Mediu m	Unlimited	e.g. Banking system
Centralized, based on validation	Private, Permissioned	Single organization	High	Unlimited	e.g. Government, Notary

Fig. 2. Common terminology for blockchain constructs

3 Designing a Blockchain Ontology

An important development in the history of databases in the early '70s was the separation of implementation choices from the database conceptual model (the principle of data independence). We believe that a similar separation is highly needed for the blockchain domain. We propose to adopt the distinction axiom of Enterprise Ontology as ontological basis for this separation.

The distinction axiom of Enterprise Ontology distinguishes three basic human abilities: performa, informa, and forma [15]. The *forma* ability concerns the form aspects of communication and information. Production acts at the forma level are datalogical in nature: they store, transmit, copy, destroy, etc. data. The *informa* ability concerns the content aspects of communication and information. Production acts at the forma level are infological in nature, meaning that they reproduce, deduce, reason, compute, etc. information, abstracting from the form aspect. The *performa* ability concerns the bringing about of new, original things, directly or indirectly by communication. Communicative acts at the performa level are about evoking or evaluating commitment; these communicative acts are realized at the informa level by means of messages with some propositional content.

The distinction axiom is highly relevant for the blockchain. Following the three abilities, we distinguish three ontological layers (Fig. 3). We start from the datalogical layer that describes blockchain transactions at the technical level in terms of blocks and code. From there, we make an infological abstraction in order to describe the blockchain transactions as effectuating an (immutable) open ledger system. This layer aims to abstract from the various implementations that exist today or will be developed in the future. To describe the economic meaning of the infological transactions we use the essential layer. This is the preferred level of specification for a blockchain application as it abstracts from the implementation choices.

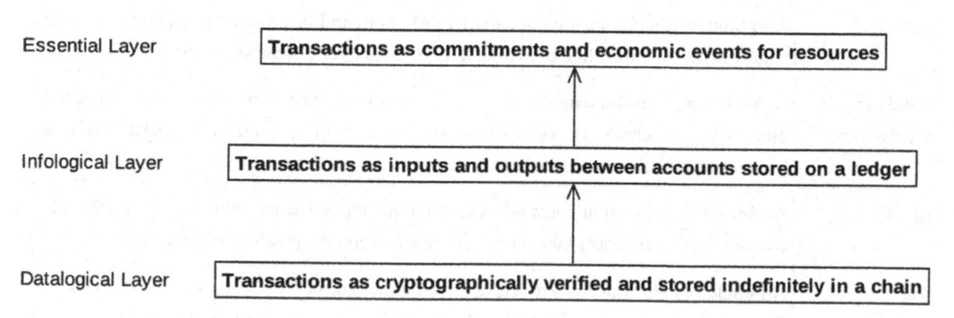

Fig. 3. Enterprise ontology layers applied to blockchain transactions

3.1 Datalogical Blockchain Ontology

In most of the publications on blockchain, the concept is described in terms of the technology that is used, that is, in terms of blocks, miners, mainchains (the blockchain), sidechains (a chain that communicates with the mainchain for enhanced functionality) etc. This technological basis is to be positioned at the datalogical level, the level of data structures and data manipulation. To build a blockchain domain ontology for this level we have used taxonomies as identified in cryptocurrency [4], blockchain research [22] and technical implementations by blockchain- and cloud providers [5].

Several specialized ontology languages are available nowadays, but one of most wide-spread modeling approaches is Object Management Group's Unified Modeling Language (UML) together with its associated Object Constraint Language (OCL) [23], so this is why we have chosen to use it for the first version of our blockchain ontology. First, an overview is provided for the UML classes that are used to construct the domain ontology for blockchain at the datalogical abstraction layer (Fig. 4). The chain concept is not included as it will be expanded in a separate taxonomy.

Class	Explanation
Actor	An **actor** is a virtual ID which (for any individual or organization) that owns a wallet
Wallet	A wallet initiates transactions on the blockchain and receives the transaction output.
Transaction	A **transaction** is a request to the blockchain nodes that contains an input, amount and output (The Blockchain) or custom data like code (altchain).
Node	A **node** is an entity in the blockchain network that either proves (public transactions) or validates (hybrid or private transactions) and subsequently adds it to a block with a unique hash. The hash will be used by the next transaction as the input. Nodes receive rewards for every successful transaction that is added to the block.
Miner	A **miner** is an anonymous node (e.g. server) that cryptographically proofs a public transaction to be valid using a proving mechanism like Proof of Work, Proof of
	Resource, Proof of State, Proof of Activity, etcetera
Mining Mechanism	A **mining mechanism** is a mechanism to mine transactions in public blockchains, altchains or sidechains.
Validator	A **validator** is a non-public node that) validates hybrid or private transactions based on validation mechanisms like byzantine fault tolerances or double spending.
Validating Mechanism	A **validating mechanism** is a mechanism to validate transactions in non-public blockchains, altchains or sidechains. An example of a validation mechanism is a byzantine fault tolerance mechanism.
Block	A **block** is a transaction container with a unique block header, which cryptographically commits to the contents of the block, a timestamp and the previous block header.
Uncle	An **uncle** is a block that is very close to being the "correct" next block in the blockchain. By mining and rewarding for uncles, the proofing process becomes more reliable.
Cousin	A **cousin** is a block that is very close to being the "correct" next uncle in the blockchain. By mining and rewarding for cousins, the proofing process becomes more reliable.
Runtime	A **runtime** (or cryplet) enables secure interoperation and communication between blockchain middleware and clouds like Microsoft Azure, Amazon AWS and others.
Middleware	**Middleware** is software that is included in the blockchain and enables third parties to interact with blockchain records to provide services like identity management

Fig. 4. Datalogical domain ontology classes for the blockchain

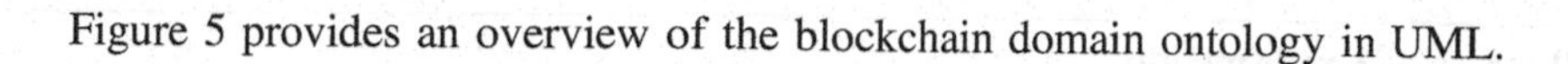

Figure 5 provides an overview of the blockchain domain ontology in UML.

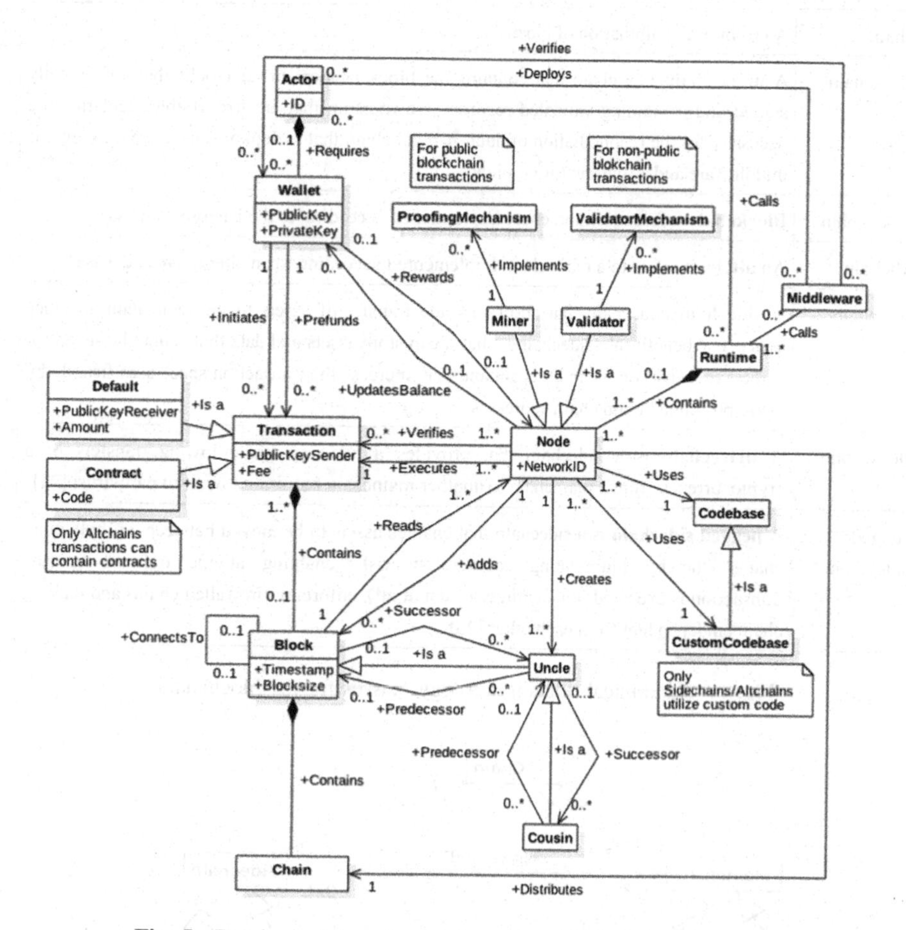

Fig. 5. Datalogical domain ontology for a blockchain transaction

Central to the domain ontology are the wallet, the transaction and the node. Each blockchain concept relies on these concepts, whereby a transaction can either be simple or contain smart contract code. Interactions with the blockchain (from outside the ecosystem) occur through nodes (via runtime and middleware) by means of API's and sockets, or via sidechains directly, which is our next focus.

For readability purposes, the ontological structure of a chain has been detailed in a dedicated view, to explain the nature of the blockchain ecosystem. Within this taxonomy, the following objects can be distinguished (Fig. 6).

Figure 7 shows the datalogical taxonomy for chains and chain interactions. A chain can be either a mainchain or a sidechain. Sidechains are always related to one or more mainchains for enhanced functionality. In this overview, a Blockchain should not be confused with the blockchain as a concept, but must be read as the Blockchain as implemented by Bitcoin. Although not included in the ontology, technical off-chain

Class	Explanation
Chain	A **chain** is a combination of blocks
Mainchain	A **main chain** is a chain that contains the block headers of all blocks that are digitally signed and containing validated records of ownership that are irreversible, depleting the necessity for the reconciliation of data. A blockchain that is deployed as a service contains middleware and a runtime (or cryplets).
Blockchain	**Blockchain** refers to a main chain implemented according to the Bitcoin codebase
Altchain	An **altchain** refers to a main chain implemented according to an alternative codebase.
Sidechain	A **sidechain** is a chain that allows for the transfer of assets to the mainchain and vice versa. The benefit of a sidechain is that it can store assets and data that cannot be saved (or is too expensive) on the main chain and may increase the transaction speed significantly by using pre-mined main chain addresses.
Drivechain	A **drivechain** is a sidechain that provides a two-way peg allowing transfers of a cryptocurrency from a mainchain to another mainchain requiring low third party trust [24]
Pegged Sidechain	A **pegged sidechain** is a sidechain that enables assets to be moved between multiple main chains, thereby illuminating counterparty risk, enabling atomic transactions (the transaction is executed in its entirety or not at all), enforcing firewalled chains and making chains independent from each other [25].

Fig. 6. Datalogical domain ontology classes for the blockchain

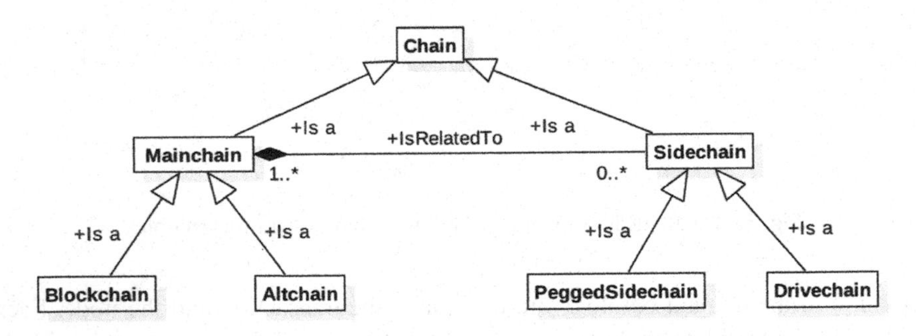

Fig. 7. Datalogical domain taxonomy for the blockchain ecosystem

solutions living outside the blockchain ecosystem may become an entity of significance in the future, as governments and enterprises build infrastructures containing non-vital information (like master data) and capable of interacting with a blockchain.

3.2 Infological Blockchain Ontology

In the 1970s, Langefors was the first to make the important distinction between information (as knowledge) and data (as representation) [26]. This separation of content and form created a new field in knowledge engineering called Information Systems Engineering or Infology, aiming to make complicated structures intellectually manageable [15].

When blockchain is described in the current literature as a "distributed ledger" [27], this is an infological characterization that abstracts from the encrypted data blocks, miners, chains, etcetera that make up the datalogical level. A transaction, in this ledger system, is not just a block of data, but a transfer of some value object (e.g. Bitcoin). A ledger consists of *accounts* (e.g. debit account), and this concept is indeed generic across the majority of blockchain providers that are part of this analysis. Accounts are not limited to have a (crypto)currency- balance or quantity, but may also refer to other types like stocks or a claim as mainchains other than Bitcoin (not taking sidechains into account) allow to register custom account types (Fig. 8).

Class	Explanation
Ledger	A **ledger** maintains a continuously growing list of timestamped transaction records, connected to a block as defined at the datalogical level
Account	An **account** sends and receives value to and from a transaction
Object	An **object type** is a custom stock or a claim (type) traded by an account via a transaction.
Transaction	A **transaction** represents the atomic inputs and outputs between accounts
Journal	A **journal** is list of transactions
RulesOfEngagement	Smart contracts (essential level) are enforced by **rules of engagement** that are implemented as blockchain code.

Fig. 8. Infological domain ontology classes for the blockchain

We made a distinction between journals and ledgers. In a traditional accounting system, journals and ledgers reside where business transactions are recorded. In essence, detail-level information for individual transactions is stored in one of several possible journals, while the information in the journals is then summarized and transferred (or posted) to a ledger. In the blockchain context, such a division can be maintained (and supported at the datalogical level by a combination of mainchain and sidechain), but it is also possible to see the ledger as an aggregated view on the journal. Anyway, the term "ledger" typically refers to a subset of all accounts. For that reason, we have modeled the ledger here as a set of accounts where we do not require every account to be part of a ledger.

Transactions must comply with rules of engagement. One axiomatic rule of engagement in Blockchain is that for each transaction, input equals output (debit = credit). Inputs and outputs in this context represent any tangible or intangible asset and are not limited to cryptocurrency (Fig. 9).

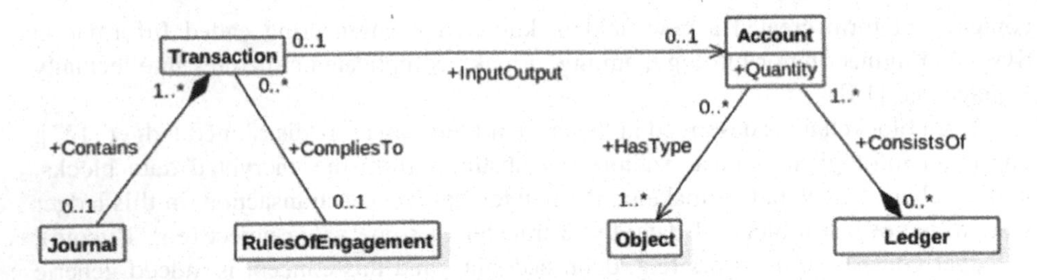

Fig. 9. Infological ontology for a blockchain transaction

3.3 Essential Blockchain Ontology

The essential or business level is concerned with what is created directly or indirectly by communication. In the Language/Action Perspective [16], the key notion in communication is commitment as a social relationship based on shared understanding of what is right and what is true. Communicative acts typically establish or evaluate commitments. In a narrower sense, a commitment (promise, commissive) is about what an actor is bound to do (so what is right in a future situation). Such a commitment being agreed upon by two parties is a change in the social reality, as is the agreed upon fulfillment of that commitment.

Given the institutional context to be in place, an infological blockchain transaction moving some value from one account to another represents a change in the social reality, e.g. transfer of ownership. Such a change is what we identify as the essential blockchain transaction.

Enterprise Ontology is not specific about the content of the change. For that reason, we combine Enterprise Ontology with the Business Ontology of REA [29]. The REA model developed by Bill McCarthy [30] can be viewed as a domain ontology for accounting. REA intends to be the basis for integrated accounting information systems focused on representing increases and decreases of value within an organization or beyond. REA inherits the stock-flow nature of accounting, but lifts the syntactic structure of accounts to a semantic level of resources and events.

The accounting perspective is quite appropriate in the blockchain context. Blockchain is facilitating and recording (in an immutable and transparent way) value transfers between economic actors in a shared data environment while accountants (and their customers) are interested in reliable information on these transfers and the resulting value positions of actors.

REA atomic constituents of processes are called economic *events*. Economic events are carried out by *agents* and affect a certain *resource*, like a (crypto) currency or physical good. The relationship between an economic event and a resource is called *stock-flow*. REA presents five generalized stock-flows: produce, use, consume, give and take. These stock-flows can generate value flows by conversion (produce, use and consume) or exchange (give and take). In the REA independent view, the give, use and consume stock-flows are process inputs (provide) and produce and take are process outputs (receive). The duality axiom says that provides and receives are always in balance. For instance, in a physical conversion process, some resources are used or

Class	Explanation
Agent	An **agent** is individual or organization that controls resources and can initiate a transaction or commitment
Resource	A **resource** is an asset with a certain economic value controlled by an agent
Stock-flow event	**Stock-flow events** represent the provide or receive of a resource
Transaction	A (business) **transaction** is a process that changes the economic reality (exchange or conversion) consisting of increment and decrement stock-flow events
Economic Exchange	An **economic exchange** is a transaction that changes the economic reality by means of exchange
Economic Conversion	An **economic conversion** is a transaction that changes the economic reality by means of conversion
Commitment	**Commitments** are promises of future stock-flow events that are fulfilled with the execution of these events
Smart Contract	A contract is an agreement between agents consisting of mutual commitments. A **smart contract** is a contract in which the commitment fulfillment is completely or partially performed automatically.

Fig. 10. Essential (business) domain ontology classes for the blockchain

consumed in the process of producing other resources. In our blockchain ontology, we will use the term "transaction" to represent such a combination of provide and receive events (Fig. 10).

REA also includes the notion of *contract* as a bundle of reciprocal commitments. Following REA and Enterprise Ontology, we have both transactions and commitments. Transactions can exist on their own, for instance, an instant bitcoin transfer from onc party to another, but also be part of a contract. A special feature of a *smart* contract (originally introduced by Szabo [28]) is that at least some of the commitments are executed automatically. In this case, the commitments are *self-fulfilling*; the committed transactions are irreversibly saved on the blockchain and executed once certain conditions are matched. This is a very powerful concept as the contract no longer has to rely on trust or complicated trade procedures (Fig. 11).

Business transactions are realized in the blockchain by a set of infological transactions, typically one for each outflow/inflow pair. Commitments are also realized by infological transactions – in his case, a transfer to a commitment type account. The fulfillment is realized by a transfer from that commitment type account. The difference between conversions and exchanges is that in the latter case, the provided resource is the same as the received resource, while they are different in the former case.

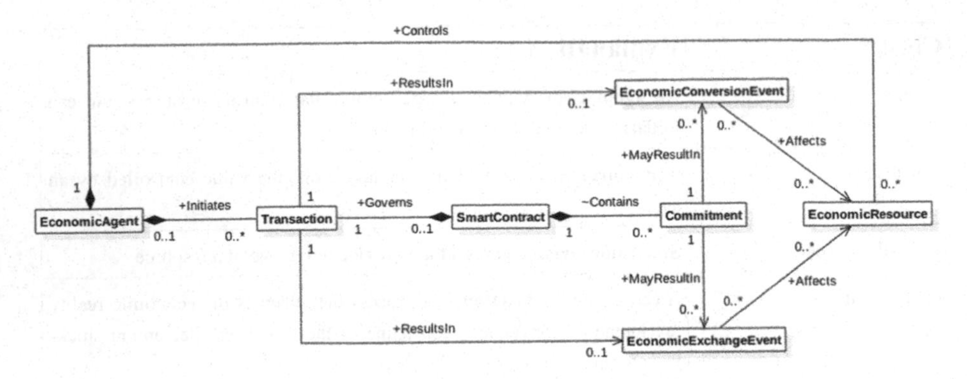

Fig. 11. Essential ontology of a blockchain transaction

4 Discussion

This paper applied the concept of abstraction on the blockchain concept utilizing Enterprise Ontology. The chosen structure aimed to explain blockchain with maximum separation of concern with regards to substance, context and audience. It turns out that a blockchain transaction, regardless of its complex ecosystem and cryptographical ingredients at the datalogical layer, shows significant infological and essential conceptual similarities with traditional economic transactions as used today.

However, although the concepts are not different, their properties change. It makes a difference when mutable records are replaced by immutable records, and when the fulfilment of commitments is left to the infrastructure rather than to the voluntary acts of the parties. Figure 12 summarizes a comparison between blockchain and traditional transaction systems.

	Blockchain	**Traditional**
Essential	Communication success based on non-tamperable infrastructure	Communication success based on subjective and objective trust (control procedures)
Infological	Performative transactions integrating descriptive and prescriptive transactions	Descriptive transactions (to be verified) and prescriptive transactions (to be realized and evaluated)
Datalogical	Immutable records (based on consensus mechanism), stored outside the company	Mutable records (to be protected), stored within the company

Fig. 12. Comparison between blockchain and traditional transaction systems

At the datalogical level, the difference is not only that records become immutable, but also that the transaction databases get positioned in between companies, rather than inside companies, thus removing data redundancy that exists today (although another form of redundancy is introduced in the consensus mechanisms). On the infological level, control procedures are not relevant anymore. An interesting feature of blockchain transactions is that they are not just a description of some transfer (e.g. of Bitcoins) but the very existence of the transfer depends on this description. This performative property also applies to other transactions, like service deliveries, when the blockchain is tightly coupled with IoT services, and to commitments (their bare existence). At the essential level, smart contracts also add the automatic fulfillment of commitments, and more in general, there is a change in what makes the communication successful: trust, perhaps grounded in control procedures, or the impersonal and non-tamperable infrastructure.

5 Conclusion

This paper describes an initial blockchain ontology on three levels. As such, it supports a better understanding of this disruptive technology. It also can be used to support application development, as it suggests to specify the blockchain application on the business level first. In our view, it should be possible then to generate the blockchain implementation automatically, with some design parameters to be set. For the specification of the business level, in terms of contract languages and graphical formats, it is possible to draw on already proven modeling approaches.

In the context of this paper, we have not been able to do an extensive validation of the ontology yet, so the proposed model should be seen as an initial one. Validation is pivotal to test and improve the capability of our ontology to reduce blockchain's ambiguity and inconsistency. Apart from the formal verification using top ontologies like DOLCE, further validation is to be done with applications as well as by establishing mappings to the various blockchain implementations that exist. We cannot claim that the present model is complete, but at least it provides a first reference point.

The current ontology does not stop the need for further research on blockchain technology of course. On the contrary, an important next step is to understand and formalize interactions between mainchains, sidechains and off-chains within or across the public, private and hybrid domain (blockchain zoning), to mention one issue. Separating the goal – immutable transactions, smart contracts – from the implementation can help to better explore all implementation variants without dogmatism.

References

1. Swanson, T.: Consensus-as-a-service: a brief report on the emergence of permissioned, distributed ledger systems (2015)
2. Pilkington, M.: Blockchain technology: principles and applications. In: Olleros, F.X., Zhegu, M. (eds.) Research Handbook on Digital Transformations. Edward Elgar, Northampton (2016)
3. Buterin, V.: On Public and Private Blockchains, crypto renaissance salon, 7 August 2015
4. Glaser, F., Bezzenberger, L.: Beyond cryptocurrencies – a taxonomy of decentralized consensus systems. In: 23rd European Conference on Information Systems (ECIS 2015) (2015)

5. Gray, M.: Introducing Project Bletchley (Microsoft), June 2016
6. Tschorsch, F., Scheuermann, B.: Bitcoin and Beyond. Cryptology ePrint Archive IACR, Berlin, p. 464 (2015)
7. Chaum, D.: Blind signatures for untraceable payments. In: Chaum, D., Rivest, R.L., Sherman, A.T. (eds.) Advances in Cryptology, pp. 199–203. Springer, New York (1983)
8. Scott, B: Visions of a Techno-Leviathan: The Politics of the Bitcoin Blockchain. E-International Relations, June 2014
9. Böhme, R., Christin, N., Edelman, B., Moore, T.: Bitcoin: economics, technology, and governance. J. Econ. Perspect. **29**(2), 213–238 (2015)
10. Wright, A., De Filippi, P.: Decentralized Blockchain Technology and the Rise of Lex Cryptographia, March 2015
11. Guarino, N., Oberle, D., Staab, S.: What is an ontology? In: Staab, S., Studer, R. (eds.) Handbook on Ontologies. IHIS, pp. 1–17. Springer, Heidelberg (2009). doi:10.1007/978-3-540-92673-3_0
12. Noy, N., McGuinness, D.: Ontology development 101: a guide to creating your first ontology. In: Semantic Web Working Symposium (2001)
13. Guarino, N.: Formal ontology and information system. In: Proceedings of FOIS (1998)
14. Andersson, B., et al.: Towards a reference ontology for business models. In: Embley, D.W., Olivé, A., Ram, S. (eds.) ER 2006. LNCS, vol. 4215, pp. 482–496. Springer, Heidelberg (2006). doi:10.1007/11901181_36
15. Dietz, J.: Enterprise Ontology. Springer, Berlin (2006)
16. Weigand, H., de Moor, A.: Argumentation semantics of communicative action. In: Aakhus, M., Lind, M. (eds.) Proceedings of the 9th International Working Conference on the Language-Action Perspective of Communication Modelling (LAP 2004), pp. 159–178 (2004)
17. Nuffel, D., Mulder, H., Kervel, S.: Enhancing the formal foundations of BPMN by enterprise ontology. In: Albani, A., Barjis, J., Dietz, J.L.G. (eds.) CIAO!/EOMAS-2009. LNBIP, vol. 34, pp. 115–129. Springer, Heidelberg (2009). doi:10.1007/978-3-642-01915-9_9
18. Den Haan, J.: Modeling an Organization using Enterprise Ontology, thesis TU Delft (2009)
19. Wang, Y., Albani, A., Barjis, J.: Transformation of DEMO metamodel into XML schema. In: Albani, A., Dietz, J.L.G., Verelst, J. (eds.) EEWC 2011. LNBIP, vol. 79, pp. 46–60. Springer, Heidelberg (2011). doi:10.1007/978-3-642-21058-7_4
20. Nandwani, K: Why Blockchain Matters (2016)
21. Mainelli, M., Smith, M.: Sharing ledgers for sharing economies: an exploration of mutual distributed ledgers (aka blockchain technology). J. Finan. Perspect.: FinTech **3**(3), 38–69 (2015)
22. Christidis, K., Devetsikiotis, M.: Blockchains and smart contracts for the internet of things. In: Special Section on the Plethora of Research in Internet of Things (IoT), 23 April 2016
23. Cranefield, S., Purvis, M.: UML as an Ontology Modelling Language, The Information Science: Discussion Paper Series, Number 99/01, January 1999
24. Lerner, S.: Drivechains, Sidechains and Hybrid 2-way peg Designs (2016)
25. Back, A., Corallo, M., Dashjr, L., Friedenbach, M., Maxwell, G., Miller, A., Poelstra, A., Timón, J., Wuille, P.: Enabling Blockchain Innovations with Pegged Sidechains (2014). https://blockstream.com/sidechains.pdf
26. Goldkuhl, G.: Information as action and communication. In: Dahlbom, B. (ed.) The Infological Equation, Essays in honour of Börje Langefors. Gothenburg Studies in Information Systems. Gothenburg University, Gothenburg (1995). (also: Linkoping Univ report LiTH-IDA-R-95-09)
27. UK Government Office for Science: Distributed Ledger Technology: Beyond the Blockchain (2015)

28. Szabo, N.: Formalizing and securing relationships on public networks. First Monday **2**(9) (1997)
29. Hunka, F., Zácek, J.: A new view of REA state machine. Appl. Ontol. **10**(1), 25–39 (2015)
30. McCarthy, W.: The REA accounting model: a generalized framework for accounting systems in a shared data environment. Acc. Rev. **LVII**(3), 554–578 (1982)

Accommodating Openness Requirements in Software Platforms: A Goal-Oriented Approach

Mahsa H. Sadi[1(✉)] and Eric Yu[1,2]

[1] Department of Computer Science, University of Toronto, Toronto, Canada
{mhsadi, eric}@cs.toronto.edu
[2] Faculty of Information, University of Toronto, Toronto, Canada

Abstract. Open innovation is becoming an important strategy in software development. Following this strategy, software companies are increasingly opening up their platforms to third-party products. However, opening up software platforms to third-party applications raises serious concerns about critical quality requirements, such as security, performance, privacy and proprietary ownership. Adopting appropriate openness design strategies, which fulfill open-innovation objectives while maintaining quality requirements, calls for deliberate analysis of openness requirements from early on in opening up software platforms. We propose to treat openness as a distinct class of non-functional requirements, and to refine and analyze it in parallel with other design concerns using a goal-oriented approach. We extend the Non-Functional Requirements (NFR) analysis method with a new set of catalogues for specifying and refining openness requirements in software platforms. We apply our approach to revisit the design of data provision service in two real-world open software platforms and discuss the results.

Keywords: Ecosystems · Open platforms · Software design · Requirements

1 Introduction

Open innovation is becoming an increasingly important strategy in software development. Following this strategy, software development organizations open up their processes and software platforms to external developers in order to use external ideas, knowledge and paths to markets (as well as the internal ones) to advance their technology [1]. External developers become part of a software ecosystem offering complementary products and services for the open platforms [2–5].

However, opening up software platforms to third-party products is recognized as one of the most difficult transitions in software product development. While openness has the potential to create momentum for the widespread adoption and support of the platform in the market, it may lead to losing overall control of the platform [2]. Moreover, opening up platforms to third-party applications raises serious concerns about critical quality requirements, such as security, performance, proprietary ownership of the platform and its complementary applications. Yet, there is no systematic method to address these concerns in opening up platforms.

E. Dubois and K. Pohl (Eds.): CAiSE 2017, LNCS 10253, pp. 44–59, 2017.
DOI: 10.1007/978-3-319-59536-8_4

A successful transition to an open platform relies on adopting openness design strategies that can fulfill open innovation objectives while preserving the quality of the platform and complementary applications and services. Adopting such balanced design strategies calls for deliberate analysis of the requirements that openness introduces on the design of software platforms from early on in the transition process. Nevertheless, openness is only one design concern among many that should be accommodated in software platforms. Effective openness design strategies should optimally fulfill all of these concerns.

Example. Consider a common design scenario in opening up software platforms: *providing data service to third-party applications*. The design includes decisions about how a platform communicates data with third-party applications and how third-party applications communicate data with each other. Three design alternatives can be considered for opening up platform data to third-party applications; namely: (1) *Centralized data provision (CDP)*: Platform centrally checks every data communications between third-party applications; (2) *Semi-centralized data provision (SDP)*: A mediator (either the platform or the end-user) decides whether and under what conditions third-party applications can communicate directly; and (3) *Decentralized data provision (DDP)*: Third-party applications communicate data directly without any central control.

To choose an appropriate design strategy to open up platform data, *performance* can be a critical concern for a specific platform. Considering this, *centralized data provision* is not an appropriate design since central data control imposes additional load on the platform and increases data access time for third-party applications. *Data integrity* can be another requirement for the platform. In this regard, *centralized data provision* performs well since every data operation is performed under direct control of the platform, helping eliminate inconsistencies in simultaneous data read and write operations. Comparably, *semi-centralized data provision* also works well enough if platform is the mediator and if the platform decides to control critical data operations itself. *Decoupling third-party applications* is also important for the *open* platform since with the increase of third-party applications, it will be difficult to maintain the platform and prevent potential erroneous and malicious data communications. Considering this, *centralized data provision* is the most effective design since it minimizes the coupling of third-party applications. *Increasing adoptability of the platform* among external developers can be one main reason for opening up the platform. However, *centralized data provision* creates "*accessibility*" barriers for the platform since third-party applications should be checked and permitted by the platform to be installed and access their required run-time data. This difficulty negatively impacts the platform adoptability.

To choose the most appropriate openness design strategy, systematic methods are required that help decide between these competing and interacting requirements.

Contributions. We propose to treat openness as a distinct class of non-functional requirements, and to refine and analyze it in parallel with other concerns in designing software platforms using a goal-oriented requirements modeling language [6]. The proposed approach allows to specify and refine the business requirements behind openness, the technical quality requirements that openness imposes on the design of software platforms, and the concerns that openness introduces on other quality requirements. The refined requirements are used as criteria for selecting optimal design alternatives. To facilitate specification and analysis of openness requirements, we propose three types of catalogues: (1) *Openness requirements specification and refinement catalogues*; (2) *Openness operationalization catalogues*; and (3) *Openness correlation catalogues*. The catalogues encode alternative paths for refining and operationalizing openness requirements, which can be customized for a particular design context. We apply our proposed approach to revisit the design of data provision service in two real-world open software platforms and discuss the results.

2 The Proposed Approach

We consider openness as a concern that should be met in the design of platforms functionalities [7]. We describe openness as a soft goal (i.e. an objective that can be fulfilled to various degrees) and refine it using contribution links. We assess the fulfillment degree of openness requirements in alternative design mechanisms using the goal-oriented forward evaluation procedure [6].

To deal with openness requirements, we customize the Non-Functional Requirements (NFR) analysis method [6]. The customized approach is comprised of seven main steps, which can be performed iteratively: **(1)** Specifying and refining openness requirements; **(2)** Specifying and refining other design concerns; **(3)** Prioritizing the requirements; **(4)** Identifying possible alternative operationalizations; **(5)** Evaluating fulfillment degree of the identified requirements in each operationalization; **(6)** Analyzing potential trade-offs; and **(7)** Selecting an appropriate design mechanism.

To facilitate specification and analysis of openness as a class of non-functional requirements, we extend NFR with a new set of catalogues, namely *openness catalogues*. Openness catalogues are of three main types: **(1)** *Openness requirements specification and refinement catalogues*; **(2)** *Openness requirements operationalization catalogues*; and **(3)** *Openness correlation catalogues*. These catalogues are used in the related steps described above, and provide extensible and customizable patterns for specifying, refining and operationalizing openness requirements in the design of software platforms.

In the following, we present instances from each type of the openness catalogues. To save space, we omit the details about the complete definition and refinement of the items in the presented catalogues, and the sources from which the items are extracted.

Openness Requirements Specification and Refinement Catalogues. These catalogues help characterize and refine the specific requirements and concerns that openness introduces on the design of software platforms. Openness requirements catalogues are of three types: **(1)** *Business-level openness requirements catalogues*. **(2)** *System-level openness requirements catalogues*; and **(3)** *General design concerns catalogues*.

System-Level Openness Requirements Catalogues. These catalogues characterize general technical and quality requirements that should be met in the design of open platforms. Three instances of system-level openness requirements catalogues are shown in Fig. 1. For example, the first catalogue (Fig. 1a) identifies that openness introduces seven types of requirements on the design of software platforms, including "*accessibility*" and "*extensibility*". From this catalogue, requirements specification paths can be generated, such as: "*To open up a platform, the platform needs to be accessible to third-party applications*", or "*To open up a platform, the platform design needs to be extensible*". The second catalogue (Fig. 1b) identifies that "*accessibility*" requirement can be refined in four ways, including "*accessibility [functionality or service]*" and "*accessibility [data]*". From this catalogue, more detailed requirements specifications can be generated, such as "*To open up a platform, platform data need to be accessible to third-party applications*". The third catalogue (Fig. 1c) identifies that "*extensibility*" requirement introduces six types of requirements on a platform design, including "*composability [Platform]*" and "*deployability [Third-party applications]*", each of which needs to be further refined into more fine-grained requirements. From this catalogues, refinement paths can be generated such as "*To make a platform design extensible, the platform needs to be composable*", and subsequently "*To make a platform composable, third-party applications should be decoupled from the platform and from each other*".

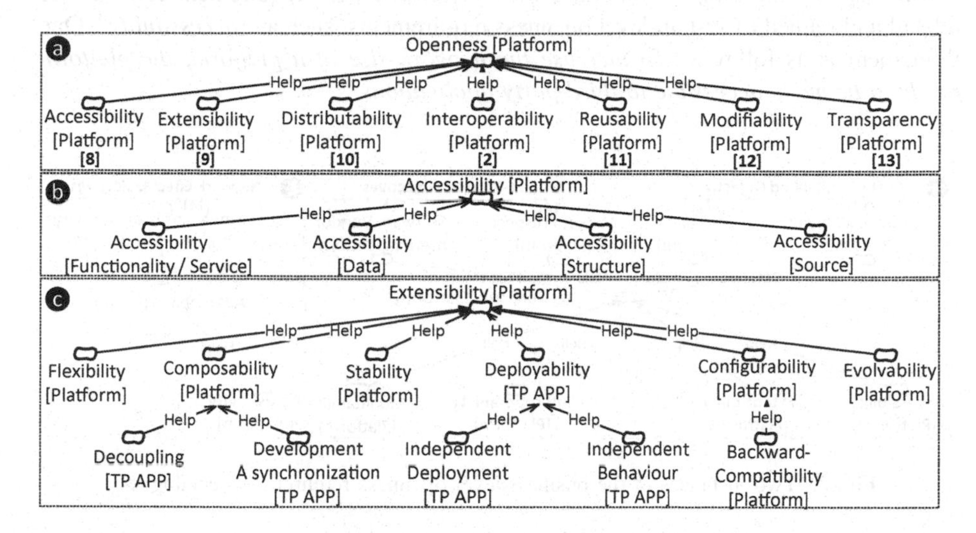

Fig. 1. Three instances of the system-level openness requirements catalogues

To develop system-level openness requirements catalogues, two steps are performed: (1) The content of the catalogues is extracted from the Software Engineering literature discussing technical requirements in open software platforms. (2) The requirements are classified, related, and refined using two types of non-functional requirement refinement [6]: topic refinement (e.g. "*Accessibility*" catalogue) and type refinement (e.g. "*Openness*" and "*Extensibility*" catalogues). To structure the content, related elements of the goal-oriented requirements modeling language are used. "*Soft goal*" element is used to represent non-functional requirements, and "*Help*" contribution link is used to relate and refine the requirements.

Business-Level Openness Requirements Catalogues. These catalogues characterize general non-technical requirements in open software platforms and relate them to system-level openness requirements. Non-technical requirements include the business and organizational incentives that drive the need for openness as well as the social requirements that should be met in open software platforms. Each business-level openness requirements catalogue has two parts: a set of non-technical requirements and the related technical requirements. Two instances of these catalogues are depicted in Fig. 2. For example, the first catalogue (Fig. 2a) identifies that "*Stickiness*" and "*Market Presence*" are two non-technical requirements in open software platforms. Stickiness refers to the degree that a software platform supports its continued use by a user instead of switching to a competitor platform [14]. "*Stickiness*" can be further related to more fine-grained business requirements such as "*Network size*". Network size refers to the number of complementary application and services that support a platform [15]. From this catalogue, specifications and refinement paths can be generated, such as "*One objective in opening up a software platform is to increase the stickiness of the platform.*", and then "*To increase the stickiness of a platform, the network size of the platform should grow.*" "*Network size*" requirement can then be related and refined to system-level openness requirements, such as "*accessibility*". One refinement is as follows: "*To increase the network size of a platform, the platform needs to be made accessible to third-party applications.*"

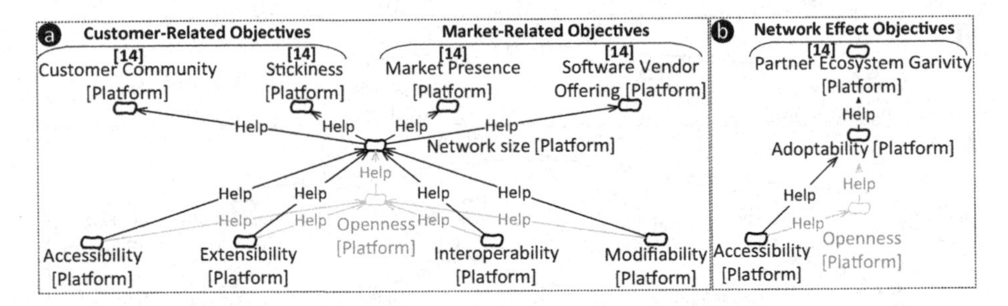

Fig. 2. Two instances of the business-level openness requirements catalogues

To develop business-level openness catalogues, three steps are taken: (1) The content of the catalogues is extracted from a set of Business and Software Engineering literature discussing open innovation, and the business, organizational, and social needs that it introduces on the development of software platforms. (2) The requirements are described using soft goals, and categorized, related and refined using "*help*" contribution links. Since business-level openness requirements are often described as openness business objectives, the notion of soft goal is conceptually close for describing these requirements. (3) The last row of refinement in each business-level openness catalogue is related to a set of first-row refinements in the system-level openness requirements (i.e. Figure 1a) using "*help*" contribution links. Contribution links allow to smoothly refine and relate the business-level requirements into the system-level requirements.

General Design Concerns Catalogues. These catalogues characterize general concerns and requirements raised in opening up software platforms. These concerns may have synergistic or conflicting relationships with openness requirements, and need to be refined and operationalized in parallel with openness requirements in designing software platforms. Two instances of this group are shown in Fig. 3. For example, the first catalogue (Fig. 3a) identifies "*security*" as a general concern in opening up software platforms and also characterizes the specific types of security requirements (such as "*integrity*" and "*availability*") that are potentially impacted by openness requirements. From this catalogue, specifications can be generated, such as "*Security needs to be assured in opening up a platform*". Then this requirement can be further refined as follows: "*To assure platform security, integrity of the platform data should be preserved.*"

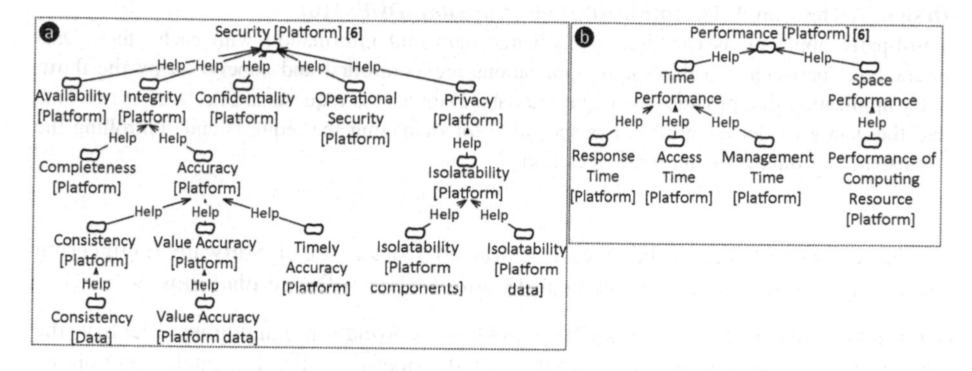

Fig. 3. Two instances of the general design concerns catalogues

The content of this group of catalogues is extracted from a set of Software Engineering and Business literature discussing problems, concerns, and requirements in opening up software platforms. The content is then structured similar to the previous catalogues. Some requirements in this group, such as security and performance overlap with existing NFR catalogues [6]. The existing catalogues have been reused and customized according to the specific context of open software platforms.

Openness Requirements Operationalization Catalogues. Operationalization catalogues identify the system functionalities that should be specifically designed to open up platforms to third-party products. They also enumerate alternative mechanisms and patterns for designing these functional requirements. Each openness operationalization catalogue has two parts: (a) *Design objectives*: the specific functionality that need to designed or implemented; and (b) *Design alternatives*: Alternative mechanisms to realize the design objective. An instance of the openness operationalization catalogues is illustrated in Table 1. The catalogue is related to the design of "*Data provision and communications service*". The catalogue elaborates on three generic alternative mechanisms for designing this functionality, namely: (1) *Centralized data provision*; (2) *Semi-centralized data provision*; (3) *Decentralized data provision*.

Table 1. One instance of the openness requirements operationalization catalogues

Design Objective: To provide data service to third-party applications
Design Mechanism 1: Centralized Data Provision (CDP) [16] The platform controls every data and information interactions between third-party applications and the platform, and between one third-party application and another. In this design, all data is stored and exchanged through a single API in the platform. Data is accessed through the platform API either by explicit get/set operations or publish/subscribe at run-time. An API identifies available data at run-time.
Design Mechanism 2: Semi-Centralized Data Provision (SDP) [17] Third-party applications can communicate data directly in some cases. Third-party applications declare what data they need at install-time. The requests are initially submitted to a mediator (i.e. end-user or platform). The mediator decides to allow data communications directly or not. If yes, third-party applications can communicate directly. If no, the mediator decides to control data read operations, data write operations or both.
Design Mechanism 3: Decentralized Data Provision (DDP) [10] Third-party applications can directly exchange data and information with each other. Data interactions between two third-party applications are controlled and supervised by the third-party application that provides the requested data. Data access requests are declared at run-time and the data provider application is responsible for managing the requests and controlling the consistency of data read and write operations.

The content of these catalogues is extracted from a set of Software Engineering research resources discussing technical design of open software platforms.

Openness Correlation Catalogues. Openness correlation catalogues identify the impact of each openness design alternative (in the operationalization catalogues) on the fulfillment of the related openness requirements (in the specification and refinement catalogues). An instance of a correlation catalogue is shown in Fig. 4. For example, one *security* concern in designing data provision service can be data integrity ("*Integrity [platform data]*"). This requirement can be further decomposed into "*accuracy [data]*" and then "*consistency [data]*". The presented catalogue identifies that "*centralized data provision*" design alternative meets the requirement of data consistency. In contrast, the other two alternatives of "*semi-centralized data provision*" and "*decentralized data provision*" violate this requirement. Another requirement that may be important in opening up a platform is "*accessibility [platform]*", which can be further refined into "*accessibility [data]*". The catalogue identifies that "*centralized data provision*" has a negative impact on the accessibility of platform data. In contrast, the other two alternatives have a positive impact on this requirement.

To develop correlation catalogues, two steps are performed: (1) The related requirements that are affected by each alternative operationalization are selected from the requirement refinement catalogues. (2) The positive or negative impact of the alternative on fulfilling the related alternatives is assessed. The assessment is done based on expert knowledge from the design alternatives and must be accompanied by a sound reasoning or evidence. The alternative mechanisms are assessed against the last row of refinement for each related requirement, and are described using "*help*" or "*hurt*" contribution links. A detailed example of an assessment is provided in [7].

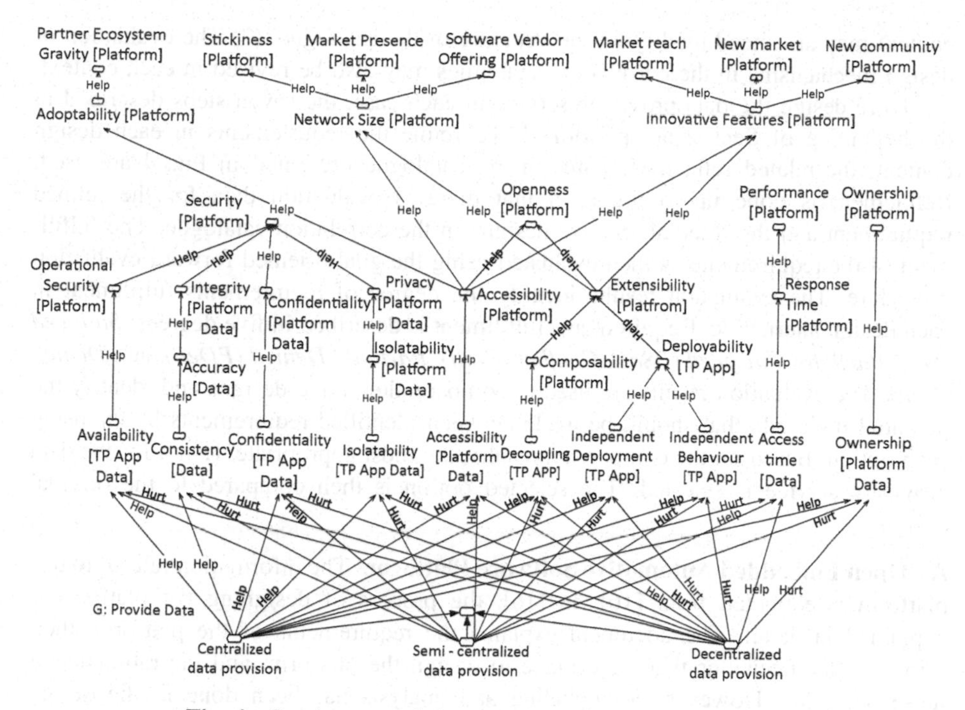

Fig. 4. One instance of the openness correlation catalogues

3 Application of the Proposed Approach

We use the proposed approach to revisit the high-level architectural design of data provision service in two real-world open software platforms. Both platforms are embedded operating systems. The first platform is an operating system controlling the electronic units of a vehicle and the second one is an operating system for smartphone devices.

To apply the proposed approach on each design case, two preparatory steps have been taken: (1) The documents containing information about the design of each platform have been collected from the literature. (2) The information required for applying the proposed approach has been extracted from the collected documents. The extracted information is of two types: (a) the important design requirements for each case; i.e. the requirements that openness introduces and other general concerns that should be considered in opening up each platform; and (b) the priority of each design requirement. Where the required information was absent or not explicitly mentioned, we have augmented the information based on our own understanding from the case. Augmented information is distinguished from the extracted information using "*".

To use the catalogues, two preparatory steps need to be performed. (1) The domain requirements are matched with the requirements items available in the catalogues. If the wording of a requirement is different, the most similar requirement item in the catalogues is selected. If no similar item is found, the correct placement of the requirement is found and the related catalogue is augmented with new the content. Adding new content may also need modifying the structure of the catalogue. (2) The evaluation of design mechanisms in the correlation catalogues may also be revised in each context.

To re-design the data provision service in each case, the seven steps described in the beginning of Sect. 2 are performed. To refine the requirements in each design context, the related refinement paths in the catalogue presented in Fig. 4 are used. Refinement is done up to the level that there is evaluation data for the refined requirement and the three alternative designs in the correlation catalogue. The fulfillment of the requirements is then evaluated using the goal-oriented forward evaluation procedure. The evaluation results identify the degree of requirements fulfillment in each design alternative. Requirements fulfillment is described in five degrees: *Satificed (Sat), Partially Satisficed (PSat), Conflict (Conf), Partially Denied (PDen),* and *Denied (Den).* The evaluation results are used to compare alternative designs and identify the potential trade-offs that should be made between identified requirements by choosing each option. Based on the comparison results, the most appropriate design for the data provision service is selected. The selected option is then compared to the original design.

An Open Embedded Automotive Software Platform. The information related to this platform is extracted from [16]. In [16], the process of designing the platform is explained in detail. The document explains the requirements of the platform, their priorities, the decisions that were made to design the platform, and the rationale for those decisions. However, no modeling and analysis has been done in the design process. All the information required for our analysis was available in the document.

The platform is an operating system sitting on top of the electronic hardware of a vehicle to control the vehicle electronic units. The platform has to deal with safety critical functionalities and data. Thus it should be highly dependable. The platform has been opened to different types of third-party applications, such as applications developed by certified developers and applications developed by undirected developers. Third-party applications sit on top of the platform and add functionality to it. Examples of these additional functionalities include: automatic control of the speed of the vehicle or displaying the speed of the vehicle in the display. To perform such operations, third-party applications may need read or write access to data (such as speed and lateral acceleration data), controlled by the platform or other third-party applications.

The important design requirements of the platform and their priorities are described in Table 2. The related paths in the catalogue of Fig. 4 that help specify and refine the requirements as well as their fulfillment in each alternative design are shown in Fig. 5.

Table 3 summarizes the fulfillment of key requirements in each design alternative. As shown, "*centralized data provision*" outperforms the other two alternatives in fulfilling all the requirements except performance. In contrast, the other two alternatives partially satisfice performance. However, "*semi-centralized data provision*" violates two openness requirements of "*composability*" and "*deployability*", and "*decentralized data provision*" underperforms in the fulfillment of all the other requirements.

Although "*centralized data provision*" fulfills four of the five important design requirements and achieves the highest rank among the three alternatives, it has negative impact on the performance of the platform. Centralized control over all data

Table 2. Design requirements for the open embbedded automotive platform

Design requirements	Text description
Openness requirements	
Type: *"Composability"* Priority: *"High"*	"The software platform must fulfil a set of properties *to allow the* ***decoupling of applications*** and ***eliminate*** *the need for* ***development synchronization***. The architecture should allow development, integration and validation of applications independent of other applications. Non-technical users cannot do this themselves, it must be provided for by application and/or platform developers."
Type: *"Deployability"* Priority: *"High"*	"The applications must be possible *to* ***be deployed independently*** *of each other*, and the ***product behavior must not depend on the order in which applications are installed***. There must also be a deployment infrastructure in place which fulfils necessary integrity requirements."
General design concerns	
Type: *"Dependability"* Priority: *"High"*	"Many embedded domains have *stringent dependability requirements*; i.e. ***real-time requirements*** *for the execution of individual applications*, ***integrity requirements***, ***high availability***, and *mechanisms to* ***eliminate*** *undesired* ***feature interaction*** if several applications interact with the same actuators."

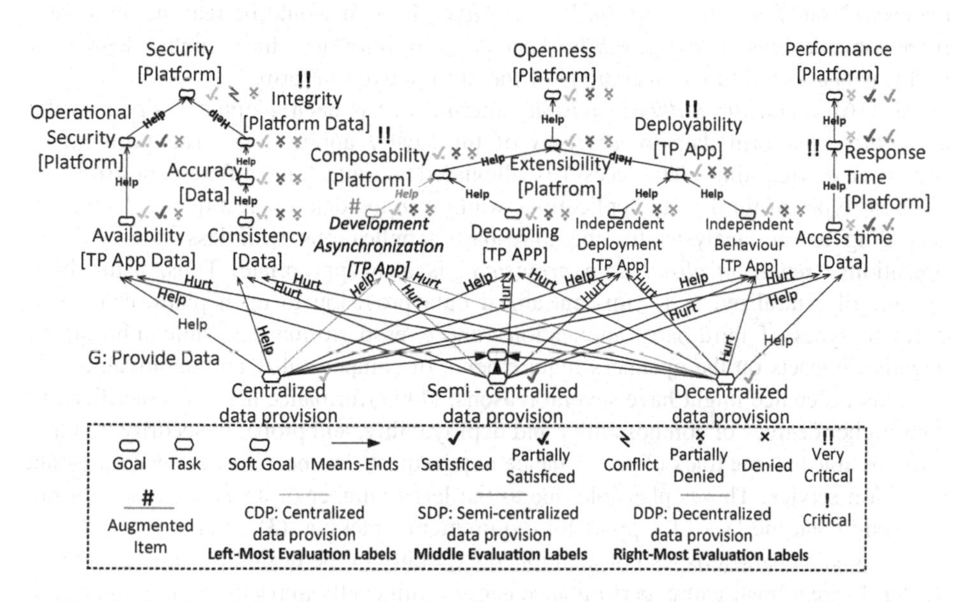

Fig. 5. Specification, refinement, and evaluation of the important design requirements

interactions creates a bottleneck in the platform. In case of several simultaneous data read and write requests, this design creates a queue of requests that should be checked by the platform and increases the waiting time of data operations. However, the automotive platform is in charge of safety-critical and real-time operations. Considering this, performance is not a negligible requirement.

Table 3. Fullfillment of the important requirements in design alternatives for data provision

Requirements	Security		Openness		Performance
	OS	IY	CP	DP	RT
Priority	H	H	H	H	H
CDP	PSat	PSat	PSat	PSat	PDen
SDP	PSat	PDen	PDen	PDen	PSat
DDP	PDen	PDen	PDen	PDen	PSat

OS: Operational Security [Platform]; **IY**: Integrity [Platform Data]; **CP**: Composability [TP Application]; **DP**: Deployability [TP Application]; **RT**: Response Time [Platform]; **H**: High (Very Critical)

In comparison, "*semi-centralized data provision*", though violating two openness requirements of "*composability*" and "*deployability*", alleviates the load of platform by delegating the control of *some* data interactions to the related third-party applications. Since critical third-party applications are developed by certified developers, the platform can easily decide to control which data operations, delegating the control of less critical data interactions to the related third-party applications. Considering this, semi-centralized control does not negatively impact the integrity and security of the platform data. Accordingly, we assess the final impact of "*semi-centralized data provision*" on "*Security [Platform]*" as positive. Thus, it would be reasonable to sacrifice some degrees of "*composability*" and "*deployablity*" to achieve higher degrees of performance for real-time operations of the automotive platform.

In [16], "*centralized data provision*" alternative has been adopted to open up the automotive platform data to *all types* of third-party applications. The problem of performance (real-time data access) is alleviated via attaching different priorities to different types of third-party applications waiting in the data request queue. However, according to our analysis, for the third-party applications with less safety-critical operations "*semi-centralized data provision*" is also appropriate. Thus, using both options of centralized and semi-centralized data provision to open platform data to different types of third-party applications improves performance, while minimizing negative impacts on the openness requirements of composability and deployability.

This difference might have several reasons: (1) Performance has been sacrificed to gain higher degrees of composability and deployability, and probably security. (2) It is also possible that the track of performance requirements has been lost in designing data provision service. This is plausible due to the large number of decisions made during the design and the lack of support for requirements tracking. (3) Alternatively, due to some domain characteristics not mentioned explicitly in the design document, such as the hardware infrastructure, performance is not significantly impacted by the bottleneck of centralized data provision.

An Open Embedded Mobile Operating System Platform. Different pieces of information related to the design of the mobile platform have been collected from [2, 15, 17]. Some requirements and priorities have been added based on our understanding from the context, which are distinguished by "*".

The platform is an operating system sitting on top of the hardware device of a smartphone to control its functionalities. The platform hosts native and non-native applications. Third-party applications add a wide range of functionalities that could be of potential interest to various mobile users. Development of mobile applications is highly knowledge-intensive. Thus, mobile application development is usually open to a wide range of third-party developers. Third-party applications may need read or write access to platform data or the data generated by other third-party applications.

The requirements of the mobile platform and their priorities are described in Table 4. The related specification and refinement paths from the catalogue of Fig. 4 and the fulfillment degree of the requirements in each design alternative are shown in Fig. 6.

Table 5 summarizes the fulfillment of the identified requirements in each design alternative. As shown, "*centralized data provision*" underperforms in fulfilling all the *high-priority* requirements, namely "*accessibility*", "*adoptability*", "*partner ecosystem gravity*", "*innovative features*", and "*performance*". Interestingly, this alternative outperforms in fulfilling *medium-priority* requirements, such as "*composability*", "*deployability*" and "*ownership*". In contrast, the other two design alternatives equally satisfice *high-priority* design requirements. However, "*semi-centralized data provision*" performs better in fulfilling "*privacy [data]*" requirement.

Table 4. Design requirements for the open mobile platform

Design requirements	Text description
Openness requirements	
Type: *"Innovative Products"* Priority: *"High"*	"In many knowledge intensive domains, users and external parties play an ***important*** role in ***developing innovative products***. The mobile operating system providers benefit from emerging external innovations because ***having a high number of applications*** increases *the* ***attractiveness*** *of the platform for* ***potential customers***. Having large number of customers lead to a bigger market share in the mobile application market." [15]
Type: *"Partner Ecosystem Gravity"* Priority: *"High"*	"Third-party developers have to be considered as ***important*** players in the mobile ecosystems. While not every application can be considered innovative, ***a larger pool of developers will provide more innovative output***. The ***network size of developers and end users*** *(i.e. network effects)* will be a significant factor for application developers in selecting which mobile ecosystem to join." [15]
Type: *"Low Entry Barriers"* (Accessibility) Priority: *"High"*	"***Entry barriers of*** *both monetary and* ***technical nature****, including entry barriers for application market, development resource needs and programing languages*, will be ***a significant factor*** for developers in selecting which mobile platform to join. Openness and entry barriers include aspects of hardware, software and market in open platforms." [15]

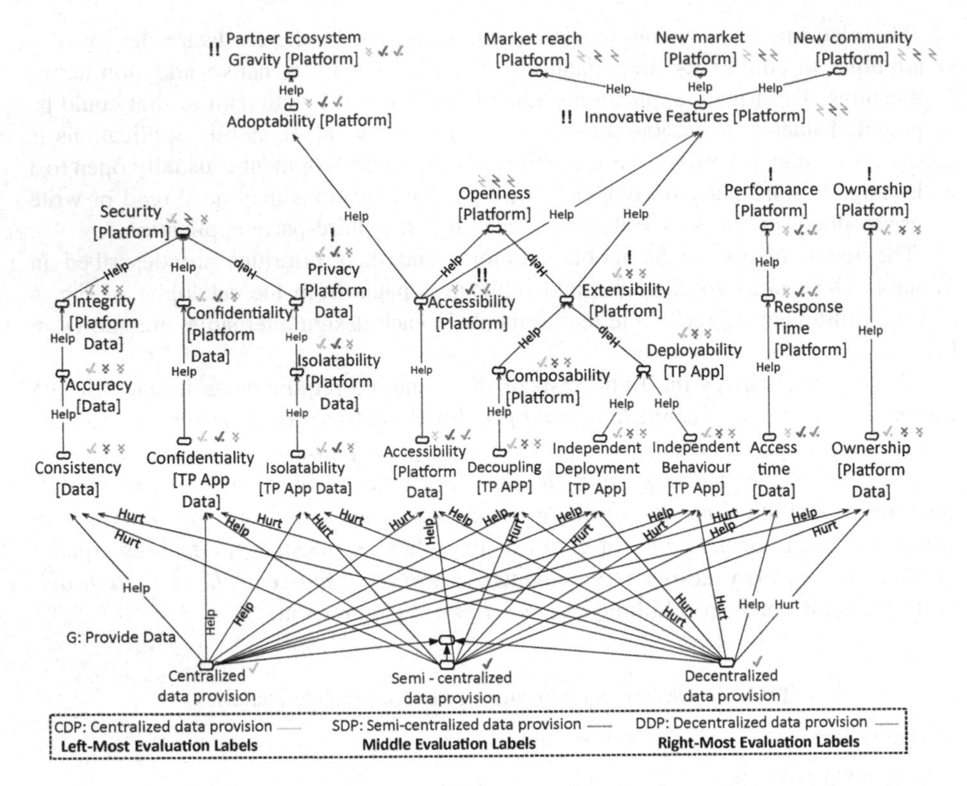

Fig. 6. Specification, refinement, and evaluation of the important design requirements

Table 5. Fullfillment of the important requirements in design alternatives for data provision

Requirements	Security	Openness: system-level			Openness: business-level		Performance	Ownership
	*PV	AC	*CP	*DP	PEG	ICF	*PR	* OW
Priority	*M	H	*M	*M	H	H	*H	*M
CDP	PSat	PDen	PSat	PSat	PDen	^ Conf → PDen	PDen	PSat
SDP	PSat	PSat	PDen	PDen	PSat	^ Conf → PSat	PSat	PDen
DDP	PDen	PSat	PDen	PDen	PSat	^ Conf → PSat	PSat	PDen

PV: Privacy [Platform Data]; **AC**: Accessibility [Platform]; **CP**: Composability [Plat]; **DP**: Deployability [TP App]; **PEG**: Partner Ecosystem Gravity [Platform]; **ICF**: Innovative and Complementary Features; **PR**: Performance; **OW**: Ownership; **H**: High (Very Critical); **M**: Medium (Critical); ^: Conflict is resolved to partially denied or partially satisficed.

Although "*semi-centralized data provision*" satisfices all the high-priority requirements and achieves the highest score from among the three design alternatives, its implementation has negative impact on two *openness* requirements of "*composability*" and "*deployability*". It also violates "*data ownership*" requirement. Nevertheless, composability and deployability are two important technical quality attributes for an open platform. Decoupling third-party applications from each other and reducing their dependencies plays an important role in the maintainability and controllability of the platform. Specifically when the size of a platform and its complementary applications and services grow, which is usually the case for an open mobile platform. Moreover, the ownership of platform data is not a negligible requirement for a platform owner.

However, "*accessibility*" and the impact it has on the "*adoptability*" and '*innovative features*" is strategically critical to the success of a mobile platform in the market, specifically in a fierce competition with other platforms. Thus, it would be reasonable to sacrifice some degrees of the *system-level openness requirements* to gain more support from innovative and complementary applications (the *business-level openness requirements*), specifically in a knowledge-intensive domain as mobile applications.

The result of our analysis indicates that "*semi-centralized data provision*" is the best option from among the three alternatives to open up mobile platform data to third-party applications. This result is consistent with real-world implementation of open mobile platforms such as Android [17]. In Android, third-party applications declare the data they require from the platform and other third-party applications at install time. The access is permitted by the end user (i.e. end user is the mediator).

4 Discussion

Our goal was to provide a method to determine appropriate design strategies for opening up software platforms to third-party applications. We proposed to treat openness as a non-functional requirement and to use a goal-oriented approach to refine and analyze openness in parallel with other requirements. The refined requirements are used to select optimal design options. We have developed a set of catalogues that facilitate reasoning about openness requirements.

We applied the proposed approach to revisit the design of data provision service in two real-world open software platforms: an automotive platform and a mobile platform. Our goal was to determine the most appropriate openness design strategy for each case. In the first case, our analysis identifies that a combination of centralized and semi-centralized data provision can be used to open up the platform data to different types of third-party applications. This result is slightly different from the original design of the platform, which is only centralized data provision. We aim to discuss the results of our analysis with the original designers in a future interview. In the second case, our results are consistent with the design of open mobile platforms, such as Android. The analysis justifies the accessibility of mobile platforms to external applications. Moreover, the analysis shows that system-level openness requirements can be sacrificed to fulfill business-level openness requirements. Finally, in both cases there is no design option that can fulfill all the identified requirements. In each case, trade-offs should be made. Therefore, it is crucial to detect and analyze the trade-off points.

The proposed approach allows to reason about openness as a distinct requirement. This approach complements recent research efforts on the development of open software platforms, which either focus on the technical design of the platforms, including API development (e.g. [9, 13, 18]) or on the business aspect (e.g. [2, 19]).

This paper presents only one instance of a complete openness correlation catalogue that we have developed. The complete definition and refinement of the requirements and operationalizations in the presented catalogues in addition to other catalogues will be published in a future work.

To improve the applicability of the proposed approach, three issues need to be further addressed: (1) The catalogues and the models developed for a specific domain become complex too quickly. To handle this complexity, automated support is required. (2) The evaluation procedure to select optimal design strategies needs to be made efficient via omitting exhaustive evaluations of all the options. (3) The evaluation procedure should allow to assess the final impact of selecting multiple operationalizations on the fulfillment of the identified requirements in a design process.

Further research is needed to extend and validate the content of the proposed catalogues and to compare the proposed approach with peer requirements analysis methods for software systems, such as Architecture Trade-Off Analysis Method (ATAM) [20].

5 Conclusion

We proposed a goal-oriented approach for analyzing openness requirement in software platforms. The proposed approach is supported by a set of catalogues that facilitate specification and refinement of openness requirements. We presented instances of these catalogues herein. Specification and analysis of requirements is essential for adopting effective openness design strategies that are "*open enough*" to benefit from the contributions of third-party applications and at the same time possess the quality of "*closed*" systems. Adopting such balanced strategies is crucial for the viability and sustainability of open platforms. Further research is needed to assess the effectiveness of the proposed approach and catalogues in case studies of open platform projects.

References

1. Chesbrough, H.W.: Open Innovation: The New Imperative for Creating and Profiting from Technology. Harvard Business Press, Boston (2006)
2. Boudreau, K.: Open platform strategies and innovation: Granting access vs. de-volving control. Manag. Sci. **56**(10), 1849–1872 (2010)
3. West, J.: How open is open enough? Melding proprietary and open source platform strategies. Res. Policy **32**(7), 1259–1285 (2003)
4. Jansen, S., Brinkkemper, S., Souer, J., Luinenburg, L.: Shades of gray: opening up a software producing organization with the open software enterprise model. J. Syst. Softw. **85** (7), 1495–1510 (2012)
5. Sadi, M.H., Yu, E.: Analyzing the evolution of software development: from creative chaos to software ecosystems. In: IEEE Eighth International Conference on Research Challenges in Information Science (RCIS), pp. (1–11) (2014)

6. Chung, L., Nixon, B.A., Yu, E., Mylopoulos, J.: Non-functional Requirements in Software Engineering, vol. 5. Springer Science & Business Media, Heidelberg (2012)
7. Sadi, M.H., Yu, E.: Modeling and analyzing openness trade-offs in software platforms: a goal-oriented approach. In: International Working Conference on Requirements Engineering: Foundation for Software Quality, pp. 33–49 (2017)
8. Anvaari, M., Jansen, S.: Evaluating architectural openness in mobile software platforms. In: Proceedings of the Fourth European Conference on Software Architecture: Companion Volume, pp. 85–92 (2010)
9. Bosch, J., Bosch-Sijtsema, P.: From integration to composition: on the impact of software product lines, global development and ecosystems. J. Syst. Softw. **83**(1), 67–76 (2010)
10. Scacchi, W.: Free/open source software development: recent research results and methods. Adv. Comput. **69**, 243–295 (2007)
11. Bosch, J.: Architecture challenges for software ecosystems. In: Proceedings of the Fourth European Conference on Software Architecture: Companion Volume, pp. 93–95 (2010)
12. Baresi, L., Di Nitto, E., Ghezzi, C.: Toward open-world software: issue and challenges. Computer **39**(10), 36–43 (2006)
13. Cataldo, M., Herbsleb, J.D.: Architecting in software ecosystems: interface translucence as an enabler for scalable collaboration. In: Proceedings of the Fourth European Conference on Software Architecture: Companion Volume, pp. 65–72 (2010)
14. Popp, K.M.: Goals of software vendors for partner ecosystems–a practitioner's view. In: Software Business, pp. 181–186 (2010)
15. Koch, S., Kerschbaum, M.: Joining a smartphone ecosystem: application developers' motivations and decision criteria. Inf. Softw. Technol. **56**(11), 1423–1435 (2014)
16. Eklund, U., Bosch, J.: Architecture for embedded open software ecosystems. J. Syst. Softw. **92**, 128–142 (2014)
17. Shabtai, A., Fledel, Y., Kanonov, U., Elovici, Y., Dolev, S., Glezer, C.: Google android: a comprehensive security assessment. IEEE Secur. Priv. **2**, 35–44 (2010)
18. Christensen, H.B., Hansen, K.M., Kyng, M., Manikas, K.: Analysis and design of software ecosystem architectures–towards the 4S telemedicine ecosystem. Inf. Softw. Technol. **56** (11), 1476–1492 (2014)
19. Ghazawneh, A., Henfridsson, O.: Balancing platform control and external contribution in third-party development: the boundary resources model. Inf. Syst. J. **23**(2), 173–192 (2013)
20. Kazman, R., Klein, M., Barbacci, M., Longstaff, T., Lipson, H., Carriere, J.: The architecture tradeoff analysis method. In: Proceedings of Fourth IEEE International Conference on Engineering of Complex Computer Systems, ICECCS 1998, pp. 68–78 (1998)

Development of Mobile Data Collection Applications by Domain Experts: Experimental Results from a Usability Study

Johannes Schobel[1(✉)], Rüdiger Pryss[1], Winfried Schlee[2], Thomas Probst[1], Dominic Gebhardt[1], Marc Schickler[1], and Manfred Reichert[1]

[1] Institute of Databases and Information Systems, Ulm University, Ulm, Germany
{johannes.schobel,ruediger.pryss,thomas.probst,dominic.gebhardt, marc.schickler,manfred.reichert}@uni-ulm.de

[2] Department of Psychiatry and Psychotherapy, Regensburg University, Regensburg, Germany
winfried.schlee@gmail.com

Abstract. Despite their drawbacks, paper-based questionnaires are still used to collect data in many application domains. In the QuestionSys project, we develop an advanced framework that enables domain experts to transform paper-based instruments to mobile data collection applications, which then run on smart mobile devices. The framework empowers domain experts to develop robust mobile data collection applications on their own without the need to involve programmers. To realize this vision, a configurator component applying a model-driven approach is developed. As this component shall relieve domain experts from technical issues, it has to be proven that domain experts are actually able to use the configurator properly. The experiment presented in this paper investigates the mental efforts for creating such data collection applications by comparing novices and experts. Results reveal that even novices are able to model instruments with an acceptable number of errors. Altogether, the QuestionSys framework empowers domain experts to develop sophisticated mobile data collection applications by orders of magnitude faster compared to current mobile application development practices.

Keywords: Process-driven applications · End-user programming · Experimental results

1 Introduction

Self-report questionnaires are commonly used to collect data in healthcare, psychology, and social sciences [8]. Although existing technologies enable researchers to create questionnaires electronically, the latter are still distributed and filled out in a *paper-and-pencil* fashion. As opposed to paper-based approaches, electronic data collection applications enable full automation of data processing (e.g., transfering data to spreadsheets), saving time and costs, especially in the

E. Dubois and K. Pohl (Eds.): CAiSE 2017, LNCS 10253, pp. 60–75, 2017.
DOI: 10.1007/978-3-319-59536-8_5

context of large-scale studies (e.g., clinical trials). According to [15], approximately 50–60% of the data collection costs can be saved when using electronic instead of paper-based instruments. Besides this, the electronic instruments do not affect psychometric properties [5], while enabling a higher quality of the collected data [14]. In this context, [12] confirms that mobile data collection applications allow for more complete datasets compared to traditional paper-based ones. Additionally, the collected data can be directly stored and processed, whereas paper-based approaches require considerable manual efforts to digitize the data. Note that this bears the risk of errors and decreases data quality. In general, electronic questionnaires are increasingly demanded in the context of studies [11]. However, the development of mobile data collection applications with contemporary approaches requires considerable programming efforts. For example, platform-specific peculiarities (e.g., concerning user interfaces) need to be properly handled. Furthermore, profound insights into mobile data collection scenarios are needed. Especially, if more sophisticated features are required to guide inexperienced users through the process of data collection, hard-coded mobile applications become costly to maintain. Note that adapting already deployed and running mobile applications is challenging, as the consistency of the data collected needs to be ensured.

To relieve IT experts from these challenges and to give control back to domain experts, the *QuestionSys* framework is developed. The latter aims at supporting domain experts in collecting large amounts of data using smart mobile devices. QuestionSys offers a user-friendly configurator for creating flexible data collection instruments. More precisely, it relies on process management technology and end-user programming techniques. Particularly, it allows domain experts without any programming skills to graphically model electronic instruments as well as to deploy them to smart mobile devices. Furthermore, the framework provides a lightweight mobile process engine that executes the individually configured questionnaires on common smart mobile devices.

To demonstrate the feasibility and usability of the QuestionSys framework, this paper presents results from a controlled experiment evaluating the configurator component we implemented. For this purpose, subjects were asked to create data collection instruments. Altogether, the results indicate that domain experts are able to properly realize mobile data collection applications on their own using the configurator. The paper is structured as follows: In Sect. 2, fundamentals of the QuestionSys framework are introduced. Section 3 presents the conducted experiment, while Sect. 4 discusses experimental results. Related work is discussed in Sect. 5; Sect. 6 summarizes the paper.

2 Mobile Data Collection with QuestionSys

This section introduces the fundamental concepts of the QuestionSys framework. In particular, we focus on the configurator component, which will be evaluated in the presented experiment.

2.1 The QuestionSys Framework

The main goal of the QuestionSys framework is to enable domain experts (e.g., physicians, psychologists) that have no programming skills to develop sophisticated data collection instruments as well as to deploy and execute them on smart mobile devices. In particular, development costs shall be reduced, development time be fastened, and the quality of the collected data be increased. Moreover, changes of already running data collection applications shall be possible for domain experts themselves without the need to involve IT experts [21].

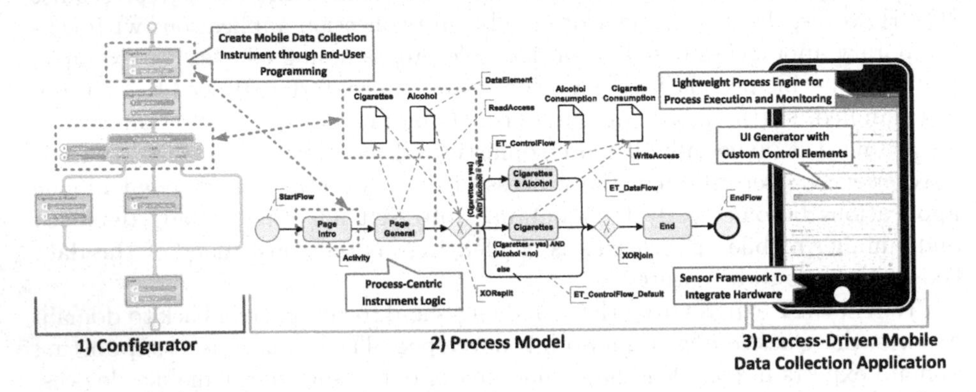

Fig. 1. The QuestionSys approach: (1) modeling a data collection instrument; (2) mapping it to an executable process model; (3) executing it on a smart mobile device.

In order to enable domain experts to develop flexible mobile applications themselves, a model-driven approach is introduced. This approach allows describing the logic of an instrument in terms of an *executable process model* (cf. Fig. 1). The latter can then be interpreted and executed by a lightweight process engine running on smart mobile devices [20]. By applying this approach, process logic and application code are separated [17]. The process model acts as a schema for creating and executing *process instances* (i.e., questionnaire instances). The process model itself consists of process activities as well as the control and data flow between them. Gateways (e.g., `XORsplit`) are used to describe more complex questionnaire logic. Following this model-driven approach, both the content and the logic of a paper-based instrument can be mapped to a process model. *Pages* of an instrument directly correspond to *process activities*; the *flow* between them, in turn, matches the *navigation logic* of the instruments. *Questions* are mapped to *process data elements*, which are connected to activities using `READ` or `WRITE` data edges. These data elements are used to store answers to various questions when executing the instrument on smart mobile devices. Altogether, QuestionSys applies fundamental BPM principles in a broader context, thus enabling novel perspectives for process-related technologies.

To properly support domain experts, the QuestionSys framework considers the entire *Mobile Data Collection Lifecycle* (cf. Fig. 2). The *Design & Modeling*

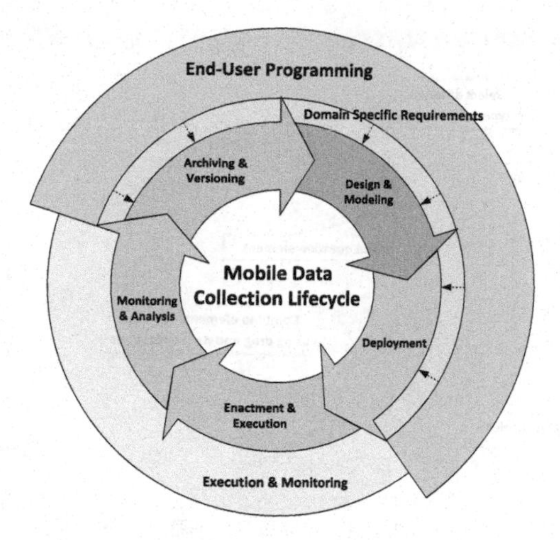

Fig. 2. Mobile data collection lifecycle

phase allows designing sophisticated data collection instruments. During the *Deployment* phase, the modeled instrument is transferred to and installed on registered smart mobile devices. In the *Enactment & Execution* phase, multiple instances of the respective mobile data collection instrument may be executed on a smart mobile device. The *Monitoring & Analysis* phase evaluates the collected data in real-time on the smart mobile device. Finally, different releases of the data collection instrument can be handled in the *Archiving & Versioning* phase. In order to address domain-specific requirements on one hand and to support domain experts on the other, technologies known from end-user programming are applied [21]. The presented study focuses on the configurator component of the presented framework. The latter covers the *Design & Modeling*, *Deployment* and *Archiving & Versioning* phases of the lifecycle.

2.2 Configurator Component

The configurator component we developed (cf. Fig. 3) applies techniques known from end-user programming and process management technology to empower domain experts to create flexible data collection instruments on their own. Due to lack of space, this component is only sketched here [19]:

(a) Element and Page Repository View (cf. Fig. 3a). The element repository allows creating basic elements of a questionnaire (e.g., headlines and questions). The rightmost part shows the editor, where particular attributes of the respective elements may be edited. Note that the configurator allows handling multiple languages. It further keeps track of different element revisions. Finally, created elements may be combined to pages using drag and drop operations.

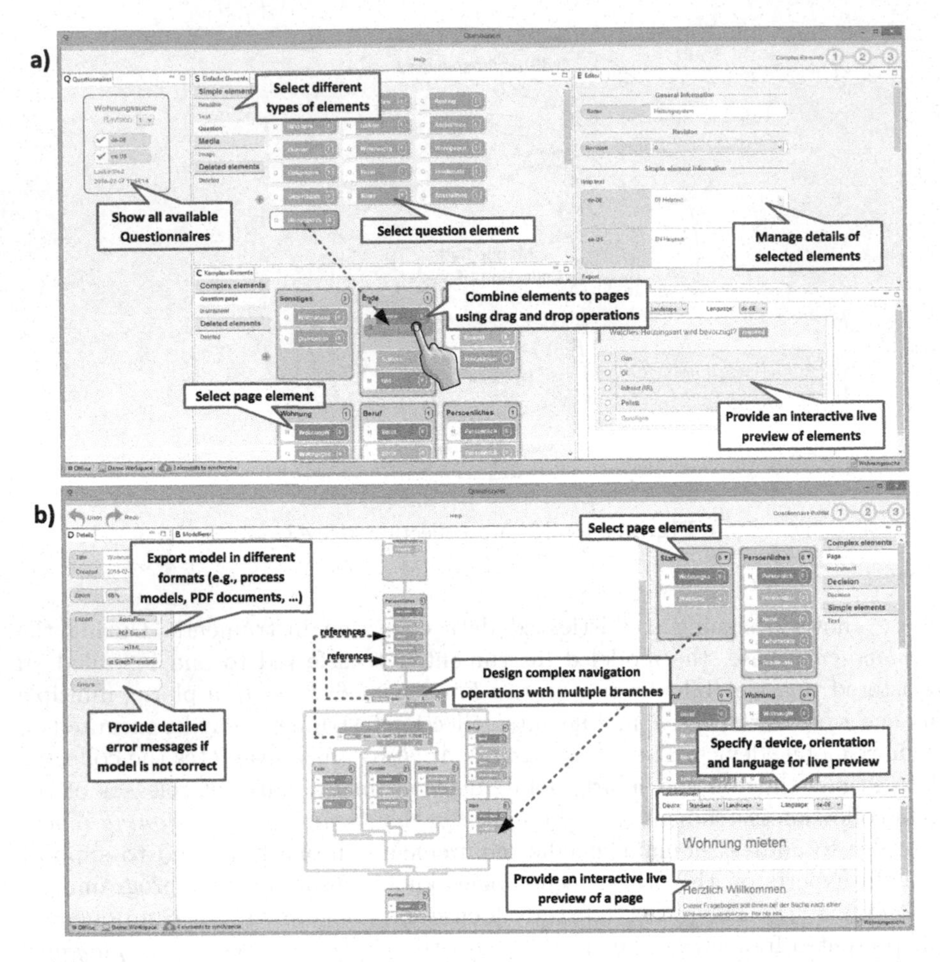

Fig. 3. The QuestionSys configurator: (a) combining elements to pages; (b) modeling a data collection instrument.

(b) Modeling Area View (cf. Fig. 3b). Domain experts may use previously created pages and drag them to the model in the center part. Furthermore, they are able to model sophisticated navigation operations to provide guidance during the data collection process. The graphical editor, in turn, strictly follows a correctness-by-construction approach; i.e., it is ensured that created models are executable by the lightweight process engine that runs on heterogeneous smart mobile devices. When deploying the model to smart mobile devices, it is automatically mapped to an executable process model.

Altogether, the configurator component and its model-driven approach allow domain experts to visually define data collection instruments. Thus, development time can be reduced and data collection applications can be realized more easily.

3 Experimental Setting

In order to ensure that domain experts are able to properly work with the configurator component, the overall concept presented in Sect. 2 needs to be evaluated. This section presents a controlled experiment, whose goal is to evaluate the feasibility and usability of the configurator component. In particular, we provide insights into the subjects and variables selected. Finally, we present the experimental design. Note that the latter constitutes a valuable template for conducting mental effort experiments on mobile data collection modeling approaches in general. Furthermore, when using the presented experimental setting, gathered results may indicate further directions on how to integrate mobile data collection with existing information systems.

3.1 Goal Definition

When developing an application, various software developing models (e.g., waterfall, V-model, SCRUM) may be chosen. Although these models include *testing* or *validation* phases, it cannot be guaranteed that end-users *accept* the final software product. Therefore, additional aspects need to be covered. For example, ISO25010 defines main software product quality characteristics, like *functional suitability*, *performance efficiency*, *usability*, and *security* [16]. The experiment presented in this paper, focuses on the usability of the presented configurator component. In particular, the experiment investigates whether domain experts understand the provided modeling concept and, therefore, are able to work properly with the configurator. For the preparation of the experiment, the *Goal Question Metric* (GQM) [2] is used in order to properly set up the goal (cf. Table 1). Based on this, we defined our research question:

Research Question

Do end-users understand the modeling concept of the questionnaire configurator with respect to the complexity of the provided application?

The subjects recruited for the experiment are students from different domains as well as research associates. [9] discusses that students can act as proper substitutes for domain experts in empirical studies. We do not require specific skills or knowledge from the subjects. The conducted experiment considers two *independent variables* (i.e., factors). First, we consider the *experience level* of the

Table 1. Goal Definition

Analyze	the questionnaire configurator
for the purpose of	evaluating the concept
with respect to the	intuitiveness of the modeling concept
from the point of	developers and researchers
in the context of	students and research associates in a controlled environment.

respective subjects with its two levels *novice* and *expert*. We assign subjects to one of the two groups based on answers regarding prior experience in process modeling given in the demographic questionnaire. In applied settings, novices would be domain experts with little experience in process modeling and experts would be domain experts with more experience in process modeling. Another variable we consider is the *difficulty level* of the task to be handled by the subjects (i.e., *easy* and *advanced* levels). As a criterion for assessing the complexity of a task, we decide to focus on the number of pages and decisions as well as the number of branches of the instrument to be modeled.

Two *dependent variables* are selected to measure an effect when changing the above mentioned factors. The experiment focuses on the *time needed* to solve the respective tasks as well as the *number of errors* in the resulting data collection instrument. We assume that prior experience in process modeling directly influences the subject's time to complete the tasks. In particular, we expect that experts are significantly faster than novices when modeling instruments. In order to automatically measure both dependent variables, a logging feature is added to the configurator. This feature, in turn, allows generating an execution log file containing all operations (i.e., all modeling steps) of respective subjects. We further record snapshots (i.e., images) of the data collection instrument modeled by a subject after each operation in order to allow for a graphic evaluation as well. The errors made are classified manually based on the submitted model and are weighted accordingly. Finally, hypotheses were derived (cf. Table 2).

3.2 Experimental Design

To be able to quickly react to possible malfunctions, the study is conducted as an offline experiment in a controlled environment. For this scenario, the computer lab of the Institute of Databases and Information Systems at Ulm University is prepared accordingly. The lab provides 10 workstations, each comparable with respect to hardware resources (e.g., RAM or CPU cores). Each workstation is equipped with one monitor using a common screen resolution. Before the

Table 2. Derived Hypotheses

H_a0	Novices are not slower when solving advanced tasks compared to easy tasks
H_a1	Novices are significantly slower when solving advanced tasks compared to easy tasks
H_b0	Experts are not slower when solving advanced tasks compared to easy tasks
H_b1	Experts are significantly slower when solving advanced tasks compared to easy tasks
H_c0	Novices do not make more errors when solving advanced tasks compared to easy tasks
H_c1	Novices make significantly more errors when solving advanced tasks compared to easy tasks
H_d0	Experts do not make more errors when solving advanced tasks compared to easy tasks
H_d1	Experts make significantly more errors when solving advanced tasks compared to easy tasks
H_e0	Novices are not slower than experts when solving tasks
H_e1	Novices are significantly slower than experts when solving tasks
H_f0	Novices do not make more errors than experts when solving tasks
H_f1	Novices make significantly more errors than experts when solving tasks

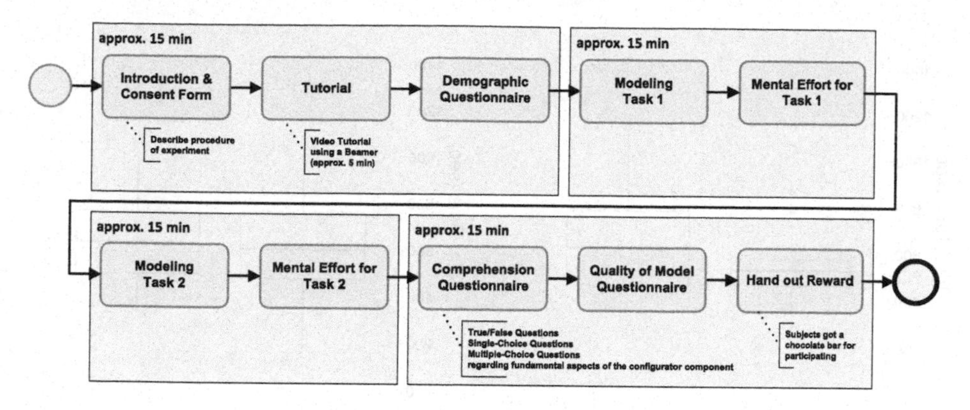

Fig. 4. Experiment design

experiment is performed, respective workstations are prepared carefully. This includes re-installing the configurator component and placing the consent form, task descriptions, and mental effort questionnaires beside each workstation.

The procedure of the experiment is outlined in Fig. 4: The experiment starts with welcoming the subjects. Afterwards, the goal of the study is described and the overall procedure is introduced. Then, the subjects are asked to sign an informed consent form. Next, we provide a 5 min live tutorial to demonstrate the most important features of the configurator component. Up to this point, the subjects may ask questions. Following this short introduction, the subjects are asked to fill in a demographic questionnaire that collects personal information. Afterwards, subjects have to model their first data collection instrument using the configurator, followed by filling in questions regarding their mental effort when handling respective task. Then, subjects have to model a second instrument (with increasing difficulty) and answer mental effort questions again. Thereby, subjects need to answer comprehension questions with respect to fundamental aspects of the developed configurator component. In the following, one final questionnaire dealing with the quality of the modeled data collection instruments has to be answered. Altogether, the experiment took about 60 min in total[1].

4 Evaluation

A total of 44 subjects participated in the experiment. Prior to analyzing the results, data is validated. [23] states that it has to be ensured that all subjects understand the tasks as well as the forms to be processed. Furthermore, invalid data (e.g., due to non-serious participation) has to be detected and removed. Two datasets need to be excluded due to invalidity (one participant aborts the study during Task 2) and doubts regarding the correctness of demographic information

[1] The dataset can be found at https://www.dropbox.com/s/tjte18zfu1j4bfk/dataset.zip.

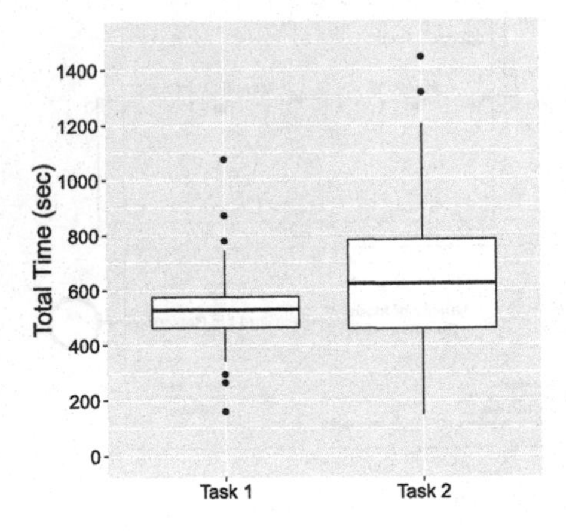

Fig. 5. Total time (novices)

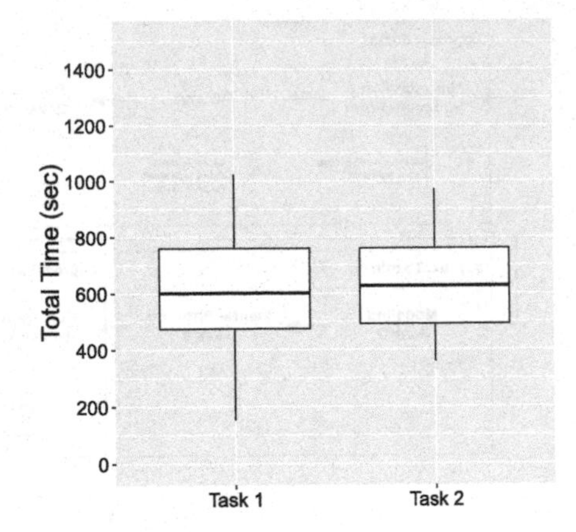

Fig. 6. Total time (experts)

(> 20 years of process modeling experience). After excluding these datasets, the final sample comprises 42 subjects. Based on their prior experience in *process modeling*, subjects are divided into two groups. Applying our criterion (*have read no more than 20 process models or have created less than 10 process models within the last 12 months*) finally results in 24 *novices* and 18 *experts*. Most of the subjects receive between 15 and 19 years of education up to this point. As no special knowledge is required for participating (besides prior experience in *process modeling* to count as *expert*), we consider the collected data as valid with respect to the goal of the study.

First, the *total time* (sec) subjects need to complete both modeling tasks is evaluated (cf. Table 3). Overall, novices need less time than experts to complete respective tasks. This may be explained by the fact that novices are not as conscientious as experts. Possibly, novices do not focus on all details needed to create data collection instruments. Next, the difference in the median is approximately 80 sec. for Task 1. The time to complete Task 2, however, barely differs for both groups. Furthermore, both groups need less time for modeling Task 1. Given the fact that Task 2 is more complex than the first one, this can be explained as well. Figs. 5 and 6 present boxplots for the total time needed. Note that the plot for novices indicates outliers in both directions. All outliers are carefully analyzed to check whether they need to be removed from the dataset. However,

Table 3. Total time and number of errors when handling tasks (median values)

	Total time (sec)		Number of errors	
Group	Task 1	Task 2	Task 1	Task 2
Novices	528.61	620.97	4	1
Experts	601.08	625.98	1	1

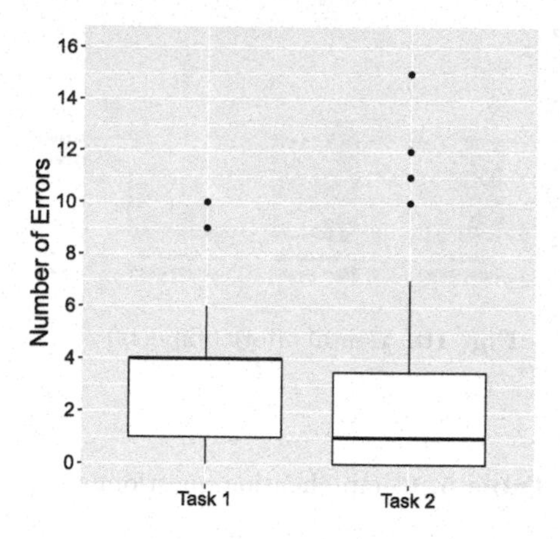

Fig. 7. Number of errors (novices)

Fig. 8. Number of errors (experts)

when considering other aspects (e.g., the number of errors), it can be shown that the outliers represent valid datasets and, therefore, must not be removed.

Second, the *number of errors* in the resulting models are evaluated (cf. Table 3). As expected, experts make fewer errors than novices in the context of Task 1. Considering the results for the time needed, one can observe that novices are faster, but produce more errors than experts when accomplishing Task 1. When modeling Task 2, however, both groups can be considered the same. This may be explained by the fact that experts have prior knowledge with respect to process modeling. Furthermore, it is conceivable that some kind of *learning effect* has taken place during Task 1 as novices make fewer errors when performing the second one. Boxplots in Figs. 7 and 8 show results for each task. Again, outliers can be observed in the group of novices.

Third, *mental effort* and *comprehension* questionnaires are evaluated with respect to the previously mentioned variables. Recall that each subject has to fill in a short questionnaire after handling a certain task (cf. Table 4, top part). Figures 9 and 10 show respective medians. The calculated score (median value)

Table 4. Mental effort questionnaires

Question	Answers
The mental effort for creating the questionnaire model was considerably high	7 Point Likert-Scale
The mental effort for changing elements was considerably high	7 Point Likert-Scale
I was able to successfully solve the task	7 Point Likert-Scale
Do your models represent the questionnaires in the given tasks?	7 Point Likert-Scale
Are there significant aspects that are missing in your models?	7 Point Likert-Scale
Do your models represent the logic of the given questionnaires exactly?	7 Point Likert-Scale
Are there any significant errors in your models?	7 Point Likert-Scale
Would you change your models if you were allowed to?	7 Point Likert-Scale

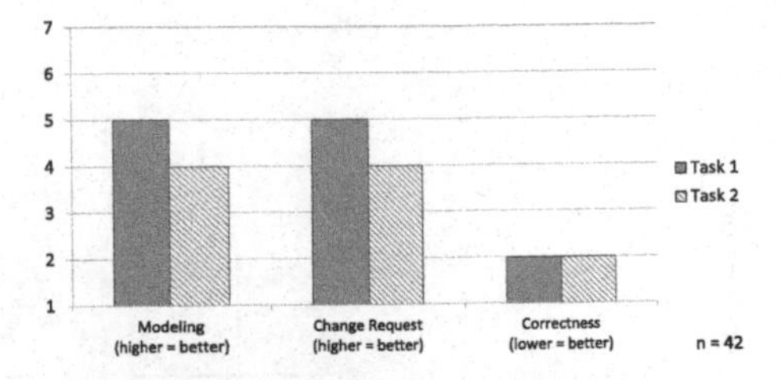

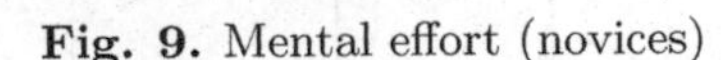
Fig. 9. Mental effort (novices)

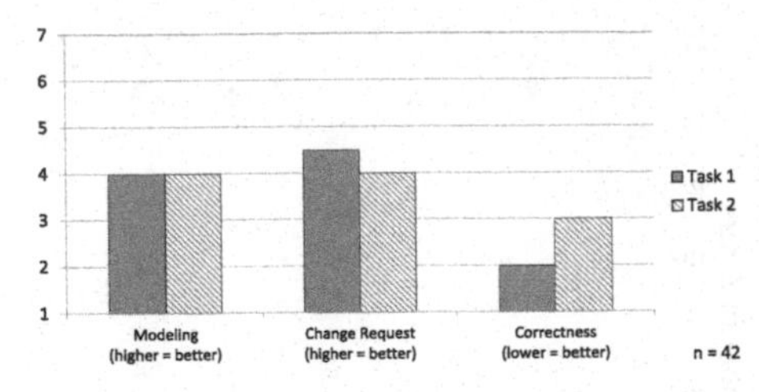

Fig. 10. Mental effort (experts)

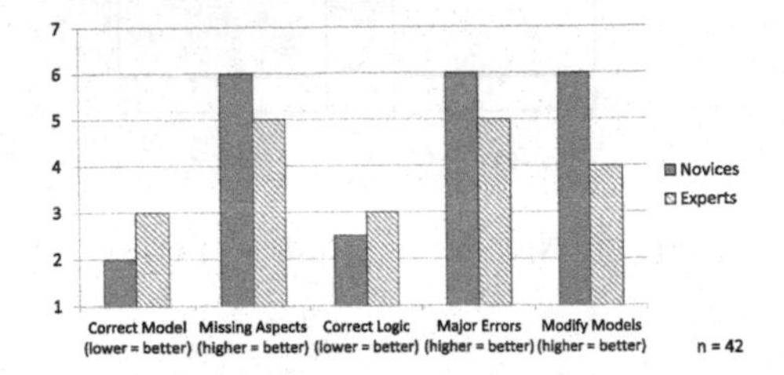

Fig. 11. Quality of models

Table 5. Comprehension questionnaire

Group	Score (median)
Novices	20.5 out of 25
Experts	21.5 out of 25

for the comprehension questionnaire is shown in Table 5. We consider the results for both the mental effort and comprehension questionnaire as reasonable. Table 4 (bottom part) shows the questions for rating the model quality when completing the experiment (cf. Fig. 11). When combining answers of the subjects (e.g., how satisfied they are with their own models) with the analysis of the errors made, results are convincing. Interestingly, novices rate their models better compared to experts. Note that from 84 data collection instruments in total (Task 1 and Task 2 combined), 43 models (21 models from novices and 22 from experts) have zero or one error. The results regarding mental effort, comprehension, and model quality questionnaires as well as the submitted instrument models do not differ largely among the two groups. Therefore, our results indicate that the modeling concept of the developed configurator component is intuitive and end-users with relatively low prior process modeling experience are able to use the configurator.

The collected data is further checked for its normal distribution (cf. Fig. 12). The first graph shows a quantile-quantile (Q-Q) graph plotting the quantiles of the sample against the ones of a theoretical distribution (i.e., normal distribution). The second graph presents a histogram of probability densities including the normal distribution (i.e., blue) and density curve (i.e., red line).

Considering the presented results, several statistical methods are used to test the hypotheses described in Sect. 3.1 (with p-value $\leq \alpha$ (0.05)). For normally distributed datasets, *t-Tests* are applied. Non-normally distributed datasets are tested with *One-Tailed Wilcoxon(-Mann-Whitney) Tests* [23]. When applying the tests, H_a showed significant results (p-value = 0.046). The other tests, however, show non-significant results (with p-value > 0.05) and the corresponding null hypotheses are accepted. Besides the hypothesis that novices are

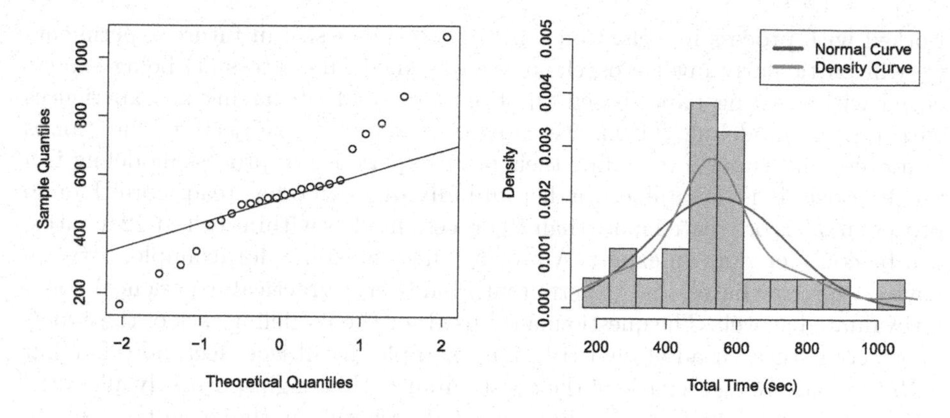

Fig. 12. Distribution of total time for Task 1 (novices) (Color figure online)

significantly slower in solving more advanced tasks, all other alternative hypotheses have to be rejected. In particular, the one stating that experts are faster than novices (i.e., hypothesis H_e1) cannot be confirmed. Considering the errors in the context of Task 1, however, novices make more errors. This may be explained by the fact that subjects having no prior experience in process modeling are not as conscientious as subjects with more experience. Novices, in turn, possibly not focus on details needed to model data collection instruments properly. The latter may be addressed by conducting an *eye-tracking* experiment with respective subjects. Furthermore, the assumption that experts make fewer errors than novices (i.e., hypothesis H_f1) cannot be confirmed. Although there is a difference in the descriptive statistics in Task 1, the difference does not attain statistical significance. In summary, results indicate that the prior experience of a subject does not affect the modeling of data collection instruments. In particular, the experiment shows that users without prior experience may gain sufficient knowledge within approximately 60 min (total time of the experiment) to model data collection applications themselves. Moreover, the learning effect between the first and second task have to be addressed more specifically in a future experiment.

To conclude, the results indicate the feasibility of the modeling concept. Overall, 43 out of 84 created instruments have been completed with zero or only one error. Given the fact that none of the subjects had ever used the application before, this relatively low number of errors confirms that the application can be easily used by novices. Hence, the QuestionSys configurator is suited to enable domain experts create mobile data collection applications themselves.

Threats to Validity. First of all, *external*, *internal*, *construct* and *conclusion validity*, as proposed in [7], were carefully considered. However, any experiment bears risks that might affect its results. Thus, its levels of validity need to be checked and limitations be discussed. The selection of involved subjects is a possible risk. First, in the experiment, solely subjects from Computer Science (34) and Business Science (8) participated. Second, 36 participants have already worked with process models. Concerning these two risks, in future experiments we will particularly involve psychologists and medical doctors (1) being experienced with creating paper-based questionnaires and (2) having no experiences with process modeling. Third, the categorization of the subjects to the groups of novices and experts regarding their prior experience in process modeling is a possible risk. It is debatable whether an individual, who has read more than 20 process models or created more than 10 process models within the last 12 months, can be considered as an expert. A broader distinguishing, for example, between novices, intermediates, and experts (with long-term practical experience) could be evaluated as well. The questionnaires used for the modeling task of the experiment constitute an additional risk. For example, if subjects feel more familiar with the underlying scenario of the questionnaire, this might positively affect the modeling of the data collection instrument. Furthermore, the given tasks might have been too simple regarding the low number of modeling errors. Hence, additional experiments should take the influence of the used questionnaires as well as their complexity into account. In addition, we address the potential learning effect when modeling data collection instruments in more detail. Finally, another limitation of the present study is the relatively small sample size of $N = 42$ participants. However, the sample is large enough to run meaningful inferential statistical tests, though their results can only be seen as preliminary with limited external validity. Therefore, we will run another experiment to evaluate the configurator component with a larger and more heterogeneous sample.

5 Related Work

Several experiments measuring mental efforts in the context of process modeling are described in literature. Common to them is their focus on the resulting process model. For example, [13] evaluates the process of modeling processes itself. Furthermore, [22] identifies a set of fixation patterns with eye tracking for acquiring a better understanding of factors that influence the way process models are created by individuals. The different steps a process modeler undertakes when modeling processes are visually presented in [6]. However, in our study the process models represent data collection instruments. Therefore, additional aspects have to be modeled that are normally not important for process models (e.g., different versions of elements). On the other hand, these aspects may increase overall mental efforts during modeling. Consequently, our experiment differs from the ones conducted in the discussed approaches.

Various approaches supporting non-programmers with creating software have proven their feasibility in a multitude of studies. For example, [10] provides an environment allowing system administrators to visually model script applications. An experiment revealed the applicability of the proposed approach. In turn, [3] introduces a graphical programming language, representing each function of a computer program as a block.

Regarding the systematic evaluation of configurators that enable domain experts to create flexible questionnaires on their own, only few literature exists.

For example, [1] evaluates a *web-based configurator for ambulatory assessments* against *movisensXS*. More precisely, two studies are described. On one hand, the configurator component is assessed by two experts. On the other, 10 subjects evaluate the respective client component capable of enacting the configured assessment. Both studies, however, rely on standardized user-experience questionnaires (e.g., *System Usability Scale* [4]) to obtain feedback. The results are limited due to the low number of subjects. In [18], a web-based application to create and coordinate *interactive information retrieval* (IIR) experiments is presented. The authors evaluate their application in two ways: First, usability analyses are performed for the application backend by a human computer interaction researcher and a student. Both confirm an easy-to-use user interface. Second, the frontend is evaluated by performing an IIR experiment with 48 participants. Thereby, the time to complete tasks is measured by the application and participants are asked to provide feedback on how they rate their performance. Though these studies focus on the usability of the developed applications, our study pursues a different approach as it evaluates the configurator by observing correctness aspects when solving specific tasks. To the best of our knowledge, when using a configurator application for modeling data collection instruments, no similar approaches are available so far.

6 Summary and Outlook

This paper investigated the questionnaire configurator of the QuestionSys framework with respect to its usability. The configurator, in turn, shall enable domain experts to create mobile data collection applications on their own. To address the usability of the configurator, a controlled experiment with 44 participants was conducted. For the experiment, the participants were separated into two groups, based on their background knowledge and experience in process modeling. To evaluate differences between both groups, we focused on the total time needed to solve specific tasks as well as the number of errors in the submitted models. We showed that user experience in process modeling has minimal effects on the overall understanding of the configurator. Furthermore, the subjects gained respective knowledge to use the configurator in adequate time. One could argue that a learning effect took place. However, contrary to our expectations, the study showed that there are no significant differences in working with the configurator regarding the experience the user has with process modeling. In order to evaluate the results with respect to domain differences, we plan a large-scale study with subjects from multiple domains. Currently, we are recruiting subjects from Psychology and Business Science. Furthermore, we address the learning effect observed and, therefore, rerun respective studies multiple times with the same subjects. The results obtained in this study confirm the intuitiveness and improve the overall user-experience of the developed configurator component. Altogether, the QuestionSys approach will significantly influence the way data is collected in large-scale studies (e.g., clinical trials).

References

1. Bachmann, A., Zetzsche, R., Schankin, A., Riedel, T., Beigl, M., Reichert, M., Santangelo, P., Ebner-Priemer, U.: ESMAC: a web-based configurator for context-aware experience sampling apps in ambulatory assessment. In: 5th International Conference on Wireless Mobile Communication and Healthcare, pp. 15–18 (2015)
2. Basili, V.R.: Software Modeling and Measurement: The Goal/Question/Metric Paradigm (1992)
3. Begel, A., Klopfer, E.: Starlogo TNG: an introduction to game development. J. E-Learn. (2007)
4. Brooke, J., et al.: SUS - a quick and dirty usability scale. Usability Eval. Ind. **189**(194), 4–7 (1996)
5. Carlbring, P., Brunt, S., Bohman, S., Austin, D., Richards, J., Öst, L.G., Andersson, G.: Internet vs. paper and pencil administration of questionnaires commonly used in panic/agoraphobia research. Comput. Hum. Behav. **23**(3), 1421–1434 (2007)
6. Claes, J., Vanderfeesten, I., Pinggera, J., Reijers, H.A., Weber, B., Poels, G.: A visual analysis of the process of process modeling. Inf. Syst. e-Bus. Manag. **13**(1), 147–190 (2015)
7. Cook, T.D., Campbell, D.T., Day, A.: Quasi-Experimentation: Design and Analysis Issues for Field Settings, vol. 351. Houghton Mifflin, Boston (1979)
8. Fernandez-Ballesteros, R.: Self-report questionnaires. Compr. Handb. Psychol. Assess. **3**, 194–221 (2004)
9. Höst, M., Regnell, B., Wohlin, C.: Using students as subjects - a comparative study of students and professionals in lead-time impact assessment. Empirical Softw. Eng. **5**(3), 201–214 (2000)
10. Kandogan, E., Haber, E., Barrett, R., Cypher, A., Maglio, P., Zhao, H.: A1: end-user programming for web-based system administration. In: Proceedings of 18th ACM Symposium on User Interface Software and Technology. ACM (2005)
11. Lane, S.J., Heddle, N.M., Arnold, E., Walker, I.: A review of randomized controlled trials comparing the effectiveness of hand held computers with paper methods for data collection. BMC Med. Inform. Decis. Mak. **6**(1), 1 (2006)
12. Marcano Belisario, J.S., Jamsek, J., Huckvale, K., O'Donoghue, J., Morrison, C.P., Car, J.: Comparison of self-administered survey questionnaire responses collected using mobile apps versus other methods. The Cochrane Library (2015)
13. Martini, M., Pinggera, J., Neurauter, M., Sachse, P., Furtner, M.R., Weber, B.: The impact of working memory and the process of process modelling on model quality: investigating experienced versus inexperienced modellers. Sci. Rep. **6**, 1–11 (2016)
14. Palermo, T.M., Valenzuela, D., Stork, P.P.: A randomized trial of electronic versus paper pain diaries in children: impact on compliance, accuracy, and acceptability. Pain **107**(3), 213–219 (2004)
15. Pavlović, I., Kern, T., Miklavčič, D.: Comparison of paper-based and electronic data collection process in clinical trials: costs simulation study. Contemp. Clin. Trials **30**(4), 300–316 (2009)
16. Rafique, I., Lew, P., Abbasi, M.Q., Li, Z.: Information quality evaluation framework: extending ISO 25012 data quality model. World Acad. Sci. Eng. Technol. **65**, 523–528 (2012)
17. Reichert, M., Weber, B.: Enabling Flexibility in Process-Aware Information Systems: Challenges, Methods, Technologies. Springer, Heidelberg (2012)

18. Renaud, G., Azzopardi, L.: SCAMP: a tool for conducting interactive information retrieval experiments. In: IIiX, pp. 286–289 (2012)
19. Schobel, J., Pryss, R., Schickler, M., Reichert, M.: A configurator component for end-user defined mobile data collection processes. In: Demo Track of the 14th International Conference on Service Oriented Computing, October 2016
20. Schobel, J., Pryss, R., Schickler, M., Reichert, M.: A lightweight process engine for enabling advanced mobile applications. In: Debruyne, C., et al. (eds.) OTM 2016. LNCS, vol. 10033, pp. 552–569. Springer, Cham (2016). doi:10.1007/978-3-319-48472-3_33
21. Schobel, J., Pryss, R., Schickler, M., Ruf-Leuschner, M., Elbert, T., Reichert, M.: End-user programming of mobile services: empowering domain experts to implement mobile data collection applications. In: IEEE 5th International Conference on Mobile Services. IEEE Computer Society Press, June 2016
22. Weber, B., Pinggera, J., Neurauter, M., Zugal, S., Martini, M., Furtner, M., Sachse, P., Schnitzer, D.: Fixation patterns during process model creation: initial steps toward neuro-adaptive process modeling environments. In: 2016 49th Hawaii International Conference on System Sciences (HICSS), pp. 600–609. IEEE (2016)
23. Wohlin, C., Runeson, P., Höst, M., Ohlsson, M.C., Regnell, B., Wesslén, A.: Experimentation in Software Engineering. Springer Science & Business Media, Heidelberg (2012)

Business Process Alignment

Checking Process Compliance on the Basis of Uncertain Event-to-Activity Mappings

Han van der Aa[1(✉)], Henrik Leopold[1], and Hajo A. Reijers[1,2]

[1] Department of Computer Sciences, VU University Amsterdam, Amsterdam, The Netherlands
{j.h.vander.aa,h.leopold,h.a.reijers}@vu.nl

[2] Department of Mathematics and Computer Science, Eindhoven University of Technology, Eindhoven, The Netherlands

Abstract. A crucial requirement for compliance checking techniques is that observed behavior, captured in event traces, can be mapped to the process models that specify allowed behavior. Without a mapping, it is not possible to determine if observed behavior is compliant or not. A considerable problem in this regard is that establishing a mapping between events and process model activities is an inherently uncertain task. Since the use of a particular mapping directly influences the compliance of a trace to a specification, this uncertainty represents a major issue for compliance checking. To overcome this issue, we introduce a probabilistic compliance checking method that can deal with uncertain mappings. Our method avoids the need to select a single mapping, but rather works on a spectrum of possible mappings. A quantitative evaluation demonstrates that our method can be applied on a considerable number of real-world processes where traditional compliance checking methods fail.

Keywords: Compliance checking · Event-to-activity mapping · Process mining · Matching · Uncertainty

1 Introduction

Compliance management supports organizations by ensuring that their processes satisfy legal requirements and are executed in an efficient manner [27]. *Compliance checking* techniques (cf. [3,20,26]) play an important role in this regard [17]. These techniques enable organizations to automatically check whether business processes are executed according to their specifications. Specifically, they check if any observed behavior, as recorded in an IT system and represented in the form of an *event trace*, conforms to the allowed process behavior, as captured in a *process model* [5]. A crucial requirement for compliance checking is that the events contained in an event log can be related to the activities of a process model [25]. Without knowing the relations between events and model activities, it is not possible to determine if the behavior within an event trace conforms to

E. Dubois and K. Pohl (Eds.): CAiSE 2017, LNCS 10253, pp. 79–93, 2017.
DOI: 10.1007/978-3-319-59536-8_6

the behavior specified by a process model. Despite this dependence of compliance checking techniques on the existence of such a, so-called, *event-to-activity mapping*, these mappings are often not readily available [8].

Furthermore, actually establishing event-to-activity mappings is a highly complex task. The effort required to *manually* perform this task is hardly manageable in practical scenarios, due to the task's combinatorial complexity [9]. *Automated* mapping techniques also face considerable challenges. These challenges are caused by, among others, cryptic event names, noncompliant behavior, and noise [7]. As a result, automated mapping techniques often cannot provide a certain solution to the mapping problem. In fact, the task of establishing event-to-activity mappings is conceptually equivalent to *matching* tasks found in the fields of *schema matching* and *process matching*. Such matching tasks have been shown to be inherently uncertain [14,28]. Due to this uncertainty, the goal of mapping techniques becomes choosing the *best* mapping from the potential ones [18]. Hence, there is always the risk that the selected mapping is wrong, i.e. that the selected mapping does not correctly capture the relations between event traces and a process model. In the context of compliance checking, selecting an incorrect mapping is particularly harmful. If the selected mapping is incorrect, the results obtained through compliance checking based on this mapping cannot be trusted.

To overcome this issue, this paper presents a compliance checking method that can be applied in spite of an uncertain mapping of events onto activities. Our method assesses the compliance of a trace by considering the entire spectrum of potential mappings, rather than focusing on a single one. To capture this spectrum, we build on the notion of *probabilistic behavioral spaces*. These behavioral spaces provide a means to capture behavioral uncertainty, i.e. varying interpretations on described process behavior, in a structured manner. We originally introduced this notion to capture behavioral uncertainty caused by ambiguity in textual process descriptions [2]. We extend the original notion with probabilistic information in the current paper and apply it in the context of mapping uncertainty. These probabilistic behavioral spaces can be used for compliance checking without the need to resolve uncertainty, i.e. without the need to select a single event-to-activity mapping from a number of alternatives. As a result, our compliance checking method avoids the risks associated with the selection of an incorrect mapping. A quantitative evaluation demonstrates that this method can be used to obtain comprehensive compliance checking results for a considerably higher number of processes than traditional methods.

The remainder of this paper is structured as follows. Section 2 motivates the problem of compliance checking in the context of uncertain event-to-activity mappings. Then, Sect. 3 provides some necessary preliminary definitions. Section 4 describes our compliance checking method. We evaluate the usefulness of our method in Sect. 5. Finally, we consider streams of related research in Sect. 6 and conclude the paper in Sect. 7.

2 Problem Illustration

In this section, we illustrate the problem of compliance checking in the context of mapping uncertainty. The goal of compliance checking is to determine if behavior captured in *event traces* is allowed by the behavior specified in the form of a *process model*. An event trace captures an execution sequence of events. These events correspond to the *actual* behavior of a process, because they are extracted from information systems that record the execution of process steps. By contrast, process models are used in compliance checking scenarios to specify the *allowed* behavior of a process. A crucial prerequisite for compliance checking is that the events in event traces can be related to the activities of a process model. For example, given an event trace $t = <e_1, e_2, e_3, e_4, e_5>$ and the process model M depicted in Fig. 1, the events in t must be mapped to activities in model M. Otherwise, it is impossible to understand which activities have occurred in reality and, thus, whether or not t complies with M.

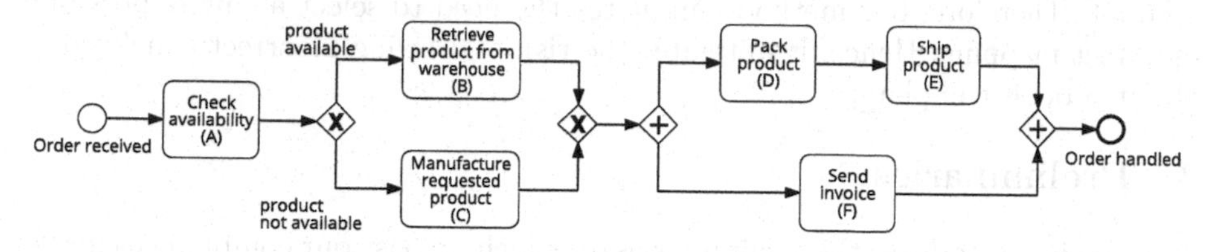

Fig. 1. Example of a BPMN process model

Unfortunately, establishing a correct mapping between events and activities is a considerable challenge. Existing techniques addressing this task can at best indicate potential mappings and their likelihoods, instead of providing a definite solution [8,9]. The reason why mapping techniques fail to provide definite solutions is that the information they can take into account when constructing mappings often does not suffice to identify relations with certainty. As an example, consider an event with the label "*Product obtained*". By considering the labels, it is not possible to determine with certainty whether this event corresponds to activity B ("*Retrieve product from warehouse*") or to activity C ("*Manufacture requested product*"). Both of these activities *obtain* a product, but in a different way. Even more problematic are the commonly observed event labels with cryptic database field names such as *CDHDR* or *I_SM_E* [9]. In these cases, not even advanced linguistic analysis tools are able to identify reliable mappings.

The inability of techniques to reliably establish event-to-activity mappings leads to mapping uncertainty. As a result, mapping techniques generally construct a number of *potential* mappings without being able to determine with certainty which mapping is correct. Since existing compliance checking techniques require a single event-to-activity mapping, mostly the mapping with the highest likelihood is selected as a basis for compliance checks. However, there is always the risk that this selected mapping is incorrect and that, consequently, compliance checking results based on the selected mapping are incorrect as well.

To illustrate the risk of selecting a single mapping in the context of mapping uncertainty, assume that trace t corresponds to the activity sequence

$\sigma = <A, B, C, E, F>$. This means that t is *not* compliant with model M, because M does not allow for the activities B and C to be executed in the same process instance, while σ contains both of these. Further assume that, due to mapping uncertainty, a mapping technique returns two possible mappings, one corresponding to the *noncompliant* sequence σ, but the other to the *compliant* sequence $\sigma' = <A, B, D, E, F>$. In this scenario, the ability to correctly identify the noncompliance of t to M fully depends on the ability to select the appropriate mapping from the two alternatives. In case the mapping corresponding to σ' is selected, then t will be considered to be compliant with M, event though in reality the process behavior contained in t does *not* comply to the allowed behavior specified by M.

The previous example illustrates that compliance checking results based on the selection of a single, potentially incorrect mapping are not trustworthy. To provide a comprehensive solution to this problem, this paper introduces a compliance checking method that takes the entire set of potential mappings into account. Therefore, our method eliminates the need to select a single, possibly incorrect mapping. Hence, it mitigates the risk of drawing incorrect conclusions about process compliance.

3 Preliminaries

This section introduces the preliminaries on which we base our compliance checking method. For the purposes of this paper, we use the *behavioral profile relations* from [24] to capture and compare behavior contained in event traces and process models. These behavioral relations build on a *weak order relation* $\succ$. For a single event trace $t = <e_1, \ldots, e_n>$ over a set of event classes E_t, the relation $\succ_t \subseteq (E_t \times E_t)$ contains all pairs $(x, y) \in (E_t \times E_t)$ such that there exist two indices $j, k \in 1, \ldots, m$ with $j < k \leq m$ for which holds that $e_j = x$ and $e_k = y$. Intuitively, the weak order relation contains any pair (x, y) for which an occurrence of event class x precedes an occurrence of event class y. A *behavioral profile* derives three distinct behavioral relations from this weak order relation: strict order, exclusiveness, and interleaving order. Definition 1 provides a formal definition for the behavioral profile of a single event trace.

Definition 1 (Behavioral Profile – Trace). *Let t be an event trace over a set of event classes E_t and with a weak order relation $\succ_t$. Then a pair of event classes $(x, y) \in E_t \times E_t$ is in at most one of the following relations:*

- *The* strict order relation $\rightsquigarrow_t$, *iff* $x \succ_t y$ *and* $y \not\succ_t x$;
- *The* exclusiveness relation $+_t$, *iff* $x \not\succ_t y$ *and* $y \not\succ_t x$;
- *The* interleaving order relation $||_t$, *iff* $x \succ_t y$ *and* $y \not\succ_t x$;

The set $BP_t = \{\rightsquigarrow_t, +_t, ||_t\}$ *is the* behavioral profile *of* t.

For a process model M, a behavioral profile BP_M is computed in a similar manner as for an event trace. The difference is that $\succ_M$ contains all pairs (x, y) for which there is an event trace t possible in M such that $(x, y) \in \succ_t$. Therefore, the behavioral profile of a process model builds on an aggregation of the weak order relation of all its possible traces. Definition 2 formally describes this.

Definition 2 (Behavioral Profile – Process Model). *Let M be a process model with an activity set A_M and with a weak order relation $\succ_M$. Then an activity pair $(x, y) \in A_M \times A_M$ is in at most one of the following relations:*

- *The* strict order relation $\rightsquigarrow_M$, *iff* $x \succ_M y$ *and* $y \not\succ_M x$;
- *The* exclusiveness relation $+_M$, *iff* $x \not\succ_M y$ *and* $y \not\succ_M x$;
- *The* interleaving order relation $||_M$, *iff* $x \succ_M y$ *and* $y \not\succ_M x$;

The set $BP_M = \{\rightsquigarrow_M, +_M, ||_M\}$ *is the* behavioral profile *of* M.

The behavioral profile relations form the basis of our compliance checking method. Given an event trace t and a process model M, we can determine the compliance of t with M by comparing the relations in BP_t to those in BP_M. It is crucial to understand the different nature of the behavioral profile of a trace and of a process model. BP_t provides information on *observed* behavioral relations for a single trace, whereas BP_M describes *constraints* for these traces. Therefore, to perform a compliance check, we do not check if the behavioral relations in BP_t and BP_M are equal. Rather, we check if the relations in BP_t are allowed within the relations in BP_M. This can be achieved by considering the *subsumption* of behavioral profile relations, as introduced in [26]. The subsumption predicate $S(R, R')$ determines if a relation type R of a process model subsumes a relation R' of a trace. $S(R, R')$ is defined as given by Definition 3. In this definition, the short-hand notation $x \rightsquigarrow^{-1} y$ is used to denote that $y \rightsquigarrow x$.

Definition 3 (Subsumption Predicate). *Given two behavioral relations* $R, R' \in \{\rightsquigarrow, \rightsquigarrow^{-1}, +, ||\}$, *the* subsumption predicate $S(R, R')$ *is satisfied iff* $(R \in \{\rightsquigarrow, \rightsquigarrow^{-1}\} \wedge R' = +)$ *or* $R = R'$ *or* $R = ||$.

Intuitively, the notion of subsumption builds on the different *strengths* of behavioral profile relations. For example, due to parallelism in the model M of the running example, the behavioral profile of M contains the relation $D \; || \; F$. However, in the behavioral profile of a trace, parallelism cannot be observed, because only a single execution of each of these activities should occur, e.g. $t = <D, F, E>$. Therefore, BP_t contains the relation $D \rightsquigarrow F$. Even though the two behavioral profile relations are not equal, it is clear that t does not violate the constraints expressed by M, because $D \rightsquigarrow F$ is a valid order in which D and F can be executed. This compliance is accounted for by the subsumption predicate, since the predicate $S(||, \rightsquigarrow)$ is satisfied. Similarly, an exclusion relation $c+d$ in a trace does not violate a strict order relation $c \rightsquigarrow d$ in a model.

A trace t is compliant with a process model M if all behavioral profile relations in BP_t are subsumed by the relations in BP_M. Definition 4 captures this for the situation when a mapping between the events of t and activities of M is known.

Definition 4 (Trace to Process Model Compliance). *Let M be a process model with an activity set A and* $t = <e_1, \ldots, e_n>$ *an event trace containing the activities* $A_t \subseteq A$. *Trace t complies with process model M if for each activity pair* $(x, y) \in (A_t \times A_t)$ *the relation in t is subsumed by the relation in M, i.e. the* compliance predicate *compl*(t, M) *is satisfied* iff $\forall R \in BP_t \cup \{\rightsquigarrow_t^{-1}\}, BP_M \cup \{\rightsquigarrow_I^{-1}\}$, *it holds* $(xRy \wedge xR'y) \implies S(R, R')$.

Next, we describe our compliance checking method that employs the compliance notion provided by Definition 4.

4 Compliance Checking Method

This section describes our method for compliance checking in the context of uncertain event-to-activity mappings. The two-step method we propose takes as input an event trace t, a process model M, and an uncertain mapping between the events of t and the activities M. Note that the question of how to obtain the mapping is not the focus of this paper, but it can be determined using techniques from e.g. [7,8,23]. In the first step, the method uses the uncertain mapping to generate a so-called *probabilistic behavioral space* for t. In the second step, we use this probabilistic behavioral space to perform a compliance check. In the remainder of this section, we describe the relevant concepts and steps of our method in detail.

4.1 From Uncertain Mapping to Probabilistic Behavioral Space

In the first step of our method, we generate a probabilistic behavioral space for an event trace. The notion of probabilistic behavioral spaces, in the remainder also simply referred to as *behavioral spaces*, provides the foundation to reason about process compliance in the context of uncertain event-to-activity mappings. The idea underlying this notion is that an uncertain event-to-activity mapping results in multiple views on what process behavior, in terms of process model activities, is described by a single event trace. A probabilistic behavioral space captures these views in a structured manner. To describe the generation of behavioral spaces, we first define *regular* and *uncertain* event-to-activity mappings.

For a given trace $t = <e_1, \ldots, e_n>$ over a set of event classes E_t and a process model M with an activity set A_M, we use $EA(t, M)$ to denote a single event-to-activity mapping between the events in t and the activities in A_M. The mapping $EA(t, M)$ consists of a number of *correspondences* between individual events and activities. Each correspondence $e \sim a \in (E_t \times A_M)$ denotes a mapping relation between an event e and an activity a. For example, given a trace $t = <e_1, e_2, e_3>$ a mapping $EA(t, M) = \{e_1 \sim a, e_2 \sim b, e_3 \sim c\}$ indicates that trace t corresponds to the execution of the sequence of process model activities $<a, b, c>$. We shall refer to such a sequence of process model activities as a *trace translation* of event trace t, because it represents a translation of the trace's events into process model activities. Definition 5 formalizes this notion. Note that, for the sake of readability, we here focus on one-to-one relations between events and activities in a trace translation. However, our compliance checking method also works on trace translations which are based on one-to-many or many-to-many mappings between events and activities.

Definition 5 (Trace translation). *Given an event trace* $t = <e_1, \ldots, e_n>$ *with a set of event classes* E_t*, a process model* M *with an activity set* A_M*,* *and an event-to-activity mapping* $EA(t, M) \subseteq (E_t \times A_M)$ *we define a* trace translation *as* $\sigma(t) = <a_1, \ldots, a_n>$*, where for each* $0 < i \leq n$*, it holds that* $e_i \sim a_i \in EA(t, M)$.

We use $\mathbb{EA}(t, M)$ to denote an uncertain event-to-activity mapping between an event trace t and a process model M. $\mathbb{EA}(t, M)$ consists of a number of event-to-activity mappings, where each $EA_i \in \mathbb{EA}$ represents a potential way to map the events in t to the activities in A_M. Therefore, each mapping $EA_i \in \mathbb{EA}$ yields a different trace translation for t. Together, these translations represent the spectrum of process behavior that might be contained in t, i.e. the behavioral space of an event trace. Since each mapping can be associated with a probability, we include a probabilistic component in our definition of a behavioral space, as captured in Definition 6.

Definition 6 (Probabilistic Behavioral Space). *Given an event trace* $t = <e_1, \ldots, e_n>$ *with a set of event classes* E_t*, a process model* M *with an activity set* A_M*, and an uncertain event-to-activity mapping* $\mathbb{EA}(t, M)$*, we define a* probabilistic behavioral space *as a tuple* $PBS_t = (\Sigma(t), \phi)$*, with:*

- $\Sigma(t)$*: the set of* trace translations *of trace* t *over the activity set* A *as given by the event-to-activity mappings in* $\mathbb{EA}(t, M)$*;*
- $\phi : \Sigma_t(A) \rightarrow [0, 1]$*: a function that assigns a probability to each trace translation in* $\Sigma(t)$*.*

The set $\Sigma(t)$ comprises the set of potential trace translations of trace t over the activity set A, where each translation $\sigma_i \in \Sigma(t)$ is based on a mapping $EA_i \in \mathbb{EA}(t, M)$. The probability function ϕ assigns a probability p_i to each translation $\sigma_i(t) \in \Sigma(t)$. These probabilities can generally be based on the confidence of an event-to-activity mapping technique. For instance, a technique based on the semantic similarity scores, such as [8], can quantify the probability as the product of the similarity scores associated with each correspondence in the trace translation. If no such probabilities are available, the most straightforward solution is to assign an equal probability $p_i = 1 \ / \ |\Sigma_t|$ to each translation.

4.2 Using Behavioral Spaces for Compliance Checking

In this section, we illustrate the usefulness of probabilistic behavioral spaces for compliance checking in the context of uncertain event-to-activity mappings. The goal of compliance checking is to determine if the behavior in a trace t is allowed by the behavioral specification of a process model M. Since uncertain event-to-activity mappings lead to multiple views on the process model behavior contained in a trace (i.e. its trace translations), different translations can lead to different compliance checking results. By using probabilistic behavioral spaces, we can perform compliance checks in spite of such different translations. In the remainder of this section, we demonstrate how to perform compliance checking using behavioral spaces by introducing a probabilistic compliance measure. Furthermore, we discuss the valuable diagnostic information that these compliance checks can provide.

To perform our compliance checks, we introduce a compliance metric that quantifies the compliance of a probabilistic behavioral space PBS_t to a process model M. The metric combines the compliance assessments for individual trace translations with probabilistic information. The metric determines for each trace translation $\sigma \in \Sigma(t)$ in a behavioral spaces whether it is compliant or not. This is achieved by computing the behavioral profile BP_σ for a trace translation σ as described in Sect. 3. Since a trace translation contains a subset of the activities of a process model, we can proceed to determine if σ complies with a model M by comparing BP_σ with BP_M according to Definition 4. By taking the sum of the probabilities associated with all compliant translations, we obtain the probability that a trace t is compliant with a model M. Definition 7 formalizes this metric.

Definition 7 (Behavioral Space Compliance). *Let t be a trace with a probabilistic behavioral space $PBST(t) = (\Sigma(t), \phi)$ and BP_M a behavioral profile for a process model M with activity set A_M. Then we define:*

- *$\Sigma_C(t) \subseteq \Sigma(t)$ as the set of trace translations in $\Sigma(t)$ compliant with BP_M;*
- *$ProbCompl(t, M) = \sum_{\sigma \in \Sigma_C(t)} \phi(\sigma)$: as the* behavioral space compliance *of trace t to model M, where $\phi(\sigma)$ captures the probability of translation σ.*

Two interesting properties of this compliance metric are worth considering in more detail. First, when compared to traditional compliance checking, the metric provides probabilistic instead of binary results. In traditional compliance scenarios, i.e. without uncertainty, a trace is either compliant or noncompliant. In the scenario with uncertainty, traces are either compliant, noncompliant, or *potentially compliant.* Figure 2 visualizes this.

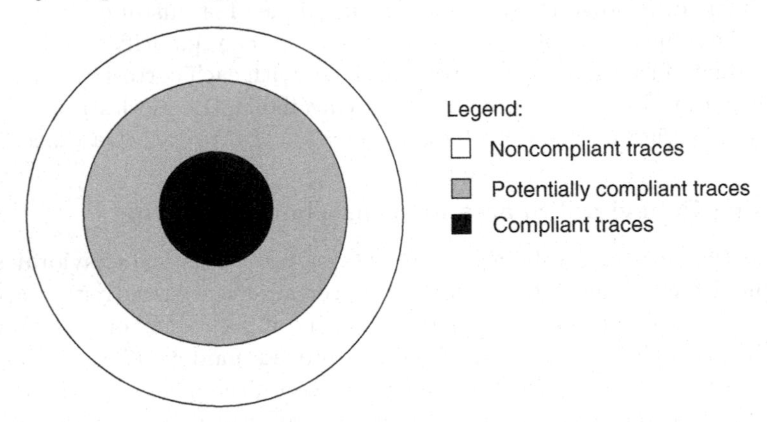

Fig. 2. Three types of compliance assessments for probabilistic compliance checking.

Potentially compliant traces are those traces for which some trace translations are compliant with a process model, whereas others are noncompliant. The compliance of these traces is associated with a certain probability $0 < p < 1$. Take, for instance, the trace $t_1 = <e_1, e_2, e_3, e_4, e_5>$ and its two translations from the running example, $\sigma_1(t_1) = <A, B, D, E, F>$ and $\sigma_2(t_1) = <A, B, C, E, F>$. Assume that $\sigma_1(t_1)$ is associated with a probability of 0.8 and $\sigma_2(t_1)$ with probability 0.2. Given that $\sigma_1(t_1)$ is compliant with M and $\sigma_2(t_1)$ is noncompliant, the trace t_1 is potentially compliant with M, with a probability of 0.8. Therefore, we know that t_1 is is more likely to be compliant than not. Furthermore, we also know the mapping conditions under which t_1 is compliant or noncompliant. Namely, t_1 is compliant if the correspondence $e_3 \sim D$ holds, whereas the trace is noncompliant if $e_3 \sim C$ is true. This is the kind of diagnostic information we referred to earlier, which can be useful because it provides insights into which aspects of an uncertain mapping lead to uncertainty in compliance checking results for observed behavior.

The second interesting property of the compliance metric is that, despite its probabilistic nature in the presence of mapping uncertainty, the metric $ProbCompl(t, M)$ often still yields non-probabilistic results. To illustrate this, consider a (partial) trace $t_2 = <e_1, e_2, e_3>$ with translations $\sigma_1(t_2) = <B, A, D>$ and $\sigma_2(t_2) = <B, C, D>$. Although mapping uncertainty has resulted in two trace translations, $ProbCompl(t_2, M)$ yields a non-probabilistic results since neither of the translations are compliant with model M. Therefore, it is certain that t_2 is noncompliant. In a similar fashion, a (partial) trace $t_3 = <e_1, e_2, e_3>$, with translations $\sigma_1(t_3) = <A, B, D>$ and $\sigma_2(t_3) = <A, C, D>$ can be said to be compliant with certainty. No matter if e_2 corresponds to activity B or C, the trace is compliant. Such cases occur in particular when activities are *behaviorally equivalent* compared to each other. In this case, B and C have such equivalence, because they present proper alternatives for each other.

The previous example illustrates that our compliance checking method can be used to determine compliance with certainty in situations where traditional compliance checking methods would not be able to make trustworthy compliance assessments. In Sect. 5, we demonstrate the usefulness of this property in practical settings.

5 Evaluation

In this section, we present an evaluation that we conducted to demonstrate the capabilities of the proposed compliance checking method for uncertain event-to-activity mappings. The goal of this evaluation is to assess how the impact of mapping uncertainty on the compliance checking task can be reduced by using our method. To achieve this, we compare results obtained through our method against results obtained by using a traditional compliance checking method. We apply these methods on a collection of real-world process models and accompanying event logs. Specifically, we evaluate for how many traces in these event logs the two methods can provide compliance checking results with certainty.

5.1 Test Collection

To perform the evaluation, we use a collection of real-world business process models from the *BIT process library*, first analyzed in an academic context by Fahland et al. [13]. The BIT process library consists of 886 process models from various industries, including the financial services and telecommunications domains. The same collection that has been used to test several event-to-activity mapping approaches [7,9], which motivates our choice for it. Hence, we believe that results obtained by using this collection present a realistic view on the applicability of the event-to-activity mapping approach against which we compare our compliance checking method. Furthermore, due to the size of the collection and its broad coverage of real-world process models, the collection seems well-suited to achieve a high external validity of the results.

From the test collection, we omitted any process model with soundness issues such as *deadlocks* or *livelocks*. Furthermore, we omitted a number of large models for which the event-to-activity mapping approach was not able to produce a results due to memory shortage. Note that the same filtering steps are also applied in [7]. As a result of the filtering, a collection of 598 process models remains available for usage in our evaluation.

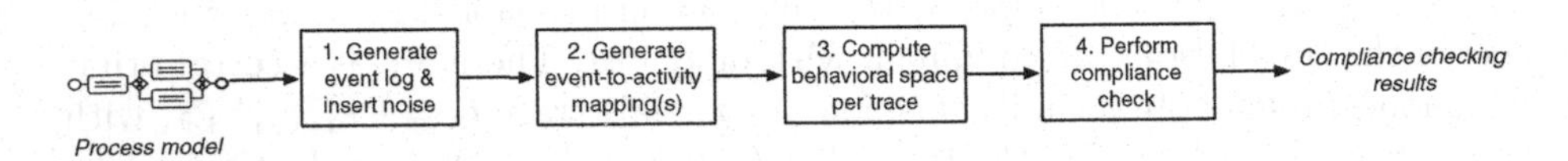

Fig. 3. Overview of the evaluation setup

5.2 Setup

Figure 3 depicts the steps of our evaluation approach. To perform these steps, we employ the *ProM6 framework*, which provides a vast amount of so-called *plug-ins* that implement process mining techniques[1]. For the first two steps of our approach we use existing plug-ins for event-to-activity mapping techniques, as described in [7]. For step 3 and 4, we have implemented the generation of behavioral spaces and our proposed method for compliance checking as a plug-in, which is available as part of the *BehavioralSpaces* package in ProM6.

Step 1 of the evaluation approach first generates an event log or each of the 598 process models in the filtered test collection. Staying true to the evaluation of [7], we generate a log containing 1000 traces for each model. For process models that include loops, we generate traces with a maximum length of 1000 events. Since we are interested in compliance checking, we transform these fully compliant logs into partially non-compliant logs. We achieve this by using a *noise-insertion* plug-in in ProM. This plug-in randomly adds noise to a log (i.e. possible noncompliance) by shuffling, duplicating, and removing events for a given percentage of traces. In this manner, we generate six different event logs, respectively containing noise in 0, 20, 40, 60, 80, and 100% of the traces.

[1] See www.promtools.org for more information and to download the framework.

In step 2, we take a process model and an accompanying event log and use the mapping technique from [7] to establish an event-to-activity mapping. We have selected this particular technique because it returns all potential mappings in case of uncertainty. Furthermore, the technique is relatively robust in the context of noncompliant behavior. In case the approach can compute a single mapping, i.e. there is no mapping uncertainty, we can conclude that for this process model and event log, traditional compliance checking techniques suffice to determine the compliance of all traces in the log. If the mapping approach returns multiple possible mappings, i.e. there is mapping uncertainty, we continue with the third step of the evaluation.

Step 3 computes a behavioral space for a trace based on an (uncertain) event-to-activity mapping $\mathbb{EA}$ established in the previous step. We obtain a behavioral space by creating a trace translation for each of the potential event-to-activity mappings included in $\mathbb{EA}$.

Lastly, in step 4 we assess if we can determine the compliance or noncompliance of a trace despite the presence of mapping uncertainty. We achieve this by computing the *ProbCompl* metric for the behavioral space of a trace t. If this metric returns a compliance level of 0.0 or 1.0, we know the compliance of t with certainty. For other values, the consideration of behavioral spaces does not suffice to determine the compliance in a certain manner, though we still obtain probabilistic and diagnostic information on its compliance.

5.3 Results

Figure 4 presents the results of our evaluation experiments. The figure illustrates for what percentage of traces deterministic compliance checking results are obtained by our proposed method and traditional methods.

For noise level 0, where all traces in the event logs are compliant with the process models, we can observe that the mapping approach can only establish an event-to-activity mapping for 70.2% of the models in the collection. Since none of the traces are noncompliant in this log, these issues are caused by activities which are behaviorally identical to each other. An example of this is seen for activities B and C of the running example. Because of these issues, traditional compliance checking techniques can only assess the compliance of 70.2% of the traces. However, by using behavioral spaces, we can still determine the compliance of a trace with certainty when mapping uncertainty is caused by such behavioral equivalent activities. Hence, by using our proposed compliance checking method, we can determine the compliance of traces with certainty in 100% of the cases. Due to its relative robustness to noise, the mapping approach obtains the same results for logs in which 20% of the traces contain noisy behavior. Therefore, the results obtained by our method are equal for this set of logs.

The results change for higher noise levels. For these sets of logs, the mapping approach fails to establish certain event-to-activity mappings for increasing numbers of processes. At 40% noise, the approach fails to establish certain mappings for 62.2% of the processes. This means that traditional compliance

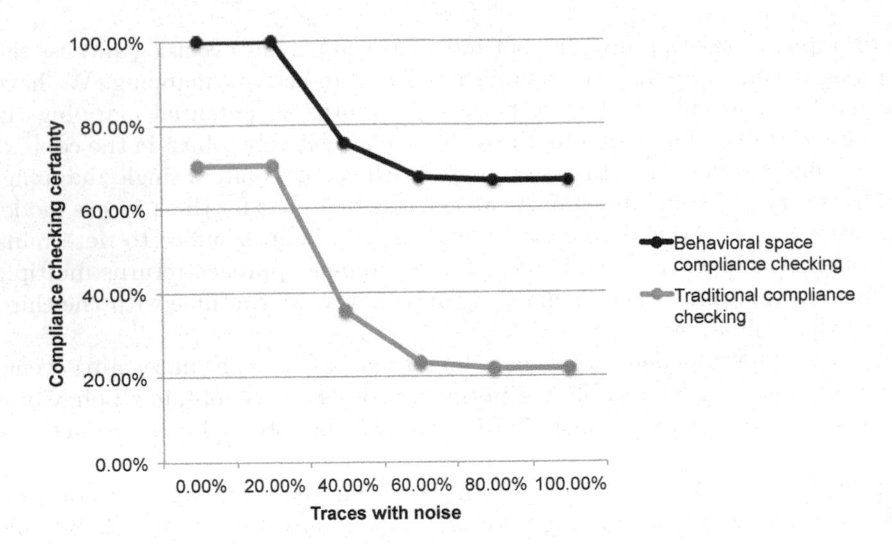

Fig. 4. Overview of the evaluation setup

checking techniques can only make compliance assessments in 36.8% of the cases. By contrast, our compliance checking method still succeeds to determine the compliance of 75.5% of the traces with certainty. The gap between our compliance checking method and traditional methods is even bigger for noise levels of 60% and higher. As Fig. 4 illustrates, the performance of the mapping approach and, thus, also of both compliance checking methods stabilizes for these noise levels. However, traditional compliance checking methods can only determine compliance for approximately 22.0% of the traces. By contrast, our proposed compliance checking method still provides deterministic results for 66.4% of the traces, i.e. for 3 times as many traces.

In summary, traditional compliance checking techniques become less and less useful. For high noise levels, they can provide results for as little as 22.0% of the traces. While the certainty obtainable through compliance checking with behavioral spaces is also affected by the increased levels of noise, the impact is much smaller. Therefore, we can conclude that in practical scenarios our compliance checking method is much wider applicable than traditional compliance checking methods.

6 Related Work

The work presented in this paper primarily relates to two major research streams: process matching and conformance checking.

Techniques for *process matching* concern the establishment of links between process concepts in different artifacts. The most commonly addressed use case for this is process model matching, where links are established between activities and events in different process models [10]. So-called process model matchers address this task by exploiting different process model features, including natural language [12], model structure [11], and behavior [15]. Therefore, they use similar techniques as the works, considered throughout this paper, that relate events to process model activities. Similar to the event-to-activity mapping task, it has been found that model-model matching is also inherently uncertain [16]. Other process matching techniques focus on different use cases, such as the alignment of natural language texts to process models [1] and the alignment of events from different event logs [19].

Process compliance checking techniques are applied in various application scenarios, including process querying [6], legal compliance [22], and auditing [4]. A plethora of techniques exist for this purpose (cf. [3,5,20,21]). In this paper, we have used techniques that perform compliance checks based on behavioral profile relations, introduced in [26]. These techniques are computationally highly efficient, which makes them an ideal choice for compliance checking in the context of the potentially vast number of translations per trace. Other commonly used techniques perform compliance checks based on so-called *alignments*. These techniques, introduced in [3,5], provide different diagnostic information than compliance checks based on behavioral profiles. Furthermore, the compliance checks can be considered to be more accurate in certain situations, because behavioral profile relations abstract from certain details of process behavior. However, these techniques are computationally much more demanding than the highly efficient compliance checks based on behavioral profiles. For the purpose of efficiency, recent advances in decomposed compliance checking present a promising direction [20]. Since the interpretations in a behavioral space generally have considerable overlaps, such techniques could be useful in order to reduce the computation time required for compliance checking.

7 Conclusion

In this paper, we introduced a compliance checking method that can be used in the presence of uncertain event-to-activity mappings. Our method considers all potential mappings generated by automated mapping approaches. As such, it can provide compliance checking results without the need to select a single, possibly incorrect mapping to base compliance checks on. Therefore, it avoids the risk of drawing incorrect compliance conclusions. A quantitative evaluation based on a large collection of real-world process models demonstrated that our method can provide deterministic compliance checking results for a considerable amount of situations where traditional compliance checking methods fail.

Our proposed method has to be considered in light of a considerable limitation. Namely, the obtained compliance checking results are dependent on the quality of the generated event-to-activity mappings. Most importantly, its results can be negatively affected if the correct mapping is not included in the set of potential mappings generated by any approach. Still, by applying our method, we eliminate the need to select a mapping from the set of potential methods. Hence, our method significantly reduces the possibility of drawing incorrect conclusions.

In future work, we intend to extend the coverage of our compliance checking method. For example, we want to provide instantiations based on other notions of compliance, such as alignment-based compliance or by considering data associated with events. Furthermore, we want to investigate possibilities to use our compliance checking method to improve existing event-to-activity mapping techniques or to support selection among potential mappings.

References

1. Van der Aa, H., Leopold, H., Reijers, H.A.: Comparing textual descriptions to process models - the automatic detection of inconsistencies. Inf. Syst. **64**, 447–460 (2016)
2. Van der Aa, H., Leopold, H., Reijers, H.A.: Dealing with behavioral ambiguity in textual process descriptions. In: La Rosa, M., Loos, P., Pastor, O. (eds.) BPM 2016. LNCS, vol. 9850, pp. 271–288. Springer, Cham (2016). doi:10.1007/978-3-319-45348-4_16
3. Van der Aalst, W.M.P., Adriansyah, A., van Dongen, B.F.: Replaying history on process models for conformance checking and performance analysis. Wiley Interdisc. Rev.: Data Mining Knowl. Discov. **2**(2), 182–192 (2012)
4. Accorsi, R., Stocker, T.: On the exploitation of process mining for security audits: the conformance checking case. In: Proceedings of the 27th Annual ACM Symposium on Applied Computing, pp. 1709–1716. ACM (2012)
5. Adriansyah, A., van Dongen, B., van der Aalst, W.: Conformance checking using cost-based fitness analysis. In: 2011 15th IEEE International on Enterprise Distributed Object Computing Conference (EDOC), pp. 55–64. IEEE (2011)
6. Awad, A., Decker, G., Weske, M.: Efficient compliance checking using BPMN-Q and temporal logic. In: Dumas, M., Reichert, M., Shan, M.-C. (eds.) BPM 2008. LNCS, vol. 5240, pp. 326–341. Springer, Heidelberg (2008). doi:10.1007/978-3-540-85758-7_24
7. Baier, T., Ciccio, C., Mendling, J., Weske, M.: Matching of events and activities - an approach using declarative modeling constraints. In: Gaaloul, K., Schmidt, R., Nurcan, S., Guerreiro, S., Ma, Q. (eds.) CAISE 2015. LNBIP, vol. 214, pp. 119–134. Springer, Cham (2015). doi:10.1007/978-3-319-19237-6_8
8. Baier, T., Mendling, J., Weske, M.: Bridging abstraction layers in process mining. Inf. Syst. **46**, 123–139 (2014)
9. Baier, T., Rogge-Solti, A., Weske, M., Mendling, J.: Matching of events and activities - an approach based on constraint satisfaction. In: Frank, U., Loucopoulos, P., Pastor, Ó., Petrounias, I. (eds.) PoEM 2014. LNBIP, vol. 197, pp. 58–72. Springer, Heidelberg (2014). doi:10.1007/978-3-662-45501-2_5
10. Cayoglu, U., Dijkman, R.M., Dumas, M., Fettke, P., Garcıa-Banuelos, L., Hake, P., Klinkmüller, C., Leopold, H., Ludwig, A., Loos, P., et al.: The process model matching contest 2013. In: 4th International Workshop on Process Model Collections: Management and Reuse (PMC-MR 2013) (2013)
11. Dijkman, R.M., Dumas, M., Van Dongen, B.F., Käärik, R., Mendling, J.: Similarity of business process models: metrics and evaluation. Inf. Syst. **36**(2), 498–516 (2011)
12. Ehrig, M., Koschmider, A., Oberweis, A.: Measuring similarity between semantic business process models. In: Proceedings of the Fourth Asia-Pacific Conference on Comceptual Modelling, vol. 67, pp. 71–80 (2007)

13. Fahland, D., Favre, C., Koehler, J., Lohmann, N., Völzer, H., Wolf, K.: Analysis on demand: instantaneous soundness checking of industrial business process models. Data Knowl. Eng. **70**(5), 448–466 (2011)
14. Gal, A.: Uncertain schema matching. Synth. Lect. Data Manag. **3**(1), 1–97 (2011)
15. Kunze, M., Weidlich, M., Weske, M.: Behavioral similarity – a proper metric. In: Rinderle-Ma, S., Toumani, F., Wolf, K. (eds.) BPM 2011. LNCS, vol. 6896, pp. 166–181. Springer, Heidelberg (2011). doi:10.1007/978-3-642-23059-2_15
16. Kuss, E., Leopold, H., Van der Aa, H., Stuckenschmidt, H., Reijers, H.A.: Probabilistic evaluation of process model matching techniques. In: Comyn-Wattiau, I., Tanaka, K., Song, I.-Y., Yamamoto, S., Saeki, M. (eds.) ER 2016. LNCS, vol. 9974, pp. 279–292. Springer, Cham (2016). doi:10.1007/978-3-319-46397-1_22
17. Ly, L.T., Maggi, F.M., Montali, M., Rinderle-Ma, S., van der Aalst, W.M.P.: Compliance monitoring in business processes: functionalities, application, and tool-support. Inf. Syst. **54**, 209–234 (2015)
18. Madhavan, J., Bernstein, P.A., Domingos, P., Halevy, A.Y.: Representing and reasoning about mappings between domain models. In: AAAI/IAAI 2002, pp. 80–86 (2002)
19. Mannhardt, F., de Leoni, M., Reijers, H.A.: Extending process logs with events from supplementary sources. In: Fournier, F., Mendling, J. (eds.) BPM 2014. LNBIP, vol. 202, pp. 235–247. Springer, Cham (2015). doi:10.1007/978-3-319-15895-2_21
20. Munoz-Gama, J., Carmona, J., Van Der Aalst, W.M.: Single-entry single-exit decomposed conformance checking. Inf. Syst. **46**, 102–122 (2014)
21. Ramezani, E., Fahland, D., Van der Aalst, W.M.P.: Where did i misbehave? Diagnostic information in compliance checking. In: Barros, A., Gal, A., Kindler, E. (eds.) BPM 2012. LNCS, vol. 7481, pp. 262–278. Springer, Heidelberg (2012). doi:10.1007/978-3-642-32885-5_21
22. Sadiq, S., Governatori, G., Namiri, K.: Modeling control objectives for business process compliance. In: Alonso, G., Dadam, P., Rosemann, M. (eds.) BPM 2007. LNCS, vol. 4714, pp. 149–164. Springer, Heidelberg (2007). doi:10.1007/978-3-540-75183-0_12
23. Senderovich, A., Rogge-Solti, A., Gal, A., Mendling, J., Mandelbaum, A.: The ROAD from sensor data to process instances via interaction mining. In: Nurcan, S., Soffer, P., Bajec, M., Eder, J. (eds.) CAiSE 2016. LNCS, vol. 9694, pp. 257–273. Springer, Cham (2016). doi:10.1007/978-3-319-39696-5_16
24. Smirnov, S., Weidlich, M., Mendling, J.: Business process model abstraction based on behavioral profiles. In: Maglio, P.P., Weske, M., Yang, J., Fantinato, M. (eds.) ICSOC 2010. LNCS, vol. 6470, pp. 1–16. Springer, Heidelberg (2010). doi:10.1007/978-3-642-17358-5_1
25. Van Der Aalst, W., et al.: Process mining manifesto. In: Daniel, F., Barkaoui, K., Dustdar, S. (eds.) BPM 2011. LNBIP, vol. 99, pp. 169–194. Springer, Heidelberg (2012). doi:10.1007/978-3-642-28108-2_19
26. Weidlich, M., Mendling, J., Weske, M.: Efficient consistency measurement based on behavioral profiles of process models. IEEE Trans. Softw. Eng. **37**(3), 410–429 (2011)
27. Weidlich, M., Polyvyanyy, A., Desai, N., Mendling, J., Weske, M.: Process compliance analysis based on behavioural profiles. Inf. Syst. **36**(7), 1009–1025 (2011)
28. Weidlich, M., Sagi, T., Leopold, H., Gal, A., Mendling, J.: Predicting the quality of process model matching. In: Daniel, F., Wang, J., Weber, B. (eds.) BPM 2013. LNCS, vol. 8094, pp. 203–210. Springer, Heidelberg (2013). doi:10.1007/978-3-642-40176-3_16

Aligning Modeled and Observed Behavior: A Compromise Between Computation Complexity and Quality

Boudewijn van Dongen[1(✉)], Josep Carmona[2], Thomas Chatain[3], and Farbod Taymouri[2]

[1] Eindhoven University of Technology, Eindhoven, The Netherlands
b.f.v.dongen@tue.nl

[2] Universitat Politècnica de Catalunya, Barcelona, Spain
{jcarmona,taymouri}@cs.upc.edu

[3] LSV, ENS Cachan, CNRS, Inria, Université Paris-Saclay, Cachan, France
chatain@lsv.ens-cachan.fr

Abstract. Certifying that a process model is aligned with the real process executions is perhaps the most desired feature a process model may have: aligned process models are crucial for organizations, since strategic decisions can be made easier on models instead of on plain data. In spite of its importance, the current algorithmic support for computing alignments is limited: either techniques that explicitly explore the model behavior (which may be worst-case exponential with respect to the model size), or heuristic approaches that cannot guarantee a solution, are the only alternatives. In this paper we propose a solution that sits right in the middle in the complexity spectrum of alignment techniques; it can always guarantee a solution, whose quality depends on the exploration depth used and local decisions taken at each step. We use linear algebraic techniques in combination with an iterative search which focuses on progressing towards a solution. The experiments show a clear reduction in the time required for reaching a solution, without sacrificing significantly the quality of the alignment obtained.

Keywords: Process mining · Conformance checking · ILP · Heuristics · Alignments

1 Introduction

The current trend to store all kinds of digital data has made organizations to become more than ever data-oriented, thus dependent on the available techniques to extract value from the data. *Process mining* is an emerging field which focuses on analyzing the data corresponding to process executions, with the purpose of extracting, analyzing and enhancing evidence-based process models [1]. The application of process mining techniques is magnified in the field of *Business Process Management*, where in the last couple of years we have seen important vendors incorporating process mining capabilities to their products.

E. Dubois and K. Pohl (Eds.): CAiSE 2017, LNCS 10253, pp. 94–109, 2017.
DOI: 10.1007/978-3-319-59536-8_7

One of the current challenges for process mining techniques is the computation of an *alignment* of a process model with respect to observed behavior [2]. Intuitively, given a trace representing a real process execution, an optimal alignment provides the best trace the process model can provide to mimic the observed behavior. Then observed and model traces are rendered in a two-row matrix denoting the synchronous/asynchronous moves between individual activities of model and log, respectively. Alignments are extremely important in the context of process mining, since they open the door to evaluate the metrics that asses the quality of a process model to represent observed behavior: *fitness* and *generalization* [2] and precision [3]. Additionally, alignments are a necessary step to enhance the information provided in a process model [1].

The current algorithmic support to compute alignments is either too complex [2] or heuristic [4]. The former is defined as a search for a minimal path on the product of the state space of the process model and the observed behavior, an object that is worst-case exponential with respect to the size of the model. This hampers the application of the techniques from [2] in case of medium/large instances. In contrast, the techniques in [4] are very efficient both in time and memory requirements, but cannot guarantee a solution always.

This paper presents an algorithm for computing alignments whose nature is in between the two aforementioned techniques. As in [4], we ground the technique on the resolution of *Integer Linear Programming* (ILP) models that guide the search for solutions while constructing the derived alignment. However, the techniques of this paper ensure the derivation of an alignment by requiring the feasibility of individual steps computed, in contrast to the recursive approach applied in [4]. As in [2], the algorithm is defined on the synchronous product between the observed trace and the process model, and we use part of the ILP model (the tail of the solutions obtained at each step) as an underestimate of the cost to reach a solution. The crucial element of our approach is to incrementally construct the alignment by "jumping" over the space of solutions in a depth-first manner, using ILP models as oracles to guide the search. The approach is implemented in the open-source platform `ProM`, and experiments are provided which witness the distinctive capabilities of the proposed approach with respect to the state-of-the-art technique to compute alignments.

2 Related Work

The seminal work in [2] proposed the notion of alignment, and developed a technique to compute optimal alignments for a particular class of process models. For each trace σ in the log, the approach consists on exploring the synchronous product of model's state space and σ. In the exploration, a shortest path is computed in the statespace of synchronous product, using the A^* algorithm, once costs for model and log moves are defined. The approach is implemented in `ProM`, and can be considered as the state-of-the-art technique for computing alignments. Several optimizations have been proposed to the basic approach: for instance, the use of ILP techniques on each visited state to prune the search space [2].

In contrast to [2], the technique presented in [4] fully resorts in the resolution of ILP models together with a recursive partitioning of the input trace. This technique computes *approximate alignments*, a novel class of alignments where deviations can be explained between sets of transitions, instead of singletons as in [2]. The techniques in [4] can be a good alternative when a precise information is not required and instead an approximation suffices.

Decompositional techniques have been presented [5,6] which, instead of computing alignments, focus on the problem of *deciding* whether a given trace fits a process model or not. The underlying idea is to split the model into a particular set of transition-bordered fragments which satisfy certain conditions, and local alignments are then computed for each one of the fragments, thus providing a upper bound on the cost of an alignment. In contrast, the technique presented in this paper does not split the model, hence enabling the computation of alignments at a global (model) level. Furthermore, our technique can be applied in the context of decisional techniques for the computation of local alignments a fitting trace is guaranteed to be identified as such.

Few techniques exist in the literature to consider also other perspectives beyond control-flow for the alignment computation [7]. In spite of the clear benefit of considering a multi-perspective view on the problem, these techniques cannot handle medium to large instances due to their algorithmic complexity. In fact, the available implementations of such techniques use a two-stage approach, where they first align the control flow and then consider the data/resources in a second stage after which optimality cannot be guaranteed. Therefore, our work can be applied directly in the first stage with some further loss of optimality.

In this paper, we focus on Petri nets as the modelling language. In [2] alignments are introduced for the turing complete class of models called inhibitor nets. The work in this paper easily extends to that class by adding constraints requiring a place to be empty before firing a transition. Since transformations exist for most modelling languages into Petri nets (or inhibitor nets) our work can be applied to these classes as well when doing the transformations explicitly. However, our techniques cannot directly be translated to existing work where alignments are computed directly on other model classes, such as declarative models [8,9] or using different log notions, such as partially ordered logs [10,11] as no ILP formulation exists for these cases.

3 Preliminaries

A *Petri Net* [12] is a 3-tuple $N = \langle P, T, \mathcal{F} \rangle$, where P is the set of places, T is the set of transitions, $P \cap T = \emptyset$, $\mathcal{F} : (P \times T) \cup (T \times P) \rightarrow \{0, 1\}$ is the flow relation. A marking is an assignment of non-negative integers to places. If k is assigned to place p by marking m (denoted $m(p) = k$), we say that p is marked with k tokens. Given a node $x \in P \cup T$, its pre-set and post-set (in graph adjacency terms) are denoted by $^\bullet x$ and $x^\bullet$ respectively. A transition t is *enabled* in a marking m when all places in $^\bullet t$ are marked. When a transition t is enabled, it can *fire* by removing a token from each place in $^\bullet t$ and putting a token to each place in $t^\bullet$. A marking m' is *reachable* from m if there is a sequence of firings $t_1 t_2 \dots t_n$ that transforms m into m', denoted by $m[t_1 t_2 \dots t_n\rangle m'$. A sequence of transitions $t_1 t_2 \dots t_n$ is a *feasible sequence* if it is firable from the initial marking m_0.

Workflow processes can be represented in a simple way by using Workflow Nets (WF-nets). A WF-net is a Petri net where there is a place *start* (denoting the initial state of the system) with no incoming arcs and a place *end* (denoting the final state of the system) with no outgoing arcs, and every other node is within a path between *start* and *end*. The transitions in a WF-net are labeled with tasks or are used for routing purposes (so-called silent transitions or τ transitions). For the sake of simplicity, the techniques of this paper assume models are specified with *sound* labeled WF-nets, i.e. models without lifelocks and with only a single deadlock indicating that the model's execution has terminated.

Definition 1 (Net System, Full Firing Sequences). *A net system is a tuple $SN = (N, m_{start}, m_{end})$, where N is a Petri net and the two last elements define the initial and final marking of the net, respectively. The set $\{\sigma \mid (N, m_{start})[\sigma\rangle(N, m_{end})\}$ denotes all the full firing sequences of SN.*

Note that in this paper, we assume that the set of all full firing sequences is not empty, i.e. the final marking is reachable from the initial marking.

Let $N = \langle P, T, \mathcal{F}\rangle$ be a Petri net with initial marking m_0. Given a feasible sequence $m_0 \xrightarrow{\sigma} m$, the number of tokens for a place p in m is equal to the tokens of p in m_0 plus the tokens added by the input transitions of p in σ minus the tokens removed by the output transitions of p in σ:

$$m(p) = m_0(p) + \sum_{t \in {}^\bullet p} |\sigma|_t \; \mathcal{F}(t,p) - \sum_{t \in p^\bullet} |\sigma|_t \; \mathcal{F}(p,t)$$

The *marking equations* for all the places in the net can be written in the following matrix form: $m = m_0 - \mathbf{N}^- \cdot \widehat{\sigma} + \mathbf{N}^+ \cdot \widehat{\sigma}$, where $\mathbf{N} = \mathbf{N}^+ - \mathbf{N}^- \in \mathbb{Z}^{P \times T}$ is the *incidence matrix* of the net: $\mathbf{N}^-(p,t) = \mathcal{F}(p,t)$ corresponds to the consumption of tokens and $\mathbf{N}^+(p,t) = \mathcal{F}(t,p)$ corresponds to production of tokens. If a marking m is reachable from m_0, then there exists a sequence σ such that $m_0 \xrightarrow{\sigma} m$, and the following system of equations has at least the solution $\vec{x} = \widehat{\sigma}$

$$\vec{m} = \vec{m_0} - \mathbf{N}^- \cdot \vec{x} + \mathbf{N}^+ \cdot \vec{x} \tag{1}$$

If (1) is infeasible, then m is not reachable from m_0. The inverse does not hold in general: there are markings satisfying (1) which are not reachable. Those markings (and the corresponding Parikh vectors) are said to be *spurious* [13].

For well-structured Petri nets classes Eq. (1) characterizes reachability. It goes beyond the scope of this paper to elaborate on the exact classes of models for which this is the case. However, in this paper, we assume that the models we consider belong to this class.

Next to Petri nets, we formalize event logs and traces.

Definition 2 (Trace, Event Log, Parikh vector). *Given an alphabet of events* $T = \{t_1, \ldots, t_n\}$, *a trace is a word* $\sigma \in T^*$ *that represents a finite sequence of events. An* event log $L \in \mathcal{B}(T^*)$ *is a multiset of traces*[1]. $|\sigma|_a$ *represents the number of occurrences of a in* σ. *The Parikh vector of a sequence of events* σ *is a function* $\widehat{\ }: T^* \to \mathbb{N}^n$ *defined as* $\widehat{\sigma} = (|\sigma|_{t_1}, \ldots, |\sigma|_{t_n})$. *For simplicity, we will also represent* $|\sigma|_{t_i}$ *as* $\widehat{\sigma}(t_i)$.

The main metric in this paper to asses the adequacy of a model in describing a log is *fitness* [1], which is based on the reproducibility of a trace in a model:

Definition 3 (Fitting Trace). *A trace* $\sigma \in T^*$ *fits* $SN = (N, m_{start}, m_{end})$ *if* σ *coincides with a full firing sequence of* SN, *i.e.,* $(N, m_{start})[\sigma\rangle(N, m_{end})$.

Hence an optimal alignment may be fitting or not, depending on whether the model can mimic exactly or not the behavior observed. Computing alignments is a complex task. In [2] the foundational work was presented to construct alignments by depth-first search using an A^* algorithm. The algorithm presented there relies on two fundamental concepts:

- A synchronous product Petri net, which is a combination of the original model being aligned and a Petri net representation of the (partially ordered) trace in the log, and
- The marking equation of that synchronous product.

The core alignment question is formalized as follows: Given a synchronous product with a penalty function assigning a non-negative penalty to each transition firing, find a firing sequence from the initial marking to the final marking with the lowest total penalties.

Consider the example model in Fig. 1. This model is a simple parallelism between transitions B and C after A and before D. Now, consider the trace $<C, D>$ translated into a trace net as shown in Fig. 2. Obviously, this trace does not fit the model, as transitions A and B are missing from it. Conceptually, the alignment problem first constructs a so-called synchronous product which is shown in Fig. 3. Here, the two black transitions are synchronous combinations of equally labeled transitions in the model and the trace, i.e. they have the same input and output places in both the model and the trace net. The alignment algorithm then finds the shortest execution sequence from the initial state to the final state, where the firing of each transition has an associated cost. Typically, the black transitions, called *synchronous moves* have the lowest cost, while the model transitions, called *model moves* and the trace net transitions, called *log moves*, have higher costs. For this example, the cheapest firing sequence would be $<A, C, B, D>$ as depicted in the upper row (model trace) of the alignment of Fig. 4. For this alignment, the white transitions A and B have been fired as model moves, and the black transitions C and D have fired as synchronous moves.

[1] $\mathcal{B}(A)$ denotes the set of all multisets of the set A.

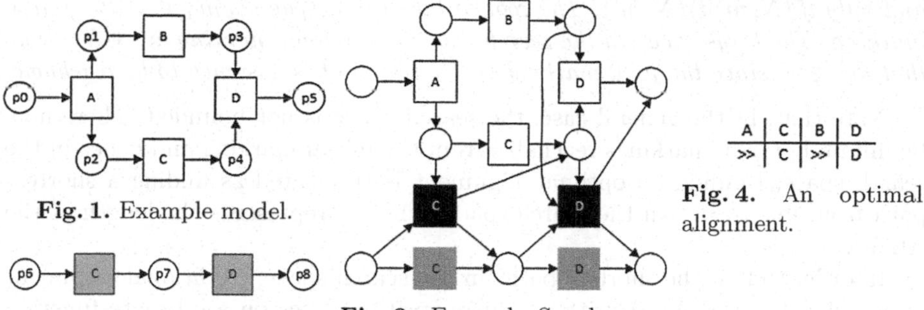

Fig. 1. Example model.

Fig. 2. Example trace net.

Fig. 3. Example Synchronous Product.

Fig. 4. An optimal alignment.

The marking equation used for the example synchronous product model in Fig. 3 is shown below. Here, the columns corresponding to each transition in the incidence matrix are labeled with m, s, or l for (m)odel, (s)ynchronous, or (log) move.

$$\begin{array}{c} \\ p0\\ p1\\ p2\\ p3\\ p4\\ p5\\ p6\\ p7\\ p8 \end{array}
\begin{array}{c} m_i \\ \left(\begin{array}{c} 1\\0\\0\\0\\0\\0\\1\\0\\0 \end{array}\right) \end{array}
-
\begin{array}{c} \begin{array}{cccccccc} A_m & B_m & C_m & D_m & C_s & D_s & C_l & D_l \end{array} \\ \left(\begin{array}{cccccccc}
1&0&0&0&0&0&0&0\\
0&1&0&0&0&0&0&0\\
0&0&1&0&1&0&0&0\\
0&0&0&1&0&1&0&0\\
0&0&0&1&0&1&0&0\\
0&0&0&0&0&0&0&0\\
0&0&0&0&1&0&1&0\\
0&0&0&0&0&1&0&1\\
0&0&0&0&0&0&0&0
\end{array}\right) \end{array}
\cdot \vec{x} +
\begin{array}{c} \begin{array}{cccccccc} A_m & B_m & C_m & D_m & C_s & D_s & C_l & D_l \end{array} \\ \left(\begin{array}{cccccccc}
0&0&0&0&0&0&0&0\\
1&0&0&0&0&0&0&0\\
1&0&0&0&0&0&0&0\\
0&1&0&0&0&0&0&0\\
0&0&1&0&1&0&0&0\\
0&0&0&1&0&1&0&0\\
0&0&0&0&0&0&0&0\\
0&0&0&0&1&0&1&0\\
0&0&0&0&0&1&0&1
\end{array}\right) \end{array}
\cdot \vec{x} =
\begin{array}{c} m_f \\ \left(\begin{array}{c} 0\\0\\0\\0\\0\\1\\0\\0\\1 \end{array}\right) \end{array}$$

In the remainder of the paper, we consider the synchronous product model as the starting point and we use the partitioning of the transitions into synchronous moves, log moves and model moves.

Definition 4 (Alignments, Optimal Alignments). *Let* $N = \langle P, T, \mathcal{F} \rangle$ *be a synchronous product Petri net where* $T = T^s \cup T^l \cup T^m$ *can be partitioned into sets of transitions corresponding to synchronous moves, log moves and model moves respectively and let* $(N, m_\perp, m^\top)$ *a corresponding net system. Furthermore let* $c : T \to \mathbb{R}^+$ *a cost function. An alignment is a full firing sequence* $\sigma_a \in \{\sigma \mid (N, m_\perp)[\sigma\rangle(N, m^\top)\}$ *of this system. An optimal alignment is an alignment* σ_a *such that for all* $\sigma \in \{\sigma \mid (N, m_\perp)[\sigma\rangle(N, m^\top)\}$ *holds that* $c(\sigma_a) \leq c(\sigma)$.

Traditional algorithms search for alignments using a depth-first search method over a search graph in which each node represents a partial firing sequence of the system and each edge the firing of a transition.

Definition 5 (Search space). *Let* $N = \langle P, T, \mathcal{F} \rangle$ *be a synchronous product Petri net where* $T = T^s \cup T^l \cup T^m$ *can be partitioned into sets of transitions corresponding to synchronous moves, log moves and model moves respectively and let* $(N, m_\perp, m^\top)$ *a corresponding net system. Furthermore let* $c : T \to \mathbb{R}^+$ *a cost function. The alignment search space is defined as* $S = (V, E, c)$, *with* $V = \{m \mid (N, m_\perp)[\sigma\rangle(N, m)\}$ *and* $E \subseteq V \times T \times V$ *such that* $(m, t, m') \in E$ *if* *and only if* $(N, m)[t\rangle(N, m')$. *The root of the search space is* $m_\perp \in V$ *the initial marking. The target node in the search space is the final marking* $m^\top \in V$. *Note that* $m^\top \in V$ *since the final marking of a system net is assumed to be reachable.*

Note that, in the general case, the search space is not bounded. There may be infinitely many markings reachable from the initial marking and hence in the search space. Finding an optimal alignment is translated as finding a shortest path from $m_\perp$ to $m^\top$ in the search space, where c represents the length of the edges[2].

In order to find the shortest path[3] in the search space, traditional alignment approaches use the A^* algorithm. This algorithm relies on a estimate function that underestimates the remaining costs from the current node to one of the target nodes. The cost between nodes m and m' in V can be underestimated by the marking equation (cf. Sect. 3) in the following way:

Definition 6 (Underestimating the costs). *Let* $S = (V, E, c)$ *be a search space and* $m_c \in V$ *the current marking reached in the graph. We know that if there exists a* σ' *such that* $(N, m_c)[\sigma'\rangle(N, m^\top)$ *then* $m_c + \mathbf{N} \cdot \widehat{\sigma'} = m^\top$.

Therefore, the solution to the linear problem minimize $c(\varsigma)$ *such that* $\overrightarrow{m_c} + \mathbf{N} \cdot \widehat{\varsigma} = \overrightarrow{m^\top}$ *provides an underestimate for the cost of* σ', *i.e.* $c(\varsigma) \leq c(\sigma')$.

If no solution exists, the final marking cannot be reached, which implies that part of the search space is not relevant or in other words a correct underestimate for the remaining distance is infinite.

This approach to finding alignments has been implemented in ProM and has been extensively used in many applications. However, there are two problems with this approach. Firstly, the search space can be very large (although only a finite part needs to be considered). Typically, the search space size is exponential in the size of the synchronous product model which is the product of the original model and the trace to be aligned. Secondly, computing estimates is computationally expensive. This can be done both using Linear Programming and Integer Linear Programming, where the latter provides more accurate estimates. In practice however, both techniques are equally fast as the increase in precision when doing Integer computations allows the A^* algorithm to visit fewer nodes.

4 ILP Techinques to Compute Alignments

4.1 Computing Optimal Alignments Using ILP

In this paper, we take a fundamentally different approach as we incrementally construct (possibly suboptimal) alignments. We do so, by "jumping" trough

[2] Since the cost function c does not allow for 0-length, there are no loops of length 0 in the graph. In the available implementations of the alignment problem, this is hidden from the end-user when instantiating the cost function, but an $\epsilon > 0$ is used in the core computation.

[3] Note that there may be more than one shortest path. Where we talk about the shortest path, we mean any shortest path.

the synchronous product model in a depth-first manner until we reach the final marking. Once the final marking is reached, we terminate the search. Effectively, from a given marking, we fire a total of x transitions such that these x firings are locally optimal with respect to the cost function c and we reach the next node in the search space, from where we continue our search. However, before discussing our algorithm, we first consider a method for computing optimal alignments of a given maximal length using the marking equation.

The marking equation allows us to formalize x transition executions at once by taking the consumption matrix for each step and the marking equation for all preceding steps in the following way:

Property 1 (Marking equation for executing x transitions). Let $N = \langle P, T, \mathcal{F} \rangle$ be a Petri net, m_0, m_f two reachable markings of the net and let $\sigma = \langle t_0, \ldots, t_{x-1} \rangle$ be a trace such that $(N, m_0)[\sigma\rangle(N, m_f)$. Furthermore, for $0 < i \leq x$, let m_i be such that $(N, m_0)[\langle t_0, \ldots, t_i \rangle\rangle(N, m_i)$. Using the marking equation and general properties of transition firing, we know the following properties hold:

- $\overrightarrow{m_f} = \overrightarrow{m_0} - \mathbf{N}^- \cdot \widehat{\sigma} + \mathbf{N}^+ \cdot \widehat{\sigma}$ as the sequence σ is executable,
- for $0 < i \leq x$ holds that $\overrightarrow{m_i} = \overrightarrow{m_{i-1}} - \mathbf{N}^- \cdot \widehat{\langle t_{i-1} \rangle} + \mathbf{N}^+ \cdot \widehat{\langle t_{i-1} \rangle}$, i.e. the marking equation holds for each individual transition in the sequence,
- for $0 \leq i < x$ holds that $\overrightarrow{m_i} - \mathbf{N}^- \cdot \widehat{\sigma_{0..i}} + \mathbf{N}^+ \cdot \widehat{\sigma_{0..i-1}} \geq 0$, i.e. before firing of each transition there are sufficient tokens to fire that transition.

The properties above are fundamental properties of Petri nets and the marking equation. They give rise to a new algorithm to find alignments of a given length.

Definition 7 (Up To Length x Alignment as ILP problem). *Let $N = \langle P, T, \mathcal{F} \rangle$ be a synchronous product Petri net and let $(N, m_\perp, m^\top)$ a corresponding net system. Furthermore let $c : T \to \mathbb{R}^+$ a cost function. Let $\overrightarrow{\theta_0}, \ldots, \overrightarrow{\theta_{x-1}}$ be a set of x vectors of dimension $|T|$ as the optimal solution to the following $\{0,1\}$ ILP problem:*

$$\text{minimize}_{\Sigma} \quad \sum_{0 \leq i < x} c(\overrightarrow{\theta_i}) \tag{2}$$

$$\text{subject to} \quad \overrightarrow{m_\perp} + \sum_{0 \leq j < x} \mathbf{N} \cdot \overrightarrow{\theta_j} = \overrightarrow{m^\top} \tag{3}$$

$$\forall_{0 \leq i < x} \quad \overrightarrow{\theta_i} \cdot \overrightarrow{1}^T \leq 1 \tag{4}$$

$$\overrightarrow{m_\perp} + \sum_{0 \leq j < i} \mathbf{N} \cdot \overrightarrow{\theta_j} - \mathbf{N}^- \cdot \overrightarrow{\theta_i} \geq 0 \tag{5}$$

$$\forall_{0 < i < x} \quad \overrightarrow{\theta_{i-1}} \cdot \overrightarrow{1}^T \geq \overrightarrow{\theta_i} \cdot \overrightarrow{1}^T \tag{6}$$

An optimal solution to the problem above constitutes a full firing sequence σ of length $l = \sum_{0 \leq i < x} \overrightarrow{\theta_i} \cdot \overrightarrow{1}^T$ of the net N in the following way: for each $0 \leq i < l$

holds that $\sigma_i = t \equiv \vec{\theta}(t) = 1$, *i.e. the sequence* σ *is made up of those transitions which correspond to the variables taking value* 1 *in this system. Note that for* $l \leq i < x$ *holds that* $\vec{\theta_i} \cdot \vec{1}^T = 0$.

The target function shown as Eq. 2 above sums the costs of firing transitions in the net. Equation 4 ensures that each vector corresponds to at most one firing of a transition and Eq. 5 ensures that firing all transitions t_j preceding transition t_i from the initial marking produces sufficient tokens in every place to enable transition t_i. Equation 6 ensures that in any solution the vectors $\vec{\theta} = \vec{0}$ are grouped together and finally, Eq. 3 ensures that the final marking is reached after firing at most k transitions.

Before showing how the ILP definition above can be extended to find alignments up to length k, we first show that any optimal alignment σ indeed corresponds to an optimal solution to this ILP for $k = |\sigma|$.

Theorem 1. *Let* $N = \langle P, T, \mathcal{F} \rangle$ *be a synchronous product Petri net and let* $(N, m_\perp, m^\top)$ *a corresponding net system. Furthermore let* $c : T \to \mathbb{R}^+$ *a cost function and* σ *an optimal alignment of* N. *We show that there is an optimal solution to the k-alignment ILP for* $k \geq |\sigma|$ *corresponding to* σ, *i.e. the ILP-alignment problem provided us with optimal alignments.*

Proof. The proof consists of two parts. First, we show that σ translates into a solution of the ILP. Then, we show that there cannot be a more optimal solution as this would imply there is a more optimal alignment.

Let $\Theta = \{\vec{\theta_0}, \ldots, \overrightarrow{\theta_{|\sigma|-1}}\}$ be a set of vectors, such that for all $0 \leq i < |\sigma|$ holds that $\vec{\theta_i}(t) = 1$ if and only if $\sigma_i = t$, otherwise $\vec{\theta_i}(t) = 0$. We show that this is a solution to the ILP of Definition 7 by enumerating the constraints:

- **(4)** For all $0 \leq i < |\sigma_a|$ it trivially holds that $\vec{\theta_i} \cdot \vec{1}^T = 1$,
- **(5)** Since σ is a full firing sequence, we know that for each $0 \leq i < |\sigma|$ holds that $(N, m_\perp)[\sigma_{0..i-1}\rangle(N, m)$ for some marking m in which transition σ_i is enabled. Furthermore, the marking equation states that $\overrightarrow{m_\perp} + \mathbf{N} \cdot \widehat{\sigma_{0..i-1}} = \vec{m}$ and $\vec{m} - \mathbf{N}^- \cdot \widehat{\langle \sigma_i \rangle} \geq 0$.
  The definition $\vec{\theta_i}$ leads to the fact that $\sum_{0 \leq j < i} \vec{\theta_j} = \widehat{\sigma_{0..i-1}}$, hence we conclude that $\overrightarrow{m_\perp} + \mathbf{N} \cdot \sum_{0 \leq j < i} \vec{\theta_j} = \vec{m}$ and $\vec{m} - \mathbf{N}^- \cdot \theta_i \geq 0$. Combining this yields $\overrightarrow{m_\perp} + \sum_{0 \leq j < i} \mathbf{N} \cdot \vec{\theta_j} - \mathbf{N}^- \cdot \theta_i \geq 0$ for all $0 \leq i < |\sigma|$,
- **(6)** Since all vectors $\vec{\theta_i}$ contain one element equal to 1 this is trivially true,
- **(3)** Similar to the proof for Eq. 5, this equation is satisfied.

The set of vectors Θ indeed is a solution to the ILP corresponding to the full firing sequence σ. Now we prove that no better solution to the ILP exists by contradiction. Assume there is a solution $\Theta' = \{\vec{\theta'_0}, \ldots, \overrightarrow{\theta'_{|\sigma|-1}}\}$ which is a solution to the ILP with a lower target function than Θ. We know we can construct a $\sigma' = \langle t_0, \ldots, t_{l-1} \rangle$ for Θ' with length $l \leq |\sigma|$ (Definition 7). Furthermore, we know σ' is a full firing sequence. Since $\sum_{0 \leq i < |\sigma'|} c(\vec{\theta'_i}) < \sum_{0 \leq i < |\sigma|} c(\vec{\theta_i})$ and the relation between σ and Θ, we know that $c(\sigma') < c(\sigma)$. However, this violates the definition of σ being an optimal alignment. □

The ILP formulation above allows us to compute an optimal alignment if we know an upper bound k for the length of such an alignment. Unfortunately, such an upper bound cannot be given in advance as this would require knowledge of the alignment sought. Furthermore, the large number of variables in this ILP (the number of transitions in the synchronous product model times the length of the alignment) makes this ILP intractable in any real life setting.

4.2 Computing Alignments Without Optimality Guarantees

To overcome the limitations of not knowing the length of the alignment and the intractability of the ILP computation, we introduce an algorithm for incrementally computing alignments. The core idea of this algorithm, which again relies heavily on the marking equation, is the following. We use an ILP problem that constructs an exact prefix of an alignment of relatively short length (for example $x = 10$ transitions) and estimates the remainder of the alignment in the same way the A^* techniques do. Then, we execute the exact prefix of relatively small length x, compute the resulting marking and repeat the computation until we reach the target marking.

Definition 8 (k of x prefix Alignment as ILP problem). *Let $N = \langle P, T, \mathcal{F} \rangle$ be a synchronous product Petri net where $T = T^s \cup T^l \cup T^m$ are the partitions of T and let $(N, m_\perp, m^\top)$ a corresponding net system. Furthermore let $c : T \to \mathbb{R}^+$ a cost function. We assume $k \leq |T^l|$.*

Let $\Theta = \{\vec{\theta_0}, \ldots, \vec{\theta_x}\}$ be a set of $x+1$ vectors of dimension $|T|$ as the optimal solution to the following ILP problem:

$$\text{minimize} \quad \sum_{0 \leq i \leq x} c(\vec{\theta_i}) \tag{7}$$

$$\text{subject to} \quad \vec{m_\perp} + \sum_{0 \leq j \leq x} \mathbf{N} \cdot \vec{\theta_j} = \vec{m^\top} \tag{8}$$

$$\sum_{t \in T^s \cup T^l} \sum_{0 \leq i < x} \theta_i(t) \geq k \tag{9}$$

$$\forall_{0 \leq i < x} \quad \vec{\theta_i} \cdot \vec{1}^T \leq 1 \tag{10}$$

$$\vec{m_\perp} + \sum_{0 \leq j < i} \mathbf{N} \cdot \vec{\theta_j} - \mathbf{N}^- \cdot \vec{\theta_i} \geq 0 \tag{11}$$

$$\forall_{0 < i < x} \quad \vec{\theta_{i-1}} \cdot \vec{1}^T \geq \vec{\theta_i} \cdot \vec{1}^T \tag{12}$$

$$C \cdot \vec{\theta_{x-1}} \cdot \vec{1}^T \geq \vec{\theta_x} \cdot \vec{1}^T \tag{13}$$

An optimal solution to the problem above constitutes a firing sequence σ of length $l = \sum_{0 \leq i < x} \vec{\theta_i} \cdot \vec{1}^T$ of the net N identical to Definition 7. Note that the constant C in Eq. 13 is a sufficiently large constant, for example $C = |T|^2$. A specific value for C can be identified, but this is beyond the scope of the paper.

Algorithm 1. Sequential Alignment

```
1  function Align (N, m_c, m^⊤, e, l, x, k);
   Input  : A net N, the current marking m_c, the target marking m^⊤, the last
            estimate for the remaining cost e, the number of events to be
            explained l and two parameters x and k with k ≤ x and k ≤ e
   Output: A firing sequence σ
2  if m_c = m^⊤ then
3  |  return ⟨⟩
4  else
5  |  Solve Θ = {θ⃗_0, ..., θ⃗_x} as the optimal solution to the k of x ILP of
   |  Definition 8 and let σ be the firing sequence derived from θ⃗_0 ... θ⃗_{x-1}
6  |  c' = Σ_{0≤i<x} c(θ⃗_i)
7  |  e' = c(θ⃗_x)
8  |  if θ⃗_x ≠ 0⃗ ∧ c' + e' ≥ 2 · e then
9  |  |  return Align(N, m_c, m^⊤, e, l, x + 1, min(k + 1, l))
10 |  else
11 |  |  compute m as m⃗ = m⃗_c + Σ_{0≤i<x} N · θ⃗_i
12 |  |  k' = Σ_{t∈T^s∪T^l} Σ_{0≤i<x} θ_i(t)
13 |  |  return (σ ∘ Align(N, m, m^⊤, e', l − k', x, min(k, l)))
14 |  end
15 end
```

The difference between Definitions 7 and 8 is relatively small, but significant. The added vector $\overrightarrow{\theta_x}$ in the solution does not represent a single transition execution. Instead, it represents the "tail" of the alignment, i.e. the resulting firing sequence σ is no longer a *full* firing sequence as it is not guaranteed to reach the target marking. Instead, it reaches some intermediate marking m and $\overrightarrow{\theta_x}$ is a vector underestimating the cost for reaching the final marking from m identical to the underestimate function in A^* as defined in Definition 6. Once the optimal solution to the ILP is found, the marking m reached after executing σ is taken as a new final marking and the problem is reinstantiated with that marking as initial marking.

The second important difference is the k used solely in Eq. 9. This equation ensures that σ contains at least k transitions from the set of synchronous moves or log moves, i.e. it guarantees progress as it is a property of a synchronous product that there are no loops in the log move and synchronous move possible.

Using the k of x ILP we present the sequential alignment algorithm as Algorithm 1 and using the algorithm outlined in Algorithm 1 we define an (k, x) sequential alignment.

Definition 9 ((k, x) - Sequential Alignment). *Let $N = \langle P, T, \mathcal{F} \rangle$ be a synchronous product Petri net where $T = T^s \cup T^l \cup T^m$ are the partitions of T and let $(N, m_\perp, m^\top)$ a corresponding net system. $\sigma = Align(N, m_\perp, m^\top, \inf, |T^l|, x, k)$ is an (k, x) sequential alignment, where $k \leq |T^l|$ and $k \leq x$.*

The sequential alignment algorithm is a recursive algorithm. It starts by solving a k of x ILP problem which for which a solution is assumed to exist. After solving the ILP, the solution is compared to the previous estimate (the cost of $\overrightarrow{\theta_x}$). If the new optimal solution deviates too much from the expected solution $e' + c' \geq 2 \cdot e$ and the $\overrightarrow{\theta_x}$ is non zero, i.e. the final marking is not reached, then we go into a backtracking phase. We try again, with increased value of x (and k if applicable). If the initial ILP cannot be solved, i.e. no solution exist, backtracking can also be used. However, we typically assume our process models to be sound workflow models.

It is easy to see that the algorithm terminates, i.e. either the final marking $m^{\top}$ is reached, or the value of x is increased until it equals the length of the shortest path from the current marking to the final marking in which case the solution of the k of x ILP becomes optimal and $\overrightarrow{\theta_x} = \overrightarrow{0}$.

4.3 Quality of Alignments

The sequential alignment algorithm presented in Algorithm 1 is guaranteed to terminate and to return an alignment. However, it is not guaranteed to return an optimal alignment. This is due to the fact that the marking equation used for the $\overrightarrow{\theta_x}$ vector does not correspond to an actual realizable sequence. Instead, as in the original A^* approach, is merely underestimates the optimal costs to reach the final marking. As such, sub-optimal decisions may be made in each prefix. In particular, this is the case if the model contains many so-called "transition invariants", the simplest case of which are structured loops of activities.

Even if a trace perfectly fits the model, extreme cases can be devised where the sequential algorithm may construct sub-optimal alignments (although this requires the introduction of duplicate labels), while at the same time, for some classes of model and log combinations, optimality can be guaranteed. Hence, overall, it is impossible to say anything about the quality of the delivered alignment in advance. However, as the experiments in the next section show, in practical cases, the alignments are of high quality and the reduced time complexity is well worth the trade-off.

In our experiments, which we present in the next section, we considered the relative error of the costs as a measure for the quality. This relative error is defined as the cost of the sequential alignment exceeding the cost of the optimal alignment as a fraction of the cost of the optimal alignment.

5 Evaluation

In order to assess the quality of the proposed technique, we conducted various experiments. In this section, we show one of these experiments on a real-life dataset and model. The dataset used deals with the treatment of sepsis patients in a hospital [14]. There are 1050 cases with in total 15214 events over 16 activities. There are 74 unique sequences of activities in the log and the model used contains 19 labeled transitions and 30 unlabeled routing transitions. The model

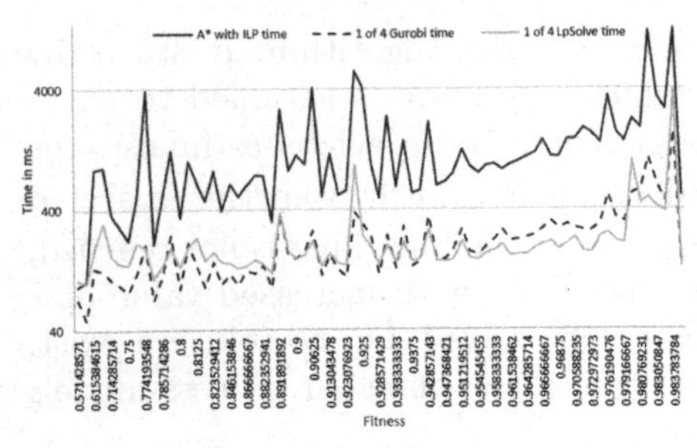

Fig. 5. Comparison of computation times.

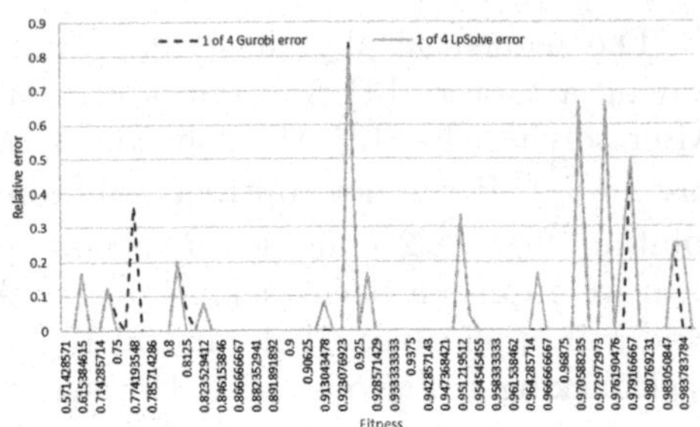

Fig. 6. Relative error of 1-of-4 alignments.

is free-choice and contains both loops and parallel constructs, i.e. it belongs to the class of models considered in this paper.

The experiments were conducted on a Core i7-4700MQ CPU with 16GB of memory, of which at most 8GB of memory were allocated to the Java virtual machine. In the interest of fairness, all algorithms were executed in single-threaded mode[4].

Figures 5 and 6 show the analysis time of aligning this log on the given model using three techniques, namely (1) the baseline traditional A^*, (2) our approach using Gurobi [15] as a backend ILP solver and (3) our approach using LpSolve [16] as a backend solver[5]. The x-axis shows the fitness of the trace (based on the baseline which guarantees optimal alignments) and for each trace, both computation time and relative error in total costs for the alignment returned are plotted. The time is plotted on the left-hand logarithmic axis and the error on the right-hand axis.

As shown in Fig. 5, the computation time of alignments using our approach is orders of magnitude lower than when using A^*. However, in some cases, sub-optimal solutions may be returned which are up to 84% off in terms of the total costs as shown in Fig. 6. The overall error on the entire log is 7,87% for Gurobi and 7,05% for LpSolve. The differences between the two solvers are explained by their local decisions for optimal solutions which may lead to different choices in the alignments. For two other models in the same collection, the results are even better, with at most an 6.7% cost overestimation.

What is important to realize is that the larger errors in the cost coincide with higher computation times in the A^* implementation. Inspection of the specific cases shows that these cases suffer from the property that the estimator used in A^*, which coincides with our $\overrightarrow{\theta_x}$, performs poorly. In the A^* case, optimality

[4] The classical A^* approach can be executed in multi-threaded mode, in which case multiple traces are aligned at once. Furthermore, the Gurobi solver can also be used in multi-threaded mode, which only affects the branch-and-bound phase of the solving.

[5] We did not compare our approach to [4] since the latter does not always produce a real alignment.

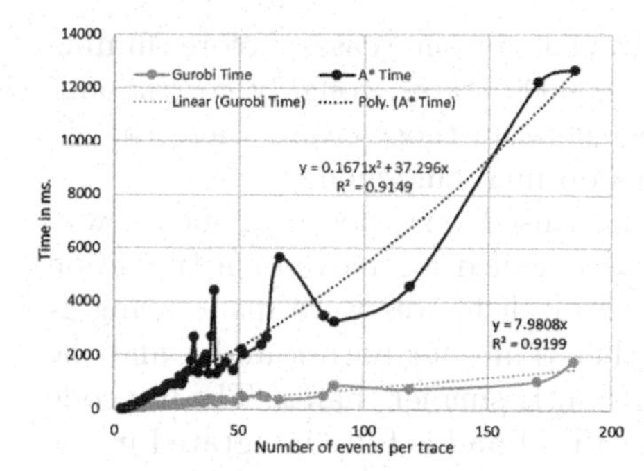

Fig. 7. Time to compute alignments vs. length of the original trace.

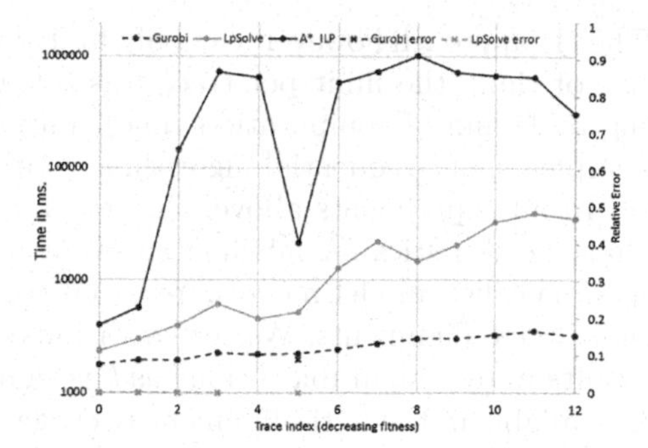

Fig. 8. Comparison of computation time and error of A^* with 1-of-4 alignments.

is still guaranteed, but at a cost of performance, while in our approach, the "wrong" decision is made for the alignment, leading to errors.

Figure 5 suggests that, when cases become more fitting, the computation becomes more expensive. However, this result is misleading as the numbers are not corrected for the length of traces, i.e. the traces that are better fitting in this dataset are typically longer. Therefore, in Fig. 7 we show the relation between the trace length and the computation time for both A^* and for our approach using Gurobi.

Figure 7 shows that our approach scales linearly in the length of the trace. This is expected since, for longer traces, more ILPs need to be solved. However, these ILPs are all of equal size and, since they have the same structure, of comparable complexity.

In the A^* case, we see that there is a considerably larger influence of the trace length to the time do compute alignments. The time complexity of A^* depends on two factors, namely the size of the synchronous product's statespace and the accuracy (and time complexity) of the internal heuristic used. The size of the synchronous product's statespace is the product of the model's statespace and the length of the trace, hence this also scales linearly in the trace length. The internal heuristic used in A^* is comparable to our tail computation for $\overrightarrow{\theta_x}$ which, for most Petri nets, is a fairly good heuristic. As such, the performance of A^* is polynomial[6] in a linearly growing graph, which is exactly what's shown in the figure.

To emphasize the importance of our work even further, we show results on a well-known, artificial benchmark example in Fig. 8. This example was taken from [17] where a model is presented with 239 uniquely labeled transitions and massive parallelism. Here, we clearly see that our approach, both using LpSolve or Gurobi, can be used to find alignments for all traces within a couple of seconds.

[6] In this case quadratic, but in general, the quality of the heuristic used in A^* degrades with the number of semi-positive transition invariants in the model, but that discussion is beyond the scope of this paper.

The A^* approach however, can only find alignments in some cases, before running out of time (the limit per trace was set at 200000 states, roughly corresponding to 15 min of computation time). Furthermore, in those cases where the A^* completes, our sequential algorithms returns optimal alignments.

In all experiments above, the cost function used was chosen in such a way that the penalties for labeling an event as a so-called log move or a transition as a so-called model move were equal to 1 and all figures were made using 1-of-4 prefix alignments. We tested various other values for both k and x and the results were comparable as long as k is significantly smaller than x. The full code is available in the anti-alignment package in ProM and is fully integrated in the conformance checking framework therein.

6 Conclusions

Alignments are a well-known basis for further analysis when comparing process models to event logs, but traditional alignment techniques suffer from computational complexity and the unpredictable nature of the computation time. In this paper, we presented an incremental approach to compute alignments for a given log and model using ILP.

Our approach is heuristic in nature, i.e. the result is not guaranteed to be optimal, but the computation time is shown to be linear in the length of the input trace (around 8 ms per event in our experiments on a high-end laptop computer) and the error in the final results, while depending on the parameters, is shown to be reasonable.

In the paper, we introduce the theoretical foundations of our work, we present the algorithm with proof of termination and we show experimental results on real-life cases. We compare our implementation using both a freely available ILP solver as well as an industrial ILP solver with the state-of-the-art in alignment computation.

All datasets and implementations used in this paper are freely available for download and the software is integrated in the process mining tool ProM.

References

1. van der Aalst, W.M.P.: Process Mining - Discovery, Conformance and Enhancement of Business Processes. Springer, Heidelberg (2011)
2. Adriansyah, A.: Aligning observed and modeled behavior. Ph.D. thesis, Technische Universiteit Eindhoven (2014)
3. Adriansyah, A., Munoz-Gama, J., Carmona, J., van Dongen, B.F., van der Aalst, W.M.P.: Measuring precision of modeled behavior. Inf. Syst. E-Bus. Manag. **13**(1), 37–67 (2015)
4. Taymouri, F., Carmona, J.: A recursive paradigm for aligning observed behavior of large structured process models. In: La Rosa, M., Loos, P., Pastor, O. (eds.) BPM 2016. LNCS, vol. 9850, pp. 197–214. Springer, Cham (2016). doi:10.1007/978-3-319-45348-4_12

5. van der Aalst, W.M.P.: Decomposing Petri nets for process mining: a generic approach. Distrib. Parallel Databases **31**(4), 471–507 (2013)
6. Munoz-Gama, J., Carmona, J., van der Aalst, W.M.P.: Single-entry single-exit decomposed conformance checking. Inf. Syst. **46**, 102–122 (2014)
7. Mannhardt, F., de Leoni, M., Reijers, H.A., van der Aalst, W.M.P.: Balanced multi-perspective checking of process conformance. Computing **98**(4), 407–437 (2016)
8. de Leoni, M., Maggi, F.M., van der Aalst, W.M.P.: An alignment-based framework to check the conformance of declarative process models and to preprocess event-log data. Inf. Syst. **47**, 258–277 (2015)
9. Burattin, A., Maggi, F.M., Sperduti, A.: Conformance checking based on multi-perspective declarative process models. Expert Syst. Appl. **65**, 194–211 (2016)
10. Lu, X., Mans, R., Fahland, D., van der Aalst, W.M.P.: Conformance checking in healthcare based on partially ordered event data. In: Proceedings of the 2014 IEEE Emerging Technology and Factory Automation, ETFA 2014, Barcelona, Spain, 16–19 September 2014, pp. 1–8 (2014)
11. Lu, X., Fahland, D., van der Aalst, W.M.P.: Conformance checking based on partially ordered event data. In: Fournier, F., Mendling, J. (eds.) BPM 2014. LNBIP, vol. 202, pp. 75–88. Springer, Cham (2015). doi:10.1007/978-3-319-15895-2_7
12. Murata, T.: Petri nets: properties, analysis and applications. Proc. IEEE **77**(4), 541–574 (1989)
13. Silva, M., Terue, E., Colom, J.M.: Linear algebraic and linear programming techniques for the analysis of place/transition net systems. In: Reisig, W., Rozenberg, G. (eds.) ACPN 1996. LNCS, vol. 1491, pp. 309–373. Springer, Heidelberg (1998). doi:10.1007/3-540-65306-6_19
14. Mannhardt, F.: Sepsis Cases - Event Log. Eindhoven University of Technology. Dataset (2016). http://dx.doi.org/10.4121/uuid:915d2bfb-7e84-49ad-a286-dc35f063a460
15. Gurobi Optimization, I.: Gurobi optimizer reference manual (2016)
16. Berkelaar, M., Eikland, K., Notebaert, P.: lpsolve : Open source (Mixed-Integer) Linear Programming system
17. Munoz-Gama, J., Carmona, J., van der Aalst, W.M.P.: Conformance checking in the large: partitioning and topology. In: Daniel, F., Wang, J., Weber, B. (eds.) BPM 2013. LNCS, vol. 8094, pp. 130–145. Springer, Heidelberg (2013). doi:10.1007/978-3-642-40176-3_11

Multi-party Business Process Resilience By-Design: A Data-Centric Perspective

Pierluigi Plebani[1](✉), Andrea Marrella[2], Massimo Mecella[2], Marouan Mizmizi[1], and Barbara Pernici[1]

[1] Politecnico di Milano - DEIB, Piazza Leonardo da Vinci 32, 20133 Milan, Italy
{pierluigi.plebani,marouan.mizmizi,barbara.pernici}@polimi.it
[2] Sapienza Università di Roma - DIAG, via Ariosto 25, 00185 Roma, Italy
{marrella,mecella}@diag.uniroma1.it

Abstract. Nowadays every business organization operates in ecosystems and cooperation is mandatory. If, on the one side, this increases the opportunities for the involved organizations, on the other side, every actor is a potential source of failures with impacts on the entire ecosystem. For this reason, *resilience* is a feature that multi-party business processes today must enforce. As resilience concerns the ability to cope with unplanned situations, managing the critical issues is usually a run-time task.

The aim of this work is to emphasize *awareness on resilience* in multi-party business processes also at design-time, when a proper analysis of involved data allows the process designer to identify (possible) failures, their impact, and thus improving the process model. Using a data-centric collaboration-oriented language for processes, i.e., OMG CMMN – Case Management Model and Notation, as modeling notation, our approach allows the designer to model a flexible business process that, at run-time, results easier to manage in case of failures.

Keywords: Process resilience · Artifact-centric modeling · Levels of resilience · CMMN - Case Management Model and Notation

1 Introduction

The adoption of service oriented architectures and workflow automation (a.k.a. orchestration), while enabling and making easier the integration among heterogeneous systems, has also reduced the difficulties in digitizing the communications among different organizations. As a result, digital business ecosystems have been proposed as a paradigm for enabling the cooperation among these organizations [20]; they can be conceptualized in terms of *multi-party business processes*: every actor performs some internal tasks (private view) and communicates with the other actors if some information is needed to perform the internal tasks or if some results need to be notified to make the others able to perform their own tasks (external view, also referred to as choreography). Although

E. Dubois and K. Pohl (Eds.): CAiSE 2017, LNCS 10253, pp. 110–124, 2017.
DOI: 10.1007/978-3-319-59536-8_8

this communication is a great opportunity for organizations, the resulting interdependencies are also difficult to manage, especially when some failures occur: a party could stop working for internal reasons and all the parties which depend on the information that the failing one is responsible for, might fail as well, creating a domino-effect.

A proper design of *resilient business processes* becomes fundamental. Generally speaking, resilience concerns the ability for a system to cope with unplanned situations in order to keep carrying out its mission [6]. In particular, making a multi-party business process resilient means to help the organization to cope with the complexity of the processes and to avoid, limit or mitigate possible failures that might affect the technological infrastructure as well as the involved organizational structure [4].

Usually, satisfying resilience requirements is considered as a mainly run-time issue, as it is related to the ability to cope with *unplanned situations*. In the literature [22], several approaches have been proposed to keep business processes running even when some unplanned exceptions occur, by enacting countermeasures. If we focus on *what to do* in case of failure, this approach seems to be the only possibility. However, if we focus on *what is affected* when a failure occurs, some improvements can be done also at design-time.

The aim of this work is to propose a *design-time and data-centric approach* for improving the resilience of multi-party business processes. Data are considered as "first class citizens" of our approach, as their unavailability might determine the failure of the processes. Depending on the data characteristics and the impacts of their possible unavailability, we propose a way to classify process models in terms of resilience by defining a set of *levels of resilience*. To achieve this goal, instead of focusing on the process activities (control flow), thus modeling the process using an activity-centric notation like OMG BPMN – Business Process Model and Notation, we adopt OMG CMMN – Case Management Model Notation [21] as a basic notation, and we enhance it to better cope with the data life-cycle definition in a process.

The rest of the paper is organized as follows: Sect. 2 introduces a motivating case study – to be used all along the paper – in which resilience aspects are considered. Section 3 defines the concept of resilience in multi-party business processes and proposes an approach to specify different levels of resilience. Section 4 defines the modeling approach based on CMMN able to support the definition of business processes according to the proposed levels of resilience. Section 5 illustrates the relevant literature related to resilient processes, and Sect. 6 presents a critical discussion about our approach, threat to validity and possible extensions.

2 Motivating Example

Smart devices have been adopted by several organizations to increase the effectiveness of business processes. For instance, in the logistics domain, smart devices provide real-time monitoring of goods transportation in terms of their position or state (e.g., temperature, humidity). Although the advantages of the adoption of smart devices are clear, there are also some side-effects in terms of system reliability. In fact, smart devices are prone to failure due to their limitations in terms of computational power and energy autonomy. Moreover, in some cases they are operating in extreme conditions (e.g., meteorological stations on top of mountains), thus they might stop working without any previous notice.

Implications of the use of sensors in processes are illustrated through the example shown in Fig. 1, illustrating a real case study involving the *ShopAnalyser* company and *Shop Inc.*, one of its clients.

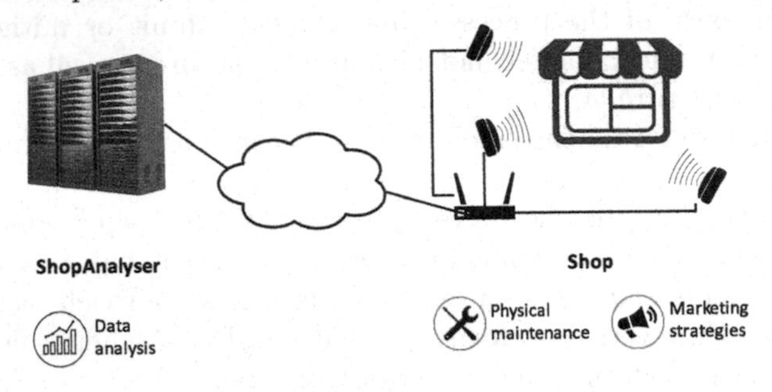

Fig. 1. Running example overview.

The ShopAnalyser company offers products and services to physical shops/commercial centers willing to monitor and analyze the behavior of their customers while they are walking inside their premises. To this aim, ShopAnalyser sells innovative sensors able to capture the probe packets periodically sent by cellphones and to localize and track the position of cellphones. In this way, assuming that a cellphone belongs to exactly one customer, the sensor is able to track the behavior of the customer inside the area and, correlating the MAC addresses, it realizes when the same customer periodically visit the shop. The analytics required to understand the customers' behaviors are offered by ShopAnalyzer as a service to all the shops which buy its sensors. More specifically, ShopAnalyzer produces one report every week to the shops, and they use these reports as a basis for defining or improving their marketing strategies.

Shop Inc. decides to acquire sensors and the analytics service from ShopAnalyzer. The owner of Shop Inc., through its maintenance personnel, is responsible for the installation and physical maintenance of the sensors: ShopAnalyser delivers the sensors to Shop Inc., which installs them in the shop and configures them to send collected data to the data center of ShopAnalyser. Some status leds are embedded in the sensors to make the owners of the shops aware about possible malfunctioning: problems in the behavior of the sensors, when the probe packets sent by the cellphones are not collected correctly (in this case the Shop informs the ShopAnalyser, which will enact some repair action, such as sending substituting sensors), or to signal connection problems (i.e., the sensor are working, however the data cannot be sent to ShopAnalyser). ShopAnalyser is responsible for the data analysis, which produces a weekly report, and for the identification of the sensors malfunctioning which cannot be detected directly by the shops, i.e., data captured by sensors and sent to the data center which are unrealistic (e.g., one hundred cellphones identified in the same tiny shop at the same time).

Although some actions are in place to cope with the malfunctioning of sensors, in the case study the focus is mainly on signaling possible failures: e.g., if a sensor stops working then a replacement is provided; if the network connection is interrupted, then the ISP – Internet Service Provider – is called to resume the connection. Actually, these occurring failures could have a more significant impact as they affect the data availability. In fact, during the down time, an amount of sensor data is not collected so it is not represented in the data set used for the analysis. As a consequence, the report used for marketing purposes might become not realistic.

To model multi-party business processes, as the one of the case study, activity-centric modeling languages such as BPMN are usually adopted. Even if this type of languages results more intuitive for the process designers, this approach has some limitations wrt specifying process resilience. As an example, the order of activities during exception handling is loosely specified: when addressing process resilience, the designer should specify recovery activities, and the order in which they are performed is usually decided at run-time based on considerations about the status of the process. Other approaches, as declarative modeling, rely on an open-world assumption, thus leaving room for supporting situations that cannot be planned at design-time [9]. In this work we adopt an artifact-based language, i.e., CMMN – Case Management Model and Notation [21], which aims to become the de-facto standard for artifact-based modeling. However, as discussed in the next section, also this language has some limitations when defining the data aspects, thus next sections will also propose some possible extensions.

Figure 2 presents the CMMN model of the ShopAnalyser case study[1]. The outer box "Shop Improvement" represents the *case plan model*, i.e., the complete behavior of the process. Inside the case plan model, there are three *stages*: "Sensor data acquisition", "Data analysis", and "Marketing analysis". Stages can be informally defined as a group of *tasks* (drawn as rounded boxes) organized according to an implicit or explicit control flow. Stages could also be decorated with *entry* and/or *exit conditions* represented, respectively, by an empty or filled diamond that specifies Boolean expressions predicating on data managed by the tasks in the stage or some events to occur. When these conditions become true, the stage opens (in case of entry condition) or terminates (in case of exit condition). Entry and exit conditions can be applied to tasks, stages, and case plan models. As an example, the "Reading values" task starts only when the sensors have been installed. The "Data analysis" stage opens every week and terminates when a new report is produced by the "Data mining" task. Finally, once the conversion rate[2] obtained by executing all the activities is considered suffi-

[1] The following discussion of the CMMN diagram does not intend to be exhaustive. For a complete description of the standard, the reader should refer to the official specification document [21].

[2] In marketing, the conversion rate measures the ratio between visitors and effectively paying customers. Therefore it is a measure of the goal of Shop Inc.

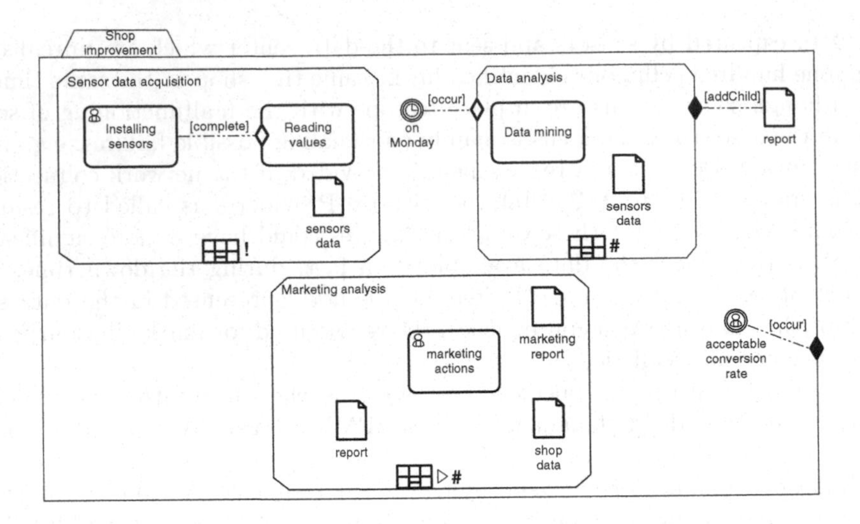

Fig. 2. CMMN diagram of the case study process

cient, then the business process concludes. Finally, *case plan items* (i.e., "Sensors data", "Report", and "Shop data") are included in the stages which use them. It is worth noting that, according to the reported diagram, since the moment in which the sensors have been installed, the sensor reading task keeps running till the time in which the expected conversion rate has been achieved. At the same time, the marketing analysis is not coordinated with the other activities as it is performed by analysing the reports produced by the ShopAnalyser.

3 Multi-party Business Process Resilience

During the process enactment unplanned situations might occur. Depending on the nature of the raised issues, the magnitude of their impact varies and one or more activities may be involved. At the same time, different countermeasures can be taken to mitigate these negative effects. As an example, as for many reasons the sensors might not be able to communicate with ShopAnalyser, an alternative source of information about the number of clients in the shops might be considered, to be able to equally infer customers' behaviors in the reports. Alternative ways to collect such information may include the ability of counting the number of persons entering the shop, which might be available from other unrelated applications, such as video surveillance. In this way, ShopAnalyser will not have gaps in the analysis, but only lower quality data. Other ways to improve the final reports may include algorithms to fill in the gaps of sensor information, based for instance on sales prediction algorithms applied when sensor data have not been collected.

Similarly to what is usually done in emergency management [17,27], where a *preparedness phase* aims to improve the systems by learning from the previous emergencies, we propose an approach which helps the process designers in improving their process models by considering the previous experiences in failures generated by data unavailability. In particular, we propose an approach to categorize resilience characteristics, then to define resiliency levels, and to model the resilience improvement aspects from a modeling perspective.

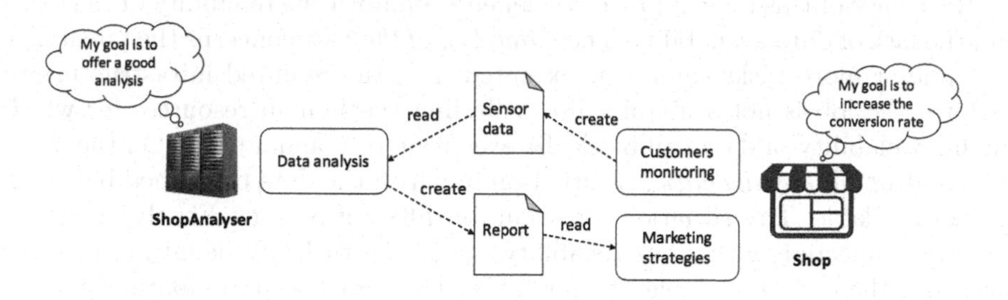

Fig. 3. Problem setting

3.1 Data Perspective on Resilience

As previously introduced, our approach analyzes the multi-party business process resilience from a *data perspective*: data dependencies among the involved parties and relationships between process activities and data are taken into account to identify the *sources of possible failures*, and how the process can be better modeled to make it resilient with respect to these failures.

To this aim, in order to set the boundaries of our problem, we define a multi-party business process in terms of (see Fig. 3):

- *Parties*: actors involved in the process. Each of them participates in the business process to achieve a personal goal. All the parties are interested in making the process up and running without problems, as their personal goals also depends on the resilience of the whole process. As an example, Shop Inc. wants to make the marketing strategy more effective by increasing the conversion rate. On the other side, ShopAnalyser wants to sell a good service to its customers. Although the concept of *role* that is related to process participants is included in the CMMN standard, no graphical notation able to explicitly include parties is defined as of today. In this paper, we do not address this issue of lack of graphical constructs for parties, thus we do not propose any extension concerning the modeling of parties.
- *Tasks*: a task is a unit of work performed by a party, which consumes data as input and produces data as output. The data produced by a task must be required by at least another party. In multi-party business processes, we are more interested in the dependencies among the parties, rather than to internal executions of processes by each party, thus we are not including tasks which are internal to a single party.

- *Data*: units of storage used by the data producer to store/write data and by the data consumer to read such data. Producers and consumers are parties performing tasks. Data can also be used to verify the entry and exit conditions, thus to realize when a stage or task starts or terminates.

Resilience of this type of processes depends on both the reliability of the tasks and the lack of data availability. The *reliability of the task* concerns the possibility that one or more tasks cannot be executed: i.e., the required infrastructure to perform the job is not available, also including the human resources for which the unavailability of data can block the execution of manual tasks. On the other side, *lack of data availability* is a situation in which the data consumed by a task are not available. This situation can occur for different reasons. Firstly, it may be directly connected to the task reliability, as all the tasks by definition produce data and these data are relevant for at least one of the participating parties, and problems on tasks may have also the side effect to make data unavailable. Moreover, there are situations in which tasks are properly working, but the returned data, although available, do not have a sufficient quality level to enable processing, thus they can be considered unavailable. Completeness, timeliness, and accuracy are some of quality parameters through which we can define the acceptable level of data quality for considering the data available [5]. For this reason, the definition of the data could be coupled with the definition of quality levels that are considered acceptable for a task that is using such data.

3.2 Levels of Resilience

Having bounded our space of analysis and identified the possible sources of failure, we aim to classify multi-party business processes in terms of their degree of resilience. We define levels of resilience on the basis of the ability of the multi-party process to adjust the possible unexpected failures. As it will be discussed in Sect. 5, other proposals in the literature have been put forward to define resilience for processes, e.g., [28]. However, here we do not focus on the structure of the process or its components and instances, but we aim to classify the way resilience can be considered and obtained, in terms of preparedness to unexpected events which might be caused or have impact on data availability. In particular, the following four levels of designed resilience have been identified:

- **Level 0 – None.** At this level business processes are designed without taking into account the data unavailability that might cause failures during the execution. As a consequence, also countermeasures to be adopted in case of critical situations are not defined. The designed process only reflects the wishful scenario where it is assumed that all the parties correctly execute their tasks and all the data are transferred among them as expected. Although a process design of this type can be useful to define the agreement between the parties, no support is given to the resilience.
- **Level 1 - Failure-awareness.** A first step for improving the process design is to make the process aware that there are possible sources of failure, so there

will be the need to make it resilient. In this work, we consider failures caused by data unavailability, which might impact on one or more tasks of the same party that is producing such data, or tasks performed by other parties. For this reason, failure-aware business processes are designed to have a clear map of which are the relevant data subject to failures, as well as the impact of these failures. The analysis of potential failures depends on several factors: amount of data, how the data are collected, how the data are stored. As an example, data stored on a local server have a probability of failure that is lower than data stored on a smart device connected to a wireless network. Similarly, if data created by one party and used by several parties becomes unavailable, the impact of this failure will be greater than the one produced by data created and consumed by the same party.

- **Level 2 – Identifying alternatives for data and goals.** For processes classified in this level, the model of the process makes an initial attempt to overcome possible failures, whose nature and impact have been defined with the previous level. In more detail, there are two aspects to be taken into account:
  - *Alternative Data*: based on the information about the source of failures and the potential impact of these failures, the designer can decide to include in the process model the alternative data. In this way, starting from the data having more probability of failures and greater impact, the designer has to specify if there are alternative data sources and how to reach them. A more precise model requires an analysis of the gap between the quality of the data in the original data source with respect to the quality of the data in the alternative data source. For instance, in case the sensors installed in Shop Inc. stops working, the process model indicates as an alternative source other services, e.g. installed door counter and/or Google Popular Times or even historical data stored in a different, but accessible, place. The issue of quality of data has been extensively addressed in traditional information systems, e.g., [5], but the quality of big data (which includes sensor-generated data) is still to be precisely defined [10].
  - *Alternative Goal*: as the process resilience implies to mitigate the effect of a failure, a possible mitigation include revising the initial expectations of the process to achieve a given goal. The designer defines, for each party, a new goal that represents a status that can terminate the execution of the process in an acceptable way. If the initial goal corresponds to the optimal goal, the alternative goal could be considered as a best-effort goal. As an example, ShopAnalyser realizing that the data coming from the sensors contain errors, instead of releasing full reports with all details, it can decide to release for a reduced-price an incomplete report.

It is worth noting that the business process models at this level do not prescribe any specific actions to cope with the failures at run-time. For this reason, a model at this level only supports who is in charge of executing the process, to select, in case of failures, new data sources as well as to decide to

consider satisfactory the result of the execution even if the initial goal is not possible to be fulfilled, accepting a weaker goal.
- **Level 3 – Defining alternative actions.** At this level, processes have been designed by considering also actions to be taken in case of failures. Design-time mechanisms are conceived to be able to (semi)-automatically move the process to an acceptable state when unexpected or unplanned failures occur. Based on the information about the alternatives (both data and goal), the designer can embed in the business process how these alternatives could be effectively managed. New tasks can be added to the process to express the activities to be performed in order to improve the quality of the data alternatives to a quality level equivalent to the original service. Taking as example the problems of missing data, the previous level suggests to include the door counter and the Google Popular Times in the list of possible alternatives. At this level, the process designer should specify if the alternative data should be considered as they are produced, or if additional actions must be taken, e.g., to combine both services into a reliable assessment of the indoor occupancy for Shop Inc.

With these levels of resilience, we aim at supporting the process designer in understanding if the resilience is modeled, and if there is room to improve the process model by specifying possible alternative solutions. As an example, once the designer understands that the modeled processes are at level 0, the first step should be to start considering the evolution of the data in the process.

4 Modeling Resilience

In this section we discuss, for each level previously introduced, which is the practical impact of using CMMN as modeling language. In this way, we are able to highlight which are the current possibly missing constructs and their semantics. Moreover, we propose an extension of CMMN able to improve the specification of which data are used and in which way, in order to better analyze the possible failures and the impacts. Concerning the extensions proposed hereafter, at this stage, we do not intend to be complete and formal. Our attempt is to verify that CMMN has the potentiality for being used to model resilient business processes. A precise definition of the new constructs will be considered in future work.

Level 0 - None. CMMN standard is sufficient to express the basic scenario where resilience is not considered at all. The model of the business process for the ShopAnalyser case study, shown in Fig. 2, belongs to this level.

Level 1 - Failure Awareness. One of the main shortcomings of CMMN is the poor semantics about data. In the current version, data are defined in terms of *CaseFileItems* with no restrictions about the format and the nature of the represented data. On the one side, this allows maximum flexibility in modeling various scenarios. On the other side, no information about the link between tasks and data is provided, unless data are attached to the entry and exit conditions as predicates in the boolean expressions.

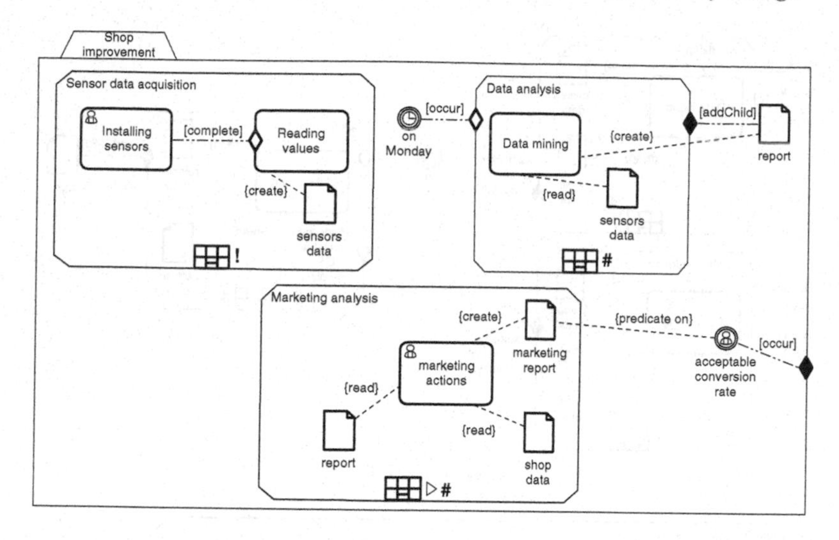

Fig. 4. Level 1 (failure awareness) compliant process model.

To overcome this limitation, we propose to extend CMMN allowing the connections between tasks and CaseFileItems also be annotated with the actions performed on the data: e.g., *create, read, update, delete.* It is also possible to link the data to the events that are defined in terms of these data (i.e., to predicate on). The use of this extension in the case study is shown in Fig. 4. The new elements in the model allow the designer to identify the data that might have impact in case of their unavailability, e.g., the lack of sensors' data will have more impact than the lack of the shops' data, as the former can cause a domino effect affecting all the tasks in the process.

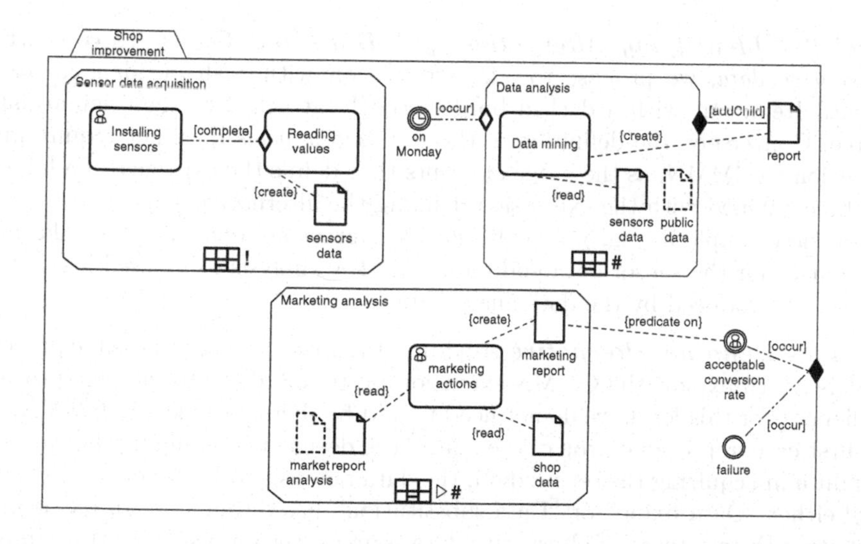

Fig. 5. Level 2 compliant process model.

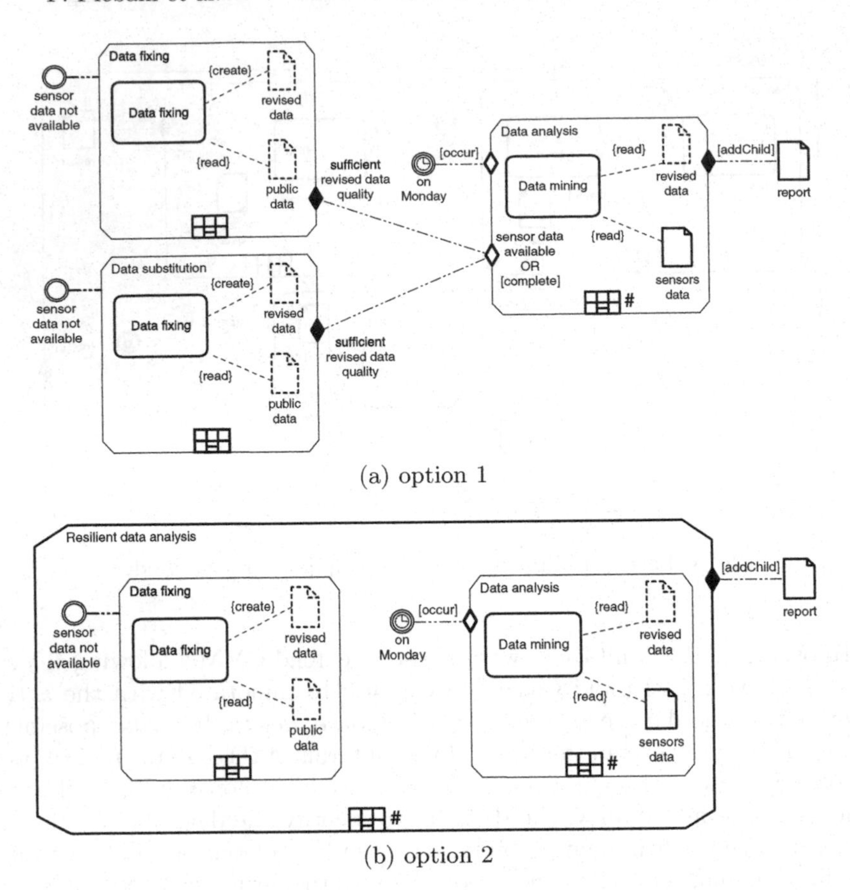

(a) option 1

(b) option 2

Fig. 6. Level 3 compliant process models.

Level 2 - Identifying Alternatives for Data and Goals. To cope with *alternative data*, we propose to add a new icon with a shape identical to a CaseFileItem, but with a dashed border strictly attached to the original data source. Conversely, the definition of the *alternative goals* does not require any extension to CMMN, as the usage of events that define the existence of a failure can be combined with the expression defining the alternative goal.

In the example in Fig. 5, two alternative sources are defined: public data as alternative for the sensor data and public market analysis to be used instead of the report produced by the data analysis task.

Level 3 - Defining Alternative Actions. Figure 6 shows two possible process models which exploit the CMMN extension proposed above to increase process resilience. For this level, we do not need to add further constructs to CMMN. In the first case, reported on top of the figure, the designer is assuming that in case of failure in acquiring the sensor data, the data analysis task cannot be executed until either "Data fixing" or "Data substitution" has terminated. In particular, exploiting the existence of alternative data sources, the data substitution simply replaces the data source. This task can be considered concluded only if the quality of the data now provided is considered sufficient for the data analysis. On the other side, the data fixing implements data quality algorithms to improve the data quality as required by the data analysis. It has to be noted that, according to this model, the data analysis potentially might never start.

The process designer could also propose a different approach, shown in the lower part of the figure, where the data fixing and data analysis are included in the same stage. In this case, data analysis and data fixing work in parallel trying to achieve a common goal, i.e., the report delivery.

5 Related Work

Research on *resilient systems* encompasses several disciplines, such as psychology [29], ecology [11], sociology [3] and engineering [14]. In information systems, *resilience engineering* has its roots in the study of safety-critical systems [14], i.e., systems aimed to ensure that organizations operating in turbulent and interconnected settings achieve high levels of safety despite a multitude of emerging risks, complex tasks, and constantly increasing pressures. A system is considered as resilient if its capabilities can be adapted to new organizational requirements and changes that have not been explicitly incorporated into the existing system's design [19]. In the BPM field, cf. [19,23], this means that respective business processes are able to automatically adapt themselves to such changes. Over the last years, change management in BPM has been mainly tackled through the notions of *process flexibility* [22] and *risk-aware BPM* [25,26].

On the one hand, research on process flexibility has focused on four major flexibility needs, namely *(i) variability* [12,13], *(ii) looseness* [2,16], *(iii) adaptation* [18,24], and *(iv) evolution* [7,8]. The ability to deal with changes makes process flexibility approaches a required but not sufficient mean for the building of resilient BPM systems. In fact, there exists a (seemingly insignificant but) relevant gap between the concepts of flexibility and resilience: (i) process flexibility is aimed at producing "reactive" approaches that reduce failures from the outset or deal with them at run-time if any "known" disturbance arises; (ii) process resilience requires "proactive" techniques accepting and managing change "on-the-fly" rather than anticipating it, in order to allow a system to address new emerging and unforeseeable changes with the potential to cascade. On the other hand, while relatively close to the concept of risk-aware BPM, which evaluates operational risks on the basis of historical threat probabilities (with a focus on the "cause" of disturbances and events), resilient BPM shifts attention on the "realized risks" and its consequences, to improve risk prevention and mitigation, and therefore aim at complementing conventional risk-aware approaches.

Surprisingly, the fact is that there exists only a limited number of research works investigating resilience of BPM systems [4,30,31], and they are all at conceptual level. For example, the work of Antunes and Mourao [4] derives a set of fundamental requirements aimed at supporting resilient BPM. The approach of Zahoransky et al. [31] investigates the use of process mining [1] to create probability distributions on time behavior of business processes. Such distributions can be used as indicators to monitor the level of resilience at run-time and indicate possible countermeasures if the level drops. Finally, the work [30] provides a support framework and a set of measures based on the analysis of previous process executions to realize and evaluate resilience in the BPM context.

If compared with the aforementioned works, our research aims at providing concrete indicators to measure the resilience of a multi-party business process by focusing on the data exchanged between the activities composing the process, an aspect neglected in the existing approaches to process resilience. We believe that such indicators can provide a reliable mean for evaluating in advance the impacts of potential disturbances and improving decision making at run-time.

6 Discussion

The levels of resilience presented in this paper, and the practical guidelines on how to achieve them during the design of processes, namely by precisely modeling in CMMN, are a concrete methodological tool to support process designers to be aware of how resilient are the processes they are working on. At design-time, it is important to be aware of failures, and to identify data and goal alternatives, in order to be able to design alternative actions. On the one side, flexible approaches cope with exceptional situations during run-time, but only a deep awareness during design-time can make really the process *resilient-by-design*.

Clearly our work should be extended and validated in many aspects. However we consider it as an important starting point in deeply investigating how to make better resilient processes. On the one side, a precise formalization of the modeling constructs to be used in order to achieve each level, and patterns to be used, is crucial in order to make the overall approach effective. On the other side, a validation is needed, in which to compare, by adopting empirical approaches [15], processes at different levels and the real resilience they achieve during enactment. Measuring resilience of multi-party business processes is not an easy task, and no measurable indicators exist nowadays in this context. Our aim is to be able to correlate our levels with a qualitative notion of "a process is more resilient of another one", and this is only possible through a large collection of case studies (models and execution traces) on top of which to perform quantitative correlation analysis. To this aim, the levels of resilience introduced in this paper go in the direction of providing a reference framework which represents an important input to the research and practitioners' community. In fact, adopting and extending a well known standard, i.e., CMMN, gives the opportunity to develop approaches able to provide this quantitative analyses.

7 Concluding Remarks

In this paper we have discussed the concept of multi-party resilient processes, and we have presented a possible way of classifying them on the basis of four levels, based on how data and goals are taken into account when considering possible ways to cope with changes. The originality of the proposed approach is in considering resilience at design-time, during process modeling, and not mainly as a run-time issues, when exceptions and anomalous events should be faced during enactment. We have shown a practical way to achieve the levels during modeling, by using and extending the newly introduced standard CMMN for artefact-centric processes. After discussing relevant work, we have provided a discussion about the limitations and possible extensions of our work, which is a promising initial step towards defining effective resilient processes.

Acknowledgments. This work is partly supported by the Italian projects Social Museum e Smart Tourism (CTN01_00034_23154), NEPTIS (PON03PE_00214_3), RoMA - Resilience of Metropolitan Areas (SCN_00064), ITS2020 (CTN01_00176_166195), and by the Sapienza project "Data-aware Adaptation of Knowledge-intensive Processes in Cyber-Physical Domains through Action-based Languages".

References

1. van der Aalst, W.M.P.: Process Mining: Data Science in Action. Springer, Heidelberg (2016)
2. van der Aalst, W.M.P., Pesic, M., Schonenberg, H.: Declarative workflows: Balancing between flexibility and support. Comput. Sci. - R&D **23**(2), 99–113 (2009)
3. Adger, W.N.: Social and ecological resilience: are they related? Prog. Hum. Geogr. **24**(3), 347–364 (2000)
4. Antunes, P., Mourõ, H.: Resilient business process management: framework and services. Expert Syst. Appl. **38**(2), 1241–1254 (2011)
5. Batini, C., Scannapieco, M.: Data and Information Quality - Dimensions, Principles and Techniques. Springer, Heidelberg (2016)
6. Caralli, R.A., Allen, J.H., White, D.W.: CERT Resilience Management Model: A Maturity Model for Managing Operational Resilience. Addison-Wesley, Boston (2010)
7. Casati, F., Ceri, S., Pernici, B., Pozzi, G.: Workflow evolution. Data Knowl. Eng. **24**(3), 211–238 (1998)
8. Dadam, P., Rinderle, S.: Workflow evolution. In: Liu, L., Özsu, M.T. (eds.) Encyclopedia of Database Systems, pp. 3540–3544. Springer, Heidelberg (2009)
9. Fahland, D., Lübke, D., Mendling, J., Reijers, H.A., Weber, B., Weidlich, M., Zugal, S.: Declarative versus imperative process modeling languages: the issue of understandability. In: Halpin, T., Krogstie, J., Nurcan, S., Proper, E., Schmidt, R., Soffer, P., Ukor, R. (eds.) BPMDS/EMMSAD-2009. LNBIP, vol. 29, pp. 353–366. Springer, Heidelberg (2009). doi:10.1007/978-3-642-01862-6_29
10. Firmani, D., Mecella, M., Scannapieco, M., Batini, C.: On the meaningfulness of "Big Data Quality". Data Sci. Eng. **1**(1), 6–20 (2016)
11. Gunderson, L.H.: Ecological resilience-in theory and application. Ann. Rev. Ecol. Syst. **31**, 425–439 (2000)
12. Hallerbach, A., Bauer, T., Reichert, M.: Capturing variability in business process models: the Provop approach. J. Softw. Maint. Evol. Res. Pract. **22**(6–7), 519–546 (2009)
13. vom Hallerbach, A., Bauer, T., Reichert, M.: Configuration and management of process variants. In: Brocke, J., Rosemann, M. (eds.) Handbook on Business Process Management. International Handbooks on Information Systems, vol. 1, pp. 237–255. Springer, Heidelberg (2010)

14. Hollnagel, E., Woods, D.D., Leveson, N.: Resilience Engineering: Concepts and Precepts. Ashgate Publishing, Ltd., Farnham (2007)
15. Johannesson, P., Perjons, E.: An Introduction to Design Science. Springer, Heidelberg (2014)
16. Marrella, A., Lespérance, Y.: Synthesizing a library of process templates through partial-order planning algorithms. In: Nurcan, S., Proper, H.A., Soffer, P., Krogstie, J., Schmidt, R., Halpin, T., Bider, I. (eds.) BPMDS/EMMSAD-2013. LNBIP, vol. 147, pp. 277–291. Springer, Heidelberg (2013). doi:10.1007/978-3-642-38484-4_20
17. Marrella, A., Mecella, M., Russo, A.: Collaboration on-the-field: suggestions and beyond. In: 8th International Conference on Information Systems for Crisis Response and Management (ISCRAM) (2011)
18. Marrella, A., Mecella, M., Sardiña, S.: Intelligent process adaptation in the SmartPM system. ACM TIST **8**(2), 25 (2017)
19. Müller, G., Koslowski, T.G., Accorsi, R.: Resilience - a new research field in business information systems? In: Abramowicz, W. (ed.) BIS 2013. LNBIP, vol. 160, pp. 3–14. Springer, Heidelberg (2013). doi:10.1007/978-3-642-41687-3_2
20. Nachira, F., Nicolai, A., Dini, P., Le Louarn, M., Rivera Leon, L. (eds.): Digital Business Ecosystems. European Commission DG Information Society and Media, Office for Official Publications of the European Communities, Luxembourg (2007). ISBN 92-79-01817-5
21. OMG: Case Management Model and Notation, Version 1.0, May 2014. http://www.omg.org/spec/CMMN/1.0
22. Reichert, M., Weber, B.: Enabling Flexibility in Process-Aware Information Systems - Challenges, Methods, Technologies. Springer, Heidelberg (2012)
23. Rosemann, M., Recker, J.: Context-aware process design exploring the extrinsic drivers for process flexibility. In: 7th International Workshop on Business Process Modeling, Development, and Support (BPMDS) (2006)
24. Sadiq, S.W., Orlowska, M.E.: On capturing exceptions in workflow process models. In: Abramowicz, W., Orlowska, M.E. (eds.) BIS 2000, pp. 3–19. Springer, London (2000)
25. Suriadi, S., Weiß, B., Winkelmann, A., et al.: Current research in risk-aware business process management: overview, comparison, and gap analysis. Commun. Assoc. Inf. Syst. **34**(1), 933–984 (2014)
26. Tjoa, S., Jakoubi, S., Goluch, G., Kitzler, G., Goluch, S., Quirchmayr, G.: A formal approach enabling risk-aware business process modeling and simulation. IEEE Trans. Serv. Comput. **4**(2), 153–166 (2011)
27. Van De Walle, B., Turoff, M., Hiltz, S.R.: Information Systems for Emergency Management. M.E. Sharpe, Armonk (2009)
28. de Vrieze, P., Xu, L.: Resilience analysis of collaborative process management systems. In: Afsarmanesh, H., Camarinha-Matos, L.M., Lucas Soares, A. (eds.) PRO-VE 2016. IAICT, vol. 480, pp. 124–133. Springer, Cham (2016). doi:10.1007/978-3-319-45390-3_11
29. Yates, T.M., Masten, A.S.: Fostering the Future: Resilience Theory and the Practice of Positive Psychology. Wiley, Hoboken (2004)
30. Zahoransky, R.M., Brenig, C., Koslowski, T.: Towards a process-centered resilience framework. In: 10th International Conference on Availability, Reliability and Security (ARES), pp. 266–273. IEEE (2015)
31. Zahoransky, R.M., Koslowski, T., Accorsi, R.: Toward resilience assessment in business process architectures. In: Bondavalli, A., Ceccarelli, A., Ortmeier, F. (eds.) SAFECOMP 2014. LNCS, vol. 8696, pp. 360–370. Springer, Cham (2014). doi:10.1007/978-3-319-10557-4_39

User Knowledge Discovery

Identifying Domains and Concepts in Short Texts via Partial Taxonomy and Unlabeled Data

Yihong Zhang[1(✉)], Claudia Szabo[2], Quan Z. Sheng[3], Wei Emma Zhang[2], and Yongrui Qin[4]

[1] School of Computer Science and Engineering, Nanyang Technological University, Singapore, Singapore
yihong.zhang@ntu.edu.sg

[2] School of Computer Science, The University of Adelaide, Adelaide, Australia
{claudia.szabo,wei.zhang01}@adelaide.edu.au

[3] Department of Computing, Macquarie University, Sydney, Australia
michael.sheng@mq.edu.au

[4] School of Computing and Engineering, University of Huddersfield, Huddersfield, UK
y.qin2@hud.ac.uk

Abstract. Accurate and real-time identification of domains and concepts discussed in microblogging texts is crucial for many important applications such as earthquake monitoring, influenza surveillance and disaster management. Existing techniques such as machine learning and keyword generation are application specific and require significant amount of training in order to achieve high accuracy. In this paper, we propose to use a multiple domain taxonomy (MDT) to capture general user knowledge. We formally define the problems of domain classification and concept tagging. Using the MDT, we devise domain-independent pure frequency count methods that do not require any training data nor annotations and that are not sensitive to misspellings or shortened word forms. Our extensive experimental analysis on real Twitter data shows that both methods have significantly better identification accuracy with low runtime than existing methods for large datasets.

Keywords: Text classification · Concept extraction · Unsupervised method · Twitter

1 Introduction

Popular microblogging services such as Twitter can generate as many as 600 million short texts in a day[1]. Similar to real world human conversations, these short texts, henceforth called *tweets*, cover all types of topics, including politics, sports, weather, product promotion, and interesting personal discoveries. Exploiting such *mixed-domain* data for the information needs of a *narrow domain* can prove extremely useful for identifying crucial information. Existing work in

[1] http://www.tweetstats.com/.

E. Dubois and K. Pohl (Eds.): CAiSE 2017, LNCS 10253, pp. 127–143, 2017.
DOI: 10.1007/978-3-319-59536-8_9

this field usually requires selecting small portions of data from a large, mixed-domain data body. For example, as a service such as Twitter allows public access to all its data[2], certain portions of this data have been collected for applications in narrow domains, including earthquake monitoring [15], influenza surveillance [2], election result prediction [18,19], ideal point estimation [1], and rumor detection [5,9].

In domain applications such as the above, the required data represents an extremely small portion of the collected datastream. For example, in a work attempting to capture disaster and crime events from tweets, the authors find that only 0.05% data in all collected data is related to the application [7]. Thus the first step in existing approaches is to filter the required data from mixed-domain, unclassified data. In [15], earthquake-related tweets are classified. In [19] tweets related to two candidates are collected. In [9], only tweets related to the bombing incident are selected. The techniques for such filtering range from machine learning based approaches [13,15], to keyword generation [11] and clustering [20]. However, most of the filtering solutions are designed specifically for the corresponding application, and are not suitable for other domains or applications. In this paper, we focus on providing an information extraction solution that can be tailored to different specific applications based on existing domain knowledge.

Our approach relies on the insight that a narrow domain information consumer has some initial but not complete knowledge of the data, including knowledge about the key elements or topics within the domain, which is quite often the case when a domain expert in an organization wants to build an information system based on text data. This knowledge often can be translated into a taxonomy. For example, in a previous work [21], short text messages containing the keyword "shooting" are collected for detecting shooting crimes, where distinctions must be made about the meaning of "shooting", such as in "shooting photo", "shooting gun", or "shooting basketball". Users may note that "photo" is a "imaging product" and "gun" is a "weapon". They may also note the domain background, that "gun" is used in a "crime", while "ball" is used in a "game". We can construct a Multiple Domain Taxonomy (MDT) that contains these two kinds of relationships, namely, *is_a*, and *in_a*, to represent user knowledge. We show that using the concepts and relationships defined in a partially constructed MDT, we can effectively provide functions such as message domain classification and key concept recognition.

Given the MDT, we use a pure frequency approach on unlabeled data to identify the domain and concepts in the short text, as we describe in detail in the Sect. 3. There are several advantages using this approach. First, a pure frequency approach that does not involve grammar-based NLP (Natural Language Processing) techniques is language independent, and suitable for processing informal microblog messages. Unlike formal texts, microblog messages are filled with common misspellings and word shortening that cannot be found in a dictionary, but can be captured by frequency-based analysis with large data.

[2] https://dev.twitter.com/streaming/firehose.

Second, it is an unsupervised approach that does not require annotating data. As Twitter allows free access to one percent of its data traffic, one can easily collect millions of tweets in a day, very few of which, however, can be manually annotated. Our approach takes advantage of the large number of unlabeled data and effectively improves the identification accuracy. Finally, our approach does not require an external knowledge source. Since existing knowledge sources such as Wikipedia[3] only provide information for more common concepts, the use of external knowledge sources generally limits the applicability of the method. Instead, our approach considers the unlabeled data as the context of the key terms and provides similar accuracy improvement effect. To summarize, we make the following contributions:

- We formally define the problem of domain classification and concept tagging given an existing taxonomy called MDT. We propose MDT as a new type of taxonomy based on the reality of narrow domain information consumption from mixed-domain data.
- We propose an unsupervised, pure-frequency approach for solving identification of domain and concepts in short texts. Our approach does not require annotation of training data and captures common misspellings and word shortenings, thus is suitable for processing informal social media messages. Our approach is also a general solution that is applicable in any narrow domain, and except for the partial MDT that requires some initial knowledge of data to construct, our approach does not need any external input.
- We test our approach extensively using real Twitter data. Our results show that the proposed domain classification method achieves much higher accuracy than existing classification methods, with up to 52% precision increase; our concept tagging method similarly achieved relatively high accuracy.

2 Related Work

Given the emerging popularity of social media, short text classification has been widely studied. Sriram et al. [16] propose a classification method to identify pre-defined message categories, such as news, opinions, and deals. Targeting such categories, their method is a supervised learning approach based on text features such as opinion words, time-event phrases, and the use of dollar sign. Li et al. [7] propose a classification method to find the Crime and Disaster Events (CDE). They use a supervised classifier that incorporates features that include hashtag, URL, and CDE-specific features such as time mention. They found that including CDE features provides about 80% accuracy versus 60% accuracy without them. These works are proposing classification solutions with presumed target domains are often considering specific domain characteristics. However, as we will show in our experiments, such solutions are usually not applicable with a different target domain. Olteanu et al. [11] propose a method for filtering relevant information based on keywords, and claim that the method can be applied to any

[3] https://en.wikipedia.org/.

domain. Their method generates discriminative keywords based on labeled data, and the discriminative strength is measured using PMI and frequency. However, their experiments show poor performance, with the proposed method providing almost no accuracy improvement over simple keyword filtering.

Some research exploits the message categories inherently associated with the messages. Ritter et al. [14] propose a method to automatically generate message types in addition to message classification. Based on the event messages and related phrases, the event type of each message is determined based on the distribution of name entity and time. The event messages and related phrases, however, are initially classified under a broad "event" label, which is first extracted using a supervised method based on signal words such as "announcement" and "new", and thus may not be applicable depending on the application domain. Lucia and Ferrari [8] propose an unsupervised message classification method based on expanding lexical meanings using external knowledge sources. They automatically generate message categories based on existing type definitions provided by knowledge sources such as YAGO[4]. Most works that automatically generate message categories, however, tend to result only in general categories such as sports, politics, and religion, and are insufficient for more specific classification needs in a particular domain.

Name and entity recognition (NER) has been widely studied in computational linguistics, and well known solutions have been developed, such as StanfordNER[5] and OpenNLP[6]. Traditional NER solutions, however, focus only on pre-defined term categories, such as person, organization, and location [3,12]. Recently, some solutions are proposed to tag names and entities without predefined categories. Tuan et al. [17] propose a method to find the taxonomy relations between unlabeled terms in data. In addition to string inclusion method and lexical-based rules, their method calculates subsumptions of contexts between terms, which rely on existing tools to extract *(Object, Verb, Subject)* triples. Their method achieves high precision recognizing taxonomy relations in formal texts such as journal papers and government reports. However, it is unlikely their method can be applied to informal texts, since there is no existing tool to effectively extract structures from such texts. Topics extracted from topic models can also be regarded as concepts for a short text. Li et al. [6] propose a topic model, GPU-DMM, for extracting topics from short texts. The method enriches the topic model with learned word embeddings. Semantically related words under the same topic are promoted during the sampling process by using a GPU model. However, this method highly depends on the word embeddings, which requires long time to learn and may not provide the specified categories. The work by Han et al. [4] has a similar aim to our work. They propose a frequency-based approach to link name mentions in texts to a concept in a knowledge graph, based on local compatibility and evidence propagation over the graph. Their

[4] http://www.mpi-inf.mpg.de/departments/databases-and-information-systems/research/yago-naga/yago/.

[5] http://nlp.stanford.edu/software/CRF-NER.shtml.

[6] http://opennlp.apache.org/.

method, however, relies on a pre-defined knowledge graph that has articles associated with each entity and thus is difficult to tailor to a specific classification task in a user-defined domain. Our proposed method, on the other hand, can work on user-defined domains and only requires a handful of domain concepts.

3 Domain Classification and Concept Tagging

We define the Multiple Domain Taxonomy (MDT) as a taxonomy with two types of relationships[7], namely, *domain association* and *taxonomy association*, denoted as *in_a* and *is_a*. *Domain associations* define the domain to which a concept belongs. *Taxonomy associations* define taxonomical hierarchies between concepts. One such MDT is shown in Fig. 1. In this example, the domains are `crime` and `imaging activity`, which could both present in a text dataset regarding a *shooting*. The concepts of suspect and victim are defined as "*in a*" crime, and camera "*is a*" tool "*in a*" imaging activity.

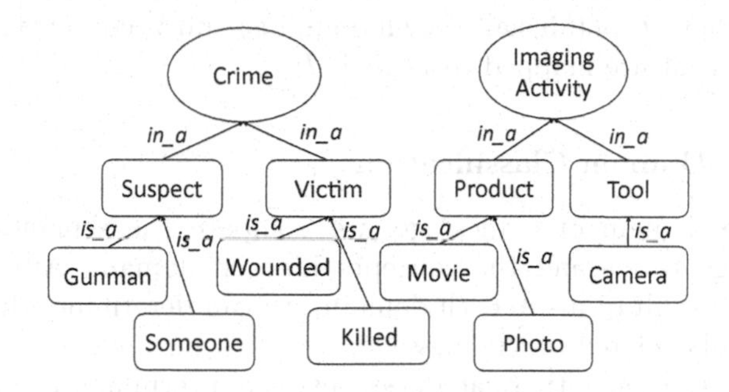

Fig. 1. An example multiple domain taxonomy

We define a multiple domain taxonomy as $MDT = \{D, V, I, S\}$, where D is the set of domains, V is the taxonomy vocabulary, and each $c \in V$ is a concept. $I = V \mapsto D$ is the mapping of *in_a* relationship between concepts and domains, and $S = V \mapsto V$ is the mapping of *is_a* relationship that describes the hierarchy of concepts. Here we consider if $\{c_1 \mapsto d\} \in I$, and $\{c_2 \mapsto c_1\} \in S$, then $\{c_2 \mapsto d\} \in I$, in other words, if a parent concept belongs to a domain, all its children concepts also belong to the same domain. In this way we do not need to explicitly define *in_a* relationship for lower level concepts.

3.1 Problem Statement

We show that using a partial MDT constructed with some initial knowledge of that data, we can solve the problem of message domain classification and concept

[7] We refer to the MDT as a taxonomy due to the simple nature of the relationships defined.

tagging. The problem of domain classification looks at determining the domain for a message given a number of known domains. The problem of concept tagging looks at tagging unknown terms in a message with a concept label. An example of a tagged message would look like: "`I took a photo[IMAGING:PRODUCT] of my girlfriend[IMAGING:TARGET] with my new camera[IMAGING:TOOL]`". We note that the text transformation is straightforward once we identify the compatible taxonomy concept for the term. We formally define the two problems as the following:

Problem 1 (Domain Classification). Given a number of possible domains $D = \{d_1, ..., d_l\}$, and the message m consisting of terms $\{t_1, ..., t_k\}$, find the domain association of m, such that $\{m \mapsto d\}$ for some $d \in D$.

Problem 2 (Concept Tagging). Given a number of concepts V, and a number of terms in a message m, $T_m = \{t_1, ..., t_k\}$, find a taxonomy association for each t such that $\{t \mapsto c\}$, for some $c \in V$.

For solving the problems, we assume a $MDT = \{D, V, I, S\}$ has been constructed, such that D contains all known domains, and V contains an incomplete list of concepts that are mapped to D with I.

3.2 Message Domain Classification

To classify the domain of a message, we compare the semantic relatedness between message terms and the concepts in each domain. After aggregating the relatedness for all terms in each domain, we can determine which domain is more semantically related to the message.

To calculate the semantic relatedness between a term and a concept, we use a method proposed by Milne and Witten [10], which utilizes the presence of the term and the concept in the unlabeled data, and calculates the semantic relatedness score (SRS) as following:

$$SRS(t,c) = 1 - \frac{log(max(|T|,|C|)) - log(|T \bigcap C|)}{log(|W|) - log(min(|T|,|C|))} \quad (1)$$

where t and c are the term and the concept, T and C are the sets of all messages that contain t and c, respectively, and W is the entire dataset.

We use the highest SRS obtained when matching the term with different domain concepts as the domain score for the term. After retrieving the SRS for each term in a domain, we calculate a message score for the domain (DS):

$$DS(m,d) = \sum_{i=1}^{k} max(SRS(t_k, c_j), \forall \{c_j \mapsto d\} \in I) \quad (2)$$

where the message m consists of terms $\{t_1, ..., t_k\}$.

We calculate a domain score for each domain. Then the predicted domain for m is the domain that provides the highest domain score, $\arg\max_i DS(m, d_i)$.

3.3 Concept Tagging

We approach the concept tagging problem by finding the *compatible* concept in the taxonomy for a term. If a term is compatible with a concept, then it can inherit its taxonomy associations. For example, if we find "film" is compatible with "movie", and "movie" is defined as a product in the taxonomy, then we can consider "film" is also a product. To calculate the concept compatibility, we take into account the message contexts, which is formed from the words surrounding the term and the concept. We argue that if a term is in the same domain as the concept, and the context they appear in are similar, then it is very likely they are compatible.

The context of a term is usually represented as a number of words neighboring the keyword. Traditionally, the position of context words is ignored, and the context words are considered interchangeable. However, we found that the position of context words contains crucial information and should not be overlooked. For example, suppose we have two message, "He took a new photo of the house", and "the house of cards took a new view on US politics". In this example, if we ignore the position, the two terms "photo" and "cards" have the same context, but they are certainly semantically incompatible. Based on this insight, in our solution we take into account the position of context words.

To calculate the context similarity between a term and a concept, we first set a context width parameter q, which defines how many neighboring words will be considered as the context. From a number of unlabeled messages that contains the term, we extract a set of words at each position between $p-q$ and $p+q$, where p is the position of the term in the message. A total of $2q$ sets will be extracted, denoted as $Q_t^1, ..., Q_t^{2q}$. Similarly we extract the context word sets for the compared concept, $Q_c^1, ..., Q_c^{2q}$. The context similarity is thus calculated based on the similarity of context words in the same position:

$$contextSimilarity(t, c) = \frac{\sum_{i=1}^{2q} sim(Q_t^i, Q_c^i)}{2q} \tag{3}$$

where $sim(Q_1, Q_2)$ is a similarity function that compares two cluster of words.

From existing work, we choose a similarity function proposed by Unankard et al. [20], which is based on term frequency and cosine similarity:

$$sim(Q_1, Q_2) = \frac{\sum_i tf(Q_1, t_i) \times tf(Q_2, t_i)}{\sqrt{\sum_i tf(Q_1, t_i)^2} \times \sqrt{\sum_i tf(Q_2, t_i)^2}} \tag{4}$$

where $t_i \in T$ is all the terms in $Q_1 \bigcup Q_2$, and $tf(Q, t)$ is the term frequency of term t in set Q.

To tag a term t in a message m, first we determine the domain for m using the method described above. Then we obtain all concepts that belong to the domain, $c_d \in V$ that satisfies $\{c_d \mapsto d\} \in I$. We then calculate the context similarity between the term and each concept, and find the concept that produces the highest context similarity, c_{max}. Finally we consider t and c_{max} compatible, and assign $\{t \mapsto c_p\}$ for any $\{c_{max} \mapsto c_p\}$, in other words, allowing t inherit the taxonomy association that c_{max} has.

We need to note that the identified concepts can be added into the MDT, based on the identified domain and compatible concepts, and thus the MDT can be iteratively improved. As more data being processed, and more concepts added to the ontology, we expect a better recognition performance of our system with the improved MDT. In this work, however, we focus on the first iteration of this process. We will explore iterative MDT improvement with identified concepts in future works.

3.4 Improving Computational Efficiency

It is computationally expensive to collect context and calculate similarity for every concept-term pair in large unlabeled datasets. For example, for 100,000 unlabeled messages and $q = 3$, a total of 600,000 words will be compared for each pair. To improve efficiency, we compute some term frequency information at the start of the system and store it in a memory heap to quickly estimate the significance of context similarity between a term and a concept, thus eliminating most contextual comparisons between insignificant pairs.

We call our runtime reduction technique *reverse contextualizing* (RC). First we compute the significance between a concept c and a context word w in position i. We collect the context of c in position i as Q_c^i, the significance of a context word w is calculated as:

$$sig(c, w, i) = \frac{tf(Q_c^i, w)}{|Q_c^i|} \tag{5}$$

This score shows the percentage of a context word in all words appearing in the concept's context at the given position. Then for each context w, we also collect its contexts, with the reversed position of $2q - i$, as Q_w^{2q-i}. For each term t of this reversed context set of w, the significance is calculated as:

$$sig(t, w, i) = \frac{tf(Q_w^{2q-i}, t)}{|Q_w^{2q-i}|} \tag{6}$$

Finally we compute a significance score between concept c and term t as:

$$sig(c, t) = 100 \times \sum_{i=1}^{2q} \sum_{w \in |Q_c^i|} sig(c, w, i) + sig(t, w, i) \tag{7}$$

As an example, suppose $q = 3$ and $i = q + 1$. Then for concept *police*, we calculate significance of contextual word *shooting* in the position next to the concept as *sig*(“*police*”, “*shooting*”, $q+1$), based on the frequency of the phrase “police shooting”. Then for word *shooting*, we calculate the significance of its context word *kids* in the position previous to the word as *sig*(“*kids*”, “*shooting*”, $q + 1$), based on the frequency of phrase “kids shooting”. Finally based on two calculation results we obtain significance score between *police* and *kids*.

We compute this score for each pair of concept and term appearing in the same position in the data with respect to context words, and store it in memory. We also set a significance threshold τ. When tagging a term in a message, we first retrieve the significance score between the term and the concept, $sig(c, t)$, and only when $sig(c, t) > \tau$ we proceed to calculate the actual context similarity.

4 Experimental Analysis

We have presented our domain and concept identifying method as an effective unsupervised method. We expect our method to achieve better accuracy than current supervised and unsupervised methods, while keep low computational cost. We conduct experiments on real Twitter data to validate our approach. First we test the accuracy of our domain classification method. Then we test the accuracy of our concept tagging method. Finally we study the runtime of our approach, and provide insights into the impact of different training data size and pre-computation on computational costs.

4.1 Datasets

Our experiments are conducted on two sets of real Twitter data. The first dataset, called the *shooting* dataset, is collected using the Twitter Filter API[8] during September and October, 2014. The dataset has about 2 million tweets containing the keyword *shooting*. After removing retweets, we obtain a set of 284,343 tweets. We examine the data and discover that the tweets are mainly related to four domains, namely, *crime*, *imaging*, *game*, and *metaphor*. After deciding the domains, we label a number of tweets according to their domains. The labeled data contains 1,083 tweets.

The second dataset is called the *crisis* dataset and is a publicly available dataset[9] introduced by Olteanu et al. [11]. It contains sets of tweets related to 26 natural disasters and other crisis events and labeled and unlabeled tweets. There are two types of labels, based on whether the tweet is related and informative, and based on the source of the tweet, respectively. We use only related tweets. Combining tweets for all 26 events, we obtain 201,078 unlabeled tweets, and 3,646 labeled tweets. The labeled tweets contain five categories, namely, *eyewitness*, *business*, *government*, *media*, and *ngo*.

For each dataset we manually construct an MDT shown in Table 1. Both MDTs have a flat structure, with the first level as domains, and the second and third levels as concepts. Between domains and concepts, *in_a* relationships are defined. Between second and third levels of concepts, *is_a* relationships are defined. We have not spent more than two hours per MDT. For the crisis dataset, the five domains are taken from the five categories of labeled data.

[8] https://dev.twitter.com/streaming/reference/post/statuses/filter.
[9] http://crisislex.org/.

Table 1. MDT used in the experiments

Shooting dataset		
crime	actor	police, officer, cops, somebody, someone, gunman
	victim	wounded, killed
	weapon	gun, handgun
	location	office, street, house, crib, backyard, block
imaging	product	movie, film, photo, video, commercial, ad
	maker	cameraman, director, assistant, production, crew
	target	wedding, party, girlfriend
	location	studio, set, indoor, outdoor
	tool	camera, script, iphone, canon
game	type	games, range, ball, hoops, dice, ranch, duck, clay, match
	result	won, wins, lost, losses, leads, point, foul
	participant	player, team, shooter, guard, opponent
metaphor	object	star, pain, slugs
	target	foot, moon, face, wall, myself
	environment	sky, space, ecstasy, fantasy
Crisis dataset		
eyewitness	observation	windy, raining, baha, ulan, habagat
	reaction	my, friend, everyone, scary, hope, think
	location	house, backyard, outside
business	person	customers, ceo, employees
	unit	company, stores, plant, site, railway, google
	operation	sales, schedule, license
government	sector	public, federal, fdny, cpa, rfs, fbi, ntsb, mta, gov
	service	warning, hotlines, forms, school
	person	governor, premier, police, commissioner
media	type	blog, news, article, journal, press, tv, video, paper
	agent	bbc, reuters, cnn, fox, yahoo, times
	report	says, reports, kills, victims, accused, missing, hits, reported, coverage, source, update, story
ngo	organization	communities, centre, redcross, members
	activity	donating, fundraising, volunteering, charities
	support	donations, goods, money, aide

4.2 Results for Domain Classification

In the first set of experiments, we test the domain classification accuracy for our approach. We first focus on the first domain for the two datasets, namely, *crime* in the shooting dataset, and *eyewitness* in the crisis dataset. We focus on these two domains because *crime* and *eyewitness* are more desirable information, and have been the topic in several studies [7,22].

We compare our approach with three baselines. The first is *accept all* which considers all messages as positive. The *accept all* method would always achieve the highest recall of 1.0. The second baseline, proposed by Sriram et al. [16], is a supervised method based on eight features and the Naive Bayes model. The eight features include author name, use of slang, time phrase, opinionated words, and word emphasis, presences of currency signs, percentage signs, mention sign at the beginning and the middle of the message. The evaluation is based on the five-fold cross validation. The Sriram classifier is shown to be effective in classifying tweets into categories such as news, opinions, deals and events, but has not been tested in other applications. The third baseline (PA) is from our previous work [22]. It is an unsupervised approach that incorporates lexical analysis and user profiling. This method is shown to be effective for filtering personal observations from tweet messages.

The classification accuracy of the first domain in two datasets achieved by three baselines and our MDT-based approach is shown in Table 2. As can be seen from the results, our approach achieves extremely high precision comparing to the baselines. For classifying *crime* domain, it achieves 0.92 precision, which is a 52% increase from the baseline methods, as well as 0.78 f-value, a 27% increase from the baseline methods. For classifying *eyewitness*, it also achieves a high precision of 0.73, a 9% increase from the baseline method, and 6% increase in f-value. The PA method is designed to distinguish observation messages according to their source, and thus it achieves a low accuracy classifying *crime* as it includes messages from various sources; for *eyewitness*, it achieves the highest accuracy among baseline methods. Our MDT-based method, nevertheless, surpasses the PA method both in precision and recall for classifying *eyewitness*.

Table 2. Classification accuracy of the first domain

	Accept all	Sriram	PA	MDT
`Shooting dataset`				
Precision	0.30	0.40	0.31	**0.92**
Recall	**1**	0.71	0.49	0.68
f-value	0.46	0.51	0.38	**0.78**
`Crisis dataset`				
Precision	0.14	0.32	0.64	**0.73**
Recall	**1**	0.52	0.50	0.54
f-value	0.24	0.40	0.56	**0.62**

We also look at other domains. Table 3 shows the classification accuracy across four domains for the shooting dataset. As can be seen from the result, classification on other domain also achieves high accuracy as the crime domain, indicated by similar f-values. However, the *crime* domain do provide the highest precision, mainly due to that it is a narrower domain that can be better identified with a simple taxonomy.

Table 3. Classification accuracy for the shooting dataset

	Crime	Imaging	Game	Metaphor
Precision	0.92	0.82	0.67	0.67
Recall	0.68	0.68	0.78	0.91
f-value	0.78	0.75	0.72	0.77

4.3 Results for Concept Tagging

In the second set of experiments, we test the accuracy of our concept tagging approach. We conduct two experiments. In the first experiment, which we call *take-out-one* experiment, the leaf level concepts in the MDT are taken out one-by-one and put back to the MDT using our approach. For example, for the shooting MDT, we first take out the *police* concept, and then use the proposed tagging method to match it with the MDT, now without the *police* concept. This process is run for every concept in the MDT. For the shooting MDT, 71 concepts are tested. For the crisis MDT, 80 concepts are tested. The proportion of correctly tagged concept with respect to different training data sizes is shown in Table 4. From the results we can see that the take-out-one experiment reaches a very high precision. With only 15,000 training data, we have over 0.95 precision for the shooting MDT, and over 0.92 precision for the crisis MDT. According to this result, we can confidently tag a concept with a MDT even with a small number of training data, if it is known that the concept must be compatible with the MDT.

Table 4. Precision in take-out-one experiment

Training size	5k	10k	15k	20k	25k	30k
Shooting	0.915	0.943	0.955	0.955	0.955	0.985
Crisis	0.850	0.875	0.925	0.925	0.962	0.987

In the next experiment, we run concept tagging on the raw data. We take 10,000 tweets from the shooting dataset and 3,000 tweets from the crisis dataset, and employ our concept tagging method. We use 30k training data, which should provide optimal effectiveness based on to the previous experiment. The detected taxonomy and the context similarity score are recorded for each tagged term, and thus a large number of tagged terms are generated. Table 5 shows the terms with the highest context similarity score for the second-level concepts.

Table 5. Top terms for second-level concept

Tagged tweet	Term	Concept	Score
Shit crazy ppl[CRIME:ACTOR] shooting omg :(	ppl	actor	0.496
On set wishes to Tyneea C and Romarni C shooting for baby[IMAGING:PRODUCT] milk product commercial - enjoy girlz!	baby	product	0.381
I enjoy shooting pool[GAME:TYPE]	pool	type	0.431
Like a shooting star, I will go the distance. I will search the world[METAPHOR:TARGET]. I will face its harm and I don't care how far	world	target	0.455
The windows are shaking at home[EYEWITNESS:LOCATION], the wind is crazy!! And it's getting worse - #GoldCoast #bigwet	home	location	0.487
Bid now on this one of a kind SIGNED canvas print of our @RedRocksOnline poster. ALL proceeds[BUSINESS:OPERATION] go to #Coflood relief:	proceeds	operation	0.512
BBC News - In pictures[MEDIA:TYPE]: Brazil nightclub fire	pictures	type	0.653
AB relief Cards are available today - if you are in Sunnyside, please go to Queen[GOVERNMENT:PERSON] Elizabeth High School! #yycflood	Queen	person	0.355
Raise funds[NGO:SUPPORT] for #Boston or West #Texas tonight if #party planning - (Between 6pm and 11pm, ET, Tuesday April 30th)	funds	support	0.694

We can identify some errors in the above tagging, such as identifying *baby* instead of *baby milk product commercial* as the shooting target, and *Queen* in *Queen Elizabeth High School* as a person. Such errors are caused by the limitation of not considering multi-word terms, which we will explore in the future. It is worth noting that word shortenings such as *ppl* are captured correctly.

To evaluate the overall accuracy, we manually check all the tagged terms with a context similarity score above 0.3. There are 296 terms and 554 terms that satisfy this requirement in the shooting and crisis test data, respectively. The tagging accuracy of these terms with respect to different context similarity score range is shown in Table 6. As a comparison, we also show the expected accuracy if we randomly choose a second-level concept for tagging.

We can obtain around 50% tagging accuracy for terms that generate a context similarity score >0.3. The low accuracy is possibly due to many terms that do not have a taxonomy relationship with the MDT but still have similar context with the concepts, such as time and location words. This problem can be overcome by, for example, adding the time-related concepts to the MDT. Nevertheless, comparing to randomly assigning tags, our approach achieves much higher tagging accuracy.

Table 6. Tagging accuracy in different context similarity score range

Context similarity	>0.3	>0.35	>0.4	>0.45	Random
Shooting	0.44	0.46	0.48	0.57	0.014
Crisis	0.55	0.567	0.60	0.64	0.012

4.4 Runtime Analysis

We test the effectiveness of our runtime reduction technique (RC). We measure the runtime of concept tagging for the 1,083 shooting tweets, with different training data sizes and two τ values. The results are shown in Fig. 2. All experiments are run on a desktop computer with a 3.7 GHz eight-core Intel Xeon CPU, 15.6 GB memory, and Ubuntu 16.04.

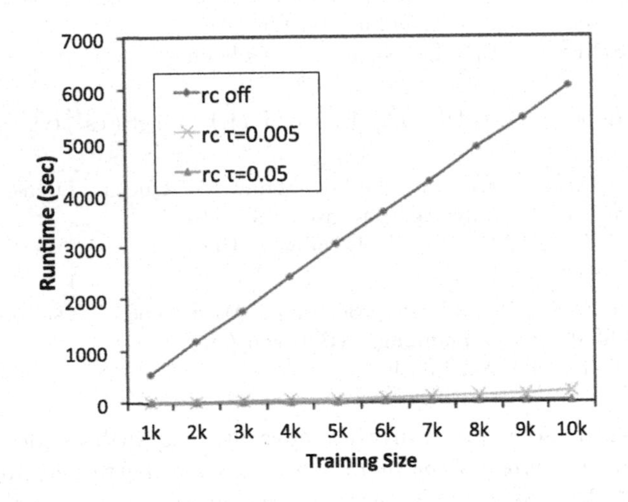

Fig. 2. Runtime with different RC options

As we can see from the figure, our RC technique effectively removes most of the computation in the otherwise computation-heavy concept tagging task. Using 5k training data, the runtime without RC is 3,045 s, while with RC the runtime is 72 s for $\tau = 0.005$ and 23 s for $\tau = 0.05$. Using 10k training data, the runtime without RC is 6,065 s, while with RC the runtime is 202 s for $\tau = 0.005$ and 49 s for $\tau = 0.05$. In both cases, the runtime is reduced to a few hundredth of the original runtime. Looking at the absolute values, using 10k training data, with which we have seen satisfactory tagging accuracy, the average tagging time for a single tweet is 5.98 s without RC, but only 0.04 s with RC ($\tau = 0.05$). With the improved tagging speed, our concept tagging method becomes suitable even for realtime tweet processing.

5 Discussion

One of the hurdles of deploying our approach is the construction of the MDT. It is nearly impossible to extract narrow domain information from a large, mixed-domain data without any manual input. Comparing to training data annotation in supervised approaches, though, we consider that constructing a MDT requires much less effort, and translates knowledge in an efficient manner. We can also see that the extraction accuracy varies depending on the quality of the MDT. In our experiments, the extraction accuracy for the *shooting* data is higher than the *crisis* dataset, most likely because we have more experience with the first dataset than with the latter, and thus constructed a more representative MDT for the first dataset. Adding identified concepts to the MDT can improve the system performance, but manually checking is required given the errors in concept recognition we discussed in the previous section. Based on our experiences, adding wrong or ambiguous concept will not improve identification accuracy, but rather decrease it.

Currently our method only considers single-word concepts, but in reality many concepts are expressed in multiple words, and we will run into error if we cannot recognize them, for example, "video camera". This can be done by generating all possible bi-grams and multi-grams from data, as existing works have suggested [8].

6 Conclusion

Social media produces significantly large volume of data covering a wide range of topics, and there is an increasing need of extracting information for narrow domain applications from large, mixed-domain datasets. However, currently most applications develop classification and extraction solutions tailored to a narrow domain, and are usually unsuitable for use in other applications and domains. Developing individual solutions is expensive including efforts to develop algorithms and annotate training data for supervised solutions. We therefore focus on a general solution that can be easily tailored to narrow domain needs and does not require training data annotation and other manual involvement.

In this paper, we propose Multiple Domain Taxonomy (MDT), a representation of mixed-domain data. We show that using a partially constructed MDT, we can effectively classify and extract key concepts from short text messages. The MDT can be constructed with some initial knowledge of the data, and can be quickly tailored to narrow domain needs. Our approach is frequency-based and unsupervised. It is robust to common misspellings and word shortenings, and does not require training data annotation. The effectiveness of our approach is verified extensively using real datasets, and comparing to baseline methods such as the Sriram classifier and the PA method, our approach increased the accuracy by up to 52%. In the future, we plan to further improve the concept tagging accuracy, as well as investigating the case of multi-word concepts.

References

1. Barberá, P.: Birds of the same feather tweet together: Bayesian ideal point estimation using Twitter data. Polit. Anal. **23**(1), 76–91 (2015)
2. Dredze, M., Paul, M.J., Bergsma, S., Tran, H.: Carmen: a Twitter geolocation system with applications to public health. In: AAAI Workshop on Expanding the Boundaries of Health Informatics Using AI, pp. 20–24 (2013)
3. Finin, T., Murnane, W., Karandikar, A., Keller, N., Martineau, J., Dredze, M.: Annotating named entities in Twitter data with crowdsourcing. In: Proceedings of the NAACL HLT 2010 Workshop on Creating Speech and Language Data with Amazon's Mechanical Turk, pp. 80–88. Association for Computational Linguistics (2010)
4. Han, X., Sun, L., Zhao, J.: Collective entity linking in web text: a graph-based method. In: Proceedings of the 34th International ACM SIGIR Conference on Research and Development in Information Retrieval, pp. 765–774. ACM (2011)
5. Kwon, S., Cha, M., Jung, K., Chen, W., Wang, Y.: Prominent features of rumor propagation in online social media. In: Proceedings of 13th International Conference on Data Mining, pp. 1103–1108 (2013)
6. Li, C., Wang, H., Zhang, Z., Sun, A., Ma, Z.: Topic modeling for short texts with auxiliary word embeddings. In: Proceedings of the 39th International ACM SIGIR Conference on Research and Development in Information Retrieval, pp. 165–174. ACM (2016)
7. Li, R., Lei, K.H., Khadiwala, R., Chang, K.-C.: TEDAS: a Twitter-based event detection and analysis system. In: Proceedings of 28th International Conference on Data Engineering, pp. 1273–1276 (2012)
8. Lucia, W., Ferrari, E.: Egocentric: ego networks for knowledge-based short text classification. In: Proceedings of the 23rd ACM International Conference on Information and Knowledge Management, pp. 1079–1088. ACM (2014)
9. Maddock, J., Starbird, K., Al-Hassani, H., Sandoval, D.E., Orand, M., Mason, R.M.: Characterizing online rumoring behavior using multi-dimensional signatures. In: Proceedings of the ACM Conference on Computer Supported Cooperative Work and Social Computing, pp. 228–241 (2015)
10. Milne, D., Witten, I.H.: Learning to link with Wikipedia. In: Proceedings of the 17th ACM Conference on Information and Knowledge Management, pp. 509–518. ACM (2008)
11. Olteanu, A., Castillo, C., Diaz, F., Vieweg, S.: CrisisLex: a lexicon for collecting and filtering microblogged communications in crises. In: Proceedings of the 8th International AAAI Conference on Weblogs and Social Media, pp. 376–385 (2014)
12. Poibeau, T., Kosseim, L.: Proper name extraction from non-journalistic texts. Lang. Comput. **37**(1), 144–157 (2001)
13. Popescu, A.-M., Pennacchiotti, M.: Detecting controversial events from Twitter. In: Proceedings of the 19th ACM International Conference on Information and Knowledge Management, pp. 1873–1876 (2010)
14. Ritter, A., Etzioni, O., Clark, S., et al.: Open domain event extraction from Twitter. In: Proceedings of the 18th ACM SIGKDD International Conference on Knowledge Discovery and Data Mining, pp. 1104–1112. ACM (2012)
15. Sakaki, T., Okazaki, M., Matsuo, Y.: Earthquake shakes Twitter users: real-time event detection by social sensors. In: Proceedings of the 19th International World Wide Web Conference, pp. 851–860 (2010)

16. Sriram, B., Fuhry, D., Demir, E., Ferhatosmanoglu, H., Demirbas, M.: Short text classification in Twitter to improve information filtering. In: Proceedings of the 33rd International ACM SIGIR Conference on Research and Development in Information Retrieval, pp. 841–842 (2010)
17. Tuan, L.A., Kim, J.-J., Kiong, N.S.: Taxonomy construction using syntactic contextual evidence. In: Proceedings of the 2014 Conference on Empirical Methods in Natural Language Processing, pp. 810–819 (2014)
18. Tumasjan, A., Sprenger, T.O., Sandner, P.G., Welpe, I.M.: Predicting elections with Twitter: what 140 characters reveal about political sentiment. In: Proceedings of the Fourth International Conference on Weblogs and Social Media, pp. 178–185 (2010)
19. Unankard, S., Li, X., Sharaf, M., Zhong, J., Li, X.: Predicting elections from social networks based on sub-event detection and sentiment analysis. In: Benatallah, B., Bestavros, A., Manolopoulos, Y., Vakali, A., Zhang, Y. (eds.) WISE 2014. LNCS, vol. 8787, pp. 1–16. Springer, Cham (2014). doi:10.1007/978-3-319-11746-1_1
20. Unankard, S., Li, X., Sharaf, M.A.: Emerging event detection in social networks with location sensitivity. World Wide Web **18**(5), 1393–1417 (2015)
21. Zhang, Y., Szabo, C., Sheng, Q.Z.: Sense and focus: towards effective location inference and event detection on Twitter. In: Wang, J., Cellary, W., Wang, D., Wang, H., Chen, S.-C., Li, T., Zhang, Y. (eds.) WISE 2015. LNCS, vol. 9418, pp. 463–477. Springer, Cham (2015). doi:10.1007/978-3-319-26190-4_31
22. Zhang, Y., Szabo, C., Sheng, Q.Z.: Improving object and event monitoring on Twitter through lexical analysis and user profiling. In: Cellary, W., Mokbel, M.F., Wang, J., Wang, H., Zhou, R., Zhang, Y. (eds.) WISE 2016. LNCS, vol. 10042, pp. 19–34. Springer, Cham (2016). doi:10.1007/978-3-319-48743-4_2

User Interests Clustering in Business Intelligence Interactions

Krista Drushku[1,2(✉)], Julien Aligon[2,3], Nicolas Labroche[2], Patrick Marcel[2], Veronika Peralta[2], and Bruno Dumant[1]

[1] SAP Research, Levallois Perret, France
{krista.drushku,bruno.dumant}@sap.com
[2] University of Tours, Blois, France
{julien.aligon,nicolas.labroche,
patrick.marcel,veronika.peralta}@univ-tours.fr,
krista.drushku@etu.univ-tours.fr
[3] University of Toulouse 1 Capitole, Toulouse, France
julien.aligon@ut-capitole.fr

Abstract. It is quite common these days for experts, casual analysts, executives or data enthusiasts, to analyze large datasets using user-friendly interfaces on top of Business Intelligence (BI) systems. However, current BI systems do not adequately detect and characterize user interests, which may lead to tedious and unproductive interactions. In this paper, we propose to identify such user interests by characterizing the intent of the interaction with the BI system. With an eye on user modeling for proactive search systems, we identify a set of features for an adequate description of intents, and a similarity measure for grouping intents into coherent interests. We validate experimentally our approach with a user study, where we analyze traces of BI navigation. We show that our similarity measure outperforms a state-of-the-art query similarity measure and yields a very good precision with respect to expressed user interests.

Keywords: User interest · Feature construction · Clustering · BI analyses

1 Introduction

BI system users range from executives to data enthusiasts who share a common way of interaction: they navigate large datasets by means of sequences of analytical queries elaborated through user-friendly interfaces. For example, users may express their information needs via keywords, and let the system infer from them the most probable formal queries (generally MDX or SQL) to be sent to the underlying data sources (generally data warehouses or databases). As information needs do not have a status per se, it usually takes many interactions with the system to satisfy an information need, and the overall session is often a tedious process, especially in the case when the information need is not even clear for the user. This bears resemblance with web search where users typically

E. Dubois and K. Pohl (Eds.): CAiSE 2017, LNCS 10253, pp. 144–158, 2017.
DOI: 10.1007/978-3-319-59536-8_10

need to repeatedly query the search engine to determine whether there is an interesting content.

Being able to automatically identify user interests from BI interactions is a challenging problem that has many potential applications: collaborative recommendation (of data or dashboards), repetitive task prediction, alert raising, etc. that would participate in reducing the tediousness of the analysis. The difficulty of this problem lies in the fact that user interests are hidden in the interactions, and two users with the same interest would probably interact with the system differently. As in web search where users may have no idea of the retrieval algorithm, BI user are generally ignorant of the data sources and the formal queries they trigger. However once logged, all this information (keywords, sources, formal queries, etc.) provide a rich basis for discovering user interests.

In web search, state-of-the-art approaches [6,12,16] characterize user interests by means of features extracted from user traces, and classify them to group queries related to the same information needs. We consider that an interaction relies on a sequence of keyword queries over some data sources. Each keyword query produces an ordered set of formal queries suggested from the set of keywords. One of these formal queries, chosen by the user, is evaluated over the data source and the answer retrieved is displayed to the user. All this (keyword query, suggestions and chosen query) is called an observation. We extract a set of features that describe each observation of all user interactions. To group observations into coherent user interests, we first use supervised classification to define a similarity measure that basically assigns a weight to each of the features. Then, we use our measure with an off-the-shelf clustering algorithm to group observations.

If our approach is inspired by the work Guha et al. did in the context of web search [6], it deviates from it on major aspects. First we present our own formal model tailored to BI interactions and we address a specific type of intents. Consistently, we use a specific set of features. Contrarily to [6] we focus more on the expressiveness of the model rather than on specific optimizations for scaling to web data volumes. Finally, our approach is automatic and we present our own evaluation of it, that includes a user study.

More precisely, our contributions include:

- a simple formal model of BI interactions,
- the identification of a set of features for characterizing BI user interests,
- the learning of a similarity measure based on these features,
- an approach to automatically discover user interests based on our measure and an off-the-shelf clustering algorithm,
- an extensive set of experiments for the tuning and validation of our approach, the comparison of our measure with a state-of-the-art metric tailored for OLAP queries [3], and the study of its behaviour in various practical situations.

The paper is organized as follows: Sect. 2 presents our formal model of BI interactions and user interests. Section 3 details the set of features used to characterize user interests and our algorithm for discovering coherent cross-interaction interests. Section 4 presents our experimental validation. Section 5 gives an overview of related work and Sect. 6 concludes the paper.

2 Formal Model of BI Interactions

This section presents our model of BI interaction. Given the proximity of BI interactions in modern BI systems and web searches, our modeling of BI interactions is inspired by the modeling of web search sessions. Note that the generation of formal (MDX or SQL) queries from keywords is out of the scope of this paper.

2.1 BI Questions, Suggestions and Queries

Let D be a database schema, I an instance of D and Q the set of formal queries one can express over D. For simplicity, in this paper, we consider relational databases under a star schema, queried with multidimensional queries [14]. Let A be the set of attributes of the relations of D. Let $M \subset A$ be a set of attributes defined on numerical domains called measures. Let $H = \{h_1, \ldots, h_n\}$ be a finite set of *hierarchies*, each characterized by (1) a subset $Lev(h_i) \subset A$ of attributes called levels, (2) a *roll-up* total order $\succeq_{h_i}$ of $Lev(h_i)$. Let $adom(I)$ be the set of constants of the instance I of D. We call a **database entity** an element of the set $A \cup adom(I)$. The result (or answer) of a query q over a database instance I is denoted $q(I)$.

Let T be a countably infinite set of keywords named tokens. A **BI question** (or question for short) K, is a set of tokens entered by a user. Each token can be matched with the entities in $A \cup adom(I)$ to generate queries. To simplify, we describe a multidimensional query q in Q as a set of query parts, as in [2]. A **query part** is either a level of a hierarchy in H used for grouping, a measure in M, or a simple Boolean predicate of the form $A = v$ involving an attribute A.

For example, starting from BI question *"Revenue for France as Country"* the following tokens {*"Revenue"*, *"France"*, *"Country"*} can be identified by excluding stop words. Then, a query may contain the following query parts: *Revenue* is a measure, *Country* a level in a hierarchy, and *France* is a constant, resulting in *Country* = *France* being a Boolean predicate.

If a query part p is a selection predicate of the form $A = v$, or a grouping attribute A, we use $level(p)$ to denote attribute A. Given two query parts p_1 and p_2, $FD(p_1, p_2)$ denotes that there is a functional dependency $level(p_1) \rightarrow level(p_2)$. Given two queries q_1 and q_2, the boolean expression $OP(q_1, q_2)$ indicates if they differ in at most one query part. This allows to detect OLAP operations when users navigate along hierarchies or change selection conditions.

As keywords are entered, a BI system might on the fly suggest further tokens to complete the current ones, letting the user choose among them, as in web search engines. The underlying idea is that a suggestion completes the original BI question in order to obtain a well-formed query over a database. We formalize the notion of suggestions as follows. A **suggestion** S is a triple $\langle K, D, q\rangle$ where

K is a BI question, D is a database schema (called source) and q is a query over D. For short, given a suggestion $S = \langle K, D, q \rangle$, we note $tokens(S)$, $source(S)$ and $query(S)$ for referring to K, D and q respectively.

2.2 Observations, Interactions and User Interests

In web search, search histories (i.e., interactions with a search engine) are analyzed to identify coherent information needs, as basis for recommendation generation. For instance, Guha et al. [6] propose to model information needs as sequences of observations, an observation being a search engine query with its associated web results (Search Engine Result Page or SERP for short) and clicks. We adapt the model of [6] to model contexts of BI interactions. This adaptation relies on the following simple analogy: (i) the search engine query corresponds to the BI question, (ii) the SERP corresponds to the set of suggestions associated with the BI question, and (iii) a click on one SERP link corresponds to the choice of a suggestion and hence to the evaluation of the query associated with the suggestion.

Formally, an **observation** o is a triple $o = \langle K, S, s \rangle$ where K is a question, $S = \{s_1, \ldots, s_n\}$ is a set of suggestions for question K, and $s \in \{s_1, \ldots, s_n\}$ is the suggestion selected by the user. Given an observation o, we note K^o the question K of o, $suggestions(o)$ its set of suggestions, and $chosen(o)$ the chosen suggestion. We note $query(o) = query(chosen(o))$, the query of the chosen suggestion, and $result(o) = query(o)(I)$, the result set of the query over a data source instance I. In addition, we annotate each observation o with a binary property indicating the expertise of the user who interacted with the system, denoted $expertise(o)$. For example, consider the question "Revenue for France" of an observation o. There are several suggestions proposed, whose respective questions are: "Revenue for France as Country", "Revenue for France as Market Unit", "Revenue Closed for France as MU/Country/Super Reg", "Revenue Closed for France as Country", etc. Assuming the first suggestion is chosen by the user, it is chosen(o) and the result of the formal query $query(o)$ is $result(o)$.

An **interaction** of length v is a sequence of v observations $i = \langle o_1, \ldots, o_v \rangle$ that represents the user interaction with the BI system. E.g., other questions as: "revenue for France 2010" or "revenue for France 2015" or "revenue closed for France" can follow our question K to create a complete interaction of the user with the system, analyzing the economic growth of France.

Without loss of generality and to keep the formalism simple, we assume that an observation is part of only one interaction. The function $interaction(o)$ returns the interaction to which o belongs. Given two observations o_x and o_y in an interaction, we say that o_y refines (is a **refinement** of) o_x if o_x precedes o_y and either $K^{o_x} = K^{o_y} \cup \{t\}$ or $K^{o_y} = K^{o_x} \cup \{t\}$ or $K^{o_y} = K^{o_x} \setminus \{t\} \cup \{t'\}$, where $t, t' \in T$.

A **user interest** is a finite set $U = \{o_1, \ldots, o_n\}$ of observations that represents one particular information need.

Table 1 presents the basic characteristics we use in our features to describe user interests. Note that $\cup^B$ denotes bag union (preserving duplicates to compute

Table 1. Basic characteristics of user interests

Characteristics	Definition	Interpretation
$questions(U)$	$\cup_{o \in U}\{K^o\}$	All the questions
$tokens(U)$	$\cup^B_{o \in U} K^o$	All the tokens
$suggestions(U)$	$\cup_{o \in U} suggestions(o)$	All the suggestions
$chosenSuggest(U)$	$\cup_{o \in U} chosen(o)$	All the chosen suggestions
$queries(U)$	$\cup^B_{o \in U}\{query(o)\}$	All the chosen queries
$qParts(U)$	$\cup^B_{o \in U} query(o)$	All the chosen query parts
$interactions(U)$	$\cup^B_{o \in U} interaction(o)$	All the interactions
$results(U)$	$\cup_{o \in U} result(o)$	All the results
$sources(U)$	$\cup_{o \in U} source(chosen(o))$	All the sources
$expertise(U)$	$\cup_{o \in U} expertise(o)$	All the expertises
$refTok(U)$	$\{t \in tokens(U) \mid \exists o, o' \in U,$ $t \in (K^o \setminus K^{o'}), o$ refines $o'\}$	Tokens that refine other ones
$matchTok(U, P)$	$\{t \in tokens(U) \mid \exists p \in P,$ $matches(t, p)\}$	Tokens that match a given set of query parts

frequencies), P is a set of query parts and $matches(t, p)$ is a binary function indicating if token t matches query part p.

3 Characterizing and Clustering User Interests

Following [6], we formalize the problem of discovering coherent user interests as a clustering problem, for which a similarity measure is learned over a set of descriptive features. These features allow to group observations (and user interests) not only based on their intentions expressed by the BI question, but also based on their objectives as expressed by the chosen suggestion, and on their knowledge as provided by the evaluation of the chosen query. To compare two user interests, a global similarity is computed as a weighted sum of feature-based similarity measures. We first define the set of features we consider, together with their similarities, then explain how the features are weighted and how contexts are clustered.

3.1 User Interest Description Features

To provide the best characterization of user interest, we define a set of candidate features, that we subsequently analyze to identify those maximizing the accuracy from the user's perspective. We considered three groups of features. The first group of features relates to the BI questions and suggestions (features 1–6). The second group relates to the chosen suggestions, and especially their query parts (features 7–9). Both groups proved effective in identifying interests in the context of Web searches [6]. The third group consists of specific BI features, and relates to formal queries and their answers (features 10–15).

Table 2. Features considered

#	Feature	Formal definition	Similarity
1	Frequency of tokens	$freq(tokens(U_1))$	Cosine
2	Frequency of refining tokens	$freq(refTok(U_1))$	Cosine
3	Suggestions	$suggestions(U_1)$	NormInt.
4	BI questions	$questions(U_1)$	NormInt.
5	U_1 questions that are sub-questions in U_2	$\{K \in questions(U_1) \mid \exists K' \in questions(U_2), K' \subset K\}$	MaxFrac.
6	U_1 questions in the same interaction as a question in U_2	$\{K^o \mid o \in U_1, \exists o' \in U_2, interactions(o) = interactions(o')\}$	MaxFrac.
7	Frequency of chosen query parts	$freq(qParts(U_1))$	Cosine
8	Frequency of tokens of U_1 that match chosen query parts of U_2	$freq(matchTok(U_1, qParts(U_2)))$	Cosine
9	Chosen suggestions	$chosenSuggest(U_1)$	NormInt.
10	Levels in chosen query parts	$\{Level(p) \mid p \in qParts(U_1)\}$	Jaccard
11	Tuples retrieved by chosen queries	$results(U_1)$	NormInt.
12	Queries in U_1 that differ by one query part from a query in U_2	$\{q \in queries(U_1) \mid \exists q' \in queries(U_2), OP(q, q')\}$	MaxFrac.
13	Sources	$sources(U_1)$	MaxFrac.
14	Attributes of U_1 functionally identifying attributes in U_2	$\{level(p) \mid p \in qParts(U_1) \exists p' \in qParts(U_2), FD(p, p')\}$	MaxFrac.
15	Expertise of users	$expertise(U_1)$	MaxFrac.

Table 2 details the features by giving their formal definition and the feature-based similarity measure used for comparing two user interests. The definition is given for a user interest $U_1 = \{o_1^1, \ldots, o_n^1\}$ to be compared to user interest $U_2 = \{o_1^2, \ldots, o_m^2\}$. Given a bag of elements x, $freq(x)$ is a vector counting the number of occurrences of each element of x. For each feature, we propose a similarity measure that is the most suited for it (e.g., cosine for vectors of frequencies, Jaccard for sets). The definition of similarity measures MaxFrac and NormInt are drawn from [6]. MaxFrac measures the maximum fraction of observations of each user interest that match an observation in the other user interest. Given two interests U_1 and U_2, it is defined by: $MaxFrac(U_1, U_2) = max(\frac{|O_1^s|}{|O_1|}, \frac{O_2^s}{|O_2|})$, where O_i^s are the observations that satisfy some property s over the total number of observations O_i of U_i. NormInt is a version of Jaccard similarity, that aims at evaluating the number of features two user interests share. It is defined by $NormInt(U_1, U_2) = \frac{|F_1 \cap F_2|}{min(|U_1|, |U_2|)}$, where F_i are the features of U_i and $|U_i|$ is the number of the set of features for the ith user interest.

3.2 Clustering User Interests

Grouping observations into user interests, and then grouping similar user interests, requires addressing two problems: (i) determining a similarity measure between user interests and (ii) finding a clustering algorithm that can work on the sole basis of this similarity.

Regarding problem (i), our aim is to distinguish among the candidate features presented above those who are the most suitable to identify coherent interests from a user standpoint. To this end, we formalize the problem as a classification task, which proved effective in [6,15]. We use a simple linear combination of feature-based similarity score. The similarity $S(U_1, U_2)$ between user interests U_1 and U_2 is defined by:

$$S(U_1, U_2) = \sum_{i=1}^{n} w_i v_i(U_1, U_2) \tag{1}$$

where n is the number of features, v_i is the similarity measure indicated in Table 2 for feature i and ω_i is a weight representing this feature's importance in the comparison. To set the weights ω_i we use an off-the-shelve SVM linear classifier paired with some ground truth knowledge about user interests to learn the predictive value of the feature. More precisely, for a feature i, the weight ω_i is set to the conditional probability that two observations correspond to the same user interest knowing that they coincide on feature i. This way we solve the tuning problem of finding an appropriate balance between all the features based on the interests that are to be discovered.

Problem (ii) is addressed by experimenting with off-the-shelves well-known and trusted relational clustering algorithms implementing different strategies: centroid-based clustering, connectivity-based clustering and density-based clustering, as explained in the next Section.

4 Experiments

Our objective is to determine a metric based on the features introduced in Sect. 3.1 that allows, when paired with a clustering algorithm, to group user observations into clusters that reflect accurately user interests. In this regard, the first experiment aims at determining and validating the best subset of features from the set presented in Table 2. Then, a comparative experiment with the state-of-the-art similarity measure for OLAP sessions proposed in [3] shows the effectiveness of our proposal in the particular context of user interests discovery. Incidentally, our experiments also reveal that considering the reference metric [3] as a feature in our similarity measure in some cases improves the overall quality of our approach.

Finally, we propose several side experiments to further validate our approach: (i) sensitivity to the clustering algorithm, (ii) behaviour of our metric when confronted to observations or clusters of observations related to a business need, (iii) behaviour of our metric when confronted to unseen business needs, and (iv) behaviour of our metric in detecting intra-interaction interests.

4.1 Experimental Protocol

Data Set. The data used for our experiments consists in navigation traces of 14 volunteers of SAP covering a range of skills in data exploration, classed, based on their position in the company, in two expertise groups: beginners and expert users. In order to evaluate to which extent actual user interests were discovered by our method, we set 10 business needs (named Q_1 to Q_{10}), each corresponding to a specific user interest. Users were asked to analyze some of the 7 available data sources to answer each of the 10 business needs, using a SAP prototype that supports keyword-based BI queries[1]. The business needs were grouped in different business cases like: *"For each European country, detect which genres of films did not reach the expected sales"* or *"In which Income Group would you classify a candidate country with a GDP of \$6 billion?"*. In order to be more realistic, business needs were defined expecting some overlap in terms of accessed data and queries. In the context of user interest discovery, the business needs Q_1 to Q_{10} serve as our ground truth, our objective being to cluster together observations (potentially from different user interactions) that addressed the same business need.

Table 3. Analysis of business needs

	Q_1	Q_2	Q_3	Q_4	Q_5	Q_6	Q_7	Q_8	Q_9	Q_{10}
Difficulty	Low	Med	Med	Med	Low	High	Low	Low	Med	High
Number of interactions	19	11	10	10	10	8	9	9	9	8
Number of queries	84	65	60	41	50	43	61	51	26	49
Number of relevant queries	34	26	30	16	26	10	27	24	24	9
Queries/interaction	4.4	5.9	6.0	4.1	5.0	5.4	6.8	5.7	2.9	6.1
Relevant queries/interaction	1.8	2.4	3.0	1.6	2.6	1.25	3.0	2.7	2.7	1.1

In total, our data set named COMPLETE hereafter contains 23 user interactions, each one possibly concerning several business needs, accounting for 530 queries. Table 3 describes, for each business need, its difficulty, estimated by an expert (in terms of time, number of queries and exploited sources expected in its resolving), the number of interactions devised for solving it, the number of queries and the number of queries perceived as relevant by users in their own activity. In order to have several difficulty settings, we also build two reduced data sets named REDUCED 1 and 2, each corresponding to 4 business needs and 4 distinct data sources, which in turn removes most of the potential overlap. Each of them contains 225 observations. Importantly, REDUCED 1 and 2 are not related to the same business needs. When dealing with these data sets only 4 well separated clusters are to be found, contrary to the COMPLETE data set in which 10 clusters with overlap are expected.

[1] Patent Reference: 14/856,984: BI Query and Answering using full text search and keyword semantics.

Evaluation of Results. Our objective is to build groups of observations that are only related to a single user interest. The main indicator of success in our case is thus the precision of the clustering when compared to the theoretical grouping of observations provided by the business questions. At a second level, recall allows to determine to which extent each cluster covers all of the observations related to a user interest. Finally, we classically use the Adjusted Rand Index (ARI) to evaluate the overall quality of the clustering. The values of this index range from around 0 (when the clustering performs badly and produces a partition close to a random clustering) and 1 (when the clustering is perfect) [4].

Metric Learning. The feature weights are learned over 50% of all observations chosen randomly, with a balance in the number of observations per business needs. Our objective is two-fold and aims at finding the smallest subset of features to avoid any problem of over-fitting when the number of dimensions increases, while still maximizing the quality of the discovery of user interests. To this aim, we tested several subsets of features and trained the weights of the metric with a linear SVM algorithm as presented in Sect. 3.2 on the sole basis of these features. The subsets of features are selected as follows. We consider all 15 features described in Table 2 and learn the metric. The linear SVM outputs weights that traduce the relative importance of each feature. It is thus possible to order features by the absolute value of their weights. This ranking allows to form subsets of features starting from those with only highly weighted features to subsets that cover more widely the whole set of features. In order to limit to a few subsets, we give results for the following subsets. $G2 = \{1, 3, 7, 8, 9\}$, $G3 = G2 \cup \{5, 10, 11, 13, 14\}$ and ALL respectively include the features with the highest relative importance (the top-5, top-10 and all features). We also constitute a group $G1 = \{7, 8, 9, 10, 13\}$ that includes top-5 features selected by repetitively adding to the group those features that increase precision, similarly to [6]. Note that G3 includes both G1 and G2. Finally, groups $G4 = \{1, 2, 3, 4, 5, 6\}$ and $G5 = \{7, 8, 9, 10, 12, 13, 14\}$ are specific groups of features related only to keywords (G4) and query parts (G5).

Clustering Algorithms. As no hypothesis can a priori be made on the shape of expected groups of observations, we use in our tests various clustering algorithms that are representative of the diversity of common methods from the literature. The only constraint imposed by the formulation of our problem is that these methods must be relational i.e., only based on the expression of a distance or dissimilarity between pairs of data instances. The first method is the PAM algorithm [8] that is a k-medoids algorithm that finds hyperspherical clusters centered around the k most representative observations. We also use agglomerative hierarchical clustering algorithms [7] with single and complete linkage criterion to either allow for elongated or compact clusters. Finally, we use the traditional DBSCAN algorithm [5] that is not restricted to a specific shape of cluster but constraint clusters to share the same density of points.

Implementation. Our approach is implemented in Java but also uses Python Scikit Learn [11] linear SVM to learn the weights of our similarity measure and R clustering packages `cluster` for k-medoids and hierarchical clustering, as well as `fpc` for DBSCAN.

4.2 Results

Determining the Best Subset of Features. Table 4 shows that the quality of the discovered groups of observations heavily depends first on the subset of features as expected, but also on the clustering algorithm used. It can be seen that approaches like the hierarchical clustering with single link criterion and DBSCAN algorithms that allows for elongated clusters achieve very poor precision results ($Prec = 0.11$). This can be explained by the fact that these two algorithms are sensitive to potential overlapping between clusters. In our case, similarities between user interests cause early unwanted merging between groups of observations. The stability in precision traduces the fact that these two approaches constantly built a majority of mono-observation clusters and one cluster with almost all the observations, whatever the group of features considered. At the opposite, clustering algorithms that favor compact clusters like the hierarchical clustering with complete link or the k-medoids PAM algorithms perform better. PAM performs significantly better than the hierarchical complete link algorithm, knowing that standard deviations (not reported here for the sake of clarity) do not exceed 10^{-2} and are most of the time around 10^{-3}. Finally, when considering only PAM, it can be seen that the subset of features $G2$ outperforms all the others. Interestingly, these features are those that had the most discriminating behaviour based on the SVM weights observed on all our 15 features (see Sect. 4.1). Adding more features only slightly increases recall. Other strategies (not mixing features from different specific groups or using the strategy of [6]) can dramatically harm precision. It is also important to note that subset $G2$ does not include BI specific features, which indicates that enough semantics is beared by the other features in detecting user interests. From the previous findings, we define $G2$ as the set of features and we use PAM clustering in the remaining tests, unless otherwise stated.

Table 4. Clustering results with distinct subset of features on COMPLETE data set. For short, *Rec*, *Prec* and *ARI* denote respectively recall, precision and ARI scores.

Features	H. Single			H. Complete			PAM			DBSCAN		
	Rec.	Prec.	ARI	Rec.	Prec.	ARI	Rec.	Prec.	ARI	Rec.	Prec.	ARI
ALL	0.96	0.11	0.002	0.49	0.34	0.315	0.52	**0.46**	0.42	0.82	0.11	0.008
G1	0.90	0.11	0.0004	0.67	0.12	0.026	0.43	**0.40**	0.35	0.86	0.11	0.006
G2	0.92	0.11	−0.0001	0.68	0.11	0.006	0.51	**0.50**	0.44	0.73	0.11	0.017
G3	0.97	0.11	0.001	0.38	0.28	0.23	0.52	**0.47**	0.43	0.77	0.11	0.007
G4	0.96	0.11	−0.0005	0.67	0.14	0.06	0.47	**0.29**	0.26	0.85	0.11	−0.0008
G5	0.91	0.11	0.0004	0.39	0.28	0.23	0.45	**0.42**	0.37	0.75	0.11	0.01

G2 Metric Behaviour. While our metric is learned on observations, our experimental protocol aims at grouping together observations participating in the analysis of a business need. To understand the behaviour of our G2 metric, we tested how it degrades when applied to analyses and then to observations. Analyses are defined as sets of observations participating to answering the same need. This is unlikely to be detected in practice, and this information was explicitly asked to the users when they answered the different needs. Obviously, as shown in Table 5, when applied on analyses, our metric achieves optimal to very good performance. In the easiest case, when user interests are clearly distinct from each others and rich information is provided to our algorithm with analyses rather than observations, the clustering fits perfectly, with precision, recall and ARI scores equal to 1. Interestingly when we cluster analyses based on the metric learned on observations, the results are identical to the previous results. On the contrary, learning metric weights on the basis of analyses (although not realistic) does not conduct to good clusters of observations, with significantly lower scores. As a conclusion, this experiment validates our choice of learning weights on observations and our choice of the G2 features. It is left to future work to address the problem of evaluating the metric on a mixed clustering situation with observations or groups of observations at the same time.

Table 5. Behaviour of G2 set of features with PAM clustering when learning weights over observations or analysis. Column *"Weighting"* indicates whether weights are learned over observations or analysis.

Input	Weighting	Complete			Reduced 1		
		Recall	Precision	ARI	Recall	Precision	ARI
Observations	Observations	0.51	0.50	0.44	0.70	0.64	0.54
Analyses	Analyses	0.80	0.74	0.74	1.0	1.0	1.0
Analyses	Observations	0.80	0.74	0.74	1.0	1.0	1.0
Observations	Analyses	0.44	0.42	0.36	0.61	0.59	0.45

Comparative Experiments. Table 6 shows how our metric compares to a reference metric from the literature [3] designed for OLAP queries. This metric has been validated by user tests that showed its effectiveness in grouping queries in accordance to what a human expert would have done. Table 6 reveals 2 distinct behaviours depending on whether we consider the COMPLETE data set or the REDUCED 1 (where clusters are well separated). With the COMPLETE data set, our metric with G2 features performs better than the other metrics as it only relies on the most discriminating features. Indeed, we know from the protocol that groups of observations heavily overlap. Thus, our metric, based on SVM, cannot find a proper linear separation between observations related to different user interests. In this particular context, adding more features makes the problem even more complex to solve for SVM as it has to determine a compromise solution over 15 dimensions rather than 5 in the case of G2 features, and with only a few training instances. On the contrary, with the REDUCED 1 set of observations,

Table 6. Comparison of our metric based on G2 features with other metrics when paired with PAM clustering. ALL denotes the set of 15 features, [3] is the state-of-art metric and "+" indicates a metric with added features and corresponding weights.

Features	Complete			Reduced 1		
	Recall	Precision	ARI	Recall	Precision	ARI
ALL	**0.52**	0.46	0.42	**0.73**	**0.64**	**0.56**
G2	0.51	**0.50**	**0.44**	0.70	**0.64**	0.54
Metric [3]	0.39	0.20	0.14	0.41	0.33	0.10
ALL + [3]	0.40	0.40	0.32	**0.78**	**0.65**	**0.63**
G2 + [3]	0.45	0.43	0.38	0.69	0.62	0.52

groups are clearly separable, the problem is much easier for the linear SVM and adding features may help finding a better solution by fine tuning the separation hyper plane. Consequently, in this case, slightly better results may be achieved with other features than G2's. However, we expect our approach to be the most efficient in any scenarios and the hypothesis that clusters of observations are clearly separated is too strong for us. Thus, the metric based on G2 features seems to be the most appropriate among those that we evaluated but also when compared to state-of-the-art metric like [3].

Handling Unseen Business Needs. In this experiment, we study how our method handles previously unseen business needs and how general is the metric learned on the G2 features. To this aim, we consider both REDUCED data sets and use one to train the metric and the other to test with PAM clustering. Recall that reduced data sets cover different business needs, with no overlap among them. Results in Table 7 show that our metric is indeed general and can adapt to new business needs as there is no drop in performance between each of the generalization tests. Moreover, the results are comparable to those observed in previous tests as reported in Table 6. Finally, it can be seen that testing on REDUCED 2 leads to better results than with REDUCED 1. This is expected as REDUCED 2 contains observations related to business need Q9 that has more relevant queries than Q10 contained in the REDUCED 1 data set (see Table 3).

Table 7. Generalization of our approach. Each test correspond to the training of the metric and discovery of user interests on different subsets of business needs.

Training	Testing	Recall	Precision	ARI
REDUCED 2	REDUCED 1	0.76	0.67	0.61
REDUCED 1	REDUCED 2	0.73	0.71	0.62

Discovering Intra-interaction Interests. To illustrate one practical interest of our metric, we conducted a test that consists of successively increasing the number of clusters and we checked how many users of different expertise are

Table 8. Increasing the number of clusters to detect intra-interaction interests. Dense UI indicates the number of clusters with more than 5 different users. Expertise indicates the number of clusters with both types of users (beginners and experts).

# Clusters	Recall	Precision	ARI	Dense UI	Expertise
10	0.35	0.86	0.41	10 (100%)	0 (100%)
15	0.24	0.90	0.31	14 (93.3%)	1 (93.33%)
20	0.20	0.92	0.26	14 (70%)	2 (90%)
25	0.18	0.92	0.24	13 (52%)	6 (76%)
30	0.17	0.95	0.23	13 (43.3%)	11 (63.33%)
35	0.16	0.95	0.22	12 (34.3%)	16 (54.29%)
50	0.14	0.96	0.19	11 (22%)	30 (40%)

represented in each cluster. The aim is to show that our metric is good not only at grouping observations that participate to the resolution of a particular business need, but also at identifying parts of the resolution that are shared by users with different expertises. To emphasize on the evolution of precision (which indicates the coherence of clusters), we use the (G2 + [3]) configuration, which is a good compromise in previous experiment, and test on the well separated REDUCED 1 data set, starting with 10 clusters. The results reported in Table 8 show how the mixing of users decreases while precision increases (and consequently recall and ARI decrease) as we increase the number of clusters. It can be noted that for high precisions, the composition of clusters in terms of users with different expertises remains very acceptable. For instance, when precision reaches 95%, more than 63% of clusters have users with different expertise. In other words, this shows that our metric can be used to identify shared sub-tasks (or intra-interaction interests) where some experts' queries could be recommended to beginner users having to solve the same business need.

5 Related Work

Analyzing web search sessions for personalizing user experience has attracted a lot of attention, varying in models for session, similarities and clustering algorithms [9]. As user's information needs span multiple search sessions, state-of-the-art approaches attach importance to both intra and inter-session similarities. Various forms of user interests have been defined, like contextual intent, task repetition or long term interests, and methods have been proposed to identify them. Sun et al. [13] are interested in contextual intent. Contextual intent attaches importance to context with a particular emphasis on external physical environment, and complex context-intent relationships are modeled. Consequently, intent tracking is done in real-time. In our work, we are not interested in modeling context, nor real-time tracking, but in user interest in certain data to answer a particular business question, which is generally context-independent. Song and

Guo [12] address the problem of predicting task repetition, i.e., whether a task represents one-time information need or exhibits recurrent patterns. A feature-based approach is used to train a deep neural network classifier to recognize the characteristics of task repetition patterns. The features incorporate information on queries, clicks, and attach a particular importance on time, with the underlying assumption that similar users often perform similar activities at similar time. A similar approach is proposed by Guha et al. [6]. The goal is to discover new intent and obtain content relevant to users' long-term interests. They develop a classifier to determine whether two search queries address the same information need. This is formalized as an agglomerative clustering problem for which a similarity measure is learned over a set of descriptive features (the stemmed query words, top 10 web results for the queries, the stemmed words in the titles of clicked URL, etc.). One advantage of this approach is that it allows to build contexts that span over several user sessions or only a portion of one session. Thus, contexts provide insights on short and long terms information needs and user habits, to build accurate user profiles.

To the best of our knowledge, our work is the first attempt to automatically discover BI users' interests in a multi-user environment. Some collaborative recommendation approaches for BI exist, but they are limited to clustering OLAP queries or sessions without treating user interest as a first class citizen (see e.g., [1]). A similarity measure tailored for OLAP queries is proposed in [3]. This work also reviews query similarity measures described in the literature, and showed through user studies that the proposed measure better respects the similarity perceived by users over the other measures. This led us to compare our measure to that one. Nguyen et al. [10] deal with discovering the most accessed areas of a relational database. Their notion of user interest relies on the set of tuples that are more frequently accessed, and is expressed as selection queries (mostly range queries). They use DBSCAN to cluster user interests. Their similarity metric relies on Jaccard coefficient of the accessed tables and on overlapping of predicates. Being tailored for range queries, their metric is inappropriate for OLAP queries that are mostly dimensional (i.e., point based), due to the nature of the hierarchical dimensions used to select data. In particular, consistently with the study of [3], the query log used for our tests feature no range queries.

6 Conclusion

We have presented an approach for identifying coherent interests of BI users with various expertise querying datasources by means of keyword-based analytical queries. Our approach relies on the identification of discriminative features for characterizing BI interactions and on the learning of a similarity measure based on these features. We have shown through user tests that our approach is effective in practice and could benefit beginner analysts whose interests match those of expert users. Overall, our results show that keyword-based interaction systems provide semantically rich user traces well adapted to the detection of coherent BI user interest.

Building upon these results, our long term goal is to go beyond keyword-based interaction systems. We envision the implementation of an intelligent assistant that raises alerts when the datasources are refreshed or when user information needs and expertise change. To this end, our future works include the development of interest and skill-based recommendation approaches and their validation via larger user studies.

References

1. Aligon, J., Gallinucci, E., Golfarelli, M., Marcel, P., Rizzi, S.: A collaborative filtering approach for recommending OLAP sessions. DSS **69**, 20–30 (2015)
2. Aligon, J., Golfarelli, M., Marcel, P., Rizzi, S., Turricchia, E.: Mining preferences from OLAP query logs for proactive personalization. In: Eder, J., Bielikova, M., Tjoa, A.M. (eds.) ADBIS 2011. LNCS, vol. 6909, pp. 84–97. Springer, Heidelberg (2011). doi:10.1007/978-3-642-23737-9_7
3. Aligon, J., Golfarelli, M., Marcel, P., Rizzi, S., Turricchia, E.: Similarity measures for OLAP sessions. KAIS **39**(2), 463–489 (2014)
4. Desgraupes, B.: Clustering indices. Technical report, University Paris Ouest - Lab Modal'X, April 2013
5. Ester, M., Kriegel, H.-P., Sander, J., Xu, X.: A density-based algorithm for discovering clusters in large spatial databases with noise. In: KDD, USA, pp. 226–231. AAAI Press (1996)
6. Guha, R., Gupta, V., Raghunathan, V., Srikant, R.: User modeling for a personal assistant. In: WSDM, Shanghai, China, pp. 275–284 (2015)
7. Kaufman, L., Rousseeuw, P.: Finding Groups in Data: An Introduction to Cluster Analysis. Wiley, New York (1990)
8. Kaufman, L., Rousseeuw, P.: Clustering by means of medoids. In: Statistical Data Analysis Based on the L1 Norm, pp. 405–416. Elsevier (1987)
9. Mobasher, B.: Data mining for web personalization. In: Brusilovsky, P., Kobsa, A., Nejdl, W. (eds.) The Adaptive Web. LNCS, vol. 4321, pp. 90–135. Springer, Heidelberg (2007). doi:10.1007/978-3-540-72079-9_3
10. Nguyen, H.V., et al.: Identifying user interests within the data space - a case study with skyserver. In: EDBT, pp. 641–652 (2015)
11. Pedregosa, F., et al.: Scikit-learn: machine learning in Python. J. Mach. Learn. Res. **12**, 2825–2830 (2011)
12. Song, Y., Guo, Q.: Query-less: predicting task repetition for nextgen proactive search and recommendation engines. In: WWW, pp. 543–553 (2016)
13. Sun, Y., Yuan, N.J., Wang, Y., Xie, X., McDonald, K., Zhang, R.: Contextual intent tracking for personal assistants. In: SIGKDD, pp. 273–282 (2016)
14. Vaisman, A.A., Zimányi, E.: Data Warehouse Systems - Design and Implementation. Data-Centric Systems and Applications. Springer, Heidelberg (2014)
15. Wang, H., Song, Y., Chang, M.-W., He, X., White, R.W., Chu, W.: Learning to extract cross-session search tasks. In: WWW (2013)
16. Yang, L., Guo, Q., Song, Y., Meng, S., Shokouhi, M., McDonald, K., Croft, W.B.: Modeling user interests for zero-query ranking. In: Ferro, N., Crestani, F., Moens, M.-F., Mothe, J., Silvestri, F., Nunzio, G.M., Hauff, C., Silvello, G. (eds.) ECIR 2016. LNCS, vol. 9626, pp. 171–184. Springer, Cham (2016). doi:10.1007/978-3-319-30671-1_13

Analysis of Online Discussions in Support of Requirements Discovery

Itzel Morales-Ramirez[1(✉)], Fitsum Meshesha Kifetew[2], and Anna Perini[2]

[1] INFOTEC, Av. San Fernando 37, 14050 Tlalpan, Mexico City, Mexico
itzel.morales@infotec.mx
[2] Software Engineering Research Unit, Fondazione Bruno Kessler, Via Sommarive, 18, 38100 Trento, Italy
{kifetew,perini}@fbk.eu

Abstract. Feedback about software applications and services that end-users express through web-based communication platforms represents an invaluable knowledge source for diverse software engineering tasks, including requirements elicitation. Research work on automated analysis of textual messages in app store reviews, open source software (OSS) mailing-lists and user forums has been rapidly increasing in the last five years. NLP techniques are applied to filter out irrelevant data, text mining and automated classification techniques are then used to classify messages into different categories, such as bug report and feature request. Our research focuses on online discussions that take place in user forums and OSS mailing-lists, and aims at providing automated analysis techniques to discover contained requirements. In this paper, we present a speech-acts based analysis technique, and experimentally evaluate it on a dataset taken from a widely used OSS project.

Keywords: Requirements engineering · Linguistic analysis · Sentiment analysis · Automated classification techniques · Speech-acts

1 Introduction

Social media, together with other web-based communication platforms, including app stores, user forums, mailing-lists, wikis, newsgroups, and blogs are becoming popular means for users of software applications and services to express their quick feedback or engage in online discussions upon their usage experience. The large amount of online data that is accumulated represents an invaluable knowledge source for customer support, software maintenance and evolution, as well as requirements engineering tasks.

The challenges posed by the analysis and exploitation of online data for such purposes is attracting the attention of the software engineering research community. A recent survey [17] on advances and trends in App Store analysis for software engineering points out a huge growth in the number of research works on this topic from 2010 to 2015.

E. Dubois and K. Pohl (Eds.): CAiSE 2017, LNCS 10253, pp. 159–174, 2017.
DOI: 10.1007/978-3-319-59536-8_11

Taking the requirements engineering (RE) perspective, the term *Crowd-based Requirements Engineering (CrowdRE)* [1] has been proposed to indicate the set of concepts, methods and techniques necessary to collect, analyse and manage requirements expressed by members of a crowd of users in the form of online feedback. An ontology for online user feedback has been proposed [20] which characterises the user feedback communication process, the diverse formats in which user feedback can be expressed and the type of information that can be extracted from this feedback. Such ontology helps understand which type of analysis techniques are needed to process online user feedback.

Focusing on the analysis of online textual feedback, Natural Language Processing (NLP) techniques [16] are first applied to filter out irrelevant data. Text mining, such as sentiment analysis and topic modelling, and automated classification techniques are then used to identify feedback that can fall into different categories, such as *bug report* and *feature request* [15,23], and serve as input to release planning tools at support of app developers to identify which new feature to include in the next release [26]. Manual analysis and supervised machine learning techniques are applied to investigate tweets related to software applications so as to characterise their relevance to software engineers and to non-technical stakeholders [11].

Our research focuses on feedback provided through online discussions related to software applications, such as those that take place in issue tracking systems and open source software (OSS) mailing-lists. According to user feedback ontology [20], they can be considered as explicit, directed feedback in which the sender reveals her intention and can affect the receivers' attitude about a subject, through the specific *speech-acts* [24] she uses in her comments. That is the structure of the sentences through which this feedback is expressed and can provide useful information about the intention of the user who expressed it and helps better interpret the user's experience that generated it. In order to capture such users' intentions, other text mining techniques, different from sentiment analysis and topic modelling, needs to be exploited.

In a previous work [18] we explored the applicability of the Speech-act theory [24] to develop a technique for supporting the analysis of OSS mailing-list discussions. *Speech-act* analysis has already been applied to the analysis of online discussions, for example, to investigate most frequent intentions expressed in status messages by users of social networks [3], and in the online teaching domain to understand students' intentions expressed in their queries to teachers [9], or during discussions with peers [14]. In these works, the *speech-acts* that are used in conversations about the specific domain under consideration are first identified, and then used during manual annotation of the conversations, which is performed by independent annotators.

In this paper, we present a revised version of our *speech-act* based analysis technique that we contrast and combine with sentiment analysis when processing online feedback about software applications with the purpose of identifying relevant information for discovering requirements. Specifically, we consider the following research questions:

RQ1: What are the speech-acts expressed in online discussions that may lead to discover requirements?
RQ2: Can the speech-acts be used as a parameter[1] *to classify defect reports, and feature or enhancement requests?*

We answer these questions by analysing online discussions taken from the issue tracking system of the Apache OpenOffice (AOO) community.

The contributions of our research work can be summarised as follows. We provide: (a) insights of a new analysis technique that considers *speech-acts*, in contrast and in combination with sentiment analysis; and (b) interpretation of the *speech-acts* expressed in discussions about software. In addition we provide (c) a new dataset of 6568 threads (40872 comments) from the issue tracking system of AOO, wherein each sentence has been annotated with an intention.

The rest of the paper is organised as follows. In Sect. 2 we present two motivating scenarios that help illustrate how we intend to apply the proposed techniques in a practical setting. In Sect. 3, we first give a brief background of the natural language processing analysis techniques that we rely on, we describe the dataset we used in our linguistic analysis, then state the research questions and the approach we followed to answer them. The analyses are detailed in Sect. 4 and the main findings are discussed is Sect. 5. In Sect. 6 we describe main related work. Conclusion and future work are given in Sect. 7.

2 Motivating Scenarios

We consider two scenarios where online discussions are present in the context of software maintenance and evolution. The first one concerns the analysis of comments from issue tracking systems in large OSS projects, like OpenOffice. In this scenario we imagine that an analyst has to analyse tens of messages per day, approximately. The second scenario is taken from a real case study that is considered in the context of the SUPERSEDE[2] project, which aims at creating an entire set of integrated methods and tools to enable a feedback-driven approach to software lifecycle management. This case study concerns a small company, where the help-desk responsible, a highly experienced person, manages tens of user feedback per months, which are collected through different channels, building an effective bridge between end users and product developers.

2.1 Scenario 1: Open Source Project, User Feedback Analysis for Software Maintenance and Evolution

In OSS communities, collaborators work in a distributed way and the number of contributors can be up to 100,000[3]. There are many developers, analysts and

[1] We use the term parameter as synonym of feature in a machine learning classification approach to avoid confusion with the term feature, which indicates a software application requirement or property, whenever necessary.
[2] http://www.supersede.eu.
[3] http://www.slideshare.net/blackducksoftware/open-source-by-the-numbers.

users that are involved and interested in maintaining and evolving software such as web servers, IDEs, productivity suites, etc. Some developers that work for companies are contributors of open source since companies use open source as core, such as operating systems, databases and development tools[4]. The contributors convey their concerns, for example any bug, new features, or they suggest modifications. There is a continuous exchange of messages that must be read, analysed, replied and considered for making a decision and put it into action. We refer to some of these messages as user feedback, specifically those messages that come from users of the software and that must be read by the OpenOffice volunteers.

The user feedback is collected through e-mail, forum, or issue tracking systems. This implies an asynchronous communication developed as a chain of written messages in natural language (e.g. "One of my spreadsheets is no longer showing in my documents"). Sometimes there are messages expressing a praise that motivates volunteers to continue their work to improving the OSS, other times there are only complaints. The important point is that OSS volunteers form a special kind of community that achieves the maintenance and evolution of software in a distributed setting with a continuous online communication.

The high amount of feedback sent by users is processed manually by any available volunteer, but sometimes it takes the involvement of other specialists to solve the issue that are better suited to deal with such an information. The idea of providing a tool to support the filtering of feedback and redirect it to the right role (analyst or developer) may be crucial to save time.

2.2 Scenario 2: SUPERSEDE User Feedback Analysis for Software Maintenance and Evolution

SEnerCon is a partner of the SUPERSEDE project. It is a small company with more than 25 years of experience in the domain of energy efficiency management, which employs about 15 software developers and engineers. SEnerCon provides several web applications including: (1) an application that enables end-users' (house owners) to monitor and analyse their energy consumption, called interactive Energy Saving Account - iESA; and (2) applications that guide and advise the end-users on how to save energy in every day life through behavioural or technical changes.

The iESA application counts thousands of users. Most of the features of the application are free, and the only obligation for users is to register and accept that their data (including usage logs) are used and analysed by the company upon anonymisation.

SEnerCon collects hundreds of user feedback per month gathered through five main channels, namely contact form, e-mail, hotline, forum and app stores. The end-users express their feedback using natural language text. According to the helpdesk, the end users may prefer to use a forum rather than a dedicated feedback channel because "they might perceive to get a broader audience in

[4] http://www.slideshare.net/blackducksoftware/2016-future-of-open-source-survey-results.

the forum and make them think that SEnerCon will pay more attention to a feedback elaborated through discussions in a forum".

The analysis of end-user feedback is performed by the help-desk who can ask for clarifications, this analysis can motivate the inclusion of new tickets in the issue tracking system that is used by the development team to keep record of pending issues, which can be addressed during maintenance or product evolution.

Specifically, the help-desk reads the user comments from the forum, try to understand if it is an information request he may answer directly, a complaint for something not working properly or if they contain suggestions for new features. This task seems not so effort demanding considering that feedback arrives at a rate of 2 to 5 per day, but it seems to require a strong experience to manage user feedback about the product in order to make it in an efficient and effective way. This becomes evident when the help-desk takes a holiday, and it is "almost impossible to find some one who can perform his task at an acceptable level".

Having a tool that *(i)* suggests if a comment could be motivated by a bug to fix; a new feature to be considered for next release, or new ideas to be further analysed; *(ii)* indicates which bug/feature requests are more important; and *(iii)* indicates if a request is related to previously addressed requests, will provide great help to enable a user-feedback driven evolution of the software product.

3 Speech Act Based Analysis of Online Discussion

3.1 Background

The use of NLP techniques in software engineering is quite popular due to the use of natural language text in key artefacts, such as requirements, test cases, and comments in code, and, more generally, to the fact that most of the information handled by practitioners is textual-based, as highlighted in the technical briefing by Arnaoudova et al. [2]. In our work we focus on artefacts that contain conversations between stakeholders, such as between end-users and the help-desk team, or between users and developers, thus the dialogue structure, which rests on dialogue acts, can provide relevant information. Dialog acts can be studied using the *speech-act* theory of Searle [24]. In a nutshell, *speech-acts* theory claims that when a person says something she/he attempts to communicate certain things to the addressee, which affect either their believes and/or their behaviour. Dialog acts represent the meaning of an utterance at the level of illocutionary force [25][5].

The interesting part of understanding dialog acts or *speech-act* is that they constitute the basis of communication and the application can be, for example, a meeting summariser needs to keep track of who said what to whom, and a conversational agent needs to know whether it was asked a question or ordered to do something [22,25].

In the work of Novielli and Strapparava [22] the approach can be easily extended to other languages by simply redefining the seeds (lexical cues) used in the definition of the dialogue act profiles and by using a POS-tagger and

[5] An illocutionary force refers to the pronouncing of a statement with an intention.

a morphological analyser trained on the target language. While the work of Stolcke et al. [25] developed a probabilistic approach to dialogue act modelling for conversational speech and tested on a large speech corpus (both works use the Switchboard corpus of human-human conversational telephone speech [10]).

The NLP framework used in this work is GATE (General Architecture for Text Engineering) which is a Java suite of tools [6], developed by the University of Sheffield in UK, for building and deploying software components to process human language. GATE can support a wide range of NLP tasks for Information Extraction (IE). IE refers to the extraction of relevant information from unstructured text, such as entities and relationships between them, thus providing facts to feed a knowledge base [5]. GATE is widely used both in research and application work in different fields (e.g. cancer research, web mining, law). This tool is composed of three main components for performing language processing tasks, namely the *Language Resources* component that represents entities such as lexicons, corpora or ontologies; the *Processing Resources* component, which contains a library of executable procedures, such as parsers, generators or ngram modellers; and the *Visual Resources* component that provides visualisation and editing functions that are used in GUIs.

3.2 Dataset: OpenOffice Online Discussions

The collection of the data was through a request done to the OO community via the mailing list dev@openoffice.apache.org on August 1st, 2013. We asked for a dump of the dataset corresponding to certain parameters such as: comments of the threads referring to the Writer application, issue type should be *Defect* and *Feature* or *Enhancement*, and the final parameter was to obtain the discussions of the last year (i.e. between the years 2012–2013). The provided data was a total of 6568 threads in the format of XML files, we parsed these files and stored them in a MySql database for a better manipulation of the information contained in the comments. Each thread contains at least one comment, but some can have more than one hundred comments. The total number of comments is 40872 and we divided each comment into sentences in order to store each one in the database for its later analysis. During the parsing of sentences we removed text enclosed into HTML elements *<* and *>* considering the text as noise; we applied some regex patterns to remove dates, identify links and unify them into a unique codification (i.e. http://www.); we eliminated common contractions and file extensions. Smiley faces or sad faces were replaced by the words SMILEY and SAD, respectively. Other elements, for example –, =, -, *"* .. are removed from the text; or double elements replaced for one, for example *?? to ?*.

We use this data because the members are very active in collaborating and communicating through written messages. Moreover, we are exploring a new type of dataset instead of the commonly used from App stores. In addition to this, the data refers to online discussions (threads) whose first comment has the characteristic of being already labelled by members of the community.

Besides this, we believe the data contains *speech-acts* which are more complex than sentiments and that can provide extra information useful to developers or requirements analysts. Another important characteristic of the dataset is that it has other properties such as *status* of the issue (e.g. confirmed, unconfirmed), *priority* (e.g. P1-highest priority), *severity* (e.g. blocker, critical) that together constitute a combined property called *importance.*

3.3 Approach

We have two research questions to explore a new dimension of analysis that we call *speech-acts* based analysis.

- *RQ1 What are the speech-acts expressed in online discussions that may lead to discover requirements?*
- *RQ2 Can the speech-acts be used as parameters to classify defect reports, and feature or enhancement requests?*

To answer *RQ1* we use NLP tools such as the Stanford CoreNLP[6], GATE framework[7] and SentiWordNet[8]. We used the Stanford CoreNLP to break the comments into sentences and to get the overall sentiment per sentence. The GATE framework has been used to perform the analysis of *speech-acts* on each sentence and determine the category to which it may belong. The categories of *speech-acts* have been described in [19] and the classification is determined by applying some lexico-syntactic rules, which includes a list of keywords. Finally, SentiStrength[9] was used to evaluate the sentiment of the nouns, verbs and adjectives contained in each sentence.

We obtain the relative frequency of the sentences that are classified into *speech-acts* and plot their distribution. We are interested in knowing the distribution of the *speech-acts* in the comments labelled as *Defect* and *Feature* or *Enhancement.* This would let us know which types of *speech-acts* are highly frequent in Defect, Feature or Enhancement comments.

We answer *RQ2* by considering *speech-acts* expressions and verbs as features of machine learning algorithms, along with the sentiment of verbs, nouns, adjectives and the overall sentiment of a sentence. Specifically, we considered elements such as the number of times *speech-acts* appear in a sentence, the number of times a verb related to specific *speech-acts* appear in a sentence, the number of positive or negative adjectives, as well as the verbs with an associated sentiment. We formulated 41 features in total to be used by machine learning algorithms and applied the well-known metrics Precision and Recall.

Moreover, we investigate the correlation of the type of *speech-acts* and the importance of the comments. The importance is constituted by the *priority* (e.g. P1-highest priority), and *severity* (e.g. blocker, critical). For example, the priority P1 blocker is considered the highest in importance. We then determine the significance of associating *speech-acts* and the importance of comments by applying the chi-squared test.

[6] http://stanfordnlp.github.io/CoreNLP/.
[7] https://gate.ac.uk/.
[8] http://sentiwordnet.isti.cnr.it/.
[9] http://sentistrength.wlv.ac.uk/.

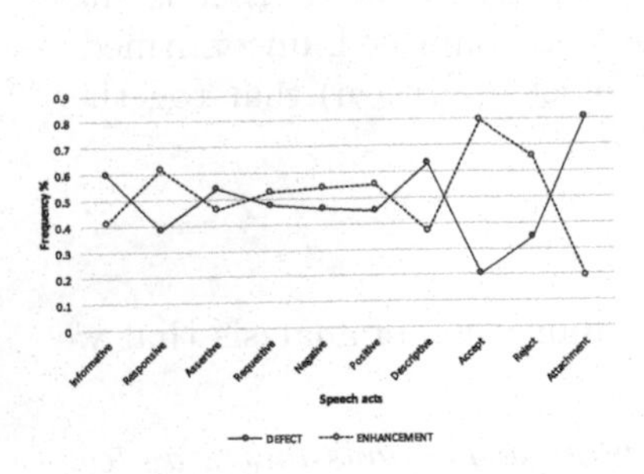

Fig. 1. *Speech-acts* annotated with GATE

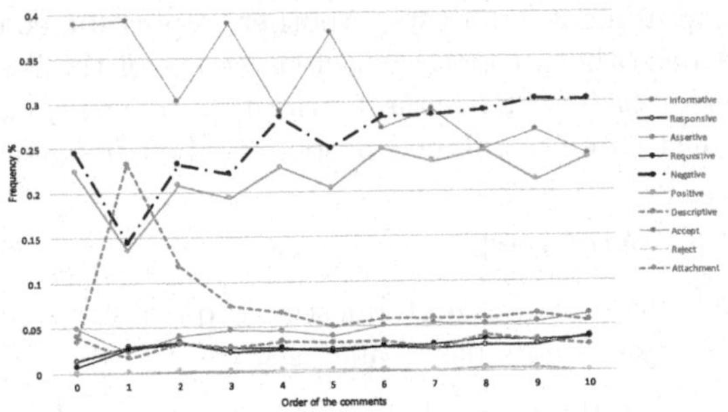

Fig. 2. Distribution of *speech-acts* by the order of the comments, for defect reports

4 Analysis Results

RQ1. What are the *speech-acts* expressed in online discussions that may lead to discover requirements?
Figure 1 reports the distribution of *speech-acts* that have been found in the online discussions of OO[10], using the GATE tool to annotate them. The y-axis shows the percentage of *speech-acts* and the x-axis shows the types of *speech-acts*. We merged the classes Feature and Enhancement, the other class corresponds to Defect.

There is a mirror effect of the lines and there are interesting peaks for each one of the classes. On one hand, we can see that for the class Enhancement the *speech-acts Responsive*, *Negative*, *Positive*, *Accept* and *Reject* have more presence in the discussions. This could mean that members tend to give more responses and engage in the discussions through accepting (80%) or rejecting (66%) new ideas. We also can assume that the participation increases and sentiments are exposed more frequently when the members discuss an Enhancement and that the description of the new feature or enhancement is fully described in the discussion if we consider that there are discussions with more than 100 comments[11].

On the other hand, the discussions regarding a Defect contain the *speech-acts Informative*, *Assertive*, *Descriptive* and *Attachment*. The interpretation we give to this is that it is mandatory to describe (65%) and give details (i.e., attachments with 80%) when there is a problem such that there is no need of further discussion and the Assertive *speech-acts* also emphasises it, for example by stating "I have a problem with...", that is why the *speech-acts* Accept and Reject are not so relevant when discussing a Defect. We also see the presence of sentiments, however they do not make a big difference between positive or negative sentiments.

Figure 2 shows a plot of the different types of *speech-acts* but along the order of how the comments were posted for the Defect reports. This is for all the

[10] The dataset is available at http://se.fbk.eu/technologies/speechactsanalysis.
[11] For instance https://bz.apache.org/ooo/show_bug.cgi?id=3395.

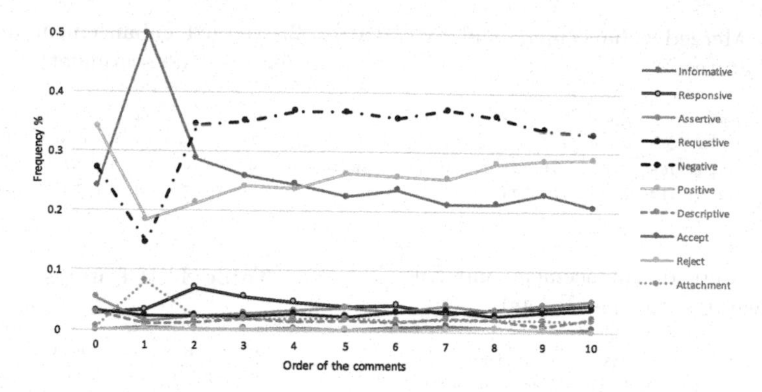

Fig. 3. Distribution of *speech-acts* by the order of the comments, for enhancement and feature requests

threads and we only took a snapshot until the 10th comment. The y-axis displays the percentage of *speech-acts* annotated and the x-axis corresponds to the order of the comments. It is worth to notice how the initial comment (order equal to zero) contains more Informative *speech-acts*, then it decreases but showing some peaks. While the immediate comment after the initial one shows a peak, with a distribution of 23% Attachment and 39% Informative. After comment number 1 the *speech-act* Attachment decreases. The sentiments Negative and Positive have a high presence in the first comment >20% but after that they decrease and later the Negative sentiment goes up and overpasses the Positive and Informative. The other *speech-acts* remain below 5% approximately.

On the other side, Fig. 3 displays the distribution of *speech-acts* for Enhancement and Feature requests, where the Positive *speech-act* has the highest percentage of 35%, followed by Negative and Informative *speech-acts*. The following comments show three interesting peaks, where the distribution is 50% for the Informative *speech-act*, and Negative and Positive sentiments are below 20%. Then, starting from comment 2 the Negative sentiment overpasses the others and keeps a distribution above 30%.

RQ2. Can the *speech-acts* be used as parameters to classify defect reports, and feature or enhancement requests?
We identified 41 features, 7 of them correspond to the *speech-acts*, 13 correspond to the sentiment of a sentence (number of positive and negative verbs, nouns, adjectives, their sentiment score, and the overall sentiment of a sentence). The rest 21 features are, for instance, number of verbs, nouns, adjectives, sentence length, number of question marks, exclamation marks, number of brackets, the number of identified code lines, among others. We trained three machine learning algorithms (Random Forest-RF, J48, SMO) in Weka[12] using these features for classifying the comments labelled as Feature, Enhancement and Defect. We performed a sensitivity analysis by excluding the *speech-acts* features or the

[12] http://www.cs.waikato.ac.nz/ml/weka/.

Table 1. Merged enhancement and feature, 41 features

	RF			J48			SMO		
	P	R	F-M	P	R	F-M	P	R	F-M
Enhancement	.70	.66	**.68**	.66	.62	.64	.61	.77	.68
Defect	.72	.76	**.74**	.68	.72	.70	.74	.56	.64

Table 2. Merged enhancement and feature, 28 features (no sentiment)

	RF			J48			SMO		
	P	R	F-M	P	R	F-M	P	R	F-M
Enhancement	.66	.66	.66	.69	.64	.66	.59	.81	**.68**
Defect	.70	.70	.70	.70	.75	**.72**	.75	.50	.60

Table 3. Merged enhancement and feature, 34 features (no speech acts)

	RF			J48			SMO		
	P	R	F-M	P	R	F-M	P	R	F-M
Enhancement	.68	.64	**.67**	.63	.60	.61	.58	.82	.68
Defect	.70	.74	**.73**	.66	.70	.68	.75	.48	.59

Table 4. 41 features

	RF			J48			SMO		
	P	R	F-M	P	R	F-M	P	R	F-M
Feature	.50	.02	.04	.08	.04	.06	0	0	0
Enhancement	.65	.62	**.63**	.59	.57	.58	.59	.66	.62
Defect	.70	.78	**.74**	.67	.71	.69	.69	.68	.69

sentiment features. Moreover, we merged the comments labelled as feature and enhancement into one class, i.e. Enhancement.

We see in Table 1 that the Random Forest algorithm gives better results compared to J48 and SMO, but it is important to notice that comments labelled as Feature and Enhancement have been merged into Enhancement. The F-Measure (F-M) for Enhancement is .68 and for Defect is .74. Moreover, we use the 41 features, i.e. the *speech-acts* and sentiment features. In Table 2 we see that J48 performs better for Defect comments with a F-M of .72 while the SMO performs better for Enhancement comments with .68, but in this case we removed the features related to sentiments, resulting in 28 features.

Table 3 presents the results of merging Enhancement and Feature and removing the features related to the *speech-acts*. In this case we train the three algorithms with 34 features and the best results for Defect and Enhancement are F-M .67 and .73, respectively. Although, SMO performs better for Enhancement comments with F-M of .68.

In Table 4 we show the results of using the 41 features without merging the Enhancement and Feature comments. The RF algorithm performs better but only for Enhancement with F-Measure .63 and .74, while .04 for Feature. This is mainly due to the small number of comments in the dataset labelled as Feature.

Table 5 shows the results of using the 28 features of *speech-acts* and the best results are given by the J48 algorithm. Again the only good F-M results are for Enhancement .61 and Defect .73. Finally, in Table 6 we apply the 34 features, dropping those related to *speech-acts*. For the Enhancement comments the best F-M result is .62 given by the SMO and for Defect .72.

Table 5. 28 features (no sentiment)

	RF			J48			SMO		
	P	R	F-M	P	R	F-M	P	R	F-M
Feature	.14	.02	.03	.08	.01	.02	0	0	0
Enhancement	.61	.61	.61	.63	.60	**.61**	.58	.64	.60
Defect	.70	.74	.71	.69	.76	**.73**	.68	.66	.67

Table 6. 34 features (no speech acts)

	RF			J48			SMO		
	P	R	F-M	P	R	F-M	P	R	F-M
Feature	.33	.02	.03	.08	.05	.06	0	0	0
Enhancement	.63	.58	.60	.55	.56	.58	.53	.74	**.62**
Defect	.70	.77	**.72**	.65	.70	.67	.71	.54	.62

The chi-squared test to determine the significance of associating *speech-acts* and categories of issues (i.e. Defect, Enhancement or Feature) to the level of *importance* assigned to the comment has been applied for the Defect comments and the merged comments classified as Enhancement or Feature. For Defect comments we have a p-value $<2.2e{-16}$ and for Enhancement and Feature a p-value $= 1.65e{-05}$, indicating that both results are significant and that *speech-acts* could be used to determine the importance associated with a comment.

5 Discussion

Regarding the results of our first research question, we can observe that there is a likelihood that certain types of *speech-acts* are more used when reporting a Defect than an Enhancement issue. We found for instance that 80% of the time the *speech-act* Attachment is expressed for reporting Defects. When an Enhancement or Feature has been reported, between 80% and 60% of the time there is a discussion about accepting or rejecting the ideas exposed by the participants in the discussion.

On one side, although the percentage of the *speech-acts* Responsive, Requestive and Positive is not higher in Enhancement comments than in Defects, we believe that the combination of Requestive and Positive *speech-acts* give a hint of a possible requirement. On the other side the *speech-acts* Informative, Assertive, and Descriptive are more representative for Defect issues.

Besides the combination of *speech-acts*, we saw that there is a trend of such *speech-acts* along the order of the comments. For example, in Defect issues the first comment (#0) contains more Informative, Negative and Positive speech acts, while in the second comment (#1) the Attachment is provided along with the Informative *speech-act*. When it comes to the Enhancement and Feature comments, in the first one the Positive, Negative and Informative *speech-acts* are more present. But the presence of Negative and Positive *speech-acts* drops, while the Informative increases and the Attachment appears as well.

When we use the *speech-acts* as features for training algorithms we notice that by using the *speech-acts* along with sentiment features we get good results when merging Enhancement and Feature comments, instead of just using either *speech-acts* or sentiment features.

Although there is a minimal difference of 1% when we reduce the features by dropping the *speech-acts*, we also know that the amount of Feature comments is not enough for getting good results. Regarding the result of the chi-squared test, of associating *speech-acts* and the importance, we need to investigate further how to recognise which are the types of *speech-acts* that are present for high importance of Defect reports and the same for Enhancement and Feature reports.

5.1 Threats to Validity

Here we discuss the main threats to validity [27]. *Conclusion validity* threats concern issues that affect the ability to draw the correct conclusion on the observed phenomenon. The results reported in this work give a positive exploitation of *speech-acts*, but we know the dataset must be extended to other years.

Internal validity threats concern the possible confounding elements that may hinder a well performed experiment. Our *speech-acts* based analysis rests on rules which are not extensive but can be improved and the dataset has been already labelled by the OpenOffice community, which means there is not biased in assigning the categories of Defect, Feature or Enhancement.

Construct validity threats concern the relationship between theory and observation. So far there is no theory explaining any correlation between *speech-acts* and categories of issues reported in online discussions related to software applications. Our method of analysis represents a first hypothesis of such relationship.

External validity threats concern extending the validity of observations outside the context. We need to apply the method on other datasets such as the SEnerCon scenario and compare with the results we have obtained until now.

6 Related Works

Research on automated analysis techniques of online discussions at support of requirements engineering tasks has increased significantly, especially in the last five years [17]. The main objective of the proposed analysis techniques is the classification of user comments into bug reports, feature requests, or polarity of sentiments.

For instance, Fang and Zhan [8] apply sentiment analysis on a dataset of 5.1 million product reviews from Amazon. Their approach consists of removing all subjective content (i.e. all sentiment sentences containing at least one positive or negative word). The sentences are tokenised and POS tagged in order to identify adjectives, adverbs, and verbs which are words that mainly convey sentiment.

Worth mentioning is the work of Carreño and Winbladh [4] that aims at analysing comments from users of software applications. Information extraction techniques and topic modelling are exploited to automatically extract topics, and to provide requirements engineers with a user feedback report, which will support them in identifying candidate new/changed requirements.

The research work by Keertipati et al. [13] uses four attributes to be exploited to do the prioritisation, i.e. frequency of a feature, rating, emotions and deontics. They propose three prioritisation approaches: (1) individual attribute-based - when ranking features based on their frequency, the ratings are not considered; (2) weighted approach - enables the combination of two or more attributes in the prioritisation; (3) regression-based approach and data-driven approach to examine influential variables for determining the severity of reviews.

The work of Guzman et al. [12] presents an approach called DIVERSE that aims at recognising the diversity of opinions on a set of App reviews. Moreover, this approach also helps developers and analysts recognise conflicting opinions regarding a feature. The evaluation is performed on a dataset of 170,829 App reviews and a truth set of 2800 manually labelled reviews.

Di Sorbo et al. [7] propose an approach that consists of a two level classification model which considers the users' intentions and review topic of app reviews. Moreover, they propose a summariser called SURF that automatically extracts topics, classifies the intention and group sentences covering the extracted topics for recommending software changes.

Manual analysis and supervised machine learning techniques are applied to investigate the usage and content of about 11 million tweets related to 22 software applications, and their relevance to software engineers and to non-technical stakeholders (such as other users) [11]. Among the main findings, the proportion of information that is relevant for software engineers is small compared to the volume of tweets, thus motivating the development of automated filtering and classification techniques for the exploitation of such online data for requirements engineering purposes.

Finally, a recent work [21] reports a study about the source of requirements in OSS projects by analysing mailing-list discussions along different dimensions including role of participants (pheripherical vs. core participants), and sentiment of end-users. Classification techniques (specifically Naive Bayes algorithm), and sentiment analysis are exploited.

Besides NLP techniques to filter out irrelevant information, these works combine text mining, sentiment analysis and classification techniques. To our knowledge none exploit models of the online discussion which relies on speech-acts. While this may be less relevant for short user feedback, such as tweets and app reviews, in our opinion for online discussions, such as user forum and mailing-list threads, understanding discussants' intentions, which are revealed by the speech-acts they use, could improve feedback classification.

7 Conclusion

In this paper we presented a method for the analysis of online discussions about software products that take place in issue tracking systems. This method aims at supporting a user-feedback driven software evolution approach. The method uses a linguistic technique called *speech-acts* based analysis. To characterise it we proposed two research questions that we answered by applying it to a dataset of the OpenOffice community, which contains 40872 comments that were extracted from the issue tracking system.

The first question investigated the correlation between the use of certain *speech-acts* and categories of issues (e.g. Enhancement, Defect) regarding the software the online discussions are arguing about. With the second question we understand if *speech-acts* used in these comments may provide a relevant parameter for classifying online discussions into Defects, or Feature and Enhancement requests.

We found that there is an association between types of speech acts (e.g. Informative, Responsive, Requestive, etc.) and categories of issues (e.g. Enhancement, Defect). We investigated the distribution of *speech-acts* for the first ten comments for Defect and Enhancement, and identified common patterns on how conversations about these issues are started and evolve throughout the discussion threads.

We used the *speech-acts* and the sentiment as parameters for training three machine learning algorithms (Random Forest, J48 and SMO) and classify comments into Enhancement, Feature and Defect. Considering the merged Enhancement and Features comments category, resulted in a F-Measure of 0.68 for the merged category and 0.74 for Defect.

In future work, we plan to apply our analysis on user feedback from real world software application, such as SEnerCon's iESA (see Sect. 2), and validate findings with the company's development team. In particular will investigate if our approach could help the team identify relevant feedback that got ignored by manual analysis. Furthermore, we plan to investigate the correlation between *speech-acts* and characteristics of the OpenOffice dataset such as importance, priority and severity.

Acknowledgement. We thank Rob Weir for providing the OpenOffice dataset. This work is a result of the SUPERSEDE project, funded by the H2020 EU Framework Programme under agreement number 644018. The first author is partially funded by INFOTEC under the project "081-022-00-FORTALECIMIENTO E INVERSIÓN".

References

1. Adam, S., Seyff, N., Perini, A., Metzger, A.: Message from the chairs. In: 2015 IEEE 1st International Workshop on Crowd-Based Requirements Engineering (CrowdRE), pp. iii–iv, August 2015. doi:10.1109/CrowdRE.2015.7367580
2. Arnaoudova, V., Haiduc, S., Marcus, A., Antoniol, G.: The use of text retrieval and natural language processing in software engineering. In: Proceedings of the 37th, ICSE 2015, pp. 949–950. IEEE Press (2015)
3. Caleb, C., Schrock, D., Dauterman, P.: Speech act analysis within social network sites' status messages. In: 59th International Communication Association Conference, vol. 20, May 2009
4. Carreño, L.V.G., Winbladh, K.: Analysis of user comments: an approach for software requirements evolution. In: Notkin, D., Cheng, B.H.C., Pohl, K. (eds.) ICSE, pp. 582–591. IEEE/ACM (2013)
5. Cowie, J., Lehnert, W.: Information extraction. Commun. ACM **39**(1), 80–91 (1996)
6. Cunningham, H., Maynard, D., Bontcheva, K., Tablan, V., Aswani, N., Roberts, I., Gorrell, G., Funk, A., Roberts, A., Damljanovic, D., Heitz, T., Greenwood, M.A., Saggion, H., Petrak, J., Li, Y., Peters, W.: Text Processing with GATE (Version 6) (2011). ISBN: 978-0956599315. http://tinyurl.com/gatebook
7. Di Sorbo, A., Panichella, S., Alexandru, C.V., Shimagaki, J., Visaggio, C.A., Canfora, G., Gall, H.C.: What would users change in my app? summarizing app reviews for recommending software changes. In: Proceedings of the 2016 24th ACM SIGSOFT International Symposium FSE, pp. 499–510. ACM (2016)
8. Fang, X., Zhan, J.: Sentiment analysis using product review data. J. Big Data **2**(1), 1–14 (2015)
9. Feng, D., Shaw, E., Kim, J., Hovy, E.H.: An intelligent discussion-bot for answering student queries in threaded discussions. In: International Conference on Intelligent User Interfaces, pp. 171–177. ACM (2006)

10. Godfrey, J.J., Holliman, E.C., McDaniel, J.: SWITCHBOARD: telephone speech corpus for research and development. In: Acoustics, Speech, and Signal Processing, ICASSP-1992, vol. 1, pp. 517–520 (1992)
11. Guzman, E., Alkadhij, R., Seyff, N.: A needle in a haystack: what do Twitter users say about software? In: IEEE 24th International Conference in Requirements Engineering, pp. 96–105 (2016)
12. Guzman, E., Aly, O., Bruegge, B.: Retrieving diverse opinions from app reviews. In: 2015 ACM/IEEE International Symposium on Empirical Software Engineering and Measurement (ESEM), pp. 1–10, October 2015
13. Keertipati, S., Savarimuthu, B.T.R., Licorish, S.A.: Approaches for prioritizing feature improvements extracted from app reviews. In: Proceedings of the 20th International Conference EASE, pp. 33:1–33:6. ACM, New York (2016)
14. Kim, J., Chern, G., Feng, D., Shaw, E., Hovy, E.: Mining and assessing discussions on the web through speech act analysis. In: Proceedings of the Workshop on Web Content Mining with Human Language Technologies (2006)
15. Maalej, W., Nabil, H.: Bug report, feature request, or simply praise? On automatically classifying app reviews. In: 2015 IEEE 23rd International Requirements Engineering Conference (RE), pp. 116–125. IEEE (2015)
16. Manning, C.D., Surdeanu, M., Bauer, J., Finkel, J., Bethard, S.J., McClosky, D.: The Stanford CoreNLP natural language processing toolkit. In: Association for Computational Linguistics (ACL) System Demonstrations, pp. 55–60 (2014)
17. Martin, W., Sarro, F., Jia, Y., Zhang, Y., Harman, M.: A survey of app store analysis for software engineering. IEEE Trans. Softw. Eng., 1, 5555 (2016). doi:10.1109/TSE.2016.2630689
18. Morales-Ramirez, I., Perini, A.: Discovering speech acts in online discussions: a tool-supported method. In: Joint Proceedings of the CAiSE 2014 Forum, volume 1164 of CEUR Workshop Proceedings, pp. 137–144. CEUR-WS.org (2014)
19. Morales-Ramirez, I., Perini, A., Ceccato, M.: Towards supporting the analysis of online discussions in OSS communities: a speech-act based approach. In: Nurcan, S., Pimenidis, E. (eds.) CAiSE Forum 2014. LNBIP, vol. 204, pp. 215–232. Springer, Cham (2015). doi:10.1007/978-3-319-19270-3_14
20. Morales-Ramirez, I., Perini, A., Guizzardi, R.S.S.: An ontology of online user feedback in software engineering. Appl. Ontol. **10**(3–4), 297–330 (2015)
21. Neulinger, K., Hannemann, A., Klamma, R., Jarke, M.: A longitudinal study of community-oriented open source software development. In: Nurcan, S., Soffer, P., Bajec, M., Eder, J. (eds.) CAiSE 2016. LNCS, vol. 9694, pp. 509–523. Springer, Cham (2016). doi:10.1007/978-3-319-39696-5_31
22. Novielli, N., Strapparava, C.: Dialogue act classification exploiting lexical semantics. In: Conversational Agents and Natural Language Interaction: Techniques and Effective Practices, pp. 80–106. IGI Global (2011)
23. Panichella, S., Di Sorbo, A., Guzman, E., Visaggio, C.A., Canfora, G., Gall, H.C.: How can i improve my app? Classifying user reviews for software maintenance and evolution. In: IEEE International Conference on Software Maintenance and Evolution (ICSME), pp. 281–290. IEEE (2015)
24. Searle, J.R.: Speech Acts: An Essay in the Philosophy of Language, vol. 626. Cambridge University Press, Cambridge (1969)
25. Stolcke, A., Coccaro, N., Bates, R., Taylor, P., Van Ess-Dykema, C., Ries, K., Shriberg, E., Jurafsky, D., Martin, R., Meteer, M.: Dialogue act modeling for automatic tagging and recognition of conversational speech. Comput. Linguist. **26**(3), 339–373 (2000)

26. Villarroel, L., Bavota, G., Russo, B., Oliveto, R., Penta, M.D.: Release planning of mobile apps based on user reviews. In: Proceedings of the 38th International Conference on Software Engineering, pp. 14–24. ACM (2016)
27. Wohlin, C., Runeson, P., Höst, M., Ohlsson, M.C., Regnell, B., Wesslén, A.: Experimentation in Software Engineering: An Introduction. Kluwer Academic Publishers, Norwell (2000)

Business Process Performance

Discovering Causal Factors Explaining Business Process Performance Variation

Bart F.A. Hompes[1,2(✉)], Abderrahmane Maaradji[3], Marcello La Rosa[3], Marlon Dumas[4], Joos C.A.M. Buijs[1], and Wil M.P. van der Aalst[1]

[1] Eindhoven University of Technology, Eindhoven, The Netherlands
{b.f.a.hompes,j.c.a.m.buijs,w.m.p.v.d.aalst}@tue.nl
[2] Philips Research, Eindhoven, The Netherlands
[3] Queensland University of Technology, Brisbane, Australia
{abderrahmane.maaradji,m.larosa}@qut.edu.au
[4] University of Tartu, Tartu, Estonia
marlon.dumas@ut.ee

Abstract. Business process performance may be affected by a range of factors, such as the volume and characteristics of ongoing cases or the performance and availability of individual resources. Event logs collected by modern information systems provide a wealth of data about the execution of business processes. However, extracting root causes for performance issues from these event logs is a major challenge. Processes may change continuously due to internal and external factors. Moreover, there may be many resources and case attributes influencing performance. This paper introduces a novel approach based on time series analysis to detect cause-effect relations between a range of business process characteristics and process performance indicators. The scalability and practical relevance of the approach has been validated by a case study involving a real-life insurance claims handling process.

Keywords: Process mining · Performance analysis · Root cause analysis

1 Introduction

Improving process performance can lead to significant cost and time savings, and to better service levels (e.g. better response times). Accordingly, process performance analysis and optimization has been an active field of research in recent years [1,2]. Business process performance is generally affected by a plethora of factors. For example, the waiting time for a procedure in a hospital may depend on the amount of scheduled staff; the duration of a credit check in a credit approval process might depend on the number of clients waiting to be approved; the waiting time for a payment receipt might depend on the time of day, etc. It is often not known to process owners which factors affect which performance indicators. Consequently, it is hard to identify the best actions to be taken when performance is unsatisfactory. For instance, when process owners have a limited set of resources available, it is often not known to which tasks these resources

E. Dubois and K. Pohl (Eds.): CAiSE 2017, LNCS 10253, pp. 177–192, 2017.
DOI: 10.1007/978-3-319-59536-8_12

should be allocated in order to redress the performance issues. The latter is especially important in processes that have a high level of variability and do not follow a fixed process model.

Although several techniques have been proposed to automatically discover process performance bottlenecks and deviations based on event data (e.g. [1,2]), little research has gone into the automated discovery of causal factors of business process performance. As a result, a number of hypotheses typically have to be tested manually in order to identify causal factors for process performance issues. Additionally, factors can have both a direct and indirect effect on process performance. For example, factors may influence other factors that in the end influence performance. Hence, new analysis techniques are required that are able to discover such chains of causal relations between causal factors and the performance indicators of interest.

In this paper, we propose a technique that, given an event log of a business process, generates a graph of causal factors explaining process performance. The technique identifies causal relations between a range of business process characteristics and process performance indicators such as case duration (a.k.a. cycle time) and activity waiting time. In order to detect causal relations, we test for Granger causality [3], a statistical test that is widely used for causal analysis of time series in a range of fields, e.g. economics and neuroscience [4,5]. The idea is that values for performance indicators are seen as time series. A factor is said to be causal to another when past values of this factor provide information that can help predict the other factor above and beyond the information contained in the past values of the latter factor alone. This idea is illustrated in Fig. 1.

Given the large number of factors that may affect process performance and their possible combinations, one of the main bottlenecks when extracting a causal graph is to prune down the number of causal relations to be tested. To this end, the paper proposes an approach to prune the space of causal relations in order to identify a manageable subset of candidate causal relations. The proposed approach has been validated via a case study involving an insurance claims handling process at a large Australian insurer.

The remainder of this paper is structured as follows. Section 2 discusses related work. Section 3 introduces preliminary definitions. Our causal discovery approach is detailed in Sect. 4 and validated in Sect. 5. The paper is concluded with views on future work in Sect. 6.

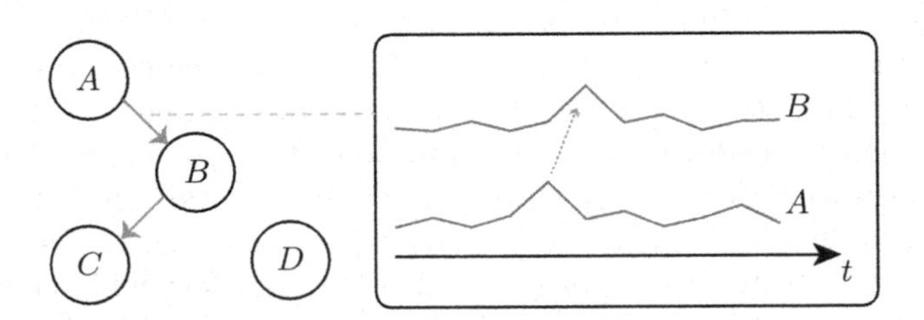

Fig. 1. Factor A causes B which in turn causes C, whereas factor D does not have any observed effect. In order to improve C, A and B should be improved.

2 Related Work

Techniques that exploit process execution data collected by information systems have gained increased interest from both industry and the research community. Model-based techniques such as alignments compare the observed behavior with either a discovered or manually designed process model and can be used for conformance checking as well as performance analysis [1]. An extensive literature review of process measures that can be used in this context can be found in [2].

Other studies addressed the interplay between different perspectives of a business process in order to provide more targeted insights. The method proposed in [6] for example aims at identifying cases that might exceed certain deadlines based on predefined process risk indicators such as activity duration. If a case contains at least one outlier value of the defined indicators, the case is labeled as being at risk. A framework for inferring new event and case attributes is proposed in [7]. Inferred attributes are subsequently used as cause-effect variables in a decision tree classifier in order to discover business rules. A related technique is proposed in [8], where process characteristics are correlated using decision tree learning. This approach is extended in [9] with a technique for recommending business decisions based on risk. The authors of [10] use decision tree learning to find process paths and contexts that lead to improved performance. In [11], the notion of process cubes is proposed. Process cubes are based on the OLAP data cube concept, and define a set of actions and operations that can be used to explore event data based on different business process perspectives. A similar framework is presented in [12].

Though the methods described above have their individual merits and applications, they provide limited insight into what cause-effect relationships might exist in event data. In [13], the authors establish the need for techniques that are able to provide actionable insights, rather than merely showing low-level analytical insights, and provide a framework to aid in this translation. In our work, we hypothesize that causal factors can be discovered for and between performance indicators, and test this hypothesis statistically using an established technique from the time series domain.

Whereas existing techniques focus mainly on finding differences in performance and on general statistics, in this paper, we focus on supporting business process decision making by discovering and providing the causal factors for business process performance. Actionable insights can then be obtained by looking at causal factors. We base our idea on methods proposed in [14] where we proposed a technique that automatically discovers statistically significant differences in performance between different contexts. This paper specifically considers the time dimension, which allows for more elaborate analysis, including the cause-effect relations focused on in this paper.

3 Preliminaries

The executed *events* of multiple *cases* of a *process* are usually recorded by some *information system*. These so-called event logs serve as input for any process mining technique. Typically, different attribute values are recorded for these events, such as the time they took place, which activity was performed, and which resources were involved. Definitions for universes and event bases used in this paper are based on those in [11].

Definition 1 (Universes). *$\mathcal{U}_V$ is the universe of possible attribute values (e.g. strings, numbers, etc.). $\mathcal{U}_S = \mathcal{P}(\mathcal{U}_V)$ is the universe of value sets*[1]. *$\mathcal{U}_H = \mathcal{P}(\mathcal{U}_S)$ is the universe of value set collections (set of sets), and $\mathcal{T} \subseteq \mathcal{U}_V$ is the universe of time stamps.*

Note that $v \in \mathcal{U}_V$ is a single value (e.g. $v = 10$), $S \in \mathcal{U}_S$ is a set of values (e.g. $S = \{gold, silver, bronze\}$), and $H \in \mathcal{U}_H$ is a collection of sets. For example, $H = \{\{Bob, John\}\{Mary, Sue\}\}$, or $H = \{\{x \in \mathbb{N} \mid x < 12\}, \{x \in \mathbb{N} \mid 12 \leq x < 55\}, \{x \in \mathbb{N} \mid x \geq 55\}\}$. Any $t \in \mathcal{T}$ represents a unique time stamp (e.g. 2016-1-4 9:15). Time stamps can have different levels of granularity (e.g. week, hour, millisecond).

Definition 2 (Event base). *An event base $EB = (E, P, \pi)$ defines a set of events E, a set of event properties P, and a function $\pi \in P \rightarrow (E \nrightarrow \mathcal{U}_V)$. For any property $p \in P$, $\pi(p)$ (denoted π_p) is a partial function mapping events onto values. If $\pi_p(e) = v$, then event $e \in E$ has a property $p \in P$ and the value of this property is $v \in \mathcal{U}_V$. If $e \notin dom(\pi_p)$, then event e does not have property p and we write $\pi_p(e) = \perp$.*

The set E refers to individual events, recorded by some information system. The event base can either consist of a single event log, or, alternatively, multiple event logs can be combined to create an aggregated event base. Note that $e \in E$ is a unique identifier and function π is needed to attach meaning to e. P is the set of properties that events may or may not have. For example, $P = \{$*case, age, type, activity, instance, time, resource, transition, cost*$\}$ corresponds to the columns in Table 1. Here, $\pi_{case}(1) = 1$, $\pi_{activity}(1) = A$, $\pi_{resource}(1) = John$, etc. An execution of an activity in the process is represented by one or more events that are associated with a lifecycle state transition for the activity instance. These states are used to calculate performance information such as activity durations and waiting times. Events belonging to the same activity instance have the same value for the instance property.

Given an event base, one can derive additional event properties. For example, different event properties can be aggregated together to form new properties, e.g. $\pi_{ar} = (\pi_{activity}, \pi_{resource})$. Alternatively, functions that operate on other properties can be defined. For example, function $\pi_{agegroup}(e) = \frac{(\pi_{age}(e) \ - \ \pi_{age}(e) \ div \ 20)}{20}$ can be used to group events for cases in age groups of 20 years, etc. Such derived event properties may also be based on other events. For example, $\pi_{case\ start}(e) = min\{\pi_{time}(e') \mid e' \in E \wedge \pi_{case}(e') = \pi_{case}(e)\}$. We use these calculated properties to create specific projections of the event base, in order to define potential causal factors for business process performance.

[1] $\mathcal{P}(Y)$ denotes the powerset of a set Y, i.e. $X \in \mathcal{P}(Y) \iff X \subseteq Y$.

Table 1. Example event log L_1. Events can be characterized by multiple properties.

Case id	Case attributes		Event id	Event attributes				
	Age	Type		Time	Activity	Transition	Resource	Instance
1	33	Gold	1	2016-1-4 8:00	A	Start	John	1
			2	2016-1-4 9:15	A	Complete	John	1
			3	2016-1-4 10:12	B	Complete	Bob	2
			4	2016-1-4 14:00	C	Start	Sue	3
			5	2016-1-4 14:05	C	Complete	Sue	3
2	27	Silver	6	2016-1-6 10:43	A	Start	Bob	4
			7	2016-1-6 11:00	A	Complete	Bob	4
			8	2016-1-7 09:33	B	Complete	John	5
			9	2016-1-7 09:35	C	Start	Sue	6
			10	2016-1-7 09:35	C	Complete	Sue	6
3	18	Silver	11	2016-1-7 9:27	A	Start	John	7
			12	2016-1-7 10:40	A	Complete	John	7
			13	2016-1-7 15:03	B	Complete	Bob	8
4	$\perp$	Gold	14	2016-1-7 12:10	A	Start	Bob	9
			15	2016-1-7 12:24	A	Complete	Bob	9
			16	2016-1-8 08:47	B	Complete	John	10
5	41	Silver	17	2016-1-8 15:32	A	Start	Bob	11
			18	2016-1-8 15:51	A	Complete	Bob	11
...	...	...	...	...	...	...	...	...

4 Method

Our causal factor detection approach consists of three main steps, as shown in Fig. 2. In the first step, the event base is systematically decomposed into a directed acyclic graph, in which each node represents a collection of events that share certain business process characteristics and can be considered a potential causal factor (Subsect. 4.1). Nodes in this so-called *decomposition graph* are connected by an edge when the target node is the result of further decomposition of the source node using any (additional) process characteristic. In the second step, this decomposition graph is converted into a so-called *inclusion graph* (Subsect. 4.2). The edges of the inclusion graph represent candidate causal relations between factors (nodes), and will be used in the third and final step. In the causal discovery step, we test for causality between factors in a pair-wise manner (Subsect. 4.3). For every pair of connected nodes in the inclusion graph, the performance values for events in each node are converted into time series and tested for causality. This three-step approach results in a graphical causal model referred to as a *causality graph*.

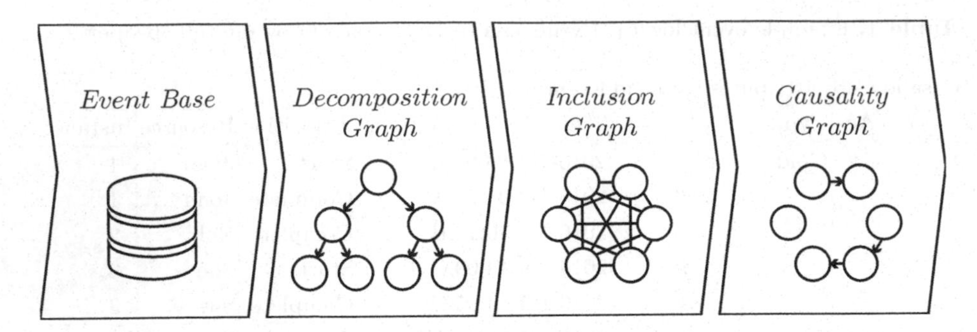

Fig. 2. The steps of our approach (from left to right). A decomposition graph is created from the event base (step 1). Next, it is converted into an inclusion graph (step 2). From the inclusion graph, a causality graph is discovered (step 3).

4.1 Systematic Decomposition

The first step in the approach takes as input the complete event base and returns as output a so-called decomposition graph in which each node represents a set of events that share certain process characteristics. For example, a decomposition can be made by differentiating between activity names, the resource that was responsible for the execution of an event, the type of case, etc. It also possible to differentiate by any combination of properties, as discussed in Sect. 3.

The decomposition step works as follows. We decompose the event collection E in an event base $EB = (E, P, \pi)$ by the set of event properties P using function π. As such, any combination of values for the event properties in P is considered to be a unique process characteristic. Conceptually, our goal is to test whether process performance of a certain set of events that share one or multiple process characteristics causes process performance of another set of events sharing other process characteristics. For example, one such test could test whether the waiting time of all *Pay invoice* activities with a cost greater than *100* causes the case duration for *Gold* customers. If causality is confirmed, it can be said that the former is a causal factor of the latter. Consequently, when the case duration for *Gold* customers is unsatisfactory, process optimization efforts should be directed towards improving the waiting time of activities *Pay invoice* in which the cost was greater than *100*. Formally, decomposition graphs are defined as follows.

Definition 3 (Decomposition graph). *Let $EB = (E, P, \pi)$ be an event base. $G_D(EB) = (N, R_D)$ denotes a decomposition graph over EB, where:*

- $N = \Big\{\Big(E', \{P_1, \ldots, P_n\}\Big) \in \mathcal{P}(E) \times \mathcal{P}(P) \;\Big|\; E' \neq \varnothing \wedge$
  $\exists_{v_1,\ldots,v_n \in \mathcal{U}_V} E' = \{e \in E \mid \forall_{1<i<n} \pi_{p_i}(E) = v_i\}\Big\}$ *is the set of nodes, and*
- $R = \Big\{\Big((E_1, P_1), (E_2, P_2)\Big) \in N \times N \;\Big|\; P_1 \subseteq P_2 \wedge E_2 \subseteq E_1\Big\}$ *the set of edges.*

Note that each decomposition graph is a directed acyclic graph with a root node $(E, \varnothing)$. All events in a node in the decomposition graph share a common value for

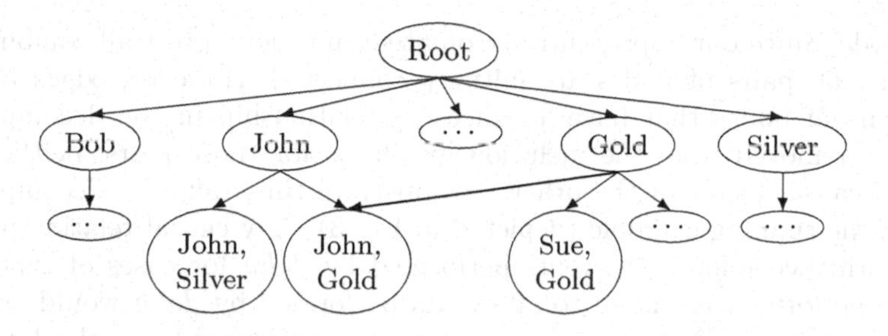

Fig. 3. The decomposition graph created from the event base EB_1. Only selected nodes and edges are shown for sake of simplicity.

each property defined for that node. Additionally, directed edges exist between any pair of nodes for which it holds that the set of properties defined for the source node is included in the set of properties of the target node, and the set of events of the target node is a subset of the set of events of the source node. Note that as only observed values are considered, the decomposition graph is finite. Additionally, context functions can be used to discretize continuous values.

For example, consider the event base $EB_1 = (L_1, P, \pi)$ created from event log L_1 in Table 1, the event properties $P = \{resource, type\}$, and function π. Applying the decomposition step for this event base leads to a decomposition graph as illustrated in Fig. 3. Here, the node labeled *"John, Gold"* holds all events that were performed by resource *John* for cases of type *Gold*, i.e. events 1, 2, and 16. These events are in the intersection of the sets of events in the nodes labeled *"John"* (events 1, 2, 8, 11, 12, 16) and *"Gold"* (events 1, 2, 3, 4, 5, 14, 15, 16).

4.2 Candidate Causal Factor Selection

The second step in the approach takes as input the decomposition graph and produces as output a so-called inclusion graph in which each edge represents a candidate causal relation. Formally, inclusion graphs are defined as follows.

Definition 4 (Inclusion graph). *Let $EB = (E, P, \pi)$ be an event base. $G_I(G_D(EB)) = (N, R_I)$ denotes an inclusion graph over a decomposition graph $G_D(EB) = (N, R_D)$, where:*

- $N = \Big\{\Big(E', \{P_1, \ldots, P_n\}\Big) \in \mathcal{P}(E) \times \mathcal{P}(P) \;\Big|\; E' \neq \varnothing \wedge$ $\exists_{v_1,\ldots,v_n \in \mathcal{U}_V} E' = \{e \in E \mid \forall_{1<i<n} \pi_{p_i}(E) = v_i\} \Big\}$ *is the set of nodes, and*
- $R_I = \Big\{\Big((E_1, P_1), (E_2, P_2)\Big) \in N \times N \;\Big|\; \Big((E_1, P_1), (E_2, P_2)\Big) \notin R_D^+ \wedge$ $\Big((E_2, P_2), (E_1, P_1)\Big) \notin R_D^+\Big\}$ *the set of edges.*

Every edge in the inclusion graph represents one candidate causal relation in the data. The performance related to events of the source node of such an edge is a potential causal factor for the performance related to events of the target node. Since our approach is automated, in order to test all combinations of factors, all pairs of nodes are initially connected. However, edges between those pairs of nodes that have an ancestry relationship in the decomposition graph are removed from the inclusion graph, as for those pairs, neither node can be a causal factor of the other. To illustrate this, take the decomposition graph of the running example (depicted in Fig. 3). Any causal relation between the performance related to events performed by *John* for cases of type *Gold*, with the performance related to all events performed by *John* would not have any logical meaning. Note that we are testing a time-lagged causal relationship rather than a compositional relationship (i.e. we do not aim to find which factor contributes most), rather we look at which factor has predictive power over another.

In order to reduce the risk of discovering spurious causalities, and in order to optimize the performance of the causality detection technique, the inclusion graph can be pruned further by removing nodes and/or edges that do not make sense from a business point of view. Multiple such pruning techniques can be constructed, from domain knowledge-based manual selection to automatic clustering and filtering of the data represented by the nodes. Any further pruning of the inclusion graph however falls beyond the scope of this paper.

4.3 Discovering Causality

Once the inclusion graph has been created, it serves as input for the causality discovery step, where individual pairs of nodes in the inclusion graph are checked for cause-effect relationships.

For many years, the concept of causality has received continuing interest in various domains of research. Over the years, the concept has evolved, and as a result, a variety of definitions have been proposed, many of which have a statistical foundation. Techniques such as structural equation modeling [15] and Bayesian networks [16] have been widely used to assess cause-effect relationships between a set of observable and latent variables. In [17], for example, dynamic Bayesian network inference is used to discover causal relations in biological data. However, these techniques are generally more applicable for confirmatory causality analysis based on predefined hypotheses.

Other techniques have been proposed to find causal relationships in case no a-priori knowledge is available about the causal structure in the data [18,19]. These techniques often return a set of causal models which are either hard to interpret, assume the input data to be of a certain restrictive form, or do not consider the time perspective in the data. For business process performance analysis however, the time perspective is of particular importance. In the context of econometric models, Granger has introduced a framework for testing predictive causality that can be used to discover causality between two time series and can be used to create graphical models of causality [3–5,20,21]. In this paper, in order to detect causal factors for business process performance, we test for Granger causality between time series that represent business process performance of different potential causal factors.

Business Process Performance. We define business process performance indicators as functions over events. Different performance functions can have different input and output. Whereas most performance analysis techniques will take only a collection of events as input, other functions can be constructed that take additional input as well. For example, the fitness of a specific case to a process model [1] can be a useful performance function when finding causal factors for non-conformance or when looking for root causes for protocol violations. In this paper, we limit the domain of performance functions to a set of events and the range to timed real values. However, our approach can easily be extended and integrated in situations that require performance functions with different input and output.

Definition 5 (Performance function). *I defines a set of performance indicators. A performance function is a function $\theta \in I \rightarrow (E \nrightarrow \mathbb{R} \times \mathcal{T})$ where for any performance indicator $i \in I$, $\theta(i)$ (denoted θ_i) is a partial function mapping events onto timed real values. If $\theta_i(e) = (r,\ t)$ (denoted r_t), then the performance of event $e \in E$ is $r \in \mathbb{R}$ and the associated time stamp is $t \in \mathcal{T}$. If $e \notin dom(\theta_i)$, then event e does not have a value for performance indicator i and we write $\theta_i(e) = \perp$.*

Typical performance functions are case duration, activity duration, activity waiting time, activity sojourn time, etc. Below, we give definitions for the case duration (Eq. 1), activity sojourn time (Eq. 2) and activity duration (Eq. 3). Other performance functions can be defined analogously.

$$\begin{aligned}\theta_{caseduration}(e) = \Big(&max\{\pi_t(e') \mid e' \in E \wedge \pi_c(e') = \pi_c(e)\} - \\ &min\{\pi_t(e') \mid e' \in E \wedge \pi_c(e') = \pi_c(e)\}, \\ &max\{\pi_t(e') \mid e' \in E \wedge \pi_c(e') = \pi_c(e)\}\Big)\end{aligned} \tag{1}$$

$$\begin{aligned}\theta_{activityduration}(e) = \Big(&max\{\pi_t(e') \mid e' \in E \wedge \pi_i(e') = \pi_i(e)\} - \\ &min\{\pi_t(e') \mid e' \in E \wedge \pi_i(e') = \pi_i(e)\}, \\ &max\{\pi_t(e') \mid e' \in E \wedge \pi_i(e') = \pi_i(e)\}\Big)\end{aligned} \tag{2}$$

$$\begin{aligned}\theta_{activitysojourntime}(e) = \Big(&max\{\pi_t(e') \mid e' \in E \wedge \pi_i(e') = \pi_i(e)\} - \\ &max\{\pi_t(e') \mid e' \in E \wedge \pi_c(e') = \pi_c(e) \wedge \pi_i(e') \neq \pi_i(e) \\ &\pi_t(e') \leq min(\pi_t(e'') \mid e'' \in E \wedge \pi_i(e'') = \pi_i(e))\}, \\ &max\{\pi_t(e') \mid e' \in E \wedge \pi_i(e') = \pi_i(e)\}\Big)\end{aligned} \tag{3}$$

where $\pi_t = \pi_{time}$, $\pi_c = \pi_{case}$ and $\pi_i = \pi_{instance}$.

Time Series. By applying a performance function to a collection of events we obtain a set of timed real values. These values can be represented as a time series, which form the basis of the Granger causality detection technique.

Definition 6 (Time series). *Let $\mathcal{U}_{TS}$ be the universe of time series. Any time series $S \in \mathcal{U}_{TS} = \{s_t \mid s \in \mathbb{R} \wedge t \in \mathcal{T}\}$ defines a time-ordered collection of real values.*

In business processes, the measurements of most process performance indicators arrive at irregular time intervals. In order to perform the Granger causality test, time series regularization needs to be performed. Therefore, we regularize the time series by re-sampling to a common measurement interval. To this end, values for time intervals that do not have any recorded values are imputed (e.g. by linear interpolation), and values for intervals with multiple values are aggregated (e.g. averaged). During analysis, a threshold must be set to avoid a high number of imputed values relative to the number of actual values.

Causality Detection. Each edge in the inclusion graph indicates a candidate causal relation between the source and target nodes. This relation is tested for Granger causality. A time series $S \in \mathcal{U}_{TS}$ is said to Granger cause another time series $S' \in \mathcal{U}_{TS}$ if the past values of S help predict future values of S' better than the past values of S' can predict itself. Three steps are needed to perform the Granger test (denoted $G_{S \to S'}$). First, a linear univariate autoregressive model of S' is fitted.

$$s'_t = \sum_{k=1}^{L} a'_k \cdot s'_{t-k} + \epsilon'_t, \tag{4}$$

Here, L is the lag of Granger test, $t = L+1, \ldots, |S'|$, a' is a vector of parameters for Eq. 4, and ϵ' is the residual. Next, a bivariate linear autoregressive model for S' including the past values of S is fitted as well:

$$s'_t = \sum_{k=1}^{L} a_k \cdot s'_t - k + \sum_{k=1}^{L} b_k \cdot s_{t-k} + \epsilon_t, \tag{5}$$

Here, a and b are vectors of parameters for Eq. 5, and ϵ is the residual. The residuals of Eqs. 4 and 5 can be estimated using a maximum likelihood estimator (in this paper we use the ordinary least squares estimator). Finally, the Granger-Sargent statistic is computed as follows.

$$G_{S \to S'} = \frac{(\epsilon' - \epsilon)/L}{\epsilon/(|S'| - 2L)}. \tag{6}$$

Informally, a large value for $G_{S \to S'}$ indicates that the past information in S is useful for predicting the future values of S'. The Granger-Sargent test is performed to test the null hypothesis of no causality. If the returned p-value is less than the test threshold (typically 5%), S is said to "Granger cause" S'.

4.4 Interpretation

It is worth mentioning here that any statistical causality technique, including ours, discovers only statistically plausible causal structures, and causal factors that are extraneous to the event data cannot be detected.

Complexity. The time-complexity of the approach is bounded by the number of nodes in the inclusion graph times the number of pair-wise tests performed, i.e. $O\Big(\sum_{i=0}^{|P|}\binom{|P|}{i}\cdot P^2_{2|I|}\Big)$. This can be reduced to $O\Big(|P|^{2|P|+2}\cdot|I|!\Big)$. However, it should be noted that as explained in Subsect. 4.2, many combinations will not be tested due to their ancestry relationship. Therefore, this upper bound is purely theoretical, and not representative for the real-world complexity.

5 Case Study

The approach presented in this paper has been implemented in the process mining tool ProM[2], and evaluated with a case study using a dataset provided by one of Australia's largest insurance providers. The obtained results were interpreted and validated by a domain expert from this company who is involved in process standardization and optimization efforts. The results were found to provide sensible and actionable insights related to business process performance.

The process that was analyzed is a variant of an automotive claims handling process for which events are recorded by a claims handling system. The provided dataset consists of 17,474 events that have been recorded for 2,577 claims (cases), spanning a total of 13 months. There are 14 distinct activities in the process, and information is recorded about which of the 739 resources was involved in the execution of activities. The total runtime of our technique on this real-life dataset is in the order of several minutes (on modern hardware).

The following subsections correspond to the different steps involved in our causality detection approach, as described in Sect. 4. We complete this section with a discussion on the result.

5.1 Systematic Decomposition

In order to decompose the event collection into a decomposition graph, the following process characteristics were used. We used the activity name as different activities can clearly have different influences on process performance. Additionally, in the process in question, not every activity is mandatory, i.e. not every activity was recorded for every case. As many resources are involved in this process, their performance is an interesting potential cause for the selected performance indicators. Thus, besides the activity name, we used the resource that executed the activity as a process characteristic. In order to have enough measurements per causality analysis, nodes that contained less than 250 events or less than 250 values in their respective time series were filtered out. In total, the obtained decomposition graph contains 25 nodes and 27 edges (after filtering).

5.2 Candidate Causal Factor Selection

From the decomposition graph obtained in the previous step, an inclusion graph was created by applying the technique described in Subsect. 4.2. No additional

[2] See http://promtools.org and the *RootCauseAnalysis* package for more information.

graph pruning techniques were used other than the (automatic) removal of edges between nodes for which an ancestry relation exists in the decomposition graph. The resulting inclusion graph contained 1,161 edges, representing 1,161 candidate causal relations per performance function.

5.3 Discovering Causality

In the dataset provided by the insurance company, only events referring to the completion of activities were available. Consequently, the activity duration could not be calculated, as no events representing the beginning of activities were recorded. We selected the case duration and the activity sojourn time, as defined in Sect. 4.3, as business process performance indicators.

Considering the time-granularity of the recorded data, the time series for the two performance functions for each candidate factor were re-sampled to daily intervals in order to obtain regular time series. When multiple values were available for any given period, the average value was taken. Missing values were replaced by linearly interpolated values. As a filtering step, time series for which more than one out of ten values were imputed were not considered in the analysis. In the Granger causality test, the maximum lag value was set to 7, in order to incorporate time-lagged effects of up to one week. The resulting causality graph showed a total of 16 causal relations involving 11 factors. Out of these, 11 relations between 10 factors were selected for further analysis and explanation in this paper, and can be seen in Fig. 4.

5.4 Discussion of Results

Visual analysis of the selected causal relations discovered by our technique showed five main observations.

Observations 1: One part of the causality graph consists of a set of three activities for which the sojourn times are all causal factors for the sojourn time of the *close claim* activity.

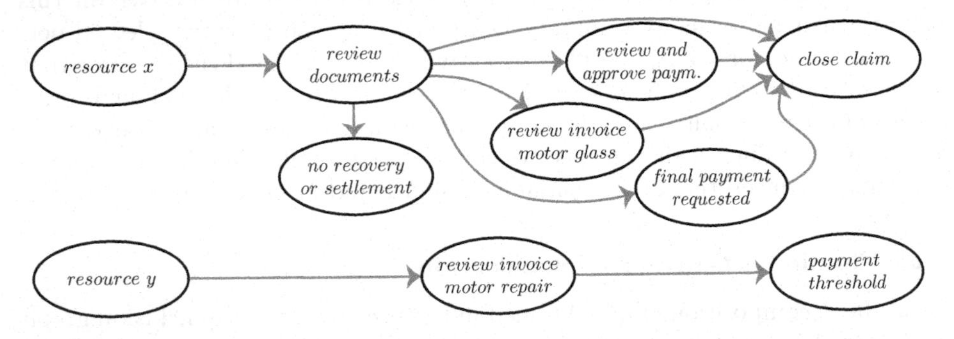

Fig. 4. The causality graph obtained by applying the technique on the insurance claims dataset. Five main observations are found.

Observations 2: The sojourn time of these three activities resulted to be caused by the sojourn time of an activity representing the *review of documents*.

Observations 3: In turn, the causal factor of the sojourn time for this activity was the sojourn time of any activity performed by a *specific resource* (resource x in Fig. 4). On close inspection of the event log, we found that the *close claim* activity was the last activity in about 30% of cases, and that the identified resource was in the top five resources that frequently performed this activity.

Observations 4: Remarkably, the *review document* node also caused the sojourn time of a fifth activity ('no recovery or settlement'), which did not seem to cause the performance of the *close claim* activity.

Observations 5: Finally, one node in the causality graph involves the sojourn time of an activity representing the *review invoice* for the vehicle repair. This factor seems to be caused by the sojourn time of a *specific resource* (resource y in Fig. 4), and is itself a causal factor for the sojourn time of an activity representing some *payment threshold being reached.*

The domain expert was presented with these five observation and was asked to validate the results. With respect to the observations 1, 2 and 3, the explanation given by the domain expert is that claims can only be closed once a checklist of other activities has been completed. The activities on this list correspond to the activities for which the sojourn time was found to be a direct causal factor for the sojourn time of the *close claim* activity. Since the resource names were made anonymous in our dataset, the specific resource could not be identified. However, the domain expert suggested that the identified resource could be an over-utilized person with a validation role, hence the effect on the sojourn time (which includes both waiting and processing time).

Based on the identified factors and the explanation provided by the domain expert, we have suggested (i) to make use of an early-knockout strategy rather than waiting until the claim is about to be closed to check all activities [22], and (ii) to allocate more resources for the validations, or to remove workload from the resources involved in the validation.

Additionally, the activity of which the performance was caused by the sojourn time of the *review document* activity but that did not cause the performance of the *close claim* activity (observation 4), was found to be an activity in which repair costs were recovered from a third-party insurance company. In such cases, the claim may be closed (i.e. this activity is not on the checklist).

Finally, with respect to observation 5, the domain expert explained that the repair of vehicles in this process is performed by a third party. As such, occasionally, an invoice needs to be reviewed. For cases in which this invoice exceeds a certain threshold, a resource having the manager role is involved. Since the performance of this resource is a causal factor, it might indicate an over-utilization. Discussing these cause-effect factors with the domain expert lead to the following recommendations: (i) allocate more resources to review invoices, and/or (ii) increase the threshold for the total amount on the invoice, in order to decrease the number of invoices that need to be reviewed by a manager.

6 Conclusions and Future Work

We proposed a novel technique to automatically discover root causes for business process performance issues such as bottlenecks from event data. To the best of our knowledge, this is the first technique of its kind. The technique supports a range of business process characteristics to perform the analysis and information from additional inputs such as process models may be used to provide specific performance insights. A case study on a real-life dataset showed that the technique has practical relevance and can be used to provide actionable insights to analysts.

One limitation of the current implementation of our technique is that the original definition for Granger causality does not account for latent confounding effects and does not capture instantaneous and non-linear causal relationships. In future work, we would like to explore extensions or alternative causality detection techniques, such as those defined on a structure of relations rather than on pairwise connections. The performance of the technique can be improved by further pruning the inclusion graph by means of clustering and filtering techniques. We would also like to investigate how obtained insights can be used for monitoring, prediction and recommendation of business process performance optimization strategies.

Acknowledgments. This research is funded by the Australian Research Council (grant DP150103356), the Estonian Research Council (grant IUT20-55) and the RISE_BPM project (H2020 Marie Curie Program, grant 645751).

References

1. van der Aalst, W.M.P., Adriansyah, A., van Dongen, B.F.: Replaying history on process models for conformance checking and performance analysis. Wiley Interdisc. Rev.: Data Min. Knowl. Discov. **2**(2), 182–192 (2012)
2. González, L.S., Rubio, F.G., González, F.R., Velthuis, M.P.: Measurement in business processes: a systematic review. Bus. Process Manag. J. **16**(1), 114–134 (2010)
3. Granger, C.W.J.: Some recent development in a concept of causality. J. Econometrics **39**(1), 199–211 (1988)
4. Kamiński, M., Ding, M., Truccolo, W.A., Bressler, S.L.: Evaluating causal relations in neural systems: Granger causality, directed transfer function and statistical assessment of significance. Biol. Cybern. **85**(2), 145–157 (2001)
5. Roebroeck, A., Formisano, E., Goebel, R.: Mapping directed influence over the brain using Granger causality and fMRI. Neuroimage **25**(1), 230–242 (2005)

6. Pika, A., van der Aalst, W.M.P., Fidge, C.J., ter Hofstede, A.H.M., Wynn, M.T.: Predicting deadline transgressions using event logs. In: Rosa, M., Soffer, P. (eds.) BPM 2012. LNBIP, vol. 132, pp. 211–216. Springer, Heidelberg (2013). doi:10.1007/978-3-642-36285-9_22
7. Suriadi, S., Ouyang, C., van der Aalst, W.M.P., ter Hofstede, A.H.M.: Root cause analysis with enriched process logs. In: Rosa, M., Soffer, P. (eds.) BPM 2012. LNBIP, vol. 132, pp. 174–186. Springer, Heidelberg (2013). doi:10.1007/978-3-642-36285-9_18
8. de Leoni, M., van der Aalst, W.M.P., Dees, M.: A general process mining framework for correlating, predicting and clustering dynamic behavior based on event logs. Inf. Syst. **56**, 235–257 (2016)
9. Conforti, R., de Leoni, M., La Rosa, M., van der Aalst, W.M.P., ter Hofstede, A.H.M.: A recommendation system for predicting risks across multiple business process instances. Decis. Support Syst. **69**(1), 1–19 (2015)
10. Ghattas, J., Soffer, P., Peleg, M.: Improving business process decision making based on past experience. Decis. Support Syst. **59**, 93–107 (2014)
11. van der Aalst, W.M.P.: Process cubes: slicing, dicing, rolling up and drilling down event data for process mining. In: Song, M., Wynn, M.T., Liu, J. (eds.) AP-BPM 2013. LNBIP, vol. 159, pp. 1–22. Springer, Cham (2013). doi:10.1007/978-3-319-02922-1_1
12. Vogelgesang, T., Appelrath, H.-J.: PMCube: a data-warehouse-based approach for multidimensional process mining. In: Reichert, M., Reijers, H.A. (eds.) BPM 2015. LNBIP, vol. 256, pp. 167–178. Springer, Cham (2016). doi:10.1007/978-3-319-42887-1_14
13. Tan, S., Chan, T.: Defining and conceptualizing actionable insight: a conceptual framework for decision-centric analytics. In: Australasian Conference on Information Systems (2015)
14. Hompes, B.F.A., Buijs, J.C.A.M., van der Aalst, W.M.P.: A generic framework for context-aware process performance analysis. In: Debruyne, C., et al. (eds.) OTM 2016. LNCS, vol. 10033, pp. 300–317. Springer, Cham (2016). doi:10.1007/978-3-319-48472-3_17
15. Bollen, K.A.: Structural Equations with Latent Variables. Wiley, Hoboken (2014)
16. Jensen, F.V.: An Introduction to Bayesian networks, vol. 210. UCL Press, London (1996)
17. Yu, J., Smith, V.A., Wang, P.P., Hartemink, A.J., Jarvis, E.D.: Advances to bayesian network inference for generating causal networks from observational biological data. Bioinformatics **20**(18), 3594–3603 (2004)
18. Shimizu, S., Hoyer, P.O., Hyvarinen, A., Kerminen, A.: A linear non-gaussian acyclic model for causal discovery. J. Mach. Learn. Res. **7**, 2003–2030 (2006)
19. Richardson, T.: A polynomial-time algorithm for deciding Markov equivalence of directed cyclic graphical models. In: Proceedings of the Twelfth International Conference on Uncertainty in Artificial Intelligence, pp. 462–469. Morgan Kaufmann Publishers Inc., Burlington (1996)
20. Granger, C.W.J.: Investigating causal relations by econometric models and cross-spectral methods. Econometrica **37**(3), 424 (1969)

21. Dahlhaus, R., Eichler, M.: Causality and graphical models in time series analysis. In: Oxford Statistical Science Series, pp. 115–137 (2003)
22. van der Aalst, W.M.P.: Re-engineering knock-out processes. Decis. Support Syst. **30**(4), 451–468 (2001)

Enriching Decision Making with Data-Based Thresholds of Process-Related KPIs

Adela del-Río-Ortega[1](✉), Félix García[2], Manuel Resinas[1], Elmar Weber[3], Francisco Ruiz[2], and Antonio Ruiz-Cortés[1]

[1] Universidad de Sevilla, Seville, Spain
adeladelrio@us.es
[2] Universidad de Castilla La Mancha, Ciudad Real, Spain
[3] Cupenya, B.V., Amsterdam, The Netherlands

Abstract. The continuous performance improvement of business processes usually involves the definition of a set of process performance indicators (PPIs) with their target values. These PPIs can be classified into lag PPIs, which establish a goal that the organization is trying to achieve, though are not directly influenceable by process performers, and lead PPIs, which are influenceable by process performers and have a predictable impact on the lag indicator. Determining thresholds for lead PPIs that enable the fulfillment of the related lag PPI is a key task, which is usually done based on the experience and intuition of the process owners. However, the amount and nature of currently available data make it possible for data-driven decisions to be made in this regard. This paper proposes a method that applies statistical techniques for thresholds determination successfully employed in other domains. Its applicability has been evaluated in a real case study, where data from more than a thousand process executions was used.

Keywords: Thresholds · Process-related KPIs · Process performance indicators · Case study · Decision making · Decision support

1 Introduction

In process-oriented organisational settings, the evaluation of process performance plays a key role in obtaining information on the achievement of their strategic and operational goals. To carry out this evaluation, a performance measurement system (PMS) is implemented, so that business processes (BPs) can be continuously improved [1]. The implementation of this PMS includes the definition of

This work has received funding from the European Commission (FEDER), the European Union's Horizon 2020 research and innovation programme under the Marie Sklodowska-Curie grant agreement No. 645751 (RISE_BPM), Spanish, Andalusian and Castilla La Mancha R&D&I programmes (grants P12–TIC-1867 (COPAS), TIN2015-70560-R (BELI) and PEII-2014-050-P (INGENIOSO)).

E. Dubois and K. Pohl (Eds.): CAiSE 2017, LNCS 10253, pp. 193–209, 2017.
DOI: 10.1007/978-3-319-59536-8_13

a set of PPIs, their target values, and associated alarms that warn whenever certain predetermined value, named threshold [2], is exceeded [3]. These PPIs are quantifiable metrics that allow the efficiency and effectiveness of BPs to be evaluated and can be computed directly from data generated during their execution, either at an instance level (single-instance PPIs) or at a process level, i.e., computed applying certain functions to the execution data gathered from a set of instances (multi-instance PPIs) [4].

Based on these PPIs, several methodologies have been developed to continuously improve the process performance. One of the best known is based on the concept of lag and lead indicators [5]. Performance indicators defined for a business process can be broadly classified into two categories, namely: lag and lead indicators, also known as outcomes and performance drivers respectively. The former establishes a goal that the organization is trying to achieve and is usually linked to a critical success factor. For instance, one could have a PPI for a manuscript management process that specifies that its cycle time should be less than 40 working days in order to keep customer (author) satisfaction. However, the problem of lag indicators is that they tell the organization whether the goal has been achieved, but they are not directly influenceable by the performers of the process. On the contrary, lead indicators have two main characteristics. First, they are predictive in the sense that if the lead indicators are achieved, then it is likely the lag indicator is achieved as well. Second, they are influenceable by the performers of the process, meaning that they should be something that the performers of the process can actively do or not do. For instance, if we think that one major issue that prevents fulfilling the lag indicator is assigning the manuscript to an employee with a large queue of work and we know we can control the queue of work of each employee up to a certain point (e.g. by balancing the work amongst all employees), then reducing the workload could be a lead indicator for the cycle time lag indicator defined above. Each lag indicator may have one or more lead indicators that are influenceable by the process performers and help to predict its value. Therefore, if thresholds are established for those lead indicators, the focus will be on fulfilling lead indicators, which are actionable, and this will enable the fulfillment of the lag indicator.

Determining these thresholds appropriately is, thus, one of the key parts of the methodology. This is usually done based on the experience and intuition of the process owners. However, nowadays, the amount and nature of available data (e.g. event logs) make it possible for data-driven decisions to be made in this regard. Unfortunately, although a number of works to identify relationships between process characteristics and PPIs have been proposed in the last years, e.g. [4,6–8], the identification of proper thresholds for a PPI (lead) in order to support the achievement of another PPI (lag) has not been tackled up to date.

The goal of the presented research is to provide a method to determine the aforementioned thresholds, focusing on single-instance PPIs. To this end, we build on a set of statistical techniques successfully used in other domains for threshold determination [9–11]. In particular, we propose the use of Receiver Operating Characteristic (ROC) curves and the Bender method. While the former allows the pursued thresholds to be determined, the latter provides ranges of values with the associated probabilities of fulfilling the target value. This information is specially useful when the changes required to reach the identified threshold cannot be implemented, since it gives hints on the risk taken.

In order to evaluate this approach, we have performed a case study in the context of the manuscript management process of an international publishing company. In this case, data from the execution of more than a thousand of instances of the selected business process are used to study the relationship between the workload, a lead indicator that measures how busy an employee is, and its cycle time, which is a lag indicator of the process. In this scenario, not only a threshold for the workload is identified, which allows for the achievement of the cycle time target value established. Furthermore, if the actions required to keep the workload under that threshold are not possible, our method provides information about the probabilities of achieving the cycle time target value depending on the range the workload value is located in.

The remainder of this paper is structured as follows. Section 2 discusses related work on both the problem and solution domains. Section 3 describes the method for threshold determination we propose. In Sect. 4, this method is applied in a case study to validate its usefulness. Finally, we conclude the paper and discuss future research directions in Sect. 5.

2 Related Work

This section describes previous research related to the work presented in this paper. Two main streams can be distinguished. One is focused on the problem domain and includes techniques developed to identify relationships between performance indicators. The other is focused on the solution domain and comments on some proposals for the definition of measures and associated thresholds.

2.1 Proposals for the Identification and Definition of PPI Relationships

Concerning the problem domain related research stream, there are a number of proposals that are focused on establishing relationships between PPIs. In particular, within the performance measurement context, there are some works that use different techniques, including correlation analysis or principal component analysis [6,12], for this purpose. In the context of process performance evaluation, there also exist some approaches to define relationships between PPIs such as: Popova and Sharpanskykh [7], where a variant of the first order sorted predicate language is employed to define cause, correlation or aggregation relationships; del-Río-Ortega et al. [4], which extracts PPI relationships with BP elements from their definition through description logic; Diamantini et al. [13], that allows for the explicit definition of algebraic relationships between PPIs using semantic techniques, or de Leoni et al. [8], who use decision and regression trees to correlate process or event characteristics. In addition, other approaches

[6,14] have been presented to quantify these relationships in magnitude and direction, providing information to determine their importance depending on whether the relationships are weak or strong. Although these works provide mechanisms to define and, somehow, quantify relationships between PPIs, none of them allow for the extraction of thresholds for PPIs from execution data. Our approach can be seen, therefore, as complementary to these previous works. Based on the PPI relationships identified with them, and given some objective to fulfill, our approach can provide thresholds for the influencing PPIs that lead to the achievement of the objective.

2.2 Thresholds Definition Proposals

Measurement of business processes is a vast research area and, in related literature, we can find numerous definitions of measures which support business process evaluation from both perspectives: modelling [15,16] and execution [4,7,17]. However, to facilitate a better decision making process from the assessment of the measurement results, it is necessary the specification of limit values or thresholds which indicate whether or not the measurement results are acceptable.

In this context, the research on thresholds associated with business process measures is more limited. Traditionally, the definition of thresholds has been applied in other disciplines such as medicine [9]. On the other hand, in the software engineering area, we can find several proposals mainly focused on measures for object oriented systems [10,11,18]. Several techniques are used for that purpose, including the mean and standard deviation, Bender Method, ROC curves, Linear Regression, clustering algorithms (k-means) and machine learning based methods.

From the business process modelling perspective, the application of techniques for threshold definition has been applied in [2,19,20]. In these works, thresholds for understandability, modifiability and correctness measures of BPMN models are extracted. To do so, Bender method, ROC curves and a new algorithm based on ANOVA called ATEMA are applied. In addition, the application of extracted thresholds to suggest improvement guidelines for business process models in a case study is presented in [21]. This research constitutes the background of the present work, which aims to apply the same threshold extraction techniques in the context of business process execution. The thresholds in this case are extracted from execution data and are aimed at assuring the fulfillment of a given PPI. To the best of our knowledge, there exists no previous work in this direction.

3 Threshold Determination Method

The method we propose is based on the concept of lag and lead indicators [5].

Specifically, our method takes as input the lag PPI, the set of performance indicators that, according to the knowledge of domain experts, can be considered lead PPIs for that particular lag PPI and the values for those lag and lead PPIs computed from a set of process executions. This method includes the following steps: (1) preprocessing; (2) checking the relationship; (3) threshold extraction with Roc Curve; (4) application of the Bender Method to determine probabilities of errors for threshold ranges; (5) threshold validation. In the following, we describe these steps, which are performed for a pair lag PPI-lead PPI, and need to be repeated as may times as lead indicators provided as input.

3.1 Preprocessing

This step is twofold: first, some information need to be gathered in the format it will be required by the statistical techniques that will be applied, and second we need to divide our input data set (with the PPI values) into two. Regarding the former, we need to define a Boolean variable that represents the fulfillment of the lag indicator. In particular, for every process instance considered, we assign this variable the value 1 if the lag PPI is fulfilled, and 0 otherwise. We will refer to this variable as $fulfilledLagPPITargetValue$. As for the latter, we need to split our data set into two groups, one group will be used to define the thresholds and the other to validate them.

3.2 Checking the Relationship

The second step is to prove that the values of the lead PPI do actually have an influence on the fulfillment of the lag PPI. Actually, this is a required step for the two techniques we use later on. ROC curves and the Bender method involve a two-step approach. The first step is about estimating the discriminator function, that allows the aforementioned influence to be checked, and the second is the determination of thresholds and the associated probabilities, that will be described in the following steps (Subsects. 3.3 and 3.4).

We utilize *logistic regression* for estimating a discriminator function, in which the p-value should be lower than 0.05 to confirm that an influence exists. Logistic regression is a statistical model for estimating the probability of binary choices [22]. In our case, we are interested in the binary variable defined in the previous step whose range is $\{fulfillment, non - fulfillment\}$. The idea of a logistic regression is that this probability can be represented by the odds. This is the ratio of fulfillment probability divided by probability of non-fulfillment. The logistic regression estimates the odds based on the logit function, which is:

$$logit(p_i) = ln(\frac{p_i}{1-p_i}) = \alpha + \beta_1 x_{1,i} + \ldots + \beta_k x_{k,i}, \quad (1)$$

where α is called the intercept and β_1, β_2, β_3, etc., are called the regression coefficients of independent variables $x_{1,i}$, $x_{2,i}$, $x_{3,i}$ respectively. In our case we only consider one independent variable for every repetition of the steps, which corresponds to the lead PPI under analysis, i.e. $k = 1$, and observations from i business process instances.

3.3 Threshold Extraction with ROC Curve

"Receiver Operating Characteristics (ROC) curves provide a pure index of accuracy by demonstrating the limits of a test's ability to discriminate between alternative states" (fulfillment/non-fulfillment) [23]. In order to define an ROC curve, two variables need to be specified: one binary, which is the previously defined $fulfilledLagPPITargetValue$ variable, whose values correspond to the fulfillment or not fulfillment of the lag PPI target value; and another continuous, which is the estimated fulfillment probability function from the logistic regression of the lead PPI. In a ROC curve, the true positive rate (sensitivity) is plotted in function of the false positive rate (1-specificity). Each point in the ROC curve represents a pair of sensitivity and 1-specificity corresponding to a particular decision threshold, i.e. it represents the classification performance of any potential threshold.

Table 1. Confusion matrix for lead PPI and threshold.

Classified	Actual	
	Fulfillment	Non-fulfillment
Lead PPI $\leq$ threshold	True positives (TP)	False positives (FP)
Lead PPI $>$ threshold	False negatives (FN)	True negatives (TN)

The determination of the best threshold builds on the confusion matrix (Table 1), for which sensitivity and specificity values are calculated as follows: sensitivity = true positive (TP) rate = TP/(TP+FN), specificity = true negative (TN) rate = TN/(FP+TN), where TP is true positives, FN is false negatives, FP is false positives, and TN is true negatives. A TP is found when the assessment of a value of the lead PPI in relation to the threshold indicates that the lag PPI is likely to be fulfilled in that process instance, and that in fact it does have been fulfilled. Something similar, but with the non-fulfillment, happens to the TN, the assessment of a value of the lead indicator in relation to the threshold indicates that the lag indicator is likely to not be fulfilled in that process instance, and that in fact it has not been fulfilled. On the other hand, an FN indicates that the prediction says that for that value of the lead indicator the lag indicator is not fulfilled while indeed it is. Finally, an FP indicates that the process instance is predicted to fulfill the lag indicator and, actually, it has not fulfilled it.

The test performance is assessed using the Area Under the ROC Curve (AUC). AUC is a widely-used measure of performance of classification [24]. It ranges between 0 and 1, and can be used to assess how good threshold values are at discriminating between groups. According to [22], there exist rules of thumb for assessing the discriminative power of the lead indicator based on AUC. An AUC < 0.5 is considered no good, poor if $0.5 \leq AUC < 0.6$, fair if $0.6 \leq AUC < 0.7$, acceptable if $0.7 \leq AUC < 0.8$, excellent if $0.8 \leq AUC < 0.9$ and outstanding if $0.9 \leq AUC < 1$. The standard error or p-value is estimated using a 95% confidence interval. The test checks if the AUC is significantly different from 0.5.

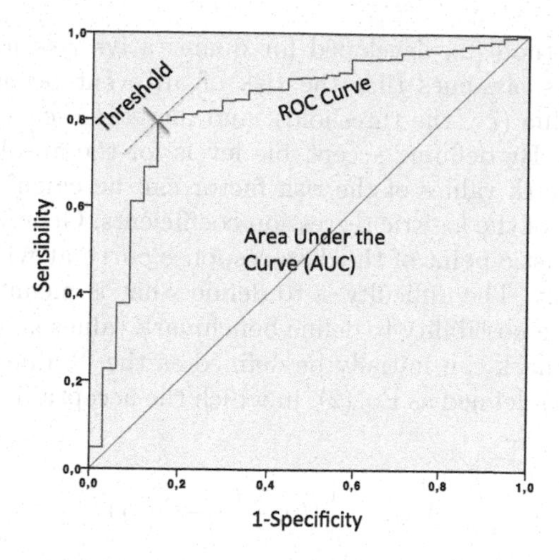

Fig. 1. ROC Curve and threshold.

Then, we can determine a threshold value for the lead PPI based on the ROC curve, but for doing so, wee need a criterion. The purpose is to maximize sensitivity and specificity, while at the same time [22] minimizing false positives and false negatives. Following [2,20], where sensitivity and specificity are considered to be equally important, we select the best threshold as depicted in Fig. 1. The best threshold is the point with the greatest distance from the 0.5 diagonal (that corresponds to a test without any ability to discriminate between the two alternatives).

Due to the involvement of humans in the process execution, one would not expect the same accuracy of predictions as in natural sciences like physics or chemistry [25]. Therefore, it is important to reflect upon the probability of errors associated with this threshold. This probability can be obtained by means of the Bender method as described in the following Subsect. 3.4.

3.4 Application of the Bender Method to Determine Probabilities of Errors for Threshold Ranges

The goal of this step is manifold. First we are interested in determining the probability associated to the threshold obtained in the previous step through the application of ROC curves. In addition, there are situations in which it is not possible to apply the changes required to reach that threshold. In those cases, it is important to provide the decision makers with information about the risk taken accepting other values lower or greater (depending if the threshold is a maximum or a minimum respectively) than the threshold. Therefore, this step also aims at providing other threshold values, or ranges, associated with different probabilities of the lag PPI fulfillment. To this end, the Bender method is applied.

The Bender method [9], developed for quantitative risk assessment in epidemiological studies, assumes that the risk of an event occurring is constant below a specific value (i.e. the threshold), and increases according to a logistic equation otherwise. By defining acceptable levels for the absolute risk, the corresponding benchmark values of the risk factor can be calculated by means of nonlinear functions of the logistic regression coefficients. Generally, a benchmark value is a characteristic point of the dose-response curve at which the risk of an event rises so steeply. The difficulty is to define what is meant by "so steeply". According to [9], one possibility to define benchmark values is based on the logistic curve. A benchmark can initially be defined as the "Value of an Acceptable Risk Level" (VARL) defined as Eq. (2), in which the acceptable risk level is given by a probability p_0.

$$VARL = \frac{1}{\beta}(ln(\frac{p_0}{1-p_0}) - \alpha) \tag{2}$$

$$p_0 = \frac{e^{\alpha+\beta x}}{1+e^{\alpha+\beta x}} \tag{3}$$

In Eq. 2, p_0 represents the probability of an event occurring. This value is indicated by the person who is applying that method and it can vary from 0 to 1. For example, applied to our case, $p_0 = 0.7$ indicates that there is a probability of 0.7 the lead PPI to be considered as appropriate, i.e., to lead to the fulfillment of the lag PPI. On the other hand, α and β are coefficients of a logistic regression equation, as was indicated in Eq. (1). The independent variable in the logistic regression model is the lead PPI for which we want to determine the threshold. The dependent variable must be a binary variable, in our case the $fulfilledLagPPITargetValue$ variable, that evaluates if the lag PPI was fulfilled or not.

We can then use this method to determine the probability associated to the threshold obtained through the application of ROC curves as follows. From the formula of Eq. 2 we can obtain Eq. 3 to calculate that probability, where x is the threshold value previously obtained, and α and β the coefficients also previously obtained. If, for instance, the resulting probability is 0.9, it means that when the lead indicator is lower or equal to the threshold obtained (considering it a maximum), there is a 90% of probability that the lag indicator is fulfilled.

Furthermore, as stated above, we can apply this method to identify other threshold values associated with different probabilities of the target value fulfillment, enriching the information provided to the manager to make a decision. For this purpose, the Bender method requires the definition of p_0, which indicates the probability of considering a BP instance as fulfilling lag indicator. Since there is no recommendation that can be used to configure this variable, we propose 9 values between 0 and 1 with the idea of obtaining a wide group of results. Therefore p_0 starts in 0.1, and 0.1 is added successively until reaching 0.9. Thus, we associate ranges of probability (from 10% to 90%) to different values of the lead PPI (see Table 4 to see the result in our case study).

3.5 Threshold Validation

In order to check the validity of the threshold obtained, we propose the application of cross-validation to that threshold. To this end, the second data set must be used. It is important to highlight that it contains information related to process instances different from those used for threshold determination.

We propose to approach the cross-validation of the thresholds by calculating precision and recall measures for assessing the quality of the prediction, as it is applied for evaluating a search result in information retrieval field [26]. *Precision* is the ratio of true positives to the sum of true and false positives ($Precision = TP/(TP + FP)$) [27]. In our context, this is the ratio of correctly predicted lag PPI fulfillments based on a threshold value in relation to all predicted lag PPI fulfillments. *Recall* is the ratio of true positives to the sum of true positives and false negatives ($Recall = TP/(TP + FN)$) [27]; i.e., the ratio of correctly predicted lag PPI fulfillments based on a threshold value in relation to all actual Lag PPI fulfillments.

To achieve accurate predictions, a technique should achieve both high precision and recall. However, an intrinsic relationship between precision and recall exists: increasing one of them may decrease the other. To combine precision and recall in a single value, literature thus recommends using measures such as the F-measure [28] (also known as F-score or F-1), which is defined in Eq. 4.

$$F\text{-}measure = \frac{2 \times Precision \times Recall}{Precision + Recall} \tag{4}$$

The above measures do not reflect a prediction technique's ability in predicting true negatives [29]. To complement our evaluation, we also propose to include specificity and accuracy measures. *Specificity* (Spec), as explained in Sect. 3, is calculated as the ratio of true negatives to the sum of false positives and true negatives ($Spec = TN/(FP + TN)$), and indicates how many actual non-fulfillments were correctly predicted as non-fulfillments. Finally, the *accuracy* (Acc) is a widespread measure of effectiveness, to evaluate a classifier's performance [30] and it is calculated as the sum of true positives and true negatives to the sum of true and false positives and true and false negatives ($Acc = (TP + TN)/(TP + FP + TN + FN)$), in other words, it is the percentage of correctly classified instances. Precision, recall, F-measure, specificity and accuracy are measures that are appropriate for computing the effectiveness of search results [26,29].

4 Evaluation with a Case Study

In order to evaluate the applicability of our approach, we conducted a case study. It was carried out in the context of an international publishing company[1] aiming at improving its core business processes. In particular, we focused on one of them,

[1] No further information can be provided about the company and its business processes due to privacy reasons.

the process associated to the management of manuscripts from the moment they are received by the editor to their publication (or rejection), trying to identify the relationship between cycle time and workload, as required by the publishing company quality manager. In this process, when a new instance arrives, the manager has to assign it to an employee, so manager's primary job is to divide the work optimally over her team. Currently, a manager is given an overview of his/her employee's progress using a report tool. This tool contains information like the number of instances his/her employees are working on or the subtasks durations. When assigning a given instance to an employee, the manager has to estimate how long this employee will take to finish the process (i.e. the cycle time). In order to help the manager to decide which employee will finish the process faster, it would be desirable to have information available to identify those PPIs or performance measures that have an influence on the value of the cycle time.

The guidelines proposed by Runeson and Höst [31] and Brereton et al. [32] were followed to design and conduct the case study, which is described in the following subsections.

4.1 Case Study Design

We carried out a holistic case study [33], with a single-case, in a single organization and in a single project of the organization. The object of the study was the improvement of the performance of the manuscript management process of this publishing company, and the main objective was to provide the publishing company's managers with additional performance information so that they can divide tasks between employees optimally, obtaining the pursued target value for cycle time. In this context, the cycle time was identified as a lag PPI and the workload as a lead PPI. Thus, the research question for this case study can be defined as follows: *"How does workload influence cycle time and what thresholds can be established for it to assure the fulfillment of the cycle time PPI?"*.

Regarding the case selected, the reasons for this selection are mainly two: first, the quality responsible was particularly interested in improving this process since it is one of the most critical processes from a customer/user point of view and can directly lead the company to success or failure; and second, a huge amount of execution data was available for the analysis. Furthermore, its lag PPI cycle time is very relevant for customer satisfaction according to the quality department of the company. Though there are probably other factors apart from the workload that influence the time it takes to an editor to complete the process, we focused on the workload because we were specifically asked to look at the relationship between workload and cycle time.

4.2 Data Collection and Analysis

The study presented in this paper consists of the application of our method to the execution data retrieved from 1080 process instances of the selected BP. Using insights from a business analytics platform[2], we collected data from the object BP and the computation of workload and cycle time values for each execution. In particular, in the case of workload, the initial definition used was the *begin workload*, i.e., the number of process instances an employee is working on at the start of a new instance. However, we had to change it since, after a first analysis of the data, no apparent connection was found between the defined workload and the duration of a process instance (its cycle time). Instead, the *average workload* was used for this study. It can be defined as the weighted average of the number of instances an employee is working on during a process instance. Regarding cycle time, their values were obtained in milliseconds, as this is the unit provided by the information systems that gather the execution data in the publishing company. Finally, a pursued target value for the cycle time PPI was also provided by the quality department.

1. **Preprocessing**
   The Boolean variable in this case corresponds to the fulfillment of the lag PPI cycle time. The values of this variable were obtained by comparing the cycle time value of each BP instance with the target value established. We assign this variable the value 1 when the cycle time value is lower or equals to its target value, and 0 in other case. In addition, the data set described above was divided into two groups. The values from 700 BP instances were used for threshold extraction, and the values from the remaining 380 BP instances for threshold validation. Table 2 shows the average (μ) and standard deviation (γ) values for workload and cycle time in these two datasets. Workload values represent process instances (PI), and Cycle time values appear in milliseconds, as obtained from the execution data, and in weeks, for readability reasons.

Table 2. Average and standard deviation for workload and cycle time in the two datasets.

Dataset	Workload (PI)		Cycle time (ms)		Cycle time (weeks)	
	μ	γ	μ	γ	μ	γ
Extraction	29.46	12.72	5.43 E9	3.71 E9	8.98	6.14
Validation	25.65	13.67	4.95 E9	3.52 E9	8.19	5.82

2. **Checking the relationship**
   Here we have to prove that workload values do have an influence on the fulfillment of the cycle time target value. So as to apply logistic regression, we are interested in the binary variable $fulfilledCTTargetValue$ with the range $\{fulfillment, non-fulfillment\}$, the independent variable $Workload$, and observations from $i = 700$ business process instances.

[2] Its identity is not revealed for confidentiality restrictions.

Applying the logistic regression to our particular data, we obtain the coefficients (the intercept α and the only regression coefficient β in our case) represented in Table 3. The results show that there exists a correlation between both variables, the workload and the fulfillment of the cycle time target value, and that it is statistically significant, given the resulting p-value for the model of $0.000 < 0.05$. This proves that the workload have an influence on the cycle time.

Table 3. Coefficients of the logistic regression applied to our data.

Coeficients	Value	Std. error	p-value
α	7.994	1.068	0.000
β	−0.137	0.025	0.000

3. **Threshold extraction with ROC Curve**
The ROC curve obtained from our data is depicted in Fig. 1. The resulting AUC value is 0.833, and the p-value 0.000 (<0.05), so the discriminative power of the workload can be considered excellent and significantly different from 0.5 from a statistical point of view. Now, we can determine a threshold value for the workload based on the ROC curve, selecting the point with the greatest distance from the 0.5 diagonal. In this case, this **threshold is 39.68**, which means that for a process instance assigned to an employe working on more than 39.68 instances on average during that instance, will likely not fulfill the pursued cycle time.
4. **Application of the Bender Method to determine probabilities of errors for threshold ranges**
For the application of the Bender method in our case, the independent variable in the logistic regression model is the workload for which we want to determine the threshold, and the dependent variable is $fulfilledCTTargetValue$. From Eq. 3 we get a **probability of 0.93**. This can be interpreted as "if the employee's workload is lower than or equal to 39,68, there is a 93% of probability that she finishes the BP instance in less than the target value of the cycle time".
Furthermore, as stated above, we can apply this method to identify other threshold values associated with different probabilities of the target value fulfillment. Table 4 depicts this information for our case and can be interpreted as follows. For a given instance, If the workload is approximately 74, then the probability of fulfilling the cycle time target value for that instance is 10%, which indicate that the workload is not appropriate at all. Conversely, if the workload is about 48, there is a probability of 80% that the BP instance fulfills the cycle time target value.
5. **Threshold validation**
Finally, the calculations of the different measures defined in Sect. 3.5 in our case study result in the values contained in Table 5. From all the BP instances

Table 4. Workload thresholds with associated probabilities extracted with the Bender method.

Probability of considering the cycle time fulfilled	10%	20%	30%	40%	50%	60%	70%	80%	90%
Workload	74.39	68.47	64.54	61.31	58.35	55.39	52.17	48.23	42.31

Table 5. Values for Precision, Recall, F-measure, Specificity and Accuracy for the extracted threshold.

Precision	Recall	F-measure	Specificity	Accuracy
0.98	0.87	0.92	0.59	0.86

predicted as fulfilling the cycle time target value, 98% of the cases actually fulfilled it. In addition, from all the BP instances that really fulfilled the cycle time target value, 87% were correctly predicted. The lowest value is obtained for the specificity. In this case, from all the non-fulfilments, about 60% are correctly predicted. As for the accuracy, 86% of the cases were correctly predicted. Though there is no existing benchmark to which compare these values, they can be considered acceptable values taking into account they are in general high values. Taking these results into consideration, this approach can be used as a predictive model that supports the decision-making process of the managers in the publishing company, and can be improved in the future with data extracted from further process executions.

4.3 Interpretation of Results

The threshold obtained for the workload can be used to provide a more confident answer to the research question put forth in Sect. 4.1. This information supports managers during the assignment of new manuscripts to editors as follows. When a new manuscript needs to be assigned, the corresponding manager will check workload values for his/her editors, and will select the one with the lowest value. When possible, this workload value should be lower than 39.68, which is the obtained threshold. Otherwise, two options are available: either hiring new editors, which is not the common case at all; or taking certain risk. Our approach also provides information in this direction thanks to the results obtained from the Bender method (c.f. Sect. 3.4). If the manuscript is assigned to an editor with a workload about 48, the probability to fulfill the cycle time target value is 80%, if the workload is closer to 52, the probability of fulfillment is closer to 70%, and so on. In this way, the manager is aware of the risk taken when necessary.

These provided thresholds can serve as a starting point for application in practice, and they should be continuously gauged according to feedback obtained from the practical experience derived from its usage as well as from data produced in future process executions.

4.4 Threats to Validity

In the context of the presented case study, the following types of validity threats can be considered. With regards to the *conclusion validity*, the size of the sample data used to perform the case study is of 1080 execution instances (700 for threshold extraction and 380 for validation), which is a considerable size for these cases, however, the study could be enriched by varying the sizes of the partitions and the samples.

In relation to *construct validity*, which is about reflecting our ability to measure what we want to measure, the measures used in this study (workload and cycle time) are relevant measures used in related literature, and they were measured or computed according to definitions in the related literature (e.g. [34]).

Internal validity concerns whether the effect measured is due to changes caused by the researcher, or from some other unknown cause. The possible threats to internal validity were: ROC curves are used and a possible disadvantage is that the discrimination (sensitivity, specificity) is not the only criterion for a good prediction. A curve with a larger AUC (which is apparently better) could be obtained even though the alternative may show superior performance over almost the entire range of values of the classification threshold. This has been mitigated with the validation of the obtained threshold. In addition, the application of ROC curves mitigates some negative aspects of other statistical techniques which require the setting of several input parameter values, which has the risk of obtaining unrealistic results for a bad setting of such parameters. In addition, ROC curves have a more intuitive interpretation of the results. With regard to the application of the Bender method, the main limitation could be the need of a binary variable as input which requires dichotomization in cases in which this binary variable is not available, with the consequent loss of information. This was not our case, as a binary variable was used as input.

Finally, regarding *external validity*, which describes the possibility of generalizing its results, in this research real data have been used from a representative business process of a company and a useful threshold has been obtained to support decision making in such process, which reinforces its validity. However, the main threat is related to the fact that each business process is particular in each organisation, and the same happens with the PPIs defined for each business process and their associated target values. In other words, the extracted threshold is context-dependent and it is not generalizable to other business processes or companies, but the threshold determination method used in this research could be reused for obtaining thresholds for other representative processes in this company, or even in other companies and domains whenever enough execution data is available. Actually, the organization where our case study was carried out presents several characteristics of organizations that would be interested in applying the same method. For example, there is a set of representative BPs with associated PPIs, from which execution data is recorded on different information systems and from where it is possible to be gathered. Another important characteristic is that the publishing company already has a quality department, which is a key factor for providing key information about PPIs and objectives to be fulfilled.

5 Conclusions and Future Work

In this paper we proposed a method to extract thresholds for lead PPIs that allow the fulfillment of a lag PPI. This method was validated through a case study performed in the context of an international publishing company, using 700 process instances to extract the threshold and 380 for its validation. The extracted thresholds and associated probabilities allow the publishing company managers to decide how to regulate workload levels to achieve the desired cycle time target value, and when to assume certain risks, being aware of the exact risk, according to the probabilities provided.

This method for threshold determination can be also applicable to other domains such as SLAs, where a guarantee term is provided, and It must be fulfilled to avoid penalties. This guarantee term could be seen as the lag PPI and is defined on the basis of other measures, which would be analogous to our lead PPIs. This is part of our future work. Furthermore, we plan to define a tool to support the methodology presented, extend it for multi-instance PPIs and apply it to other different domains.

References

1. Parmenter, D.: Key Performance Indicators (KPI): Developing, Implementing, and Using Winning KPIs. Wiley, Hoboken (2010)
2. Sánchez-González, L., García, F., Ruiz, F., Mendling, J.: A study of the effectiveness of two threshold definition techniques. In: 16th International Conference on Evaluation & Assessment in Software Engineering, EASE 2012, pp. 197–205 (2012)
3. Wetzstein, B., Leitner, P., Rosenberg, F., Dustdar, S., Leymann, F.: Identifying influential factors of business process performance using dependency analysis. Enterp. IS **5**(1), 79–98 (2011)
4. del Río-Ortega, A., Resinas, M., Cabanillas, C., Ruiz-Cortés, A.: On the definition and design-time analysis of process performance indicators. Inf. Syst. **38**(4), 470–490 (2013)
5. McChesney, C., Covey, S., Huling, J.: The 4 Disciplines of Execution: Achieving Your Wildly Important Goals. Simon and Schuster, New York (2012)
6. Rodriguez, R.R., Saiz, J.J.A., Bas, A.O.: Quantitative relationships between key performance indicators for supporting decision-making processes. Comput. Ind. **60**(2), 104–113 (2009)
7. Popova, V., Sharpanskykh, A.: Modeling organizational performance indicators. Inf. Syst. **35**(4), 505–527 (2010)
8. de Leoni, M., van der Aalst, W.M.P., Dees, M.: A general process mining framework for correlating, predicting and clustering dynamic behavior based on event logs. Inf. Syst. **56**, 235–257 (2016)

9. Bender, R.: Quantitative risk assessment in epidemiological studies investigating threshold effects. Biometrical J. **41**(3), 305–319 (1999)
10. Shatnawi, R., Li, W., Swain, J., Newman, T.: Finding software metrics threshold values using ROC curves. J. Softw. Maint. Evol. **22**(1), 1–16 (2010)
11. Catal, C., Alan, O., Balkan, K.: Class noise detection based on software metrics and ROC curves. Inf. Sci. **181**(21), 4867–4877 (2011)
12. Youngblood, A.D., Collins, T.R.: Addressing balanced scorecard trade-off issues between performance metrics using multi-attribute utility theory. Eng. Manag. J. **15**(1), 11–17 (2003)
13. Diamantini, C., Genga, L., Potena, D., Storti, E.: Collaborative building of an ontology of key performance indicators. In: Meersman, R., Panetto, H., Dillon, T., Missikoff, M., Liu, L., Pastor, O., Cuzzocrea, A., Sellis, T. (eds.) OTM 2014. LNCS, vol. 8841, pp. 148–165. Springer, Heidelberg (2014). doi:10.1007/978-3-662-45563-0_9
14. Patel, B., Chaussalet, T., Millard, P.: Balancing the NHS balanced scorecard!. Eur. J. Oper. Res. **185**(3), 905–914 (2008)
15. Sánchez-González, L., García, F., Ruiz, F., Piattini, M.: Toward a quality framework for business process models. Int. J. Coop. Inf. Syst. **22**(01), 1350003 (2013)
16. Mendling, J.: Metrics for Process Models: Empirical Foundations of Verification, Error Prediction, and Guidelines for Correctness. LNBIP, vol. 6. Springer, Heidelberg (2008)
17. Delgado, A., Weber, B., Ruiz, F., de Guzmán, I.G.R., Piattini, M.: An integrated approach based on execution measures for the continuous improvement of business processes realized by services. Inf. Softw. Technol. **56**(2), 134–162 (2014)
18. Herbold, S., Grabowski, J., Waack, S.: Calculation and optimization of thresholds for sets of software metrics. Empir. Softw. Eng. **16**(6), 812–841 (2011)
19. Sánchez-González, L., García, F., Ruiz, F., Mendling, J.: Quality indicators for business process models from a gateway complexity perspective. Inf. Softw. Technol. **54**(11), 1159–1174 (2012)
20. Mendling, J., Sánchez-González, L., García, F., Rosa, M.L.: Thresholds for error probability measures of business process models. J. Syst. Softw. **85**(5), 1188–1197 (2012)
21. Sánchez-González, L., García, F., Ruiz, F., Piattini, M.: A case study about the improvement of business process models driven by indicators. Softw. Syst. Model., 1–30 (2015). doi:10.1007/s10270-015-0482-0
22. Hosmer, D., Lemeshow, S.: Applied Logistic Regression. Wiley, Hoboken (2004)
23. Zweig, M.H., Campbell, G.: Receiver-operating characteristic (ROC) plots: a fundamental evaluation tool in clinical medicine. Clin. Chem. **39**(4), 561–577 (1993)
24. Hand, D.J.: Measuring classifier performance: a coherent alternative to the area under the ROC curve. Mach. Learn. **77**(1), 103–123 (2009)
25. Morasca, S., Ruhe, G.: Introduction: knowledge discovery from empirical software engineering data. Int. J. Softw. Eng. Knowl. Eng. **09**(05), 495–498 (1999)
26. Baeza-Yates, R.A., Ribeiro-Neto, B.A.: Modern Information Retrieval. ACM Press/Addison-Wesley, New York/Boston (1999)
27. Olson, D.L., Delen, D.: Advanced Data Mining Techniques, 1st edn. Springe, Heidelberg (2008). Incorporated
28. Salfner, F., Lenk, M., Malek, M.: A survey of online failure prediction methods. ACM Comput. Surv. **42**(3), 10:1–10:42 (2010)
29. Metzger, A., Leitner, P., Ivanovic, D., Schmieders, E., Franklin, R., Carro, M., Dustdar, S., Pohl, K.: Comparing and combining predictive business process monitoring techniques. IEEE Trans. Syst. Man Cybern.: Syst. **45**(2), 276–290 (2015)

30. Michie, D., Spiegelhalter, D.J., Taylor, C.C., Campbell, J. (eds.): Machine Learning, Neural and Statistical Classification. Ellis Horwood, Upper Saddle River (1994)
31. Runeson, P., Höst, M.: Guidelines for conducting and reporting case study research in software engineering. Empir. Softw. Eng. **14**(2), 131–164 (2009)
32. Brereton, P., Kitchenham, B., Budgen, D.: Using a protocol template for case study planning. In: Proceedings of EASE 2008, BCS-eWiC (2008)
33. Yin, R.: Case Study Research: Design and Methods. Applied Social Research Methods. SAGE Publications, Thousand Oaks (2009)
34. Nakatumba, J.: Resource-aware business process management: analysis and support. Ph.D. thesis, Eindhoven University of Technology (2014)

Characterizing Drift from Event Streams of Business Processes

Alireza Ostovar(✉), Abderrahmane Maaradji, Marcello La Rosa, and Arthur H.M. ter Hofstede

Queensland University of Technology, Brisbane, Australia
{alireza.ostovar,abderrahmane.maaradji,m.larosa,a.terhofstede}@qut.edu.au

Abstract. Early detection of business process drifts from event logs enables analysts to identify changes that may negatively affect process performance. However, detecting a process drift without characterizing its nature is not enough to support analysts in understanding and rectifying process performance issues. We propose a method to characterize process drifts from event streams, in terms of the behavioral relations that are modified by the drift. The method builds upon a technique for online drift detection, and relies on a statistical test to select the behavioral relations extracted from the stream that have the highest explanatory power. The selected relations are then mapped to typical change patterns to explain the detected drifts. An extensive evaluation on synthetic and real-life logs shows that our method is fast and accurate in characterizing process drifts, and performs significantly better than alternative techniques.

1 Introduction

Business processes evolve over time in response to different types of change, such as changes in regulations, competition, supply, demand, technological capabilities, as well as seasonal effects. Some process changes are intentional and planned ahead, while others may occur without being noticed or documented, such as changes resulting from ad-hoc workarounds initiated by individuals in emergency situations, or changes that are due to the replacement of human resources. Over time, these changes may affect process performance, and more generally hinder process improvement initiatives.

In this regard, there is a need for techniques and tools that can discover and characterize, as soon as possible, *process drifts* [13], i.e. statistically significant changes in the behavior of business processes. Accordingly, several techniques have been proposed to detect and localize process drifts from process execution logs (*event logs*) recorded by supporting IT systems [2,5,6,13,14,17]. However, detection and localization of a process drift does not provide, per se, enough insight to undertake a process improvement initiative, unless the drift is characterized, i.e. unless one can understand *what* has changed in the process behavior. To the best of our knowledge, there has not been any attempt to provide a systematic solution for characterizing process drifts.

E. Dubois and K. Pohl (Eds.): CAiSE 2017, LNCS 10253, pp. 210–228, 2017.
DOI: 10.1007/978-3-319-59536-8_14

In this paper, we propose a fully automated online method for characterizing process drifts from event streams. For each detected drift, we perform a statistical test to measure the statistical association between the drift and the distributions of the α^+ relations of process behavior extracted from the event stream before and after the drift. We then rank the relations based on their relative frequency change, and try to match them with a set of predefined change templates. The best-matching templates are then reported to the user as the changes underpinning the drift. We extensively evaluated the accuracy of our method by simulating event streams from artificial and real-life logs. The results show that the approach is fast and highly accurate in characterizing common change patterns, and performs significantly better than state-of-the-art techniques for log delta analysis and model-to-model comparison.

The paper is structured as follows. Section 2 discusses related work. Section 3 introduces the proposed method while Sects. 4 and 5 present its evaluation on synthetic and real-life logs, respectively. Section 6 concludes the paper.

2 Related Work

The literature abounds of methods for detecting process drifts [2,5,6,13,14,17]. These methods are based on the idea of extracting features (e.g. patterns) from the process behavior recorded in event logs or in event streams. For example, Bose et al. [5] rely on a statistical test over feature vectors. The user is asked to specify which features to be used for drift detection, implying that they have a-priori knowledge of the possible nature of the drift. In our previous work we introduced two online drift detection methods based on streams of traces [13] or streams of events [17]. The basic idea is to monitor the distribution of a specific feature representing process behavior over two juxtaposed time windows sliding over the trace (event) stream in order to detect a process drift. However, as already remarked, all the above methods only focus on process drift detection, and while some can also localize with high accuracy the drift in the log, none can actually characterize the drift detected.

A possible approach to characterize process drifts is to compare the two process models automatically discovered from the sublogs (or substreams) before and after the drift point. In [3], Armas-Cervantes et al. identify behavioral differences between two process models using canonically reduced event structures. Despite the set of retrieved differences being complete, the accuracy of this approach for process drift characterization highly depends on the quality of the discovered process models. In fact, techniques for automated process discovery are not designed to create overfitting models, i.e. models that do not generalize the behavior of the log [1]. So these models may intentionally add behavior. In addition, these models may be underfitting, i.e. they may not be able to fully capture the process behavior recorded in the log, hence missing behavior [1], especially if the process behavior captured in the log is highly varied. To avoid the possible bias introduced by automated process discovery techniques, one can use log delta analysis techniques, i.e. perform the comparison directly at the level of the log, rather than at the level of the model extracted from the log. In this context, Van Beest et al. [4] propose a technique to detect behavioral differences between two event logs and explain them via natural language statements, by extracting event structures from logs. This technique may be applied for drift characterization by using the two event sublogs (substreams) extracted from before and after the drift point. In the evaluation of our method, we experiment both with the technique for model-to-model comparison in [3], in combination with state-of-the-art techniques for automated process discovery, as well as with the technique for log-to-log comparison in [4].

Drift detection has also been studied in the field of data mining [10], where a widely studied challenge is that of designing efficient learning algorithms that can adapt to data that evolves over time (a.k.a. concept drift). In this context, the term *drift characterization* is often used to refer to the identification of the drift nature, e.g. sudden or gradual [20], as well as the identification of features that explain the drift. For instance, in [18], brushed parallel histograms are used for visualizing concept drifts in multidimensional problem spaces. However, the methods developed in this context deal with simple structures (e.g. numerical or categorical variables and vectors thereof), while in business process drift characterization we seek to characterize changes in more complex structures, specifically behavioral relations between process tasks, such as concurrency, conflicts and loops. Thus, methods from the field of concept drift characterization in data mining cannot be readily transposed to business process drift characterization.

3 Drift Characterization Method

The purpose of process drift characterization is to identify the differences in the process behavior before and after the drift point that best explain the drift. In [17], the α^+ binary relations are shown to be suitable for capturing process behavior, in particular in the context of highly variable business processes. These behavioral relations and their frequencies are extracted from the time window containing the most recent events of the stream. As a preprocessing operation, each time this window slides, a snapshot of the process behavior is captured and stored as a *data point*. Each binary relation actually represents a dimension of the stored data point, while the frequency of this relation is the scalar in this dimension. Sliding the window along the event stream provides us with a set of data points representing snapshots of the pre-drift and post-drift process behaviors. These data points are used as input to our two-stage characterization method.

In Stage 1 we measure the statistical association of each of the α^+ relations with the drift using an information gain metric. Those relations that are significantly associated with the drift are then ordered based on their explanatory power with respect to the drift. In Stage 2, the resulting ordered list of relations is fed to a template matching algorithm, where we find the best-matching templates that characterize the drift. The identified templates are then reported to the user in natural language. An overview of our method is shown in Fig. 1. The rest of this section describes the method in detail.

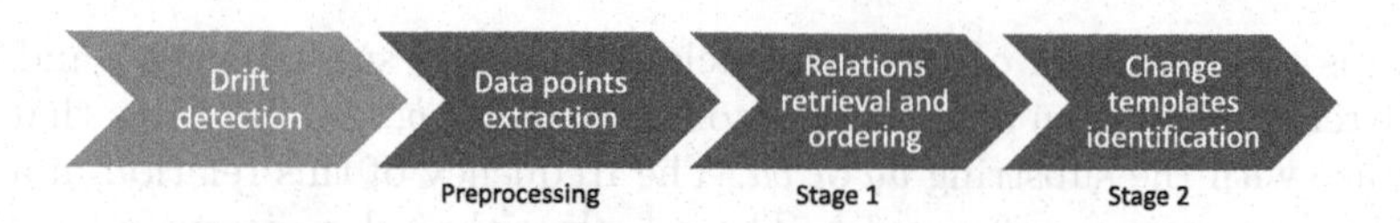

Fig. 1. Overview of our method for process drift characterization.

3.1 Preliminaries

Event logs are at the core of all process mining techniques. An event log is a set of traces, each capturing the sequence of events originated from a given process instance. Each event represents an occurrence of an activity. The configuration where these events are read individually from an online source is known as event streaming. An event stream is a potentially infinite sequence of events, where events are ordered by time and indexed. Events of the same trace do not need to be consecutive in the event stream, i.e. traces can be "overlapping". Formally:

Definition 1 (Event log, Trace, Event stream). Let L be an *event log* over the set of labels $\mathcal{L}$, i.e. $L \in \mathbb{P}(\mathcal{L}^*)$. Let $\mathcal{E}$ be the set of event occurrences and $\lambda : \mathcal{E} \rightarrow \mathcal{L}$ a labelling function. An *event trace* $\sigma \in L$ is defined in terms of an order $i \in [0, n-1]$ and a set of events $\mathcal{E}_\sigma \subseteq \mathcal{E}$ with $|\mathcal{E}_\sigma| = n$ such that $\sigma = \langle \lambda(e_0), \lambda(e_1), \ldots, \lambda(e_{n-1}) \rangle$. An *event stream* is a partial bijective function $S : \mathbb{N}^+ \rightarrow \mathcal{E}$ that maps every element from the index $\mathbb{N}^+$ to $\mathcal{E}$.

In this paper, we use the α^+ relations, as an extension of the α relations, to capture the behavior of a process. The α-algorithm defines three exclusive relations: *conflict*, *concurrency* and *causality*. The α^+-algorithm adds two more relations: *length-two loop* and *length-one loop*. The α^+ relations are formally defined as follows:

Definition 2 (α^+ Relations from [15]**).** Let L be an event log over $\mathcal{L}$. Let a,b $\in \mathcal{L}$:

- $a \triangle_L b$ if and only if there is a trace $\sigma = l_1 l_2 l_3 ... l_n$ and $i \in 1, ..., n-2$ such that $\sigma \in L$ and $l_i = l_{i+2} = a$ and $l_{i+1} = b$,
- $a \diamond_L b$ if and only if $a \triangle_L b$ and $b \triangle_L a$,
- $a >_L b$ if and only if there is a trace $\sigma = l_1 l_2 l_3 ... l_{n-1}$ and $i \in 1, ..., n-2$ such that $\sigma \in L$ and $l_i = a$ and $l_{i+1} = b$,
- $a \rightarrow_L b$ if and only if $a >_L b$ and $(b \not>_L a$ or $a \diamond_L b)$,
- $a \#_L b$ if and only if $a \not>_L b$ and $b \not>_L a$, and
- $a \parallel_L b$ if and only if $a >_L b$ and $b >_L a$, and $a \not\diamond_L b$.

A length-two loop relation, including a and b, is denoted with $a \triangle_L b$. The frequency of this relation in a log is the number of occurrences of the substring *aba*. A causality relation from a to b is denoted with $a \rightarrow_L b$. The frequency of this relation in a log is the number of occurrences of the substring *ab*. A parallel relation between a and b is denoted with $a \parallel_L b$. The frequency of this relation in a log is the minimum of the frequencies of the two substrings, ab and ba. A conflict relation between a and b is denoted with $a\#_L b$, and indicates that there is no trace with the substring ab or ba. The frequency of this relation in a log is the sum of occurrences of a and b. The α^+-algorithm also discovers length-one loop relations (denoted as $\circlearrowleft$) as a pre-processing operation. For example, there is a length-one loop including the activity a in a log if there is a trace with the substring aa. The frequency of this relation in a log is the number of occurrences of the substring aa.

3.2 Preprocessing: Data Points Extraction

For drift detection, we use our technique in [17], which works in online settings with event streams of highly-variable business processes. This technique has been shown to be the state of the art in process drift detection, both in terms of detection accuracy and detection delay. However, our characterization method can in principle be used on top of any process drift detection technique.

Our detection technique captures process behavior by extracting α^+ binary relations in two juxtaposed windows of the same size, namely *reference* and *detection* windows, sliding along the event stream. The most recent events are equally divided into these two windows, where the reference window contains the less recent events, and the detection window contains the more recent ones. The size of these windows is adjusted using a formula based on the maximum number of distinct activity labels within the two windows. This adaptive window sizing ensures that there are enough events in each window for accurately capturing the process behavior.

We use the detection window as a snapshot of the most recent process behavior. Each time this window slides with the stream on arrival of a new event, we extract α^+ relations and their frequencies and store them as a multidimensional data point in a buffer, namely *characterization buffer*. Each α^+ relation represents a dimension of this data point. By sliding the detection window the new data points are added to the head of the buffer. As a drift is detected, the *P–value* of the statistical test (e.g. *G–test* in [17]) drops below the detection threshold (drift point). At this point we stop inserting any new data point into the characterization buffer. We then remove the last w (window size at drift point) data points from the head of the characterization buffer, as these data points may include the post-drift process behavior. This results in a set of recent data points that only encode the process behavior from the pre-drift area. We retain these data points for characterizing the detected drift.

The *P–value* remains below threshold until the process behaviors within the two reference and detection windows become statistically similar. In other words until the process behavior, reflected in the event stream, starts to stabilize. Therefore, we call the point where *P–value* returns to above the detection threshold a *stabilization point*. This is where we start inserting new data points into the characterization buffer, as the detection window only includes the behavior from the post-drift process. We continue extracting data points from the event stream with the next n incoming events. We define n as the *characterization delay*, as it indicates the delay that is needed after the stabilization point to characterize the drift. Similarly, we consider only the n most recent pre-drift data points for drift characterization. In Sect. 4.2, we perform an experiment to determine the suitable characterization delay that leads to a hight accuracy of retrieving and ordering the relevant binary relations. The behavioral relations extraction, explained above, is illustrated in Fig. 2.

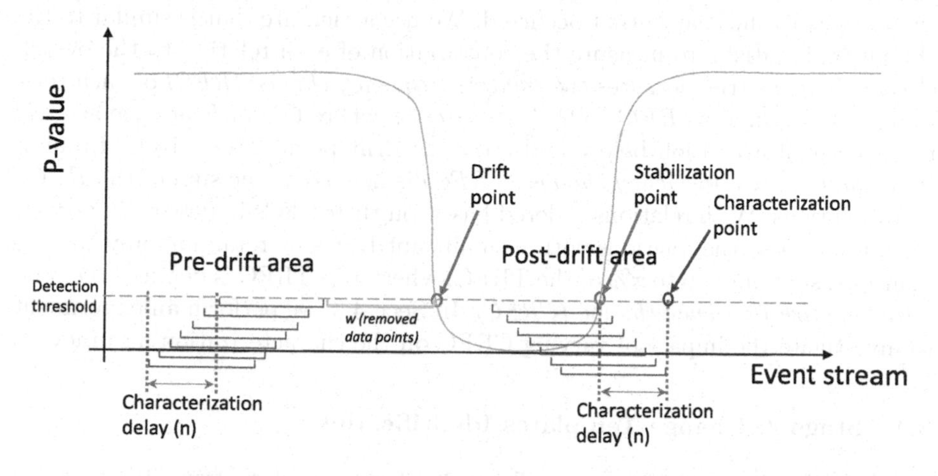

Fig. 2. From drift detection to drift characterization.

3.3 Stage 1: Relevant Binary Relations Retrieval and Ordering

The purpose of the first stage of our approach is to identify and order the α^+ binary relations that are statistically associated with the detected drift. In other words, we would like to measure the explanatory power of each relation with respect to the detected drift. We approach this issue as a classification problem with the α^+ binary relations, extracted from the event stream, as the explanatory variables, and the binary target variable defined with the labels *pre-drift* and *post-drift*. One might first opt for a logistic regression model because of its additive and interpretability properties. However, the logistic regression requires the least correlation between the independent variables (multicollinearity problem [16]). Such a requirement cannot be guaranteed, particularity in our case where the binary relations come from the same process (model). We opted for a less restrictive classification approach, namely decision tree, where we use K-sample permutation test (KSPT) in order to measure the statistical association between each individual explanatory variable (here a binary relation) and the target variable (the drift classification variable). Similarly to the *information gain*, the permutation test allows us to measure the mutual information between two variables. We opted for the permutation test since it is more suitable for small sample sizes [9]. We perform a pairwise permutation test to measure the significance of the statistical association of each binary relation with the target variable (drift). This latter is encoded with the value 0 (resp. 1) for the pre-drift (resp. post-drift) behavior. If the null hypothesis is rejected, we discard the relation as it is not significantly associated with the drift.

As suggested in [9], the KSPT can be applied to identify the relevant features, then an appropriate distance measure is used to order the selected features. Indeed, despite identifying the relations that are found to be statistically associated with our binary drift target variable, some relations may contribute more than others to the change that occurred. We use a measure that is similar to the chi-squared statistic to measure the contribution of each relation to the overall change. This metric measures the *relative frequency change (RFC)* of each relation, and is defines as $RFC = {(O-E)^2}/{max(O,E)}$, where O and E are the average frequencies of a relation before and after the drift point, respectively. In addition, *total relative frequency change (TRFC)* is defined as the sum of the $RFCs$ of all relations. With relations ordered based on their RFCs in descending order, we can filter out the relations with insignificant RFCs by retaining only the top relations, summing up to $x\%$ of the TRFC, where $x\%\cdot$ TRFC is defined as *cumulative relative frequency change (CRFC)*. In Sect. 4.3, we perform an experiment to investigate the impact of varying CRFC on the characterization accuracy.

3.4 Stage 2: Change Templates Identification

The output of the Stage 1 is a list of relations ordered based on their explanatory power (RFC) with respect to the drift, where the first ordered relation and the last ordered relation have the highest and the lowest explanatory power, respectively. In the stage 2, we aim to match the relations with the typical change patterns that may characterize the drift the best. For that we define a set of templates based on the change patterns defined in [21]. These templates, summarized in Table 1, describe different generic change operations commonly occurring in business process models, such as adding/removing an activity, making an activity loopable, swapping two activities, or parallelizing two sequential activities. Each template is represented based on α^+ binary relations. We try to match the process relations, obtained from Stage 1, with the binary relations of the predefined templates. Using a matching confidence

Table 1. Change templates from [21].

Code	Simple change template	Cat.
sre	Add/remove activity between two process fragments	I
pre	Add/remove activity to/from parallel branch	I
cre	Add/remove activity to/from conditional branch	I
cp	Duplicate activity	I
rp	Substitute activity	I
sw	Swap two activities	I
sm	Move activity to between two process fragments	I
pm	Move activity into/out of parallel branch	I
cm	Move activity into/out of conditional branch	I
cf	Make activities conditional/sequential	R
pl	Make activities parallel/sequential	R
cd	Synchronize two activities	R
lp	Make activity loopable/non-loopable	O
cb	Make activity skippable/non-skippable	O
fr	Change branching frequency	O

metric we find the best matching between templates and the process relations. In the rest, we explain our template matching algorithm in detail.

Example 1. *As a running example, let us assume the output of the stage 1 of our method is the ordered relation list of* $\langle$ $e \rightarrow f$: $-$, $e \parallel f$: $+$, $e \rightarrow g$: $+$, $d \rightarrow f$: $+$, $a \rightarrow b$: $-$, $f \rightarrow g$: $\searrow$, $d \rightarrow e$: $\searrow$, $b \rightarrow c$: $-$, $a \rightarrow c$: $+$$\rangle$, *where* $+$ *(resp.* $-$*) indicates that the relation appeared (resp. disappeared) after the drift, and* $\nearrow$ *(resp.* $\searrow$*) indicates that the frequency of the relation increased (resp. decreased) after the drift.*

In the remainder of this paper, unless otherwise indicated, we use both "feature" and "relation" to refer to an α^+ binary relation between two activity labels. A *feature set* is used to represent the α^+ relations before or after the drift, and is defined as follows.

Definition 3 (Feature Set). Let $\mathcal{L}$ be a set of activity labels, and $\mathcal{T} := \{\rightarrow, \|, \#, \circlearrowleft, \triangle\}$ a set of binary α^+ relations symbols, denoting causality, concurrency, conflict, length one and two loops, respectively. A *feature set* $F\colon \mathcal{L} \times \mathcal{L} \rightarrowtail \mathcal{T}$ is a partial function that yields the type of α^+ relation between two labels.

Two feature sets, will be used to represent the sets of the discovered features before and after a given drift point, along with a classification of a feature frequency change before and after the drift point. The classification only considers the relations that existed both before and after the occurrence of the drift, in our example $\{f \rightarrow g, d \rightarrow e\}$. A relation is classified as increasing ($\nearrow$), decreasing ($\searrow$) or not applicable ($\perp$), depending on whether its frequency increased, decreased, or remained unchanged. A relation that disappeared (resp. appeared) after the drift does not need to be classified as it only belongs to the pre-drift (resp. post-drift) feature set. All the features existing before and after the drift are ordered in terms of their explanatory power. The two feature sets from before and after the drift, the classification and the ordering functions form a *drift feature set* which constitutes the output of the first stage of our method. Formally, a drift feature set is defined as follows:

Definition 4 (Drift Feature Set). Let $\mathcal{O} := \{\nearrow, \searrow, \perp\}$ be a set of feature frequency change types. A *drift feature set* is a tuple $D := \langle F_{pre}, F_{post}, \mathit{Diff}_D, \sqsubseteq, \mathcal{L}\rangle$, where F_{pre} (resp. F_{post}) is the feature set before (resp. after) a drift, Diff_D is a classification function defined as $\mathit{Diff}_D\colon F_{pre} \cap F_{post} \rightarrow \mathcal{O}$, and $\sqsubseteq$ is a total order on $F_{pre} \cup F_{post}$.

The following function returns the index of a feature in a given drift feature set.

Definition 5 (Rank). Let $\preceq$ be a total order on a finite set $\mathcal{B}$. For all $b \in \mathcal{B}$, $\mathit{Rank}(b, \preceq, \mathcal{B}) = |\{b' \in \mathcal{B} \mid b' \preceq b\}|$.

Example 2. *With the Definition 4, Example 1 is represented as a drift feature set* $D^1 = \langle F_{pre}^{D^1}, F_{post}^{D^1}, \mathit{Diff}_D, \searrow, \mathcal{L} \rangle$, *where* $\mathcal{L} = \{a, b, c, d, e, f, g\}$, $F_{pre}^{D^1} = \{e \rightarrow f,$

$a \to b,\ f \to g,\ d \to e,\ b \to c\}$, $F^{D^1}_{post} = \{e \parallel f,\ e \to g,\ d \to f,\ f \to g,\ d \to e,\ a \to c\}$, $\sqsubseteq\ = \langle\, e \to f,\ e \parallel f,\ e \to g,\ d \to f,\ a \to b, f \to g,\ d \to e,\ b \to c,\ a \to c\rangle$, *and* $Diff_D\ = \{\,(f \to g, \searrow), (d \to e, \searrow)\}$.

Our drift characterization method aims at explaining a detected drift using predefined change templates. In this regard, we define a set of change templates representing the typical change patterns [21]. These templates are presented in Table 1. A change template is represented by a process model fragment before the change compared to another process model fragment after the change.

Consequently, a *template* is a generic way to describe a typical change pattern. It enumerates the expected sets of relations before and after the change based on a change pattern representation. The relations that are present in both process model fragments, before and after the change, need to be classified based on their expected frequency evolution in the change pattern. Besides, the importance of every relation in the change pattern is appended to the template. A template handles variables that can be instantiated with actual activity labels in a matching operation.

Definition 6 (Template). Let $\mathcal{V}$ be a set of variables, $\mathcal{T}$ a set of α^+ binary relations symbols, and $\mathcal{O}$ a set of relation frequency change types. A *template* is a tuple $T := \langle\, T_{pre}, T_{post}, Diff_T, \mathcal{S}, \mathcal{V}\rangle$ where $T_{pre} : \mathcal{V} \times \mathcal{V} \rightarrowtail \mathcal{T}$ represents the relations before the change, $T_{post} : \mathcal{V} \times \mathcal{V} \rightarrowtail \mathcal{T}$ represents the relations after the change, $Diff_T$ is a classification function defined as $Diff_T : T_{pre} \cap T_{post} \to \mathcal{O}$, and $\mathcal{S}$ is a function specifying the importance of each relation to the template T defined as $\mathcal{S} : T_{pre} \cup T_{post} \to (0, 1]$.

Example 3. *Let us assume the two change templates, parallelize activities* (T^{pl}) *and remove activity* (T^{sre}), *for our example, illustrated in the Figs. 3 and 4, respectively. With the Definition 6* $T^{pl} = \langle\{X \to Y,\ W \to X,\ Y \to Z\},\ \{X \parallel Y,\ W \to Y,\ X \to Z,\ W \to X,\ Y \to Z\},\ \{(W \to X, \searrow),\ (Y \to Z, \searrow)\},\ \{(X \to Y, 1),\ (W \to X, 1),\ (Y \to Z, 1),\ (X \parallel Y, 1),\ (W \to Y, 1),\ (X \to Z, 1)\},\ \{W, X, Y, Z\}\rangle$, *and* $T^{sre} = \langle\{X \to Y,\ Y \to Z\},\ \{X \to Z\},\ \varnothing,\ \{(X \to Y, 1),\ (Y \to Z, 1),\ (X \to Z, 1)\},\ \{X, Y, Z\}\rangle$.

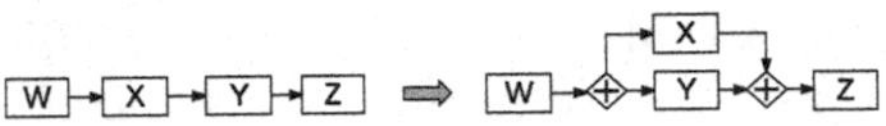

Fig. 3. Parallelize activities template (T^{pl})

Fig. 4. Remove activity template (T^{sre})

In order to explain a drift, the discovered features represented with a drift feature set are matched to a predefined template. All the variables in the template need to be mapped to a label from the drift feature set. This operation is called a *valid instantiation*, and is defined as follows:

Definition 7 (Valid Instantiation). Given a drift feature set $D := \langle F_{pre}, F_{post}, Diff_D, \sqsubseteq, \mathcal{L}\rangle$, and a template $T := \langle T_{pre}, T_{post}, Diff_T, \mathcal{S}, \mathcal{V}\rangle$, a *valid instantiation of* T *through* D is a function $\mathcal{I}_{D,T} : \mathcal{V} \rightarrow \mathcal{L}$ such that

- $T_{pre}(v_1, v_2) = t_1$ *iff* $F_{pre}(\mathcal{I}_{D,T}(v_1), \mathcal{I}_{D,T}(v_2)) = t_1$,
- $T_{post}(v_3, v_4) = t_2$ *iff* $F_{post}(\mathcal{I}_{D,T}(v_3), \mathcal{I}_{D,T}(v_4)) = t_2$, and
- $Diff_T(v_5, v_6) = \vartheta$ *iff* $Diff_D(\mathcal{I}_{D,T}(v_5), \mathcal{I}_{D,T}(v_6)) = \vartheta$

Example 4. *In our example, we can have two valid instantiations, one per template. The first instantiation* $I_{D^1,T^{pl}} = \{ W : d, X : e, Y : f, Z : g\}$, *whereas the second instantiation* $I_{D^1,T^{sre}} = \{ X : a, Y : b, Z : c\}$.

A confidence is calculated for each matching (valid instantiation) in order to assess the likelihood of such a matching. The *confidence of an instantiation* is based on the *Discounted Cumulative Gain* (DCG) measure [11], which indicates the quality of ranking relations in a drift feature set with regards to their predefined importance in a template. In our method, we consider the same importance of 1 for all the relations of a template. The confidence of an instantiation is defined as follows.

Definition 8 (Confidence in an Instantiation). Given a drift feature set $D := \langle F_{pre}, F_{post}, Diff_D, \sqsubseteq, \mathcal{L}\rangle$, a template $T := \langle T_{pre}, T_{post}, Diff_T, \mathcal{S}, \mathcal{V}\rangle$, and a valid instantiation $\mathcal{I}_{D,T} : \mathcal{V} \rightarrow \mathcal{L}$, the *confidence* $\mathcal{C}(\mathcal{I}_{D,T})$ of D matching T through $\mathcal{I}_{D,T}$ is:

$$\mathcal{C}(\mathcal{I}_{D,T}) = \sum_{(x,y,t)\in T_{pre}\cup T_{post}} \frac{\mathcal{S}(x,y,t)}{\log_2(Rank((\mathcal{I}_{D,T}(x), \mathcal{I}_{D,T}(y), t),\ \sqsubseteq,\ F_{pre}\cup F_{post}) + 1)}$$

Example 5. *In our example, the confidence of* $I_{D^1,T^{pl}}$ *is calculated as follows:* $C(I_{D^1,T^{pl}}) = \frac{1}{\log_2(1+1)} + \frac{1}{\log_2(2+1)} + \frac{1}{\log_2(3+1)} + \frac{1}{\log_2(4+1)} + \frac{1}{\log_2(6+1)} + \frac{1}{\log_2(7+1)} \approx 2.25$. *The confidence of* $I_{D^1,T^{sre}}$ *is calculated in the same way and approximates to* 0.62.

As we want to find the best-matching template among all matching templates we need to rank them based on their confidences. However, as the number of relations in different templates may not be the same, we need to normalize the confidence of an instantiation with respect to the maximal confidence of its template. Similarly to the normalized DCG (nDCG) [11], we first define the notion of *ideal confidence* of a template T as the DCG obtained after ordering relations of T based on their importance defined by $\mathcal{S}$. The *normalized confidence (nC)* of an instantiation is calculated by dividing the confidence of the instantiation by the ideal confidence of its template.

Definition 8 (continued). The *Ideal confidence* $i\mathcal{C}(T)$ of T is computed as $i\mathcal{C}(T) = \sum_{(x,y,t)\in T_{pre}\cup T_{post}} \frac{\mathcal{S}(x,y,t)}{\log_2(Rank((x,y,t),\ \geq,\ \text{range}(\mathcal{S})) + 1)}$, and the *normalized confidence* $n\mathcal{C}(\mathcal{I}_{D,T})$ of D matching T through $\mathcal{I}_{D,T}$ is computed as $n\mathcal{C}(\mathcal{I}_{D,T}) = \frac{\mathcal{C}(\mathcal{I}_{D,T})}{i\mathcal{C}(\mathcal{I}_{D,T})}$.

Example 6. *In our example,* $iC(T^{pl}) \approx 2.30$ *and* $nC(I_{D^1,T^{pl}}) \approx 0.98$*, whereas* $iC(T^{sre}) \approx 1.13$ *and* $nC(I_{D^1,T^{sre}}) \approx 0.54$*. As* $nC(I_{D^1,T^{pl}}) \geq nC(I_{D^1,T^{sre}})$*,* T^{pl} *is identified as the best-matching template with the drift feature set.*

Simultaneous Changes. Identifying one template is not enough as a process drift may involve more than one change. In order to characterize all the simultaneous changes, each time that a best-matching template with the drift feature set is identified, we remove the features that were used for this template instantiation from the drift feature set. The new resulting drift feature set is then reused for the identification of a new best-matching template. We repeat this cycle until we cannot find any more templates that match the remaining features within the drift feature set. It is worth mentioning that if there are two *overlapping* changes in the process, i.e. changes that share a non-empty set of features, only the one with higher nC can be matched with a template. This is because each time we find a best-matching template we remove the matched features from the drift feature set. This limits the ability of the proposed method to the identification of non-overlapping simultaneous changes.

Example 7. *In our example, as there is no feature shared between* $I_{D^1,T^{pl}}$ *and* $I_{D^1,T^{sre}}$*, both change templates can be identified. The identified templates,* T^{pl} *and* T^{sre}*, are then reported to the user using the two following statements, respectively:*

- *Before the drift, activity "e" preceded "f", while after the drift, they are in parallel.*
- *Activity "b" has been removed from between activities "a" and "c" after the detected drift.*

Time Complexity. Given the number of data points $2n$, where n is the characterization delay, and the maximum possible number of α^+ relations $|\mathcal{L}|^2$, where $\mathcal{L}$ is the label set, the complexity of our drift characterization method is the maximum of the worst-case complexities of the following sequential operations: (i) performing KSPT between the α^+ relations and a binary target variable ($O(2n \cdot |\mathcal{L}|^2)$), (ii) computing the average frequencies and RFCs of the relations ($O(2n \,.\, |\mathcal{L}|^2)$), (iii) ordering the relations ($O(|\mathcal{L}|^2 \cdot \log(|\mathcal{L}|^2))$), and (iv) template identification $O(|\mathcal{L}|^2 \cdot m \cdot |\mathcal{L}|^2!)$[1]. Hence, the time complexity of our method is $O(|\mathcal{L}|^2 \cdot m \cdot |\mathcal{L}|^2!)$. This time complexity is a theoretical upper-bound, however in practice the number of relations rarely approaches $|\mathcal{L}|^2$, and not all permutations are verified for the template identification operations (relations are first filtered based on their types, e.g. causality).

[1] Matching a template of k relations to a drift feature set of $|\mathcal{L}|^2$ relations requires iterating over all possible permutations (${}^nP_k = |\mathcal{L}|^2!/(|\mathcal{L}|^2-k)!$). The upper-bound complexity of this operation is $O(|\mathcal{L}|^2!)$. Next, to identify the best-matching template, we iterate over the number of predefined templates m. Finally, we need to match simultaneous changes which in the worse case are $|\mathcal{L}|^2$ (where each template has only one relation). The upper-bound time complexity of identifying multiple non-overlapping templates is $O(|\mathcal{L}|^2 \cdot m \cdot |\mathcal{L}|^2!)$.

4 Evaluation on Synthetic Logs

We implemented the proposed method as an extension of the *ProDrift 2.0* plugin for the Apromore platform.[2] This tool is fed with an event stream replayed from an event log, and reports, for each detected drift, its characterization as a verbalization in natural language, based on the applicable templates. We used this tool to evaluate the effectiveness of our method with different parameters settings. In the rest of this section we discuss the setup of the experiments and a two-pronged evaluation to assess the effectiveness of the relevant relations retrieval and ranking with respect to each individual template, and the accuracy of template identification. Finally, we compare our method with model-to-model comparison in combination with automated process discovery, as well as log-to-log comparison.

4.1 Setup

We generated a synthetic dataset using the same approach and CPN[3] base model in [17] that represents a highly variable process. For each simple change template in Table 1, we generated a log featuring 9 drifts, each injected by alternatively activating and deactivating the template within the base model. For instance, for the template "sre" we alternatively added or removed an activity to or from the process model. For the particular change template "lp", three logs were generated with length-one, length-two and length-three loops, and the reported results for this template were averaged over these three logs. This resulted in 17 logs, each containing 10,000 traces with nine equidistant drifts of the same change template. To evaluate the characterization of drifts in the context of simultaneous changes, we organized our change templates in three categories: Insertion ("I"), Resequentialization ("R") and Optionalization ("O") (cf. Table 1). Limited to two and three simultaneous cross-category changes, these categories make four possible scenarios of simultaneous changes ("IR", "IO", "RO", "RIO"). For each such scenarios two logs were generated by randomly selecting single templates from different categories. For instance, a drift from the simultaneous changes scenario of "IR" could simultaneously add a new activity ("I") and a loop back ("R") in two different locations of the process. This resulted in eight logs for the simultaneous changes setting. All in all, the dataset contained 25 logs for both single and simultaneous changes.[4]

In these experiments, we used our technique in [17] to detect drifts, because this technique works in online settings with event streams of highly-variable business processes and has been shown to be the state of the art in process drift detection, both in terms of detection accuracy and detection delay (cf. Sect. 2).

[2] Available at http://apromore.org/platform/tools.

[3] http://cpntools.org.

[4] All the CPN models used for this simulation, the resulting synthetic logs, and the detailed evaluation results are available with the software distribution.

4.2 Impact of Characterization Delay on Relations Ordering

In Stage 1 of our method, the KSPT is used to retrieve the relations that are significantly associated with the drift, and discard the irrelevant ones. Then, the retrieved binary relations are ordered based on their RFCs with respect to the TRFC that occurred in the drift. For each detected drift, the ground truth (ideal case) is that the relations related to the injected drift template are correctly identified and placed in the top of the returned ordered list. However, some spurious relations may affect the relations ordering. We use the *normalized discounted cumulative gain (nDCG)* to evaluate the accuracy of the relations ordering. The nDCG is a relative measure where a value of 1.0 indicates that the ordered list corresponds to the ground truth, while 0.0 indicates that none of the relations related to the injected drift template have been retrieved. This measure is also used for computing the confidence of a template matching, as explained in Sect. 3.3.

In the first experiment, we study how the accuracy of the ordered binary relations list is impacted by changing the characterization delay. We vary the characterization delay from 200 to 1,000 events, and report the mean and the standard deviation of the nDCG over all the simple change templates, where each template was evaluated separately over nine injected drifts (cf. Fig. 5). In this experiment, we do not apply any filtering on the ordered binary relations list (CRFC = 100%· TRFC).

Not surprisingly, for a characterization delay of 200 events, the KSPT does not have enough data to identify the relevant binary relations causing the drift, which leads to a relatively low average nDCG of around 0.84 and a standard deviation of 0.19 over all templates. Consequently, spurious relations, most often resulting from a slight change in a branching probability, appear in the ordered relations list. However, we observe that the accuracy of the relations ordering increases when the characterization delay grows and eventually plateaus at an average of 0.98 with a standard deviation of 0.02. As expected, the more data points are fed to the KSPT, the more accurate is the statistical association between the explanatory variable (here an individual binary relation) and the target variable (the drift classification variable), and the better the estimation of the RFC for ordering the relations is. However, the characterization delay cannot grow indefinitely, hence, we select 500 events as a trade-off between a short characterization delay and a high characterization accuracy (fewer spurious relations). This value is used as the default delay in the remaining experiments.

We note that the characterization delay does not only indicate how many events our method needs to fetch from the event stream to obtain an accurate characterization, but it also allows us to infer the minimum inter-drift distance that our method can handle. In other terms, the next potential drift must occur at least after a number of events equal to this characterization delay (+ one detection window) after the stabilization point (cf. Fig. 2) in order to be accurately characterized.

4.3 Impact of Relation Filtering on Characterization Accuracy

As introduced in Sect. 3.3, the ordered relations list resulting from Stage 1 can be filtered based on the CRFC to discard the relations with insignificant RFCs. Thus, only the top relations that sum up their CRFC to a certain proportion of the TRFC are retained. The filtered list is then fed to the template identification stage to find the best-matching templates with the relations. In this experiment, we study how the filter affects the accuracy of template identification. We vary the CRFC threshold (x%) from 70% to 100% (no filtering), and report the *F-score* of the template identification averaged over the 25 synthetic logs. The F-score is measured as the harmonic mean of *recall* and *precision*, where recall measures the ratio of correctly identified change templates of a specific type over the total number of injected templates of the same type, and precision measures the ratio of correctly identified change templates of a specific type over the total number of identified templates of that same type. Figure 6 shows the average accuracy over all templates and per single change, double and triple simultaneous changes.

As expected, we observe that the F-score increases as the CRFC threshold increases. When the threshold is low, many relations are filtered out, and if only one relation corresponding to an injected template is discarded then its corresponding template will not be matched. On the other hand, when the threshold increases, more relations remain in the filtered list, thereby increasing the likelihood of matching the relevant template, leading to a higher recall. However, when no relations are filtered out (threshold = 100%), spurious relations will be matched with the frequency template "fr". This will impact the precision, explaining the drop in the average F-score at the threshold value of 100%. As an example, for the change template parallel move "pm" (with 8 relations), the output of the first stage of our method was an ordered list of 50 relations. A filter threshold of 70% retains only the top five relations out of 50, leading to a recall of 0 for this template. On the other hand, a threshold of 90% retains the top nine relations, leading to a recall of 1. In the remaining experiments we use a CRFC threshold of 95% that is suitable for both single and simultaneous changes.

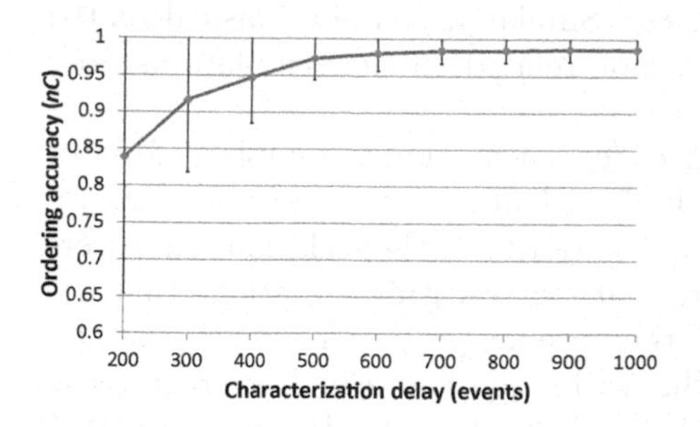

Fig. 5. Impact of characterization delay on relevant relations retrieval and ordering

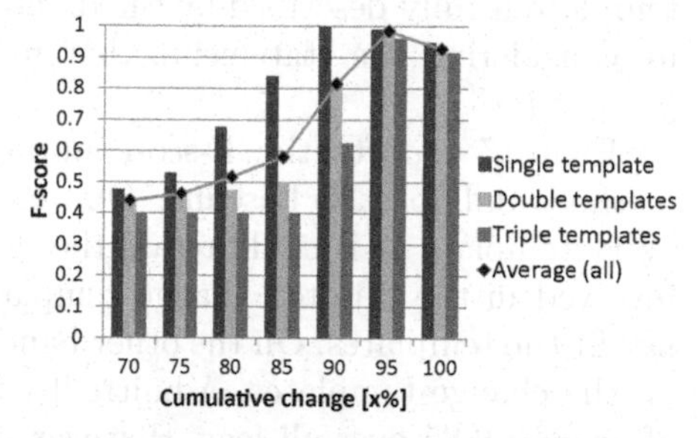

Fig. 6. Impact of relation filtering on characterization accuracy

4.4 Comparison with Baseline

As discussed in Sect. 2, a possible approach to process drift characterization is to apply automated process discovery before and after the drift point, and compare the resulting process models. We first conducted an exploratory experiment using a sample artificial log with a single injected drift. After drift detection, we extracted the pre-drift and post-drift sublogsand fed these to two state-of-the-art automated process discovery techniques: Inductive Miner [12] and BPMN Miner [7]. The resulting models, obtained from each technique, were then compared using the model-to-model technique in [3]. The comparison between the pair of models discovered by the Inductive Miner did not finish after six hours of execution. This is explained by the over-generalization introduced by the Inductive Miner in the discovered models. In the particular situation of a highly variable process, this miner tends to produce a model close to the so-called *flower model.* This causes the model-to-model comparison technique to explore the combination of all the possible execution paths from the two models. using BPMN Miner, the model comparison technique produced many incorrect differences. This false positives are due to the two models being underfitting. For instance, if the discovered pre-drift model misses to represent a particular process behavior, the comparison technique mistakenly reports this behavior as being added after the drift. Based on these results, we decided to discard this approach as a baseline to benchmark our method.

We then evaluated the possibility of using the log-to-log comparison technique in [4] as a baseline. This technique is designed to compare logs with complete traces, while in our setting the pre-drift and post-drift sublogs are extracted from an event stream, and hence contain many incomplete traces. As a first attempt, we fed the log comparison technique with the two sublogs before and after the drift as is, but as expected, the comparison led to a large number of misleading differences. We then decided to only use complete traces within the two sublogs. This was possible as we knew the start and end activities of the process. However, in an online setting such activities may not be known. For each change template, we evaluated the accuracy of the differences returned by the technique manually. We calculated recall by considering the missing differences for a given template as false negatives, so that a recall of 1 is obtained if a template is fully described by the differences. Similarly, precision was calculated by considering the statements that were not related to the template as false positives.

Figure 7 reports the F-score obtained for each change template for our method and for the baseline. Our method had almost a perfect F-score for every template as it could retain the (great majority of the) relations that were involved in the injected change template, without returning relations that did not fit the templates. On the other hand, the baseline produced a low F-score for all the change templates. Admittedly, this technique had a high average recall of around 0.85 over all logs. However, its precision was very low due to a high number of false positives (wrong differences returned). Indeed, the two sublogs capture partial process behavior, which, even if similar at the event level, is quite variable at the trace level. This was exacerbated by the high variability of the process. These results are in line with the findings in [17] on drift detection (the step preceding the drift characterization). In the latter study, we showed that techniques based on (abstraction of) complete traces such as [13] do not perform well when detecting drifts in highly variable logs and that finer-grained features such as the $\alpha+$ relations are more suitable to capture process behavior in high variability settings.

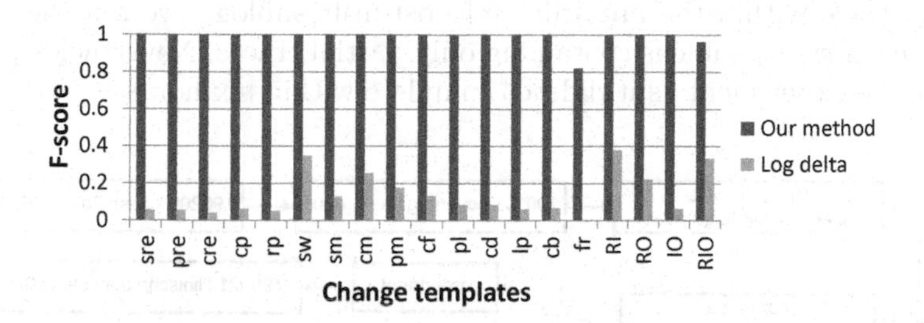

Fig. 7. F-score per change template, obtained with our method vs. [4].

We conducted all the experiments on an Intel i7 2.20 GHz with 16 GB RAM (64 bit), running Windows 7 and JVM 7 with standard heap space of 4 GB. The time required to extract, order, and then match the α^+ relations to the predefined templates for each drift ranged from a minimum of 410 ms to a maximum of 660 ms with an average of 530 ms. The baseline method took on average 15 s to report the differences between the pre-drift and post-drift sub-logs.

5 Evaluation on Real-Life Log

We further evaluated our method on the BPI Challenge (BPIC) 2011.[5] We chose this log, which records patient treatments in a Dutch hospital, because of its high trace variability (~70%). We prepared the log by filtering out infrequent behavior using the noise filter in [8] with its default settings. This operation resulted in a log with 1,121 traces, of which 798 are distinct, and 42 activity labels. In [17], we had detected two drifts from this filtered log, using our technique for drift detection. The two drifts were supported by the observation of a sudden increase, and a subsequent decrease in the number of events while the number of active cases was decreasing.

We applied our method for drift characterization in order to identify the change templates that explain these two drifts. Two frequency change templates were identified to characterize the first drift, while the second drift was explained by one frequency change template. This template was symmetric to the first frequency change template, identified for the first drift. After investigation, we found that the probability of the branch which was identified by the change

[5] http://dx.doi.org/10.4121/uuid:d9769f3d-0ab0-4fb8-803b-0d1120ffcf54.

template as increasing (resp. decreasing) after the first (resp. second) drift point included five activities in a loopback. The increase from 34% to 46% (resp. decrease from 46% to 34%) in the upper branch probability of the identified frequency change template is, in fact, the cause of the increased (resp. decreased) number of events after the first (resp. second) drift. Figure 8 depicts the identified template, with the activity labels in their original language.

As discussed in Sect. 4.4, the baseline technique for log-to-log comparison [4] is designed to compare logs with complete traces. However, since there was no complete trace within the pre-drift and post-drift sublogs, we ran the baseline technique using the sublogs containing only partial traces. Nevertheless, we had to abort the experiment as it did not complete within six hours.

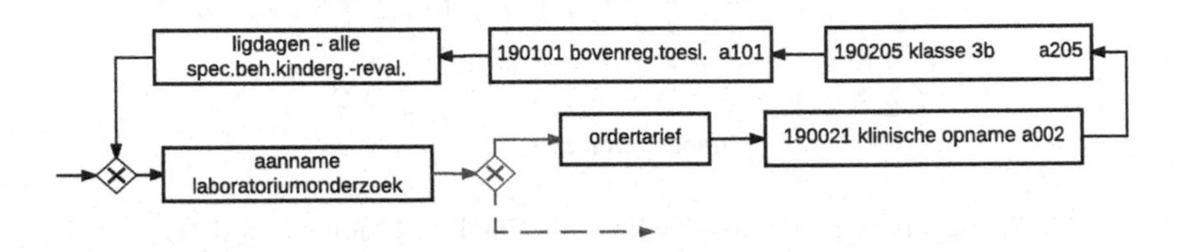

Fig. 8. Identified template for drift 1 in BPIC 2011 log.

6 Conclusion and Future Work

We proposed a systematic online drift characterization method based on event streams. The method can characterize multiple simultaneous changes so long as they do not overlap in terms of process behavior. The strength of our method resides in the features used to encode the process behavior and its well-grounded statistical approach, that allow us to deal with highly variable processes. The collection of change templates that we use to describe a drift is based on a well-established categorization of typical change patterns. We do not claim this collection to be complete, but it can easily be extended.

We extensively evaluated our method using both highly variable synthetic logs as well as a real-life log. The results on the syntetic logs show high accuracy, low characterization delay and low time performance. And despite the lack of a ground truth to validate our findings on the real-life log, the results were supported by various observations from the log. In addition, the method outperforms state-of-the-art techniques for model-to-model comparison, in combination with automated discovery techniques, as well as techniques for log-to-log comparison.

A first avenue for future work is to provide a visual description of the identified templates as a simple and effective way to communicate the nature of the drift, as in [3]. Another avenue is to characterize more sophisticated changes such as overlapping or nested changes. A third avenue is to combine collocated relations to support process fragments (subprocesses), such as single-entry-single-exit fragments or local process fragments [19]. Finally, the characterization may be extended to other process aspects, such as process data and resources.

Acknowledgments. This research is partly funded by the Australian Research Council (grant DP150103356).

References

1. van der Aalst, W.M.P.: Process Mining: Discovery, Conformance and Enhancement of Business Processes. Springer, Heidelberg (2011)
2. Accorsi, R., Stocker, T.: Discovering workflow changes with time-based trace clustering. In: Aberer, K., Damiani, E., Dillon, T. (eds.) SIMPDA 2011. LNBIP, vol. 116, pp. 154–168. Springer, Heidelberg (2012). doi:10.1007/978-3-642-34044-4_9
3. Armas-Cervantes, A., Baldan, P., Dumas, M., García-Bañuelos, L.: Behavioral comparison of process models based on canonically reduced event structures. In: Sadiq, S., Soffer, P., Völzer, H. (eds.) BPM 2014. LNCS, vol. 8659, pp. 267–282. Springer, Cham (2014). doi:10.1007/978-3-319-10172-9_17
4. van Beest, N.R.T.P., Dumas, M., García-Bañuelos, L., La Rosa, M.: Log delta analysis: interpretable differencing of business process event logs. In: Motahari-Nezhad, H.R., Recker, J., Weidlich, M. (eds.) BPM 2015. LNCS, vol. 9253, pp. 386–405. Springer, Cham (2015). doi:10.1007/978-3-319-23063-4_26
5. Bose, R.P.J.C., van der Aalst, W.M.P., Zliobaite, I., Pechenizkiy, M.: Dealing with concept drifts in process mining. IEEE Trans. NNLS **25**, 154–171 (2014)
6. Carmona, J., Gavaldà, R.: Online techniques for dealing with concept drift in process mining. In: Hollmén, J., Klawonn, F., Tucker, A. (eds.) IDA 2012. LNCS, vol. 7619, pp. 90–102. Springer, Heidelberg (2012). doi:10.1007/978-3-642-34156-4_10
7. Conforti, R., Dumas, M., García-Bañuelos, L., Rosa, M.L.: BPMN miner: Automated discovery of BPMN process models with hierarchical structure. Inf. Syst. **56**, 284–303 (2016)
8. Conforti, R., La Rosa, M., ter Hofstede, A.H.: Filtering out infrequent behavior from business process event logs. IEEE Trans. Knowl. Data Eng. **29**, 300–314 (2016)
9. Frank, E., Witten, I.H.: Using a permutation test for attribute selection in decision trees. In: International Conference on Machine Learning. Morgan Kaufmann (1998)
10. Gama, J., Žliobaitė, I., Bifet, A., Pechenizkiy, M., Bouchachia, A.: A survey on concept drift adaptation. ACM Computing Surveys (CSUR) **46**, 44 (2014)
11. Järvelin, K., Kekäläinen, J.: Cumulated gain-based evaluation of IR techniques. ACM Trans. Inf. Syst. (TOIS) **20**, 422–446 (2002)
12. Leemans, S.J.J., Fahland, D., Aalst, W.M.P.: Discovering block-structured process models from event logs - a constructive approach. In: Colom, J.-M., Desel, J. (eds.) PETRI NETS 2013. LNCS, vol. 7927, pp. 311–329. Springer, Heidelberg (2013). doi:10.1007/978-3-642-38697-8_17
13. Maaradji, A., Dumas, M., La Rosa, M., Ostovar, A.: Fast and accurate business process drift detection. In: Motahari-Nezhad, H.R., Recker, J., Weidlich, M. (eds.) BPM 2015. LNCS, vol. 9253, pp. 406–422. Springer, Cham (2015). doi:10.1007/978-3-319-23063-4_27
14. Martjushev, J., Bose, R.P.J.C., van der Aalst, W.M.P.: Change point detection and dealing with gradual and multi-order dynamics in process mining. In: Matulevičius, R., Dumas, M. (eds.) BIR 2015. LNBIP, vol. 229, pp. 161–178. Springer, Cham (2015). doi:10.1007/978-3-319-21915-8_11
15. de Medeiros, A.A., van Dongen, B.F., van der Aalst, W.M.P., Weijters, A.: Process mining: extending the α-algorithm to mine short loops. Technical report (2004)

16. Menard, S.: Applied Logistic Regression Analysis. Sage, Thousand Oaks (2002)
17. Ostovar, A., Maaradji, A., La Rosa, M., ter Hofstede, A.H.M., van Dongen, B.F.V.: Detecting drift from event streams of unpredictable business processes. In: Comyn-Wattiau, I., Tanaka, K., Song, I.-Y., Yamamoto, S., Saeki, M. (eds.) ER 2016. LNCS, vol. 9974, pp. 330–346. Springer, Cham (2016). doi:10.1007/978-3-319-46397-1_26
18. Pratt, K.B., Tschapek, G.: Visualizing concept drift. In: Proceedings of the Ninth ACM SIGKDD International Conference on Knowledge Discovery and Data Mining. ACM (2003)
19. Tax, N., Sidorova, N., van der Aalst, W.M., Haakma, R.: Heuristic approaches for generating local process models through log projections. In: IEEE Symposium on Computational Intelligence and Data Mining (CIDM) (2016)
20. Webb, G.I., Hyde, R., Cao, H., Nguyen, H.L., Petitjean, F.: Characterizing concept drift. Data Mining Knowl. Discov. **30**, 964–994 (2016)
21. Weber, B., Reichert, M., Rinderle-Ma, S.: Change patterns and change support features-enhancing flexibility in process-aware information systems. DKE **66**, 438–466 (2008)

Big Data Exploration

Massively Distributed Environments and Closed Itemset Mining: The DCIM Approach

Mehdi Zitouni[1,2](✉), Reza Akbarinia[1], Sadok Ben Yahia[2], and Florent Masseglia[1]

[1] INRIA, Montpellier, France
{Mehdi.Zitouni,Reza.Akbarinia,Florent.Masseglia}@inria.fr
[2] Faculté des Sciences de Tunis, LIPAH-LR 11ES14, Université de Tunis ElManar, Tunis, Tunisia
Sadok.Benyahia@fst.rnu.tn

Abstract. Data analytics in general, and data mining primitives in particular, are a major source of bottlenecks in the operation of information systems. This is mainly due to their high complexity and intensive call to IO operations, particularly in massively distributed environments. Moreover, an important application of data analytics is to discover key insights from the running traces of information system in order to improve their engineering. Mining closed frequent itemsets (CFI) is one of these data mining techniques, associated with great challenges. It allows discovering itemsets with better efficiency and result compactness. However, discovering such itemsets in massively distributed data poses a number of issues that are not addressed by traditional methods. One solution for dealing with such characteristics is to take advantage of parallel frameworks like, *e.g.*, MapReduce. We address the problem of distributed CFI mining by introducing a new parallel algorithm, called DCIM, which uses a prime number based approach. A key feature of DCIM is the deep combination of data mining properties with the principles of massive data distribution. We carried out exhaustive experiments over real world datasets to illustrate the efficiency of DCIM for large real world datasets with up to 53 million documents.

Keywords: Distributed information systems · Data analytics · Closed frequent itemsets

1 Introduction

In the past few years, advances in hardware and software technologies have made it possible for the users of information systems to produce large amounts of transactional data. Although data mining has become a fairly well established field now, its applications in massively distributed environment poses a number of thriving challenges which are a well-known source of bottlenecks for the operation of distributed information systems. This is particularly the case of frequent itemset mining (FIM) [1]. FIM allows discovering important correlation for massive sets of data and reveal key insights for numerous applications, ranging from

E. Dubois and K. Pohl (Eds.): CAiSE 2017, LNCS 10253, pp. 231–246, 2017.
DOI: 10.1007/978-3-319-59536-8_15

marketing, to scientific data analytics, and including the optimization of information systems. Actually, discovering the relationship between features in the running traces of a system, for its optimization, is an active research topic [2,3].

Unfortunately, mining only frequent itemsets generates an overwhelming number of itemsets. This makes their interpretation almost impossible and affects the reliability of the expected results.

Several studies were conducted to define and generate condensed representations of frequent itemsets in the past few years. In particular, closed frequent itemsets (CFI in short) [4] have received much attention with very general proposals. Existing algorithms for mining CFI flag out good performance when the input dataset is small or the support threshold is high. However, when the database increases in size or the support threshold turns to be low, both memory usage and communication costs become hard to bear. Some early efforts tried to speed up the mining algorithms by running them in parallel [5], using frameworks such as MapReduce [6] or Spark [7], that allow to make powerful computing and storage units on top of ordinary machines. In [8], Wang et al. propose an approach for mining closed itemsets using MapReduce, but it suffers from the lack of scalability.

In this paper, we propose a new parallel algorithm named *Distributed Closed Itemset Mining* (DCIM) for enumerating CFIs using MapReduce. In DCIM, we develop a new approach based on mathematical techniques. The items from the database are transformed into prime numbers, and CFIs are generated by using only division and multiplication operations. When the scale of datasets gets large, such operations could cause an overwhelming computing and memory utilization. To overcome this issue, we propose insightful optimization techniques that allow extracting CFI from even very large datasets. The main contributions of this paper are as follows:

- We propose a numerical representation of transactional datasets using a new transformation technique. This transformation is embedded in the algorithm for a very low additional cost.
- We design an efficient parallel algorithm for CFI mining by deeply combining MapReduce functionalities with the properties of CFI.
- We exploit the mathematical properties of our numerical representation and provide optimizations both at the architecture level as well as on the computing nodes.
- We carry out exhaustive experiments on real world databases to evaluate the performance of DCIM. The results suggest that our algorithm significantly outperforms the pioneering algorithms in CFI mining over large real world datasets with up to 53 millions articles.

The rest of this paper is organized as follows. In Sect. 2, we describe some related works. In Sect. 3, we present some preliminary notions they would be of help for defining the problem. In Sect. 4, we introduce our DCIM algorithm. The results of our experimental evaluations are reported in Sect. 5. Finally, in Sect. 6 we conclude.

2 Related Work

Many research efforts [9,10] have been introduced to design parallel algorithms capable of working under multiple threads under a shared memory environment. Unfortunately, these approaches do not address the major problem of heavy memory requirement when processing large scale databases. To overcome the latter, MapReduce platform was designed to enable and facilitate the ability to distribute processing of large scale datasets on large computing clusters. In [11], the authors propose a parallel FP-Growth algorithm in MapReduce, which achieves quasi-linear speedups. However, the method presented so far suffers from either excessive amounts of data that need to be transferred and sorted and a high demand for main-memory at cluster nodes.

Moreover, having a large amount of transactional data, finding correlation between them highlights the necessity of discovering a condensed representations of items. Since the introduction of CFI in [4], numerous algorithms for mining it were proposed [12,13]. In fact, these algorithms tried to reduce the problem of finding frequent itemsets to the problem of mining CFIs by limiting the search space to only CFIs rather than the whole powerset lattice. Furthermore, they have good performance whenever the size of dataset is small or the support threshold is high. However, as far as the size of the datasets becomes large, both memory use and communication cost are unacceptable. Thus, parallel solutions are of a compelling need. But, research works on parallel mining of CFI are few. In [8] introduce a new algorithm based on the parallel FP-Growth algorithm PFP [11] that divides an entire mining task into independent parallel subtasks and achieves quasi-linear speedups. The algorithm mines CFI in four MapReduce jobs and introduces a redundancy filtering approach to deal with the problem of generating redundant itemsets. However, we don't find in the literature a work that scales for CFI mining on MapReduce with very large databases, as we tackle in this paper.

3 Preliminaries

Definition 1. *Let $I = \{i_1, ..., i_n\}$ be the set of items. A transaction dataset on I is a set $T = \{t_1, ..., t_m\}$ such that each t_i is included in I. Each t_i is called a transaction. We denote by $||T||$ the sum of sizes of all transactions in T, that is, the size of database T. A set $P \subseteq I$ is called itemset. For an itemset P, a transaction including P is called an occurrence of P, and $T(P)$ is the set of the occurrences of P. $|T(P)|$ is called the frequency of P, and denoted by $frq(P)$. For a given constant θ, called minimum support, the itemset P is frequent if $frq(P) \geq \theta$. For any itemsets P and Q such that $T(P \cup Q) = T(P) \cap T(Q)$, if $P \subseteq Q$ then $T(Q) \subseteq T(P)$. An itemset P is called closed if no other itemset Q satisfies $T(P) = T(Q)$ having $P \subseteq Q$. Given a set $S \subseteq T$ of transactions, let $I(S)$ be the set of items common to all transactions in S, i.e., $I(S) = \cap_{(T \in S)} T$. Then, we define $clo(P)$, the closure of itemset P in T, by $I(T(P)) = \cap_{(t \in T(P))} t$.*

For every pair of itemsets P and Q, the following properties hold [4]:

1. If $P \subseteq Q$, then $clo(P) \subseteq clo(Q)$.
2. If $T(P) = T(Q)$, then $clo(P) = clo(Q)$.
3. $clo(clo(P)) = clo(P)$.
4. $clo(P)$ is the unique smallest closed itemset including P.
5. An itemset P is a closed itemset if and only if $clo(P) = P$.

MapReduce is one of the most popular solutions for big data processing, in particular owe to its automatic management of parallel execution in clusters of machines. Initially proposed in [6], it has gained increasing popularity, as shown by the tremendous success of Hadoop[1], an open-source implementation.

MapReduce splits the computation in two phases, namely *map* and *reduce*, which in turn are carried out by several tasks that process the data in parallel. The idea behind MapReduce is simple and elegant. Given an input file, and two map and reduce functions, each MapReduce job is executed in two main phases. In the first phase, called *map*, the input data is divided into a set of splits, and each split is processed by a map task in a given worker node. These tasks apply the *map* function on every key-value pair of their splits and generate a set of intermediate pairs. In the second phase, called *reduce*, all the values of each intermediate key are grouped and assigned to a reduce task. Reduce tasks are also assigned to worker machines and apply the *reduce* function on the values of each key to produce the final results.

4 DCIM Algorithm

Manipulating string operations causes multiple problems when handling large scale datasets. In fact, when the support threshold turns to be low, both memory usage and communication costs become unbearable. We overcome this issue by designing a distributed solution to mine CFI using the MapReduce framework. In this section, we propose our algorithm, called DCIM, that distributes the mining process of CFI over a cluster of nodes by using a number of well specified MapReduce jobs adapted to our mining problem.

4.1 Algorithm Overview

The DCIM algorithm uses two MapReduce phases to mine CFIs in three steps which are depicted as follows.

- **Step 1:** *Splitting*: Splits T into multiple and successive parts and stores the parts on N different computers. Each part is called a *split.*
- **Step 2:** *Frequency counting*: Executing a first MapReduce job, this step is dedicated to count the support of each item in T and prune non-frequent ones. The output of this step will be a list of items sorted in descendent order, and each one is linked with a specific prime number.

[1] https://hadoop.apache.org/.

- **Step 3:** *CFI Mining*: This is the key step of DCIM that adopts the second MapReduce pass in which Map phase and Reduce phase perform different methods. Here, load balancing is a crucial concern and will call for particular care and a comprehensive approach of distribution principle.

Frequency Counting: Using a simple MapReduce count process, in this step, DCIM scans the database and computes the frequency of each item. In fact, the input key-value pair would be like $(key, value = t_i)$, with $t_i \subset T$. For each item, say $i_k \in t_i$, the mapper outputs a key-value pair $(key = i_k, value = 1)$. After all mappers instances are completed, the MapReduce infrastructure feeds the reducers with key-value pairs and the output result is represented as $(key = i_k, value_2 = \Sigma(value))$. Adding the minimum support θ as an input of the job, the set of items is pruned by discarding those who are not frequent and sorted in descending order of their supports in one list, denoted *Frequency-List*. To proceed with DCIM algorithm, each item in *Frequency-List* will receive a specified prime number.

CFI Mining: After generating the *Frequency-List*, sorted in descending order of supports, DCIM starts the second MapReduce job to extract the complete set of CFI. We detail the Map and Reduce phases below. We assume that the mining process of the algorithm is going to be on multiple Sub-Datasets. At this point, we need to deal with our data and well split the dataset, in order to satisfy the correctness and completeness of our results. To do so, a Sub-Dataset definition cited in [12] says:

Definition 2. *For a given dataset T, let i be a frequent item in T. The i-Sub-Dataset is the subset of transactions containing i, while all infrequent items, item i and items following i in the Frequency-List are omitted. And therefore, having j as a frequent item in P-Sub-Dataset, where P is a frequent itemset, the jP-Sub-Dataset is the subset of transactions in the P-Sub-Dataset containing j, while all infrequent items, item j, and items following j in local Frequency-List are omitted.*

Our splitting process is based on item-based partitioning of the dataset. In fact, the idea is based on the creation of one split S_i for every θ-frequent item $i \in$ *Frequency-List*. Thus, we extract, for each item, its appropriate Sub-Dataset. In the Map phase, the algorithm loads the *Frequency-List* of the Dataset. In each split from the inputs, the algorithm treats each transaction t_i from the split S_i. The input pair is like $(key, value = t_i)$. For each t_i, item i is omitted from the transaction t_i and the rest of items are sorted in descending order of supports by checking the *Frequency-List*. Then, DCIM generates a big integer V_{t_i} representing the transaction by multiplying all the primes representing items of the transaction. At the end, the Map phase emits the item i and the appropriates V_{t_i} as follows $(key = i, value = t_i[1], t_i[2], ..., t_i[n])$ where $n \leq ||S_i||$. Figure 1 illustrates the transformation process of our algorithm. Each item is mapped to a prime number (left part of Fig. 1), while the dataset (on the right) is transformed by prime number multiplications.

Item	frq(Item)	Prime Nb.
B	4	2
C	4	3
E	4	5
A	3	7
D	1	11

t_i	Original Tr.	Prime Nb.	V_{t_i}
1	A, C, D	7, 3, 11	231
2	B, C, E	2, 3, 5	30
3	A, B, C, E	7, 2, 3, 5	210
4	B, E	2, 5	10
5	A, B, C, E	7, 2, 3, 5	210

Fig. 1. (Left) A mapping between items and prime numbers, and (Right) a dataset T and its transformation.

When all mapper instances have completed, reducers read collections corresponding to a group of transactions in form of big integers representing the Sub-Dataset linked to item or itemset in question. Then, the mining process begins literally. Before describing the Reduce phase, some properties and definitions are of use in the remainder. Indeed, for every pair of itemsets P and Q represented respectively as two big integers X and Y, the following properties hold.

1. P is a Closed itemset extracted from a Sub-Dataset. P is discovered by concatenating the items having the same support as P (in the Sub-Dataset)
2. It is not necessary to develop a Sub-Dataset of an itemset Q included in a CFI already discovered P, such that supports of P and Q are equal.
3. $P \subseteq Q$ if the rest of division of Y by X is 0.

In previous works [14], to facilitate the exploration of Sub-Datasets and mine CFI, authors propose a new technique that defines a header table which is associated to each context. This table lists the items contained in the corresponding Sub-Dataset, sorted in descending order of their supports. However, in this current approach, extracting CFI in the reduce phase of DCIM does not need the use of this header table, and thus avoids additional process. To do so, we adopted the notion of greatest common divisor (GCD). Knowing that the GCD of two or more integers, when at least one of them is not zero, is the largest positive integer that divides the numbers without a remainder, we deduce our closure operator using the following lemma.

Lemma 1. *Let P-Sub-Dataset be the subset of transactions containing P. The greatest common divisor in P-Sub-Dataset represents the closure between all transactions.*

Proof. The closure of an itemset P is produced from the intersection between all transactions containing P. Manipulating prime numbers, the GCD between primes is unique. Thus, having all $V_t i$ from P-Sub-Dataset, extracting the closure from a set of transactions amounts to calculate the GCD between them. Hence, the GCD in P-Sub-Dataset is the closure between transactions composing P-Sub-Dataset.

Having the prime number representing the item and its transactions as a set of V_{t_i} as input for reducers, computing the closure from the Sub-Dataset is straightforward by computing the GCD of all transactions of the Sub-Dataset. Doing so, there is no further need to store supports of items contained in the Sub-Dataset. Indeed, if the closure exists, then it will undoubtedly have the same support as that of the item. By concatenating the closure to the candidate item multiplying the prime number of the item and the number representing the closure, the result of our reduce phase will be a CFI that is represented as a number which is added to the set of final results.

Load Balancing: The principles explained above are a strong basis for high performances when mining CFIs. However, a fully parallel data mining algorithms has to be deeply combined with the intrinsic characteristics of the distributed framework. We know that, in MapReduce, the reducers cannot start applying the reduce function before all mappers finish their work. Thus, when approaching the end of Map phase, there are usually nodes that are idle waiting for the others to finish. It is worth using these nodes for reducing the amount

Algorithm 1. DCIM Algorithm

1: **function** MAPPER(i, S_i)
2: Load *Frequency-List* ; Load *Primes-List*
3: **for all** $T_i \in S_i$ **do**
4: $T_i^{'} \leftarrow ORD(T_i)$ ▷ ORD : sort items from T_i
5: $PN(i) = 1$
6: **if** $T_i^{'} \neq \emptyset$ **then**
7: **for all** $j \in T_i^{'}$ **do**
8: $PN(i) \leftarrow PN(i) \times Primes\text{-}List(j)$
9: ▷ Transforms j and generates V_{t_i}
10: Emit$(Primes\text{-}List(j+1), PN(i))$
11: **end for**
12: **end if**
13: **end for**
14: **end function**
15: **function** COMBINER$(i, List\text{-}PN(i))$
16: $List\text{-}Gcd(i) \leftarrow \emptyset$; $k \leftarrow 0$
17: **for all** $PN(i)_k \in List\text{-}PN(i)$, $k < \|List\text{-}PN(i)\|$ **do**
18: $Gcd(i) \leftarrow Gcd(PN(i)_k)$ ▷ Computing GCDs
19: $k \leftarrow k + 1$
20: **end for**
21: $List\text{-}Gcd(i) \leftarrow Gcd(i)$
22: Emit$(i, List\text{-}Gcd(i))$
23: **end function**
24: **function** REDUCER$(i, List\text{-}Gcd(i))$
25: $Clos(i) \leftarrow \emptyset$; $CFI \leftarrow \emptyset$
26: **for all** $Gcd(i) \in List\text{-}Gcd(i)$ **do**
27: $Clos(i) \leftarrow Gcd(List\text{-}Gcd(i))$ ▷ Results shuffling
28: **end for**
29: $CFI \leftarrow i \cup Clos(i)$ ▷ $\cup$: Operation to join items
30: **end function**

of data that should be transferred from mappers to reducers. The main issue is to find the adequate decomposition of the problem, such that one part of the load may be given to a node that may do some pre-processing and save time to the reducers. This can be done thanks to the nice properties of the GCD, which may be divided into parts of any size. In fact, having a unique GCD for multiple integers, its computation can be done in a successive manner, while maintaining the correctness of the final results. Let us consider that we have n mappers $\{M_1, ..., M_n\}$, and on each mapper i we have $M_{i,k}$ numbers (V_{t_k}) associated to key k. Then, we can compute $\text{GCD}_{i,k}(M_i)$ the local GCD of mapper i for k on the $M_{i,k}$ V_{t_k} it contains. Later, instead of receiving $\sum_{i=1}^{n} M_{i,k} V_{t_k}$ for key k, a reducer will receive a much lower amount of numbers, corresponding to the results of this pre-computing (n, in the ideal case).

Thus, in DCIM, we anticipate the next step of calculating GCDs, avoiding heavy synchronization, and significantly reducing the computing time by performing a reduce-type function, called *combiner*, before starting the reduce phase of the proposed algorithm. Doing so, we limit the volume of data transfer between the map and reduce tasks. This function runs on the output key-value pairs of the map phase which are not immediately written to the output and already available in memory. Instead, they will be collected in lists, one list per each key value. Also, in our new algorithm, we set the combiner class as a shuffling class where all instances of Map's output are handled as a set of transactions, represented as a set of V_{t_i}. In fact, for each map output key, the combiner function is called and tries to compute the global GCD taking V_{t_i}s one by one and applies a series of GCD calculations between them. It is obvious that, besides the technical tricks, passing summarized GCDs to the reduce phase of the algorithm enhances the computation and calculation time. Pseudo-code of Map, Combiner and Reduce phases to enumerate CFIs is sketched in Algorithm 1. An example of DCIM running is presented in Fig. 2.

Illustrative Example: Figure 1 illustrates how DCIM works on a dataset T. First, having a minimum support $\theta = 2$, the frequency counting pass provides the *Frequency-List* containing items of T with their primes linked sorted in descendent order of frequencies (in case of same frequencies we applied alphabetical order on items). Then, the second MapReduce pass of DCIM is sketched in Fig. 2. Starting by the less frequent items from each transaction, DCIM decompose the V_{t_i} to construct Sub-Datasets. In the example, the first mapper took {CA} as a transaction. Having $frq(A) \leq frq(C)$, DCIM starts by dividing V_{t_1} by "7" the prime associated to {A}. The mapper provides {C} as a transaction for A-Sub-Dataset as a first result. Reciprocally, {A} is provided as a transaction for C-Sub-Dataset. The same calculations are applied for the rest of the mappers. Treating {A} as a combine inputs in the second table of the example, A-Sub-Dataset is delivered as a set of V_ts (e.g. {C} = 3, {BCE} = 30, {BCE} = 30). With a GCD = 3 which is the prime associated to {C}, {AC} is a closed frequent itemset. The same calculations are applied to itemset {AB}, taking into account its Sub-dataset as inheritance from A-Sub-dataset and so

Map Inputs (V_{t_i})	Processing V_{t_i}	Map Outputs (Sub-DS)
{CA} = {21}	21 = 3 × 7	{A} = 7 : {C} = 3
{BCE} = {30}	30 = 2 × 3 × 5	{E} = 5 : {BC} = 6
	6 = 2 × 3	{C} = 3 : {B} = 2
{BCEA} = {210}	210 = 2 × 3 × 5 × 7	{A} = 7 : {BCE} = 30
	30 = 2 × 3 × 5	{E} = 5 : {BC} = 6
	6 = 2 × 3	{C} = 3 : {B} = 2
{BE} = {10}	10 = 2 × 5	{E} = 5 : {B} = 2
{BCEA} = {210}	210 = 2 × 3 × 5 × 7	{A} = 7 : {BCE} = 30
	30 = 2 × 3 × 5	{E} = 5 : {BC} = 6
	6 = 2 × 3	{C}= 3 : {B} = 2

Combine Inputs (Sub-DS)	CFI Mining → Reduce Outputs
{A} = 7 : {3, 30, 30}	GCD(3, 30, 30) = 3 ⇒ 3 × 7 = 21
	21 = {AC} ⇒ {AC} is CFI
{AB} = 14 : {15, 15}	GCD(15, 15) = 15 ⇒ 14 × 15 = 210
	210 = {ABCE} ⇒ {ABCE} is CFI
{AE} ? → {AE} ⊆ {ABCE}	STOP
{E} = 5 : {6, 2, 6, 6}	GCD(6, 2, 6, 6) = 2 ⇒ 2 × 5 = 10
	10 = {BE} ⇒ {BE} is CFI
{EC} = 15 : {2, 2, 2}	GCD(2, 2, 2) = 2 ⇒ 2 × 15 = 30
	30 = {BCE} ⇒ {BCE} is CFI
{C} = 3 : {7, 2, 2, 2}	GCD(7, 2, 2, 2) = 1 ⇒ 1 × 3 = 3
	3 = {C} ⇒ {C} is CFI

Fig. 2. Illustrative example: map, combiner and reduce phases of DCIM

one. The process is stopped in each reducer in two cases. A first case when there is no other item to treat from mappers outputs and a second phase when there is an inclusion relation between closed itemset found and those provided before the latter.

4.2 Optimizing Strategies

The load-balancing technique presented above is a key for high performances. However, massively distributed data mining applied to very large databases calls for thorough optimizations. In this section, we provide insightful optimizing strategies for improving the performance of DCIM in practice.

Document Splitting: Collection frequencies of items can be exploited to reduce required work by splitting up every document adopting the item-based partitioning approach. The main idea is to observe the transactional dataset and fit each mapper with a group of dependent transactions. Thus, assuming i ∈*Frequency-List* a frequent item, we can split the document by searching transactions containing i concatenated to other items having the same supports as i and so on. This allows not only to have fair splits between mappers, but also reduces the time complexity of each mapper by pruning transactions not needed to extract the Sub-Dataset of the item in question.

Multiplying Big Integers: In large datasets, transforming data into numerical forms may generate big integers for which we developed special multiply operator. Before describing this operator, let us recall some definitions about big integers. A big integer X is handled thanks to its polynomial representation in a given base B as $X = x_0 \times B^0 + x_1 \times B^1 + x_2 \times B^2 + ... + x_n \times B^n$, where B usually depends on the maximal size of the basic data types and the coefficients x_i (also called limbs) are basic number data types (such as long or double in Java) and fulfill $0 < x_i < B$.

Due to the format of our final output, we treat the base B as a power of 10. It significantly reduces the memory usage of the DCIM algorithm. Given two big integers X and Y in their respective canonical forms as follows, $X = \sum_{i=0}^{m}(x_i \times B^i)$ and $Y = \sum_{i=0}^{n}(y_i \times B^i)$, the big integer $Z = X \times Y$ can be obtained thanks to $Z_i = \sum_{k+l=i}(x_k \times y_l)$.

Using these basic definitions, for large integers of size n, all the operations addition, substraction, product and division have a complexity of $O(n)$. This means that the number of basic operations on basic data storage type is proportional to n. Interestingly enough, for the classical product and division operations, the complexity is $O(n^2)$ for multiplying and dividing two integers of size n, when n becomes big, this cost becomes very handicapping. When handling huge integers, it is then of interest to try to obtain a faster algorithm for multiplication and division operations. There are some solutions proposed to overcome the above-mentioned problem, and we tried most of them. One of them is the Karatsuba algorithm [15] proposed for an efficient multiplication of big integers. Karatsuba was the first to observe that multiplication of large integer can be made faster than $O(n^2)$. However, its method is a recursive one. It reduces the number of multiplications from the four products $x_0 \times y_0, x_0 \times y_1, x_1 \times y_0$ and $x_1 \times y_1$ to three by dividing the big integers in two parts. To minimize the complexity caused by Karatsuba, a second algorithm called Toom-Cook algorithm was implemented [16]. In fact, Toom-Cook algorithm takes X and Y as two big integers, and splits them into j lower parts each of length i, and operates on the parts. As j grows, one may mix many of the multiplication sub-processing, thus reducing the overall complexity of the algorithm. The multiplication sub-operations can then be computed recursively using ToomCook multiplication again, and so on. Nevertheless, the complexity of Toom-Cook can be further reduced. Indeed, the product of two large integers of size n can be done in $O(n \log(n))$ thanks to Fast Fourier Transform techniques detailed in follow. In fact, two large integers X and Y of size at most $n-1$ can be written in the form of $X = X(B)$ and $Y = Y(B)$, where B is the base (B a power of 10) and X and Y two polynomials as $X(z) = \sum_{i=0}^{n-1}(x_i \times z^i)$ and $Y(z) = \sum_{i=0}^{n-1}(y_i \times z^i)$. Denoting by $R(z)$ the polynomial obtained by the product of $X(z)$ and $Y(z)$, we have $XY = R(B)$ and a final rearrangement on the coefficients of R(z) permits to obtain the product XY. Thus, we are lead to the problem of multiplying two polynomials of degree lower than n. A polynomial of degree lower than n is uniquely defined from its evaluations at n distinct points. Therefore, to obtain the product $R(z) = X(z)Y(z)$, it is sufficient to compute the values $R(w_k)$ at $2 \times n$ distinct points of w_k, that are computing X(w_k) and Y(w_k).

The Fast Fourier Transform idea consists in choosing for w_k the complex roots of unity Ω like $w_k = \exp(\frac{2i\Pi k}{2n}) = \Omega^k$ where $\Omega = \exp(\frac{2i\Pi}{2n})$.

Thus, FFT algorithm proceeds with a transformation technique called the Fourier Transform. For a given sequence $X = (x_0, x_1, ..., x_{2n-1})$ derived from $X(z) = \sum_{i=0}^{n-1}(x_i \times z^i)$, the algorithm computes its Fourier transform F using Ω from below as follows.

$$F(X) = (f_0, f_1, ..., f_{2n-1}) \ ; \ f_k = \sum_{j=0}^{2n-1}(x_j \Omega^{jk})$$

where the conjugate Fourier transform is :

$$\overline{F}(X) = (f_0, f_1, ..., f_{2n-1}) \ \text{ with } f_k = \sum_{j=0}^{2n-1}(x_j \Omega^{-jk}).$$

Roughly speaking, to compute the coefficients f_k of $F(X)$, the transformation performs the following steps:

1. Define two sub-sequences of size n:
   $X_0 = (x_0, x_2, ..., x_{2n-2}) \ ; \ X_1 = (x_1, x_3, ..., x_{2n-1})$
2. Compute the Fourrier transform:
   $F(X_0) = (a_0, a_1, ..., a_{n-1}) \ ; \ F(X_1) = (b_0, b_1, ..., b_{n-1})$
3. Deduce the Fourier Transform $F(X)$ with the formulas:
   $f_k = a_k + \Omega^k b_k \ ; \ f_{n+k} = a_k - \Omega^k b_k \ ; \ 0 \leq k \leq n$

We now present formally the algorithm to multiply big numbers with FFT algorithm. Let X and Y be two big integers with less than n coefficients. To compute $Z = X \times Y$ in time $O(n \log(n))$, FFT performs the following steps:

1. Compute the Fourier transform X' and Y', of size $2n$ each, of the sequences x_j and y_j : $X' = (x'_0, x'_1, ..., x'_{2n-1}) \ ; \ Y' = (y'_0, y'_1, ..., y'_{2n-1})$
2. Compute the product term by term in Z': $Z' = (z'_0, z'_1, ..., z'_{2n-1}) \ ; \ z'_i = x'_i \times y'_i$
3. Compute the inverse Fourier transform Z of Z' with the conjugate FFT process: $Z = (z_0, z_1, ..., z_{2n-1}) \equiv \frac{1}{2n}\overline{F}(Z)$

And finally, after rearrangement of the coefficients z_i, the number $Z_i = \sum_0^{2n-1}(z_i B^i)$ is equal to the product of X by Y. The algorithm consists in computing two FFTs of size $2n$ and one reverse FFT of size $2n$. Thus the product of two large integers with n digits has a complexity asymptotically equal to 3 FFTs, let's say $O(n \log(n)^3)$.

Reducing the Size of Prime Numbers: Dealing with large datasets leads us to efficiently manipulate large numbers. Thus, in addition to the efficient multiplication operator, we also tried to reduce the size of generated numbers as much as possible. In fact, when analyzing our execution logs, we observed that items with low-frequency are much more numerous than those having high support values. Thus, for performance enhancements, we tried to attribute the lower primes to items that have higher frequencies. This idea remarkably reduced the running time of our algorithm.

5 Experimental Evaluation

Setup and Implementation: To perform our experiments, we used one of the clusters of Grid5000[2] which is a large-scale and versatile test-bed for experiment-driven research on parallel and distributed computing. Our experiments were performed on a cluster with 32 nodes (384 cores in total), equipped with Hadoop 2.6.0 version. Each machine is equipped with linux operating system, 96 Gigabytes of main memory, dual-Xeon X5670 with 2.93 GHz 12 core CPUs and 320 Gigabytes SATA hard disk.

Due to lack of parallel CFI mining approaches in the literature, we compared our algorithm to our own parallel implementation of CLOSET in MapReduce. We used three Map Reduce jobs. The first job is dedicated to generate the frequency list containing all items in the dataset and for each one we associated its number of occurrences (support) and the final list was sorted in descending order of supports. The second job in CLOSET takes the entire dataset and removes all the infrequent items. Eventually, the third job achieves the CFI mining process. The latter divides the dataset in Map phase into multiple splits using the item-based partitioning approach mentioned earlier in Sect. 4.2. The Map phase finds for each frequent item its Sub-Dataset and the associates header table. The Reduce phase starts by comparing the supports of the items with the supports of the itemsets in the header table of the corresponding Sub-Dataset. Those which have the same supports, their string concatenation produces a CFI which is stored in a hash-table with its corresponding supports.

Finally, we also compared DCIM to the parallel PFP-Growth [11] implementation of the FP-Growth algorithm (PFP in short) for MapReduce. PFP is dedicated to extraction of frequent itemsets only (and the generation of frequent itemsets from closed frequents one can be done in a significant amount of time). However, this is an interesting comparison to a well-known approach of the literature. The default values for PFP in our experiments are: $Q = 30,000$ (the number of groups containing dependent transactions, for the construction of the corresponding FP-Trees from Sub-Datasets to each itemset candidates) and $K = 90$ (the number of top frequent itemsets). For more details see [11].

Datasets. We carried out our tests on two real-life datasets. The first one, called "English Wikipedia", represents a transformed set of Wikipedia articles into a transactional dataset, each line mimics an article. It contains 8 millions transactions with 7 millions distinct items, in which the maximal length of a transaction is 150, 000, and the size of the whole database is 4.7 Gigabytes. The second dataset, called "ClueWeb", consists of Web pages that were collected in January and February 2009 and is used by several tracks of the TREC conference. During our experiments, we used a part of this dataset with 53 millions transactions including 11 millions items with a maximal length of a transaction of 700,000. The size of the considered "ClueWeb" dataset is 24.9 Gigabytes.

[2] https://wiki.inria.fr/ClustersSophia/Clusters_Home.

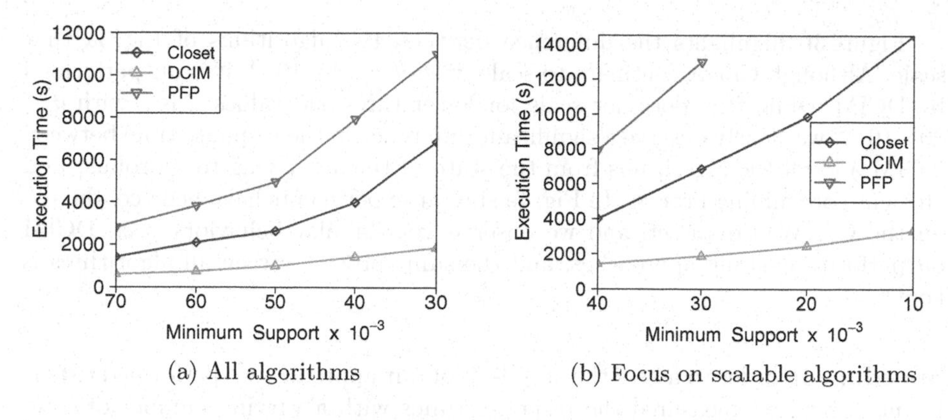

(a) All algorithms (b) Focus on scalable algorithms

Fig. 3. Runtime on the English Wikipedia dataset with a cluster of 16 nodes

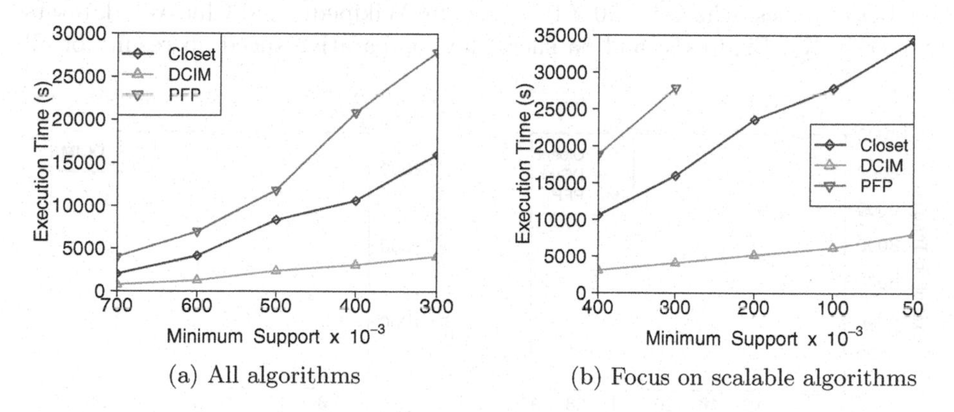

(a) All algorithms (b) Focus on scalable algorithms

Fig. 4. Runtime on the ClueWeb dataset with a cluster of 16 nodes

Runtime. Figures 3 and 4 show the results of our experiments on both English Wikipedia and ClueWeb datasets (respectively). Figure 3a reports the comparative performance of DCIM under different values of minimum support (θ) less then 1% of the overall size of the dataset. We see that DCIM sharply outperform both other algorithms. In fact, Wikipedia dataset contains a most equally number of items and transactions. Thus, as far as θ value is low, PFP and CLOSET generate too many candidates, and a lot of long Sub-datasets for each one. So, the inclusion tests and evaluations under the pruning methods used in these two algorithms causes lead as expected to poor performances. Therefore, the response time of PFP and CLOSET grows exponentially and gets quickly very high. DCIM overcomes these problems by using prime numbers to generate the Sub-datasets through division operations. Furthermore, the GCD in each Sub-dataset has eliminated the check of supports between the candidate and its deduced closure, leading to much better performances. For instance, on the wikipedia dataset, the difference in response time is 5% with a support of $\theta = 60 \times 10^{-3}$, while it grows up to 43% with a support of $\theta = 10 \times 10^{-3}$.

Figure 3b highlights the difference between the algorithms of Fig. 3a that scale. Although Closet continues to scale with $\theta = 40 \times 10^{-3}$, it is outperformed by DCIM, while PFP does not scale for lower threshold values. Also, with $\theta \leq 20 \times 10^{-3}$, we clearly observe a significant difference in the response time between DCIM and all the algorithms from the state of the art, owing to its robust and efficient core mining process. In Fig. 4a similar experiments have been conducted on the ClueWeb data set, and we observe very similar behaviors (*i.e.*, DCIM outperforms existing approaches, and the same order between all algorithms is kept).

Speedup. In order to assess the speed-up of our approach, we performed experiments where we measured the response times with a varying number of computing nodes. In Figs. 5 and 6, we performed multiple evaluations over different number of nodes, whith $\theta = 50 \times 10^{-3}$, on the Wikipedia and ClueWeb datasets (respectively). Figures 5a and 6a show the comparative speed-up results of all

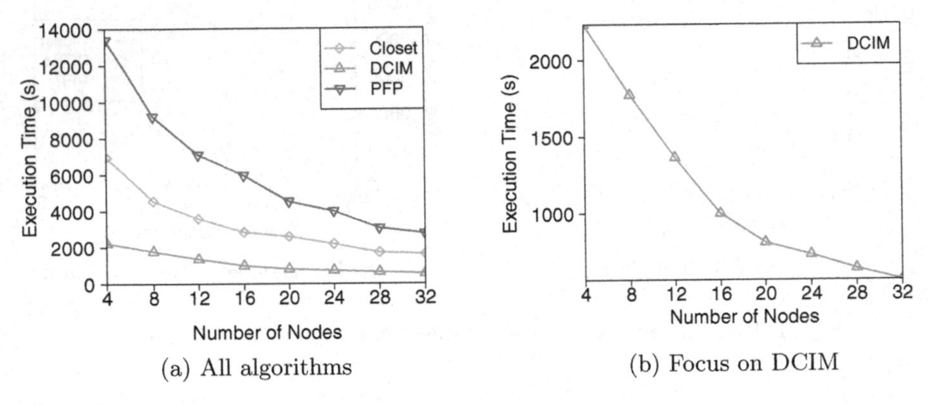

(a) All algorithms (b) Focus on DCIM

Fig. 5. Speed-up on the English Wikipedia dataset, $\theta = 50 \times 10^{-3}$

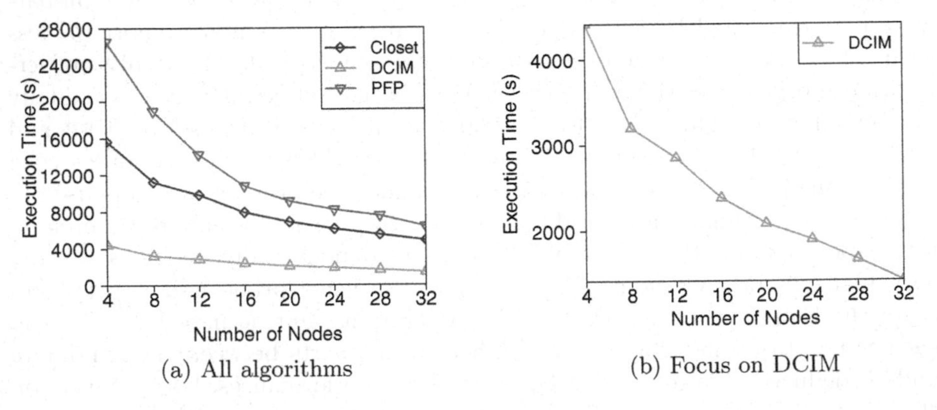

(a) All algorithms (b) Focus on DCIM

Fig. 6. Speed-up on the ClueWeb dataset, $\theta = 500 \times 10^{-3}$

algorithms, and confirm the clear advantage of DCIM for all the possible settings in the number of nodes. Figures 5b and 6b focus on the speed-up of DCIM only. This is the same number of nodes and same value of θ (and, of course, the same response times for each number of nodes), with a magnified view on DCIM. We can observe the very good speed-up of DCIM which, by taking into account parallel optmizations in its core design, benefits from an increase in the number of computing nodes.

6 Conclusion

In this paper, we proposed a reliable and efficient parallel algorithm for CFI mining namely DCIM, that shows significantly better performances than approaches from the state of the art. In addition to using prime numbers and processing big integers, we provide DCIM with optimizations designed towards massive distribution and the MapReduce framework. The results illustrate that our method outperforms other alternatives, mainly by reducing the overhead of data exchange between nodes.

Acknowledgments. This work has been partially funded by the European Commission under the CloudDBAppliance project (grant 732051) and performed in the context of the Computational Biology Institute in Montpellier.

References

1. Moens, S., Aksehirli, E., Goethals, B.: Frequent itemset mining for big data. In: Proceedings of IEEE 2013 on Big Data, Santa Clara, CA, USA (2013)
2. Gainaru, A., Cappello, F., Trausan-Matu, S., Kramer, B.: Event log mining tool for large scale HPC systems. In: Jeannot, E., Namyst, R., Roman, J. (eds.) Euro-Par 2011. LNCS, vol. 6852, pp. 52–64. Springer, Heidelberg (2011). doi:10.1007/978-3-642-23400-2_6
3. Xu, W., Huang, L., Fox, A., Patterson, D., Jordan, M.: Mining console logs for large-scale system problem detection. In: Proceedings of SysML 2008, Berkeley, CA, USA (2008)
4. Pasquier, N., Bastide, Y., Taouil, R., Lakhal, L.: Discovering frequent closed itemsets for association rules. In: Beeri, C., Buneman, P. (eds.) ICDT 1999. LNCS, vol. 1540, pp. 398–416. Springer, Heidelberg (1999). doi:10.1007/3-540-49257-7_25
5. Chen, K., Zhang, L., Li, S., Ke, W.: Research on association rules parallel algorithm based on FP-growth. In: Liu, C., Chang, J., Yang, A. (eds.) ICICA 2011. CCIS, vol. 244, pp. 249–256. Springer, Heidelberg (2011). doi:10.1007/978-3-642-27452-7_33
6. Dean, J., Ghemawat, S.: MapReduce: simplified data processing on large clusters. ACM J. Commun. **51**, 107–113 (2008)
7. Zaharia, M., Chowdhury, M., Franklin, M.J., Shenker, S., Stoica, I.: Spark: cluster computing with working sets. In: Proceedings of USENIX, HotCloud 2010, Boston, MA, USA (2010)
8. Wang, S.-Q., Yang, Y.-B., Gao, Y., Chen, G.-P., Zhang, Y.: MapReduce-based closed frequent itemset mining with efficient redundancy filtering. In: Proceedings of IEEE 2012 ICDM, Brussels, Belgium (2012)

9. Zaïane, O.R., El-Hajj, M., Lu, P.: Fast parallel association rule mining without candidacy generation. In: Proceedings of IEEE 2001 ICDM, San Jose, California, USA (2001)
10. Li, E., Liu, L.: Optimization of frequent itemset mining on multiple-core processor. In: Proceedings of VLDB 2007, Vienna, Austria (2007)
11. Li, H., Wang, Y., Zhang, D., Zhang, M., Chang, E.Y.: PFP: parallel FP-growth for query recommendation. In: Proceedings of RecSys 2008, Lausanne, Switzerland (2008)
12. Wang, J., Han, J., Pei, J.: CLOSET+: searching for the best strategies for mining frequent closed itemsets. In: Proceedings of SIG-KDD 2003, Washington, DC, USA (2003)
13. Lucchese, C., Orlando, S., Perego, R.: Fast and memory efficient mining of frequent closed itemsets. J. IEEE 2006 (2006)
14. Wang, S., Wang, L.: An implementation of FP-growth algorithm based on high level data structures of Weka-Jung framework. J. JCIT (2010)
15. Nègre, C.: Efficient binary polynomial multiplication based on optimized Karatsuba reconstruction. J. Cryptographic Eng. **4**, 91–106 (2014)
16. Zanoni, A.: Iterative Toom-Cook methods for very unbalanced long integer multiplication. In: Proceedings ISSAC 2010, Munich, Germany (2010)

Uncovering the Runtime Enterprise Architecture of a Large Distributed Organisation

A Process Mining-Oriented Approach

Robert van Langerak, Jan Martijn E.M. van der Werf(✉), and Sjaak Brinkkemper

Department of Information and Computing Science, Utrecht University, Utrecht, Netherlands
{r.p.vanlangerak,j.m.e.m.vanderwerf,s.brinkkemper}@uu.nl

Abstract. Process mining mainly focuses on analyzing a single process that runs through an organization. Often organisations consist of multiple departments that need to work together to deliver a process. ArchiMate introduced the Business Process Cooperation Viewpoint for this. However, such models tend to focus on modeling design time, and not the runtime behavior. Additionally, many approaches exist to analyze multiple departments in isolation, or the social network they form, but the cooperation between processes received little attention.

In this paper we take a different approach by analyzing the runtime execution data to create a new visualization technique to uncover cooperation between departments by means of the Runtime Enterprise Architecture using process mining techniques. By means of a real-life case study at a large logistic organization, we apply the presented approach.

Keywords: Process mining · Enterprise architecture · Data analytics · Business analytics · Runtime enterprise architecture

1 Introduction

In larger organisations, departments work jointly to deliver the services or products of that organisation. Capturing this cooperation is part of the domain of Enterprise Architecture (EA) [29]. EA consists of principles, methods, and models to design and realize an enterprise's organisational structure, business processes, information systems, and infrastructure. An important aspect within organisations is the cooperation between different departments in the overall processes of the organisation. ArchiMate [13] introduced the Business Process Co-operation Viewpoint (BPC) to model this explicitly. These models mainly focus on the design of cooperation: which processes and departments within an organisation are allowed to communicate. The runtime behaviour, i.e., whether and when communication occurs, and the possible execution orders are typically left out.

E. Dubois and K. Pohl (Eds.): CAiSE 2017, LNCS 10253, pp. 247–263, 2017.
DOI: 10.1007/978-3-319-59536-8_16

Process mining [2] offers many opportunities to assist the enterprise architect in uncovering the runtime behaviour of their EA. In process mining, many algorithms exist to discover processes (e.g. [5,8,10,16]), to check for conformance (e.g. [3,7,22]), and to enhance process models (e.g. [11,25]). Although the process is viewed from different perspectives [17], such as the case, process and resource perspective, the organisational perspective [23] has been given little attention. Approaches like PM^2 [24] and Process Diagnostics [6] focus on the overall process within an organisation, rather than focusing on how the different departments within the organisation contribute to deliver its service. Consequently, for larger organisations where multiple departments cooperate to deliver their services, current process mining techniques are hard to apply.

As a running example, consider the insurance company InsComp. The organisation has three deparments: the Policy Department, the Claim Department and the Financial Administration. InsComp delivers two services: the issuing of policies and the handling of claims, where the former is the responsibility of the Policy Department, and the latter of the Claim Department. The Claim Department sometimes asks the Policy Department to check a policy. Once a claim is approved, the Financial Administration is instructed to compensate the claim. As InsComp has a problem with the Claim Handling service, they want to obtain insights into the cooperation and functioning of the different departments and locations.

In this paper, we want to close the gap between the static descriptions created in EA and the runtime environment in which all these processes have been implemented. We do this by addressing the research question: *How can the analysis of runtime execution data facilitate the visualisation of the actual business process cooperation in enterprise architecture?* To pursue this research, we applied the objective-centered approach in Design Science Research [20], to design and evaluate visualisation techniques of runtime execution data in the field of enterprise architecture.

Based on the successful application of process mining in other fields [2,4,6,10], we propose to apply process mining techniques for the analysis of questions about the quality of the actual different departments and their cooperation. We do this by introducing the Runtime Enterprise Architecture (REA) of an organisation, which uses the runtime operation data from the processes operated within the organisation. This allows us to create new visualisations to uncover the involvement of departments, their cooperation, and their relative achievements in the process.

In the remainder of this paper we make the following contributions:

- Incorporation of the runtime behaviour of an organisation into the Business Process Co-operation Viewpoint of Enterprise Architecture (Sect. 2);
- Visualisation techniques to uncover the Runtime Business Process Co-operation View of an organisation (Sect. 3); and
- Showing the applicability and possibilities of the techniques through a case study in a large parcel distributor in the Netherlands (Sect. 4).

2 Runtime Enterprise Architectures

To model the different departments within an organisation and how these cooperate to deliver the services of an organisation, ArchiMate 3.0 [13] introduced the Business Process Co-operation Viewpoint (BPC) [15]. This viewpoint shows the relation between the business processes and their surroundings, and can be used to create a high-level design of business processes within their context and to provide insight into their dependencies [15]. The BPC viewpoint of our example organisation InsComp is shown in Fig. 1.

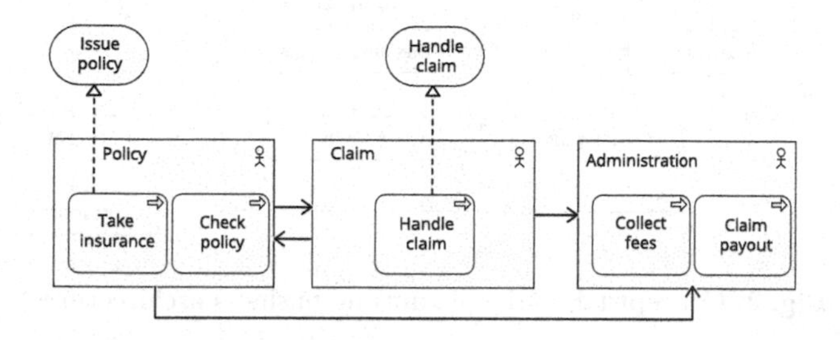

Fig. 1. Business process co-operation viewpoint

The BPC viewpoint reflects the allowed cooperations at design time. Whether in real life this blue print is always followed is a complete different question. With the logging capabilities of current Process-Aware Information Systems (PAISs), it is possible to record reality in the form of audit trails or event logs [26]. These event logs are input for process mining.

Key in process mining is that each event is related to a process instance of some businesss process. Process mining focuses on analyzing a single process, whereas in an organisation many different processes run intertwined. For this we define the *Runtime Enterprise Architecture* (REA) as the set of structures and metrics to capture and analyze the runtime behaviour of that organisation based on its Enterprise Architecture. In this paper, we focus on the dynamic behaviour of the BPC viewpoint, the Runtime Business Process Co-operation View (RBPC). As for process mining in general, this approach relies on the assumption that for each event it is known to which activity (and thus process) it belongs.

2.1 Meta-Model of the Runtime Business Process Co-operation View

The conceptual model that maps the relevant event log concepts to the concepts of the BPC viewpoint is shown in Fig. 2. On the left, the relevant elements of the BPC viewpoint are depicted. The gray elements are the default elements of ArchiMate. *Organisation* and *Department* are specializations of the ArchiMate element *Business Actor*. An *Organisation* has a hierarchical structure of *Departments*, and delivers some *Business Service*. A *Business Service* is implemented by one or more *Business Processes*. *Activities* in a *Business Process* form *Cooperation*. A *Cooperation* is always initiated by an *Activity* (relation *from*) and concluded by an *Activity* (relation *to*).

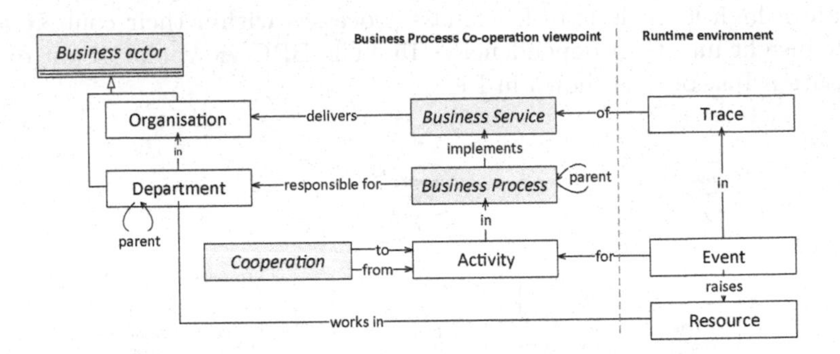

Fig. 2. Conceptual model of runtime business architectures

At runtime, *Business Services* are instantiated, resulting in *Traces*, that flow through the organisation. For a *Trace*, *Events* are raised by executing *Activities*. Possibly, the *Resource* is recorded as well. Notice that in many organisations, traces are identified by some global identifier that is used throughout the business service or organisation.

2.2 Runtime Business Process Co-operation View

At design time, different cooperations can be modelled in the BPC view. The definition of the concepts and relations are directly derived from the conceptual model in Fig. 2. Let c be a cooperation. From the conceptual model, we can define the following types of cooperations.

Intra-process A cooperation occurs within the same process, i.e. $in(from(c)) = in(to(c))$;

Inter-process A cooperation occurs between two different processes, i.e., $in(from(c)) \neq in(to(c))$;

Intra-departmental A cooperation within the same department (possibly between different processes), i.e., $responsible\_for(in(from(c))) = responsible\_for(in(to(c)))$

Inter-departmental A cooperation between different departments, i.e., $responsible\_for(in(from(c))) \neq responsible\_for(in(to(c)))$

In this model, a cooperation can be both inter-process and intra-deparmental at the same time, if the cooperation is between two business processes for which the same department is responsible.

3 Uncovering Cooperations

To obtain insight in the cooperations within an organisation, we first discuss how to discover cooperations. Next, we present a new visualisation technique for cooperations, the Runtime Business Process Co-operation View that visualises the runtime behaviour of an organisation, rather than only focusing on the design time, as is current practice in EA.

3.1 Discovering Cooperations Using Process Mining

Several techniques have been proposed in process mining to analyze both inter and intra organisations [1], such as social network analysis [23], artifact-centric techniques [21] and feature discovery [28]. Social Network Analysis (SNA) focuses on identifying nodes and their relationships [19]. A social network consists of nodes and a set of relationships or links. In [23], the authors use event logs to generate a social network of the resources within the event log. In process analysis this derived SNA can be used to identify resources in a network, and to show how these resources interact. Additionally, SNA can be used to study patterns within an organisations network and enabling organisations to use these patterns to create competitive advantages [14].

Whereas process mining relies on the assumption that each process instance belongs to the same business process, the artifact-centric approach assumes that the process instances are manipulated by artifacts [18], and tries to discover the processes and interactions of these artifacts [9,21]. Artifact-centric mining is used to discover a process by using the artifacts that are present in the process and is therefore often used to create better process models for real life or physical processes [12].

Recent research focuses on the use of process discovery techniques to construct functional architectures [28] by relating software execution data to features. In this way, it is possible to discover the communication protocols between features from the behavioural profile [27].

Each of these process mining techniques can be used to enhance the existing BPC viewpoint by updating the *Cooperations* from the event log. Next step is to visualise and quantify the cooperations found at runtime.

3.2 Visualising the Runtime Business Process Cooperation

At runtime, many different metrics are available about the business processes and their cooperations. The current visualisation of the BPC viewpoint in ArchiMate only focuses on depicting the EA at design time. Consequently, we require new visualisations to provide useful insights in the organisation.

In this paper, we introduce the Runtime Business Process Co-operation View (RBPC), which is an interactive representation of process execution data. As an example, a RBPC of InsComp is depicted in Fig. 3. The view combines a chord diagram and a sunburst diagram. Chord diagrams have been developed to visualise large sets of arcs by bundling all arcs between two nodes. Similarly, a

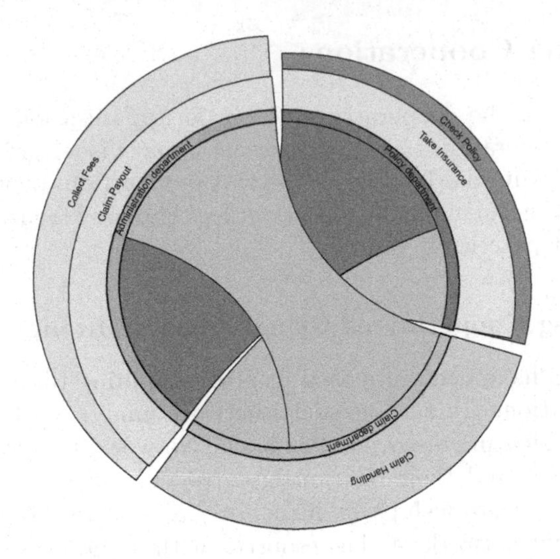

Fig. 3. Runtime business process co-operation view

sunburst diagram provides a visualisation for the frequency of elements: the size of each element is proportional to its frequency.

The view consists of two circles. The inner circle is a chord diagram that represents the cooperation between the different departments. Each part represents a department. The length of each part is determined by the centrality of the node in the social network, which is a combination of the number of cooperations each part initiated and concluded, and the size of the flows represent the volumes traveling between the nodes. The colour of the flow is determined by the node that initiates most cooperations. The outer cricle is a sunburst that indicates the percentage of process instances handled by the departments. In case the departments run multiple processes, each process is depicted as a layer, with a height proportional to the number of process instances handled by that process. In this way, the view provides a high level overview of the processes, and their cooperation, and at the same time insights in how frequent these processes have been executed.

Additionally, we can colour the outer circle with other metrics, such as the overall duration of the cooperations, or the conformance of the different processes within the department.

For the running example InsComp, an example RBPC is depicted in Fig. 3. The three parts represent the three departments, and their processes as layers in outer circle. The colour scale represents the duration time of the process. From its size in the diagram, we directly see that the Financial Department plays a large role in the organisation. Also, we see that a third of the cooperations with the Policy Department are with the Claim Department. Most cooperations of this department are with the Financial Administration. From this view, we can conclude from the flows that a third of the communication of the Policy

Department comes from the Claim Department, and from the colouring we conclude that the "Check Policy" process in the Policy Department is a bottleneck, and that in the Financial Administration the duration for the "Claim Payout" process is above average, which would explain why the Claim Handling service of InsComp requires attention.

4 Validation of the Runtime Enterprise Architecture

We aim to validate the proposed Runtime Business Process Co-operation View with a non-trivial case study in a large logistics company. The selected case organisation is one of the largest mail and parcel distributors in the Netherlands, referred to as SendIT. In 2014, the organisation addressed 2,705 million mail items and 142 million parcels. SendIT has 18 distribution centers throughout the Netherlands for the distribution of parcels. Each center represents a specific area for delivery and is responsible for that part of the distribution process. Consequently, there are 18 instances of the same departmental processes, and cooperations between all 18 distribution centers. Each center has its own facilities to record the process execution data. Each of the instances can be analyzed and compared using this data. Currently, the organisation lacks proper visualisations of the performance of the different centers, and their cooperation in the different processes. In this case study, we use the data to compare the different distribution centers on process execution and performance, and to discover the different cooperations between departmental processes.

4.1 Distribution Process and Scan Trails

Each distribution center is responsible for three main processes: sorting shifts (B), sorting routes (J), and delivery (I). The intended happy flow of the parcel delivery process is depicted in Fig. 4.

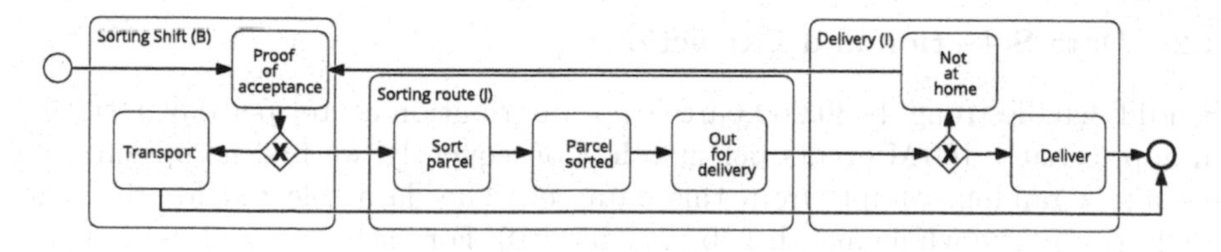

Fig. 4. Intended process model of the happy flow of the parcel delivery at SendIT

During the night, process B is executed at the centers. Each parcel is scanned, and based on the postal code, the center decides to either sort itself, or to transport it to a different center. In the morning, once all parcels of the other centers are received, each parcel is scanned again, and passed to the sorting route process (J), that determines the parcels each delivery man has to handle. Once all packages are sorted to the different routes, the delivery men start the delivery process (I). In case a parcel cannot be delivered at an address, it returns to the sorting shift.

Parcels are represented by unique barcodes. In each step of the process, the parcels are scanned, which results in adding a new scan value to its respective barcode. A scan value has its own definition and possible consequences for the further distribution of this parcel. In total there are more than 150 possible scan values. Each scan value consists of a label indicating the process (value), and the activity in that process (reason). Examples of possible scan values include entering a distribution center, with scan vallue $B1$, 'Proof of Acceptance', placing a parcel on a conveyer ($J1$), out for delivery ($J5$), and delivered ($I1$).

Table 1. Scan trail of a single package representing the most frequent happy flow

Barcode	Date	Time	Value	Reason	Description
1B1671337	10/02/2016	00:49:25	B	1	Proof of acceptance
1B1671337	10/02/2016	09:34:25	J	1	Sorted
1B1671337	10/02/2016	09:34:26	J	40	Sorted on route
1B1671337	10/02/2016	10:06:03	J	5	Out for delivery
1B1671337	10/02/2016	12:28:45	I	1	Delivered

The scan trail of a parcel is a sequence of all its scan vallues and their occurence. Each scan vallue always consists of a character and a number, together with a timestamp. Several happy flows exist for these trails: flows where nothing went wrong and the parcel was delivered. The most frequent happy flow is depicted in Table 1. For each parcel a trail can be exported from the different PAISs of the distribution centers at SendIT.

4.2 Data Selection and Extraction

SendIT handles roughly 30.000 parcels per distribution center per day, resulting in approxmatly 160 M events per month. Consequently, we had no option than to take a random sample from this data set. The data selected for this case study covers the whole month February in 2016. For each center, a dataset was created with at most 500 parcels per day. For these parcels, the scan trails were extracted and combined into a large dataset for a distribution center. The total number of events per center is depicted in Table 2. As a last step, all datasets were combined into a single dataset for analysis. This resulting dataset contains 136.575 scan trails.

Each dataset had to be prepared before it can be analyzed. An excerpt of the trail is depicted in Table 1. For example, the date and time values had to be merged into a single timestamp, as this is required by the different process

Table 2. Events per distribution center (DC). In total, the dataset contains 1.555.492 events divided over 136.575 scan trails

DC	# Events
1	111.001
2	84.309
3	85.935
4	103.887
5	72.345
6	90.116
7	81.362
8	124.722
9	66.348
10	79.234
11	74.715
12	83.476
13	85.049
14	87.188
15	80.159
16	77.148
17	88.714
18	79.784

Table 3. Structure of an event in the event logs after conversion. The Scan letter and number together form the activity name to which the event is related. The Barcode is the instance identifier.

Attribute	Example
Barcode (ID)	1B1671337
Timestamp	10/02/2016 00:49:25
Scan letter	B
Scan number	01
Combinedscan	B01
Center	LOC 3

mining tools. The Value and Reason attributes in the scan trail are merged to create the activity name for each event. Both values were added to the event log, to be able to analyze the event log on different levels of abstraction, as the Value and Reason represent the business process, and the corresponding activity, respectively. The final structure of an event is shown in Table 3.

4.3 Analysis

For the analysis of the datasets, the open source software ProM [26] is used. To exclude parcels that are not yet delivered, we filtered the dataset by removing all scan trails that do not contain an activity with an I-value. Next, multiple analyses have been executed with ProM to identify the structures and flows in the dataset. To create an overview of the entire process, the organisational process is visualised first. Next, a generic departmental process model is created from the most occurring traces in the dataset. Lastly, the subprocesses of the departmental processes are identified. By combining these models using Archimate, a static enterprise architecture is created.

The organisational model is created using the Social network miner plugin [23]. The result is depicted in Fig. 5. It is a complete graph, i.e., all distribution centers send parcels to each other.

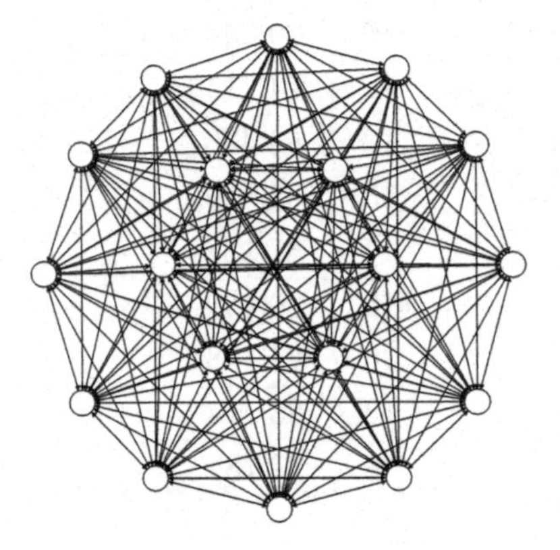

Fig. 5. Organisational model as mined with the social network miner of ProM

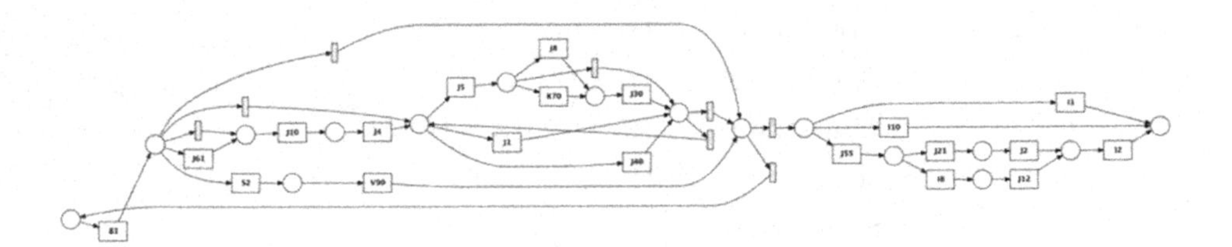

Fig. 6. 10 most occuring traces

Departmental Models. As a complete process model representing all 136.575 scan trails returns a spaghetti-like model, we decided to apply Occam's razor, and as a first step [6], created a new dataset containing only the 10 most occurring traces of the 18 distribution centers. The ten most occurring traces cover together almost 68% of all scan trails. Applying the Inductive Visual Miner [16] resulted in the Petri net as depicted in Fig. 6. The process starts with a B1 event, then the sorting process is started (J-valued events), after which the parcel is delivered (I-valued events). From the same dataset containing the 10 most frequent scan trails, we discovered for each of the processes a separate process model. The J process is depicted in Fig. 7.

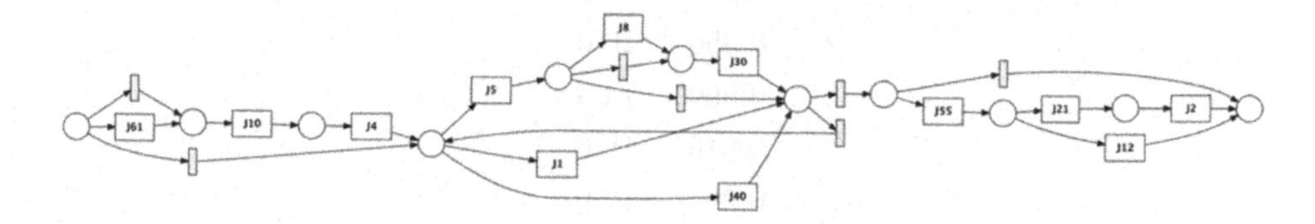

Fig. 7. Model of process J in isolation

To check the degree of conformance of the processes of the different distribution centers the logs are replayed through the petri net using the "Replay for conformance checking plugin" in ProM. This results in a fitness value per center (Table 4), indicating how well a model represents a log, on a scale from 0 (no fitness) to 1 (complete fitness). Overall, the mined process shows a high fitness (average: 0.945), indicating that our razor of only taking the 10 most occurring traces approximates the overall process very well. Additionally, we used Disco[1] to analyze the median duration time for each center. All values range between 14,3 and 23,3 h, the average is 17,4 h between first scan and delivery.

Enterprise Architecture. The Enterprise Architecture comprises the different processes, and abstracts from the detailed activities. To discover how the different processes cooperate, we decided to create an additional organisational model in which the hand-over of work is analysed between the different processes by taking the Value as resource. This resulted in the model depicted in Fig. 8(a). Based on this organisational model, it is possible to create the BPC viewpoint of the static EA of SendIT, shown in Fig. 8(b).

Runtime Business Process Co-operation View. One of the main drivers of SendIT is to compare the runtime behaviour of the different centers, and the amount of parcels that is transported between the centers. For this, we created two separate RBPC views for SendIT. Both RBPC views use the location changes of the parcels in the chord diagram, and the respective number of scan trails handled in the center for the length of the sunburst. For the colouring schema, the former is based on the median duration of scan trails, the latter is based on the fitness of the sub processes at each center.

To define the chord diagram of both RBPC views, we first analyzed the mined social network (Fig. 5), where the location changes have been defined as

[1] https://fluxicon.com/disco/.

Table 4. Fitness values and median durations in hours per distribution center (DC), calculated with the Replay for Conformance Plugin of ProM on the model depicted in Fig. 6. The fitness is a score between 0 and 1, and indicates how well the instances adhere to the given process model. The average fitness is 0.945.

DC	Fitness	Dur. (h)
1	0.911	15.8
2	0.956	16.0
3	0.960	14.3
4	0.916	18.6
5	0.964	17.9
6	0.870	15.9
7	0.957	15.8
8	0.943	16.8
9	0.954	15.1
10	0.941	19.1
11	0.954	19.6
12	0.955	23.3
13	0.968	19.7
14	0.954	18.7
15	0.952	17.6
16	0.949	15.1
17	0.948	16.0
18	0.949	17.6

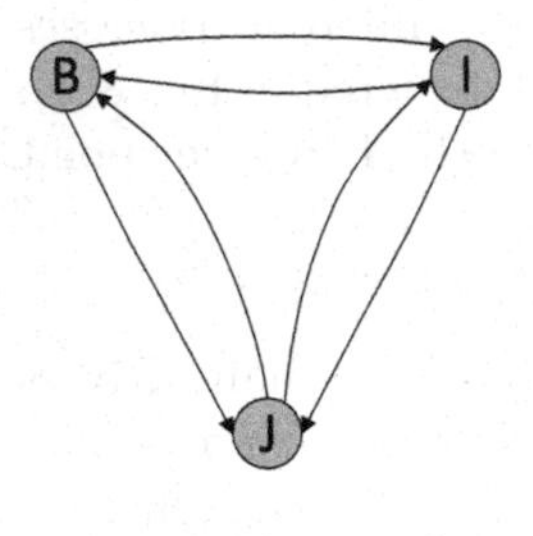

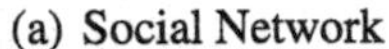
(a) Social Network

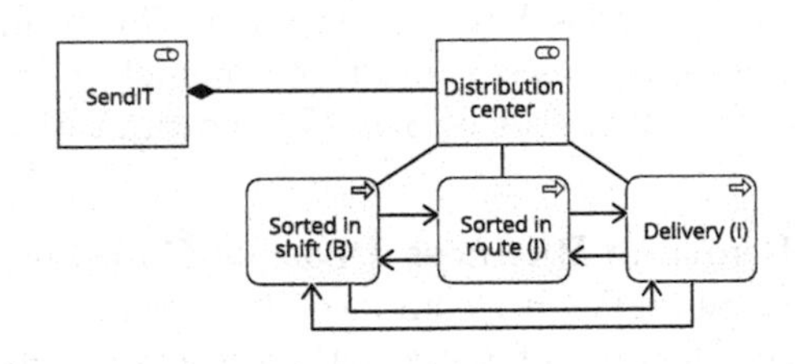

(b) Archimate BPC view

Fig. 8. The discovered BPC view of SendIT generated from the social network miner of ProM

the hand-over of work between the centers [23]. As a first step, their respective frequencies have been analyzed. As each parcel is always at exactly one location, we counted the number of consecutive event pairs with different locations.

As a next step, these numbers have been normalized using the total number of location changes. In this way, location changes become relative to each other, and all add up to 100%. Based on this data, the chord diagram is constructed.

To determine the length of each center in the RBPC views, i.e., the number of scan trails handled by the center, we analyzed for each center the ratio between parcels with a B scan vallue, i.e., the number of parcels that arrive, with the number of parcels that have an I scan vallue, i.e., the number of parcels delivered by the center. If this ratio is high, most parcels that arrive at the center are distributed in the region, i.e., the center handles many parcels, whereas if the ratio is low, most parcels are transported to different centers, thus the center handles few parcels.

Next, for each center we determine the size of the internal process by normalizing the amount of parcels each process handles with the ratio determined for that center. For example, if a center has 50% of B scan vallues, 25% of J scan vallues, and 25% of I scan vallues, parts J and I will be similar in size, and the size of B has the size of J and I combined. As each center has three processes, sorting shifts (B), sorting routes (J), and delivery (I), this results in three rings for each center in the RBPC views.

These two steps create the basis for the RBPC views using the d3 javascript framework[2]. The first RBPC view uses the median duration, as depicted in Table 4, for colouring its elements. The lowest median duration is coloured green, the highest is coloured red. Each center is assigned a gradient colour relative to the higest and lowest median durations, resulting in the view depicted in Fig. 9(a).

Analyzing the two RBPC views, we directly observe that location 6 sends out many more parcels than that it handles, as its size is large, while its length is relatively low. Location 1 handles most parcels, as it has the largest length. Another observation in Fig. 9(a) is that at 5 centers (i.e., 28%) the delivery process have a longer than average median duration (red), and that at 3 centers (i.e., 17%) the process takes shorter than average. Only at one location, the sorting to shifts process (B) takes much longer than average. Similarly, analyzing Fig. 9(b), we observe that all centers conform the B process, whereas the other two processes have more deviations. Only location 1 and 4 show outlying fitness values for the I and J processes.

4.4 Expert Validation

To validate the results and different visualisations of the RBPC, we presented the results to two stakeholders of SendIT, being a process manager and a process data analyst, who were not involved in executing the case study. The goal of the interviews was to identify the perceived usefulness of the design, and to obtain possible improvements and additional feedback. The technical details of the design were discussed, as well as the possible business applications of the solution. Additionally, the feasibility within SendIT was part of the discussion.

[2] https://d3js.org/.

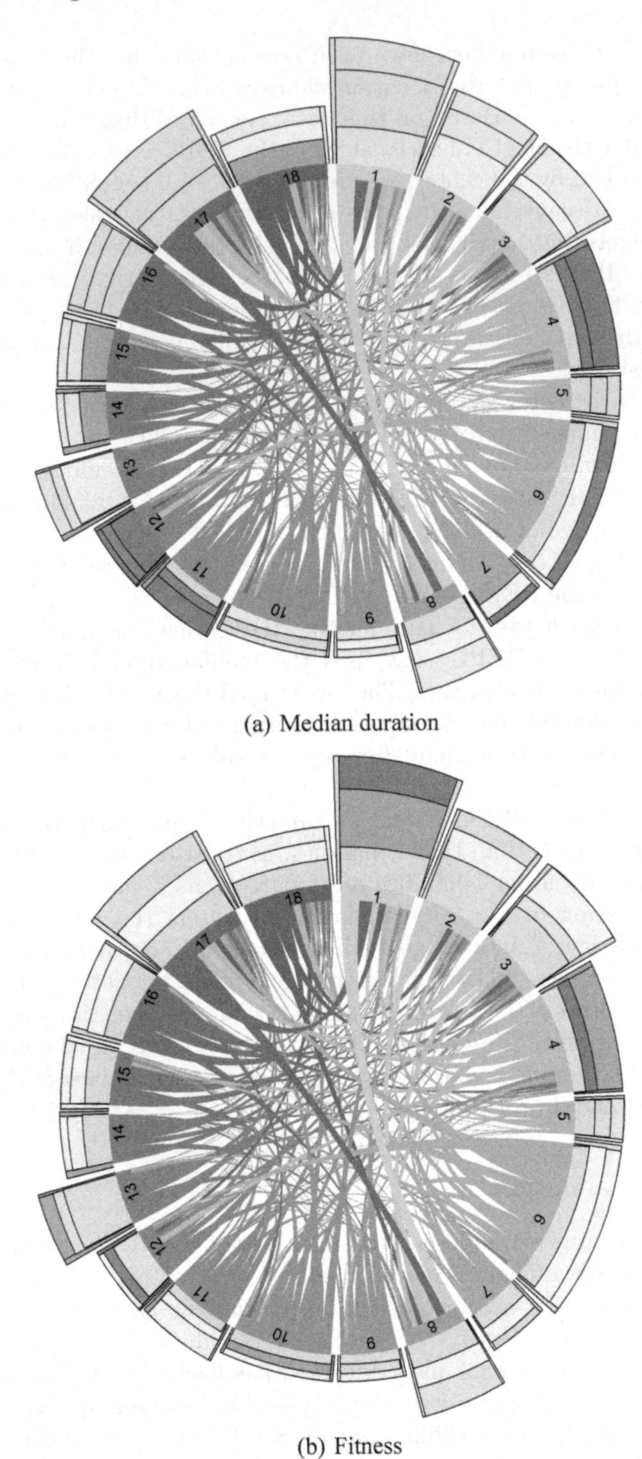

(a) Median duration

(b) Fitness

Fig. 9. Two runtime business process co-operation views of SendIT. Each part in the diagram corresponds to a department (1–18). Each layer in the deparment represents the processes B, I and J (from inner to outer layer)

The validation started with discussing the standard process mining models, which are also presented in this section. The stakeholders mentioned that these models were "interesting to see, but are not really useful in day to day practice". There is no real chance for active management using only the petri nets. However, they could be useful to get some "low level process insight".

The RBPC was perceived very useful. The idea and the ability to present real time process data to the "Operations Management Division" of the organisation was met with an enthusiastic response. This would lead to more proactive management of the distribution process throughout each day. Currently, most of the improvements actions that are undertaken are based on negative outliers of the past week. Using the RBPC on a real time basis would enable Operations management to pro-actively correct problems that occur in a distribution center.

Additionally, the RBPC could be used to bridge the gap between Operations and Organisation management. The management is not aware and not interested in low level process information. Their main objective is to fulfill the KPIs that were set for a certain period. Using the RBPC, it is possible to convert low level process data to high level process information. This information subsequently can be used to actively used when discussion the current execution and performance of the entire organisation.

Concluding, the RBPC was received positively. Some remarks were made how the RBPC could be adapted to better fit the organisation, but this is a matter of implementation that varies per organisation. The stakeholders mentioned that "in todays world the trick is to create something that can covert the abundance of data into information, so it can be used by someone who is not familiar with the data. This is what the RBPC does.".

5 Conclusions and Future Work

Current Enterprise Architecture mainly focus on modeling an organisation design-time only. In this paper, we propose the Runtime Enterprise Architecture (REA) that enhances the EA of an organisation with runtime execution data. To visualise the cooperation between departments and their process within an organisation, we propose the Runtime Business Process Co-operation viewpoint that visualises the runtime cooperation between departments and the relative volumes and quality of the different processes at the departments. The visualisation combines the chord diagram for visualising cooperations with the sunburst visualisation for the volume of the processes. The colouring schema is used to depict the quality of the processes.

To illustrate the visualisation, we applied it on one a large logistics organisation to analyze parcel transportation between departments. Initial validation at the organisation shows the perceived usefulness of the visualisation technique. Another limitation of the case study is that although the proposed visualisation technique in itself is quite general, the case study organisation had no concurrency in their processes. Generalization of the validation results therefore require further experimentation.

Many different viewpoints exist in EA modeling. In this paper we focused mainly on the Business Process Co-operation Viewpoint, but we envision the proposed techniques to be extended to different viewpoints as well. As the proof of the pudding is in the eating, we plan on fully automating the visualisation technique in ProM to perform more in-depth case studies to explore further analysis and visualisation possibilities of the technique.

References

1. van der Aalst, W.M.P.: Intra- and inter-organizational process mining: discovering processes within and between organizations. In: Johannesson, P., Krogstie, J., Opdahl, A.L. (eds.) PoEM 2011. LNBIP, vol. 92, pp. 1–11. Springer, Heidelberg (2011). doi:10.1007/978-3-642-24849-8_1
2. van der Aalst, W.M.P.: Process Mining: Discovery, Conformance and Enhancement of Business Processes. Springer, Heidelberg (2011)
3. van der Aalst, W.M.P., Adriansyah, A., van Dongen, B.F.: Replaying history on process models for conformance checking and performance analysis. Wiley Interdisc. Rev. Data Mining Knowl. Discov. **2**(2), 182–192 (2012)
4. van der Aalst, W.M.P., Reijers, H.A., Song, M.: Discovering social networks from event logs. Comput. Support. Coop. Work **14**(6), 549–593 (2005)
5. van der Aalst, W.M.P., Weijters, A.J.M.M., Maruster, L.: Workflow mining: discovering process models from event logs. Knowl. Data Eng. **16**(9), 1128–1142 (2004)
6. Bozkaya, M., Gabriels, J., van der Werf, J.M.E.M.: Process diagnostics: a method based on process mining. In: eKNOW 2009, pp. 22–27. IEEE Computer Society (2009)
7. Buijs, J.C.A.M., Reijers, H.A.: Comparing business process variants using models and event logs. In: Bider, I., Gaaloul, K., Krogstie, J., Nurcan, S., Proper, H.A., Schmidt, R., Soffer, P. (eds.) BPMDS/EMMSAD -2014. LNBIP, vol. 175, pp. 154–168. Springer, Heidelberg (2014). doi:10.1007/978-3-662-43745-2_11
8. Buijs, J.C.A.M., van Dongen, B.F., van der Aalst, W.M.P.: Discovering and navigating a collection of process models using multiple quality dimensions. In: Lohmann, N., Song, M., Wohed, P. (eds.) BPM 2013. LNBIP, vol. 171, pp. 3–14. Springer, Cham (2014). doi:10.1007/978-3-319-06257-0_1
9. Cohn, D., Hull, R.: Business artifacts: a data-centric approach to modeling business operations and processes. IEEE Data Eng. Bull. **32**(3), 3–9 (2009)
10. van Dongen, B.F., Alves de Medeiros, A.K., Wen, L.: Process mining: overview and outlook of petri net discovery algorithms. Trans. Petri Nets Other Models Concurrency **II**(5460), 225–242 (2009)
11. Fahland, D., van der Aalst, W.M.P.: Model repair - aligning process models to reality. Inf. Syst. **47**, 220–243 (2015)
12. Fahland, D., de Leoni, M., van Dongen, B.F., van der Aalst, W.M.P.: Behavioral conformance of artifact-centric process models. In: Abramowicz, W. (ed.) BIS 2011. LNBIP, vol. 87, pp. 37–49. Springer, Heidelberg (2011). doi:10.1007/978-3-642-21863-7_4
13. The Open Group. Archimate 3.0 specification (2016). http://pubs.opengroup.org/architecture/archimate3-doc/
14. Kim, Y., Choi, T.Y., Yan, T., Dooley, K.: Structural investigation of supply networks: a social network analysis approach. J. Oper. Manag. **29**(3), 194–211 (2011)

15. Lankhorst, M.: Enterprise Architecture at Work: Modeling, Communication and Analysis, vol. 36. Springer, Heidelberg (2013)
16. Leemans, S.J.J., Fahland, D., van der Aalst, W.M.P.: Discovering block-structured process models from event logs - a constructive approach. In: Colom, J.-M., Desel, J. (eds.) PETRI NETS 2013. LNCS, vol. 7927, pp. 311–329. Springer, Heidelberg (2013). doi:10.1007/978-3-642-38697-8_17
17. Mannhardt, F., de Leoni, M., Reijers, H.A., van der Aalst, W.M.P.: Balanced multi-perspective checking of process conformance. Computing **98**(4), 407–437 (2016)
18. Nooijen, E.H.J., van Dongen, B.F., Fahland, D.: Automatic discovery of data-centric and artifact-centric processes. In: Rosa, M., Soffer, P. (eds.) BPM 2012. LNBIP, vol. 132, pp. 316–327. Springer, Heidelberg (2013). doi:10.1007/978-3-642-36285-9_36
19. Otte, E., Rousseau, R.: Social network analysis: a powerful strategy, also for the information sciences. J. Inf. Sci. **28**(6), 441–453 (2002)
20. Peffers, K., Tuunanen, T., Rothenberger, M.A., Chatterjee, S.: A design science research methodology for information systems research. J. Manag. Inf. Syst. **24**(3), 45–77 (2007)
21. Popova, V., Fahland, D., Dumas, M.: Artifact Lifecycle Discovery. arXiv preprint arXiv:1303.2554, pp. 1–27 (2013)
22. Rozinat, A., van der Aalst, W.M.P.: Conformance checking of processes based on monitoring real behavior. Inf. Syst. **33**(1), 64–95 (2008)
23. Song, M., van der Aalst, W.M.P.: Towards comprehensive support for organizational mining. Decis. Support Syst. **46**(1), 300–317 (2008)
24. van Eck, M.L., Lu, X., Leemans, S.J.J., Aalst, W.M.P.: PM2: a process mining project methodology. In: Zdravkovic, J., Kirikova, M., Johannesson, P. (eds.) CAiSE 2015. LNCS, vol. 9097, pp. 297–313. Springer, Cham (2015). doi:10.1007/978-3-319-19069-3_19
25. Vázquez-Barreiros, B., van Zelst, S.J., Buijs, J.C.A.M., Lama, M., Mucientes, M.: Repairing alignments: striking the right nerve. In: Schmidt, R., Guédria, W., Bider, I., Guerreiro, S. (eds.) BPMDS/EMMSAD -2016. LNBIP, vol. 248, pp. 266–281. Springer, Cham (2016). doi:10.1007/978-3-319-39429-9_17
26. Verbeek, H.M.W., Buijs, J.C.A.M., van Dongen, B.F., van der Aalst, W.M.P.: XES, XESame, and ProM 6. In: Soffer, P., Proper, E. (eds.) CAiSE Forum 2010. LNBIP, vol. 72, pp. 60–75. Springer, Heidelberg (2011). doi:10.1007/978-3-642-17722-4_5
27. Weidlich, M., van der Werf, J.M.E.M.: On profiles and footprints – relational semantics for Petri nets. In: Haddad, S., van der Pomello, L. (eds.) PETRI NETS 2012. LNCS, vol. 7347, pp. 148–167. Springer, Heidelberg (2012). doi:10.1007/978-3-642-31131-4_9
28. van der Werf, J.M.E.M., Kaats, E.: Discovery of functional architectures from event logs. In: International Workshop on Petri Nets and Software Engineering (PNSE 2015), pp. 227–243 (2015)
29. Winter, R., Sinz, E.J.: Enterprise architecture. Inf. Syst. e-Bus. Manag. **5**(4), 357–358 (2007)

Summarisation and Relevance Evaluation Techniques for Big Data Exploration: The Smart Factory Case Study

Ada Bagozi(✉), Devis Bianchini, Valeria De Antonellis, Alessandro Marini, and Davide Ragazzi

Department of Information Engineering, University of Brescia, Via Branze, 38, 25123 Brescia, Italy
adabagozi@gmail.com

Abstract. The increasing connections of systems that produce high volumes of real time data have raised the importance of addressing data abundance research challenges. In the Industry 4.0 application domain, for example, high volumes and velocity of data collected from machines, as well as value of data that declines very quickly, put Big Data issues among the new challenges also for the factory of the future. While many approaches have been developed to investigate data analysis, data visualisation, data collection and management, the impact of Big Data exploration is still under-estimated. In this paper, we propose an approach to support and ease exploration of real time data in a dynamic context of interconnected systems, such as the Industry 4.0 domain, where large amounts of data must be incrementally collected, organized and analysed on-the-fly. The approach relies on: (i) a multi-dimensional model, that is suited for supporting the iterative and multi-step exploration of Big Data; (ii) novel data summarisation techniques, based on clustering; (iii) a model of relevance, aimed at focusing the attention of the user only on relevant data that are being explored. We describe the application of the approach in the smart factory as a case study.

Keywords: Data exploration · Big data · Multi-dimensional data model · Industry 4.0 · Cyber physical systems

1 Introduction

The research challenges raised by the abundance of real time data in Cyber-Physical Systems (CPS) have focused the attention of researchers on the collection, organisation and exploration of data as produced by interconnected systems, enabled by the widespread diffusion of IoT technologies [11]. Collected data are featured by high volumes and velocity and have outgrown the ability to be stored and processed by many traditional systems. Moreover, their value declines very quickly, making organisations' success more and more dependent on how efficiently they can turn collected data into actionable insights. For instance,

E. Dubois and K. Pohl (Eds.): CAiSE 2017, LNCS 10253, pp. 264–279, 2017.
DOI: 10.1007/978-3-319-59536-8_17

advanced Industry 4.0 capabilities, namely self-awareness, self-configuration and self-repairing, as well as *manufacturing servitization*, defined as the strategic innovation of organisations' capabilities and processes to shift from selling products to selling integrated product and service offerings, rely on data collection and sharing [10], according to the emerging "data-driven innovation paradigm" [7].

In this context, many approaches have addressed issues related to data collection and management, data analysis, data visualisation and rendering. Neverthless, Big Data exploration issues have been under-estimated. In this paper, we discuss the ingredients to enable exploration of real time data in a dynamic context of interconnected systems, where large amounts of data must be incrementally collected, organized and analysed on-the-fly. Firstly, we envision exploration as a multi-step process, where data can be browsed through iterative refinements over a set of dimensions, hierarchically modelled, that are used to organise data into a *multi-dimensional model*. Data modeling according to "facets" or "dimensions", either flat or hierarchically organized, has been recognised as a factor for easing data exploration, since it offers the opportunity of performing flexible aggregations of data [3]. On top of the multi-dimensional model, we developed a *data summarisation* approach, in order to simplify overall view over high volumes of data, and a *model of relevance*, aimed at focusing the attention of the user on relevant data only, also when the user is not able to specify his/her requirements through a query. The multi-dimensional model, the data summarisation approach and the model of relevance are the core components of our Big&Open Data Innovation framework (BODaI) and the main contributions of this paper. With respect to exploratory data analysis [13] and Data Mining [6], our approach aims at supporting exploration as a multi-step process, where the user may iteratively improve focus on relevant data, by receiving suggestions of the system based on the model of relevance. Compared to On Line Analytical Processing [5], we manage data that are incrementally collected, organized and analysed on-the-fly. Finally, with respect to traditional faceted search [14], we deal with high data volumes and velocity, that imply efficient techniques for storing and managing them. Given the importance of these research challenges in the Industry 4.0 domain, we describe the application of our approach in the smart factory as a case study.

The paper is organized as follows: Sect. 2 presents a motivating example, used to introduce the innovative aspects of our approach in the Industry 4.0 domain; in Sect. 3 we describe the multi-dimensional model and proposed data summarisation techniques; Sect. 4 provides details about the model of relevance and how this can be engaged within the multi-dimensional model in order to foster big data exploration; the architecture of BODaI framework and experimental evaluation are detailed in Sect. 5; Sect. 6 highlights cutting-edge features of our approach compared to the state of the art; finally, Sect. 7 closes the paper.

2 Motivating Example and Research Challenges

As a motivating example, we introduce here the application of our approach for exploring real time data collected from a machine produced by an Original Equipment Manufacturer (OEM). As shown in Fig. 1, the OEM produces multi-spindle machines, where spindles work independently each other on the raw material. Each spindle is mounted on a unit moved by an electrical engine to perform X, Y, Z movements. The spindle rotation is impressed by an electrical engine and its rotation speed is controlled by the machine control. Spindles use different tools (that are selected according to the instructions specified within the Part Program) in order to complete different steps in the manufacturing cycle. For each unit, we can measure the velocity of the three axes (X, Y and Z) and the electrical current absorbed by each of the engines, the value of rpm for the spindle, the percentage of power absorbed by the spindle engine (charge coefficient). Hereafter, we will refer to the measured aspects as *features*.

The aim of the OEM is to understand if it is possible to use real time data collected directly from the machine control for monitoring the spindle axle hardening over time and the tool wear. With spindle axle hardening we refer to a specific behaviour of the spindle shaft that turns hard more and more due to different possible reasons: lack of lubrication and bearing wear that may lead to possible bearing failures. Tool wear monitoring is referred to possible tool usage optimisation in order to balance the trade-off between the number of tools used and the risk of breaking the tool during operations that may lead to long downtimes.

Fig. 1. The multi-spindle machine from which real time data have been collected for exploration purposes.

This opens a set of issues, mainly related to data volumes and velocity and the considered application domain, that can be summarised as follows.

Data Modeling for Exploration. Data modeling according to "facets" (e.g., categories), evenly hierarchically organised, represents a powerful mean to enable incremental and on-the-fly data exploration. A multi-dimensional representation of data can be helpful, since it allows aggregation of data according to different dimensions (e.g., time, monitored spindle, tool used for a specific manufacturing step), that might be related to the observed problems (e.g., spindle axles hardening or tool wear), thus giving proper semantics to the collected data. Moreover, multi-dimensional model enables refinement of the exploration by following the hierarchical organisation of dimensions.

Data Summarisation. The ability of providing a compact view of the huge amount of data collected from the machine is strongly required. A data summarisation approach is recommended, where data should be observed in an aggregated way, instead of monitoring each single data record, that might be not relevant given the high level of noise in the working environment (slight variations in the measured variables). At the same time, data aggregations should be observed on the fly, given the highly dynamic nature of the application domain, and efficient computation algorithms are required to summarise data.

Data Relevance. The user who explores data needs an underlying data-model to enable fast exploration of the available data, guiding the user towards only those relevant measures that correspond to spindle hardening or tool wear problems. To this aim, it is required a model of relevance that enables to identify only relevant data on which the user must focus for managing critical situations, taking into account volumes and speed of data collection phase.

3 A Multi-dimensional Model for Big Data Exploration

3.1 Basic Definitions

The basic concept of the multi-dimensional model, on which exploration relies, is the *feature*, that is, a monitored variable (e.g., measured through sensors and machine control). Features are defined as follows.

Definition 1 (Feature). *A feature represents a monitored variable that can be measured. A feature F_i is described as $\langle n_{F_i}, u_{F_i} \rangle$, where n_{F_i} is the feature name, u_{F_i} represents the unit of measure. Let's denote with $F = \{F_1, F_2 \ldots F_n\}$ the overall set of features.*

Definition 2 (Measure). *We define a measure $X_i(t)$ a value for the feature F_i, expressed in terms of the unit of measure u_{F_i} and of the timestamp t, that represents the instant in which the measure has been taken. At a given time t, a set of measures can be identified, one for each considered feature. Therefore, we denote with vector $\boldsymbol{X}(t)$ a record of measures $\langle X_1(t), X_2(t), \ldots X_n(t) \rangle$ obtained at a given time t and synchronised with respect to the acquisition timestamp.*

Examples. In the running example, velocity of the three axes X, Y and Z, electrical current, the value of spindle rpm and percentage of absorbed power are modelled as features.

3.2 Clustering-Based Data Summarisation

Records of measures collected at a given time interval Δt are clustered. Clustering offers a two-fold advantage: (a) it gives an overall view over a set of measure records, using a reduced amount of information; (b) it allows to depict the behaviour of the system better than single records, that might be affected by noise and false outliers, in order to observe a given physical phenomenon. When dealing with real time data, collected for example in Cyber Physical Systems, we face with data streams, where data are not all available since the beginning, but are collected in an incremental way. For these reasons, an incremental, data-stream clustering algorithm has been developed, in order to extract from records of measures in a time interval Δt a set of clusters aimed at summarising collected measures. The clustering algorithm is performed in two steps: (i) in the first one, a variant of Clustream algorithm [1] is applied, that incrementally processes incoming data to obtain a *set of syntheses*; (ii) in the second step, X-means algorithm is applied [12] in order to cluster syntheses obtained in the previous step. X-means does not require an a-priori knowledge on the number of output clusters. Syntheses are defined as follows.

Definition 3 (Synthesis). *We define a synthesis of records* S *as a tuple consisting of five elements, that is,* $S = \langle N, \boldsymbol{LS}, SS, \boldsymbol{X}0, R\rangle$*, where: (i)* N *is the number of records included into the synthesis (from* $\boldsymbol{X}(t_1)$ *to* $\boldsymbol{X}(t_N)$*, where* $t_N = t_1 + \Delta t$*); (ii)* $\boldsymbol{LS}$ *is a vector representing the linear sum of measures in* S*; (iii)* SS *is the quadratic sum of points in* S*; (iv)* $\boldsymbol{X}0$ *is a vector representing the centroid of the synthesis; (v)* R *is the radius of the synthesis. In particular:*

$$\boldsymbol{LS} = \sum_{k=1}^{N} \boldsymbol{X}(t_k) \;\; SS = \sum_{k=1}^{N} \boldsymbol{X}^2(t_k) \tag{1}$$

$$\boldsymbol{X}0 = \frac{\sum_{k=1}^{N} \boldsymbol{X}(t_k)}{N} \tag{2}$$

$$R = \sqrt{\frac{\sum_{k=1}^{N}(\boldsymbol{X}(t_k) - \boldsymbol{X}0)^2}{N}} \tag{3}$$

The second step aims at clustering syntheses. Clustering is performed to minimise the distance between syntheses centroids within the same cluster and to maximise the distance between syntheses centroids across different clusters. Clusters give a balanced view of the observed physical phenomenon, grouping together syntheses corresponding to the same working status. Details about the algorithm for syntheses generation and clustering are out of the scope of this paper.

Definition 4 (Cluster). *A cluster* C *is defined as follows:* $C = \langle \boldsymbol{C}_0, \mathcal{S}_C\rangle$*, where* $\boldsymbol{C}_0$ *is the cluster centroid,* $\mathcal{S}_C$ *is the set of syntheses belonging to the cluster. We denote with* SC *the set of identified clusters.*

3.3 Dimensions

Clusters are associated with values of specific *dimensions*. Among dimensions, we mention *time*, *feature space*, *working mode* and other *domain-specific dimensions*.

Time. Time is the most important dimension. In fact, the clustering algorithm described in the previous section is computed incrementally over time. The minimum granularity of time dimension corresponds to the time interval over which clustering is performed. This means that, considering Δt as the time interval on which records of measures are grouped in syntheses, that in turn are clustered, every Δt seconds the clustering algorithm outputs a new cluster set SC built on top of the previous sets. Δt is chosen at configuration time such that $1/\Delta t$ is greater than the data acquisition frequency.

Feature Space. Feature spaces are used to represent different physical phenomena of a system that are being monitored. In the running example, the spindle hardening and the tool wear are feature spaces. A feature space conceptually represents a set of related features, whose measures are useful in order to describe the evolution over the time of monitored physical phenomena. Multiple feature spaces might be observed, and the observation of a feature might be useful to monitor more than one feature space. We denote with $FS = \{FS_1, FS_2, \dots FS_m\}$ the set of feature spaces, where $FS_j \subseteq F$ and $m \leq n$. Feature spaces can be monitored independently each others.

Working Mode. The working mode represents the conditions in which monitored cyber physical system operates. Working mode can be identified through one or more parameters. In our running example, working mode is identified by the kind of manufacturing task that is being processed, described within the Part Program of the machine, and by the machine model. Roughly speaking, working mode represents the *context* in which data analysis/comparison between collected measures might have sense. For example, comparison between the behaviour of two machines is meaningful only if two machines are executing the same Part Program and machine model is the same.

Domain-Specific Dimensions. Other dimensions can be considered depending on the specific domain of interest. In the running example, domain-specific dimensions are the monitored physical system (e.g., the spindle) and the tool used for the manufacturing process.

Dimensions can be organized in hierarchies, at different levels. Formally, we denote with $\mathcal{D} = \mathcal{D}_1 \times \mathcal{D}_2 \times \dots \times \mathcal{D}_p$ the multi-dimensional space created by p dimensions $\mathcal{D}_1, \mathcal{D}_2, \dots \mathcal{D}_p$. We denote with $\mathcal{D}_j^i$ the i-th level in the hierarchy of j-th dimension and with $d_i \in \mathcal{D}_i$ a single value of the dimension $\mathcal{D}_i$.

Example. The *time* dimension can be considered starting from the level of hour (if clustering is performed every hour), hours can be aggregated into days, days can be aggregated into months, that can be in turn aggregated into quarters, that is, `time[hour:days:month:quarters]`. Tools can be aggregated into tool types (`tool[tool:tool_type]`). Spindles can be aggregated into the machines they belong to (`monitored_system[spindle:machine]`).

3.4 Multi-dimensional Model

Our multi-dimensional model consists of an hypercube such as the one shown in Fig. 2 for the running example. Dimensions represent axes of the hypercube, that is defined as follows.

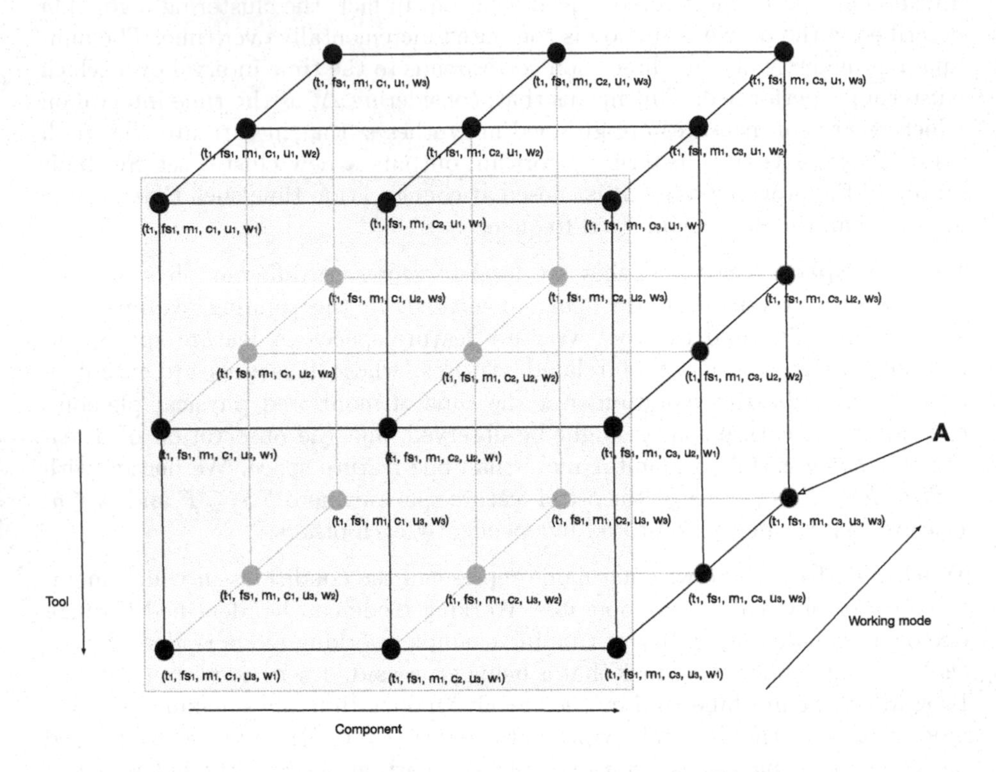

Fig. 2. The multi-dimensional data model for big data exploration.

Definition 5 (Multi-dimensional model). *We describe the multi-dimensional model as a set* $\mathcal{V}$ *nodes. Each node* $v \in \mathcal{V}$ *is described as* $v = \langle SC(d_1, d_2, \ldots d_p) \rangle$*, where* $SC(d_1, d_2, \ldots d_p)$ *represents a cluster set, obtained at fixed values for each dimension* $d_1 \in \mathcal{D}_1, d_2 \in \mathcal{D}_2 \ldots\ d_p \in \mathcal{D}_p$.

For example, in Fig. 2 the node identified as "A" represents the cluster set identified at time t_1 for machine $\mathtt{m}_1$ (spindle $\mathtt{c}_3$), that is using tool $\mathtt{u}_3$ and is working within the working mode $\mathtt{w}_3$, considering features in the feature space $\mathtt{fs}_1$. Exploration will be performed within this data structure as described in the next section.

4 Relevance-Based Big Data Exploration

The proposed approach enables exploration of real time data incrementally collected and organized, as well as aggregated on-the-fly. The user is guided by the multi-dimensional model through a set of steps according to data relevance aspects.

4.1 Model of Data Relevance

In Exploratory Computing (EC), during exploration steps data can be considered as *relevant* if they differ from an *expected status*. The latter one can be for example a normal distribution of values of a feature, as assumed in [3]. In our case, the expected status corresponds to the one of normal working conditions for monitored cyber physical systems. The expected status can be tagged by domain expert while observing the monitored system when operates normally. Let's denote with $\hat{SC}(d_1, d_2, \dots d_p)$ the cluster set identified during such condition, for dimension values fixed at $d_1, d_2, \dots d_p$.

The model of relevance adopted in our approach is based on the concept of *cluster distance*. The algorithm proposed here is inspired by [4] and has been adapted to the multi-dimensional model considered in this paper. Given two sets of clusters $SC_1 = \{C_1, C_2, \dots, C_n\}$ and $SC_2 = \{C'_1, C'_2, \dots, C'_m\}$, with size n and m respectively, we evaluate the distance between SC_1 and SC_2 by aggregating distances between each cluster belonging to SC_1 and the closest cluster belonging to SC_2 and viceversa, for symmetry purposes (see, for example, C_2 and C'_2 in Fig. 3). Formally, the distance is computed as:

$$\Delta(SC_1, SC_2) = \frac{\sum_{i=1}^{n} d(C_i, SC_2) + \sum_{j=1}^{m} d(SC_1, C'_j)}{m+n} \quad (4)$$

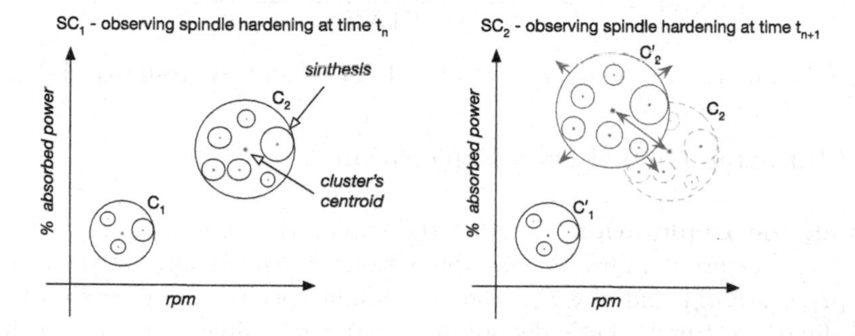

Fig. 3. Illustration of cluster's sets changes in time due to spindle hardening that may cause a decrease of rpm and an increase of the percentage of absorbed power. In the figure is showed how the cluster $C_2 \in SC_1$ changed its position, as well as its size, from time t_n to t_{n+1}; this changes may indicate an anomaly like the spindle hardening.

where $d(C_i, SC_2) = min_{j=1,\dots m} d_c(C_i, C'_j)$ and $d(SC_1, C'_j) = min_{i=1,\dots n}$ $d_c(C_i, C'_j)$ is the distance between clusters. To compute the distance between two clusters $d_c(C_i, C'_j)$, we combined different factors: (i) the distance between clusters centroids $d_{\mathbf{C}_0}(C_i, C'_j)$, to verify if C'_j moved with respect to C_i (or viceversa); (ii) the *intra-cluster distance* $d_c^{intra}(C_i, C'_j)$, to verify if there has been an expansion or a contraction of cluster C'_j with respect to C_i; (iii) the difference in number of syntheses contained in C_i and C'_j, denoted with $d_N(C_i, C'_j)$:

$$d_c(C_i, C'_j) = \alpha d_{\mathbf{C}_0}(C_i, C'_j) + \beta d_c^{intra}(C_i, C'_j) + \gamma d_N(C_i, C'_j) \quad (5)$$

where α, β and $\gamma \in [0,1]$ are weights such that $\alpha+\beta+\gamma=1$, used to balance the impact of terms in Eq. (5). To set the optimal weights, a grid procedure can be performed over α and β (γ is set with $1-\alpha-\beta$), with the value of each weight varying from 0 to 1. In our preliminary experiments, we put $\alpha=\beta=\gamma=\frac{1}{3}$.

In particular, $d_{\boldsymbol{C}_0}(C_i, C'_j)$ is computed by applying the Euclidean distance ($D0$) between clusters' centroids, according to the following formula:

$$D0 = \sqrt{(\boldsymbol{C}_0^i - \boldsymbol{C}_0^j)^2} \quad (6)$$

where $\boldsymbol{C}_0^i$ and $\boldsymbol{C}_0^j$ are centroids of C_i and C'_j, respectively. The intra-cluster distance $d_c^{intra}(C_i, C'_j)$ is obtained by recursively computing $\Delta(\mathcal{S}_{C_i}, \mathcal{S}_{C'_j})$ on the sets of syntheses of C_i and C_j, that is:

$$d_c^{intra}(C_i, C'_j) = \frac{\sum_{k=1}^{n_1} d(S_k, C'_j) + \sum_{h=1}^{n_2} d(C_i, S_h)}{n_1 + n_2} \quad (7)$$

where $S_k \in \mathcal{S}_{C_i}$, $S_h \in \mathcal{S}_{C'_j}$, $|\mathcal{S}_{C_i}| = n_1$, $|\mathcal{S}_{C'_j}| = n_2$, $d(S_k, C'_j) = min_{h=1,\dots n_2} d_s(S_k, S_h)$ and $d(C_i, S_h) = min_{k=1,\dots n_1} d_s(S_k, S_h)$. Term $d_s(S_k, S_h)$ represents the average inter-syntheses distance ($D1$):

$$D1 = \sqrt{\frac{\sum_{i=1}^{N1} \sum_{j=N1+1}^{N1+N2} (\boldsymbol{X}(t_i) - \boldsymbol{X}(t_j))^2}{N1N2}} \quad (8)$$

where $N1$ and $N2$ are the number of records in S_k and S_h, respectively.

4.2 Multi-step Guided Data Exploration

Starting the Exploration. To start the exploration, the user might specify a set d^r of preferred values for the dimensions he/she is interested in, where $d^r = \{d_1^r, d_2^r, \dots d_p^r\}$ and $d_i^r \in \mathcal{D}_i$. The user might specify preferences on a subset of dimensions in $\mathcal{D}$. Let's denote as *bounded* the dimensions on which the user expressed a preference, as *unbounded* the other dimensions. The systems identifies a subset $\mathcal{V}' \subseteq \mathcal{V}$ of nodes within the multi-dimensional model, such that the values of bounded dimensions corresponds to the one specified in d^r. The exploration will start from nodes $v \in \mathcal{V}'$. We remark here that bounded dimensions must be considered starting from selected level in the hierarchy. This means that if the user selects a specific machine, the `monitored_system` dimension is bounded at machine level, but remains unbounded at spindle level, that is, no preferences are expressed on spindles and the user is enabled to browse data among all spindles that compose the selected machine. For example, if $d^r = \langle -, \texttt{fs}_1, \texttt{m}_1, -, -, \texttt{w}_1 \rangle$, feature space, machine and working mode are the *bound* dimensions, while time, tool and spindle are the *unbound* ones: the front facade of hypercube shown in Fig. 2 groups the candidate nodes $v \in \mathcal{V}'$.

We assume that the user formulates d^r as an explicit, albeit vague exploration request, and expects the system to suggest some promising data to explore.

To this aim, we need a model of relevance to establish what data can be considered as relevant or interesting. The system uses the model of relevance in order to restrict the set of nodes from which to start the exploration among nodes $v \in \mathcal{V}'$, that is, the set of relevant data to be explored. For each node $v = \langle SC(d_1, d_2, \dots d_p) \rangle \in \mathcal{V}$, the node is considered as relevant if the clusters distance with respect to the set of clusters $\hat{SC}(d_1, d_2, \dots d_p)$ overtakes a predefined threshold, that is, $\Delta(SC(d_1, d_2, \dots d_p), \hat{SC}(d_1, d_2, \dots d_p)) \geq \delta$. Such a model of relevance enables the identification of relevant nodes also when the user does not specify any constraints in d^r, that is, he/she does not have any idea from which dimensions and data to start the exploration. In the latter case, the same relevance criteria is used, where the candidate nodes $v \in \mathcal{V}$ are all the ones in the hypercube.

How the Exploration Goes On. Starting from nodes selected in the previous step, exploration goes on through a set of different traversals that the user applies in order to move from one node to the other ones. We define a *traversal* as $\sigma(\tau_\sigma, v_i, v_j, \omega_\sigma)$, where: (i) τ_σ is the kind of traversal (among *drill-down*, *roll-up* and *sibling*), inspired by OLAP operators, as detailed below; (ii) $v_i \in \mathcal{V}$ is the starting node; (iii) $v_j \in \mathcal{V}$ is the destination node; (iv) ω_σ is a weight assigned to the traversal, computed according to the model of relevance. By using traversals it's possible to move in all directions.
Using a *drill-down* traversal the user moves towards a node $v_j \in \mathcal{V}$ by specialising any of the dimensions in $v_i \in \mathcal{V}$. An example of drill-down traversal is to move from a node labeled with $\langle t_1, \mathtt{fs}_1, \mathtt{m}_1, \mathtt{u}_1, \mathtt{w}_1 \rangle$ towards a node labeled with $\langle t_1, \mathtt{fs}_1, \mathtt{c}_2, \mathtt{u}_1, \mathtt{w}_1 \rangle$, where $\mathtt{c}_2$ (spindle) specialises $\mathtt{m}_1$ (machine) in the hierarchy of `monitored_system` dimension. Note that this means to include the spindle among the *bounded* variables and therefore to restrict the exploration space.

The *roll-up* traversal is similar. Using a *roll-up* traversal the user moves towards a node $v_j \in \mathcal{V}$ by generalising any of the dimensions in $v_i \in \mathcal{V}$. An example of roll-up traversal is to move from a node labeled with $\langle t_1, \mathtt{fs}_1, \mathtt{c}_2, \mathtt{u}_1, \mathtt{w}_1 \rangle$ towards a node labeled with $\langle t_1, \mathtt{fs}_1, \mathtt{m}_1, \mathtt{u}_1, \mathtt{w}_1 \rangle$. This also means to include the spindle among the *unbounded* variables and therefore to expand the exploration space.

Using a *sibling* traversal the user moves towards a node $v_j \in \mathcal{V}$ by changing the value of one of the dimensions in $v_i \in \mathcal{V}$. An example of sibling traversal is to move from a node labeled with $\langle t_1, \mathtt{fs}_1, \mathtt{m}_1, \mathtt{u}_1, \mathtt{w}_1 \rangle$ towards a node labeled with $\langle t_1, \mathtt{fs}_1, \mathtt{m}_2, \mathtt{u}_1, \mathtt{w}_1 \rangle$, where $\mathtt{m}_1$ and $\mathtt{m}_2$ are two machines, that is, values of the same level in the hierarchy of `monitored_system` dimension. This traversal does not change the sets of *bounded* and *unbounded* variables and therefore does not change in size the exploration space.

The model of relevance can be used here by the system to suggest more relevant nodes to move on: in particular, nodes $v_j \in \mathcal{V}$ are suggested such as $\Delta(SC(d_1, d_2, \dots d_p), \hat{SC}(d_1, d_2, \dots d_p)) \geq \delta$, where $v_j = \langle SC(d_1, d_2, \dots d_p) \rangle$.

5 Implementation and Experiments

5.1 Architecture of the BODaI Framework

Figure 4 depicts the functional architecture of the BODaI framework. The framework has been developed in Java as a modular infrastructure composed of:

- `BODaI_BigData`, that is based on NoSQL technology (MongoDB) and stores records of measures, incrementally provided by monitored physical system; the composition of a record is defined within a *Config file*; different records are processed in parallel;
- `BODaI_model`, that contains all metadata the framework relies on (hierarchies of dimensions, organisation of features within feature spaces, features metadata such as names and unit of measures), as well as cluster sets, syntheses information and computed distances used in the model of relevance for guiding the exploration; the size of this information is much lower than the total amount of collected measures and MySQL technology has been used; both the `BODaI_BigData`, and the `BODaI_model`, are accessed through the BDAO (*BODaI Data Access Objects*);
- *BSB level* (BODaI Service Bus), that manages the interactions between BDAO and the framework services;
- *Data Acquisition Service*, in charge of collecting records of measures, synchronising timestamps and storing acquired data within the `BODaI_BigData`, according to feature spaces as specified in `BODaI_model`; during acquisition data processing is strongly minimised to avoid bottlenecks in data acquisition; costly data elaboration steps are postponed in a second step, where other services (clustering, data control, cluster distance computation) are invoked in parallel;
- *Data Control Service*, *Clustering Service* and *Cluster Distance Service*, in charge of performing controls on collected records, clustering and cluster sets distance computation, respectively;
- *Notification Service*, in charge of sending a notification when an unexpected variation between distances of cluster sets has been identified; it also manages notifications raised when data control is executed.

5.2 Real Use Cases

We applied the approach described in this paper to the Industry 4.0 application domain. We considered a factory producing multi-spindle machines for various industrial sectors: automotive, aviation, water industry, etc. Specifically, the multi-dimensional model enabled to monitor axle hardening by observing changes in the values of energy consumption (spindle engine charge coefficient) for similar rpm, with reference to the tool that has been used. By detecting energy consumption differences using different tools, we identified spindle hardening as the possible anomaly that increases the energy request to perform the

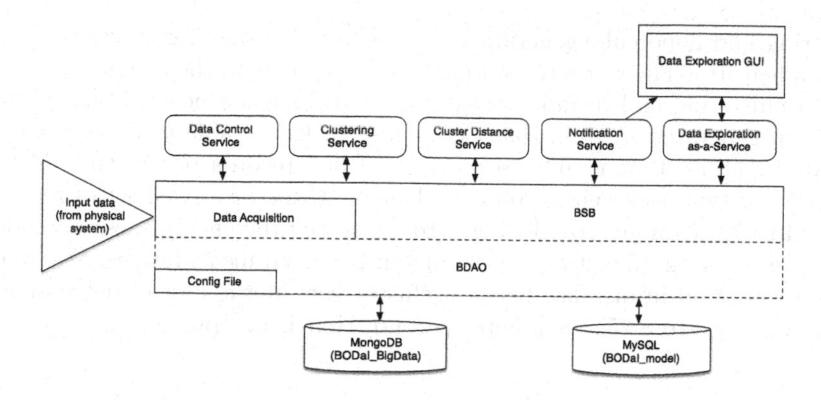

Fig. 4. The functional architecture of the BODaI framework.

manufacturing operations. If the increase in energy consumption is related only to the usage of a particular tool, this has been recognised as a symptom of a possible excessive tool wear. Next step will focus on monitoring of other variables like the absorbed electrical current on the axes X, Y, Z. The level of change in these variables may help in measuring the degree of tool wear and learning the best moment to change it before suffering a tool break and a machine downtime.

Experiments. We performed experiments in order to demonstrate the feasibility of our approach in terms of processing time and its effectiveness in providing summarised data for exploration purposes. Our evaluation focuses mostly on system performance. We collected real data from three machines, each one equipped with three spindles and different tools. On each spindle, we monitored the features listed in the motivating example: the velocity of the three axes (X, Y and Z) and the electrical current absorbed by each of the engines, the value of rpm for the spindle, the percentage of power absorbed by the spindle engine (charge coefficient). We collected 140 millions of records from the three machines. All records present a timestamp, and have been collected every 200 ms (5 records per second). We run experiments on an Intel Core i7-6700HQ, CPU 2.60 GHz, 4 cores, 8 logical cores, RAM 16 GB. As suggested in [2], during acquisition phase data processing is strongly minimised to avoid bottlenecks, by delaying clustering in a second phase. Collected records of measures have been saved within MongoDB as JSON documents grouped into collections. Each document contains a record $\boldsymbol{X}(t)$ of measures, labeled with the values of dimensions $d_1, d_2, \ldots d_p$. The structure of documents is maintained very simple, with at most one level of depth, and collection have been organised considering the time as main dimension, in order to speed up both data storage and data extraction for clustering, that is applied to records grouped with respect to the timestamps. This enabled to storage all 140 millions of records in 1 h and 14 min, with an acquisition rate of ~31,531 records per second. Experimental results depicted in Fig. 5(a) show how these tasks can be addressed given the data acquisition rate. We recall here that clustering is applied on slots of records on a time internal Δt. We tested clustering and hypercube generation on real data considering average values on 2 and 3 features. The worse response time corresponds to the case where we performed clustering and distance computation tasks when no previous syntheses had been generated. Also in that case, these tasks are able to process ~15,600 records in 11.5 s, that is able to process ~1,356 records per second. Through the tasks of syntheses generation and clustering, the processed set of records is reduced to 7,2% on average. In Fig. 5(b) we tested the effectiveness of model of relevance by simulating strong variations in collected measures. We observed an evident variation in distance between cluster sets at the cost of decreasing the processing time to ~255 records per second, that is acceptable.

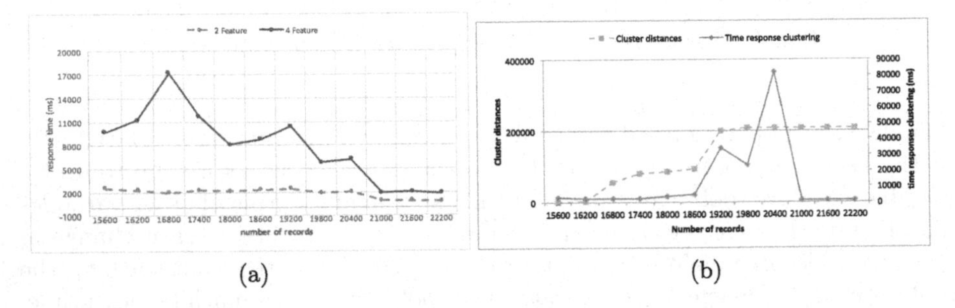

Fig. 5. Tests on efficiency of clustering and hypercube generation (a) And on the effectiveness of the model of relevance, introducing a variation in collected records (b). Number of records on X axis represent different incremental steps.

5.3 Considerations

The approach revealed to be useful in order to extract information for supporting production operator (i.e., the user of our system in this case study) in taking better decisions, thus preventing failures or increasing production efficiency. These observations are performed by operators to provide prompt maintenance services, thus avoiding long downtime periods. Using our model the operator is able to fully explore the multi-dimensional model, i.e., all data nodes can be explored using the three types of traversals introduced in Sect. 4, and it is possible to use traversals in any order and in a sequence of any length. The traversals are also intuitive, since they are inspired by the rollup, drill down and pivot operations of data cube. In addition here, we exploit the model of relevance to further reduce the exploration space. Operators can focus their attention on some relevant measures, explore them, verify the machine working conditions also according to their experience and decide to activate or not a maintenance activity. In this way, explorative approach can be used to adjust planning of maintenance interventions as scheduled through traditional, offline data mining techniques, that use historical data for their purposes. In fact, several latent factors might influence manufacturing operations and might have an impact on maintenance schedule. These factors cannot be easily detected through measured variables and the role of human actor is still of paramount importance for avoiding useless maintenance interventions, that are costly both for the OEM and for the OEM's client. The data exploration viewpoint enables to improve this task also for unexperienced maintenance operators through decisions supported by the system.

6 Related Work

Other approaches have been specifically focused on data exploration and exploratory computing research fields. Comparison criteria in this case include data characteristics (structured/semistructured/unstructured data, traditional vs big data, OLAP vs OLTP), the way data are collected (incrementally or one-step collection before starting data processing), the adopted exploration techniques, the model of relevance (if any), application of data mining or query approximation techniques, technological issues (e.g., the DBMS technology among SQL-based, NoSQL, NewSQL). The presentation of Exploratory Computing as a comprehensive approach that includes the notions of "exploration as a multi-step process", model of relevance, data summarisation, multi-dimensional data modeling is given in [3]. In this paper, authors proposed a model of relevance based on statistical distribution of data. Compared to them, our approach has a model of relevance based on clustering aimed at detecting deviations from the normal working conditions of a monitored physical system. In [9] cube exploration is discussed, in order to give OLAP-based exploration facilities that help users in navigating multi-dimensional data. No model of relevance is proposed and the aim is at foreseeing user's explorative actions in order to properly apply techniques of query approximation. Authors in [15] propose the application of query approximation techniques to big data that are incrementally collected. Here approximation methods are based on the analysis of user's action previously performed and on statistical properties of data, no model of relevance is proposed and the concept of exploration as a multi-step process has not been addressed.

In [8] an approach operating on structured data stored within a PostgreSQL database is proposed. Data are grouped according to specific criteria (e.g., all data in a given time interval, or all geographical data in the same area). These groups are referred to as *semantic windows*. The user is supported in formulating query where selection criteria and ranges of data are required. Query by sampling is applied and samples are compared against user's query to check their compliance. If sampled data are relevant with respect to the query, all data in the same semantic window are presented to the user and next queries are performed on the same data. With respect to this approach, we proposed a model of relevance for enabling exploration also when the user is not able to specify his/her requirements through a query. Moreover, we focused on big data incrementally collected and summarised.

7 Concluding Remarks

In this paper, we discussed the ingredients to enable exploration of real time data in a dynamic context of interconnected systems, where large amounts of data must be incrementally collected, organized and analysed on-the-fly: (i) a multi-dimensional model, that is suited for supporting the iterative and multi-step nature of data exploration; (ii) efficient data summarisation techniques, based on clustering, in order to simplify overall view over high volumes of data; (iii) a model of relevance, aimed at focusing the attention of the user on relevant data only, also when the user is not able to specify his/her requirements through a query. Given the importance of these research challenges in the Industry 4.0 domain, we applied our approach in the smart factory as a case study. Future development efforts will be devoted to a parallelisation of data clustering, in order to further speed up data elaboration in the multi-dimensional model, the study of data visualisation techniques, automate and operationalise knowledge extracted from data produced by the system and the development of a GUI specifically meant for data exploration. With reference to the case study, the migration of the BODaI infrastructure onto the Niagara IoT framework[1] is being implemented.

References

1. Aggarwal, C., Han, J., Wang, J., Yu, P.: A framework for clustering evolving data streams. In: Proceedings of VLDB 2003, pp. 81–92 (2003)
2. Biswas, S., Sen, J.: A proposed architecture for big data driven supply chain analytics. Int. J. Supply Chain Manag. (2016)
3. Buoncristiano, M., Mecca, G., Quintarelli, E., Roveri, D.S., Tanca, L.: Database challenges for exploratory computing. SIGMOD Rec. **44**(2), 17–22 (2015)
4. Goldberg, M., Hayvanovych, M., Magdon-Ismail, M.: Measuring similarity between sets of overlapping clusters. In: Proceedings of 2nd IEEE International Conference on Social Computing, pp. 303–308 (2010)
5. Golfarelli, M., Rizzi, S.: Data Warehouse Design: Modern Principles and Methodologies. McGraw-Hill, New York (2009)
6. Han, J., Kamber, M.: Data Mining: Concepts and Techniques. Morgan Kaufmann Publisher, Burlington (2006)
7. Hou, Z., Wang, Z.: From model-based control to data-driven control: survey, classification and perspective. Inf. Sci. **235**, 3–25 (2013)
8. Kalinin, A., Cetintemel, U., Zdonik, S.: Interactive data exploration using semantic windows. In: Proceedings of ACM SIGMOD 2014, pp. 505–516 (2014)
9. Kamat, N., Jayachandran, P., Tunga, K., Nandi, A.: Distributed and interactive cube exploration. In: Proceedings of ICDE 2014 (2014)
10. Lee, J., Kao, H.A.: Service innovation and smart analytics for industry 4.0 and big data environment. In: 6th Conference on Industrial Product-Service Systems (2014)
11. Monostori, L.: Cyber-physical production systems: roots, expectations and R&D challenges. In: 47th CIRP Conference on Manufacturing Systems, pp. 9–13 (2014)

[1] https://www.tridium.com/en/products-services/niagara4.

12. Pelleg, D., Moore, A.: X-means: extending K-means with efficient estimation of the number of clusters. In: 17th International Conference on Machine Learning, pp. 727–734 (2000)
13. Tukey, J.: Exploratory Data Analysis. Reading (1977)
14. Tunkelang, D.: Faceted Search (Synthesis Lectures on Information Concepts, Retrieval and Services). Morgan and Claypool Publishers, San Rafael (2009)
15. Wasay, A., Athanassoulis, M., Idreos, S.: Queriosity: automated data exploration. In: Proceedings of the IEEE International Congress on Big Data (2015)

Process Variability Management

Instance-Based Process Matching Using Event-Log Information

Han van der Aa[1](✉), Avigdor Gal[2], Henrik Leopold[1], Hajo A. Reijers[1], Tomer Sagi[3], and Roee Shraga[2]

[1] Department of Computer Sciences, VU University Amsterdam, Amsterdam, The Netherlands
{j.h.vander.aa,h.leopold,h.a.reijers}@vu.nl
[2] Faculty of Industrial Engineering and Management, Technion – Israel Institute of Technology, Haifa, Israel
avigal@technion.ac.il, shraga89@tx.technion.ac.il
[3] Hewlett Packard Labs, Guttwirt Industrial Park, Technion City, Haifa, Israel
ts.tomersagi@gmail.com

Abstract. Process model matching provides the basis for many process analysis techniques such as inconsistency detection and process querying. The matching task refers to the automatic identification of correspondences between activities in two process models. Numerous techniques have been developed for this purpose, all share a focus on process-level information. In this paper we introduce *instance-based process matching*, which specifically focuses on information related to instances of a process. In particular, we introduce six similarity metrics that each use a different type of instance information stored in the event logs associated with processes. The proposed metrics can be used as standalone matching techniques or to complement existing process model matching techniques. A quantitative evaluation on real-world data demonstrates that the use of information from event logs is essential in identifying a considerable amount of correspondences.

Keywords: Process model matching · Event logs · Process similarity

1 Introduction and Motivation

Process models have been established as a means to design, analyze, and improve information systems [7]. The creation, utilization, and evolution of such models is supported by a manifold of concepts and techniques that offer, for instance, re-use driven modeling support, harmonization of model variants, model-based system validation, and effective management of model repositories. Many of these techniques share a reliance on the identification of correspondences between entities of different models, also termed *process model matching* [13]. The accuracy and, therefore, usefulness of techniques supporting the creation, utilization, and

E. Dubois and K. Pohl (Eds.): CAiSE 2017, LNCS 10253, pp. 283–297, 2017.
DOI: 10.1007/978-3-319-59536-8_18

evolution of models is highly dependent on the correctness and completeness of the process model matching outcome.

In recent years, a plethora of works have addressed process model matching [1,3]. Growing alongside related fields such as *ontology alignment* and *schema matching* [15], process model matching offers innovation through the use of process-oriented information in the matching task. Existing process model matching techniques focus mainly on process information described by process models themselves. In this work we present the first matching technique that uses an important additional resource: *event logs*. Such logs offer valuable information on attributes, event durations, and other aspects that specifically relate to the *observed execution* of processes, rather than their *specification*. We propose and evaluate six new matching techniques that use event-log information and evaluate their contribution to the effective matching of processes. These techniques aim to identify correspondences that cannot be identified by just considering process model information.

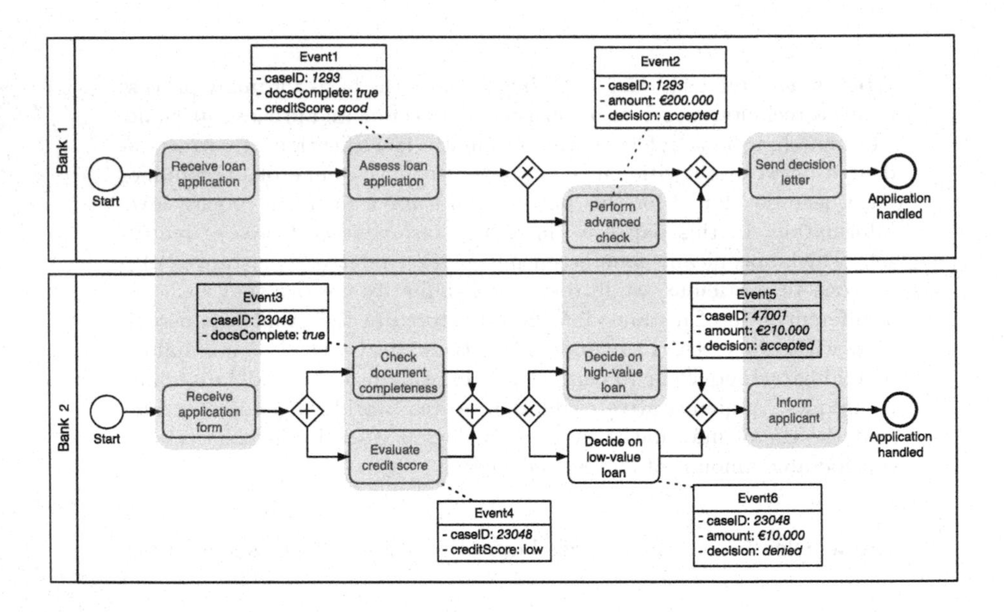

Fig. 1. Two process models and their correspondences

To illustrate the usefulness of event-log information for process model matching, consider two process models, M_1 and M_2, which depict two (simplified) processes to handle loan applications. Also consider their respective sets of activities $\mathcal{A}_1$ and $\mathcal{A}_2$. Figure 1 illustrates these models, M_1 at the top and M_2 at the bottom, and highlights their *correspondences*, i.e. the activities that represent similar behavior.

In process model matching, we wish to automatically identify these correspondences between $\mathcal{A}_1$ and $\mathcal{A}_2$. By analyzing the labels of the activity, some correspondences can be identified in a straightforward manner, such as the correspondence between `receive loan application` and `receive application form`. However, the label-based identification of other correspondences is not as straightforward, if at all possible. Consider the `assess loan application` activity in M_1 and the activities `check document completeness` and `evaluate credit score` from M_2. For the correspondences between these activities, there is no obvious syntactic or semantic relation for the contents of their labels. This makes it difficult to recognize their similarity based on textual analysis. However, the events associated with these activities provide valuable information about their similarity. `Event1` in M_1 includes attributes that describe the completeness of the filed documents and the credit score. Events `Event3` and `Event4` in M_2 are each also associated with one of these attributes. This similarity between event attributes provides a strong indication of relation between the activities, which could not be derived without considering event information.

In other cases, the names of attributes that are associated with events, by themselves, do not suffice to distinguish among potential correspondences. For example, the `decide on low-value loan` (a_m) and `decide on high-value loan` (a_n) activities from model M_2 both have events that contain an `amount` attribute. Therefore, the attribute names are not sufficient to determine which of these corresponds to the `perform advanced check` activity (a_o) in M_1. However, by analyzing the values associated with these attributes throughout an event log, this could be achieved. For instance, if events corresponding to a_n and a_o are always associated with amounts above €200.000, while a_m always has a lower amount, the correspondence between a_n and a_o can be asserted.

The main contribution of the paper is in the introduction of six conceptual notions of similarity between event classes. These *similarity notions* cover different aspects of process information stored in event logs, ranging from similarity in execution times to data-based similarity. We also discuss operationalizations of the similarity notions into *similarity measures*. In particular, we define one specific similarity measure for each of the six notions and reflect on alternative ways to operationalize them. We also offer a full-scale instance-based process model matching tool, which builds on an existing tool for schema matching.

The remainder of the paper is organized as follows. Section 2 introduces preliminary notions relevant to event logs and process model matching. Section 3 describes our proposed six similarity measures. The quantitative evaluation in Sect. 4 considers the performance of these individual similarity measures for matching, as well as their composition in matching ensembles. We discuss related work in Sect. 5 and conclude the paper in Sect. 6.

2 Preliminaries

This section introduces notions relevant to the matching techniques we present in this paper. In particular, we define event logs and process matching concepts.

An *event log* $\mathcal{L}$ comprises a set of *traces*, each representing an execution of a single process instance. Each trace $t = \langle e_1, \ldots, e_n \rangle \in \mathcal{L}$ consists of a sequence of events. We use $\mathcal{E}$ to denote the finite set of *event classes* that occur in a log. An occurrence of an event $e \in t$ for any trace $t \in \mathcal{L}$ corresponds to a specific event class, *i.e.*, $e \in E_i$ for $E_i \in \mathcal{E}$. For the purposes of this paper, we assume that for a process model M with an activity set $\mathcal{A}$ each activity $a \in \mathcal{A}$ corresponds to exactly one event class $E \in \mathcal{E}$ and vice versa. Therefore, without loss of generality, we shall refer to *activities* and *event classes* interchangeably.

We formally define *process model matching* based upon notions from [11]. For any pair of event class sets $\{\mathcal{E}_1, \mathcal{E}_2\}$, a matching task creates an $n \times n'$ *similarity matrix* $\mathcal{M}(\mathcal{E}_1, \mathcal{E}_2)$ over $\mathcal{E}_1 \times \mathcal{E}_2$. Each $M_{i,j}$ in the matrix represents a degree of similarity, usually a real number in $[0, 1]$, between the i-th event class in $\mathcal{E}_1$ and the j-th event class in $\mathcal{E}_2$. The matching task often consists of sequential steps in which different classes of matchers are applied. Here, it is important to distinguish between three classes of matchers: (i) first line matchers, (ii) ensemble matchers, and (iii) decision makers. A first line matcher (1LM) establishes a similarity matrix by directly analyzing sets of event classes, $\{\mathcal{E}_1, \mathcal{E}_2\}$. For any pair of event classes $E_1 \in \mathcal{E}_1$ and $E_2 \in \mathcal{E}_2$, each 1LM produces a score $[0, 1]$ that quantifies the similarity between E_1 and E_2 by comparing the instances of these classes according to a certain characteristic. Ensemble matchers and decision makers are both specific types of so-called *second line matchers* (2LMs). A 2LM establishes a similarity matrix from an input of one or more other similarity matrices. *Ensemble matchers* are 2LMs that combine the results of multiple 1LMs into a single similarity matrix, for example by computing a weighted average of the similarity matrices. Lastly, *decision makers* take a non-binary similarity matrix (with values in the range [0,1]), as created by a 1LM or an ensemble matcher, and convert it into a binary matrix (with values in $\{0, 1\}$). For example, if we know that each $E_1 \in \mathcal{E}_1$ corresponds to at most one event class in $\mathcal{E}_2$, a decision maker can be used to select the event class E_2 with the highest similarity scores for each E_1. We refer to this selected pair as a *correspondence* between E_1 and E_2.

3 Event-Class Similarity

This section describes how information contained in event logs can be utilized to identify correspondences among event classes. We describe six conceptual *notions* of similarity, which together provide a complete coverage of the prominent types of information contained in event logs: *ordering*, *frequencies*, *timestamps*, and *data attributes*. We consider one similarity notion for each of the first three types and, due to its versatility, three different similarity notions related to the *data attributes* associated with events. To illustrate the operationalization of these similarity notions, we introduce a corresponding similarity *measure* for each of them. Each measure produces a value in the range $[0, 1]$, where a higher score indicates a stronger similarity. These measures can be used as 1LMs, where the similarity scores obtained by the measures are used to populate a similarity matrix. The measures that we introduce can be applied without imposing any assumptions on the data. Furthermore, we also reflect on alternative measures that typically depend on certain assumptions or are computationally more complex.

3.1 Positional Similarity

The underlying idea of positional similarity is that if two event classes occur at similar stages in the execution of a process, they are more likely to be similar. For example, the final event in M_1, `Send decision letter`, is more likely to be similar to `Inform applicant`, which occurs at the end of M_2, than to `Receive application form`, which occurs at the start of the process.

Similarity Measure. We define a *relative position* (*RP*) measure that quantifies the average position at which events of a certain event class occur in traces. To account for varying trace sizes, we consider the position of an event relative to the length of a trace. Specifically, we use p_e to denote the relative position of an event e in a trace, *e.g.*, for $t = \langle a, b, c \rangle$, $p_a = 1/3$, $p_b = 2/3$ and $p_c = 3/3$. Using $\bar{p}_E$ to denote the average p_e over all instances $e \in E$, Eq. 1 provides the RP measure.

$$RP(E_1, E_2) = 1 - |\bar{p}_{E_1} - \bar{p}_{E_2}| \tag{1}$$

Alternatives. Comparing the position of events in traces provides a basic measure for structural or behavioral similarity. Techniques for process model matching exist that use more advanced similarity measures, for example those base on *graph edit distance* or *behavioral relations* [4]. Such measures can also be adapted to work on graph structures or behavioral relations derived from event-log information. Such derivation is done by techniques that automatically derive process models from event logs, i.e. so-called *process discovery* techniques.

3.2 Occurrence Similarity

The frequency with which events of a certain event class occur can provide useful information regarding its similarity to other event classes. For example, if two event classes E_1 and E_2 each occur only rarely in an event log, then E_1 and E_2 both correspond to some exceptional action, hinting at their potential similarity. In the running example, for instance, it can be expected that the majority of loan requests will be for amounts below €200,000. This means that occurrences of the `perform advanced check` and `decide on high-value loan` are relatively rare. Therefore, comparing the frequencies with which event classes occur can be a useful similarity indicator. Furthermore, the consideration of frequencies can also be used to identify a lack of similarity, for instance between event classes that occur only once per trace and those that occur multiple times.

Similarity Measure. We define a measure $FREQ$ which compares the average number of occurrences of event classes per trace. We let $\bar{f}_E$ denote this average for an event class E, and use Eq. 2 to formalize $FREQ$. Because it is possible that $\bar{f}_E > 1$, this measure is normalized to ensure a confidence score in $[0, 1]$.

$$FREQ(E_1, E_2) = 1 - \left|\frac{|\bar{f}_{E_1} - \bar{f}_{E_2}|}{\max(\bar{f}_{E_1}, \bar{f}_{E_2})}\right| \tag{2}$$

Alternatives. An alternative way to evaluate occurrence similarity is to consider the fraction of traces in which an event class occurs, rather than the average number of occurrences per trace. Furthermore, it is possible to perform statistical tests rather than compare averages. We reflect on these tests in Sect. 3.3.

3.3 Duration Similarity

The time it takes to execute activities can serve as an indicator that provides useful hints regarding their similarity. In our running example it can be expected that activities that check loans with amounts over €200,000 are extensive and, therefore, consume a significant amount of time. By contrast, the communication of the decision to the applicant can very well be automated, resulting in negligible durations. Such a considerable difference in durations can be an important indicator for dissimilarity.

Similarity Measure. A straightforward similarity measure for durations can be obtained by comparing the average durations of an event class in a log. Using $\bar{d}_E$ to denote the average duration of events of class E, Eq. 3 provides a normalized measure that returns a score in $[0, 1]$.

$$DUR(E_1, E_2) = 1 - |\frac{|\bar{d}_{E_1} - \bar{d}_{E_2}|}{\max(\bar{d}_{E_1}, \bar{d}_{E_2})}| \tag{3}$$

Alternatives. Durations can vary significantly among occurrences of the same event class. An alternative is to use statistical tests, *e.g.*, the *t-test* or *Kolmogorov-Smirnov test* [16] to compare the statistical distribution of the durations for two event classes. To apply a statistical test certain preconditions have to be met. For example, the t-test requires data to be normally distributed. Another consideration to take into account is the cost of computing the similarity. For instance, the Kolmogorov-Smirnov test is computationally intensive, which can negatively affect its applicability to matching problems.

3.4 Attribute Name Similarity

The names of attributes provide insights into the data values used or created by events. These attribute names can be useful similarity indicators to identify correspondences. Their importance is demonstrated in the motivational scenario, where event classes that produce the same attributes (e.g. the `docsComplete` attribute) are recognized to be similar to each other.

Similarity Measure. We define an attribute name similarity measure $ATTR$, which determines the level of overlap in attribute names among the attribute sets associated with two event classes. To quantify this overlap, we adapt the well-known *inverse document frequency* (idf) and *cosine similarity* measures from the field of information retrieval [18]. The idf assigns weights to the occurrence of attribute names based on how common they are in a particular context, i.e. in a process. The underlying idea is that unique attributes, such as `docsComplete` in the motivational scenario, provide better indicators of similarity than common attributes. To compute the cosine similarity measure, we convert the attribute sets of event classes into weighted vector-based representations, denoted as $\mathbf{A_E}$. The weights in these vectors reflect the idf-score associated with a given attribute.

$$ATTR(E_1, E_2) = \frac{\mathbf{A_{E_1}} \cdot \mathbf{A_{E_2}}}{\| \mathbf{A_{E_1}} \| \| \mathbf{A_{E_2}} \|} \tag{4}$$

Alternatives. The ATTR measure only considers overlap in attributes with identical names. Numerous techniques exist that can be used to also quantify the similarity between non-identical attribute names [10]. Commonly applied measures include the Levenshtein distance [22] for *syntactic* similarity, which can be used to compute the string edit distance between attribute names. *Semantic* similarity measures can be used to recognize names with similar meanings, for instance those that use synonymous terms. The most commonly used tool to quantify semantic similarity is WordNet [2].

3.5 Attribute Value Similarity

The values of an attribute, associated with events of a given event class may provide insights into similarity beyond attribute name similarity. We have identified two general scenarios for this. First, an analysis of values can be useful to determine similarity in the context of opaque or unrelated attribute names. For instance, it is difficult to relate two attributes `month` and `m` based on their labels. By contrast, if both attributes are associated with numeric values in the range 1–12 (or even month names), their similarity becomes more apparent. Second, attribute value similarity can be used to disambiguate event classes that use the same attributes. The motivational scenario provides an example of this. The event classes `decide on high-value loan` and `decide on low-value loan` in M_2 both consider an `amount` attribute. Events of the former class are associated with a higher range of values than events of the latter. Therefore, by considering the attribute values, we can identify that the former event class is more likely to correspond to `perform advanced check` in M_1, which similarly occurs only for loan requests with a high amount.

Similarity Measure. To quantify attribute value similarity for two *individual* attributes, we rely on techniques from the research area of schema matching [8], where *content-based* matching, (direct comparison of sets of attribute values) is combined with *constraint-based* matching. The latter aims to extract constraints from a set of values, such as upper and lower bounds for numerical values. For brevity, we refrain from presenting explicitly the equations used in this method. After considering the similarity of individual attributes, the similarity values obtained in this manner can be used as weights to calculate the cosine similarity between two attribute sets. Using $VAL(A_E)$ to refer to the value sets of the attributes of an event class E, we compute the VAL measure as given by Eq. 5.

$$VAL(E_1, E_2) = \frac{\mathbf{VAL(A_{E_1}) \cdot VAL(A_{E_2})}}{\| \mathbf{VAL(A_{E_1})} \| \| \mathbf{VAL(A_{E_2})} \|} \quad (5)$$

Alternatives. Various alternative techniques exist to determine the similarity between two individual attributes, including identifying and comparing data types such as zip codes or geographical names, putting constraints on values, and identifying data patterns and distributions (cf. [15]).

3.6 Prerequisites Similarity

The input data used by an event can be an important indicator of event class similarity. Intuitively, this builds on the idea that the more similar the data that is used by event classes, the more similar their purpose. For example, in the motivational scenario, events of the classes `send decision letter` in M_1 and `inform applicant` in M_2 are the only ones to occur *after* an event has produced a value for the `decision` attribute. A challenge here is that the *XES-standard*[1] for event logs does not have an explicit notion of input data. Therefore, an event log can contain information on input data in two ways. First, input data elements of an event e might be part of the attribute set of e, as seen for the `amount` attribute of the `perform advanced check` event. In this case, similarity of inputs is already covered by the aforementioned attribute name and value similarity measures $ATTR$ and VAL. However, input data can also be derived from data attributes that were created *prior* to the execution of an event, which we operationalize next.

Similarity Measure. We define a measure $PREQ$ that determines the similarity of prerequisites based on the attributes associated with prior events. Specifically, given an event e_i that occurs at position i in a trace t, we define P_{e_i} as the union of all attribute sets A_{e_j} for $0 < j < i$. P_E then denotes all attributes contained in a set P_e for $e \in E$. The similarity between two prerequisites sets P_{E_1} and P_{E_2} is then computed in a similar manner as the $ATTR$ measure.

$$PREQ(E_1, E_2) = \frac{\mathbf{P_{E_1} \cdot P_{E_2}}}{\| \mathbf{P_{E_1}} \| \| \mathbf{P_{E_2}} \|} \quad (6)$$

Alternatives. It is possible to consider the values of prerequisite attributes, rather than their names, as provided by the VAL measure, or by combining the two. Furthermore, alternative measures can consider two more factors in the similarity computation, namely frequency and proximity of prerequisite attributes. The *frequency* with which an attribute is created prior to the execution of an event $e \in E$ can be used to distinguish among mandatory and optional prerequisites. In the context of process matching, such a distinction was proposed by Sagi et al. [17]. The *proximity* between the creation of an attribute and an occurrence of an event can provide insights into their similarity. Intuitively, if an attribute is created by an event at index i in a trace, then this attribute is

[1] http://www.xes-standard.org/.

more likely to be a relevant prerequisite to its immediate sequel event e_{i+1} than it is to events that are further away. Frequency and proximity considerations can be integrated by adapting the weights of the elements of the vectors used by *PREQ* accordingly.

4 Empirical Evaluation

This section presents an empirical evaluation that demonstrates the usefulness of event-log information for process matching. We evaluate the performance of the proposed event log-based matchers as a standalone tool. Specifically, we compare the correspondences obtained by automatic matching based on our 1LMs to a *gold standard* that contains the true correspondences between event classes. Our evaluation is based on real-world data, using a test collection of 105 event log pairs.

4.1 Test Collection

To perform the evaluation, we use data from the *BPI Challenge 2015* [5], which consists of real-world event data related to the handling of construction permit applications by five Dutch municipalities. The event data describe similar processes, while their actual implementation differs considerably. To obtain a sufficiently large collection of event logs to match, we split the event data into event logs, each relating to a different subprocess (on average 17 subprocesses per municipality). After removing the logs that contain less than five event classes (to avoid trivial matching tasks), we obtain a total of 57 event logs. We create pairs of event logs that relate to the same subprocess from different municipalities. This results in a total of 105 event log pairs.

Table 1. Characteristics of the test collection

Measure	Traces	Event classes	Total corr.	True corr.	Log overlap
Average	487.0	33.0	2,533.4	30.9	87.7%
Std.dev	353.6	40.7	6,246.3	36.5	10.5%
Minimum	8	5	15	3	50.0%
Maximum	1409	172	26,832	156	100.0%

Table 1 provides an overview of the test collection. The table illustrates the great diversity between the subprocesses. This can, for example, be seen in the number of event classes per log, which ranges from 5 to 172. The *true correspondences* reflect the actual correspondences between event classes from a pair of logs, also referred to as the *gold standard.* This gold standard directly follows from the traceability between the event classes in the logs of the different municipalities. The last column in the table describes the overlap in terms of the event classes of a log pair, *i.e.*, the fraction of event classes that appear in both logs. This measure indicates that, on average, 88% of the event classes in a log also appear in the gold standard. In the most extreme case, only 50% of the event classes from a log pair correspond to each other. Table 1 highlights the fact that even though the processes are similar across the five municipalities, considerable differences exist as well. The choice for this data collection is, furthermore, motivated by the lack of event logs associated with the collections typically used to evaluate matchers, i.e. the collections of the Process Model Matching Contests [1,3].

Note that in order to provide objective evaluation results, we hide all references to the names of event classes in this test collection. In particular, we hide the names and values of the following attributes: `concept:name`, `action_code`, `activityNameEN`, and `activityNameNL`.

4.2 Setup

To conduct the evaluation, we used the Ontobuilder Research Environment (ORE), an open source schema matching tool that enables researchers to run and evaluate matching experiments. We implemented the six 1LMs (Sect. 3) in ORE and made their implementation publicly available as part of the tool.[2]

As described in Sect. 2, establishing (exact) correspondences between the event class sets $\mathcal{E}_1, \mathcal{E}_2$ of a log pair requires a similarity matrix $\mathcal{M}(\mathcal{E}_1, \mathcal{E}_2)$ and a decision maker. Here, we obtain the similarity matrices in two different manners, resulting in a two-part evaluation. In the first part, we use each of the six 1LMs separately to construct $\mathcal{M}(\mathcal{E}_1, \mathcal{E}_2)$ based on a distinct similarity measure. This part of the evaluation provides insights into the performance of the *individual* 1LMs and into the characteristics of the test collection. In the second part, we use an ensemble matcher that combines the scores of the six similarity matrices into a single matrix. By evaluating this *matching ensemble*, we obtain insights into the combined performance of the matchers and their complementary nature. We further reflect on the way in which the measures complement each other by computing correlations among the individual similarity scores.

After obtaining a similarity matrix $\mathcal{M}(\mathcal{E}_1, \mathcal{E}_2)$ we apply a decision maker on $\mathcal{M}(\mathcal{E}_1, \mathcal{E}_2)$ to obtain a set of exact correspondences, to which we will refer to as $\mathcal{C}(\mathcal{E}_1, \mathcal{E}_2)$. In particular, we apply the *maximum weighted bipartite graph match* (MWBM) [12] to establish $\mathcal{C}(\mathcal{E}_1, \mathcal{E}_2)$. This decision maker is particularly well-suited in the context of the test collection, because it establishes 1:1 correspondences between event classes.

We use the well-known precision, recall, and F1 measures to compare the automatically obtained set of correspondences $\mathcal{C}$ to the set $\mathcal{G}$ of *actual* correspondences included in the gold standard. *Precision* (*pre*) here reflects the fraction of the correspondences obtained by the matching techniques that is also included in the gold standard, whereas recall (*rec*) represents the fraction of the correspondences in the gold standard that is correctly identi-

[2] https://bitbucket.org/tomers77/ontobuilder-research-environment.

fied by the matchers. The *F1* measure represents the *harmonic mean* of precision and recall. Equations 7, 8 and 9 formally define these measures.

$$pre = \frac{\mathcal{C} \cap \mathcal{G}}{\mathcal{C}} \quad (7) \qquad rec = \frac{\mathcal{C} \cap \mathcal{G}}{\mathcal{G}} \quad (8) \qquad F1 = \frac{2 * pre * rec}{pre + rec} \quad (9)$$

4.3 Results

Table 2 presents an overview of the results obtained by using the individual 1LMs and by a matching ensemble based on all six 1LMs. We will now elaborate on the results obtained through these two methods.

Table 2. Overview of the evaluation results

FLM	Precision	Recall	F1-score
RP	.24	.25	.25
FREQ	.14	.14	.14
DUR	.13	.11	.12
ATTR	.05	.04	.04
VAL	**.27**	**.27**	**.27**
PREQ	.09	.08	.08
Ensemble	**.38**	**.38**	**.38**

Matching Results. The results presented in Table 2 show that the performance varies greatly among the various 1LMs. The lowest performance results belong to *ATTR* and *PREQ* 1LMs, which both consider similarity based on *attribute names*. These 1LMs achieve $F1$-score of .04 and .08, respectively. A post-hoc analysis of the similarity matrices generated by these 1LMs shows that, indeed, attribute names provide little discriminatory power in the context of this particular test collection. In fact, most event classes are associated with identical or nearly identical sets of attributes, which results in a similarity score of 1.0 for the vast majority of event class pairs. By contrast, *VAL* achieves the highest results with an $F1$-score of 0.27. This shows that, as opposed to the names of attributes, attribute *values* provide a substantially better indicator of similarity. Furthermore, the performance of *RP* shows that the consideration of positional similarity also provides a relatively good indicator of similarity.

The last row of Table 2 presents the results obtained by an ensemble consisting of the six 1LMs. For this ensemble, we applied a naïve weighting scheme, in which we computed the average score of the six similarity measures. The results demonstrate that the ensemble greatly outperforms individual 1LMs, achieving an $F1$-score of .38. A one-sided paired t-test reveals that this result is statistically significant ($p < 0.05$) when compared to the best performing individual

1LM (*VAL*). The improved results of the ensemble illustrate that the six 1LMs are complementary to each other and can enhance each other's performance.

Top-*k* Results. The results shown so far indicate that the use of log data for process matching is a valid approach that can identify correspondences among activities by analyzing execution data. It is also clear that the use of log data alone does not suffice for achieving an industrial-strength matching tool. An $F1$-score of about 0.4 indicates a far from random correlation between the decisions made by the ensemble and the true correspondences. Still, it requires the support of other techniques to strengthen its performance. Existing process model-based matchers represent good candidates, because they use valuable process model information (*e.g.*, activity labels), which is purposefully not used by our log-based matchers. Because numerous model-based matchers exist, each with their own strengths and weaknesses, we leave for future research the best way to tackle the combination of log-based and model-based matching techniques. Here, we investigate the obtained results in more depth and determine to what extent the log-based techniques lend themselves well to process matching.

Identified correspondences can be incorrect because often an event class has multiple correspondences with equal or near equal similarity scores as the best candidates. The selection of a single, best correspondence then becomes an arbitrary selection among a handful of correspondences. This problem relates to the inherent issue of uncertainty in the matching task. Works on *matching monotonicity* [9] have found that this uncertainty prevents matchers from identifying a correct correspondence as the one with the highest similarity measure. However, these works argue that *good* matchers should contain the *correct correspondences* among the correspondences with the highest similarity scores, *i.e.*, in the so-called top-k matches. If they succeed in this, a good matcher positions a true correspondence high enough for a human observer to confirm it after scanning only a few possible correspondences. To test this, we check for each event class whether its correct correspondence occurs within the top 3 or top 5 correspondences with the highest similarity scores.

Figure 2 presents results of the top-k analysis. For each matcher, we measure the recall of top-1, top-3, and top-5. As expected, the matching result improves significantly when the best correspondences are considered. This holds for all matchers, but with varying levels of success. The biggest gain is observed for the RP measure. There, the performance increases from a recall of 0.25 for top-1 to 0.69 and 0.78 for top-3 and top-5, respectively. As such, the RP measure performs nearly identically to the matching ensemble. The results indicate that all matchers show a monotonic behavior, though some more than others. It is interesting to see that while the top-1 performance of RP is worse than the one of VAL, a different picture is drawn for top-3 and top-5. There, RP surpasses VAL (in terms of Recall), performing just as well as the ensemble matcher. Finally, what is important to realize is that by considering the top-3 and top-5 scores users need to just evaluate approximately 4% and 7% of the total possible correspondences. These small fractions already enable the respective identification of close to 70% and 80% of the true correspondences.

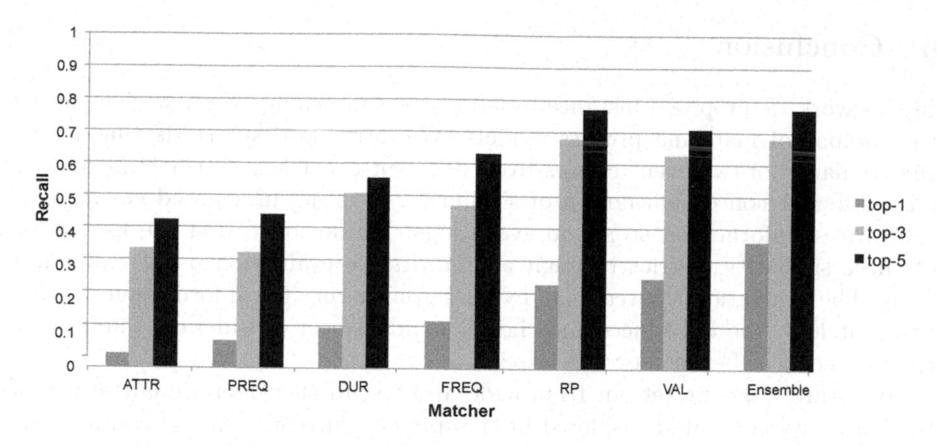

Fig. 2. Recall scores for top-k results

5 Related Work

The work presented in this paper relates to two main streams of research, namely process model matching and instance-based matching.

In the last few years, a plethora of *process model matching* approaches has been proposed [1,3]. Traditionally, they combine structural or behavioral properties with different types of textual similarity. Some rely on rather simplistic techniques such as the Levenshtein distance [20], others use WordNet for computing textual similarity [14]. Recognizing the limitations of many existing matchers in terms of performance, researchers recently started to explore alternative strategies. For instance, Klinkmüller et al. [13] improve matching results by incorporating user feedback. Weidlich et al. [21] used prediction techniques to select the most suitable matching technique for a given problem. In this work, we propose a new resource, event log data, to improve the matching results. Our experiments demonstrate that this indeed represents a promising direction.

Instance-based matching has been previously explored in the context of schema matching and the related field of ontology alignment. Engmann and Maßmann [8] used two methods to enhance their COMA++ matcher. The first, a constraint-based matcher, identifies the field types using a list of patterns and numerical constraints attempted over the instance data per attribute. An approach similar to our own *VAL* measure. Their second method applies to text-based fields taken from the same domain in which the string-similarity of all instances is compared and averaged. A similar approach is suggested by Wang et al. [19] which probe a Web query interfaces with keywords and then compare the vector-space similarity of the query result tokens. A similar approach is applied by Duan et al. [6], using *Locality Sensitive Hashing* (LSH) techniques to compare instances over very large ontologies. Zaiß et al. [23] use regular expressions to improve pattern identification of attribute domains. Our work differs from these works in that we make use of process-unique features to perform the matching task.

6 Conclusion

In this work we proposed instance-based process matching as a new element for the toolbox of matching process models. We introduced six 1LMs that assess the similarity of two event classes from different event logs. Each 1LM focuses on a different conceptual notion of similarity, resulting in a broad coverage of the process information stored in event logs. We demonstrated the usefulness of these similarity metrics through a quantitative evaluation using real-world data. The evaluation showed that by just considering the information specific to event logs, the introduced matchers can identify a considerable number of correspondences between event classes.

In future work, we set out to provide and test further operationalizations of the similarity concepts considered in this paper. Currently, we defined a single similarity metric for each of the six concepts. However, the majority of these concepts can be operationalized by implementing a variety of metrics, as discussed in Sect. 3. Furthermore, we strive to combine our event log-based matching techniques with traditional, model-based techniques for process model matching. By combining model-based matchers with the proposed log-based matchers, we will aim at achieving matching results that cannot be obtained by using either of these techniques alone.

References

1. Antunes, G., Bakhshandeh, M., Borbinha, J., Cardoso, J., Dadashnia, S., Francescomarino, C., Dragoni, M., Fettke, P., Gal, A., Ghidini, C., et al.: The process model matching contest 2015. In: 6th EMISA Workshop, pp. 127–155 (2015)
2. Budanitsky, A., Hirst, G.: Evaluating wordnet-based measures of lexical semantic relatedness. Comput. Linguist. **32**(1), 13–47 (2006)
3. Cayoglu, U., Dijkman, R.M., Dumas, M., Fettke, P., Garcıa-Banuelos, L., Hake, P., Klinkmüller, C., Leopold, H., Ludwig, A., Loos, P., et al.: The process model matching contest 2013. In: 4th International Workshop on Process Model Collections: Management and Reuse (PMC-MR 2013) (2013)
4. Dijkman, R.M., Dumas, M., Van Dongen, B., Käärik, R., Mendling, J.: Similarity of business process models: metrics and evaluation. Inf. Syst. **36**(2), 498–516 (2011)
5. Dongen, B.F.V.: BPI challenge 2015 (2015). https://doi.org/10.4121/uuid:31a308ef-c844-48da-948c-305d167a0ec1
6. Duan, S., Fokoue, A., Hassanzadeh, O., Kementsietsidis, A., Srinivas, K., Ward, M.J.: Instance-based matching of large ontologies using locality-sensitive hashing. In: Cudré-Mauroux, P., et al. (eds.) ISWC 2012. LNCS, vol. 7649, pp. 49–64. Springer, Heidelberg (2012). doi:10.1007/978-3-642-35176-1_4
7. Dumas, M., La Rosa, M., Mendling, J., Reijers, H.A.: Fundamentals of Business Process Management. Springer, Heidelberg (2012)
8. Engmann, D., Maßmann, S.: Instance matching with COMA++. In: BTW Workshops, pp. 28–37 (2007)
9. Gal, A., Anaby-Tavor, A., Trombetta, A., Montesi, D.: A framework for modeling and evaluating automatic semantic reconciliation. VLDB J. Int. J. Very Large Data Bases **14**(1), 50–67 (2005)

10. Gal, A., Weidlich, M.: Model matching - processes and beyond. In: Zdravkovic, J., Kirikova, M., Johannesson, P. (eds.) CAiSE 2015. LNCS, vol. 9097, pp. 525–526. Springer, Cham (2015). https://link.springer.com/book/10.1007/978-3-319-19069-3
11. Gal, A.: Uncertain schema matching. Synth. Lect. Data Manag. **3**(1), 1–97 (2011)
12. Galil, Z., Micali, S., Gabow, H.: An o(EV logV) algorithm for finding a maximal weighted matching in general graphs. SIAM J. Comput. **15**(1), 120–130 (1986)
13. Klinkmüller, C., Leopold, H., Weber, I., Mendling, J., Ludwig, A.: Listen to me: improving process model matching through user feedback. In: Sadiq, S., Soffer, P., Völzer, H. (eds.) BPM 2014. LNCS, vol. 8659, pp. 84–100. Springer, Cham (2014). doi:10.1007/978-3-319-10172-9_6
14. Leopold, H., Niepert, M., Weidlich, M., Mendling, J., Dijkman, R., Stuckenschmidt, H.: Probabilistic optimization of semantic process model matching. In: Barros, A., Gal, A., Kindler, E. (eds.) BPM 2012. LNCS, vol. 7481, pp. 319–334. Springer, Heidelberg (2012). doi:10.1007/978-3-642-32885-5_25
15. Rahm, E., Bernstein, P.A.: A survey of approaches to automatic schema matching. VLDB J. **10**(4), 334–350 (2001)
16. Razali, N.M., Wah, Y.B., et al.: Power comparisons of shapiro-wilk, kolmogorov-smirnov, lilliefors and anderson-darling tests. J. Stat. Model. Anal. **2**(1), 21–33 (2011)
17. Sagi, T., Gal, A., Weidlich, M.: Measuring expected integration effort in service composition. In: 2014 IEEE International Conference on Services Computing (SCC), pp. 645–652. IEEE (2014)
18. Salton, G., McGill, M.J.: Introduction to modern information retrieval (1986)
19. Wang, J., Wen, J., Lochovsky, F., Ma, W.: Instance-based schema matching for web databases by domain-specific query probing. In: Proceedings of the Thirtieth International Conference on Very Large Data Bases, vol. 30, pp. 408–419. VLDB Endowment (2004)
20. Weidlich, M., Dijkman, R., Mendling, J.: The ICoP framework: identification of correspondences between process models. In: Pernici, B. (ed.) CAiSE 2010. LNCS, vol. 6051, pp. 483–498. Springer, Heidelberg (2010). doi:10.1007/978-3-642-13094-6_37
21. Weidlich, M., Sagi, T., Leopold, H., Gal, A., Mendling, J.: Predicting the quality of process model matching. In: Daniel, F., Wang, J., Weber, B. (eds.) BPM 2013. LNCS, vol. 8094, pp. 203–210. Springer, Heidelberg (2013). doi:10.1007/978-3-642-40176-3_16
22. Yujian, L., Bo, L.: A normalized levenshtein distance metric. IEEE Trans. Pattern Anal. Mach. Intell. **29**(6), 1091–1095 (2007)
23. Zaiß, K., Schlüter, T., Conrad, S.: Instance-based ontology matching using regular expressions. In: Meersman, R., Tari, Z., Herrero, P. (eds.) OTM 2008. LNCS, vol. 5333, pp. 40–41. Springer, Heidelberg (2008). doi:10.1007/978-3-540-88875-8_19

Analyzing Process Variants to Understand Differences in Key Performance Indices

Nithish Pai Ballambettu(✉), Mahima Agumbe Suresh, and R.P. Jagadeesh Chandra Bose

Conduent Labs India, Etamin Block, 4th Floor, Wing A, Prestige Technology Park II, Bangalore 560037, India
{nithish.pai,jagadeesh.prabhakara}@conduent.com

Abstract. Service delivery organizations cater similar processes across several clients. Process variants may manifest due to the differences in the nature of clients, heterogeneity in the type of cases, etc. The organization's operational Key Performance Indices (KPIs) across these variants may vary, e.g., KPIs for some variants may be better than others. There is a need to gain insights for such variance in performance and seek opportunities to learn from well performing process variants (e.g., to establish best practices and standardization of processes) and leverage these learnings/insights on non-performing ones. In this paper, we present an approach to analyze two or more process variants, presented as annotated process maps. Our approach identifies and reasons the key differences, manifested in both the control-flow (e.g., frequent paths) and performance (e.g., flow time, activity execution times, etc.) perspectives, among these variants. The fragments within process variants where the key differences manifest are targets for process redesign and re-engineering. The proposed approach has been implemented as a plug-in in the process mining framework, ProM, and applied on real-life case studies.

Keywords: Process variants · Process comparison · Annotations · Process mining · Pair-wise · Unified process model

1 Introduction

Services organizations cater to a large number of clients on a daily basis. Service providers typically implement/deploy a service delivery framework to meet Service Level Agreements (SLAs) and closely monitor the performance and efficiency of their operations to meet stringent compliance requirements, handle cost pressures, inefficient processes and complex workflows. Subtleties specific to clients, heterogeneity in types of cases, etc. lead to process variants. For example, the way how a particular process (e.g., claims processing) is handled for *different clients* (different insurance providers) lead to process variants; in large organizations due to a lack of standardization, process variations may arise as a result of, e.g., *different teams handling the same process in different ways*; in a loan

E. Dubois and K. Pohl (Eds.): CAiSE 2017, LNCS 10253, pp. 298–313, 2017.
DOI: 10.1007/978-3-319-59536-8_19

application process, there could be *different pathways followed depending on the type of customer* (e.g., gold, platinum, etc.); in an issue management process, process variations might manifest depending on the *type of issue*.

The operational Key Performance Indices (KPIs) may vary across such process variants. For instance, two clients requiring a similar process (e.g., document verification) to be executed, may incur very different turnaround times for process completion. In some cases, this can even result in the service provider meeting SLA specifications for some variants, and violating those of others, despite the similarity in processes executed. There is a need to gain insights for such variance in performance and seek opportunities to learn from well performing process variants and leverage these learnings/insights on non-performing variants (e.g., establish best practices, standardization of processes, etc.). An important step towards this is to identify key differences that manifest among the process variants. Variants of a business process may be different in several perspectives, such as control-flow and time. For example, in the time perspective, the execution/flow time of activities/transitions across the variants may differ, in the control-flow perspective, the paths of the process flows that are most often executed may differ.

In this paper, we propose an approach for analyzing *two or more* process variants to identify key differences among them. Our approach addresses not just structural differences between the variants but also considers rich qualitative information such as the frequencies and flow times (provided as annotations) pertaining to the execution of processes. We present metrics and measures to identify significant differences, detect cascaded components (due to the propagation of differences manifested at a source), and identify most aberrant processes among the variants. The proposed approach has been implemented as a plug-in in the ProM framework[1] and tested on several real-life case studies. Our experiments reveal that this approach is able to uncover useful insights on *where* and *how* processes differ. Such insights are helpful to further explore and identify the reasons for such aberrations (understand the *why's*).

The rest of the paper is organized as follows: Related work is presented in Sect. 2. Section 3 discusses some metrics that could be used to enrich process models. Our framework for analyzing process variants is presented in Sect. 4. Section 5 discusses the implementation of the proposed approach as a ProM plug-in. Section 6 presents and discusses some experimental results. Finally, Sect. 7 concludes the paper.

2 Related Work

There has been some prior work in identifying the similarities in process graphs [4,6,10,13]. [6] presents metrics to identify the key similarities between two process graphs based on presence, absence, or changes in nodes and edges in the graphs while [4] discusses techniques to identify semantic equality between

[1] See www.processmining.org for more information and to download ProM.

process graphs when the names of the activities among processes are not provided correctly. [13] presents fast classification of process models into relevant, irrelevant, and potentially relevant, as a way to quickly identify similarities in different business processes. The aforementioned papers fail to account for the attributes/annotations of the edges in a process model. In this work, we identify the differences in the transitions (i.e., edges) in processes apart from the activities (i.e., nodes).

Structural differences among process graphs have been studied in [2,7,8,12]. While [2] uses graph distance metrics based on whether or not an edge is present between two process dependency graphs, [8] uses spectral graph analysis to detect structural changes. However, these do not consider the qualitative differences based on attributes of the nodes and/or edges in process graphs.

Differences between process variants considering attributes of nodes/edges were studied in [3,5]. [5] detects only categorical differences among attribute values i.e., it only indicates whether there is an increase/decrease/no change in attribute values but doesn't quantify the magnitude of differences. In contrast, in this paper, we quantify the magnitude of differences. [3] uncovers statistically significant differences between two process models represented as transition systems. The statistical significance of the difference is computed using Welch's two sided T-test, which assumes that the two distributions are normal. However, this assumption may not hold true in many real-life circumstances. In fact, most of the transition time annotations in the processes we have studied are observed to have non-normal distributions. In this paper, we propose a much robust difference metric using Wasserstein distance [11] based on cumulative distribution functions. Furthermore, our approach enables the analysis of multiple (more than two) process variants and also detects cascading effects in the differences.

Table 1 summarizes the result of our comparative analysis. We can see that our proposed work extends the state-of-the-art with capabilities missing in those. We evaluated the various plug-ins/tools available for process comparison on their functional and non-functional aspects. On the functional side, we checked for

- *nature of differences:* whether the tool supports the detection of structural and/or quantitative annotation differences
- *diagnostic insights:* the ability to provide diagnostic insights through interactive visualization (e.g., upon clicking on an element of the model)
- *scalability:* the ability to compare more than two variants
- *cascaded components:* the ability to detect cascaded components, i.e., propagation of differences (cf., Sect. 4)
- *flexibility:* the ability to support multiple distance measures, handle different types of annotations (e.g., scalar values, distributions, etc.)

On the non-functional side, we looked at the ease-of-use. We evaluated these tools on the basis of usability and interpretability of the outputs. In particular, we looked for interactive visualizations, drill downs and textual descriptions for the identified differences for easy consumption by the user.

Table 1. Comparison of state of the art with our approach

	Functional						Non-functional
	Nature of differences			Diagnostic insights	Flexibility	Scalability	Ease of use
	Structural differences	Annotation differences	Cascaded components				
[4,6,10,13]	✓						
[2,8,12]	✓						
[7]	✓				✓		
[5]	✓	✓					✓
[3]	✓	✓		✓			✓
Our work	✓	✓	✓	✓	✓	✓	✓

3 Process Annotation Metrics

Variants of a process can manifest themselves across several different perspectives, e.g., control-flow, performance, data, resource, etc. Process models can be enriched with rich information (as annotations) to provide deep insights. Such enriched process models can be viewed as *process maps*, analogous to cartographic maps. With effective visualization, process map can provide multiple seamless views of a process highlighting several facets w.r.t process executions, e.g., highway paths followed in a process, bottleneck flows, etc. In this section, we introduce some measures (metrics) that could be used as annotations in process maps.

Given a process model, frequency and time of execution are two measures that provide insightful information on the control-flow and performance perspectives of the process.

- **Frequency** is a control-flow measure that captures the number of times a node/edge of process map is traversed (visited) during the execution of process instances.
- **Time** is a performance measure that captures the amount of time spent during the execution of process instances. Different notions of time can be captured, e.g., execution time (of an activity), turnaround time (of an activity and process instance), flow time (between two activities), etc.

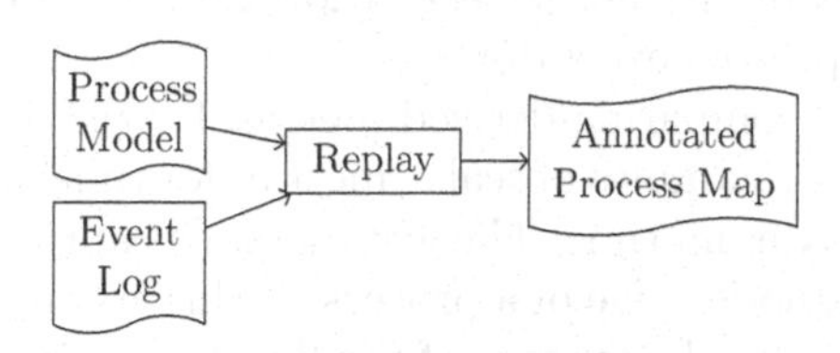

Fig. 1. Deriving metrics and annotating process maps by replaying event logs on process models.

If event logs capturing process executions are available, one can use replay techniques [1] to accumulate such metrics and use them for generating process maps as illustrated in Fig. 1. In case event logs are not available, we expect the process owners to provide these metrics (e.g., expected flow time).

Depending on the richness of process execution data and process model specification, some or several of these metrics can be computed. For example, if the event log captures the various life cycle stages of an activity (e.g., start, suspend, resume, complete, etc.), one can compute the execution time, turnaround time, waiting time, etc. If the process model specification also captures the life cycle stages of an activity (e.g., a flow from activity-start to activity-suspend, activity-suspend to activity-resume, etc.), several of the primitive time metrics can be captured as flow-time of edges (flows) in the process.

We consider three variants of the frequency measure

- *absolute frequency:* is the absolute value of the number of times a node/edge is traversed/visited during process executions.
- *trace frequency:* is the number of process instances (or traces) that visited a node/edge. Multiple visits of a node/edge within a process instance are ignored here.
- *normalized trace frequency:* is the fraction of process instances that visited a node/edge. This is helpful if the metrics are derived from event logs. This metric normalizes the differences in the number of process instances among the process executions of the variants.

Figure 2(a) depicts an issue management process with no annotations. Figure 2(b) depicts the issue management process map annotated with frequency measures. For each node/edge, there are two measures, the absolute frequency and trace frequency (enclosed in parenthesis). For example, the number of instances of execution of In Progress is 146 and these are manifested in 137 traces. It must be noted that the absolute frequency and the trace frequency for a node/edge will differ when it is visited multiple times due to the presence of a cycle/loop in a process instance. The absolute frequency of that node/edge will be the number of times it was visited in all the process instances. But the trace frequency will only count the number of process instances (or traces) in which the node/edge was present.

We consider two variants of the time measure

- *distributions:* capture the actual execution/flow time of all instances of a node/edge in the process executions.
- *scalars:* sometimes, comparing derived metrics for the distributions may provide useful insights. Examples of scalar metrics for time are average time, minimum time and maximum time. The average time captures the average execution/flow time of a node/edge of a process. If this is computed from the event log, this corresponds to the average of the flow/execution time of all instances of the node/edge manifested in the process executions. If this is to be provided by a process owner, this can correspond to the expected execution/flow time. The minimum time corresponds to the minimum flow/execution time of

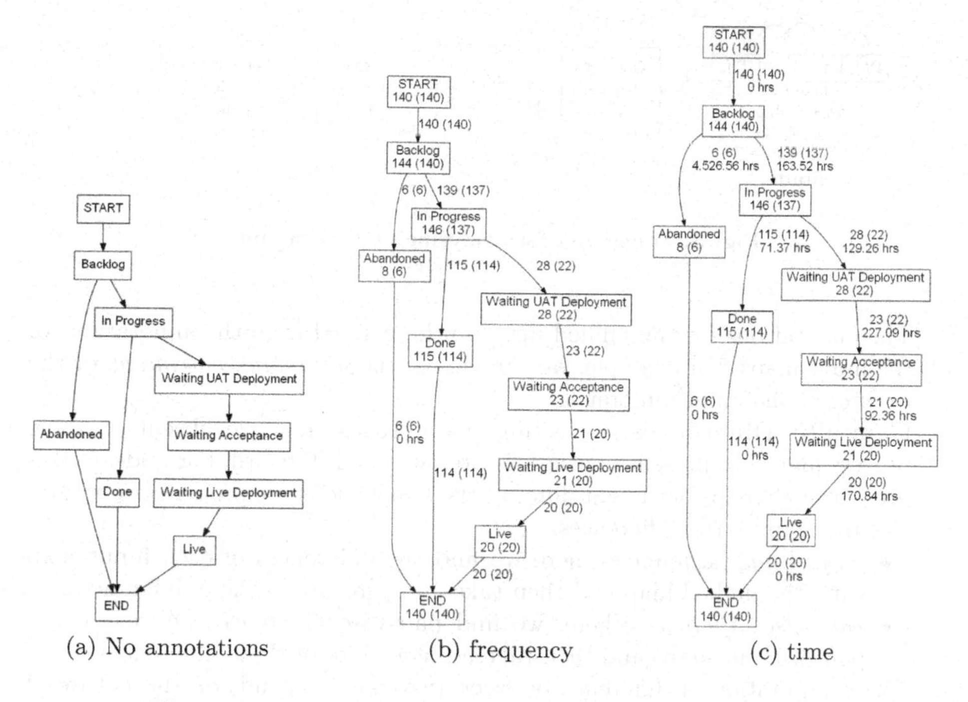

(a) No annotations (b) frequency (c) time

Fig. 2. Issue management process and its annotated versions.

all the manifestations of a node/edge in the process maps. Comparing minimum times can provide useful insights to the process owner at times. For instance, a node/edge in a process variant having twice the minimum time than the same node/edge in another variant of the process could suggest an improvement that could be made in the first variant.

Figure 2(c) depicts the issue management process map enriched with average flow time measure on the edges. For example, the average flow time between In Progress and Waiting UAT Deployment is 129.26 h.

4 Framework to Analyze Process Variants

Given a set of annotated process map variants, our framework for analyzing those variants comprises of five steps as depicted in Fig. 3.

- **Generate Unified Process Map:** To provide a global view of all process map variants, we generate a unified process map that is formed by taking a union of all nodes and edges of the input map variants. In other words, if $P_1 = (V_1, E_1), P_2 = (V_2, E_2), \ldots, P_n = (V_n, E_n)$ are the n process variants, the unified process map $P_U = (V_U, E_U)$ where $V_U = \cup_{i=1}^{n} V_i$ and $E_U = \cup_{i=1}^{n} E_i$.

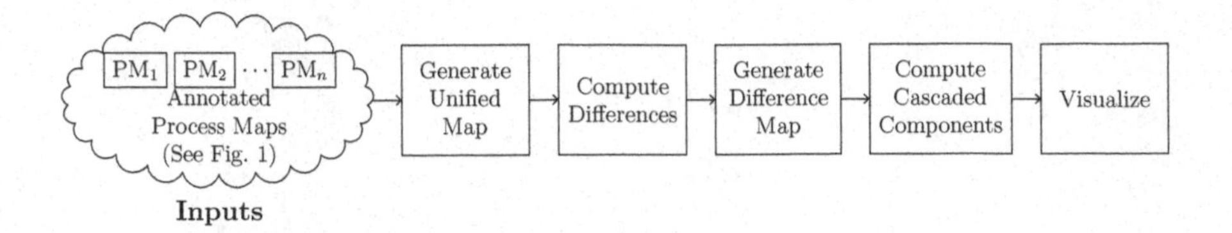

Fig. 3. Framework for analyzing process variants.

The annotations for the unified map can be derived from the annotations of the input maps. For example, we can choose the *minimum*, *maximum*, or the *average* of the input annotations.

- **Compute Differences:** Detecting nodes/edges that are absent in some process maps but present in others is pretty straightforward. For nodes/edges present in all maps but might differ in the annotations, we propose two strategies to compute the differences:
  - *unified map differences:* here we find the differences of each input map w.r.t the unified map and then take an aggregate of these differences.
  - *pair-wise differences:* here, we find pair-wise differences between every pair of input maps and then take an aggregate of these differences.

  The computation of difference between two maps depends on the nature of the annotation in the maps' nodes/edges. We suggest three different distance measures
  - *absolute difference* of an annotation is defined as the magnitude (absolute value) of the difference between the annotation values of the two maps. This measure is applicable when the annotation values are numeric and normalized, e.g., as in normalized trace frequency.
  - *relative difference* of an annotation is defined as the relative change in the values of the annotation in the two maps. Here, we choose one map as a reference.

    $$\text{rel}_{\text{diff}}(v_i, v_j) = \frac{|v_i - v_j|}{v_{\text{ref}}}$$

    where v_{ref} is the annotation value of the reference map.
    However, using this definition makes $\text{rel}_{\text{diff}}(v_i, v_j)$ asymmetric depending on the choice of reference. If the reference map is the unified process map, then the denominator is always the same (that of the unified process map). However, for pair-wise differences, we can take either of the maps as reference. In order to make it symmetric, we use the same strategy that is used to make the KL-Divergence symmetric [9], which is:

    $$\text{rel}_{\text{diff}}(v_i, v_j) = \frac{1}{2}\frac{|v_i - v_j|}{v_i} + \frac{1}{2}\frac{|v_i - v_j|}{v_j}$$

    i.e., we consider the relative difference taking both the input values as a reference and then average the differences.
    This measure is applicable when the annotation values are numeric but

not normalized, e.g., as in average flow time. In non-normalized annotations, the magnitude of the difference will not be informative. For example, the absolute difference of flow time between 1000 ms and 1002 ms and between 1 ms and 3 ms is the same. However, the latter difference might be significant than the former.

- *statistical difference* of an annotation is defined over those annotations that contain collections of values, e.g., flow time distributions. For such annotations, we propose the use of Wasserstein distance based on cumulative distribution functions (CDFs) as a distance measure, which is defined as

$$d_{\text{Wasserstein}}(V_1, V_2) = \int_{k=-\infty}^{\infty} |\mathbb{P}(x \leq k) - \mathbb{P}(y \leq k)|$$

  where x and y are random variables representing the two distributions V_1 and V_2 respectively. $\mathbb{P}(x \leq k)$ is the fraction of elements in x that are less than or equal to k.

  Intuitively, *Wasserstein distance measures the difference in the areas of the CDFs.* Figure 4(a) depicts CDFs for two populations and Fig. 4(b) depicts the Wasserstein's distance, which is captured as the difference in areas between the two cdfs (shaded region).

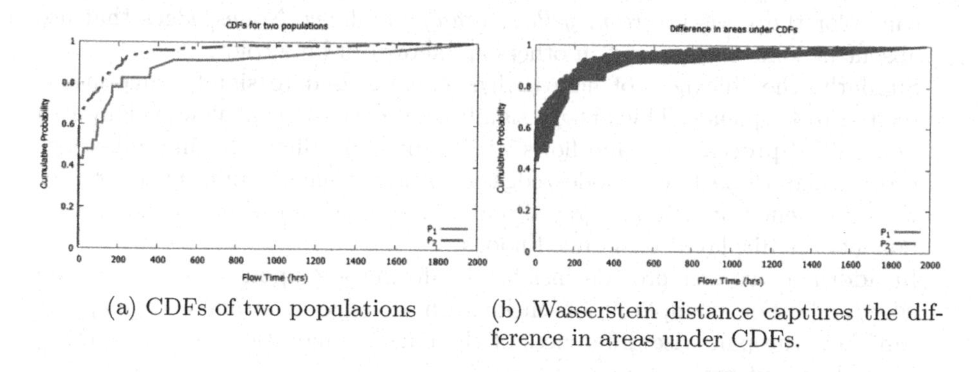

(a) CDFs of two populations

(b) Wasserstein distance captures the difference in areas under CDFs.

Fig. 4. Illustration of Wasserstein's distance.

- **Generate Difference Process Map:** The difference process map is a unified process map annotated with the differences computed for the nodes and edges. As discussed above, the differences among the input process maps can be computed either with the unified graph annotations or using pair-wise differences.
- **Compute Cascaded Components:** Control-flow differences between process maps due to a change at a single node (e.g., being executed more/less often) in a process map variant may cause a set of related nodes to also have significant differences w.r.t. frequency measure. Identifying such fragments is interesting to a business user for root-cause analysis. We discover

such cascaded effects by identifying connected components in the difference map. The basic idea in detecting cascading components is as follows. First, we identify the nodes/edges that have significant differences. Then in each process map, we consider only that view of the process map involving the nodes/edges with significant differences. For each such component, we extract those nodes/edges that have a similar annotation value as compared to the node/edge under consideration, i.e., the relative difference is below a threshold. The extracted nodes/edges are considered to be in the same cascaded fragment. The fragments containing both the components are then merged to obtain a bigger connected component of cascaded differences. The process is repeated for each node/edge in the view until no other connected component can be formed.

- **Visualize:** The unified and difference process maps are to be presented to the user in an interactive and intuitive visualization. We use *color* and *thickness* properties of graph visualization to represent the intensity of an annotation in time and frequency respectively. For the time-based annotations, we divide the range of annotation values into bins and represent them in a color spectrum ranging from green to red (with red indicating most significant value in time). For example, a red edge indicates bottleneck flow in a unified process map while it indicates the flow with the most significant difference in flow time (among process variants) in a difference map. Using four quartiles, we can color the flows in *green, yellow, orange*, and *red*. Nodes/edges that are absent in some and present in others are shown in blue color.
  Similarly, the thickness of nodes/edges can be used to signify annotations related to frequency. Thick edges signify the most frequent flows (highways) in a unified process map and flows with significant differences in a difference process map respectively. Nodes/edges that do not have significant differences w.r.t frequency or time are grayed out (made invisible) while cascaded components are displayed using filled nodes.
  In addition, we can provide insightful information upon drill-down on an edge/node. For example, upon clicking on an edge in a difference map, we can show the pair-wise differences of the edge's annotation (e.g., flow time) w.r.t the input process maps.

Detecting the Most Aberrant Process Map

Given a set of process maps, an interesting question is to find the process map that is most aberrant from the rest. Using the pair-wise difference matrix, we can rank the maps according to their contribution of differences w.r.t other maps by sorting the rows/columns according to the sum of values in each row/column. We can then answer questions such as what are the top k process maps that contribute the maximum to the differences or the process maps that contribute to p percentage of differences.

5 Implementation

The proposed framework has been implemented as a plug-in in ProM. Although our framework is generic and can be applied to process models represented in any formalism, in this implementation, we use Heuristic nets as base process models and annotate them with metrics discussed in Sect. 3. We have adapted the Heuristics miner plug-in to compute these metrics. Heuristic models are annotated with these metrics to generate Heuristic maps. Given process variants as multiple Heuristics maps, the plug-in implements the framework discussed in Sect. 4 to analyze these variants and presents the results in an interactive visualization. We can drill down into the components (nodes/edges) identified as significantly different to gain further insights into *how* the variants are different.

6 Experiments and Discussion

In this section, we discuss the results of applying the proposed framework on the event logs pertaining to an issue management process in the customer care division within a large service delivery organization. The organization is interested in analyzing the differences in product development issue management process when handling different types of products. The product development issue management process at a very high-level involves the movement of cases from backlog to in progress. Subsequently, some cases can be completed while some can be sent for user acceptance tests and then are deployed live. Cases can be abandoned at any point in time. We considered the event logs from this product issue management process related to three different products P_1, P_2, and P_3 to analyze how these variants differ. The characteristics of these logs are depicted in Table 2. Figure 5 depicts the process maps obtained by using the heuristics miner. The heuristics nets are annotated with the frequency, trace frequency, and average flow time metrics. The numbers in parenthesis at each node/edge correspond to the trace frequency of that node/edge.

Table 2. Event log characteristics of product issue management process pertaining to three products.

Log	No. cases	No. events	No. activities	No. resources
P_1	140	505	8	20
P_2	158	912	8	28
P_3	122	668	8	24

Figure 6 depicts a screenshot of the plug-in's output highlighting the difference process map and the summary of pair-wise differences between the input variants both for frequency (bottom-left diagonal matrix) and time (bottom-right). From the figure, we can see that variant P_1 is the most aberrant model

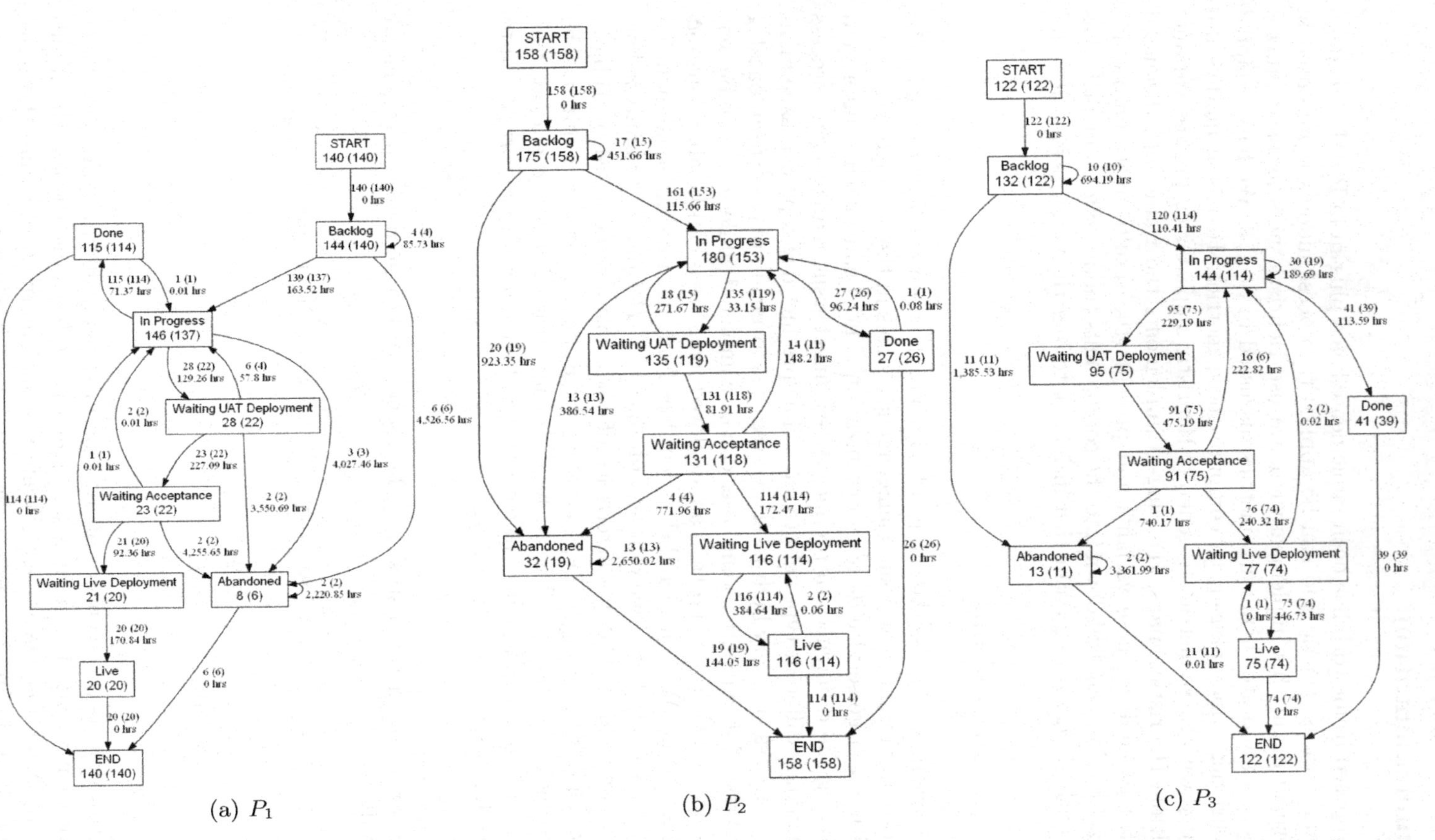

(a) P_1 (b) P_2 (c) P_3

Fig. 5. Process models discovered using heuristic nets miner and annotated with frequency, trace frequency, and average flow time metrics.

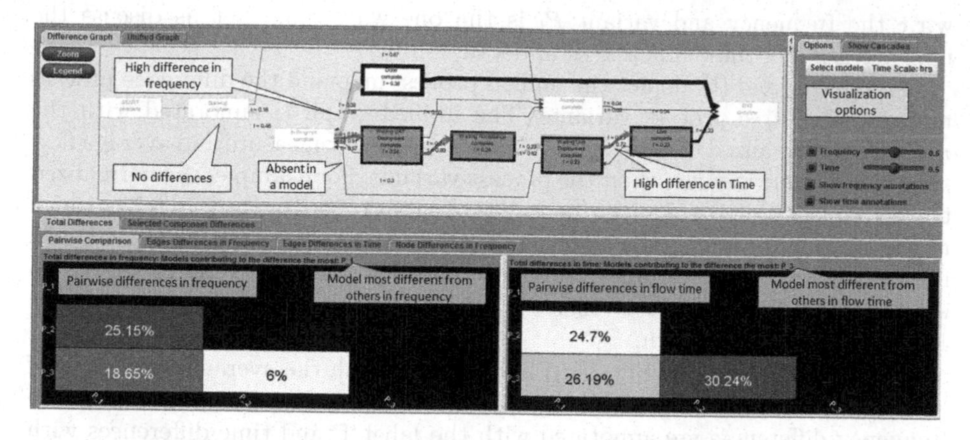

Fig. 6. Screenshot of the output of the plug-in showing the difference process map and pair-wise differences between the variants both in frequency and time.

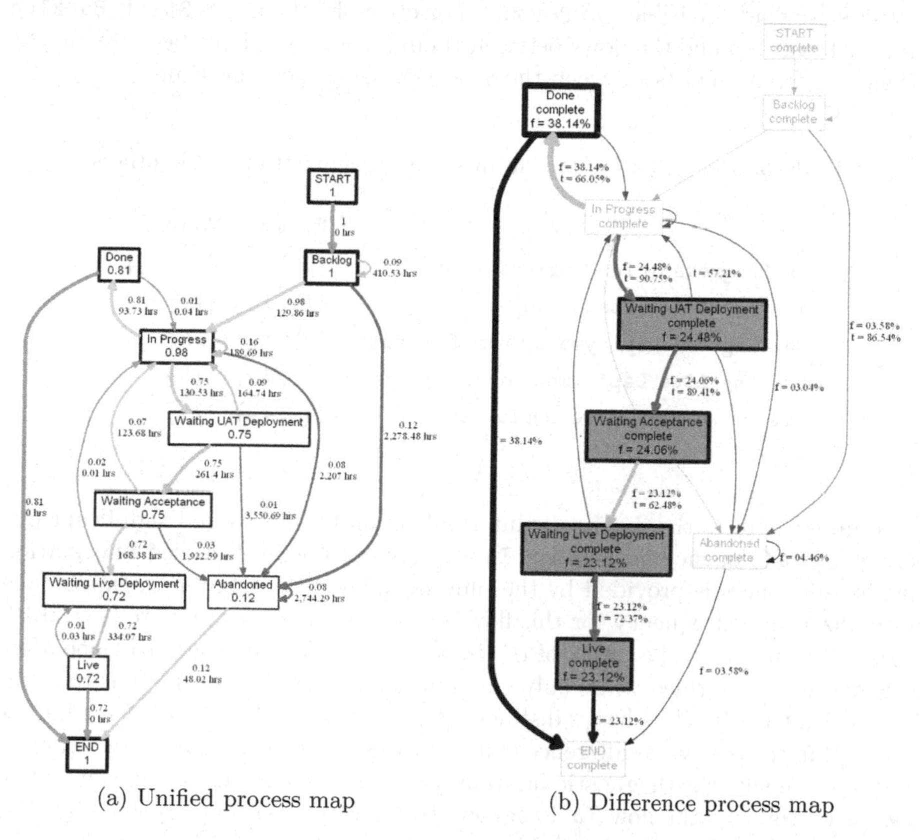

(a) Unified process map

(b) Difference process map

Fig. 7. Unified and difference process maps of the three process variants P_1, P_2 and P_3.

w.r.t the frequency and variant P_3 is the one w.r.t time. Let us discuss the interpretation of these differences in detail.

Figure 7(a) and (b) depict the unified process map and the difference process map for the three process variants. The unified graph is annotated with the *maximum* normalized trace frequency for the frequency measure and average flow time for the time measure w.r.t the process variants. For example, the normalized trace frequency metric for the node `Waiting UAT Deployment` is 0.75, which is the maximum among the normalized trace frequencies 0.16, 0.31 and 0.75 for the three process variants. Similarly, the flow time from `In Progress` to `Waiting UAT Deployment` is 130.53 h, which is the average of the flow times 129.26, 33.15, and 229.19 h.

The difference graph (Fig. 7(b)) is annotated with the average differences of each node/edge w.r.t the unified graph for both the frequency and time (the frequency differences are annotated with the label 'f' and time differences with 't'). Nodes/flows that are absent in some input variants but present in others are drawn in blue. Table 3 depicts such flows along with the variants where they manifest and where they do not. Nodes/flows that do not exhibit significant differences are made invisible (*grayed* out). For example, the nodes `Start`, `Backlog` and `In Progress` and the flows between them are all greyed out because, no significant difference exists between them both in frequency and time.

Table 3. Flows that are present in some variants but absent in others.

Flow	Present	Absent
`In Progress` to `In Progress`	$\{P_3\}$	$\{P_1, P_2\}$
`In Progress` to `Abandoned`	$\{P_1, P_2\}$	$\{P_3\}$
`Waiting UAT Deployment` to `In Progress`	$\{P_1, P_2\}$	$\{P_3\}$
`Waiting Live Deployment` to `In Progress`	$\{P_1, P_3\}$	$\{P_2\}$
`Live` to `Waiting Live Deployment`	$\{P_2, P_3\}$	$\{P_1\}$

Figure 8 depicts the diagnostic information on the uncovered significant difference w.r.t frequency for the flow `In Progress` to `Done`. Detailed information on the differences is provided by the plug-in upon clicking any edge/node. The normalized trace frequency for this flow across the three variants are 0.81, 0.16, and 0.32 respectively, i.e., 81% of the issues in P_1 takes the route to Done after In Progress is performed while only 16% and 32% of the cases take that route in P_2 and P_3. Clearly, P_1 behaves distinctly when compared to P_2 and P_3, which is reflected in the pair-wise difference matrix in Fig. 8 as the most aberrant process. Figure 10 depicts the diagnostic information on the uncovered significant difference w.r.t time for the flow `In Progress` to `Waiting UAT Deployment`. Table 4 depicts the flow time values of this flow across the three variants while Fig. 9 depicts the cumulative distribution functions (CDFs) of the sets of time values for the three variants. Clearly, we can see that the cdf of P_3 is much distinct

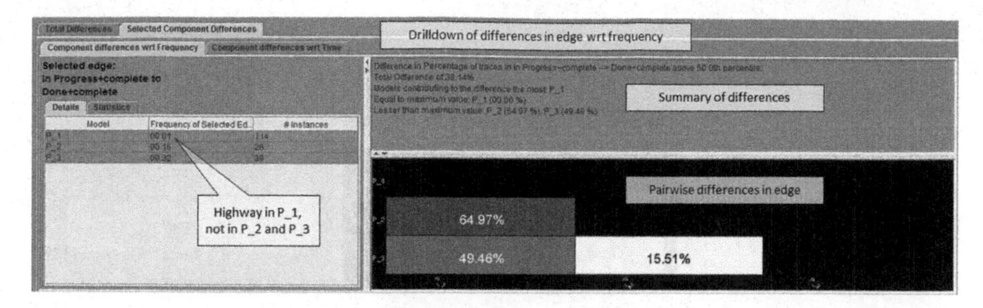

Fig. 8. Diagnostic information on the frequency difference of the flow In Progress to Done.

from that of P_1 and P_2. This is also reflected in the average and standard deviation values of P_3, which is much larger than that of P_1 and P_2. As discussed in Sect. 4, we use the Wasserstein distance to quantify the difference between the time distributions. The pair-wise differences between the variants on this particular flow is shown in Fig. 10. We can see that P_3 is reflected as the most aberrant process.

Table 4. Flow time values for the different variants.

Map	Avg	Std. dev	No. cases
P_1	129.26	278.16	28
P_2	33.15	94.52	135
P_3	229.19	819.59	95

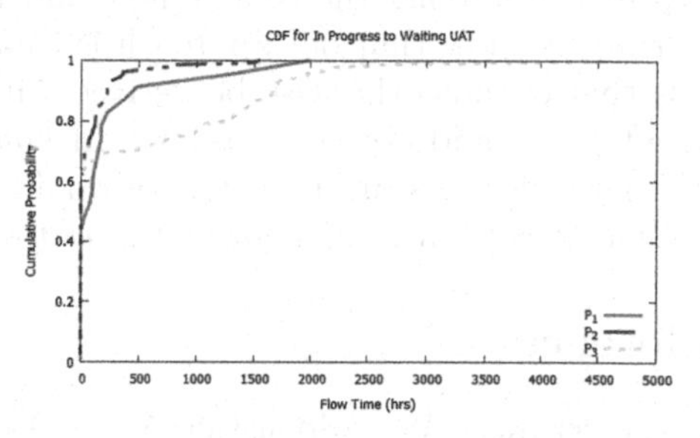

Fig. 9. Cumulative distribution functions for the different variants.

Furthermore, the difference process map highlights the cascaded component, Waiting UAT Deployment, Waiting Acceptance, Waiting Live Deployment and Live (Ref. Figure 7(b)). As discussed earlier, process P_1 exhibits distinct behavior in the flow In Progress to Waiting UAT Deployment (81% of traces in P_1 take that flow as against 16% and 32% in the other two variants). Because of this, the subsequent flows in P_1 after Waiting UAT Deployment also exhibit a significant difference. Apart from identifying the individual differences, it is insightful to identify the root-cause of the propagation of the change. Using the detection of cascaded components, we are able to identify the root-cause in this context to be the node Waiting UAT Deployment.

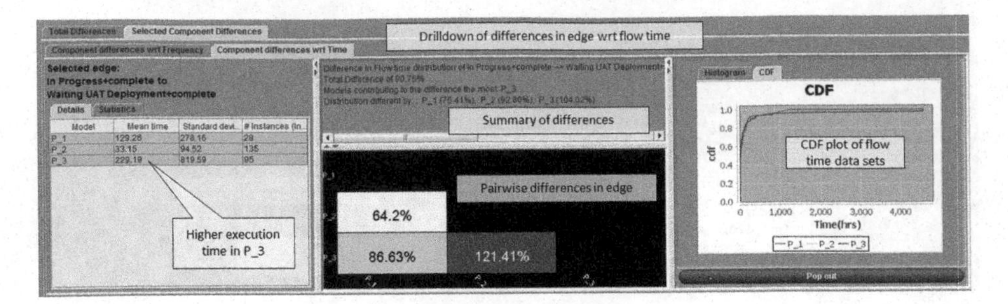

Fig. 10. Diagnostic information on the time difference of the flow In Progress to Waiting UAT Deployment.

7 Conclusions

Analyzing variants of process execution provides valuable insights on where the variants differ. Such elements are potential candidates for process reengineering/redesign efforts. One can try to learn from better performing variants and adopt them to others. In this paper, we presented an approach to analyze two or more process variants to identify nodes/flows where key differences manifest along the control-flow and time dimensions. The results of our experiments show that our approach is capable of providing insights at various levels that cannot otherwise be derived with existing tools as easily. While the present paper addresses the *where* and *how* aspects (where variants differ and how they differ), as future work, we would like to focus on *alluding root-causes* for such aberrations, i.e., address the *why's* [1].

References

1. Van der Aalst, W., Adriansyah, A., van Dongen, B.: Replaying history on process models for conformance checking and performance analysis. Wiley Interdisc. Rev.: Data Mining Knowl. Discov. **2**(2), 182–192 (2012)
2. Bae, J., Liu, L., Caverlee, J., Zhang, L.J., Bae, H.: Development of distance measures for process mining, discovery, and integration. Int. J. Web Serv. Res. **4**(4), 1 (2007)
3. Bolt, A., de Leoni, M., van der Aalst, W.M.P.: A visual approach to spot statistically-significant differences in event logs based on process metrics. In: Nurcan, S., Soffer, P., Bajec, M., Eder, J. (eds.) CAiSE 2016. LNCS, vol. 9694, pp. 151–166. Springer, Cham (2016). doi:10.1007/978-3-319-39696-5_10
4. Dijkman, R., Dumas, M., Van Dongen, B., Käärik, R., Mendling, J.: Similarity of business process models: metrics and evaluation. Inf. Syst. **36**(2), 498–516 (2011)
5. Kriglstein, S., Wallner, G., Rinderle-Ma, S.: A visualization approach for difference analysis of process models and instance traffic. In: Daniel, F., Wang, J., Weber, B. (eds.) BPM 2013. LNCS, vol. 8094, pp. 219–226. Springer, Heidelberg (2013). doi:10.1007/978-3-642-40176-3_18
6. Kunze, M., Weske, M.: Metric trees for efficient similarity search in large process model repositories. In: Muehlen, M., Su, J. (eds.) BPM 2010. LNBIP, vol. 66, pp. 535–546. Springer, Heidelberg (2011). doi:10.1007/978-3-642-20511-8_49

7. Küster, J.M., Gerth, C., Förster, A., Engels, G.: Detecting and resolving process model differences in the absence of a change log. In: Dumas, M., Reichert, M., Shan, M.-C. (eds.) BPM 2008. LNCS, vol. 5240, pp. 244–260. Springer, Heidelberg (2008). doi:10.1007/978-3-540-85758-7_19
8. Lakshmanan, G.T., Keyser, P.T., Duan, S.: Detecting changes in a semi-structured business process through spectral graph analysis. In: Workshops Proceedings of the 27th International Conference on Data Engineering, ICDE, pp. 255–260 (2011)
9. Manning, C.D., Schütze, H.: Foundations of Statistical Natural Language Processing, vol. 999. MIT Press, Cambridge (1999)
10. Montani, S., Leonardi, G., Quaglini, S., Cavallini, A., Micieli, G.: A knowledge-intensive approach to process similarity calculation. Expert Syst. Appl. **42**(9), 4207–4215 (2015)
11. Vallender, S.: Calculation of the Wasserstein distance between probability distributions on the line. Theory Prob. Appl. **18**(4), 784–786 (1974)
12. Weidlich, M., Mendling, J., Weske, M.: Propagating changes between aligned process models. J. Syst. Softw. **85**(8), 1885–1898 (2012)
13. Yan, Z., Dijkman, R., Grefen, P.: Fast business process similarity search with feature-based similarity estimation. In: Meersman, R., Dillon, T., Herrero, P. (eds.) OTM 2010. LNCS, vol. 6426, pp. 60–77. Springer, Heidelberg (2010). doi:10.1007/978-3-642-16934-2_8

Discovering Hierarchical Consolidated Models from Process Families

Nour Assy(✉), Boudewijn F. van Dongen, and Wil M.P. van der Aalst

Department of Mathematics and Computer Science,
Eindhoven University of Technology, Eindhoven, The Netherlands
{n.assy,b.v.f.dongen,w.m.p.v.d.aalst}@tue.nl

Abstract. Process families consist of different related variants that represent the same process. This might include, for example, processes executed similarly by different organizations or different versions of a same process with varying features. Motivated by the need to manage variability in process families, recent advances in process mining make it possible to discover, from a collection of event logs, a generic process model that explicitly describes the commonalities and differences across variants. However, existing approaches often result in flat complex models where it is hard to obtain a comparative insight into the common and different parts, especially when the family consists of a large number of process variants. This paper presents a decomposition-driven approach to discover hierarchical consolidated process models from collections of event logs. The discovered hierarchy consists of nested process fragments and allows to browse the variability at different levels of abstraction. The approach has been implemented as a plugin in ProM and was evaluated using synthetic and real-life event logs.

Keywords: Process mining · Consolidated process families · Hierarchical configurable models · Decomposed discovery · Configurable fragments

1 Introduction

As event data are becoming omnipresent, the importance of process mining is becoming more and more significant. Process mining allows to automatically discover, analyse and improve business processes from execution data referred to as *event logs* [1]. Traditionally, event logs are assumed to describe the execution of static and homogeneous processes. However, business requirements and regulations are continuously changing, and so are the processes. Municipalities, banks, telecommunication service providers and many others execute the same processes but with personalized features. For example, [2] reports on about 100 process variants executed by an asset management company to handle assets for institutional clients and fund distributors. This results in a family of related event logs that can be mined to discover their underlying process variants.

Discovering a collection of disconnected variants creates redundancy and turns the management and maintenance of the process family a difficult task [3].

E. Dubois and K. Pohl (Eds.): CAiSE 2017, LNCS 10253, pp. 314–329, 2017.
DOI: 10.1007/978-3-319-59536-8_20

Instead, organizations need to efficiently analyze and track changes in their processes in a unified way. Recent advances in process mining make it possible to mine process variants and to discover a generic consolidated process model (e.g. [4,5]). However, as the number of process variants increases, it becomes more common to observe partly shared behavior between a subset of the variants instead of one global behavior shared between all the variants. As a result, the discovered consolidated models may quickly become large and complex [6].

To remedy this problem, we propose an approach to discover hierarchical consolidated process models from collections of event logs. The discovered hierarchy helps in taming the complexity of consolidated models in two ways: (i) by modeling variability at different levels of abstraction (i.e. variability is shown/hidden according to the desired level of abstraction) and (ii) by expressing variability in a coarse-grained way (i.e. commonalities and differences between process fragments instead of individual elements).

Figure 1 describes the problem addressed and the desired output. Given a process family consisting of a collection of events logs, state of the art discovery approaches produce flat consolidated models as shown in Fig. 1b. The nodes' sizes give an indication about the number of variants in which the activities appear. Some edges are annotated with the logs' identifiers from which they are discovered. Clearly, the flat structure of the model and the increasing number of variants make it hard to compare variants and to track where do they agree or disagree unless applying some filtering techniques (e.g. filtering on digests [7]).

The hierarchical model discovered by our approach is shown in Fig. 1c. The hierarchical structure allows to browse the process variability at different levels of abstraction. The elements in the hierarchy refer to abstracted process fragments shared between a (sub)set of process variants. To describe fragments, we introduce the concept of *SHared-Entry SHared-Exit (SHESHE)* which is inspired from the well-know concept of Single-Entry Single-Exit (SESE) [8]. SHESHEs are independent subprocesses that are entered and exited via *shared paths*. They have well-defined interfaces through which they interact with the rest of the process. Their internal behavior encloses the variability between the entering and exiting variants. The variability abstraction is achieved by hiding the internal behavior of each fragment and by keeping the interaction of its boundaries with the rest of the process visible. Therefore, going down in the hierarchy corresponds to expanding the internal behavior of abstracted fragments. For example, in the process model shown at `Level 2`, the internal behavior of the parent at `Level 1` is expanded and the abstracted nested fragments at `Level 2` become visible.

The approach has been implemented as a plugin in ProM and was evaluated using both synthetic and real-life event logs. Experimental results show that the hierarchical structure does not only reduce the structural complexity of consolidated processes but also can improve their behavioral quality.

The paper is structured as follow. In Sect. 2, related work is discussed. Some basic definitions used throughout the paper are introduced in Sect. 3. The proposed approach is detailed in Sect. 4 through a running example. Section 5

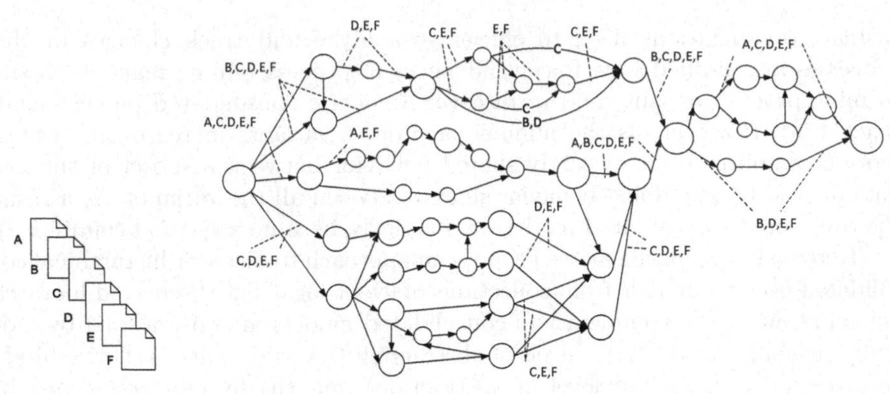

(a) Input: collection of event logs recording the execution of a process family

(b) Output of traditional approaches: a flat consolidated model where variability (commonalities vs differences) is expressed at the process elements' level; For readability, some of the edges are annotates with the logs' identifiers from which they are discovered

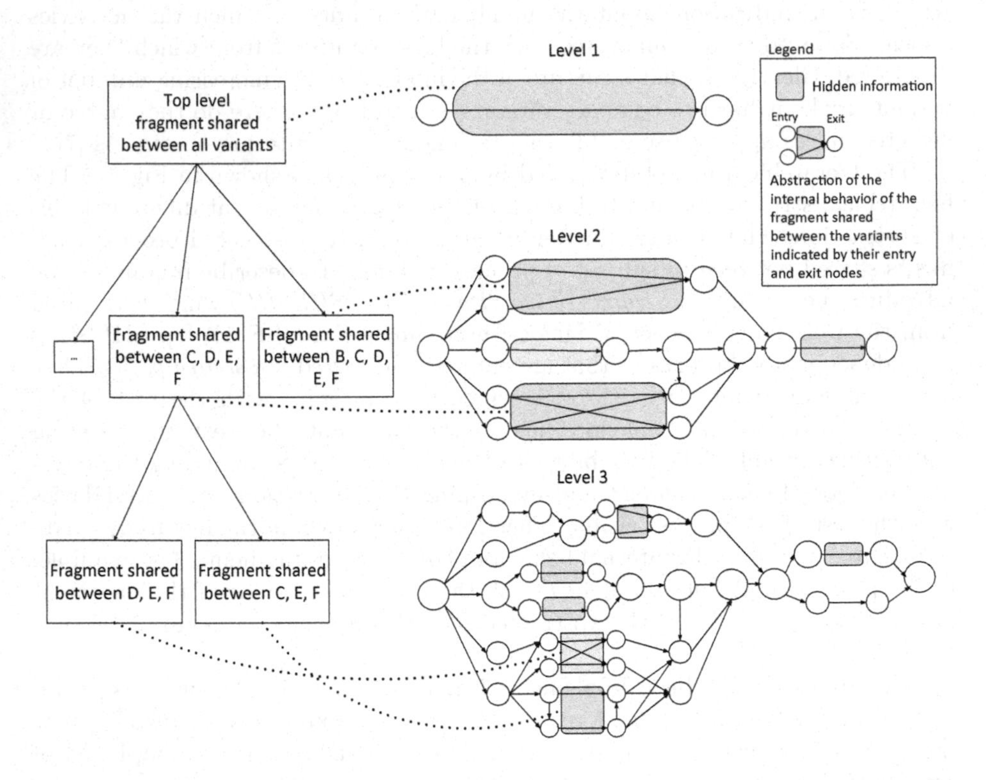

(c) Output of the proposed approach: a hierarchical consolidated model where variability is expressed at the fragment level and is shown/hidden according to the desired level of abstraction

Fig. 1. Snapshot of the problem addressed and the proposed approach

reports our experimental results. Finally, we discuss some limitations and extensions of the proposed work in Sect. 6.

2 Related Work

Process variant management is a recent research body that addresses the problem of modeling and maintaining large collections of related process variants [3]. Approaches developed in this area aim to represent the variants in a consolidated manner. For this purpose, conventional process modeling languages have been extended to explicitly support process variability modeling [9]. In this work, we adopt the configurable modeling approach [10] since it allows to explicitly represent the common and different parts in one customizable model.

To consolidate a collection of process variants, two techniques can be applied: model-merging (e.g. [2,7]) and model-mining (e.g. [4,5]). Model-merging techniques construct consolidated process models by *structurally* merging existing process variants. Model-mining techniques use process mining to discover consolidated process models from the execution behavior of process variants. All of the existing approaches produce flat models with fine-grained variability.

To overcome the complexity of consolidated models, different approaches have been proposed to abstract from the fine-grained variability expressed at the process elements' level to a coarse-grained variability expressed using domain oriented models (e.g. [11,12]). The drawback of these approaches is that they heavily rely on the domain expert knowledge. Another stream of works try to tame the complexity by localizing variability in fragments instead of entire processes (e.g. [6,13]). Subprocesses, often expressed in terms of SESE fragments, are extracted from existing process variants and are consolidated if they are similar. These techniques use model merging. The merged fragments show a local view on the variability, while in our work, we aim at providing a global view of the consolidated model and at different levels of abstraction.

Divide and conquer techniques have been also proposed to solve the complexity of discovered models. They can be grouped into two categories: case-based and activity-based. In case-based techniques, the log is split into homogeneous clusters of traces and a model is mined per cluster (e.g. [14]). The aim here is to mine a collection of simpler variants of a complex process. In this work, we deal with activity-based decomposition where traces are split into clusters of subtraces. A fragment is mined from each cluster and finally, the mined fragments are glued together into an overall model. In [15], a generic approach is presented and the principles of *correct decomposition* are discussed. The decomposition technique proposed in this paper rely on the theoretical results presented in [15].

Finally, our work can be also related to **process model abstraction** (e.g. [16,17]) and **hierarchical process discovery** (e.g. [18]). In model abstraction, the aim is to create simpler views of the process by abstracting from process details. The focus of existing works has been on defining aggregation and hiding operators that preserve some correctness criteria. The focus of our work is not on defining new abstraction operators. Instead, we aim at automatically creating different abstraction levels of the variability in a process family. For this purpose, we introduce the notion of SHESHE fragments which, by definition, allows us to achieve our goal. On the other hand, the works on hierarchical process discovery explore the information recorded in event logs in order to infer a hierarchical structure that can explain the flow of the process. In our work, we discover a hierarchical structure that explains *the flow of the variability* in a process family.

3 Preliminaries

Set, Multiset. Let S be a finite set. The multiset $B(S)$ over S is a set where elements may appear multiple times. The elements in the multiset are listed between square brackets. For example, $B = [\ ]$ is the empty multiset, $B(S) = [a, a, b, c, b] = [a^2, b^2, c]$ is a multiset over $S = \{a, b, c\}$. $\mathcal{B}(S)$ is the set of all multisets over S.

Sequence, Projection. A sequence $\sigma = \langle s_1, s_2, ..., s_n \rangle \in S^*$ is an ordered list of elements. The empty sequence is denoted as $\langle\ \rangle$. The projection of σ on a subset $S' \subseteq S$ denoted as $\sigma_{\restriction S'}$ is a subsequence of σ containing only the elements of S'. For example $\langle a, a, b, d \rangle_{\restriction \{a,d\}} = \langle a, a, d \rangle$. Projection is also defined for multisets. For example, $[a^3, b^2, c]_{\restriction \{a,b\}} = [a^3, b^2]$.

Event Log. An event log is a multiset of traces. A trace is a sequence of activities describing the lifecycle of a particular process instance. Let $\mathcal{A} \subseteq \mathcal{U}_A$ be a set of activities in some universe of activities. A trace $\sigma \in \mathcal{A}^*$ is a sequence of activities. $L \in \mathcal{B}(\mathcal{A}^*)$ is an event log. We denote by $A_L = \{a \in \sigma \mid \sigma \in L\}$ the set of activities occurring in L.

Causal Graph. A causal graph $C_L = (A_L, E_L)$ constructed from an event log L is a graph showing the causal relations between the log activities. Most process mining algorithms build such a graph in a preprocessing step by scanning the event log to see how many times an activity a_1 is followed by another activity a_2. If this occurs above a certain threshold, then it is assumed that a_1 causally precedes a_2 (i.e. $(a_1, a_2) \in E_L$). The selection of an appropriate threshold is out of scope of this paper. In this work, we assume that C_L is constructed using an existing algorithm. We also assume that C_L is connected.

Configurable Process Models. Configurable process models allow to explicitly represent the common and different parts in one customizable process model. They need to be configured to specific requirements by (de)selecting (ir)relevant parts. The essence of configuration can be captured in terms of two operators, *hiding* and *blocking* [10]. Hiding an activity corresponds to skipping it. In other words, the activity is either removed or renamed to a silent step. Blocking an activity corresponds to disabling it, i.e. the path from the activity cannot be taken anymore. There exist several extensions to existing process modeling notations. They all share the same configuration basis but differ according to the language notation. In this work, we use Petri nets as a process modeling notation since a great number of the process mining techniques assume or generate Petri nets. However the results are not restricted to this notation.

4 Proposed Approach

In this section, we first present a running example (Sect. 4.1) that will be used to illustrate the three steps of our discovery approach (Sects. 4.2, 4.3 and 4.4).

4.1 Running Example

We consider a scenario of four different variants of a loan process: home, student, business and small. Example event logs corresponding to these variants are as follow: $L_1 = [\langle a,b,c,d,e,h,i,j,l,k,m,n,o,p,w\rangle^{47}, \langle a,b,d,c,e,h,i,j,k,l,m,n,o,q, w\rangle^{28}, \langle a,b,d,c,e,h,i,k,j,l,m,n,o,p\rangle^{25}]$; $L_2 = [\langle a,b,r,s,t,u,v,w\rangle^{50}]$; $L_3 = [\langle a, b,c,d,f,g,e,h,n,w\rangle^{48}, \langle a,b,d,c,f,g,e,h,n,w\rangle^{52}]$; $L_4 = [\langle a,b,r,s,t,v,s,u,v,o, p,q,w\rangle^{48}, \langle a,b,r,s,u,v,o,q,p,w\rangle^{52}]$. Figure 2 shows the causal graphs of the four event logs. To ease the understanding of the processes, we split and annotate them with the names of different phases. There are in total 22 distinct activities. Three activities appear in all the four event logs and 13 activities appear in different subsets of the logs.

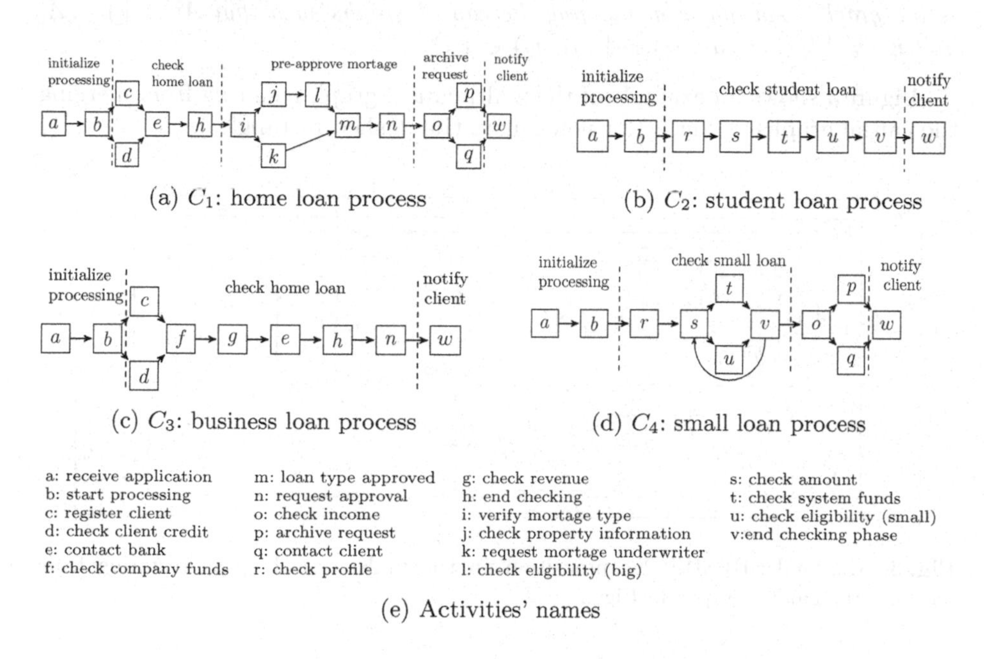

Fig. 2. The causal graphs of four event logs of different loan process variants

Our approach for discovering a hierarchical consolidated model consists of three main steps:

1. An integrated representation of the causal graphs is created and is referred to as *multi causal graph* (Sect. 4.2);

2. The multi causal graph is decomposed into a hierarchical structure of nested SHESHE fragments. For this, we formally introduce the concept of SHESHE and their induced hierarchical structure (Sect. 4.3);
3. The abstraction of SHESHE fragments is generated and the event logs are mined accordingly to discover a hierarchical consolidated model (Sect. 4.4).

4.2 Multi Causal Graph Construction

Given a collection of event logs $L_1, \ldots, L_n \in \mathcal{B}(\mathcal{A}^*)$, we first unify the start and end of all the event logs by adding start (ST) and end (ET) activities to all the traces. Then, we construct a causal graph C_i for each event log L_i. The causal graphs are merged into a multi-causal graph. Edges in the multi causal graph have different identities according to the causal graph from which they originate. In this work, we assume that activities having the same labels are identical.

Definition 1 (Multi causal graph). *Let $\mathfrak{L} = \{L_i \mid i \geq 2\}$ be a collection of events logs with unique start (ST) and end activities (ET) and $C_i = (A_i, E_i)$ a causal graph constructed for each $L_i \in \mathfrak{L}$. A multi causal graph $C^\circ = (A^\circ, E^\circ)$ is the graph resulting from merging the causal graphs such that $A^\circ = \bigcup_{i\geq 2} A_i$ and $E^\circ = \bigcup_{i\geq 2} \{((a_1, a_2), i) \mid (a_1, a_2) \in E_i\}$.*

Figure 3 shows an example of the multi causal graph resulting from merging the causal graphs in Fig. 2 (for now ignore the dashed rectangles).

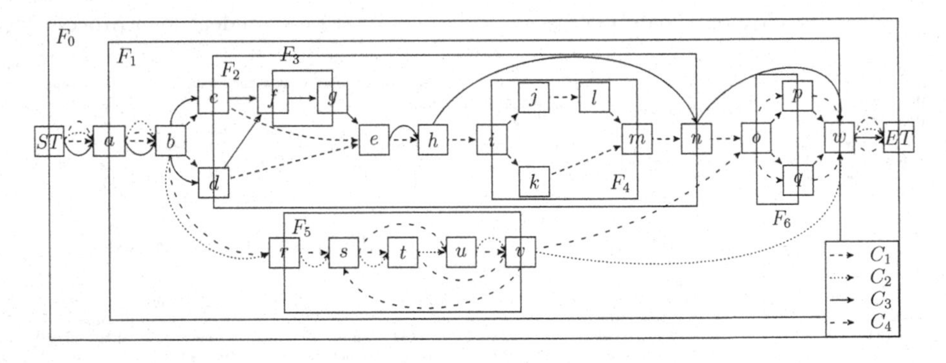

Fig. 3. Maximal SHESHE decomposition on the multi causal graph resulting from merging the causal graphs in Fig. 2

4.3 SHESHE Decomposition

The second step of our approach is to find a hierarchical decomposition of the multi causal graph in terms of fragments organized in a *hierarchical containment* relationship. To define fragments, we introduce the concept of *SHared-Entry SHared-Exit (SHESHE)*. SHESHE fragments are subprocesses with well-defined interfaces through which they interact with the rest of the process. They represent parts in the process where variants *enter and exit through the same interfaces.* In the following, we give some definitions to introduce a SHESHE.

Let $\mathfrak{L} = \{L_i \mid i \geq 2\}$ be a collection of event logs with unique start (ST) and end (ET) activities; $C_1, \ldots, C_n$ be the casual graphs constructed for each $L_i \in \mathfrak{L}$ and $C^\circ = (A^\circ, E^\circ)$ be the multi causal graph constructed from $C_1, \ldots, C_n$.

Definition 2. *Let $F \subseteq E^\circ$ be a non empty set of weakly connected edges. We define the following notations:*

- *The shareability level of F: $id(F) = \{i \mid ((a_1, a_2), i) \in F\}$;*
- *The edges with the identifier i in F: $F_{\restriction i} = \{((a_1, a_2), i') \in F \mid i' = i\}$;*
- *The set of activities: $act(F) = \bigcup_{((a_1,a_2),i) \in F} \{a_1, a_2\}$;*
- *The complement of F in E°: $\overline{F} = E^\circ \setminus F$;*
- *For an activity $a \in act(F)$, the following is defined:*
  - *The incoming edges that belong to F: $in(a, F) = \{((a_1, a), i) \in F\}$;*
  - *The incoming edges that do not belong to F: $\overline{in}(a, F) = in(a, \overline{F}) = \{((a_1, a), i) \in \overline{F}\}$;*
  - *The outgoing edges that belong to F: $out(a, F) = \{((a, a_1), i) \in F\}$;*
  - *The outgoing edges that do not belong to F: $\overline{out}(a, F) = out(a, \overline{F}) = \{((a, a_1), i) \in \overline{F}\}$;*
  - *The edges connected to a: $conn(a, F) = in(a, F) \cup \overline{in}(a, F) \cup out(a, F) \cup \overline{out}(a, F)$.*

The activities in F can be split into three categories: local if the activity is connected only to activities in F, boundary if it is connected to elements not in F, and shared boundary if, in addition to being boundary, the activity is connected only to edges having the identifier included in the shareability level of F. This latter category allows us to introduce the concept of SHESHE.

Definition 3 (Local, boundary, shared boundary). *Let $F \subseteq E^\circ$ be a non empty set of weakly connected edges such that $ST, ET \notin act(F)$. The local, boundary and shared boundary nodes in F are defined as following:*

- *$lact(F) = \{a \in act(F) \mid \overline{in}(a, F) \cup \overline{out}(a, F) = \emptyset\}$;*
- *$bact(F) = \{a \in act(F) \mid a \notin lact(F)\}$;*
- *$sact(F) = \{a \in bact(F) \mid id(conn(a, F)) = id(F)\}$.*

For example, in Fig. 3, the set of edges represented by the fragment F_5 has: $lact(F_5) = \{s, t, u\}$, $bact(F_5) = \{r, v\}$ and $sact(F_5) = \{r, v\}$. The boundary activities in F can be further classified into entry and exit activities. In [8], SESEs are defined as sets of edges having *single entry* and *single exit* activities. In this work, we define SHESHEs as sets of edges having *shared entry* and *shared exit* nodes. Roughly speaking, a shared entry is a shared boundary through which it is possible for every variant to enter inside the region represented by F. The same holds for a shared exit. For example, in Fig. 3, c and d are shared entries for F_2 since both variant 1 (which corresponds to L_1) and variant 3 can enter F_2 through them; n is a shared exit, since both variants can exit F_2 through it. The formal definition of shared entry and exit nodes is given in Definition 4.

Definition 4 (Shared entry and exit nodes). *Let $F \subseteq E^\circ$ be a non empty set of weakly connected edges such that $ST, ET \notin act(F)$. A node $a \in sact(F)$ is a shared entry iff:*

1. $id(\overline{in}(a, F)) = id(out(a, F)) = id(F)$ *and*
2. $[(\forall_{i \in id(F)}\ \overline{out}(a, F)_{\restriction i} = \emptyset \vee in(a, F)_{\restriction i} = \emptyset)$ *or*
3. $(id(\overline{out}(a, F)) = id(in(a, F)) = id(F))]$.

$a \in sact(F)$ is a shared exit iff:

1. $id(\overline{out}(a, F)) = id(in(a, F)) = id(F)$ *and*
2. $[(\forall_{i \in id(F)}\ \overline{in}(a, F)_{\restriction i} = \emptyset \vee out(a, F)_{\restriction i} = \emptyset)$ *or*
3. $(id(\overline{in}(a, F)) = id(out(a, F)) = id(F))]$.

We denote by $entry(F)$ and $exit(F)$ the set of entry and exit nodes respectively.

The first requirement of a shared entry states that the set of identifiers of the incoming edges that do not belong to F should be equal to the set of identifiers of the outgoing edges that belong to F, which in turn, should be equal to the shareability level of F. This requirement ensures that all variants can enter F through the entry node. Since we do not impose single entry nodes, the second and third requirement ensure that the entry node can either be only an entry (i.e. no variant can exit through this node) or a shared exit (i.e. all variants have the possibility to exit the node).

Definition 5 (Shared-Entry Shared-Exit). *Let $F \subseteq E^\circ$ be a non empty set of weakly connected edges such that $ST, ET \notin act(F)$. F is a shared-entry shared-exit iff: $act(F) = lact(F) \cup entry(F) \cup exit(F)$.*

A SHESHE fragment allows to localize the variability between a subset of variants. As all involved variants can enter and exit through its entry and exit nodes, the fragment can be treated as a black box (similar to a macro activity) and the variability can be expressed at the fragment level. Blocking a fragment corresponds to blocking the subprocess executed by the corresponding variants. On the process elements' level, this requires only to blocking the fragment interfaces (i.e. entry and exit activities). On the other hand, any local configuration inside the fragment does not affect its interfaces and therefore is independent from outside. Examples of SHESHE fragments are shown in Fig. 3.

The edges formed by E° define a specific type of a SHESHE with no incoming or outgoing edges. This fragment is called the root and is not considered in any operation on SHESHEs. In this work, we are interested in a hierarchical representation of SHESHE fragments where a child fragment restricts the shareability level of its parent. This requires that SHESHE fragments do not overlap. In the following, we give some definitions to derive non-overlapping SHESHEs.

Lemma 1 (SHESHE inclusion). *Let $F_1, F_2 \subseteq E^\circ$ be two SHESHEs such that $F_1 \subseteq F_2$. The following hold: (i) $id(F_1) \subseteq id(F_2)$ and (ii) if $entry(F_1) \cap entry(F_2) \neq \emptyset$ or $exit(F_1) \cap exit(F_2) \neq \emptyset$ then $id(F_1) = id(F_2)$.*

Lemma 2 (SHESHE union). *Let $F_1, F_2 \subseteq E^\circ$ be two SHESHEs and $F = F_1 \cup F_2$ be their union such that F is weakly connected. F is a SHESHE iff $id(F_1) = id(F_2)$ or $F_1 \subseteq F_2$.*

Many of the SHESHEs in a multi causal graph are *less informative*. For instance, in Fig. 3, $F_1' = \{((e,h),1),((e,h),2)\} \subset F_1$ [1] has the same shareability level $\{1,2\}$ as F_1. Given F_1, F_1' does not provide any additional information. This does not hold for $F_8 \subset F_1$ as F_8 has a new restricted shareability level. In this work, we are interested in *maximal* SHESHE fragments that are the largest fragments having a specific shareability level.

Definition 6 (Maximal SHESHE). *Let $F \subseteq E^\circ$ be a SHESHE. F is maximal iff $\nexists F' \subseteq E^\circ, F' \neq F$ where $F \cup F'$ is a SHESHE and $id(F) = id(F')$.*

Proposition 1 (Non overlapping SHESHE). *Let $F, F' \subseteq E^\circ$ be two maximal SHESHEs. One of the three statements holds: (i) $F \subseteq F'$, (ii) $F' \subseteq F$ or (iii) $F \cap F' = \emptyset$.*

Proposition 1 allows to derive a hierarchical topology of the SHESHE fragments organized in a tree-like structure (Fig. 3 shows an example).

Definition 7 (SHESHE decomposition tree). *Let C° be a multi causal graph and $\mathcal{F}$ be the set of its maximal SHESHEs including E°. $D = (\mathcal{F}, \prec)$ is a tree of maximal SHESHE fragments where $\mathcal{F}$ is the set of tree nodes and $\prec \subseteq \mathcal{F} \times \mathcal{F}$ is the set of parent-child relations such that $(F_1, F_2) \in \prec$ iff $F_2 \subset F_1$ and F_1 is the smallest SHESHE containing F_2.*

4.4 Hierarchical Discovery

Given a SHESHE decomposition tree, we aim at discovering a hierarchical consolidated model that shows the fragments at different levels of abstraction. The abstraction of fragments allows to show the *most shared behavior* and to *hide the local variability* between the involved variants. For instance, given F_2 in Fig. 3, we would like to see that the variants of both L_1 and L_3 start with executing c and d; both execute the fragment represented by e and h and end with the execution of n; the fragments F_3 and F_4 are hidden since they are executed by L_3 and L_1 respectively and therefore depict a local variability. In terms of event logs, this abstraction can be achieved by projecting the traces of the logs L_1 and L_3 on the activities c, d, e, h and n and discovering the corresponding fragment. The fragment is discovered by merging the projected traces of L_1 and L_3 into one log and using existing discovery techniques (e.g. Inductive Miner).

In addition to the shared behavior, we should be able to link the discovered abstracted fragments with their children in order to create the entire process. For example, the abstracted fragment of F_2 includes the activities c, d, e, h and n; the abstracted fragment of F_3 includes f and g and the abstracted fragment

[1] This SHESHE is not shown because it is not maximal according to Definition 6.

of F_4 includes i, j, l, k and m. In order to construct the whole behavior of F_2 (i.e. non abstracted version), we should be able to link the discovered abstracted fragment of F_2 with its children. In this case two solutions are possible. The trivial one is to restart from scratch by projecting the traces of L_1 and L_3 on all the activities of F_2 and discovering their corresponding fragment. However, this solution requires an excessive and repeated work of discovery which may be expensive in case of a large number of parent-child relations in the tree.

Another more convenient solution is to include the boundary nodes of children fragments in their abstracted parent fragment. In this way the children boundary nodes act as a glue and allow to create the entire process by combining the discovered abstracted parents with their discovered abstracted children. This solution corresponds to the output of the approach shown in Fig. 4.

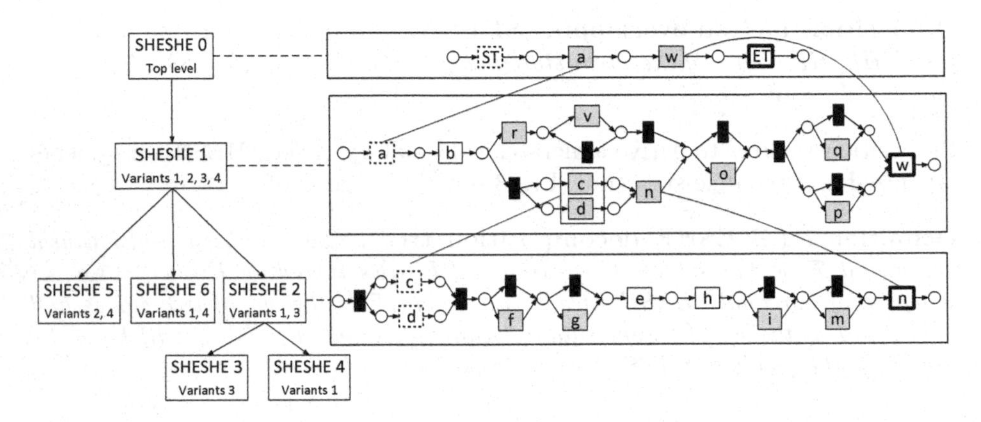

Fig. 4. Output of the discovery approach taking as input the logs of the variants in Fig. 2. Transitions with dashed line represent the entry of the SHESHE fragment; those with bold line represent the exit; gray transitions are the boundaries of the SHESHE children. The fragments are discovered using Inductive Miner

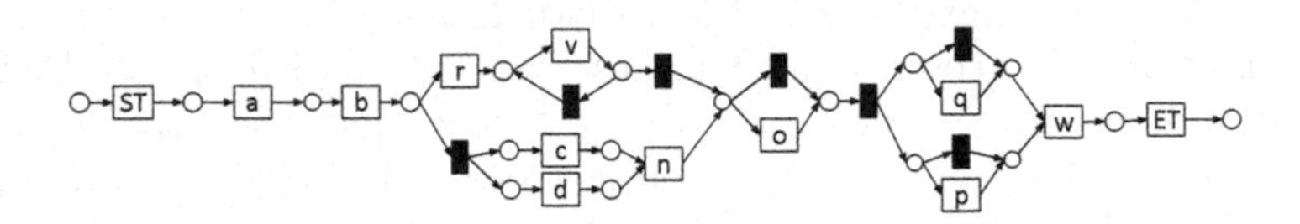

Fig. 5. A model provided at the second level of the tree in Fig. 4 by glueing the discovered fragment of SHESHE 0 and its children (in this case SHESHE 1)

The tree shows the abstracted fragments of the SHESHE decomposition tree in Fig. 3. The discovered fragments of some nodes are shown on the right-hand side. For example, the discovered fragment of SEHSHE 2 which corresponds to the abstracted version of F_2 includes the entry and exit of F_2, the shared behavior including the activities e and h as well as the boundary nodes of SHESHE 3 and SHESHE 4. Each level of the tree shows a local behavior on the abstracted SHESHE. To construct an entire process, parents and children can be recursively glued at each level using the approach presented in [15]. For example, the model shown in Fig. 5 corresponds to the entire process of the second level in the tree. It is obtained by glueing together the fragment of SHESHE 0 and its children (in this case SHESHE 1). The entire process of the third level can be obtained by glueing the entire process of the second level with the children of the third level (i.e. SHESHE 5, 6 and 2) and so on.

Having such hierarchical structure, it becomes easy to express variability by identifying the configurable elements. The tree nodes *shared between a subset of the variants* are configurable. They can be either blocked or allowed. On the process level, this corresponds to making the entry and exit activities configurable.

5 Evaluation

The approach has been implemented as a plugin in ProM[2](www.processmining.org). The plugin takes a collection of event logs as input and produces a hierarchical consolidated process model as output.

5.1 Synthetic Logs

We used event logs of four variants of a travel booking process[3]. The base process allows for booking a flight with the option of booking a hotel and/or a car in a subset of the variants. Figure 6a shows the flat configurable process model discovered using Inductive Miner (IM) with the default parameters in ProM. Because of the high variability in the logs, IM generates an underfitting model (i.e., a flower construct) which allows for any behavior. All the activities in the flower construct are configurable. This model is simple but scores very low on precision. With Heuristics Miner (HM), a better model is discovered. However, the number of configurable nodes is 21 which is still relatively high.

Figure 6b shows the hierarchical structure discovered using our approach. The tree hierarchy contains 5 configurable fragments (i.e. 5 out of 7 nodes are shared between a subset of the variants). Figures 6c and d show the discovered root fragment SHESHE 0 and the fragment SHESHE 4 using IM. Compared to the flower model in Fig. 6a, the flower construct in the root fragment is reduced and is completely broken in the child fragment.

5.2 Real-Life Logs

We used the dataset from BPI challenge 2015 [19] which corresponds to five process variants of building permit applications executed by five Dutch municipalities. We evaluated the quality, in terms of structural complexity and behavioral

[2] https://svn.win.tue.nl/repos/prom/Packages/NourAssy/.

[3] The process models and logs can be downloaded from: https://svn.win.tue.nl/repos/prom/Packages/NourAssy/Trunk/artificialLogs.

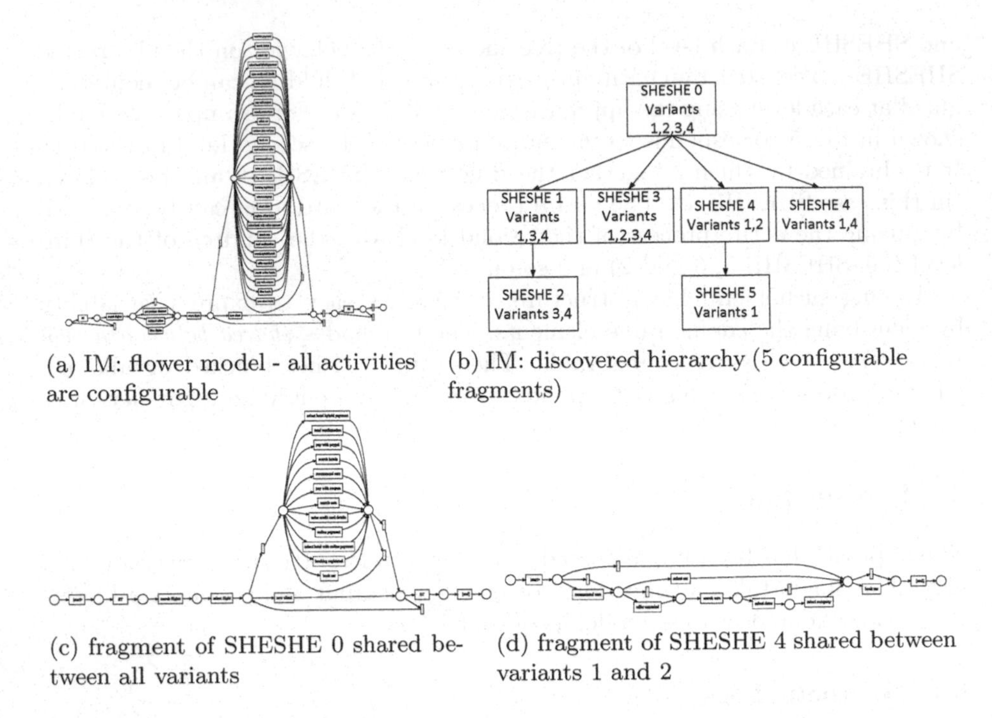

(a) IM: flower model - all activities are configurable

(b) IM: discovered hierarchy (5 configurable fragments)

(c) fragment of SHESHE 0 shared between all variants

(d) fragment of SHESHE 4 shared between variants 1 and 2

Fig. 6. (a) flat vs (b), (c) and (d) hierarchical discovered process models

accuracy, of the discovered models using traditional approaches for discovering flat models versus using our approach for discovering hierarchical models.

The structural quality of the discovered models is measured in terms of the hierarchy quality and the fragments complexity. To evaluate the quality of the hierarchy, we compute (i) the number of configurable nodes in the discovered models (# conf. nodes), (ii) the average number of configuration steps needed to derive a variant (# conf. dec.), (iii) the depth of the tree and (iv) the average number of shared variants per node (# Avg. share). Regarding the fragments' complexity, we measured their average size and compared it to the size of one flat model (Size(# arcs)). The behavioral accuracy is measured in terms of fitness, precision and generalization of the merged log against the discovered consolidated model. The results are reported in Tables 1 and 2.

The results show that, with the hierarchical discovery, the sizes of fragments in the hierarchy are greatly reduced compared to the size of one flat model. Instead of looking to one *big* process model, one can scan the hierarchy and inspect smaller fragments. On the other hand, the depth of the tree is small. This means that the decomposition was not able to find a hierarchy of nested fragments. Because of the small depth, the difference in the number of configurable nodes between the hierarchical model and the flat model is not in our favour. In the hierarchical model, the fragments shared between different variants contain shared activities but exhibit different behavior (this is explained by the high number of configurable nodes in the flat model). The reasons for this can be explained by the fact that we assumed that activities with the same labels are the same across variants. By doing so, we reduce the chance to find valid SHESHEs. Regarding the behavioral quality, we noticed that our decomposition approach was able to improve the precision of hierarchical models with a small decrease in the fitness. The decrease in the fitness is not caused by the SHESHE decomposition itself, but because of the glueing step presented in Sect. 4.4.

Table 1. Structural quality of the discovered flat vs hierarchical model

Dataset	Flat			Hierarchical				
	# conf. nodes	# conf. dec	Size	Depth	Avg. share	#conf. nodes	# conf. dec	Size frag
BPI 15	29	16.6	102	2	2.92	7	2	45.53

Table 2. Behavioral quality of the discovered flat model vs hierarchical model

		Fitness	Precision	Generalization
IM	Flat	1	0.1	1
	Hierarchical	0.86	0.57	0.97
	Hierarchical (fragment avg.)	0.99	0.84	0.44
HM	Flat	0.93	0.76	0.94
	Hierarchical	0.96	0.8	0.95
	Hierarchical (fragment avg.)	0.99	0.99	0.4

6 Conclusion

In this paper, we presented an approach for mining hierarchical consolidated models from process families. The hierarchy allows to (i) browse the variability at different levels of abstraction and to (ii) model it in a coarse-grained way. Through experimental evaluation, we showed that our decomposition approach is suitable to tame the complexity of consolidated models.

As already shown in Sect. 5, the quality of the discovered hierarchy highly depends on the way the equivalence class is defined over the logs' activities. In the present work, we simply assumed that activities with common labels are equal. However, one interesting feature of our shared-entry shared-exit fragments is that they allow to *bring structure to unstructured variability*. Therefore, in our future work, we will investigate the problem of discovering consolidated process models with structured variability. This calls for the problem of finding an equivalence class over the logs' activities that optimizes the SHESHE decomposition quality.

References

1. van der Aalst, W.M.P.: Process Mining - Data Science in Action, 2nd edn. Springer, Heidelberg (2016)
2. Reijers, H.A., Mans, R.S., van der Toorn, R.A.: Improved model management with aggregated business process models. Data Knowl. Eng. **68**(2), 221–243 (2009)
3. Dijkman, R.M., La Rosa, M., Reijers, H.A.: Managing large collections of business process models - current techniques and challenges. Comput. Ind. **63**(2), 91–97 (2012)
4. Buijs, J.C.A.M., Dongen, B.F., van der Aalst, W.M.P.: Mining configurable process models from collections of event logs. In: Daniel, F., Wang, J., Weber, B. (eds.) BPM 2013. LNCS, vol. 8094, pp. 33–48. Springer, Heidelberg (2013). doi:10.1007/978-3-642-40176-3_5
5. Li, C., Reichert, M., Wombacher, A.: Mining business process variants: challenges, scenarios, algorithms. Data Knowl. Eng. **70**(5), 409–434 (2011)
6. Milani, F., Dumas, M., Ahmed, N., Matulevicius, R.: Modelling families of business process variants: a decomposition driven method. Inf. Syst. **56**, 55–72 (2016)
7. La Rosa, M., Dumas, M., Uba, R., Dijkman, R.: Business process model merging: an approach to business process consolidation. ACM Trans. Softw. Eng. Methodol. **22**(2), 11:1–11:42 (2013)
8. Johnson, R., Pearson, D., Pingali, K.: The program structure tree: computing control regions in linear time. In: Proceedings of the ACM SIGPLAN 1994 Conference on Programming Language Design and Implementation (PLDI), pp. 171–185 (1994)
9. La Rosa, M., van der Aalst, W.M.P., Dumas, M., Milani, F.P.: Business process variability modeling: a survey. ACM Comput. Surv. **50**(1), 2:1–2:45 (2017)
10. Gottschalk, F., van der Aalst, W.M.P., Jansen-Vullers, M.H., La Rosa, M.: Configurable workflow models. Int. J. Coop. Inf. Syst. **17**(2), 177–221 (2008)
11. La Rosa, M., van der Aalst, W.M.P., Dumas, M., ter Hofstede, A.H.M.: Questionnaire-based variability modeling for system configuration. Softw. Syst. Model. **8**(2), 251–274 (2009)
12. Gröner, G., Boskovic, M., Parreiras, F.S., Gasevic, D.: Modeling and validation of business process families. Inf. Syst. **38**(5), 709–726 (2013)
13. La Rosa, M., Dumas, M., Ekanayake, C.C., García-Bañuelos, L., Recker, J., ter Hofstede, A.H.M.: Detecting approximate clones in business process model repositories. Inf. Syst. **49**, 102–125 (2015)
14. García-Bañuelos, L., Dumas, M., La Rosa, M., De Weerdt, J., Ekanayake, C.C.: Controlled automated discovery of collections of business process models. Inf. Syst. **46**, 85–101 (2014)
15. van der Aalst, W.M.P.: Decomposing Petri nets for process mining: a generic approach. Distributed and Parallel Databases **31**(4), 471–507 (2013)
16. Polyvyanyy, A., Smirnov, S., Weske, M.: The triconnected abstraction of process models. In: Dayal, U., Eder, J., Koehler, J., Reijers, H.A. (eds.) BPM 2009. LNCS, vol. 5701, pp. 229–244. Springer, Heidelberg (2009). doi:10.1007/978-3-642-03848-8_16
17. Reichert, M., Kolb, J., Bobrik, R., Bauer, T.: Enabling personalized visualization of large business processes through parameterizable views. In: Proceedings of the ACM Symposium on Applied Computing, SAC 2012, Riva, Trento, Italy, 26–30 March 2012, pp. 1653–1660 (2012)

18. Conforti, R., Dumas, M., García-Bañuelos, L., La Rosa, M.: BPMN miner: automated discovery of BPMN process models with hierarchical structure. Inf. Syst. **56**, 284–303 (2016)
19. van Dongen, B.F.: BPI challenge 2015 (2015). http://dx.doi.org/10.4121/uuid:31a308ef-c844-48da-948c-305d167a0ec1

Information Systems Transformation and Evolution

Survival in Schema Evolution: Putting the Lives of Survivor and Dead Tables in Counterpoint

Panos Vassiliadis(✉) and Apostolos V. Zarras

Department of Computer Science and Engineering,
University of Ioannina, Ioannina, Greece
{pvassil,zarras}@cs.uoi.gr

Abstract. How can we plan development over an evolving schema? In this paper, we study the history of the schema of eight open source software projects that include relational databases and extract patterns related to the survival or death of their tables. Our findings are mostly summarized by a pattern, which we call "electrolysis pattern" due to its diagrammatic representation, stating that dead and survivor tables live quite different lives: tables typically die shortly after birth, with short durations and mostly no updates, whereas survivors mostly live quiet lives with few updates – except for a small group of tables with high update ratios that are characterized by high durations and survival. Based on our findings, we recommend that development over newborn tables should be restrained, and wherever possible, encapsulated by views to buffer both infant mortality and high update rate of hyperactive tables. Once a table matures, developers can rely on a typical pattern of gravitation to rigidity, providing less disturbances due to evolution to the surrounding code.

Keywords: Schema evolution · Evolution patterns · Table survival

1 Introduction

The study of schema evolution in an attempt to dig out patterns and regularities is an important endeavor in order to understand its mechanics and plan software design and development on top of databases. However, this problem has attracted little attention by the research community so far. To a large extent, the possibility of actually studying schema evolution emerged from the availability of schema histories embedded in open source software projects, publicly available via Github. So far, research efforts [2,4–6,11] – see Sect. 2 – have demonstrated that schemata grow over time, mostly with insertions and updates, and are frequently out of synch with their surrounding code. However, we are still far from a detailed understanding of how individual tables evolve and what factors affect their evolution. In our latest work [9,10], we have performed a first study towards charting the relationship of factors like schema size and version of birth to the duration and the amount of change a table undergoes. In this paper, we continue

E. Dubois and K. Pohl (Eds.): CAiSE 2017, LNCS 10253, pp. 333–347, 2017.
DOI: 10.1007/978-3-319-59536-8_21

along this line of work by answering a fundamental question on the survival of a table that has not been answered so far: "how are survival, activity behavior and duration of a table interrelated?". To the best of our knowledge, the problem was only initially touched in [9,10] and the insights of this paper are completely novel in the related literature.

Following the research method of our previous work, we have performed a large study of eight data sets with the schema history of databases included in open source projects (see Sect. 3 for our experimental setup). Our results are detailed in Sect. 4; here, we can give a concise summary of our findings as follows. The antithesis of the durations between dead and survivor tables is striking: table deletions take place shortly after birth, resulting in short durations for the dead tables; this is to be contrasted with the large number of survivors with high (and frequently, maximum) durations. When activity profile, duration and survival are studied together, we observe the *electrolysis pattern*, named after the paradigm of positive and negative ions in electrolysis moving towards opposite directions: Not only dead tables cluster in short or medium durations, and practically never at high durations, but also, with few exceptions, the less active dead tables are, the higher the chance to reach shorter durations. In contrast, survivors are mostly located at medium and high durations and the more active survivors are, the stronger they are attracted towards high durations, with a significant such inclination for the few active survivors, that cluster in very high durations.

Why is the knowledge of patterns in life and death of tables so important? We believe that our study gives solid evidence on a phenomenon that we call *gravitation to rigidity*[1] stating that despite some valiant efforts, relational schemata suffer from the tendency of developers to minimize evolution as much as possible in order to minimize the resulting impact to the surrounding code. Section 5 discusses possible explanations on the relationship of the observed phenomena with gravitation to rigidity. Equally importantly, understanding the probability of update or removal of a table can aid the development team in avoiding to invest too much effort and code to high-risk parts of the database schema. To this end, in Sect. 5 we provide recommendations to developers, based on our findings and also suggest roads for future work.

2 Background and Related Work

The first known case study of schema evolution, published in 1993 [6], monitored the database of a health management system for 18 months, to report the overall increase of schema size over time and the percentage breakdown for different types of changes. After this study, it was only 15 years later that research was revived on the problem. The key to this revival was the existence of open source software repositories exposing all the code of a software project in all its history. Software projects based on relational databases, thus, would expose the entire history of their schema. There is a handful of works since the late '00s [2,4,5,11]

[1] *Rigidity* is used in its software engineering meaning, referring to software that is hard to evolve and maintain.

that have assessed the evolution of databases involved in open source software projects.

In [2], the authors report findings on the evolution of Mediawiki, the software that supports Wikipedia. The authors of this work, and also in the followup work on "algebrizing" schema modification operations [3] should be accredited for the public release of schema histories that they collected. Several works followed, where the authors have primarily worked on (a) the schema size, which grows over time but with progressively less rate [5], (b) the absence of total synchronization between source code and database schema, as schemata evolve [4,11], and, (c) the impact of schema change to the surrounding code [5], which requires a significant amount of code modifications. [5] is also presenting preliminary results on the timing of the schema modifications, reporting that the early versions of the database included a large part of the schema growth. A study presented in [1] verifies the observations of other works concerning the trend of increase in schema size and the reluctance in the deletion of tables.

Our recent involvement in the area is based on the study of the history of the schema of eight open source software projects. In [7], also presented in full length in [8], we have worked at the macroscopic level to study how the schema of a database evolves in terms of its size. We have found evidence that *schemata grow over time in order to satisfy new requirements, albeit not in a continuous or linear fashion, but rather, with bursts of concentrated effort interrupting longer periods of calmness and drops, signifying perfective maintenance* (Fig. 1).

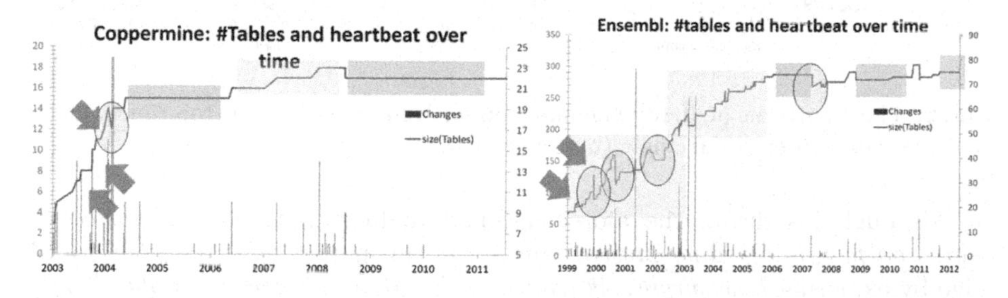

Fig. 1. Summary of [8] with schema growth over time (red continuous line) along with the heartbeat of changes (spikes) for two datasets. Overlayed darker green rectangles highlight the calmness periods, and lighter blue rectangles highlight smooth expansions. Arrows point at periods of abrupt expansion and circles highlight drops in size. (Color figure online)

Whereas all related work had focused on the study of *schema* size, in [10], also presented in full length in [9], we have worked on the identification of frequently encountered patterns on *table* properties (e.g., birth, duration, amount of change). We identified four major patterns on the relationship of such properties. The *Γ pattern* on the relationship of the schema size of a table at its birth with its overall duration indicates that tables with large schemata tend to have long durations and avoid removal. The *Comet pattern* on the relationship of the schema size of a table at its birth with its total amount of updates indicates that the tables with most updates are frequently the ones with medium schema size. The *Inverse Γ pattern* on the relationship of the amount of updates and the duration of a table indicates that tables with medium or small durations produce amounts of updates lower than expected, whereas tables with long duration expose all sorts of update behavior. The *Empty Triangle* pattern on the relationship of a table's version of birth with its overall duration indicates a significant absence of tables of medium or long durations that were removed – thus, an empty triangle – signifying mainly short lives for deleted tables and low probability of deletion for old timers (Fig. 2).

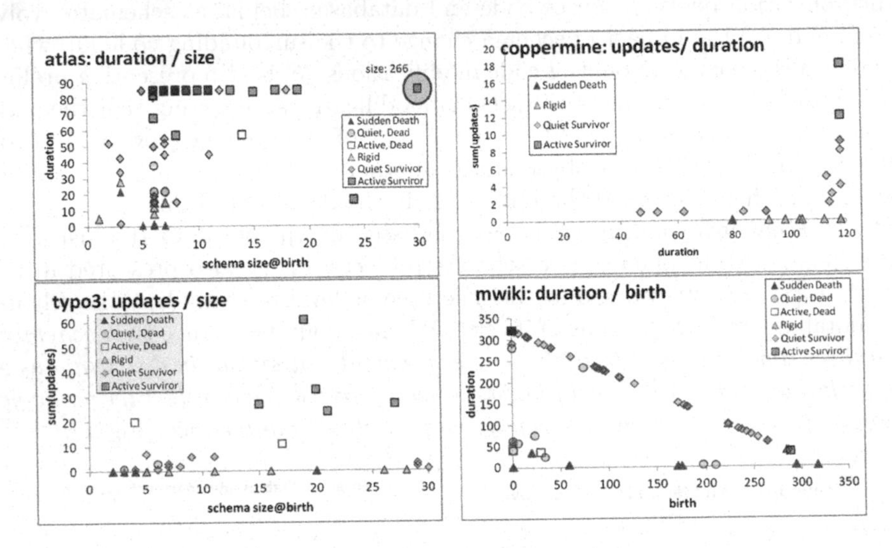

Fig. 2. The 4 patterns of [9,10]: Gamma (top left), inverse Gamma (top right), comet (bottom left) and empty triangle (bottom right).

Although insightful, the aforementioned findings *have not exhausted the search on factors affecting survival*, and so, in this paper, we extend our knowledge by exploring *how survival is related to duration and activity profile*. To the best of our knowledge this is the first comprehensive study of this kind in the literature.

3 Experimental Method

In this section, we briefly present our experimental method. Here we can only provide a self-contained, condensed description, so, we will kindly refer the interested reader to [7] for a detailed description and to our *Schema Biographies* website[2] containing links to all our results, data, code and presentations that are made publicly available to the research community.

Experimental Protocol. We have collected the version histories of 8 data sets that support open source software projects. For each dataset we gathered as

[2] http://www.cs.uoi.gr/~pvassil/projects/schemaBiographies/.

Dataset	Type	Versions	Lifetime	Tables @ Start	Tables @ End
ATLAS Trigger	[P]	84	**2** Y, 7 M, 2 D	56	73
BioSQL	[B]	46	**10** Y, 6 M, 19 D	21	28
Coppermine	[C]	117	**8** Y, 6 M, 2 D	8	22
Ensembl	[B]	528	**13** Y, 3 M, 15 D	17	75
MediaWiki	[C]	322	**8** Y, 10 M, 6 D	17	50
OpenCart	[C]	164	**4** Y, 4 M, 3 D	46	114
phpBB	[C]	133	**6** Y, 7 M, 10 D	61	65
Typo3	[C]	97	**8** Y, 11 M, 0 D	10	23

Fig. 3. Datasets used in our study

many schema *versions* (DDL files) as we could from their public source code repositories (cvs, svn, git). We have targeted only changes at the database part of the project as they were integrated in the trunk of the project. The files were collected during June 2013. For all of the projects, we focused on their release for MySQL (except ATLAS Trigger, available only for Oracle). The files were then processed by our tool, Hecate, that detected, in a fully automated way, (a) changes at the table-level, i.e., which tables were inserted and deleted, and (b) updates at the attribute-level, and specifically, attributes inserted, deleted, having a changed data type, or participation in a changed primary key.

Reported Measures. Hecate pair-wise compared subsequent files and reported the changes for each *transition* between subsequent versions. The details of each particular change along with collective statistics per table, as well as for the entire schema were also reported. An important part of the produced measures involves information on the update profile of each table, including the total number of changes it went through, the change rate etc. We have classified tables in profiles concerning (a) their *survival* (i.e., their presence in the last version of the schema history or not), characterizing them as *survivors* or *dead*, (b) their *activity behavior*, characterizing them as *rigid* (if they go through zero updates), *active* (if their rate of change is higher than 0.1 changes per transition) and *quiet* otherwise, and, (c) by the combination of the above via their Cartesian product, which we call *LifeAndDeath* profile.

Scope. Concerning the scope of the study, we would like to clarify that we work only with changes at the logical schema level (and ignore physical-level changes like index creation or change of storage engine). Also, the reader is advised to avoid generalizing our findings to proprietary databases, outside the realm of open source software.

4 Survival and Duration: How Dead Tables Differ from Survivors

In this section, we first explore whether there is a difference in the duration between survivor and dead tables. Then, we examine how table duration, survival and activity behavior interrelate.

4.1 Oppositely Skewed Durations

We have studied how the duration of tables is distributed in different duration ranges, thus creating a histogram of durations. We have discriminated between dead and survivor tables, so we have a histogram for each of these two classes. Figure 4 depicts the respective histograms. We observe a phenomenon, which we call the *oppositely skewed durations* or *opposite skews* pattern.

The Oppositely Skewed Durations Pattern. When one constructs the histograms for the durations of dead vs survivor tables one can observe a symmetry in the histograms of the two classes. *The dead tables are strongly biased towards short durations (left-heavy), often with very large percentages of them being removed very shortly after birth. In quite the opposite manner, the survivor tables are mostly gathered at the other end of the spectrum (right-heavy), i.e., at high (frequently: max) durations.*

Exceptions to the Pattern. Exceptions to the pattern do exist, albeit they do not significantly alter its validity. Coppermine's single deleted table was removed at 6 years of age. The phpBB database, which is otherwise too rigid, has 5 deleted tables that were removed at significantly larger durations than the typical in other data sets (in fact after 5 or 6 years of lifetime, all 5 being removed in the same version). The typo3 database, also has a set of 9 removed tables, again with quite high durations (7 of which had a lifetime between 4 and 8 years at the time of their removal).

Gravitation to Rigidity. We attribute the tendency to short durations for the deleted tables to the cost that deletions have for the maintenance of the software that surrounds the database. The earlier a table is removed, the smaller the cost of maintaining the surrounding code is. Thus, when the table has been involved in several queries found in several places in the code, it is always a painstaking process to locate, maintain and test the application code that uses it. At the same time, the reluctance for removals allows tables who survive the early stages to "remain safe". Thus, they grow in age without being removed. This fact, combined with the fact that the starting versions of the database already include a large percentage of the overall population of tables, results in a right-heavy, left-tailed distribution of survivor tables (for 6 out of 8 data sets, survivor durations reaching the final bucket of the respective histogram exceed 45%).

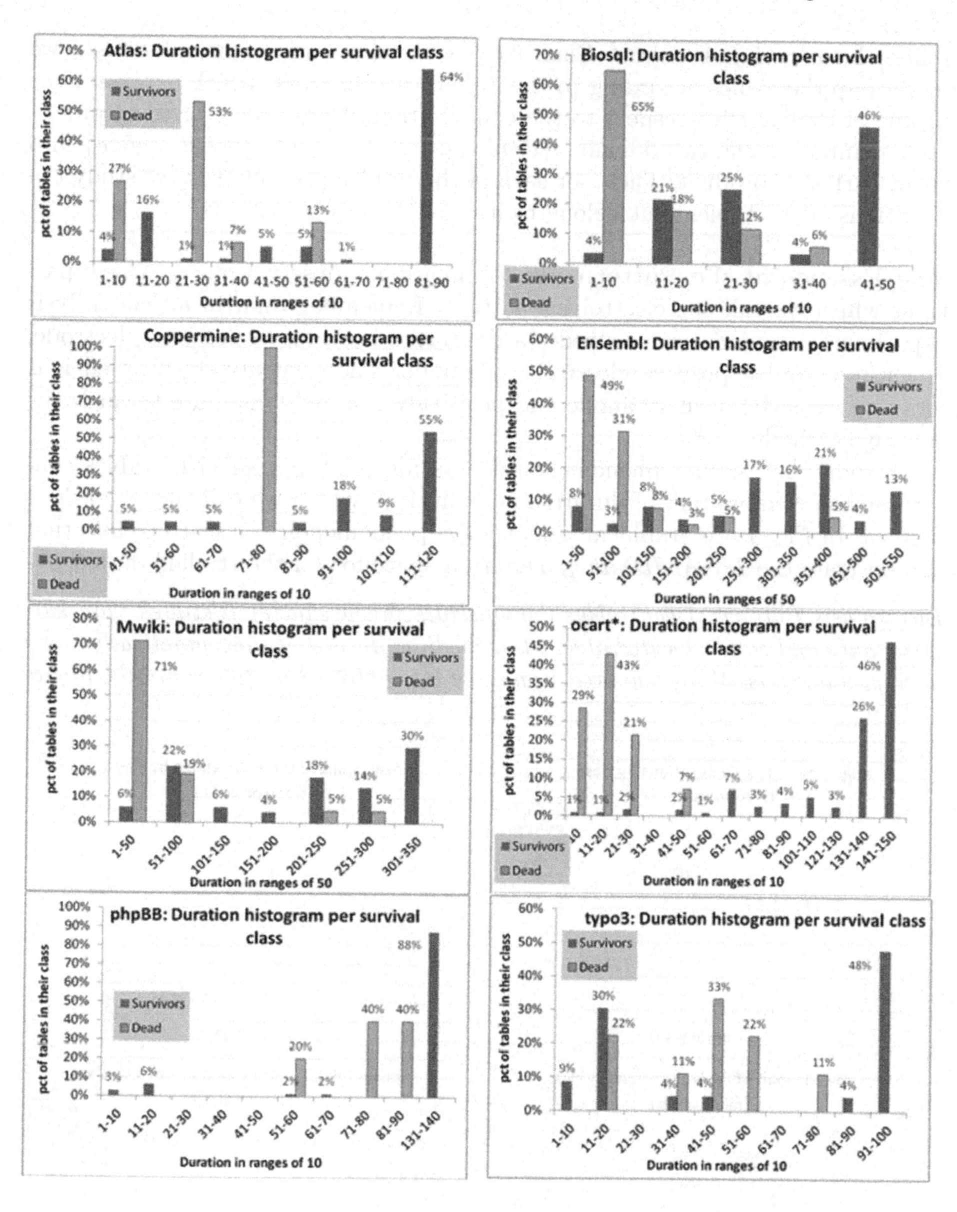

Fig. 4. Histograms of the durations of (a) dead, vs., (b) survivor tables.

4.2 The Electrolysis Pattern

What happens if we relate duration with activity? The research question that is guiding us here is to discover whether there are patterns in the way survival, duration and activity behavior relate. Our analysis is a refinement of the oppositely skewed durations pattern with activity profile information. Whereas the opposite skews pattern simply reports percentages for duration ranges, here, we refine them by *LifeAndDeath* Class too. So, in the rest of this subsection, we will group the tables according to the *LifeAndDeath* class, which expresses the profile of a table with respect to the combination of *survival* x *activity*, practically composing the two domains {*dead*, *survivor*} × {*rigid*, *quiet*, *active*} into their Cartesian product. Then, for each of the resulting six classes, we study the durations of the tables that belong to it.

The Essence of the Pattern. We formulate our observations as a new pattern, which we call the electrolysis pattern. Remember than in an electrolysis experimental device, two electrodes are inserted in water: a negative electrode, or cathode and a positive electrode, or anode. Then, negatively charged ions move towards the positive anode and positively charged ions move towards the negative cathode.

A somewhat similar phenomenon occurs for dead and survivor tables concerning the combination of duration and survival, which we call the *electrolysis pattern*. In Fig. 5, we graphically depict the phenomenon via scatter-plots that demonstrate the *LifeAndDeath* × *Duration* space for all the studied data sets.

Electrolysis Pattern: Dead tables demonstrate much shorter lifetimes than survivor ones and can be located at short or medium durations, and practically never at high durations. With few exceptions, the less active dead tables are the higher

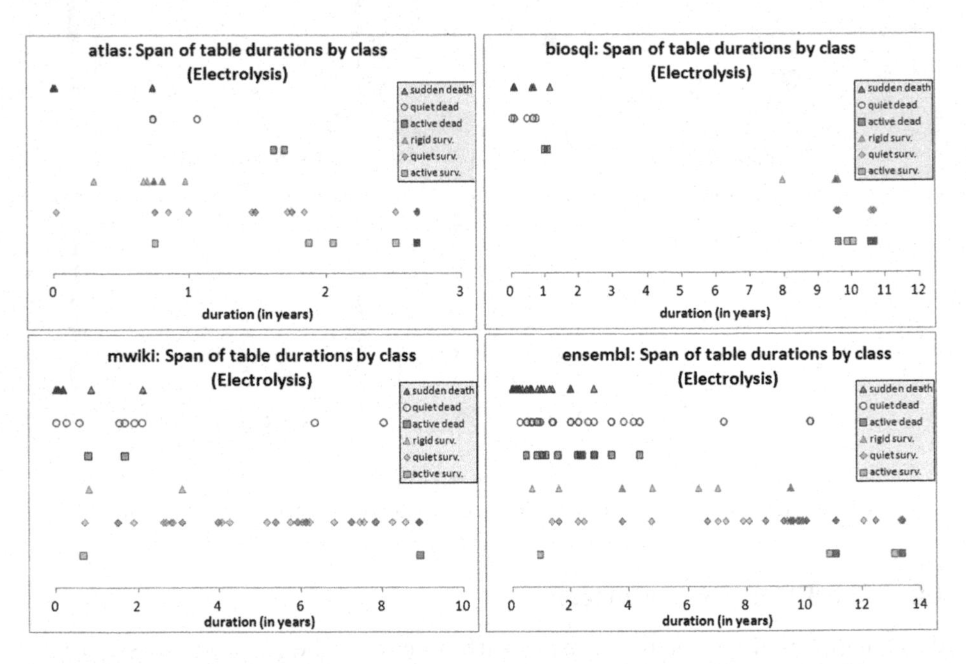

Fig. 5. The Electrolysis pattern. Each point refers to a table with (a) its duration at the x-axis and (b) its LifeAndDeath class (including both survival and activity) at the y-axis (also its symbol). Points are semi-transparent: intense color signifies large concentration of overlapping points. (Color figure online)

the chance to reach shorter durations. Survivors expose the inverse behavior i.e., mostly located at medium or high durations. The more active survivors are, the stronger they are attracted towards high durations, with a significant such inclination for the few active ones that cluster in very high durations.

Figure 5 vividly reveals the pattern's highlights. Observe:

- The total absence of dead tables from high durations.
- The clustering of rigid dead at low durations, the spread of quiet dead tables to low or medium durations, and the occasional presence of the few active dead, that are found also at low or medium durations, but in a clustered way.
- The extreme clustering of active survivors to high durations.
- The wider spread of the (quite numerous) quiet survivors to a large span of durations with long trails of points.
- The clustering of rigid survivors, albeit not just to one, but to all kinds of durations (frequently, not as high as quiet and active survivors).

One could possibly argue that the observed clusterings and time spans are simply a matter of numbers: the more populated a class is, the broader its span is. To forestall any such criticism, this is simply not the case. We give the respective numbers in the sequel of this subsection; here, we proactively mention a few examples to address this concern. Rigid dead tables are the most populated group in the dead class, yet they have the shortest span of all. The rigid survivors, who are the second most populated class of the entire population, exhibit all kinds of behaviors; yet, in most of the cases, they are disproportionally clustered and not spread throughout the different categories. Active survivors are also disproportionately clustered at high durations. Overall, with the exception of the quiet survivors that indeed span a large variance of durations, in the rest of the categories, the time span is disproportionate to the size of the population (number of points in the scatter plot) of the respective class.

In-Depth Study of Durations. To understand how tables are distributed in different durations, we have expressed table durations as percentages over the lifetime of their schema. Then, for each *LifeAndDeath* value and for each duration range of 5% of the database lifetime, we computed the percentage of tables whose duration falls within this range. Then, we proceeded in averaging the respective percentages of the eight data sets[3].

Both for lack of space and understanability reasons, we have to condense the detailed data in an easily understandable format. To summarize the detailed data, we regrouped the data in just 3 duration ranges, presented in Fig. 6: (a) durations lower that the 20% of the database lifetime (that attracts a large number of dead tables, esp., the rigid ones), to which we will refer as *low durations*, in the sequel, (b) durations higher that the 80% of the database lifetime

[3] An acute reader might express the concern whether it would be better to gather all the tables in one single set and average over them. We disagree: each data set comes with its own requirements, development style, and idiosyncrasy and putting all tables in a single data set, not only scandalously favors large data sets, but integrates different things. We average the behavior of schemata, not tables here.

	Rigid Dead	Quiet Dead	Active Dead	Rigid Surv	Quiet Surv	Active Surv	
[0-20%)	8%	5%	2%	4%	3%	1%	*23%*
[20%-80%)	3%	3%	1%	5%	13%	0%	*26%*
[80%-100%]	0%	0%	1%	14%	24%	12%	*51%*
	12%	*8%*	*3%*	*23%*	*40%*	*14%*	*100%*

Fig. 6. Indicative, average values over all datasets: for each LifeAndDeath class, percentage of tables per duration range over the total of the entire data set.

Atlas	Rigid dead	Quiet Dead	Active Dead	Rigid Surv	Quiet Surv	Active Surv
[0% -20%)	57%	0%	0%	9%	3%	0%
[20%-80%)	43%	100%	100%	91%	30%	12%
[80%-100%]	0%	0%	0%	0%	68%	88%
	100%	*100%*	*100%*	*100%*	*100%*	*100%*

Biosql	Rigid dead	Quiet Dead	Active Dead	Rigid Surv	Quiet Surv	Active Surv
[0-20%)	100%	100%	100%	0%	0%	0%
[20%-80%)	0%	0%	0%	14%	0%	0%
[80%-100%]	0%	0%	0%	86%	100%	100%
	100%	*100%*	*100%*	*100%*	*100%*	*100%*

Copperm.	Rigid dead	Quiet Dead	Active Dead	Rigid Surv	Quiet Surv	Active Surv
[0-20%)	0%			0%	0%	0%
[20%-80%)	100%			0%	23%	0%
[80%-100%]	0%			100%	77%	100%
	100%			*100%*	*100%*	*100%*

Ensembl	Rigid dead	Quiet Dead	Active Dead	Rigid Surv	Quiet Surv	Active Surv
[0-20%)	97%	65%	67%	20%	9%	9%
[20%-80%)	3%	35%	33%	80%	65%	0%
[80%-100%]	0%	0%	0%	0%	26%	91%
	100%	*100%*	*100%*	*100%*	*100%*	*100%*

Mwiki	Rigid dead	Quiet Dead	Active Dead	Rigid Surv	Quiet Surv	Active Surv
[0-20%)	90%	56%	100%	50%	9%	33%
[20%-80%)	10%	33%	0%	50%	49%	0%
[80%-100%]	0%	11%	0%	0%	42%	67%
	100%	*100%*	*100%*	*100%*	*100%*	*100%*

Ocart*	Rigid dead	Quiet Dead	Active Dead	Rigid Surv	Quiet Surv	Active Surv
[0-20%)	36%	100%		19%	13%	25%
[20%-80%)	64%	0%		41%	38%	0%
[80%-100%]	0%	0%		41%	50%	75%
	100%	*100%*		*100%*	*100%*	*100%*

phpBB	Rigid dead	Quiet Dead	Active Dead	Rigid Surv	Quiet Surv	Active Surv
[0-20%)		0%	0%	3%	9%	25%
[20%-80%)		50%	0%	0%	14%	0%
[80%-100%]		50%	100%	97%	77%	75%
		100%	*100%*	*100%*	*100%*	*100%*

typo3	Rigid dead	Quiet Dead	Active Dead	Rigid Surv	Quiet Surv	Active Surv
[0-20%)	20%	50%	0%	71%	27%	20%
[20%-80%)	80%	50%	50%	14%	18%	0%
[80%-100%]	0%	0%	50%	14%	55%	80%
	100%	*100%*	*100%*	*100%*	*100%*	*100%*

Fig. 7. For each data set, for each LifeAndDeath class, percentage of tables per duration range over the total of the LifeAndDeath class (for each data set, for each column, percentages add up to 100%).

(where too many survivors, esp., active ones are found), to which we will refer as *high durations*, and finally, (c) the rest of the durations in between, forming an intermediate category of *medium* durations.

Breakdown Per *LifeAndDeath* Class. Another research question concerns the breakdown of the distribution of tables within each *LifeAndDeath* class. In other words, we ask: *do certain LifeAndDeath classes have high concentrations in particular duration ranges*?

If one wants to measure the percentage of tables for each value of the *LifeAndDeath Class* over each duration range, we need to calculate each cell as the percentage of the specific class (e.g., each cell in the rigid dead column should measure the fraction of rigid dead tables that belong to its particular duration range). The detailed data per data set, where the value of each cell is presented as percentage over its *LifeAndDeath* class are depicted in Fig. 7.

Finally, in Fig. 8 we zoom only in (a) dead tables at the lowest 20% and (b) survivors at the highest 20% of durations. We count the number of tables, per *LifeAndDeath* class, for the respective critical duration range, and we compute the fraction of this value over the total number of tables pertaining to this *LifeAndDeath* class (columns *Rigid*, *Quiet*, *Active*). For the *Dead* and *Surv* columns, we divide the total number of dead/survivor tables belonging to the respective critical duration over the total number of dead/survivor tables overall.

	Pct of durations shorter than 20% of db life for Dead tables over the ...				Pct of durations longer than 80% of db life for Survivor tables over the ...			
	... Dead	... Rigid	... Quiet	...Active	... Surv	... Rigid	... Quiet	...Active
atlas	27%	57%	0%	0%	64%	0%	68%	88%
biosql	100%	100%	100%	100%	96%	86%	100%	100%
coppermine	0%	0%	-	-	86%	100%	77%	100%
ensembl	80%	97%	65%	67%	32%	0%	26%	91%
mediawiki	76%	90%	56%	100%	42%	0%	42%	67%
opencart*	50%	36%	100%	-	46%	41%	50%	75%
phpBB	0%	-	0%	0%	88%	97%	77%	75%
typo3	22%	20%	50%	0%	48%	14%	55%	80%

Fig. 8. Percentages of dead tables with too short durations and survivor tables with too long durations (red: above 50%, bold: above 75%, blue: below 20%, dash: no such tables). (Color figure online)

We observe that in more than half of the cells of the table in Fig. 8, the percentage reaches or exceeds 50%. This clearly demarcates the high concentrations of dead tables in low durations and of survivor tables in high durations.

Observations and Findings. Now, we are ready to quantitatively support the wording of the electrolysis pattern. We organize our discussion by *LifeAndDeath* class. Our quantitative findings for the electrolysis pattern are delineated in the rest of this subsection.

Dead Tables. We already knew from [9] that almost half the dead tables are rigid. Here, we have a clear testimony, however, that *not only are dead tables inclined to rigidity, but they are also strongly attracted to small durations.* The less active tables are the more they are attracted to short durations. *The attraction of dead tables, especially rigid ones, to (primarily) low or (secondarily) medium durations is significant and only few tables in the class of dead tables escape this rule.* Interestingly, in all our datasets, the only dead tables that escape the barrier of low and medium durations are a single table in mediawiki, another one in typo3 and the 4 of the 5 tables that are simultaneously deleted in phpBB.

- *Rigid dead tables, which is the most populated category of dead tables, strongly cluster in the area of low durations (lower than the 20% of the database lifetime) with percentages of 90%–100% in 3 of the 6 data sets* (Fig. 8). Atlas follows with a large percentage of 57% in this range. Two exceptions exist: opencart and typo3, having most of their dead tables in the medium range. There are also two exceptions of minor importance: coppermine with a single deleted table and phpBB with a focused deletion of 5 tables at a single time point.
- *Quiet dead tables, which is a category including few tables, are mostly oriented towards low durations.* Specifically, there are 5 data sets with a high concentration of tables in the area of low durations (Fig. 8); for the rest of

the data sets, the majority of quiet dead tables lie elsewhere: atlas has 100% in the medium range and phpBB is split in half between medium and large durations.
- Finally, for the very few active dead, which is a category where only six of the eight data sets have even a single table, there are two of them with 100% concentration and another one in 67% of its population in the low durations (Fig. 8). For the rest, atlas has 100% of its active dead in the medium range, phpBB 100% of the active dead in the long range (remember that phpBB has an exceptional behavior) and typo3 is split in half between low and medium durations (Fig. 7).

Survivors. *Survivors have the opposite tendency of clustering compared to the dead ones.* So, there are quite a few cases where survivor tables reach very high concentrations in high durations, and, interestingly, the more active the tables are, the higher their clustering in high durations.

- *Rigid survivors demonstrate a large variety of behaviors.* Rigid survivors are the second most populated category of tables after quiet survivors and demonstrate too many profiles of clustering (Fig. 7): one data set comes with a low-heavy profile, another 3 with a high-heavy profile, another two with a medium-heavy profile, and there is one data set split in half between early and medium durations and another one with an orientation of medium-to-high durations.
- *Quiet survivors, being the (sometimes vast) majority of survivor tables, are mostly gravitated towards large durations, and secondarily to medium ones.* In 6 out of 8 data sets, the percentage of quiet survivors that exceed 80% of db lifetime surpasses 50% (Fig. 7). In the two exceptions, medium durations is the largest subgroup of quiet survivors. Still, quiet survivors also demonstrate short durations too (Fig. 7), so overall, their span of possible durations is large. Notably, in all data sets, there are quiet survivors reaching maximum duration.
- It is extremely surprising that the vast majority of active survivors exceed 80% of the database lifetime in all datasets (Fig. 8). With the exception of three data sets in the range of 67%–75%, *the percentage of active survivors that exceed 80% of the db lifetime exceeds 80% and even attains totality in 2 cases.* Active survivor tables are not too many; however, it is their clustering to high durations (implying early birth) that is amazing. If one looks into the detailed data and in synch with the empty triangle pattern of [9], *the top changers are very often of maximum duration, i.e., early born and survivors* (Fig. 5).

Absence of Evolution. Although the majority of survivor tables are in the quiet class, we can quite emphatically say that *it is the absence of evolution that dominates.* Survivors vastly outnumber removed tables. Similarly, rigid tables outnumber the active ones, both in the survival and, in particular, in the dead class. Active tables are few and are mainly born in the early phases of the database lifetime.

5 Discussion, Take up and Future Work

Why Do We See What We See. We believe that this study strengthens our theory that schema evolution antagonizes a powerful gravitation to rigidity. The "dependency magnet" nature of databases, where all the application code relies on them but not vice versa, leads to this phenomenon, as avoiding the adaptation and maintenance of application code is a strong driver towards avoiding the frequent evolution of the database. Some explanations around the individual phenomena that we have observed can be attributed to the gravitation to rigidity:

- Dead tables die shortly after their birth and quite often, rigid: this setting provides as little as possible exposure to application development for tables to be removed.
- As dead tables do not attain high durations, it appears that after a certain period, practically within 10%–20% of the databases' lifetime, tables begin to be "safe". The significant amount of tables that stand the chance to attain maximum durations can be explained if we combine this observation with the fact that large percentages of tables are created at the first version of the database.
- Rigid tables find it hard to attain high durations (unless found in an environment of low change activity). This difficulty can be explained by two reasons. First, shortly after they are born, rigid tables are in the high-risk group of being removed. Second, rigid tables are also a class of tables with the highest migration probability. Even if their duration surpasses the critical 10% of databases lifetime where the mass of the deleted tables lies, they are candidates for being updated and migrating to the quiet class.
- Tables with high durations (i.e., early born) that survive spend their lives mostly quietly (i.e., with the few occasional maintenance changes) – again minimizing the impact to the surrounding code.
- The high concentration of the few active tables to very high durations and survival (which is of course related to early births) is also related to the gravitation to rigidity: the early phases of the database lifetime typically include more table births and, at the same time, gravitation to rigidity says that after the development of a substantial amount of code, too high rate of updates becomes harder; this results in very low numbers of active tables being born later. So, the pattern should not be read so much as "active tables are born early", but rather as "we do not see so many active tables being born in late phases of the database life".

Prediction of a Table's Life and Recommendations for Developers. How is a table going to live its life? Tables typically die shortly after their birth and quite often, rigid, i.e., without having experienced any update before. So, young rigid tables are the high risk group for being removed.

Typically, if a table surpasses infant mortality, it will likely survive to live a rigid or, more commonly, a quiet live. There is a small group of active tables, going through significant updates. Look for them in the early born survivors, as later phases of the database life do not seem to generate tables that are too active.

Overall, after a table is born, the development of code that depends on it should be kept as restrained as possible – preferably encapsulated via views that will hide the changes from the application code. After the period of infant mortality, it is fairly safe to say that unless the table shows signs of significant update activity, gravitation to rigidity enters the stage and the table's evolution will be low.

Threats to Validity. It is always necessary to approach one's study with a critical eye for its validity. With respect to the *measurement validity* of our work, we have tested (i) our automatic extraction tool, Hecate, for the accuracy of its automatic extraction of delta's and measures, and (ii) our human-made calculations. With respect to the *scope* of the study, as already mentioned, we frame our investigation to schemata that belong to open-source projects. This has to do with the decentralized nature of the development process in an open source environment. Databases in closed organizational environments have different administration protocols, their surrounding applications are possibly developed under strict software house regulations and also suffer from the inertia that their evolution might incur, due to the need to migrate large data volumes. So, we warn the reader not to overgeneralize our results to this area. Another warning to the reader is that we have worked only with changes at the logical and not the physical layer. Having said that, we should mention, however, that the *external validity* of our study is supported by several strong statements: we have chosen data sets with (a) fairly long histories of versions, (b) a variety of domains (CMS's and scientific systems), (c) a variety in the number of their commits (from 46 to 528), and, (d) a variety of schema sizes (from 23 to 114 at the end of the study); kindly refer to Fig. 3 for all these properties. We have also been steadily attentive to work only with phenomena that are common to all the data sets. We warn the reader not to interpret our findings as laws (that would need confirmation of our results by other research groups), but rather as patterns. Favorably, some very recent anecdotal evidence, in fact coming from the industrial world, is corroborating in favor of our gravitation to rigidity theory (see the blog entry by Stonebraker et al., at http://cacm.acm.org/blogs/blog-cacm/208958-database-decay-and-what-to-do-about-it/fulltext). Based on the above, *we are confident for the validity of our findings within the aforementioned scope.*

Future Work. Related literature suggests that database evolution cools down after the first versions. This has been studied for the slowdown of the birth rate, however a precise, deep investigation of the timing of the heartbeat of the database schema with all its births, deaths and updates is still pending. To our view, this practically marks the limits of analyses based on descriptive statistics. The next challenge for the research community lies in going all the way down to the posted comments and the expressed user requirements at the public repositories and try to figure out why change is happening the way it does. Automating this effort is a very ambitious goal in this context. Finally, the validation of existing research results with more studies from other groups, different software tools, hopefully extending the set of studied data sets, is imperative to allow us progressively to move towards 'laws' rather than 'patterns' of change in the field of understanding schema evolution.

References

1. Cleve, A., Gobert, M., Meurice, L., Maes, J., Weber, J.H.: Understanding database schema evolution: a case study. Sci. Comput. Program. **97**, 113–121 (2015)
2. Curino, C., Moon, H.J., Tanca, L., Zaniolo, C.: Schema evolution in wikipedia: toward a web information system benchmark. In: Proceedings of ICEIS 2008. Citeseer (2008)
3. Curino, C., Moon, H.J., Deutsch, A., Zaniolo, C.: Automating the database schema evolution process. VLDB J. **22**(1), 73–98 (2013)
4. Lin, D.Y., Neamtiu, I.: Collateral evolution of applications and databases. In: Proceedings of the Joint International and Annual ERCIM Workshops on Principles of Software Evolution (IWPSE) and Software Evolution (Evol) Workshops, IWPSE-Evol 2009, pp. 31–40 (2009)
5. Qiu, D., Li, B., Su, Z.: An empirical analysis of the co-evolution of schema and code in database applications. In: Proceedings of the 2013 9th Joint Meeting on Foundations of Software Engineering, ESEC/FSE 2013, pp. 125–135 (2013)
6. Sjøberg, D.: Quantifying schema evolution. Inf. Softw. Technol. **35**(1), 35–44 (1993)
7. Skoulis, I., Vassiliadis, P., Zarras, A.: Open-source databases: within, outside, or beyond Lehman's laws of software evolution? In: Proceedings of 26th International Conference on Advanced Information Systems Engineering - CAiSE 2014 (2014)
8. Skoulis, I., Vassiliadis, P., Zarras, A.V.: Growing up with stability: how open-source relational databases evolve. Inf. Syst. **53**, 363–385 (2015)
9. Vassiliadis, P., Zarras, A., Skoulis, I.: Gravitating to rigidity: patterns of schema evolution -and its absence- in the lives of tables. Inf. Syst. **63**, 24–46 (2017)
10. Vassiliadis, P., Zarras, A.V., Skoulis, I.: How is life for a table in an evolving relational schema? Birth, death and everything in between. In: Proceedings of 34th International Conference on Conceptual Modeling (ER 2015), Stockholm, Sweden, 19–22 October 2015, pp. 453–466 (2015)
11. Wu, S., Neamtiu, I.: Schema evolution analysis for embedded databases. In: Proceedings of the 2011 IEEE 27th International Conference on Data Engineering Workshops, ICDEW 2011, pp. 151–156 (2011)

On the Similarity of Process Change Operations

Georg Kaes(✉) and Stefanie Rinderle-Ma

Faculty of Computer Science, University of Vienna, Vienna, Austria
{georg.kaes,stefanie.rinderle-ma}@univie.ac.at

Abstract. Process flexibility is a vital part for almost any business area. Change logs are a central asset for documenting adaptations in processes, since they capture key information about associated change operations. Comparing multiple change operations offers interesting data for many analysis questions, e.g., for analyzing previously applied change operations and for supporting users in future adaptions. In this paper, we discuss different change perspectives and present metrics for comparing change operations. Their applicability and feasibility are evaluated based on a prototypical implementation and based on real world process logs.

Keywords: Business process analysis · Process change similarity · Similarity metrics

1 Introduction

Being able to adapt processes when the situation requires to do so is vital in almost any business domain. Change operations are the key concept when adapting processes. For analyzing dependencies between change operations, change processes [1] and change trees [2] can be used. On top of that, being able to compare change operations would be beneficial in the following situations [3]:

Planning Future Adaptations: When planning adaptations in certain situations, the person responsible for planning the change could analyze the adaptations which have been made before. Imagine a nursing home, where the therapy plan of each patient is represented as a process instance. Whenever a patient shows a new symptom, his and only his therapy process has to be changed in order to deal with the new problem. If two patients have problems with their digestion, some drugs could be applied for a certain amount of time, their diet plans could be changed, or some other therapies could be applied. Which type of therapy is applied usually depends on various individual circumstances, such as their medical history, pre-existing conditions, allergies etc.

Analyzing Past Change Operations: When evaluating change operations, identifying similar process change operations can add relevant information to an analysis. In a hospital, it can be analyzed in which situations similar therapies have been applied to a patient's therapy plan. Side effects of change operations

E. Dubois and K. Pohl (Eds.): CAiSE 2017, LNCS 10253, pp. 348–363, 2017.
DOI: 10.1007/978-3-319-59536-8_22

can also be compared: Think of a patient who got ill, and received some kind of treatment. Additionally, all therapies which include activities which burden the patient's immune system have to be removed. By analyzing the similarity of such side effects, the evaluation of such situations can be improved.

Both situations benefit from assessing the similarity of the involved change operations based on metrics that measure how much a change operations is similar to another one in a given context. Though literature proposes several metrics for process similarity (e.g., [4]) and instance similarity [5], metrics for change similarity have mainly be neglected so far. This paper approaches this gap based on the following research questions:

Q1: How can process change similarity metrics be defined in general? Considering which perspectives? Based on which information?
Q2: In which scenarios can different change similarity metrics be used? What are their advantages and disadvantages?

Q1 and Q2 are tackled as follows: First, we analyze the attributes of process change operations and their effects on different process perspectives, i.e., model, data, time, and resource perspective ($\mapsto$ Q1). The limitations of comparing the similarity of two process change operations solely based on their attributes is discussed in the sequel ($\mapsto$ Q2). An alternative approach is to exploit the effects of applying change operations to processes. Hence, two change similarity metrics are provided that exploit the effects on the resource and time perspective of the underlying processes ($\mapsto$ Q1). They can be useful in change scenarios where, for example, the model perspective is not available to users deciding on the change due to privacy reasons. The feasibility and applicability of these metrics is evaluated against metrics that consider the effects of change operations on the model perspective of processes ($\mapsto$ Q2).

The rest of the paper is structured as follows: Sect. 2 introduces fundamentals, perspectives, and change effects (Q1). This is followed by a discussion about a metric which focuses solely on the attributes of a process change operation (Sect. 3). In Sect. 4, we present effect-based metrics for comparing process change operations (Q2), which are evaluated in Sect. 5. Section 6 presents related work and Sect. 7 concludes our paper.

2 Fundamentals

This section introduces basic concepts of process change operation similarity.

2.1 Basic Definitions

The process schema and the process fragment are basic components of process change operations [6]. A change operation is applied to a process schema. The fragment defines what is being inserted, removed, or in any other way affected by the change operation. A process schema/fragment is defined as follows:

Definition 1 (Process Schema, Process Fragment). *A process schema* S *is defined as* $S := (N, E, D, DE, Res, Temp)$ *where*

- N *denotes a set of nodes, i.e. tasks and gateways such as XOR and parallel splits and joins*
- E *denotes the set of control flow edges,* $E \subseteq N \times N$
- D *is a set of data elements.*
- $DE \subseteq (N \times D) \cup (D \times N)$ *is a set of data edges connecting nodes with data elements (write) and data elements with nodes (read).*
- $Res : N \mapsto 2^{R \times \mathbb{N}}$ *denotes a function that assigns each activity the required number of resources, i.e.,* $Res(n) = \{(r, x) | r \in R, x \in \mathbb{N},\ r \text{ assigned to } n\}$ *where* R *is the set of all resources.*
- $Temp : N \mapsto \mathcal{N}$ *denotes the point in time associated with a node* $n \in N$.

The resource assignment $Res(n)$ determines the number of resources that are required to perform task n, for example, 2 nurses and 1 doctor for a surgery. $Temp(n)$ assigns a point in time to task n. This expression of temporal requirements in processes is simple; more powerful definitions (e.g., [7]) exist. However, for the purpose of constructing first similarity metric proposal time points are assumed as being sufficient.

In the following definition, process change operations are defined according to literature [6].

Definition 2 (Process Change Operation). *A process change operation* Δ *is defined as a tupel* $\Delta := (t, f, p, S)$ *where*

- t *denotes the type of the change* ($t \in \{INSERT, DELETE\}$).
- f *denotes the process fragment* $f := (N, E, D, DE, Res, Temp)$ *which is used by the change operation.*
- p *denotes the position of the change operation.*
- S *denotes the process schema* $S := (N, E, D, DE, Res, Temp)$ *the change operation is applied to.*

Further attributes such as rationale or the goal of the process change (cf. [8,9]) will be considered in future work. Moreover, this work focuses on INSERT and DELETE as change types. Based on these types other types such as MOVE can be expressed.

2.2 Types of Process Change Metrics

Basically, comparing process change operations can be based on the *attributes* of a change operation Δ, such as its position, goal, type or schema (cf. Definition 2) and its *effects*. The suitability of comparing change operations based on their attributes is discussed by means of an example in Sect. 3.

For comparing change effects, at first, we have to define what change effects actually are. In literature, there are multiple definitions for effects in general, depending on the context. In *Hinge et al.* [10], effects relate to process tasks and are notated in conjunctive normal form (CNF). In *Cossentino et al.* [11], effect logs contain the result of a programs state after steps have been executed. *Rinderle et al.* [8] uses the term *effects* related to change operations to describe the difference between a model S, and an adapted model S' where S' results from applying change Δ to S.

With respect to literature, the definition by *Rinderle et al.* [8] seems most suitable as it is related to change operations. However, the approach focuses mostly on the model and data perspective of the change, even though a schema definition such as in Definiton 1 comprises additional perspectives such as the resource and time perspectives of process schemas. In order to provide a more comprehensive picture on change effects, a short discussion on change effects in relation to process perspectives seems useful. Hereby we follow [6].

The *model perspective* captures the structural and behaviorial perspective of a process. In [12], the formal semantics of change patterns for the control flow of a process are defined. These formal semantics describe the effects of six groups of process adaptation patterns, such as insertion patterns, deletion patterns, or replace patterns.

The *data perspective* describes the data, or information flow of a process model. Related to a process change operation, the data perspective covers the data flow regarding the unchanged process schema, the process fragment, and the resulting process schema. [13] describes several data patterns for the groups *Data Visibility*, which defines in which parts of a process a data element can be accessed, *Data Interaction*, which defines the interaction with data elements in the process, *Data Transfer*, which focuses on the actual data flow, and *Data-based Routing*, which defines the influence of data elements on a processes execution. Analyzing the similarity of the effects of two process change operations on the data flow can yield interesting information, e.g. if some data element which is critical to the processes execution was affected by the process change or not.

The *resource perspective* covers the organizational aspects of a process such as actors, roles, and organizational units. Effects of process change operations on this perspective can be relevant when planning future changes, specifically which and how many resources are affected by the change operation (either because they have to do more work, less work, or something at a different point in time). In a nursing home, required resources for a long-running therapy can be planned and analyzed before adaptation. If resources are scarce, different adaptations can be compared in order to find the most efficient one. In this paper, we will describe a metric which focuses on comparing the effects of two process change operations on the resource flow.

The *time perspective* covers all temporal aspects of the process. It is also relevant for change operations, e.g., when the change operation has been conducted (cf. logging changes in [1]) or which due dates are defined for tasks in the change fragment. When comparing the effects of two change operations on a processes time perspective, one can analyze for how long the fragment in a process change will affect the affected schema.

Conclusion: In general both, metrics that are based on attributes or change effects can be used to measure the similarity of change operations. Table 1 summarizes what can specifically be compared using either the attributes or the effects of a change operation along the different perspectives.

Table 1. Comparing change operations based on their attributes or effects for different perspectives

↓ Perspective	Attribute based similarity of	Effect based similarity of
Model/Data:	control and data flow of the original schemas and change fragments	the change of control and data flow due to process change operations
Resource:	utilizing resources in the original schemas and change fragments	resource requirement change due to process change operations
Time:	temporal constraints of tasks in the original schemas and change fragments	temporal shifts in the resulting processes due to the process change operations

3 Comparing the Attributes of Process Change Operations

This section illustrates that a metric which is solely based on the attributes of a process change operation only yields satisfactory results, if it is tailored to the specific situation (Q2).

When comparing two process change operations $\Delta_1 := (t_1, f_1, p_1, S_1)$ and $\Delta_2 := (t_2, f_2, p_2, S_2)$, one could use the four basic attributes which define them for comparison, i.e. the operation type, the fragment, the position and the schema. For each of these values, different metrics already exist: For the process schema (sim(S_1, S_2) and fragment (sim(f_1, f_2)), techniques for the similarity of process models can be used [4,14,15]. The positions of the change operations (sim(p_1, p_2)), which are defined by the pre- and postset of the element, can be compared by adapting the node matching similarity as defined in [4]. For comparing the change operation type (sim(t_1, t_2)), which is typically a string such as INSERT or DELETE, approaches which compare string similarity [16] or equivalence could be used.

Overall, for $\Delta_1 := (t_1, f_1, p_1, S_1)$ and $\Delta_2 := (t_2, f_2, p_2, S_2)$ the following attribute-based metric can be formulated:

$$sim_{attr}(\Delta_1, \Delta_2) := w_t * sim(t_1, t_2) + w_f * sim(f_1, f_2) + w_s * sim(S_1, S_2) + w_p * sim(p_1, p_2) \quad (1)$$

where the sum of the weights $w_t + w_f + w_s + w_p = 1$.

As the following example shows, the weights which should be used for each of these values highly depend on the situation, i.e., the schema, fragment, position, and change operation type.

In Fig. 1, three process schemas for a surgery in a hospital are shown: The first one displays the process for an adult, the second for an elderly person, who can still care for himself, and the third shows the process for a child, where the parents still have the right to decide. With a few minor differences, the basic process works as follows: First, general information about the patient is being collected, then, he is prepared for surgery, the surgery is being conducted, and finally, a report is delivered.

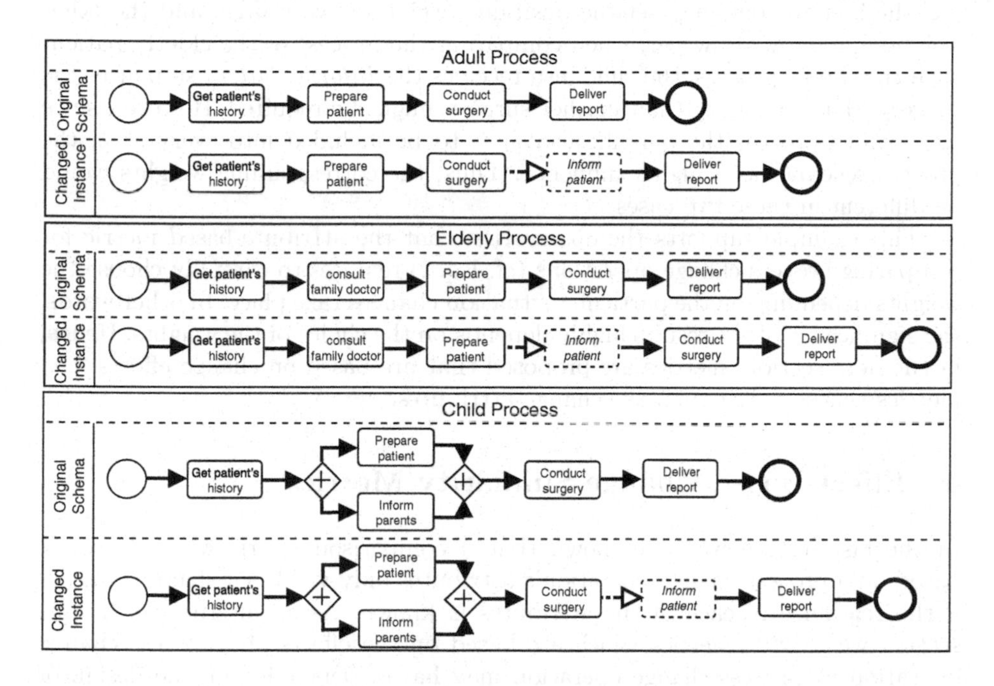

Fig. 1. Three examples of process change operations

In certain cases, adaptations to these basic processes are necessary: If a patient requires additional information *before* the surgery, an *Inform Patient* step is added to the process instance, where another doctor consults the patient. This is shown in the changed instance of the elderly process.

Sometimes, the surgery did not reach its desired goal, and another surgery will be necessary. Thus, the patient has to be informed separately *after* the surgery. For this, an *Inform Patient* step is added to the process instance *after* the surgery. This is shown in the changed instance of the adult process.

Following, the *position* of the *Inform Patient* step highly influences its semantical meaning: If it is added before the surgery, it usually just means that another doctor has to be consulted; if it is added after the surgery, it might hint that something went wrong. Thus, when comparing two change operations with the element *Inform Patient*, one may regard the weight of the position $w_{position}$ as very high, while the other weights are quite low.

When doing surgeries on children, their parents have to be included in every step of the process. Each time the patient is informed, his or her parents also have to be informed. Besides this, the *Inform Patient* step has the same semantic meaning if added before or after the surgery as for the other two processes.

When comparing the change operations of the adult and the elderly patient, the *Inform Patient* step is added for the adult after the surgery, and for the elderly person before the surgery. Since the two process schemas do not have much effect on this particular change operation, but the position does have a very high effect, one may set the position's weight as very high, and the other weights quite low. However, when comparing the process of the elderly patient with the child's process, the child also receives the *Inform Patient* step after the surgery, thus indicating that another surgery might be required. However, since in a child's process the parents also have to be included into every step, the process schema has a higher influence. Thus, the corresponding weights would be different in these two cases.

This example supports the observation that the attribute-based metric for comparing process change operations (cf. Eq. 1) requires to carefully choose the weights depending on the particular situation changes take place. In other words, the significance of the results highly depends on the choice of the weights. Hence, in the next section, metrics are proposed that are based on change effects, i.e., metrics that abstract from the change attributes.

4 Effect Based Change Similarity Metrics

In the last section we have shown that a comparison metric which is solely based on a process change operation's attributes only yields satisfactory results if the relevance of each of the attributes is known. As an alternative, in this section we provide metrics which are based on the effects of a process change operation. A process change operation may have - depending on the design of the fragment which is inserted to or deleted from the schema - effects on all process perspectives presented in Sect. 2.2.

A common scenario in which process change operations may be compared is that of some domain expert who uses the resulting data for comparing possible adaptations, or for analyzing past adaptations, as discussed in the introduction. Depending on the question at hand, different perspectives on the process fragment may be of interest. In this section we chose to set our focus on the resource and temporal perspective for two reasons: First, these perspectives can provide answers to interesting questions for a domain expert. For a practitioner such as a nurse in a nursing home the resource and temporal perspectives provide answers to questions such as *How much staff will be required* or *How long will this therapy take?* Second, metrics which are solely based on the temporal and resource perspective can be used to compare process change operations without any knowledge of the schema after the change, or about the other perspectives of the change operation's fragment. This can be relevant when the whole process cannot be accessed (a) due to privacy issues or (b) because the whole information is not relevant to the question. Think of a nursing home where a nurse has to plan the resources of the upcoming weeks: She may not have to know which steps the therapy processes contain exactly - all she needs is data about the required resources. By removing critical information about the patient's therapy processes (and reducing the information only to the resource and time perspective) this data can also be used with less data privacy issues.

4.1 Resource Perspective Metrics

In this section, we present a similarity metric for process change effects from the resource perspective, which captures all required organizational and other resources. When planning a process adaptation, it may be interesting to compare available adaptations based on the resources they require. Thus, one can choose the adaptation which requires the least resources if two or more adaptations are similar otherwise.

For this we present the aggregated resource view for process schemas and process fragments that are used for changes. This view builds the basis for creating a metric to compare the resource perspective of two change operations. For each task, a definition of resources which are connected to this task are required. The effects of a change operation $\Delta = (t, f, p, S)$ on the resources perspective of the underlying process schema S can be determined based on the resource assignments of S and the process fragment f. In order to determine the effects, the aggregated resource view of a process schema/fragment is defined as follows:

Definition 3 (Aggregated Resource View). *Let $S = (N, E, D, DE, Res, Temp)$ be a process schema. Then the aggregated resource assignment ρ_S for S is defined as*

$$\rho_S := \{(r, s) | \exists (r, x) \in \bigcup_{n \in N} Res(n) \wedge s = \sum_{n \in N, (r,x) \in Res(n)} x\}$$

Consider Change Fragment 1 ($CF1$) and Change Fragment 2 ($CF2$) to be inserted or deleted by change operations as depicted in Fig. 2 with $CF1 = (N1, E1, D1, DE1, Res, Temp)$ and $CF2 = (N2, E2, D2, DE2, Res, Temp)$. The required resources for each task are depicted in italic as attributes of the task (so for executing task A resource *nurse* is required two times, while for executing task B resource *doctor* is required once.) This leads to the following sets of tasks and aggregated resource views:

- $N1 = \{A, A, B, C\}$ and $N2 = \{A, B, C, D\}$[1]
- For $CF1$: $Res(A)$ = (nurse, 2), $Res(B)$ = (doctor, 1), $Res(A)$ = (nurse, 2), $Res(C)$ = (nurse, 1)
- For $CF2$: $Res(A)$ = (nurse, 2), $Res(C)$ = (nurse, 1), $Res(B)$ = (doctor, 1), $Res(D)$ = (assistant, 1)
- $\rho_{CF1} := \{(nurse, 5), (doctor, 1)\}$
- $\rho_{CF2} := \{(nurse, 3), (doctor, 1), (assistant, 1)\}$

[1] The sets are seen as bags due to multiple occurrence of activities.

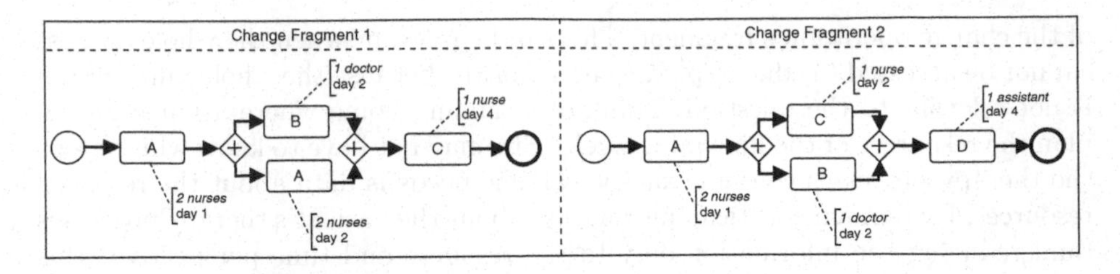

Fig. 2. Example for aggregated resource perspective in process fragments

Definition 4 (Similarity Metrics for Resource Assignment). *Let ρ_1, ρ_2 be two aggregated resource assignments. Then the similarity between ρ_1 and ρ_2 is defined as follows:*

$$sim(\rho_1, \rho_2) := \begin{cases} \frac{\sum_{\rho_1,\rho_2} \{|y_1 - y_2| | \exists(r,y_1) \in \rho_1, \exists(r,y_2) \in \rho_2\}}{\sum_{\rho_1,\rho_2} \{max(z) | \exists(r,z) \in \rho_1 \cup \rho_2\}} & if\, \rho_1 \cup \rho_2 \neq \emptyset \\ 0 & otherwise \end{cases}$$

$sim(\rho_1, \rho_2)$ relates the number of resources that are required for ρ_1 and ρ_2 to the maximum number of each required resource. For the example shown in Fig. 2 we have $\rho_1 := \{(nurse, 5), (doctor, 1)\}$ and $\rho_2 := \{(nurse, 3), (doctor, 1), (assistant, 1)\}$. Thus 4 resources are required for ρ_1 and ρ_2, i.e., 3 nurses and 1 doctor. The maximum number for each particular resource are 5 (nurse), 1 (doctor), and 1 assistant, summing up to 7. Overall, $sim(\rho_1, \rho_2) = \frac{4}{7} \approx 0.57$ for this example.

Metric $sim(\rho_1, \rho_2)$ can be calculated for the resource assignments of two fragments $f1$, $f2$ that are used by change operations $\Delta_1 = (t1, f1, p1, S1)$ and $\Delta_2 = (t2, f2, p2, S2)$. Doing so it becomes possible to measure the effects on the resource assignments of the underlying process schemas $S1$ and $S2$. It has only be further distinguished whether Δ_1 and Δ_2 insert or delete the fragments. For insertion, typically, resource assignments will be added, for deletion, resource assignments will be removed. Note that intentionally the resource assignments of the underlying schemata $S1$ and $S2$ are not considered as the metric is designed in an independent manner. The reason behind is to enable similarity calculation also for different schemas $S1$ and $S2$.

Definition 5 (Change Resource Similarity (CRS)). *Let $\Delta_1 = (t1, f1, p1, S1)$, $\Delta_2 = (t2, f2, p2, S2)$ be two change operations and ρ_1 (ρ_2) the aggregated resource assignment for $f1$ ($f2$). The Change Resource Similarity CRS between changes Δ_1 and Δ_2 is defined as follows:*

$$CRS(\Delta_1, \Delta_2) := \begin{cases} sim(\rho_1, \rho_2)\, if\, t1 = t2 \\ -sim(\rho_1, \rho_2)\, otherwise \end{cases}$$

4.2 Towards a Similarity Metric for the Timed Resource Perspective

The CRS metric compares the required resources of a process fragment. Sometimes, especially in long-running process settings, the time perspective is also relevant. Think about a nursing home planning the required resources for the next weeks: It may be interesting how two change operations affect the resource view only in a certain time frame. Definition 6 incorporates the time information into the aggregated resource view:

Definition 6 (Timed Aggregated Resource View). *Let $S = (N, E, D, DE, Res, Temp)$ be a process schema with aggregated resource view ρ_S. The timed aggregated resource view τ_S is defined as follows:*

$$\tau_S := \{(r, s, t1, t2) | (r, s) \in \rho_S, \\ t1 = min\{Temp(n) | n \in N \wedge \exists (r, x) \in Res(n)\}, \\ t2 = max\{Temp(n) | n \in N \wedge \exists (r, x) \in Res(n)\}\}$$

Informally, the timed aggregated resource view determined for each tuple in the aggregated resource view the earliest and latest point in time the associated resource was required. For the change fragments $CF1$ and $CF2$ depicted in Fig. 2, we obtain

τ_{CF1} = {(nurse, 5, 1, 4), (doctor, 1, 2, 2)} and

τ_{CF2} = {(nurse, 3, 1, 2), (doctor, 1, 2, 2), (assistant, 1, 4, 4)}.

Similarity between the timed aggregated resource views of two process schemas or fragments can be defined as follows. For comparing the temporal perspective a simple comparison between the intervals for each aggregated resource is utilized, i.e., calculating the differences between upper and lower interval limit divided by the sum of the interval lengths. This similarity value is combined with the CRS by weighing both equally. Note that if more complex temporal information is assigned to the tasks, more sophisticated similarity metrics can be used.

Definition 7 (Similarity Metrics for Timed Resource Assignment). *Let τ_1, τ_2 be two timed aggregated resource assignments for resource assignments ρ_1 and ρ_2. Then the similarity between τ_1 and τ_2 is defined as follows:*

$$sim(\tau_1, \tau_2) := \begin{cases} \frac{1}{2} * (sim(\rho_1, \rho_2) + \frac{\sum_{t1,t2} sim(t1,t2)}{max(|\tau_1|, |\tau_2|)}) & if\, \tau_1 \cup \tau_2 \neq \emptyset \\ 0 & otherwise \end{cases}$$

where $t1 = (r1, s1, l1, u1) \in \tau_1, t2 = (r2, s2, l2, u2) \in \tau_2$ *and*

$$sim(t1, t2) := \begin{cases} 1 & if\, r1 = r2 \wedge l1 = l2 \wedge u1 = u2 \\ 1 - \frac{|l1-l2|+|u1-u2|}{|u1-l2|+|u2-l1|)} & if\, r1 = r2 \\ 0 & otherwise \end{cases}$$

The metrics combines the similarity between the aggregated resource views with the more specific assessment of the resource requirements related to time. Each value can be also considered in a separated manner.

The corner cases for the metrics would be to have (a) highly similar or equal resource assignments that are due at the same time and (b) highly similar or equal resource assignments that are due at totally different times. For case (a), intuitively, the timed aggregated resource metrics yields a value close to or equal 1. For case (b) assume

$\rho_1 = \{(nurse, 3, 1, 3), (doctor, 1, 4, 5)\}$ and $\rho_2 = \{(nurse, 3, 4, 5), (doctor, 1, 6, 7)\}$. In this case $sim(\rho_1, \rho_2) = 1$. Then: $sim((nurse, 3, 1, 3), (nurse, 3, 4, 5)) = 1 - \frac{3+2}{1+4} = 0$ and $sim((doctor, 1, 4, 5), (doctor, 1, 6, 7)) = 1 - \frac{2+2}{1+3} = 0$. Hence, $sim(\tau_1, \tau_2) = 0.5$. This means that the high similarity between ρ_1 and ρ_2 is reduced by half because the same resources are required, but at totally different times.

For the example in Fig. 2, applying Definition 7 yields:

$sim((nurse, 3, 1, 2), (nurse, 5, 1, 4)) = 1 - \frac{2}{1+3} = 0.5$ and $sim((doctor, 1, 2, 2), (doctor, 1, 2, 2)) = 1$.

Then: $sim(\tau_{CF1}, \tau_{CF2}) = \frac{0.57 + \frac{0.5+1}{3}}{2} = 0.54$.

This means that the deviations in the time assignments reduce the similarity of the aggregated resource assignment a bit.

For an example where $\rho_1 = \{(nurse, 3, 2, 4)\}$ and $\rho_2 = \{(nurse, 1, 2, 4)\}$ the resource assignment similarity would yield $sim(\rho_1, \rho_2) = 0.66$.

Looking at the time requirements, $sim((nurse, 3, 2, 4), (nurse, 2, 2, 4)) = 1$ and hence $sim(\tau_1, \tau_2) = \frac{0.66+1}{2} = 0.83$.

In this case the similarity increased when incorporating the time as a different number of the same resource is required at exactly the same time.

For comparing changes along their timed aggregated resource views a first proposal for a similarity metric is as follows:

Definition 8 (Timed Change Resource Similarity (TCRS)). *Let* $\Delta_1 = (t1, f1, p1, S1)$, $\Delta_2 = (t2, f2, p2, S2)$ *be two change operations and* τ_1 (τ_2) *the timed aggregated resource assignment for* $f1$ $(f2)$. *The Timed Change Resource Similarity* $TCRS$ *between changes* Δ_1 *and* Δ_2 *is defined as follows:*

$$TCRS(\Delta_1, \Delta_2) := \begin{cases} sim(\tau_1, \tau_2)\, if\ t1 = t2 \\ -sim(\tau_1, \tau_2)\ otherwise \end{cases}$$

Looking at the different examples and corner cases above, TCRS seems to make sense. However, the observations from the metrics start to become blurred if the earliest and latest point in time a resource is required span a longer time frame. The interpretation can be different. The resources could be required rather at the beginning and the end of the process or during the entire execution of the process. Both cases would be treated the same. Hence, a more fine-granule comparison becomes necessary. This aspect will be addressed in future work.

5 Implementation and Evaluation

In this section we present the implementation and evaluation of the approach. Change logs are provided by the *Apelands* [17] data set, a game-based experimentation environment for flexible and individual process settings.

5.1 Implementation

The prototype[2] developed as a basis for our evaluation provides an interface for inspecting process models, instances (Fig. 3) and the applied change operations. The metrics discussed in this paper are shown in Fig. 4.

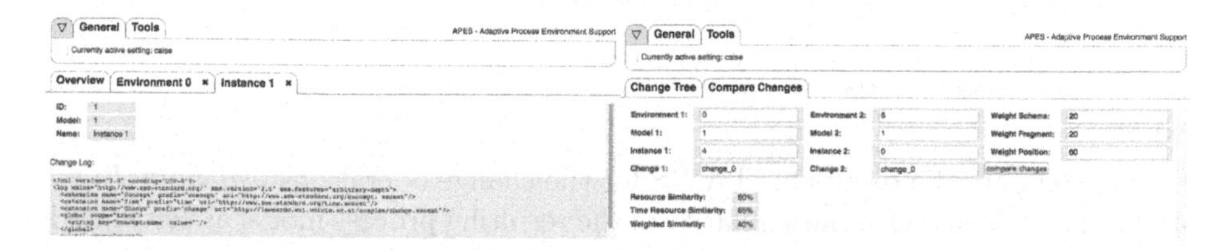

Fig. 3. Details of a process instance in the prototype

Fig. 4. Comparing two change operations in the prototype

5.2 Discussion of Applicability

Using (T)CRS, one can compare process change operations even when there is no information about the resulting process schemas or about other perspectives of the process change operations. This can be useful for cases where (a) other information is not available, e.g. due to data privacy issues or (b) if the other data is not required to the current analysis. Thus, change operation similarity based on the temporal and resource perspective alone can be used as an alternative to structural or behavioral similarity metrics. In the next section, we will show that the results from (T)CRS actually correlate with structural similarity of the process schemas after the change operation has been executed.

5.3 Comparing (T)CRS Effect Similarity with Structural Similarity

We evaluate the effect similarity of two change operations as measured by (T)CRS against *node matching similarity* (NMS) of the resulting process schemas.

For the evaluation we have used data set 1 from the Apelands project[3]. This data set contains 136 change operations for 23 different basic models, of which

[2] http://cs.univie.ac.at/project/apes.

[3] The data set can be found at http://cs.univie.ac.at/project/apes.

107 are based on the same model. Apelands is a game-based experimentation and evaluation service for flexible process settings. While playing the round-based game, players adapt process instances, thus generating process change logs. These change logs contain all perspectives required for the metrics presented in this paper, i.e. a list of required resources for each activity which can be added to a process instance, and information about the game round the activity is supposed to be executed. Listing 1.1 shows a change fragment from the game. Each contains two activities which have been planned for the next two rounds (c.f. <round/> tag). In the <resources/> Tag, the required resources are shown.

Listing 1.1. Apelands change fragment

```
<fragment>
  <call>
    <name>'Fire Elemental'</name> <round>1</round>
    <resource name="Alchemy Lab" count=''2''/>
  </call>
  <call>
    <name>'Knight'</name> <round>2</round>
    <resource name=''Barracks'' count=''2''/>
  </call>
</fragment>
```

We compare the results of (T)CRS for the change operations *which are based on the same model* with the similarity of the resulting process model as calculated by NMS. In this special case, NMS similarity of the resulting process models can be seen as the effects of the change operations from the control flow perspective. We compare a randomly chosen change operation from this data set against all other change operations. As Figs. 5 and 6 show, both CRS and TCRS correlate with NMS. In most cases, the similarity as calculated by (T)CRS is higher than NMS, since (T)CRS are based on a subset of the attributes of the process models. Attributes not considered by (T)CRS which are different do not have any effect on (T)CRS scores, but lower the NMS score. This relationship can also be seen in the fact that TCRS has a closer correlation to NMS than CRS, since it also incorporates the time-related attributes, which are not used by CRS.

Conclusion: This evaluation shows that the similarity of change operation effects as calculated by (T)CRS correlates with the similarity of the resulting process schemas. Thus, such a metric can be used to compare process change operations independent of attribute-specific weights.

Threats to Validity: Our approach was evaluated with experimental data generated from a game, not with data from several different settings in which change operations occur. Also, we did not interview domain experts about the impact of the results of our metrics. These evaluations would be interesting additions to our validation which is based on a state of the art approach from process similarity, and will be addressed as future work.

6 Related Work

Soundness notions and checks for the application of change operations to process models and instances have been subject to several approaches. Structural

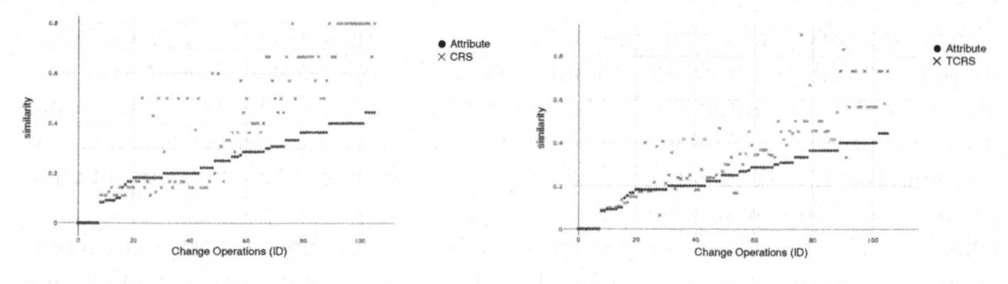

Fig. 5. Comparing CRS with the attribute similarity

Fig. 6. Comparing TCRS with the attribute similarity

soundness with respect to control and data flow has been tackled in [18], whereas correctness criteria for the behavorial soundness of change operations are provided and compared in [19]. An overview on how to define and apply change operations on business processes is provided in [6]. Other approaches have focused on the representation of change information based on change logs [8], change processes [1], and change trees [2]. Especially, change processes and change trees aim at presenting information on past change operations to users in order to support decisions on future changes, although no assessment of the similarity of change operation is provided. The most related approach is ProCycle [3] where change operations are augmented with CBR-based techniques such that users can comment on the reasons for conducting a change. Then the changes can be compared. The approach at hand is different as it does not rely on additional comments, but only considers information that is available based on the change operations themselves.

In contrast to change operation similarity, process equivalence and similarity have been analyzed frequently in current literature. [20] discusses label equivalence, attribute equivalence, position equivalence and regional equivalence for processes which execute web services. [21] uses behavioral profiles of processes to compare their similarity. Comparing these profiles leads to a behavior based matching of processes. [14] measures the similarity of two processes based on causal footprints, which consist of a set of look-back and look-ahead links. [4] defines three metrics for measuring the similarity between process models, namely (a) node matching similarity, (b) structural similarity and (c) behavioral similarity. [22] defines the difference between two process models by a difference model that is visualized based on a difference graph. Doing so, differences between models can be visually inspected. [5] proposes similarity metrics between process instances, taking into consideration different perspective as well.

7 Conclusion and Future Work

Process change operations are usually applied when the situation requires domain experts to do so. Being able to show which change operations have similar effects on a certain perspective can be interesting for the person in charge of the adaptation: When adapting therapy processes in a nursing home, using a resource perspective metric the nurse can see which therapy process fragments require similar resources. In conjunction with information about available resources for the upcoming weeks, such a clustering can facilitate the planning of process adaptations. When evaluating the effects of former process adaptations, comparison metrics can be used to create cluster of similar process change operations, thus improving analysis.

Effect metrics for other perspectives will be part of future work. Also comparing data structures based on change logs, e.g. change processes [1] and change trees [2] can be discussed based on the presented similarity metrics.

References

1. Günther, C.W., Rinderle, S., Reichert, M., van der Aalst, W.: Change mining in adaptive process management systems. In: Meersman, R., Tari, Z. (eds.) OTM 2006. LNCS, vol. 4275, pp. 309–326. Springer, Heidelberg (2006). doi:10.1007/11914853_19
2. Kaes, G., Rinderle-Ma, S.: Mining and querying process change information based on change trees. In: Barros, A., Grigori, D., Narendra, N.C., Dam, H.K. (eds.) ICSOC 2015. LNCS, vol. 9435, pp. 269–284. Springer, Heidelberg (2015). doi:10.1007/978-3-662-48616-0_17
3. Weber, B., Reichert, M., et al.: Providing integrated life cycle support in process-aware information systems. Int. J. Coop. Inf. Syst. **18**, 115–165 (2009)
4. Dijkman, R., Dumas, M., van Dongen, B., Krik, R., Mendling, J.: Similarity of business process models: metrics and evaluation. Inf. Syst. **36**, 498–516 (2011). Special Issue: Semantic Integration of Data, Multimedia, and Services
5. Pflug, J., Rinderle-Ma, S.: Process instance similarity: potentials, metrics, applications. In: Debruyne, C., et al. (eds.) OTM 2016. LNCS, vol. 10033. Springer, Cham (2016). doi:10.1007/978-3-319-48472-3_8
6. Reichert, M., Weber, B.: Enabling Flexibility in Process-Aware Information Systems - Challenges, Methods, Technologies. Springer, Heidelberg (2012)
7. Lanz, A., Reichert, M., Weber, B.: Process time patterns: a formal foundation. Inf. Syst. **57**, 38–68 (2016)
8. Rinderle, S., Reichert, M., Jurisch, M., Kreher, U.: On representing, purging, and utilizing change logs in process management systems. In: Dustdar, S., Fiadeiro, J.L., Sheth, A.P. (eds.) BPM 2006. LNCS, vol. 4102, pp. 241–256. Springer, Heidelberg (2006). doi:10.1007/11841760_17
9. Rinderle, S., Weber, B., Reichert, M., Wild, W.: Integrating process learning and process evolution – a semantics based approach. In: Aalst, W.M.P., Benatallah, B., Casati, F., Curbera, F. (eds.) BPM 2005. LNCS, vol. 3649, pp. 252–267. Springer, Heidelberg (2005). doi:10.1007/11538394_17
10. Hinge, K., Ghose, A., Koliadis, G.: Process SEER: a tool for semantic effect annotation of business process models. In: Enterprise Distributed Object Computing Conference, pp. 54–63 (2009)
11. Xu, H., Savarimuthu, B.T.R., Ghose, A., Morrison, E., Cao, Q., Shi, Y.: Automatic BDI plan recognition from process execution logs and effect logs. In: Cossentino, M., Fallah Seghrouchni, A., Winikoff, M. (eds.) EMAS 2013. LNCS, vol. 8245, pp. 274–291. Springer, Heidelberg (2013). doi:10.1007/978-3-642-45343-4_15

12. Rinderle-Ma, S., Reichert, M., Weber, B.: On the formal semantics of change patterns in process-aware information systems. In: Li, Q., Spaccapietra, S., Yu, E., Olivé, A. (eds.) ER 2008. LNCS, vol. 5231, pp. 279–293. Springer, Heidelberg (2008). doi:10.1007/978-3-540-87877-3_21
13. Russell, N., ter Hofstede, A.H.M., Edmond, D., van der Aalst, W.M.P.: Workflow data patterns: identification, representation and tool support. In: Delcambre, L., Kop, C., Mayr, H.C., Mylopoulos, J., Pastor, O. (eds.) ER 2005. LNCS, vol. 3716, pp. 353–368. Springer, Heidelberg (2005). doi:10.1007/11568322_23
14. Dongen, B., Dijkman, R., Mendling, J.: Measuring similarity between business process models. In: Bellahsène, Z., Léonard, M. (eds.) CAiSE 2008. LNCS, vol. 5074, pp. 450–464. Springer, Heidelberg (2008). doi:10.1007/978-3-540-69534-9_34
15. Becker, M., Laue, R.: A comparative survey of business process similarity measures. Comput. Ind. **63**, 148–167 (2012)
16. Levenshtein, V.I.: Binary codes capable of correcting deletions, insertions and reversals. Soviet physics doklady **10**, 707–710 (1966). (in Russian)
17. Kaes, G., Rinderle-Ma, S.: Generating data from highly flexible and individual process settings through a game-based experimentation service. In: Datenbanksysteme für Business, Technologie und Web, pp. 331–350 (2017)
18. Reichert, M., Dadam, P.: Adeptflex–supporting dynamic changes of workflows without losing control. J. Intell. Inf. Syst. **10**, 93–129 (2011)
19. Rinderle, S., Reichert, M., Dadam, P.: Correctness criteria for dynamic changes in workflow systems a survey. Data Knowl. Eng. **50**, 9–34 (2004)
20. Rinderle-Ma, S., Reichert, M., Jurisch, M.: On utilizing web service equivalence for supporting the composition life cycle. Int. J. Web Serv. Res. **8**, 41–67 (2011)
21. Kunze, M., Weidlich, M., Weske, M.: m3 - a behavioral similarity metric for business processes. In: Services und ihre Komposition (2011)
22. Kriglstein, S., Wallner, G., Rinderle-Ma, S.: A visualization approach for difference analysis of process models and instance traffic. In: Daniel, F., Wang, J., Weber, B. (eds.) BPM 2013. LNCS, vol. 8094, pp. 219–226. Springer, Heidelberg (2013). doi:10.1007/978-3-642-40176-3_18

Agile Transformation Success Factors: A Practitioner's Survey

Amadeu Silveira Campanelli[1](✉), Dairton Bassi[2], and Fernando Silva Parreiras[1]

[1] LAIS Laboratory for Advanced Information Systems, FUMEC University, Belo Horizonte, Brazil
amadeu@fumec.edu.br, fernando.parreiras@fumec.br
[2] Agile Trends, Sao Paulo, Brazil
dbassi@agiletrendsbr.com

Abstract. An agile transformation process presents challenges to organizations around the world. Research on agile success factors is not conclusive and there is still need for guidelines to help in the transformation process considering the organizational context. This research proposes a survey among practitioners to identify the difficulty to implement success factors in organizations to create a fertile environment for agile transformation. We conducted a survey with 457 practitioners resulting in 328 valid responses. The findings show that the success factors implementation difficulty rankings generated for all practitioners and for expert practitioners have a high correlation. According to expert practitioners, measurement model and changes in mindset of project managers are the hardest success factors to implement while incentives and motivation to adopt agile methods and management buy-in are the easiest to implement. The contribution of this research is a ranking organizations can use as a reference for their agile transformation processes.

Keywords: Agile transformation process · Success factors · Agile adoption challenges

1 Introduction

Organizations are searching for ways to achieve the defined business goals and overcome software development barriers. Agile methods are an option many organizations have chosen to try to reach success [1–4]. Agile methods adoption has been growing [4] and it creates the need to guide organizations through the transformation process [2,5,6]. Researches show that it is hard to adopt out of the box agile methods and that there no unique path to success [2,5–8].

During agile transformation processes (ATPs), organizations go through important changes that have deep impacts in multiple aspects: culture, hierarchy, management, environment and people [8,9]. Understanding the challenges or success factors for an agile transformation helps to prepare the organization and the people involved and increase chances of success. Agile transformation

E. Dubois and K. Pohl (Eds.): CAiSE 2017, LNCS 10253, pp. 364–379, 2017.
DOI: 10.1007/978-3-319-59536-8_23

projects that do not consider the challenges to be faced along the way do not bring positive results to the organization. It can also create rejection from the professionals involved in the ATP. Understanding the impacts of the changes in the organizational environment is an important step in the adoption process [9].

The literature is rich in agile success factors involved in an ATP [8,10–13] but there is still no direct guidelines of how to use these success factors in specific organizational contexts. The usage of success factors as a tool to help in the agile transformation initiatives can start with the awareness of how organizations and agile practitioners implement these success factors to create a fertile environment for ATPs and how hard this implementation can be.

This research intends to investigate the level of difficulty of agile success factors implementation according to practitioners point of view and to create a ranking that can be used as a reference for organizations in any stage of their ATPs. We proposed an assessment as a tool to provide awareness of the current status of agile success factors in the organization and the gaps to get to the target state defined by organization leadership. Thus, we used this assessment to conduct a survey to gather information from agile practitioners about success factor implementation in their organizations. Using the survey results as input, we applied the Rasch algorithm [14] to create a success factors implementation difficulty ranking identifying which are the hardest success factors to implement and which are the easiest ones.

The remainder of the paper is organized as follows. Section 2 provides the technical background on ATPs and success factors while Sect. 3 describes the methodology used in the research. The results of the survey and the findings are discussed in Sect. 4 and related work is summarized in Sect. 2.3. Section 5 outlines the conclusions and future work opportunities.

2 Background

This section reviews two key concepts: agile transformation process (ATP) and agile transformation success factors groups. It also provides a review of the related work found in the literature.

2.1 Agile Transformation Process (ATP)

Agile transformation process (ATP) is the process of transforming an organization into agile [15]. This process impacts all areas of the organizations. People are required to change their mindset and behavior [16,17], they need to modify the way they work as a team. Processes are affected and need to be adjusted, management style and attitudes are affected as well [15].

It is important that organizations understand the reach of the changes involved in ATP. It helps to create the awareness needed for this type of initiative, prepares the team for the upcoming challenges and increases the chances of achieving the proposed goals [10,15]. Further, organizations need to control effort and costs associated with ATP [18].

2.2 Agile Transformation Success Factors Groups

Agile transformation success factors have been studied by researchers to point paths to allow organizations to have control over their adoption process and to be able to deal with known barriers and challenges during the implementation [18].

Some researchers refer to the success factors as challenges for agile adoption (Nerur et al. [9], Conboy et al. [17] and Gregory et al. [11]) but it is basically a different view of the same factor. Success factors are the basis of the agile transformation success factors assessment since the evaluation occurs at the success factor level. During the assessment definition, we found a need for a higher level of evaluation to allow a consolidated management view of the success factors. This view is provided by the success factor groups defined in this section.

We identified multiple success factors in the literature and aggregated them according to their concepts into terms and then into a set of groups. There were multiple references to the same concepts in different articles and we used the terms we considered more representative of the concepts to aggregate all the references found. The six groups were proposed organizing the terms according to the areas of the company affected by them are summarized in Table 1: customer, management, organization, process, team and tools.

Customer Group. Customer involvement and relationship are cited by multiple researchers as a relevant factor in agile transformation [9,10,12,20]. Customers should participate of the projects in a regular basis, establish effective communication, be able to make decisions and provide feedback [9,12,19].

Management Group. Management plays an important role in the ATP supporting the team's empowerment and creating conditions for changes to take place [15,18]. Management support is a prerequisite for agile adoption [15,16] because people need to see their buy-in to feel involved, to give the expected importance to the adoption initiative and to understand that adjustments can be made to the organization and its structure to support the new proposed paradigms [10].

Organization Group. The organization is one of the main focuses of the ATP. Multiple deep changes happen at this level, covering aspects driving the professionals behavior in the company such as culture and values [9]. As software development is a knowledge based activity, learning and flexibility are important attributes for the organizations involved with ATPs.

Process Group. The process group covers the adequacy of the process to the organizational context. In ATPs, it is common to change the development process to adopt an iterative, incremental, secure, transparent and people focused process. However, it requires significant effort and a careful analysis to create a process that makes sense for the reality of the teams [9,17].

Table 1. Agile transformation success factors and groups proposed by the authors.

Group	Id	Success factor	References
Customer	SF01	Customer involvement	[10,12]
Management	SF02	Changes in management style and decentralized decision making	[10,11,13,18,19]
Management	SF03	Changes in mindset of project managers	[12,13]
Management	SF04	Management buy-in	[9,11,12,15,16,20]
Organization	SF05	Incentives and motivation to adopt agile methods	[15–17,20]
Organization	SF06	Agile champions	[15,16]
Organization	SF07	Business goals	[18]
Organization	SF08	Coaching and mentoring	[13,15,16,18,20]
Organization	SF09	Communication flow in the organization	[15]
Organization	SF10	Cultural changes	[9,11,16,19,20]
Organization	SF11	Knowledge sharing	[9–11]
Organization	SF12	New mindset and roles	[10–13,16,17,19,20]
Organization	SF13	Training	[13,15,16,20]
Process	SF14	Lightweight documentation	[11,13,19]
Process	SF15	Measurement model	[10,13,19]
Process	SF16	Process is compatible with the organizational context	[11–13]
Team	SF17	Technical activities and skills	[9,11–13,17,19]
Team	SF18	Ability to build trustworthy relationships	[11,13,19]
Team	SF19	Collaboration	[9,11,13,16,17,19,20]
Team	SF20	Distributed teams	[11,19]
Team	SF21	Self-organized teams	[13,17,20]
Team	SF22	Team involvement	[10–12,15,16,19,20]
Tools	SF23	Toolset	[9,13,19]

Team Group. Agile environments are all about people. It requires people to be involved and to participate in agile adoption since the beginning of the ATP [15]. People buy-in is a facilitator of the transformation process [10,16], involved people can help in the transformation and attract other people to be part of it [15].

Tools Group. Here we see an interesting conflict between agile values and reality. We understand that in a people-centric approach such as agile methods the individuals and interactions are highly valuable. However, in the practice, tools are important to allow teams to transition their work procedures in a more natural and productive fashion [9,13,19].

2.3 Related Work

Taylor et al. [10] proposed a minimally intrusive risk assessment to prepare small companies to adopt agile methods. The articles express concerns about the capability of small companies to survive to a failed agile adoption attempt and proposes the assessment to point directions if the organization should pursue the agile adoption or use a traditional approach for software development. This assessment can provide a direction on agile adoption per project basis. The authors used the agility/discipline assessment (ADA) developed by Boehm and Tuner [25] and they applied it to six organizations proposing adaptations to each of the contexts. The areas contemplated by the assessment were criticality, personnel, dynamism, culture, client involvement and team distribution.

Gandomani et al. [13] provided a comparison between traditional and agile software development methods and the challenges of transitioning to agile methods. They classify the challenges for agile transformation into four categories: organization and management; people; process; technology and tools. Their work also highlighted that the organization as whole is affected by this process. A strong message from their study is that all members should be involved to deal with such challenges.

Chow and Cao [12] investigated the critical success factors in agile methods adoption and proposed groups to classify critical success factors and created a model to validate how the critical success factors affects the quality, cost, scope and time of agile software development projects. The groups of factors were defined as organizational, people, process, technical and project. They conducted a survey to validate hypothesis for each of the success factors and analyzed the correlation between success factors and project success to establish critical success factors. The critical success factors according to their results are: delivery strategy, agile software engineering techniques and high qualified team.

3 Methodology

In order to reach the goals of this study, we planned the data collection and analysis starting with an assessment called “Agile Success Factors Assessment”. It was used as a questionnaire to gather data for this research. The second step was to apply the assessment as a survey to agile practitioners in an event named “Agile Trends” in the city of Belo Horizonte, Brazil on September 10th, 2016. After the event, we also published the questionnaire as a on-line survey form to be responded by agile practitioners. The third step was to apply the Rasch algorithm [14] to generate a success factors implementation difficulty ranking.

3.1 Agile Success Factors Assessment

The assessment was created using the proposed success factors and groups. We formulated phrases to represent each of the success factors and to allow their evaluation during the assessment. The main objective of the assessment is to be used as a tool to provide awareness of how the organization evaluates itself, defines its goals for the ATP and which should be the next steps in the process considering the feedback from people in the organization regarding their current state.

The assessment is composed by 23 phrases representing the success factors. The assessment has been previously tested by agile experts. In this research, the phrases were evaluated by the respondents to measure the level of implementation of that success factor for that organization.

3.2 Survey

We conducted a survey in an agile event in the city of Belo Horizonte, Brazil and we published an on-line version of the survey as well. The survey consisted of two parts. Part One was where respondents identified their years of work experience, years of agile-related experience and the position they hold in the company. The demographic questions did not identify any of the respondents or their organizations. Part Two was composed of the Agile Success Factors Assessment and two scales for the respondents to inform their current level of implementation of each success factor and their target or ideal level of implementation of the success factor based on their organizational context. The level of implementation was measured using a 5-point ordinal Likert scale. We received a total of 457 responses of which 329 questionnaires were considered valid to be analyzed.

Respondents Profile. The most common position of the respondents was "project manager". The second most common position for the respondents was "analyst" followed by "developer". Table 2 summarizes the distribution of positions among the respondents. Table 3 shows that 33.7% of the respondents declared to have 16 or more years of work experience. 250 respondents (76.0% of the total) have at least eight years of work experience. A high number of the respondents (41.6%) declared to have from one to four years of experience using agile methods and practices while 5.6% of the respondents have 11 years or more of this type of experience. 41.7% of the respondents have five or more years of experience with agile methods and practices as summarized in Table 4.

Data Analysis. Based on the success factors' current state and the target state gathered in the survey, we applied the Rasch algorithm [14] to generate the success factors implementation difficulty rankings. This approach has been used by Lahrmann et al. [14] to create maturity models in design science research. In this research, since the respondents came from different organizations, we used the median of their target state values for the success factors to create

Table 2. Distribution of the positions of the respondents.

Position	Percentage
Project manager	19.8%
Analyst	19.5%
Developer	18.5%
Consultant	14.9%
Other	13.1%
Scrum master	8.8%
Designer	2.7%
Tester	2.7%

Table 3. Distribution of the years of work experience of the respondents.

Years of work experience	Percentage
Less than 1 year	0.3%
From 1 to 4 years	5.8%
From 5 to 7 years	17.9%
From 8 to 10 years	22.2%
From 11 to 15 years	20.1%
16 or more years	33.7%

Table 4. Distribution of the years of experience of the respondents with agile methods and practices.

Years of agile methods experience	Percentage
Less than 1 year	16.7%
From 1 to 4 years	41.6%
From 5 to 7 years	25.8%
From 8 to 10 years	10.3%
11 or more years	5.6%

the desired results for the Rasch analysis. This was used in order to provide a consistent value across all the organizations evaluated as proposed by Lahrmann et al. [14].

4 Results

The intention of this research was to understand how agile practitioners perceive the level of difficulty of agile success factors implementation and create a ranking that can be used as a reference for organizations in any stage of their ATP.

After the initial analysis of the data gathered in the survey, we used the agile success factors assessment to calculate different success factors rankings based on four groups of respondents: all respondents (Group 1), respondents with eight or more years of work experience (Group 2), respondents with five or more years of agile methods experience (Group 3) and respondents with eight or more years of work experience and five or more years of agile methods experience (Group 4).

We used the data gathered segmented by group to generate a success factors implementation difficulty ranking for each of the groups. Group 1 was composed of all 329 respondents and Group 2 of 250 respondents. 137 respondents were part of Group 3 and 131 respondents composed Group 4. In this setup, one respondent could be part of all groups based on his profile information. The results for each group were compared to draw the conclusions. The intention of the groups analysis was to compare how groups ranked the success factors and check the impact of general work experience and agile methods experience on the rankings.

4.1 Group 1

We executed the Rasch algorithm using the Winsteps software [21] on the data collected for Group 1 to obtain the item calibration. The item calibration resulting of the Rasch algorithm classifies the success factors in the assessment according to their implementation difficulty. The hardest to implement success factors are at the top of the ranking. The ranking and the Rasch algorithm results for Group 1 are summarized in Table 5.

In order to validate the results from the Rasch algorithm, we used to the recommendations provided by Winsteps documentation [21] and the guidelines used by Lahrmann et al. [14]. The fit statistics values (Infit and Outfit) are around 1.00 satisfying the fit expectations and validating the results. All the execution and validation steps described for Group 1 were also used for the other groups.

Based on the results, the success factors that would be the hardest to implement are: training; measurement model; coaching and mentoring; changes in mindset of project managers and decentralized decision making; and new mindset and roles. Furthermore, the results point out the success factors that would be the easiest to implement: management buy-in; technical activities and skills; incentives and motivation to adopt agile methods; knowledge sharing; and team involvement.

4.2 Groups 2 and 3

The respondents with eight or more years of work experience composed Group 2 independently of their experience with agile methods and practices. These respondents are the ones with a considerable amount of work experience. Group 2's ranking shows that the easiest to implement success factors are: management buy-in; technical activities and skills; knowledge sharing; incentives and

Table 5. Success factors implementation difficulty ranking and Rasch algorithm results for Group 1.

Rank	Success factor	Logit	Error	Infit	Outfit
1	Training	0.77	0.07	1.11	1.11
2	Measurement model	0.72	0.07	0.93	0.9
3	Coaching and mentoring	0.64	0.07	0.84	0.86
4	Changes in mindset of project managers	0.44	0.06	0.95	0.97
5	New mindset and roles	0.42	0.06	0.58	0.57
6	Communication flow in the organization	0.32	0.06	0.76	0.78
7	Collaboration	0.23	0.06	1.00	1.04
8	Changes in management style and decentralized decision making	0.22	0.06	1.01	1.07
9	Lightweight documentation	0.17	0.06	1.42	1.64
10	Business goals	0.02	0.06	1.37	1.67
11	Distributed teams	0.01	0.06	0.92	0.89
12	Agile champions	0.00	0.06	0.99	1.05
13	Process is compatible with the organizational context	−0.01	0.06	0.99	1.02
14	Customer involvement	−0.02	0.06	1.29	1.34
15	Tool set	−0.06	0.06	0.93	0.90
16	Ability to build trustworthy relationships	−0.14	0.06	0.78	0.74
17	Cultural changes	−0.19	0.06	0.80	0.79
18	Self-organized teams	−0.22	0.06	0.92	0.86
19	Team involvement	−0.25	0.06	0.74	0.74
20	Knowledge sharing	−0.62	0.07	1.04	1.08
21	Incentives and motivation to adopt agile methods	−0.72	0.07	1.65	1.70
22	Technical activities and skills	−0.82	0.07	0.86	0.99
23	Management buy-in	−0.92	0.07	1.20	1.26

motivation to adopt agile methods; and self-organized teams. The success factors considered the hardest to implement by Group 2 were: measurement model; coaching and mentoring; training; new mindset and roles; and changes in mindset of project managers.

Group 3's respondents had five or more years of experience with agile methods and they were considered experienced practitioners. We did not consider their work experience in this analysis. The top five success factors (the hardest to implement) for this group were: measurement model; training; changes in mindset of project managers; coaching and mentoring; and new mindset and roles. The results for Group 3 presented the following success factors as the easiest to implement: incentives and motivation to adopt agile methods; management buy-in; technical activities and skills; knowledge sharing; and self-organized teams.

4.3 Group 4

Group 4 is a restrictive group being the intersection of groups 2 and 3. The 131 respondents part of this group (39.8% of the total) have work and agile methods experience to be considered experts practitioners in this study. The success factors implementation difficulty ranking for Group 4 is presented in Table 6.

The hardest to implement success factors for Group 4 are: measurement model; changes in mindset of project managers; training; coaching and mentoring; and new mindset and roles. At the bottom of Group 4's ranking, as the easiest to implement success factors we have: incentives and motivation to adopt agile methods; management buy-in; technical activities and skills; knowledge sharing; and self-organized teams. We considered Group 4's ranking as the one to be used as reference for organizations during their ATPs because it represents the view of the expert practitioners on the success factors implementation difficulty levels.

4.4 Correlation Between Rankings

After we obtained the groups' rankings, we proceeded to the correlation analysis in order to understand the correlation between the rankings of the different groups. We used the Spearman's rank correlation coefficient [22,23] to identify the correlation between the groups' rankings. The Spearman's rank correlation coefficient was calculated for all the rankings using the SPSS tool and the results are summarized in Table 7.

According to Butler [24], the critical or minimal correlation value to be accepted for the Spearman's coefficient considering the 23 observations (success factors) used in this research and applying a significance level of 0.01 in a two-tailed analysis is 0.532. All the correlation coefficients presented in Table 7 have values higher than the critical correlation value of 0.532 and they are also considered very strong correlations since the values are higher than 0.900 [22]. All the correlation coefficients were calculated considering a significance level of 0.01 that means there is a 1% chance that the relationship found happened by chance.

The strongest correlation is observed between groups 3 and 4 with a value of 0.994. This is explained by the respondents being almost the same. Group 3 has only 6 respondents that are not part of Group 4. The most relevant result in this correlation analysis is the correlation coefficient between groups 1 and 4. It represents a very high correlation level with a value of 0.957.

4.5 Discussion

In this section we will discuss the success factors found in the top 5 and bottom 5 positions of the rankings for groups 1 and 4. The correlation between these groups will also be examined. We are considering only these groups because

Table 6. Success factors implementation difficulty ranking and Rasch algorithm results for Group 4.

Rank	Success factor	Logit	Error	Infit	Outfit
1	Measurement model	0.78	0.11	1.00	0.99
2	Changes in mindset of project managers	0.56	0.11	0.93	1.06
3	Training	0.56	0.11	1.08	1.13
4	Coaching and mentoring	0.55	0.11	0.85	1.00
5	New mindset and roles	0.53	0.11	0.61	0.61
6	Collaboration	0.48	0.10	1.06	1.12
7	Communication flow in the organization	0.46	0.10	0.82	0.74
8	Lightweight documentation	0.19	0.10	1.35	1.52
9	Changes in management style and decentralized decision making	0.18	0.10	1.17	1.18
10	Customer involvement	0.07	0.10	1.28	1.32
11	Process is compatible with the organizational context	0.06	0.10	1.02	1.06
12	Agile champions	0.03	0.01	1.01	1.07
13	Distributed teams	−0.04	0.10	0.95	0.9
14	Ability to build trustworthy relationships	−0.05	0.10	0.68	0.67
15	Business goals	−0.06	0.10	1.30	1.65
16	Team involvement	−0.10	0.11	0.77	0.74
17	Tool set	−0.2	0.11	1.04	1.04
18	Cultural changes	−0.22	0.11	0.86	0.84
19	Self-organized teams	−0.32	0.11	0.87	0.79
20	Knowledge sharing	−0.72	0.11	1.02	1.07
21	Technical activities and skills	−0.82	0.12	0.86	0.85
22	Management buy-in	−0.91	0.12	1.16	1.08
23	Incentives and motivation to adopt agile methods	−1.03	0.12	1.64	1.61

Table 7. Spearman's rank correlation coefficient results for the groups of respondents with significance at the 0.01 level.

	Group 1	Group 2	Group 3	Group 4
Group 1	-	0.976	0.966	0.957
Group 2	0.976	-	0.980	0.974
Group 3	0.966	0.980	-	0.994
Group 4	0.957	0.974	0.994	-

they reflect the general sample of all respondents (Group 1) and the expert practitioners (Group 4).

Among the top 5 of the rankings we have the hardest to implement success factors (see Tables 5 and 6). Training is ranked 1st for Group 1 and 3rd for Group 4. Gandomani et al. [16] shows that lack of training is a challenge for ATPs and that training can be used to correct wrong mindsets. Chan and Thong [20] state that training can improve the person's learning about agile methods and impact the knowledge transfer to the practice. Training implementation can a challenge in organizations when you consider tight budgets, small teams and the team's work load.

As the hardest to implement success factor for Group 4 and ranked 3rd for Group 1, measurement model is a challenge in ATPs [13,19]. The lack of measurement practices can represent a limitation for the organization to understand the progress of the initiative and it will not allow comparison with the previous state of the organization. Coaching and mentoring ranked 4th in both rankings. ATPs involve multiple human factors and the people are the center of these processes [13,16]. That makes the coach role an important role in the ATP. The coach should be involved in the planning phase to provide awareness of the risks involved [15]. The challenge in using coaches is related to economic constraints and also to the acceptance of the coach by the teams.

Changes in mindset of project managers ranked 4th for Group 1 and 2nd for Group 4. The role of project manager needs to change from planner and controller to facilitator [13]. This is a considerable challenge for the formal project managers used to traditional software development and project management approaches. Their role should shift to the role of the team's facilitator of the collaboration, creativity and groups decisions.

New mindset and roles ranked 4th for Group 1 and 2nd for Group 4. ATPs require not only cultural changes but operational and technical changes that at the end will demand a change in the way people think [11]. Culture and mindset are hardest aspects to be changed in an ATP [19]. The acceptance of a new mindset and a new set of roles involves the participation of all levels of the organization to engage people in the ATP, to provide awareness and knowledge about agile methods, to create a secure environment and to encourage people to embrace the new way of thinking and working. At the bottom of the rankings we have six success factors among groups 1 and 4: management buy-in; team involvement; knowledge sharing; incentives and motivation to adopt agile methods; technical activities and skills; self-organized teams (see Tables 5 and 6).

Management buy-in is one of the most cited success factors in the literature [9,11,12,15,16,20]. Management buy-in is important to the ATP since it provides access to resources (budget, time, people, reach within the organization) and it shows to all people involved in the ATP that this is an important initiative. Team involvement was also considerate an easy to implement success factor. This shows that the respondents considered the team involvement an easy to implement success factor or that this success factor is already implemented in their organizations. That can be based in the perception the practitioners have of the benefits of agile adoption such as increased team motivation and increased team productivity [4].

Knowledge sharing is a practice already adopted by multiple companies and not exclusive of agile methods. This could explain why it is considered an easy to implement success factor. There is also the fact that knowledge sharing is a practice valued by software organizations or departments considering the high levels of complexity of existing applications and the technologies used to build these applications. Incentives and motivation to adopt agile methods play an important role engaging people in ATPs [15–17,20]. If the organization is able to provide the correct level of incentives to the people that needs to participate in ATPs, it can increase the chances of getting motivated teams and of achieving the established goals.

The investment in technical skills and activities is considered a common task for technology related professionals. These professionals are always learning new technologies and researching new ways of doing their work because of the constant evolution of the technologies available in the market. Self-organized teams ranked as an easy to implement success factor intrigued us. Self-organized teams are related to decision making, learning new skills as the person plays different roles and freedom to operate as the team wishes to get to their goals done [13,17,20]. We would need further investigation of this success factor to make sure respondents understood this concept and what it means for them in their organizations.

The correlation values between all groups are higher than 0.900 which is considered very high [22]. It is interesting to notice that even the correlation between the most divergent groups in terms of respondents profile (Groups 1 and 4) is very high. This indicates that success factors with a high rank for Group 1 would also have a high rank for Group 4 and vice-versa. The correlation between groups 1 and 4 also shows that the understanding of agile success factors among practitioners varies based on their experiences and the positions of the success factors between groups' rankings varies based on experience as well but both groups of practitioners have similar success factors as challenging to implement and consider other similar success factors easy to implement.

The assessment proposed by Taylor et al. [10] has similarities to our work: it is used to evaluate the risks of agile adoption, the goal is to involve the team members in the discussion around agile adoption and it requires a minimum overhead. Their work focuses on the choice between agile and traditional approaches at the project level while our work is focused on the preparation for an ATP and guidance for the agile success factors implementation at the organization level. Their assessment considers different aspects from the ones considered in our assessment. Our research also generated a success factors implementation difficulty ranking to be used by organizations in their ATPs.

The work of Gandomani et al. [13] work is similar to ours up to the point of the proposed success factors groups. The groups are similar between the two researches but we have aggregated terms from different references. However, their work stops at this point while, in our research, the success factors groups are used as basis for the agile transformation success factors assessment definition. We understand that our research has a practice oriented goal with the usage of the assessment and the generation of the success factors implementation difficulty ranking to serve as a road map for the ATP. Chow and Cao's work [12] has similarities with this research on the usage of the success factors groups approach, on the survey to gather data for the research and on the usage of statistical methods to analyze the data gathered. The differences are that they proposed a model to associate success factors to software development projects aspects while we used a success factor assessment and proposed the success factors implementation difficulty ranking targeting the organization as a whole and not a specific project.

The limitation of this research is that the data might not be a generalized random sample of agile practitioners. The sample population of this research might not be representative of the agile practitioners' community in general. The survey gathered anonymous data preventing data validation. The idea of the success factors implementation difficulty ranking is to represent the findings for the analyzed sample population of expert practitioners. However, we are aware that the organizational context and the people involved in the process make it rather unique and our findings can be used as a reference but might not be applicable to all cases.

5 Conclusions

In this study, we used an agile transformation success factors assessment to gather data about agile success factor implementation difficulty in a survey among agile practitioners. The analysis of the data was done using four groups of respondents: all respondents (Group 1), respondents with eight or more years of work experience (Group 2), respondents with five or more years of agile methods experience (Group 3) and respondents with eight or more years of work experience and five or more years of agile methods experience (Group 4). Group 4 was considered the group of expert practitioners. The results generated a success factors implementation difficulty ranking for each group showing which are the hardest and easiest success factors to be implemented by organizations.

The rankings presented in this study list the success factors according to the difficulty to implement them in the organization considering its context (culture, reality, goals, hierarchy). For the group of expert practitioners, the hardest to implement success factors were: measurement model; changes in mindset of project managers; training; coaching and mentoring; and new mindset and roles. Meanwhile, the easiest to implement success factors were: incentives and motivation to adopt agile methods; management buy-in; technical activities and skills; knowledge sharing; and self-organized teams.

The correlation coefficient between the rankings also showed very high correlation among all the rankings. This means that success factors with a high rank for one rankings would also have a high rank for another ranking and vice-versa.

This is an indication that both expert practitioners and non-experienced practitioners face similar challenges when implementing the success factors with some variation according the their organizational context.

The contributions of this research are the success factors implementation difficulty ranking and the correlation between the rankings. The ranking can be used as a tool to help organizations to understand the current state of agile success factors in the organization based on their team members view and to prepare for the agile transformation process. The correlation findings can be used to provide a further view of how expert and non-experienced practitioners look at the challenges in ATPs. Future work would involve using the success factors implementation difficulty ranking and the agile transformation success factors assessment in organizations to provide a diagnostic of their current state regarding success factors and use it as an input for the ATP.

Acknowledgement. This work is partially funded by the following Brazilian funding agencies: FAPEMIG, CAPES and CNPq.

References

1. Jyothi, V.E., Rao, K.N.: Effective implementation of agile practices ingenious and organized theoretical framework. IJACSA - Int. J. Adv. Comput. Sci. Appl. **2**(3), 41–48 (2011)
2. Ayed, H., Habra, N., Vanderose, B.: Am-quick: a measurement-based framework for agile methods customisation. In: 2013 Joint Conference of the 23rd International Workshop on Software Measurement and the 2013 Eighth International Conference on Software Process and Product Measurement (IWSM-MENSURA), pp. 71–80. IEEE (2013)
3. Nishijima, R.T., Santos, J.G.D.: The challenge of implementing scrum agile methodology in a traditional development environment. Int. J. Comput. Technol. **5**(2), 98–108 (2013)
4. VersionOne. 10th annual state of agile development survey (2015). http://stateofagile.versionone.com. Accessed 05 Oct 2015
5. Soundararajan, S., Balci, O., Arthur, J.D.: Assessing an organization's capability to effectively implement its selected agile method(s): an objectives, principles, strategies approach. In: 2013 Agile Conference, AGILE 2013, Nashville, TN, USA, 5–9 August 2013, pp. 22–31 (2013)
6. Gandomani, T.J., Nafchi, M.Z.: An empirically-developed framework for agile transition and adoption. J. Syst. Softw. **107**(C), 204–219 (2015)
7. Campanelli, A.S., Parreiras, F.S.: Agile methods tailoring a systematic literature review. J. Syst. Softw. **110**, 85–100 (2015)
8. Gregory, P., Barroca, L., Sharp, H., Deshpande, A., Taylor, K.: The challenges that challenge: engaging with agile practitioners' concerns. Inf. Softw. Technol. **77**, 92–104 (2016)
9. Nerur, S.P., Mahapatra, R.K., Mangalaraj, G.: Challenges of migrating to agile methodologies. Commun. ACM **48**(5), 72–78 (2005)
10. Taylor, P.S., Greer, D., Coleman, G., McDaid, K., Keenan, F.: Preparing small software companies for tailored agile method adoption: minimally intrusive risk assessment. Softw. Process: Improv. Pract. **13**(5), 421–437 (2008)

11. Gregory, P., Barroca, L., Taylor, K., Salah, D., Sharp, H.: Agile challenges in practice: a thematic analysis. In: Lassenius, C., Dingsøyr, T., Paasivaara, M. (eds.) XP 2015. LNBIP, vol. 212, pp. 64–80. Springer, Cham (2015). doi:10.1007/978-3-319-18612-2_6
12. Chow, T., Cao, D.-B.: A survey study of critical success factors in agile software projects. J. Syst. Softw. **81**(6), 961–971 (2008)
13. Gandomani, T.J., Zulzalil, H., Ghani, A.A.A., Sultan, A.B.M., Nafchi, M.Z.: Obstacles in moving to agile software development methods; at a glance. J. Comput. Sci. **9**(5), 620 (2013)
14. Lahrmann, G., Marx, F., Mettler, T., Winter, R., Wortmann, F.: Inductive design of maturity models: applying the rasch algorithm for design science research. In: Jain, H., Sinha, A.P., Vitharana, P. (eds.) DESRIST 2011. LNCS, vol. 6629, pp. 176–191. Springer, Heidelberg (2011). doi:10.1007/978-3-642-20633-7_13
15. Gandomani, T.J., Zulzalil, H., Ghani, A.A.A., Sultan, A.B.M., Shairf, K.Y.: Exploring facilitators of transition and adoption to agile methods: a grounded theory study. J. Soft. **9**(7), 1666–1678 (2014)
16. Gandomani, T.J., Zulzalil, H., Ghani, A.A.A., Sultan, A.B.M., Sharif, K.Y.: How human aspects impress agile software development transition, adoption. Int. J. Softw. Eng. Appl. **8**(1), 129–148 (2014)
17. Conboy, K., Coyle, S., Wang, X., Pikkarainen, M.: People over process: key challenges in agile development. IEEE Softw. **28**(4), 48–57 (2011)
18. Gandomani, T.J., Zulzalil, H., Ghani, A.A.A., Md. Sultan, A.B., Sharif, K.Y.: An exploratory study on managing agile transition and adoption. In: Boonkrong, S., Unger, H., Meesad, P. (eds.) Recent Advances in Information and Communication Technology. AISC, vol. 265, pp. 177–188. Springer, Cham (2014). doi:10.1007/978-3-319-06538-0_18
19. Hamid, S.S., Nasir, M.H.N.M., Othman, M.K., Ahmadi, R.: Factors limiting the implementations of agile practices in the software industry: a pilot systematic review. Indian J Sci. Technol. **8**(30) (2015). http://www.indjst.org/index.php/indjst/article/view/87111
20. Chan, F.K.Y., Thong, J.Y.L.: Acceptance of agile methodologies: a critical review and conceptual framework. Decis. Support Syst. **46**(4), 803–814 (2009)
21. Linacre, J.M.: Winsteps rasch measurement computer program 2016. http://www.winsteps.com. Accessed 20 July 2016
22. Zar, J.H.: Significance testing of the spearman rank correlation coefficient. J. Am. Stat. Assoc. **67**(339), 578–580 (1972)
23. Hauke, J., Kossowski, T.: Comparison of values of Pearson's and Spearman's correlation coefficients on the same sets of data. Quaestiones Geogr. **30**(2), 87–93 (2011)
24. Butler, C.: Statistics in Linguistics. B. Blackwell (1985). https://books.google.com/books?id=zZFlQgAACAAJ. ISBN 9780631142652, ICCN 85003885
25. Boehm, B., Turner, R.: Using risk to balance agile and plan-driven methods. Computer **36**(6), 57–66 (2003)

Crossing the Boundaries – Agile Methods in Large-Scale, Plan-Driven Organizations: A Case Study from the Financial Services Industry

Sina Katharina Weiss and Philipp Brune(✉)

Neu-Ulm University of Applied Sciences, Wileystraße 1, 89231 Neu-Ulm, Germany
sweiss@kpmg.com, Philipp.Brune@hs-neu-ulm.de

Abstract. Selecting the software development methodology best-suited for a project or organization is a fundamental decision in the context of Information Systems (IS) engineering. In many industries and organizations, agile software development models are already well-established and commonly used for this purpose. However, large-scale, plan-driven organizations face additional challenges when implementing agile methods. To analyze how such organizations could make the implementation more effective, the results of a qualitative case study performed in a large-scale financial institution are presented in this paper. Based on these results, a best-practice model for their effective implementation in a complex environment is proposed. An organization-specific agile development framework and continuous stakeholder involvement are identified as crucial success factors. In addition, a successful implementation of agile methods in practice needs to be performed by dedicated individuals and cross-functional teams should be established in order to support a common understanding across organizational boundaries.

Keywords: Agile methods · Software development · IS engineering · Large organizations · Organizational change

1 Introduction

Traditional sequential software development methods very often do not provide the necessary flexibility for todays fast changing business environment. Therefore, in the last decade the more light-weight agile methods established as a better suited alternative in many companies and industries, which helped to shorten development cycles and reduce the time-to-market of new software [24].

Consequently, in recent years the application domain of agile methods has extended from the original small and co-located teams to a wider range of organizational settings [48]. This extension also received considerable attention by researchers discussing the general applicability of agile methods in various settings. Several studies indicated the suitability of agile methods also for plan-driven and large-scale organizations [9,26], large and distributed teams [38,46] as well as strongly regulated environments [16].

E. Dubois and K. Pohl (Eds.): CAiSE 2017, LNCS 10253, pp. 380–393, 2017.
DOI: 10.1007/978-3-319-59536-8_24

Their findings suggest that especially the implementation of agile methods in large-scale, plan-driven environments comes with additional challenges and constraints [32]. In particular, agile practices need to be integrated into the existing process environment and comply with various internal and external regulations [5,16,27]. Therefore, the use of a tailored agile development framework and the creation of a common understanding across stakeholders have been suggested to be crucial success factors in this context [32,36].

However, the perception of such a tailored agile framework within a plan-driven organization and the creation of awareness and understanding with respect to it have not been studied so far. Therefore, in this paper results of a qualitative study are presented, which evaluates the role of an agile development framework within in a large-scale, plan-driven financial institution and its perception by the relevant stakeholders. I.e., the interface between agile development teams and plan-driven release management und IT operations is found to be critical and challenging. In particular, it is analyzed how organizational boundaries between the stakeholders should be designed to implement such a framework effectively across all relevant organizational functions.

The rest of this paper is organized as follows: In Sect. 2 the related work from the research literature is discussed in detail, followed by the research design of the study in Sect. 3. Section 4 describes the used qualitative data collection and analysis procedure. In Sect. 5 the proposed resulting agile implementation model is presented. The limitations of the study and an outlook to further research are illustrated in Sect. 6. We conclude with a summary of our findings.

2 Related Work

Over the last decades, various software development processes have been proposed by researchers and practitioners. First, sequential, plan-driven models such as the Waterfall model [40] became popular, where each phase of the development process needs to be completed before the next one starts, resulting in a strictly sequential order of the development activities. However, this approach fails to accomodate late changes of requirements during development, which frequently occur in todays business environment [19,22].

Driven by the need for adaptability to changing requirements, first iterative models like the Spiral model [8] were proposed, followed by evolutionary or agile methods such as Extreme Programming [6] and Scrum [42,43]. Although these agile methods have become very popular, traditional plan-driven methods are not obsolete as every method can be effective and useful depending on the project characteristics and its environment [30].

Therefore, especially in large-scale organizations it cannot be expected that all teams and projects make the transition to agile methods, which can hinder the work of agile teams [2,12,32]. Consequently, it has been found that large-scale organizations are confronted with additional challenges as they need to integrate the agile practices into their existing, complex processual and organizational environment [5,27,28].

In order to be successful, it is therefore highly important to focus on the interfaces between agile development teams and their environment and to tailor agile practices to the specific organizational requirements [5,27]. In the course of this, not only the practices of the agile teams need to be adjusted. It is also important to focus on the practices of other organizational functions as agile teams rely on them and do not work isolated [32,37]. A study by van Waardenburg and van Vliet states that the adjustment of the practices on both sides is especially important in a plan-driven environment in order to successfully implement agility. However, the study also provides evidence that the adjustments made on the agile team level should not be exaggerated, as this might lead to the loss of benefits intended to achieve by agile methods [32].

In order to achieve the continuous tailoring and improvement on both sides, especially communication is crucial [36]. Consequently, it is beneficial to plan and execute specific procedures in order to tailor agile practices to suit an organization's individual requirements. One example is the definition of clear feedback channels that provide the organization with valid information [4,37]. This approach might result in an organization-specific agile process model, which is claimed as being effective in providing guidance for agile teams [36,37].

Besides tailoring and integration on the project and organizational side, research has shown that awareness and common understanding of agile practices is essential during their implementation [4,32]. Education, training and coaching have proven to be suitable approaches in order to achieve a common ground [4,9,45]. Especially coaching of affected stakeholders should not be underestimated and be available right from the beginning of the implementation [45]. Without coaching and clear guidance, the implementation likely fails or only small plan-oriented projects just labeled "agile" are performed. Besides the actual development teams' also organizational stakeholders, such as the business side and other still plan-driven functions (like i.e. the IT operations department) should be involved when creating awareness and understanding of agile methods. If they are left out, they likely will not get actively involved in the agile process and their mindset remains traditional, which increases barriers and tension between them and the agile teams [32].

Although the current body of knowledge provides guidance for the complex process of implementing agile methods in large-scale and plan-driven environments, recommendations are rather general and isolated [9]. Correspondingly, van Waardenburg suggests that "[a] more systematic and in-depth study of the role of boundary spanning activities and artifacts could help to better align the simultaneous use of plan-driven and agile methods." [32].

Furthermore, although in general an organization-specific tailored agile development framework has been suggested as being beneficial [36], it has not investigated how the role of such a framework is perceived in organizations and how its implementation can be done effectively. In order to overcome this gap, in this paper the following research questions are addressed:

- RQ1: Is an agile development framework beneficial for the successful implementation of agile methods within a division of a large-scale, plan-driven organization?
- RQ2: How need organizational boundaries be designed when implementing an agile development framework within a division of a large-scale, plan-driven organization?

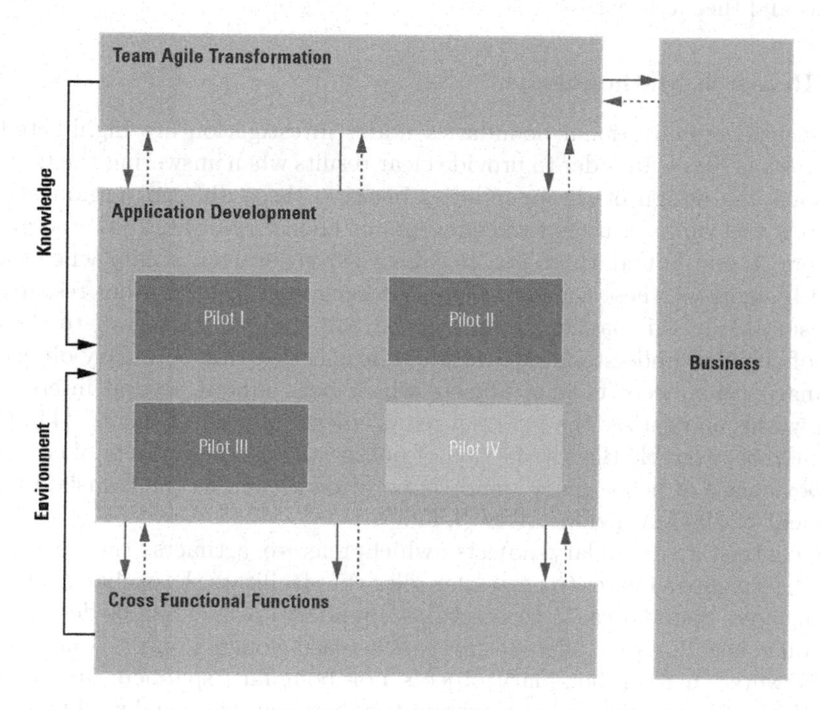

Fig. 1. Model of the unit of analysis illustrating the project context of the case study performed.

3 Research Design

3.1 Project Context

In order to collect the relevant data for the qualitative analysis, a case study was performed within a division of a large-scale financial institution currently implementing an agile development framework. The division can be characterized as a forerunner regarding agile development within this organization and therefore is embedded in a generally plan-driven environment.

The agile methodology used is based on Scrum [42], mainly because it defines clear roles and responsibilities. It is tailored to support all relevant internal and external policies in order to ensure legal and regulatory compliance. The tailored methodology was designed by a dedicated team formed for this particular purpose, including members of various functions as i.e. quality management, test management and release management. After its initial design the first version of the framework was piloted in several development teams from February 2016 onwards, before becoming mandatory for all development teams within the division in May 2016.

This project context is illustrated schematically in Fig. 1 by the model of the unit of analysis [7], including all relevant stakeholders for the implementation process and their relation.

3.2 Research Methodology

The relevant organizational boundaries under investigation are highlighted by the arrows in Fig. 1. In order to provide clear results when answering the research questions, the design of the boundaries between these different organizational functions was viewed through the concepts of boundary objects [44], boundary spanners [1] and boundary events. Besides their general suitability when focusing on boundaries, these concepts have also been identified by other researchers to be suitable in this particular context [32,33,35,38]. With regard to the creation of common understanding Star and Giesmer describe boundary objects as an "analytical concept of [...] objects which both inhibit several intersecting social worlds and satisfy the informal requirements of each of them." [44]. Consequently, they enable the satisfaction of potentially conflicting sets of concerns, the coexistence of heterogeneity and cooperation as well as the translation and alignment of different perspectives [3,44].

In contrast to boundary objects, which refer to artifacts, the concept of boundary spanners relates to particular roles that facilitate the exchange of information across boundaries [1]. In general, a boundary spanner can be described as a person connecting two different groups whereas belonging only to one of them [20]. However, neither boundary objects nor boundary spanners are effective through their mere existence at the boundary between two social worlds. Rather they have to be actively integrated. Therefore, Levina and Vaast introduced the concepts of boundary objects-in-use and boundary spanners-in-practice [26].

Beyond the concepts of boundary objects and boundary spanners, the terms boundary spanning actions [29] and boundary spanning activities can be found in current literature on the topic of boundary crossing [33,41]. Yet, they are in general attributed to a particular boundary spanning role, for example in form of the active coordination of task performance with other groups or the linking of information [29,47]. Therefore, the following study will introduce a variation of the concepts in the form of boundary events in order to also clearly cover installed training activities provided independently from one particular initiator. Such a variation is especially important in the context at hand considering the importance of training and coaching.

The two boundaries explicitly not under investigation within the unit of analysis were the boundaries between the development teams itself as well as the boundary between the IT and the business function. First, one reason for this is that the pilot projects within the division are relatively independent from other projects, which made the inter-team boundaries irrelevant. Second, the boundary between the IT and business function has already been extensively investigated by other researchers applying the chosen concepts [39]. Here, agile methods and especially the related practices of the business requirements being communicated through user stories and the prioritization of these in the product backlog were identified to support the coordination of the two social worlds and enable the creation of a common understanding [34,39].

For the qualitative analysis, the Grounded Theory Methodology (GTM) as introduced by Glaser and Strauss in 1967 was chosen [21]. Its main idea is to discover new theory based on the insights gained rather than verifying existing theory [21]. The approach is especially valuable in areas where theoretical explanation is limited [18,32], as it is the case regarding the questions addressed by the study at hand.

4 Data Collection and Analysis

Referring to the concept of theoretical sampling in the GTM [13,21], the participants were not defined prior to the start of the investigation. Instead the interview partners were selected based on information gathered during the iterations of the research process resulting in twelve interviews across all relevant groups. Table 1 shows a list of all interview partners which finally took part in the qualitative empirical study.

In line with the iterative procedure of the GTM, a specific guide for the semi-structured interviews was developed for each iteration based on the questions emerged during previous interviews. All four interview guides covered the following content:

- General information: Personal information and his or her experience with agility,
- Organization-specific agile development framework: Knowledge about its development, personal involvement in the development process, assessment of the framework and its necessity,
- Transformation process: Individual perception and assessment in general, knowledge about and assessment of specific concepts in place to support the implementation process, main facilitator for the transformation.

In addition, the agile development teams were asked about the most critical boundaries within the plan-driven organization, the concepts in place to cross these and their effectiveness. The interviewees of the cross-functional functions were asked if and/or how their processes have been adapted to suit the new agile development practice and also about the concepts and their effectiveness.

Due to the limited availability of the participants, the interviews lasted between 12 and 35 min. However, usable information was able be obtained. Each interview was immediately transcribed and analyzed. As a starting point for open coding the concepts of boundary objects, boundary spanners and boundary events were assigned to the text. However, the majority of concepts were derived from the interviews themselves, which is preferred when applying the GTM as it relates closer to the actual data [18]. After coding was performed on all data [14,17,18], in total a list of 534 codes was obtained.

After the recombination of the codes during axial coding [14,18], the influences and effects governing the implemenation of the agile development framework could be derived from the data. The resulting interconnections model is illustrated in Fig. 2.

Table 1. List of interview partners participating in the qualitative study.

Iteration		Role/ Responsibility	Corporate Membership
Iteration I	Agile 1	Coordinator Agile Transformation	since 2016
	Agile 2	Lead Framework Development	since 1997
	Agile 3	Coordinator Agile Transformation	since 1996
Iteration II	Dev 1	Scrum Master	since 2012
	Dev 2	Scrum Master	since 2016
	Dev 3	Functional Analyst	since 2001
	Dev 4	Product Owner (IT)	since 2002
Iteration III	CrossFunc 1	Release Manager	since 2015
	CrossFunc 2	Lead Production Services	since 1998
	CrossFunc 3	Test Manager/Tester	since 2013
Iteration IV	Business 1	Product Owner (Business)	since 1999
	Business 2	Product Owner (Business)	since 1997

In agreement with the literature [5,9,31], the main initial motivation to implement agile development methods was found to be the ability to react fast and flexibly to changing market requirements. However, as every development team performed agile development initially to the best of their knowledge, they were not conform with given processes and policies leading to many impediments and negative responses within the organization. Driven by that, an adapted agile development framework compliant with the corporate standards was designed, legitimizing agile practices and providing a certain degree of consistency. The design of the framework was mainly influenced by internal and external regulations, which are especially important for financial institutions. Therefore, the necessity of a division-specific agile development framework was perceived as given by all interviewees.

In line with this, Pikkarainen et al. state that companies should develop an agile development process model parallel to its implementation [36]. However, a comprehensive framework is seen as result of the pilots' experiences rather than as a starting point for the implementation of agile methods [25,36,37]. This is supported by the study at hand, as the high complexity of the framework and its adaption to original Scrum practices were perceived in a negative way by the interviewees.

Therefore, it is recommended that an agile development framework is designed in parallel to the beginning of agile methods' uasge, with its initial scope and complexity being low and as close as possible to pre-defined agile practices. Similarly this is recommended by Boehm and Turner, as they claim that it is more effective to "[b]uild up processes rather than tailoring them down." [9]. The resulting design builds the basis for feedback and consequently for building up the framework along with its implementation based on daily experiences.

Furthermore, it was stated that it is preferred that the framework presents a guideline rather than a set of strict rules. Such an approach is supported by previous findings, as for example Pikkarainen et al. state that teams should receive enough freedom to adapt agile methods to their specific needs as the full mandatory appliance of a model could cause increased resistance. This practice leads to the emergence of two learning cycles. One on the project and one on the organizational level with the latter being influenced by the feedback of the first [36].

Nevertheless, the negative assessment of the deviation from Scrum must be viewed critically as the implementation of hybrid approaches [5,49] or at least of tailored approaches [9,27] is an established standard, which the affected groups should be made aware of.

5 Resulting Implementation Model

To describe how an agile development framework could be embedded within a large-scale, plan-driven organization, the implementation model illustrated in Fig. 3 can be used. This model uses the concepts of boundary objects [44], boundary spanners [1] and boundary events.

Overall, 49 concepts were named at the relevant boundaries under investigation. However, as not only their mere existence at the boundaries between different social worlds leads to the effective creation of awareness and common understanding, it is important to take their usage into account [26].

In total, 17 boundary objects were identified, of which a detailed overview of the agile development framework in terms of roles, responsibilities, activities as well as deliverables was identified as the most effective boundary object-in-use. It is used to retrieve ideas from it or in order to review and verify the own practices. Furthermore, it served as the main foundation for feedback, with personal communication being the preferred channel. In comparison to this, a high-level overview of the framework which was also offered was rarely used.

Furthermore, 17 boundary spanners were identified at the boundaries under investigation. These are considered highly effective with regard to the creation of awareness and common understanding and therefore the effective implementation of the framework.

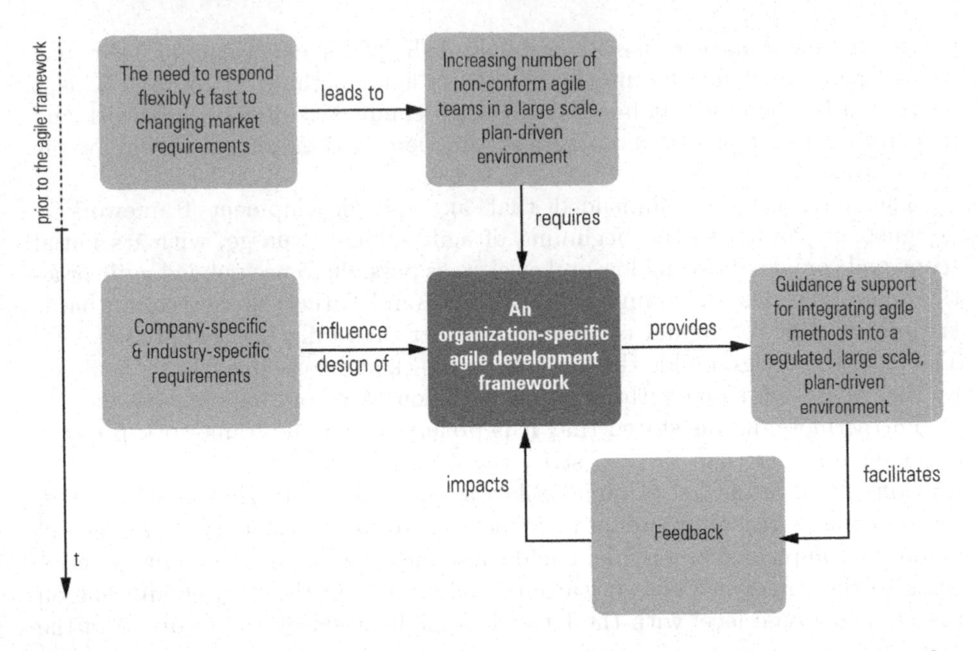

Fig. 2. Interconnections model describing the influences and effects governing the implemenation of the agile development framework as obtained from the empirical data.

Levina and Vaast in addition found that boundary objects rely on boundary spanners in-practice to be effective with regard to the crossing of boundaries [26]. The study at hand supports this, as the effectiveness of boundary crossing with respect to the framework is mainly facilitated by active roles applying, assessing and gathering feedback on it.

In the present study, the boundary spanners at the boundary between the team designing the framework and the development teams can be identified as being the Scrum Master and Product Owner as well as the core team members of the team that is designing the framework. The boundary spanning roles of the Scrum Master and Product Owner have also been identified in previous studies, but rather in the context of bridging the boundary between the business function and the development teams [39]. This is supported by the study at hand as the two roles were additionally identified as boundary spanners at the boundary to the business function and in addition at the boundary to other relevant organizational functions.

Although boundary spanners are identified as being effective with regard to the creation of common understanding, the integration of environmental roles into the actual development teams was claimed to even increase their general effectiveness. The integration of roles is in addition capable of solving the issue of the business side being a separate line organization and therefore difficult to reach with specific boundary crossing activities, as it is the case in this case study context.

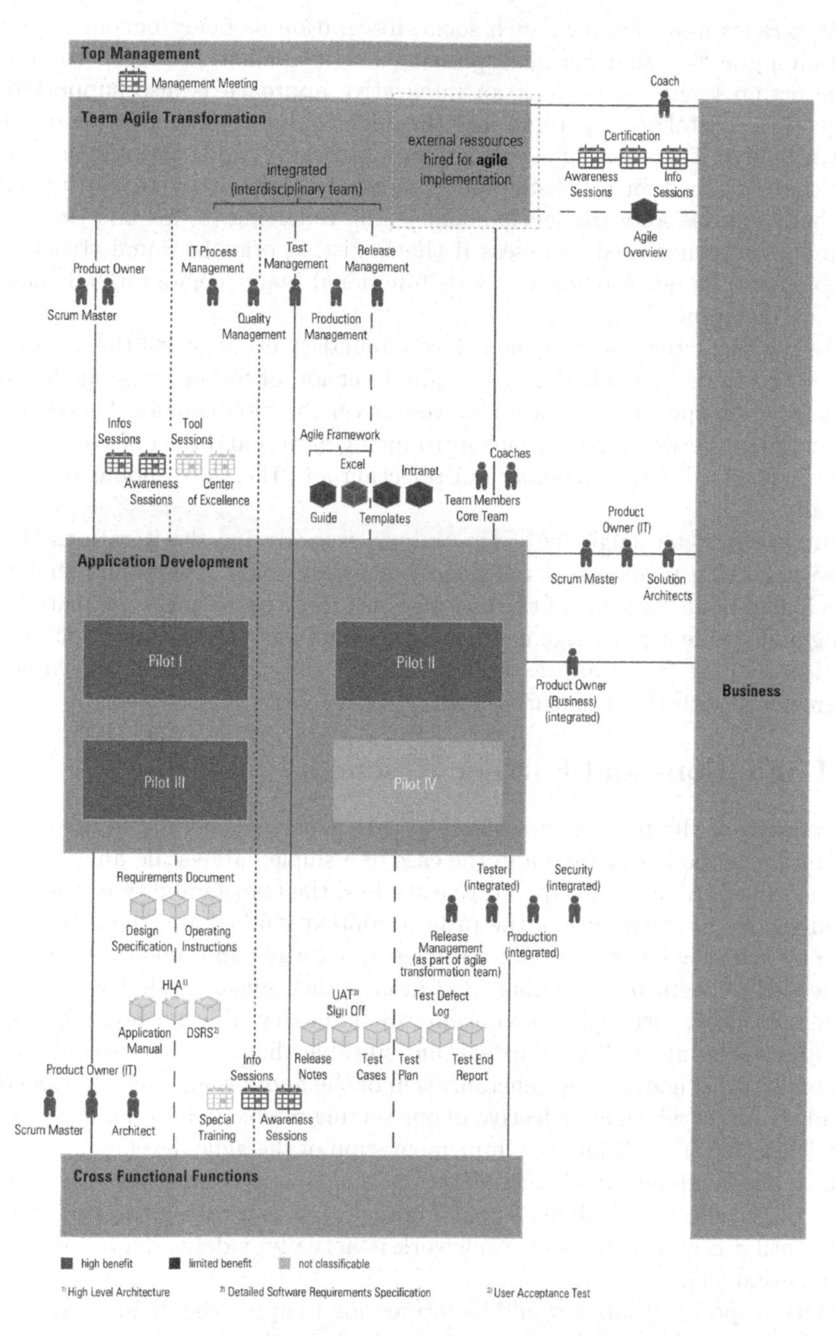

Fig. 3. Implementation model for embedding an agile development framework within a large-scale, plan-driven organization. The model uses boundary objects (cube symbols), boundary spanners (person symbols) and boundary events (calendar symbols). Colors indicate the perceived importance of the respective concepts. (Color figure online)

Pries-Hejes also identified such social integration as being beneficial and in addition argue "[...] that Scrum is plastic enough to allow such roles to be part of the Scrum team." [39]. Such an integrative approach is also supported by Fitzgerald and Stol as they argue that the added value of agile software development is limited if related organizational functions stay rigid. Consequently, they state the "[...] need for a holistic and integrated approach across all the activities that comprise software development." [15]. Referring to this and the results at hand, companies need to assess if their existing organizational structure is suitable for agile development as cross-functional teams combining all relevant roles are preferable.

Overall, the interviewees named eleven boundary events, with the most effective being sessions introducing the original version of Scrum, sessions focusing on the division-specific framework as well as certification courses. However, the differentiation between the sessions introducing Scrum and the ones introducing the framework lead to confusion and rejection and therefore should be viewed critically.

Furthermore, although six of nine interviewees during the iterations II - IV (those not being members of the agile framework team) mentioned that they participated in at least one of the two sessions, these participants indicated that strong and visible top management support would increase the adoption of agile practices and the framework as well as increase the participation, which is also in agreement with the literature [11,23].

6 Limitations and Further Research

The validity of the findings presented in this paper is generally limited by the qualitative methodology used and the case of a single, large-scale financial institution studied. As usual for qualitative studies, the transferability of the results is limited due to the nature of the project context studied and the assumptions made by the researcher. Therefore, further qualitative and quantitative studies are needed to confirm the findings and discuss their general validity.

In particular, although the concepts of boundary objects, boundary spanners and events are well established and suitable theoretical constructs in the area under investigation, the generalization of the findings may be questioned, as boundary object which are effective in one setting might limit boundary crossing in another [10]. In addition, the implementation of the agile development framework in the company under consideration is still in a comparably early stage, which might affect the validity of the findings as it can take up to two or three years until a new development framework is actually widely adopted within an organization [36].

With respect to that, it would be interesting to apply the findings to another financial institution implementing agile methods. Furthermore, other large-scale, plan-driven organizations operating in a highly regulated environment should be analyzed, i.e. from the pharmaceutical industry. In general, the applicability of agile methods in highly regulated environments should be further investigated as there is still rather limited scientific evidence for it found in the literature.

7 Conclusion

In conclusion, in this paper we qualitatively evaluated the role and effectiveness of an agile development framework in a large-scale, plan-driven organization. In particular, it was studied how organizational boundaries should be designed in order to effectively create awareness and common understanding between the relevant stakeholders. Therefore, a qualitative study using a Grounded Theory approach was performed at a division of a large-scale financial institution.

The results show that a customized agile development framework designed specifically to the needs of the organization is beneficial for the implementation of agile methods in a complex setting. This holds in particular true if this framework is designed by involving all relevant organizational stakeholders right from the beginning. This early involvement is crucial not only for the common understanding of all stakeholders but also for their motivation to apply the framework.

The evaluation revealed the importance of implementing boundary spanners at the organizational boundaries between relevant stakeholder groups. The establishment of these functional roles in the organization should be supplemented by a detailed overview of the framework and respective events introducing it to the affected stakeholders. The results indicate that organizational boundaries should be resolved as far as applicable in order to establish cross-functional agile development teams including members of all stakeholder groups relevant for the successful development of the product.

References

1. Aldrich, H., Herker, D.: Boundary spanning roles and organization structure. Acad. Manag. Rev. **2**(2), 217–230 (1977)
2. Ambler, S.W.: Agile software development at scale. In: Meyer, B., Nawrocki, J.R., Walter, B. (eds.) CEE-SET 2007. LNCS, vol. 5082, pp. 1–12. Springer, Heidelberg (2008). doi:10.1007/978-3-540-85279-7_1
3. Arias, E.G., Fischer, G.: Boundary objects: their role in articulating the task at hand and making information relevant to it. In: International ICSC Symposium on Interactive and Collaborative Computing (ICC 2000), Wollongong, pp. 567–574 (2000)
4. Bannink, S.: Challenges in the transition from waterfall to scrum - a casestudy at portbase. In: Proceedings of the 20th Twente student Conference on IT, Eschende, pp. 1–10 (2014)
5. Barlow, J.B., Giboney, J.S., Keith, J.K., Wilson, D.W., Schuetzler, R.M.: Overview and guidance on agile development in large organizations. Commun. Assoc. Inf. Syst. **29**(2), 25–44 (2011)
6. Beck, K.: Embracing change with extreme programming. IEEE Comput. Soc. **32**(10), 70–77 (1999)
7. Bhattacherjee, A.: Social Science Research: Principles, Methods, and Practices. CreateSpace Publishing, 2 edn. (2012)
8. Boehm, B.: A spiral model of software development and enhancement. Computer **21**(5), 61–72 (1988)
9. Boehm, B., Turner, R.: Management challenges to implementing agile processes in traditional development organizations. IEEE Comput. Soc. **22**(5), 30–39 (2005)

10. Carlile, P.R.: View of knowledge and boundaries: boundary objects in new product development. Organ. Sci. **13**(4), 442–455 (2002)
11. Chan, F.K.Y., Thong, J.Y.L.: Acceptance of agile methodologies: a critical review and conceptual framework. Decis. Support Syst. **46**(4), 803–814 (2009)
12. Cockburn, A., Highsmith, J.: Agile software development: the people factor. Computer **34**(11), 131–133 (2001)
13. Corbin, J., Strauss, A.: Basics of Qualitative Research, 4th edn. SAGE Publications, Thousand Oaks (2015)
14. Doering, N., Bortz, J.: Forschungsmethoden und Evaluation, 5th edn. Springer, Berlin (2016)
15. Fitzgerald, B., Stol, K.J.: Continuous software engineering and beyond: trends and challenges. In: Proceedings of the 1st International Workshop on Rapid Continuous Software Engineering - RCoSE 2014, Hyderabad, pp. 1–9 (2014)
16. Fitzgerald, B., Stol, K.J., O'Sullivan, R., O'Brien, D.: Scaling agile methods to regulated environments: an industry case study. In: 35th International Conference on Software Engineering (ICSE), San Francisco, pp. 863–872 (2013)
17. Flick, U.: Introduction Reseach Methodology. SAGE Publications Ltd., London (2011)
18. Flick, U.: An Introduction to Qualitative Research, 5th edn. SAGE Publications Ltd., London (2014)
19. Fowler, M., Highsmith, J.: The agile manifesto. Softw. Dev. **9**, 28–35 (2001). http://www.pmp-projects.org/Agile-Manifesto.pdf, http://andrey.hristov.com/fht-stuttgart/The_Agile_Manifesto_SDMagazine.pdf, http://www.pmp-projects.org/Agile-Manifesto.pdf
20. Friedman, R.A., Podolny, J.: Differentiation of boundary spanning roles: labor negotiations and implications for role conflict. Adm. Sci. Q. **37**(1), 28 (1992). http://www.jstor.org/stable/2393532?origin=crossref
21. Glaser, B.G., Strauss, A.L.: The Discovery of Grounded Theory: Strategies for Qualitative Research. Aldine Publishing Company, New York (1967)
22. Highsmith, J., Cockburn, A.: Agile software development: the business of innovation. Computer **34**(9), 120–122 (2001)
23. Hoda, R., Noble, J., Marshall, S.: Supporting self-organizing agile teams. In: Sillitti, A., Hazzan, O., Bache, E., Albaladejo, X. (eds.) XP 2011. LNBIP, vol. 77, pp. 73–87. Springer, Heidelberg (2011). doi:10.1007/978-3-642-20677-1_6
24. Kettunen, P.: Adopting key lessons from agile manufacturing to agile software product development—a comparative study. Technovation **29**(6–7), 408–422 (2009)
25. Kettunen, P., Laanti, M.: How to steer an embedded software project: tactics for selecting the software process model. Inf. Softw. Technol. **47**(9), 587–608 (2005)
26. Levina, N., Vaast, E.: The emergence of boundary spanning competence in practice: implications for implementation and use of information systems. MIS Q. **29**(2), 335–363 (2005)
27. Lindvall, M., Muthig, D., Dagnino, A., Wallin, C., Stupperich, M., Kiefer, D., May, J., Kähkönen, T.: Agile software development in large organizations. Computer **37**(12), 26–34 (2004)
28. Livermore, J.A.: Factors that impact implementing an agile software development methodology. In: Proceedings 2007 IEEE SoutheastCon, Richmond, pp. 82–86 (2007)
29. Marrone, J.A.: Team boundary spanning: a multilevel review of past research and proposals for the future. J. Manag. **36**(4), 911–940 (2010)
30. Mishra, A., Dubey, D.: Suitability analysis of various software development life cycle models. Int. J. Electron. Commun. Comput. Eng. **4**(6), 98–101 (2013)

31. Nerur, S., Mahapatra, R., Mangalaraj, G.: Challenges of migrating to agile methodologies. Commun. ACM **48**(5), 72–78 (2005)
32. van Nes, F., Abma, T., Jonsson, H., Deeg, D.: Language differences in qualitative research: is meaning lost in translation? Eur. J. Ageing **7**(4), 313–316 (2010)
33. Nguyen-Duc, A., Cruzes, D.S., Conradi, R.: On the role of boundary spanners as team coordination mechanisms in organizationally distributed projects. In: 2014 IEEE 9th International Conference on Global Software Engineering, Shanghai, pp. 125–134 (2014)
34. O'hEocha, C., Conboy, K.: The role of the user story agile practice in innovation. In: Abrahamsson, P., Oza, N. (eds.) LESS 2010. LNBIP, vol. 65, pp. 20–30. Springer, Heidelberg (2010). doi:10.1007/978-3-642-16416-3_3
35. Perneger, T.V., Hudelson, P.M.: Writing a research article. Int. J. Health Care **16**(3), 191–192 (2004)
36. Pikkarainen, M., Salo, O., Kuusela, R., Abrahamsson, P.: Strengths and barriers behind the successful agile deployment-insights from the three software intensive companies in Finland. Empir. Softw. Eng. **17**(6), 675–702 (2012)
37. Pikkarainen, M., Salo, O., Still, J.: Deploying agile practices in organizations: a case study. In: Richardson, I., Abrahamsson, P., Messnarz, R. (eds.) EuroSPI 2005. LNCS, vol. 3792, pp. 16–27. Springer, Heidelberg (2005). doi:10.1007/11586012_3
38. Pries-Heje, L., Pries-Heje, J.: Agile & distributed project management: a case study revealing why scrum is useful. In: European Conference on Information Systems (ECIS2011), Helsinki, pp. 20–28 (2011)
39. Pries-Heje, L., Pries-Heje, J.: Why Scrum works: a case study from an agile distributed project in Denmark and India. In: Agile Conference (AGILE), 2011, pp. 20–28 (2011)
40. Royce, W.W.: Managing the development of large software systems. In: ICSE 1987 Proceedings of the 9th International Conference on Software Engineering, Monterey, pp. 328–338 (1970)
41. Scheerer, A., Hildenbrand, T., Kude, T.: Coordination in large-scale agile software development: a multiteam systems perspective. In: HICSS 2014 Proceedings of the 2014 47th Hawaii International Conference on System Sciences, Auckland, pp. 4780–4788 (2014)
42. Schwaber, K.: SCRUM development process. In: Sutherland, J., Casanave, C., Miller, J., Patel, P., Hollowell, G. (eds.) Business Object Design and Implementation, pp. 117–134. Springer, London (1997)
43. Schwaber, K., Beedle, M.: Agile Software Development with Scrum, 1st edn. Prentice Hall, Upper Saddle River (2001)
44. Star, S.L., Griesemer, J.R.: Institutional ecology, 'Translations' and boundary objects: amateurs and professionals in Berkeley's Museum of Vertebrate Zoology, 1907-39. Soc. Stud. Sci. **19**(3), 387–420 (1989)
45. Sureshchandra, K., Shrinivasavadhani, J.: Moving from waterfall to agile. In: Proceedings - Agile 2008 Conference, Toronto, pp. 97–101 (2008)
46. Sutherland, J., Viktorov, A., Blount, J., Puntikov, N.: Distributed Scrum: agile project management with outsourced development teams. In: Proceedings of the 40th Hawaii International Conference on System Sciences, Waikoloa, p. 274a (2007)
47. Tushman, M.L., Scanlan, T.J.: Boundary spanning individuals: their role in information transfer and their antecendents. Acad. Manag. J. **24**(2), 289–305 (1981)
48. VersionOne Inc.: The 10th anual State of Agile report. VersionOne Incorporated (2016)
49. West, D., Grant, T.: Agile Development: Mainstream Adoption Has Changed Agility. Forrester Research, Cambridge (2010)

Business Process Modeling Readability

Structural Descriptions of Process Models Based on Goal-Oriented Unfolding

Chen Qian[1], Lijie Wen[1(✉)], Jianmin Wang[1], Akhil Kumar[2], and Haoran Li[3]

[1] School of Software, Tsinghua University, Beijing 100084, China
qc16@mails.tsinghua.edu.cn, {wenlj,jimwang}@tsinghua.edu.cn
[2] Smeal College of Business, Penn State University, 16802 State College, USA
akhilkumar@psu.edu
[3] The Affiliated School of Peking University, Beijing 100080, China
lihaoran1@stu.pkuschool.edu.cn

Abstract. Business processes are normally managed by designing, operating and analysing corresponding process models. While delivering these process models, an understanding gap arises depending on the degree of different users' familiarity with modeling languages, which may slow down or even stop the normal functioning of processes. Therefore, a method for automatically generating texts from process models was proposed. However, the current method just involves ordinary model patterns so that the coverage of the generated text is too low and information loss exists. In this paper, we propose an improved transformation algorithm named Goun to tackle this problem of describing the process models automatically. The experimental results demonstrate that the Goun algorithm not only supports more elements and complex structures, but also remarkably improves the coverage of generated text.

Keywords: Process model · Natural language text generation · Extended process structure tree · Matching · Unfolding

1 Introduction

Requirements analysis is the primary step in software development. In this step, there are two kinds of important roles named domain expert and systems analyst [3]. Through oral communications and documents, they try to thoroughly understand how business processes run. After that, a systems analyst converts what he or she has comprehended into business process models which can be expressed by Petri net, Business Process Modeling and Notation (BPMN), Event-driven Process Chains (EPC) or other modeling languages [1,8,14]. However, there is a high possibility that the domain expert lacks the confidence to understand these models, or even feels that it is too time-consuming to learn formal process modeling, which may directly lead to interruption or even abortion of the project [3]. Therefore, our research goal here is to automatically generate the corresponding natural language text for a given process model since natural language texts could be read and understood by almost everyone.

E. Dubois and K. Pohl (Eds.): CAiSE 2017, LNCS 10253, pp. 397–412, 2017.
DOI: 10.1007/978-3-319-59536-8_25

Against this background, Leopold et al. proposed a model-to-text transformation algorithm (abbr. Hen) which transforms a BPMN model into its corresponding textual description to avoid understanding gaps between different roles [3]. Hen linearized a process model by traversing its corresponding Refined Process Structure Tree (RPST) [2]. When processing the leaf nodes of the tree, a data structure - Deep Syntactic Tree - is derived to represent a natural language sentence. After refinement and realization [15], the textual description with bullet points is generated. An example for illustrating the model-to-text transformation scenario is presented next.

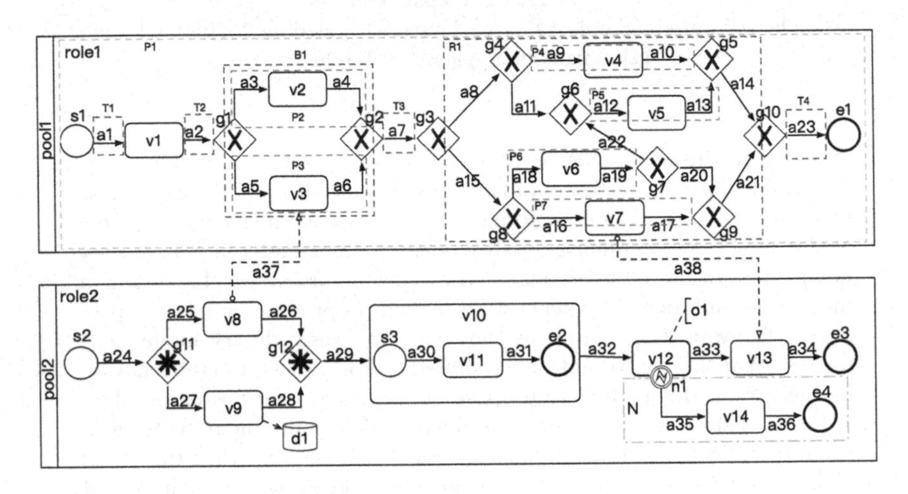

Fig. 1. A sample of BPMN 2.0 model (Color figure online)

Example 1. Taking the *pool*1 in Fig. 1 as an example, the Hen text is (for illustration, we add 9 line numbers below to mark every sentence):

1. *The 'pool1' process begins when the 'role1' does 'v1'. Then one of the following branches is executed.*
2. • *The 'role1' does 'v2'.*
3. • *The 'role1' does 'v3'.*
4. *Once one of the above branches is executed, there is a region which allows for different execution paths. One option from start to end is the following.*
5. • *The 'role1' does 'v6'. Subsequently, the 'role1' does 'v5'.*
6. *However, the region allows for a number of deviations.*
7. • *After the region begins, the 'role1' can also do 'v4'.*
8. • *After the region begins, the 'role1' can also do 'v7'.*
9. *Then, the 'pool1' process is finished.*

The sentences 1, 4 and 6 in *Example* 1 are pre-defined language templates to express the semantics of certain patterns. Note that there is a nested structure above to show the depth of a sentence using indentation with bullet points '•'.

However, to the authors' knowledge, Hen has the following four main drawbacks. First, Hen fails to generate the text when a model contains some kinds of complex elements, such as text annotation, complex gateway, message flow, or subprocess [1]. For the *pool*2 in Fig. 1, Hen fails to generate sentences for the complex gateways $g11$ and $g12$, the subprocess $v10$ and the error path N. Second, Hen only works on free-choice models and omits some descriptions of trivial paths, i.e. it suffers from information loss. For example, the Hen text in *Example* 1 is somewhat incomplete because it omits some behavior such as when only $v5$ is executed (without $v6$). Third, if we were to change the direction of $a17$ and $a16$ to create a loop structure, Hen fails to generate text for it due to the existence of the loop structure in the non-structured part (i.e. $R1$). Fourth, the generated text of non-structured part is a linear structure with limited expressive power. Based on these insights, one of our goals is to solve these drawbacks of Hen and improve the expressive power of model-to-text conversion.

Our research contributions are as follows. First, we proposed a fresh data structure to express more model patterns. Second, we developed a new linearization technique based on the basic architecture of Hen to transform a model into a structured one and then convert it into textual description, which is the biggest challenge. Third, we evaluated different methods along different dimensions and discussed the results of the comparison.

The remainder of this paper is organized as follows. Section 2 briefly introduces the definitions used in this paper. Section 3 presents the new data structure EPST to express more model patterns, while Sect. 4 introduces Goun and exemplifies it with a specific model. Later, Sect. 5 evaluates the Goun algorithm and compares it with the Hen algorithm. Finally, Sect. 6 describes related work and Sect. 7 draws our conclusions.

2 Preliminaries

This section introduces Business Process Modeling and Notation (BPMN) and Refined Process Structure Tree (RPST) [2–4].

2.1 BPMN

BPMN is a graphical process modeling language. BPMN version 2.0 contains *swimlanes* (pools, lanes), *nodes* (events, activities, gateways), *flows* (sequence flow, message flow) and *artifacts* (e.g. text annotation, data stores) [4].

Example 2. The full process model in Fig. 1 contains two pools denoted by the two large rectangles. Events are represented as circles with thin or thick borders. The corner-rounded rectangles $v1, v2$ etc. are activities. In particular, activity $v10$ is a subprocess because it can be decomposed into three nodes $s3, v11, e2$ linked by edges $a30$ and $a31$. The diamonds with 'X' symbols $g1$, $g2$, etc. are exclusive gateways which split or merge multiple branches. $d1$ and $o1$ are the data store and text annotation, respectively. The message flows $a37$ and $a38$

transfer messages between two activities belonging to different pools as shown by dotted lines. The error path N occurs if there is an error while processing $v12$. Node $v1$ precedes gateway $g1$; and $v2, v3$ follow $g1$; thus, the pre- and post-set of $g1$ are $\bullet g1 = \{v1\}$ and $g1\bullet = \{v2, v3\}$.

2.2 RPST

RPST is a kind of tree structure that indicates SESE (single entry single exit) parts of a process model. We call these parts process components. A *process component* is *canonical* iff (i.e., if and only if) it does not overlap with any other process component, meaning that any two canonical process components are either disjoint or nested. Therefore, canonical process components naturally form a hierarchy, which leads to the definition of RPST [6].

Definition 1 (Trivial, Polygon, Bond, Rigid). *Let C be a process component of a process model. C belongs to one of T, P, B or R components.*

- *C belongs to a Trivial (T) component, iff C contains only a single edge.*
- *C belongs to a Polygon (P) component, iff C contains a set of components linked consecutively.*
- *C belongs to a Bond (B) component, iff all components in C share one source node and one sink node.*
- *C belongs to a Rigid (R) component, iff C is none of T, P or B.*

Definition 2 (RPST). *The refined process structure tree (RPST) of a process model is the set of all its canonical process components.*

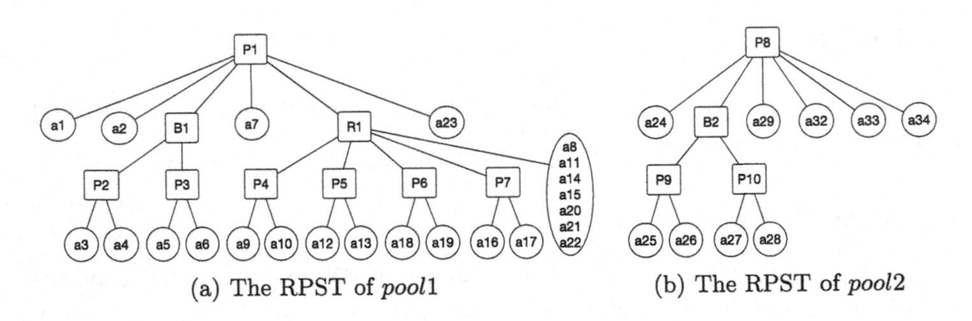

(a) The RPST of *pool1* (b) The RPST of *pool2*

Fig. 2. The two RPSTs of the two pools in Fig. 1

Example 3. In Fig. 1, the colored dotted-line rectangles represent different depths in decomposition (blue, red represent depth 1, 2, respectively). Every single node in Fig. 1 attaches to its following Trivial component. Except Trivial, the other three kinds of canonical components can be decomposed. In *pool*1, $P1$ contains six components $T1, T2, B1, T3, R1, T4$. More precisely, component $B1's$ sub-polygon components $P2, P3$ share one source node $g1$ and one sink node $g2$. $R1$ is unstructured since the edge $a22$ connects two separate branches $P5$ and $P6$, which leads to the unstructured Rigid component. Every component in a Rigid component is bounded by a gateway node such as $P4, P5, P6, P7$ and non-decomposable Trivial components such as $a8, a11$, etc. These visual decompositions naturally form a hierarchy so that we can get the undirected tree representation of a RPST in Fig. 2. For ease of representation, seven edges are shown in the same ellipse in Fig. 2(a) but, in fact, they are seven independent leaves of $R1$. The RPST of *pool*2 is generated in the same way.

3 Extending Expressive Patterns of RPST

From *Example* 3, we know that the lack of corresponding textual expressions for some of the patterns in RPST prevents Hen from generating the corresponding text, and impairs its expressive ability. Thus, we proposed a new data structure EPST and added some language templates to enhance RPST.

Definition 3 (Extended Process Structure Tree). *Extended Process Structure Tree (EPST) is a multi-tuple* $E_m = (R_S, r_O, E_R, M, O, M_S, \vartheta, \mu)$.

- R_S *is a finite set of RPSTs for all pools in the whole model.*
- r_O *is the super root node.* r_O *connects every* $r_s \in R_S$ *through edge set* E_R.
- M *is a finite set of sub-models, which contains models corresponding to a subprocess, an exceptional path, a group element, etc.*
- O *is a finite set of artifacts and data objects, i.e. text annotations, IT systems, data objects and data stores.*
- M_S *is a set of message flows that link two elements in different pools.*
- ϑ *is a function attaching a T component and a corresponding element in* M.
- μ *is a function attaching a T component and a corresponding element in* O.

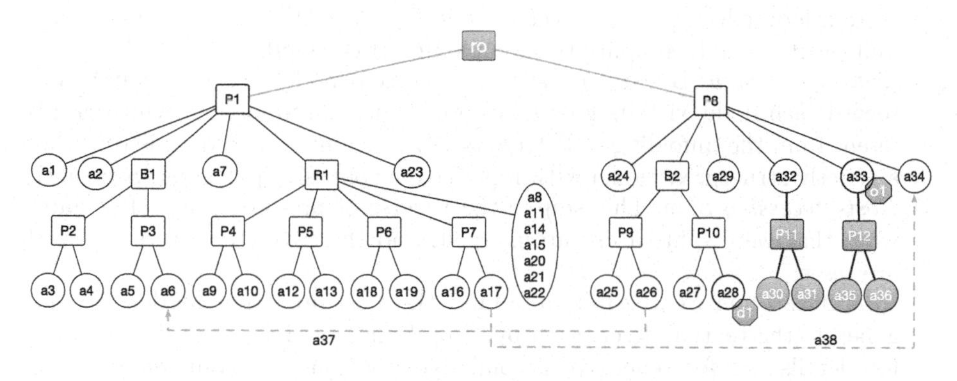

Fig. 3. The EPST of the BPMN 2.0 model in Fig. 1

Example 4. In Fig. 1, *pool2* contains patterns that RPST cannot express such as subprocess $v10$, exceptional path N, data store $d1$ and text annotation $o1$. Besides, there are two message flows transmitting messages between the two pools. The EPST of the whole model in Fig. 1 is shown in Fig. 3. In the EPST, $R_S = \{P1, P8\}$; and, $P1$ and $P8$ connect with super root node r_O. For $M = \{P11, P12\}$, $P11$ and $P12$ are respectively attached to subprocess $v10$ and error event $n1$. For $M_S = \{a37, a38\}$, $a37$ and $a38$ are message flows. For $O = \{o1, d1\}$, $o1$ and $d1$ are attached onto corresponding elements $a33$ and $a28$. Therefore, the set of patterns EPST can express is the superset of that of RPST.

4 Structural Description

Figure 4 shows the overview of Goun in which blue parts highlight our work based on the Hen architecture. As Fig. 4 indicates, the input is a process model passing through five main steps to generate the final textual description. Here, converting a random model into a well-structured one is our biggest challenge.

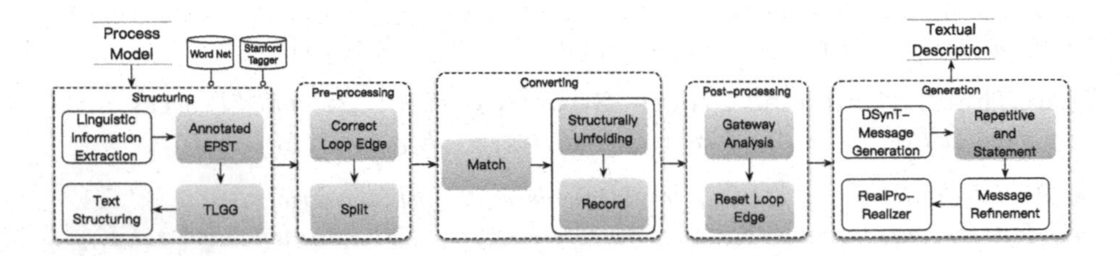

Fig. 4. The overview of Goun (Color figure online)

(1) *Structuring Step.* This step generates two main data structures of a process model, i.e. EPST and TLGG that will be introduced in this section.
(2) *Pre-processing Step.* Loop edges in a model are edges that can cause loops. For the converting step, the model should be pre-processed by reversing certain loop edges to break cycles. Splitting each MEME (multi-entry and multi-exit) aims to simplify the complexity of the model.
(3) *Converting Step.* Based on the pre-processed model, we can match and record each node with its goal nodes for structural unfolding, which is different from the unfolding of Petri nets [8]. The aim of unfolding is to create a strictly structured model with repetitive or omissive polygons (Sect. 4.4).
(4) *Post-processing Step.* This step is the reverse of pre-processing. The gateways that were split earlier are merged, and the edges that were reversed are reset.
(5) *Text generation Step.* After obtaining the post-processed model, we can generate the textual description by Deep Syntactic Tree analysis, cf. [3,15] for details. As for repetitive or omissive polygons, we complement their behavior descriptions by attaching additional messages.

In order to overcome the drawbacks of Hen in handling Rigid components, we propose the Goun algorithm. Here, we first define TLGG with respect to the top level. Goun will run recursively so that nodes on other levels can be processed in the next successive iterations.

Definition 4 (Top-Level Gateway Graph). *Given a Rigid component node in an EPST, we treat its direct children as Polygon components. A top-level gateway graph (TLGG) is a triple* $M_{TLGG} = (G, F, \nu)$ *where:*

- *G is a finite set of gateway nodes.*
- *F is a finite set of directional edges connecting two different nodes in G.*
- ν *is a binary function to mark whether a node in G can cause concurrent behavior or not.*

To illustrate, we give an example in Fig. 5(a) of a NFC (non-free choice) model with a loop structure that Hen fails to handle. This whole model belongs to a Rigid component, whose EPST is shown in Fig. 5(b). For ease of presentation, eight independent edges are shown in one ellipse on the right. Note that the light green parts in Fig. 5(b) are not at the top level of the tree. Moreover, the top level (depth = 1) components are highlighted in blue. In general, we can treat every blue EPST node as a Polygon. Thus, this Rigid component contains 11 top-level Polygons.

The TLGG of the original model is derived in Fig. 5(c). In this figure, only the concurrent (or parallel) gateway nodes are shown in purple, while the "non-concurrent" nodes (e.g. $G3, G4$) are in white. The non-top-level parts of the original model (e.g. $B1, E, F$, at level 2) are not of interest here and were removed.

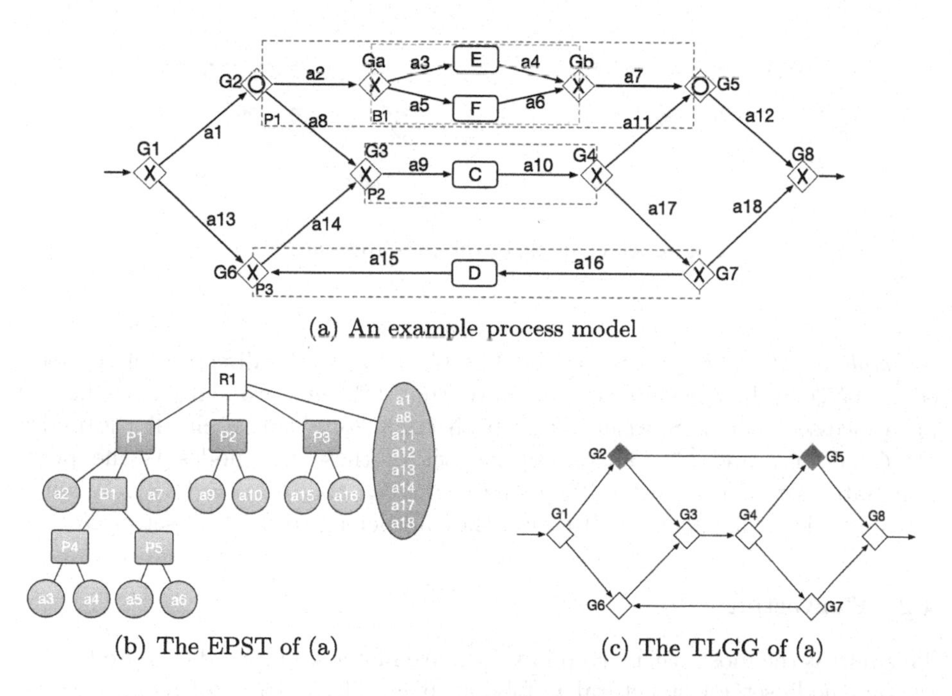

Fig. 5. An example process model and its EPST and TLGG (Color figure online)

4.1 Pre-processing

Loop edges in a model are edges which can cause loop structures [6]. In general, any edge attaches to its source node $source(a)$ and target node $target(a)$. The in- and out-degrees of a node g are $|\bullet g|$ and $|g \bullet|$.

For the conversion step, the model should be pre-processed to create an acyclic model. We trivially traverse TLGG by breadth first search (BFS) to number every node with its traversed depth (td). If there are two nodes g_i, g_j and an edge a_l, where $source(a_l) = g_i \wedge target(a_l) = g_j \wedge td(g_i) > td(g_j)$, then a_l is marked as a loop edge *and* its direction is reversed.

Further, if $|\bullet g_k| > 1 \wedge |g_k \bullet| > 1$, i.e. g_k is a MEME node, then g_k is split into two nodes g_{ka} and g_{kb}, where $|\bullet g_{ka}| = |\bullet g_k| \wedge |g_{kb} \bullet| = |g_k \bullet| \wedge (g_{ka}, g_{kb}) \in F$.

As a result, the TLGG contains no loop structure so that we can get dominators and goals from TLGG, which will be the basis of Goun.

Definition 5 (Dominator, Goal). *For a pair of nodes A, B in a TLGG, if starting from an arbitrary edge originating from A, there always exists one path ending at B, then we say that A is B's pre-dominator and B is A's post-dominator. If the post-dominator set of A is* $A_D = \{A_{D1}, A_{D2}, \ldots, A_{Dn}\}$, *and there exists* i $(1 \leq i \leq n)$ *such that* $|A_{Di} \bullet| = 0 \wedge len(A, A_{Di}) = min\{len(A, A_{Dj})\}$ *for any* j $(1 \leq j \leq n)$, *we say* A_{Di} *is a goal node of A.*

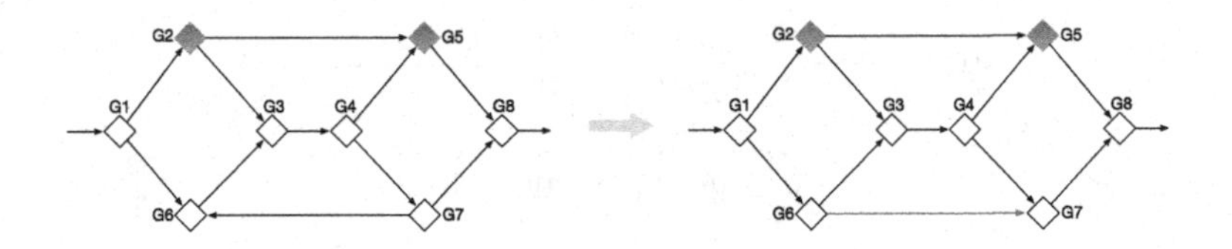

Fig. 6. An example of the pre-processing step

Example 5. After pre-processing the TLGG in Fig. 6, the direction of the loop edge $(G7, G6)$ has been reversed. Note that $G1$ has two out edges in the pre-processed model. Starting along both edges, one can reach all the nodes $G3, G4, G5, G7$ and $G8$. Therefore, the set of these five nodes is the post-dominator set of $G1$. Note that $|G8 \bullet| = 0 \Rightarrow goal(G1) = \{G8\}$. When a certain node Gi has many goal nodes, they all belong to the goal set of Gi.

4.2 Converting

This part is the most crucial step in Goun. We match and record each node with its goal node set for structural unfolding [6–8]. The purpose of matching and unfolding is to create a strictly structured model with repetitive and omissive edges (introduced in Sect. 4.4). More details are given next.

Matching. In this part, we match every valid TLGG node with its goal set. Goun begins at collecting nodes without incoming edges (*entry list*) and nodes without outgoing edges (*exit list*). For a valid entry node, there should be at least one exit node corresponding to it. If the sizes of the entry and exit lists are both equal to one, then the unique entry u and the unique exit v are matched and recorded, meaning v is the goal node of u. As for multiple exit nodes, we use a heuristic rule to guide the matching procedure. For a node u_1 and two exit nodes $v1$ and $v2$, the *len* function calculates the minimum length paths that originate from $u1$ to $v1$ and $v2$. If $len(u1, v1) < len(u1, v2)$, then $v2$ is no more a goal of $u1$.

The node matching problem is slightly similar to the parentheses matching problem. At every step, we delete matched nodes and their connecting edges. Subsequently, whether the TLGG is still reasonable should be taken into consideration. If the exit (entry) list of the remaining graph contains concurrent nodes (purple), and its entry (exit) list does not, then an unreasonable situation is said to occur. If so, we reset the deleted source nodes to keep the reasonableness of the current graph intact.

After every deletion step, a simplification operation is performed. We trivially regard ZEZE (zero entry and zero exit) and SESE nodes as invalid nodes because they both do not change the behavior of the present model and can simplify the model if removed. Thus, the algorithm checks whether an invalid node g in TLGG such that ($|\bullet g| = |g \bullet| = 0$ or $|\bullet g| = |g \bullet| = 1$) exists, and, if so, erases it.

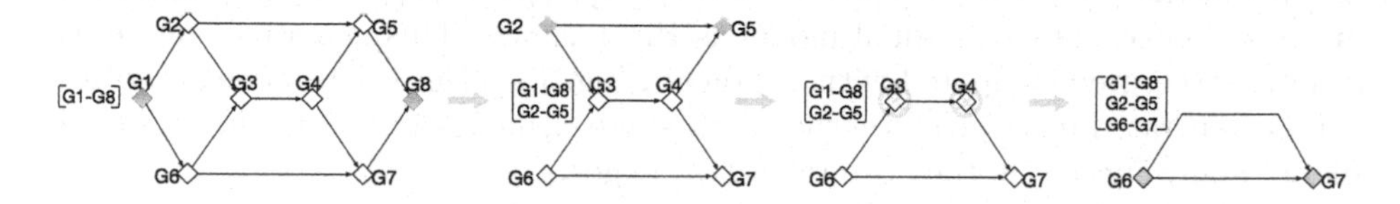

Fig. 7. An example of the matching step

In Fig. 7, $G8$ is marked as the goal node of $G1$ since they are the entry and exit nodes in the TLGG. After deleting them six nodes are left, and $G2$ and $G6$ need to be matched because they are entry nodes now. Note that $G2$ can always reach $G5$ and $G6$ can always reach $G7$, thus $goal(G2) = \{G5\}; goal(G6) = \{G7\}$. If a conflict occurs in matching, the *minimum path length first* heuristic rule should apply. In the simplification step, the SESE nodes $G3$ and $G4$ are erased. Lastly, $G7$ is marked as the goal node of $G6$; thus, the goal set is: $\{(G1, \{G8\}), (G2, \{G5\}), (G6, \{G7\})\}$.

Unfolding. Based on the matched node set, this step aims to create a structured process model with repetitive and omissive edges which is essential for structured text generation. Specifically, a *repetitive edge* is one that exists in the original model once, and in the unfolded model more than once (i.e. it is unfolded many times). An *omissive edge* exists in the original model but not in the unfolded model.

Goun begins at creating reachable paths from node u to v. In every path, it checks whether there is a goal node, and, if so, it skips all the succeeding nodes of the goal node, and continues recursive unfolding. In doing so, some nodes may be copied many times to avoid generating a Rigid component. If not, it unfolds every gateway directly. For every edge in the current path, the corresponding polygon is added.

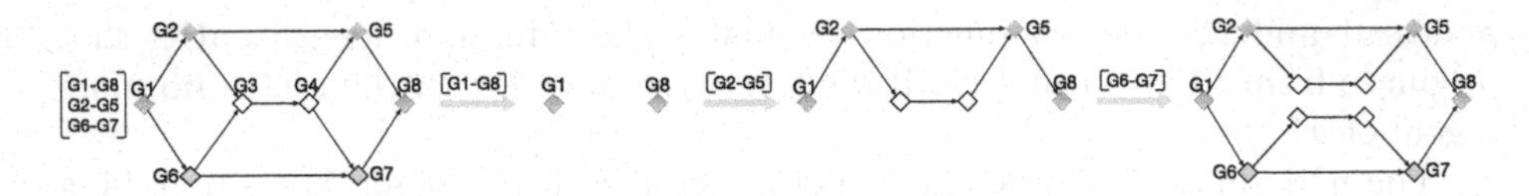

Fig. 8. An example of the unfolding step

In Fig. 8, after unfolding $(G1, \{G8\})$ (at level 1), there are two nodes (yellow) in the unfolded model. Then, after unfolding $(G2, \{G5\})$ and $(G6, \{G7\})$ (at level 2), there are ten nodes in the unfolded model. When all levels are similarly unfolded, the model is strictly structured, i.e. the EPST of it contains no Rigid components.

4.3 Post-processing

This step performs pre-processing in reverse. The gateways which were split should be merged and the edges which were reversed should be restored. Guided by the matched node set $\{(G1, \{G8\}), (G2, \{G5\}), (G6, \{G7\})\}$, we have unfolded and post-processed the original model as Fig. 9 shows. This generated model is strictly structured compared with the one in Fig. 5(a). Note that some activities can be generated twice or more; therefore, some elements appear in the unfolded model many times (i.e. they are repetitive edges).

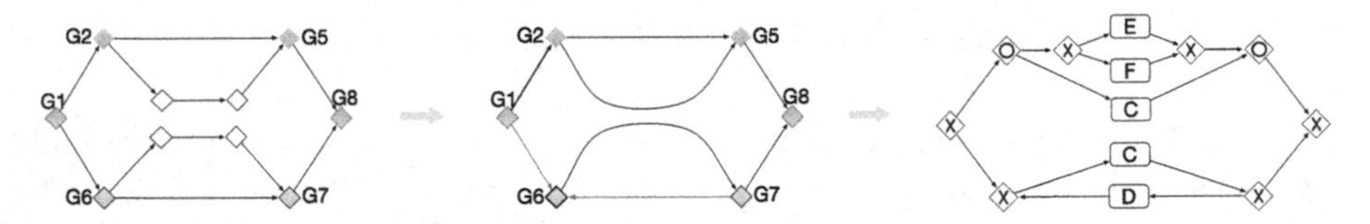

Fig. 9. An example of the post-processing step

4.4 Text Generation

Goun assumes that all generated statements capturing the new elements are correct and well-placed within the text. e.g. a text annotation should directly follow the sentence(s) of its corresponding node and be placed in parentheses.

Transformation of Trivial. After traversing an EPST until its Trivial components are found, we can generate a natural language sentence by Deep Syntactic Tree analysis of every trivial component [3,5]. Goun detects whether all elements are attached, and if so, their corresponding templates are loaded.

Adding Additional Description. Text generation consists of three further aspects as follows.

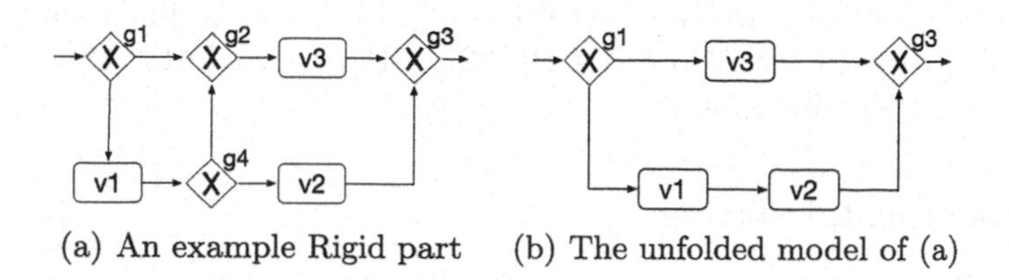

(a) An example Rigid part (b) The unfolded model of (a)

Fig. 10. An example model with an omissive edge and its unfolded model

(1) *Body text.* If the model contains no Rigid component, we can employ the traditional text generation method to solve all the components [3]. The description of this part needs to be decorated with statements for the behavior of other elements to avoid information loss.
(2) *Repetitive behavior.* From our experience, activities described more than once do not need additional language templates.
(3) *Omissive behavior.* For some models, those edges which can cause different behavior are dropped after unfolding. In Fig. 10(a), after matching $g1$ and $g3$, its unfolded model is shown in Fig. 10(b). Note that edge $(g4, g2)$ is an omissive edge since it cannot be mapped in Fig. 10(b). Accordingly, edges that cannot be mapped in the unfolded model are recorded. Every omissive edge should be clarified through a language template. Taking Fig. 10(a) as an example, the additional statement is, *"After the 'role' does 'v1', it can also do 'v3"'*.

Having described the Goun algorithm, we give an example to show how it works.

Example 6. The structured Goun text of the *pool*1 in Fig. 1 is:

01. *The 'pool1' process begins when the 'role1' does 'v1'. Then one of the following branches is executed:*
02. • *The 'role1' does 'v2'.*
03. • *The 'role1' does 'v3'.*
04. *Once one of the above branches is executed, there is a region which allows for different execution paths:*
05. *One of the following branches is executed:*
06. • *The 'role1' does 'v4'.*
07. • *The 'role1' does 'v5'.*
08. *One of the following branches is executed:*
09. • *The 'role1' does 'v6'.*
10. • *The 'role1' does 'v7'.*
11. *However, the region allows for other behavior.*
12. • *After the 'role1' does 'v6', it also can do 'v5'.*
13. *Once the region is executed, the 'pool1' process is finished.*

5 Experimental Evaluation

We have implemented Goun[1] based on an open source BPM tool named jBPT[2]. In this section, we compare Goun with Hen [3]. All the experiments were run on a Macbook Pro with Intel Core I7 CPU@2.2 GHz, 16G DDR3@1600 MHz, and OS X 10.11.4 operating system.

5.1 Experimental Setting

We created[3] artificial test cases [9] and collected real-life test cases from different sources such as books (24.6%, textbook), online tutorials (7.4%, academic), papers (27.6%, academic), modeling tools (5.9%, industry), enterprises (30.5%, industry), and so on. We divided them into 10 datasets based on their domain. Their structural characteristics vary from easy (with just one activity) to complex (with hundreds of nodes with sub-processes, message flows, boundary events, etc.). The ratio of real-life cases is 61.76%. To eliminate artificial factors as much as possible, these 130 models[4] from different sources are randomly selected and sorted. Afterwards, we run the Hen and Goun algorithms to generate two separate texts for each case. Finally, text coverage, time cost, text property and user evaluation are measured as well.

5.2 Handling Ability

We analyzed the features of the Hen and Goun algorithms, in the context of both simple and complex models, and present a qualitative comparison in Table 1 (symbols '+' for supported; '–' for not supported; '±' for partial support).

Table 1. Comparison on handling abilities of Hen and Goun

Item	Hen	Goun
Structural model	+	+
Gateway	±	+
Artifacts	–	+
Message flow	–	+
Subprocess	±	+
Text annotation	–	+
Boundary events	±	+
Loop in Rigid	–	+
NFC models	–	+

[1] https://github.com/qc529491527/ModelToText/tree/master/SourceCodes.
[2] https://code.google.com/archive/p/jbpt/.
[3] www.signavio.com.
[4] https://github.com/qc529491527/ModelToText/tree/master/TestModels.

The results show that Goun enhances the completeness of structural descriptions, and the patterns it can handle is a superset of those of Hen.

5.3 Quantitative Comparison Results

We compared the coverage rate of Hen and Goun algorithms as shown in Fig. 11 (coverage-sources graphs). The element coverage, activity coverage, gateway coverage, flow coverage, message flow coverage and artifact coverage, respectively,

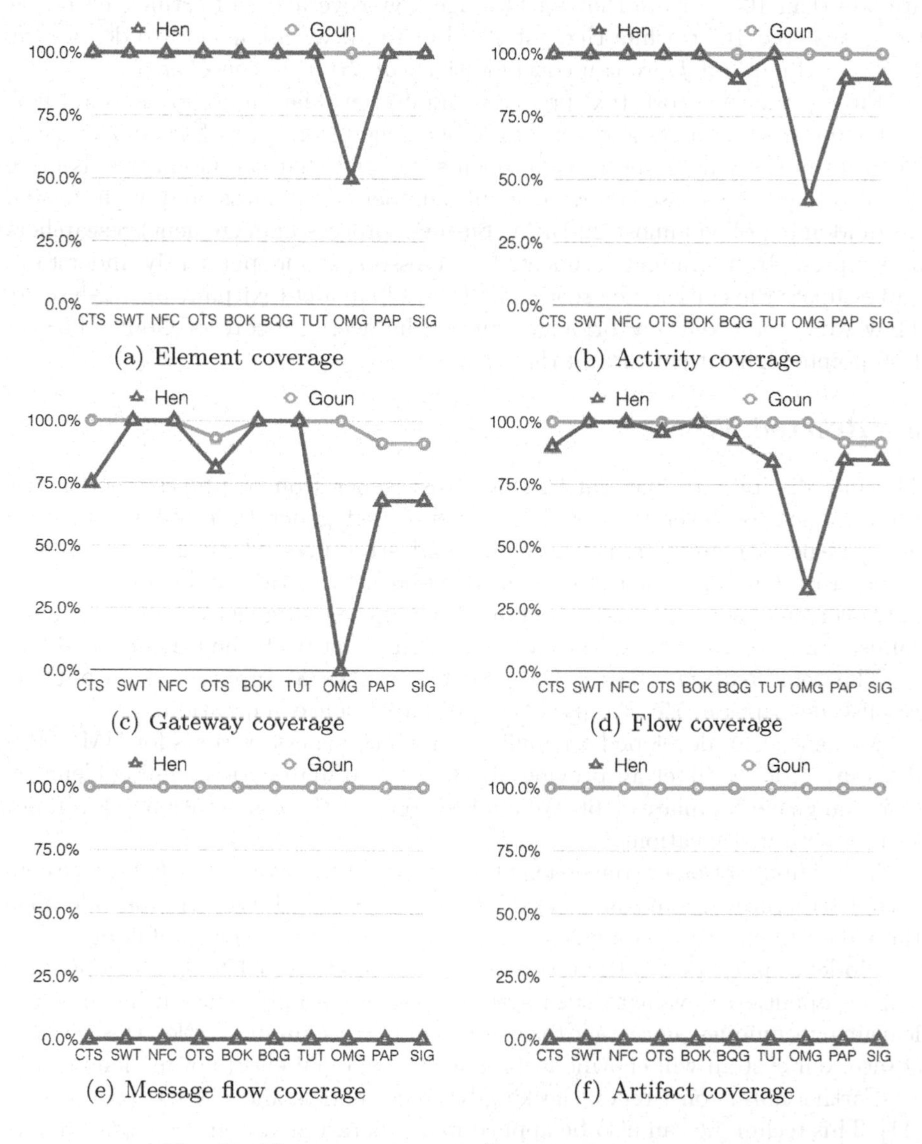

(a) Element coverage

(b) Activity coverage

(c) Gateway coverage

(d) Flow coverage

(e) Message flow coverage

(f) Artifact coverage

Fig. 11. The comparison results on text coverage rates

represent the ratio of covered elements, activities, gateways, control flows, message flows and artifacts to their maximum values. As for the BQG source in Fig. 11(c), since this set contains no gateway elements it is not shown. Next, we reverse constructed the process models from the generated text manually [12], and then compared the models with the "gold" models created manually. From the single source or total statistic, we can clearly see that the coverage rates of Goun are either equal to or more than those of Hen. The below-100% performance of Goun is explained by the fact that Goun ignores invalid gateways, i.e. SESE gateways, to avoid overfitting; thus, the coverage rates of these models are less than 100%. Note that for message flow coverage and artifact coverage, Goun achieved 100% while Hen got 0%. In sum, if we use $cov(f)$ to denote the coverage of method f, we can conclude that $cov(Hen) \leq cov(Goun)$.

Finally, the time cost, text property and user evaluation are measured. First, we tested these datasets and got an average generation time of around 1162 ms. Then, from the text property experiments, we find that the Goun text is more detailed than Hen's based on word count, number of sentences, and so on. Lastly, we randomly polled almost 22 BPM (business process management) researchers and experts, from graduate students to professors, to independently understand and evaluate the consistency scores of all the 130 model-text pairs on a 1–5 scale. They were not given any prior guidance. The average score of Goun (4.58) is 1.59 points higher than that of Hen (2.99).

6 Related Work

The interdisciplinary, natural language text generation of process model, has been studied for several years. The model-to-text generation system proposed in [3] neglects many complex elements and structures which may be used in enterprises. Our approach is developed based on the Hen architecture. It not only overcomes some drawbacks but also makes the text generation system more robust, and generates texts that are more compliant with the original models.

The tool *Realizer* takes a Deep Syntactic Tree as input, and outputs its English description [15]. We used the tool for sentence generation.

Meziane et al. developed an application which generates texts for UML class diagrams [10]. Malik et al. provide SBVR rules to map corresponding elements to its language templates [16]. We applied some of their generation rules in our system with modifications.

The simplification or conversion of model structure is valuable [6–8] since converted structures are in some ways easier to understand. Our approach applied the ideas of behavioral equivalence and proper complete prefix unfolding.

Model construction is the reverse of text generation [5,12,13]. Our approach can be applied to evaluate such systems also, especially when using machine learning techniques since raw texts are required as input. Under this circumstance, our system will enormously reduce the manual efforts of modeling.

Furthermore, consistency checking between models and texts is proposed in [11]. This technique can also be applied in a generation system to quantitatively evaluate multiple generated results.

7 Conclusion

In this paper, we proposed a new data structure EPST, and an algorithm for transforming general business process models to their textual descriptions. The EPST is an extended version of RPST since it can describe more patterns of process models. In addition, we implemented the Goun method which computes the goal sets of the original models, unfolds them into strictly structured ones and generates corresponding structured texts for them. Afterwards, test cases were collected to evaluate the Goun and Hen transformation methods along different dimensions. Experiments show that Goun not only extends the expressive patterns, but also presents a strictly structured text to readers. Furthermore, we showed that it improves the text coverage and reduces information loss.

Although the Goun technique can handle arbitrary Rigid components with loops and possesses good extensibility, the Goun texts are expressed by similar expression templates and are somewhat longer than those of Hen. In the future, we will try to decorate and shorten generated texts, and also do more extensive testing using enterprise models. In the meantime, we will give formal proofs to validate the properties and abilities of Goun. We will also employ automatic consistency checking to avoid subjective evaluation [11,13].

Acknowledgement. The work was supported by the National Key Research and Development Program of China (No. 2016YFB1001101) and the National Nature Science Foundation of China (Nos. 61472207, 61325008 and 71690231).

References

1. BPMN Task Force, Business Process Model and Notation (BPMN) Version 2.0, Object Management Group, 2011 (OMG Document Number formal 2011-01-03)
2. Vanhatalo, J., Vlzer, H., Koehler, J.: The refined process structure tree. Data Knowl. Eng. **68**(9), 793–818 (2009)
3. Leopold, H., Mendling, J., Polyvyanyy, A.: Supporting process model validation through natural language generation. IEEE Trans. Softw. Eng. **40**(8), 818–840 (2014)
4. Leopold, H., Mendling, J., Polyvyanyy, A.: Generating natural language texts from business process models. In: Ralyté, J., Franch, X., Brinkkemper, S., Wrycza, S. (eds.) CAiSE 2012. LNCS, vol. 7328, pp. 64–79. Springer, Heidelberg (2012). doi:10.1007/978-3-642-31095-9_5
5. Friedrich, F.: Automated generation of business process models from natural language input. Humboldt University at zu Berlin, Berlin, Germany, Institute of Information Systems (2010)
6. Polyvyanyy, A., Garca-Bauelos, L., Dumas, M.: Structuring acyclic process models. Inf. Syst. **37**(6), 518–538 (2012)
7. Lengauer, T., Tarjan, R.E.: A fast algorithm for finding dominators in a flowgraph. ACM Trans. Program. Lang. Syst. **1**, 121–141 (1979)
8. McMillan, K.L., Probst, D.K.: A technique of state space search based on unfolding. Form. Methods Syst. Des. **6**(1), 45–65 (1995)
9. Yan, Z., Dijkman, R., Grefen, P.: Generating process model collections. Softw. Syst. Model. **16**, 1–17 (2015)

10. Meziane, F., Athanasakis, N., Ananiadou, S.: Generating natural language specifications from UML class diagrams. Requir. Eng. **13**, 1–18 (2008)
11. van der Aa, H., Leopold, H., Reijers, H.A.: Detecting inconsistencies between process models and textual descriptions. In: Motahari-Nezhad, H.R., Recker, J., Weidlich, M. (eds.) BPM 2015. LNCS, vol. 9253, pp. 90–105. Springer, Cham (2015). doi:10.1007/978-3-319-23063-4_6
12. Schumacher, P., Minor, M., Schulte-Zurhausen, E.: Extracting and enriching workflows from text. In: 2013 IEEE 14th International Conference on Information Reuse and Integration (IRI), pp. 285–292. IEEE (2013)
13. Zhang, Z., Webster, P., Uren, V., Varga, A., Ciravegna, F.: Automatically extracting procedural knowledge from instructional texts using natural language processing. In: International Conference on Language Resources and Evaluation (2012)
14. van der Aalst, W.: Process Mining: Discovery, Conformance and Enhancement of Business Processes, 1st edn. Springer, Heidelberg (2011)
15. Lavoie, B., Rambow, O.: A fast and portable realizer for text generation systems. In: Proceedings of the fifth conference on Applied natural language processing. Association for Computational Linguistics (1997)
16. Malik, S., Bajwa, I.S.: Back to origin: transformation of business process models to business rules. In: La Rosa, M., Soffer, P., et al. (eds.) BPM Workshops 2012. LNBIP, vol. 132, pp. 611–622. Springer, Heidelberg (2013)

Aligning Textual and Graphical Descriptions of Processes Through ILP Techniques

Josep Sànchez-Ferreres, Josep Carmona(✉), and Lluís Padró

Universitat Politècnica de Catalunya, Barcelona, Spain
{jsanchezf,jcarmona,padro}@cs.upc.edu

Abstract. With the aim of having individuals from different backgrounds and expertise levels examine the operations in an organization, different representations of business processes are maintained. To have these different representations aligned is not only a desired feature, but also a real challenge due to the contrasting nature of each process representation. In this paper we present an efficient technique for aligning a textual description and a graphical model of a process. The technique is grounded on using natural language processing techniques to extract linguistic features of each representation, and encode the search as a mathematical optimization encoded using Integer Linear Programming (ILP) whose resolution ensures an optimal alignment between both descriptions. The technique has been implemented and the experiments witness the significance of the approach with respect to the state-of-the-art technique for the same task.

Keywords: Process models · Natural language processing · Integer Linear Programming

1 Introduction

Nowadays organizations store processes descriptions in various representations. The reason for this is the different nature stakeholders have: while textual descriptions of processes are well-suited for non-technical users, they are less appropriate for describing precise aspects of the underlying process [1]. In contrast, formal and graphical process notations (e.g., BPMN) are unambiguous representations which can be the basis for automating the corresponding processes within the organization [2], but they are oriented to specialized users. In this context, due to the evolving nature of processes, there is a high risk of having deviations between the different representations, a problem that may have serious consequences for any organization [3].

In the last decade, the field of *Natural Language Processing* (NLP) has grown up to a mature enough level, where the algorithmic support to analyze any text is high. Currently, there are several powerful open-source libraries that can be integrated easily to any software project, thus making linguistic analysis a reality in many contexts [4–7]. In this paper we exploit state-of-the-art NLP algorithms

E. Dubois and K. Pohl (Eds.): CAiSE 2017, LNCS 10253, pp. 413–427, 2017.
DOI: 10.1007/978-3-319-59536-8_26

to extract advanced linguistic features for the text found in both representations, so that the corresponding linguistic footprint can be mapped to a canonical form. Several similarity metrics can be defined on top of this canonical form, including weighted versions which may favor particular characteristics of process descriptions such as the action performed.

Once the similarity metric is chosen, the problem is casted as an optimization, whose solution(s) represent an assignment between tasks and sentences such that the accumulated sum of similarity is maximum. In particular, we encode the problem as an Integer Linear Programming (ILP) model whose resolution provides the optimal alignment between the text and the model.

The work of this paper is inspired by and shares the motivation of the seminal work [8,9] (see Sect. 3 for an accurate comparison of both approaches). Remarkably, although the core algorithm for searching solutions of the techniques is very different from our approach's, the quality of both approaches is similar. However, due to the simplicity of the encoding proposed, the method proposed is much faster and can deal with model-text pairs of medium/large size in a feasible time, a crucial distinctive feature of our approach with respect to [8,9]. By mapping the problem as an ILP, we clearly separate problem encoding from computation, thus allowing to easily incorporate new dimensions to consider (as we have done in this paper by incorporating actors). Notably, the technique provides a result very fast, thus widenning the application scope from post mortem or batch analysis to real-time analysis.

The research method followed in this work is *Design Science* [10], which "creates and evaluates IT artifacts intended to solve identified organizational problems".

The remainder of the paper is organized as follows: we provide a motivating example in the next section. Then, in Sect. 3 a detailed comparison with related work is reported. Preliminaries are then provided in Sect. 4, and the main contribution of the paper is presented in Sect. 5. Experiments on reference benchmarks are presented in Sect. 6. Finally, Sect. 7 concludes the paper and provides future lines for research.

2 Motivating Example

To give some intuition let us consider the example represented by the textual description and its corresponding BPMN model in Fig. 1. The technique we present derives the correct alignment between sentences 1–13 and tasks *A*-*P*, except for task *J*, as this task is not mentioned in the text.

In the simpler cases, the correct alignment between a task and a sentence can be obtained just by comparing the words in the sentences and the task labels. In this work, we aim to expand on previous techniques by considering more information about the tasks in the form of features. To better illustrate this, let us consider sentences 6 and 8, which correspond to tasks *G* and *L* respectively. When performing the comparison only by looking at the task labels, there is no clear way to distinguish *G* from *L* since they have the same label. Because of

(1) *When a visitor wants to become a member of Barcelona's ZooClub, the following steps must be taken.* (2) *First of all, the customer must decide whether he wants an individual or family membership.* (3) *If he wants an individual membership, he must prepare his personal information.* (4) *If he wants a family membership instead, he should prepare the information for its spouse and spawn as well.* (5) *The customer must then give this information to the ZooClub department.* (6) *The ZooClub enters the visitor's personal data into the system and takes the payment request to the Billing department.* (7) *The ZooClub department also forwards the visitor's information to the marketing department.* (8) *On receiving the request, the billing department also enters the visitor's personal data into their local database.* (9) *After that, the billing department sends the payment request to the bank.* (10) *The bank processes the payment information and, if everything is correct, charges the payment into user's account.* (11) *Once the payment is confirmed, the ZooClub department can print the card and deliver it to the visitor.* (12) *In the meantime, the Marketing department makes a request to mail the Zoo Club's magazine to the visitor's home.* (13) *Once the visitor receives the card, he can go home.*

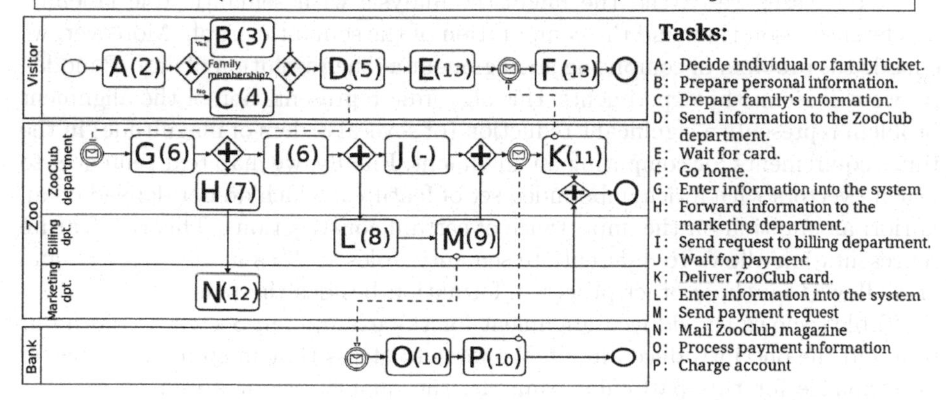

Fig. 1. Textual description and BPMN model of the Zoo business process. The correct alignment is displayed in parenthesis on the task labels.

that, there is nothing preventing both tasks from getting mapped to the same sentence. To correctly solve cases like this, semantic information is required, such as the fact that G and L are performed by different actors, so they should be assigned to sentences where the right actor is performing the task. Another helpful linguistic information can be obtained from gateways surrounding a task: Tasks following choice gateways are more likely to match sentences containing conditional statements.

3 Related Work

The contributions of this paper intersect with various works in the literature. In general, previous work can be categorized into transformations between models and text (e.g., [11,12] for UML diagrams, or [1,13] for BPMN), and schema [14] or process model [15] matching. Also, there has been work on generating process models from group stories [16] and from use-cases [17], which are less related to this work since they restrict the form of the textual description used to describe the process. For the problem considered in this paper, the transformation approches can only be applied when the source process description is unambiguous, and the transformation used does not modify the underlying process. Hence, the rest of the section considers only the work that computes alignments without requiring a transformation between process descriptions.

The seminal work [8,9] proposed an algorithm for aligning textual descriptions and process models, with the particular aim of detecting inconsistencies between both representations. Their approach consists on using a linguistic analysis that derives a bag-of-words summary (i.e., resolving anaphoric references, extracting relevant clauses or removing prepositions) of the main elements in each representation. Then, a similarity computation between these elements is applied, and finally an optimal alignment which globally maximizes the similarity is computed, using a *best-first search* technique.

In our case, we extend the linguistic analysis with semantic role labeling, coreference resolution, and the computation of the semantic graph. Moreover, we encode the problem of computing an alignment as the resolution of an ILP model. As we will see in the experiments, this algebraic representation of the alignment problem represents a significant reduction (of several orders of magnitude) in the time requirements for computing an alignment. Finally, we map text sentences to feature vectors with a rich unbounded set of features, which do not depend on an apriori assumption on the importance of certain constructions. This rich feature representation allows to differentiate semantic roles such as *actor* or *object*, and also allows to include other process information besides the task labels.

Table 1 shows the derived alignment for the example in Sect. 2, by both our tool and the one introduced in [9]. We want to stress that in spite of our better performance for this particular example, the quality of our approach and the one in [9] is similar. We believe both contributions can be naturally combined to boost the quality of the alignments derived.

Table 1. Errors in task-to-sentence alignments produced by our approach and by [9]'s for the example in Sect. 2.

Task	A	B	C	D	E	F	G	H	I	J	K	L	M	N	O	P
Groundtruth	2	3	4	5	13	13	6	7	6	–	11	8	9	12	10	10
[9]'s approach	✓	✓	3 ✗	6 ✗	✓	✓	✓	12 ✗	✓	6 ✗	✓	6 ✗	✓	✓	✓	✓
Our approach	✓	✓	✓	✓	✓	✓	✓	✓	✓	6 ✗	✓	✓	✓	✓	✓	✓

4 Preliminaries on Process Models and NLP

4.1 Graphical Process Notations

There exist a plethora of graphical notations to model processes. A full description of them is beyond the scope of this paper. In this paper we focus on BPMN, a notation that has become one of the most widely used to model business processes. However, the techniques presented can be adapted to other notations like EPCs, Petri Nets, YAWL, among others.

BPMN models are composed by three types of nodes: events, activities and gateways. *Events* (represented as circles) denote something that happens (e.g., time, messages, ...), rather than *Activities* (rounded-corner rectangles) which are something that is done. Finally, *gateways* (diamond shapes) are used to describe the control flow. These elements can be partitioned into pools or lanes, to group activities performed by the same actor (person, department, institution, etc.). An example of BPMN is shown in Fig. 1.

4.2 Natural Language Processing

Natural Language Processing (NLP) is a wide research area inside Artificial Intelligence that includes any kind of technique or application related to the automatic processing of human language. NLP goals range from simple basic processing such as determining in which language a text is written, to high-level complex applications such as Machine Translation, Dialogue Systems, or Intelligent Assistants.

However, linguistic analysis tools can be used as a means to structure information contained in texts for its later processing in applications less related to language itself. This is our case, where we use NLP analyzers to convert a textual description of a BPM into a structured representation that can be compared, mapped, or analyzed using more conventional tools.

The NLP processing software used in this work is FreeLing[1] [5], an open-source library of language analyzers providing a variety of analysis modules for a wide range of languages. More specifically, the natural language processing layers used in this work are:

Tokenization and sentence splitting: Given a text, split the basic lexical terms (word, punctuation signs, numbers, ZIP codes, URLs, e-mail, etc.), and group these tokens into sentences.

Morphological analysis: For each word in the text, find out its possible parts-of-speech (PoS).

PoS-Tagging: Determine which is the right PoS for each word in a sentence. (e.g. the word *dance* is a verb in *I dance all Saturdays* but it is a noun in *I enjoyed our dance together.*)

Named Entity Recognition: Detect named entities in the text, which may be formed by one or more tokens, and classify them as *person*, *location*, *organization*, *time-expression*, *numeric-expression*, *currency-expression*, etc.

Word sense disambiguation: Determine the sense of each word in a text (e.g. the word *crane* may refer to an animal or to a weight-lifting machine). We use WordNet [18] as the sense catalogue and synset codes as concept identifiers.

Constituency/dependency parsing: Given a sentence, get its syntatic structure as a constituency/dependency parse tree.

[1] http://nlp.cs.upc.edu/freeling.

Semantic role labeling: Given a sentence identify its predicates and the main actors in each of them, regardless of the surface structure of the sentence (active/passive, main/subordinate, etc.)

Coreference resolution: Given a document, group mentions referring to the same entity (e.g. a person can be mentioned in the text as *Mr. Peterson*, *the director*, or *he*.)

Semantic graph generation: All the information extracted by the previous analyzers can be organized in a graph depicting events (mainly coming from predicates in the text), entities (coming from detected coreference groups), and relations between them (i.e. which entities participate in which events and with which role). This graph can be converted to triples and stored in an RDF database if needed.

5 Aligning Model and Text with ILP

5.1 Overview

A general description of the approach is shown in Fig. 2. The overall process can be separated into three categories. The modules handling the text in natural language (white), the ones treating the process model (light gray) and finally, those working on feature vectors (dark gray).

As a first stage, the model task labels and the textual process description are analyzed using FreeLing to obtain a structured representation of the text. After that, a phase of feature extraction follows where the model tasks and the text sentences are both converted into a canonical feature vector representation. These vectors can then be compared by means of standard distance metrics.

Parallel to that, a chronological partial order of both the sentences in the text and the tasks in the model is computed. To find an optimal alignment between model and text, these ingredients are encoded as an ILP model, whose solution denotes an optimal alignment between tasks and sentences. That assignment is used afterwards to both present the results to the end user and compute a numerical similarity score.

5.2 Linguistic Analysis of Text and Model

We perform a full NLP analysis on the text body corresponding to the input text, as listed in Sect. 4.2. This is a distinctive aspect of our approach with respect to [8,9], since we gather the linguistic information from the semantic graph, which contains a structured semantic representation of the text.

For the process model, we extract the natural language parts contained on it (from the activities, events, gateways, arcs, lanes and pools), and then a simple lingustic analysis (up to the word sense disambiguation step) is performed.[2]

[2] In order improve the performance of the word sense disambiguator on model sentences, the sentences from the text are provided as additional context to the analyzer. This greatly improves the disambiguation step when the model and the text are sharing a common semantic domain.

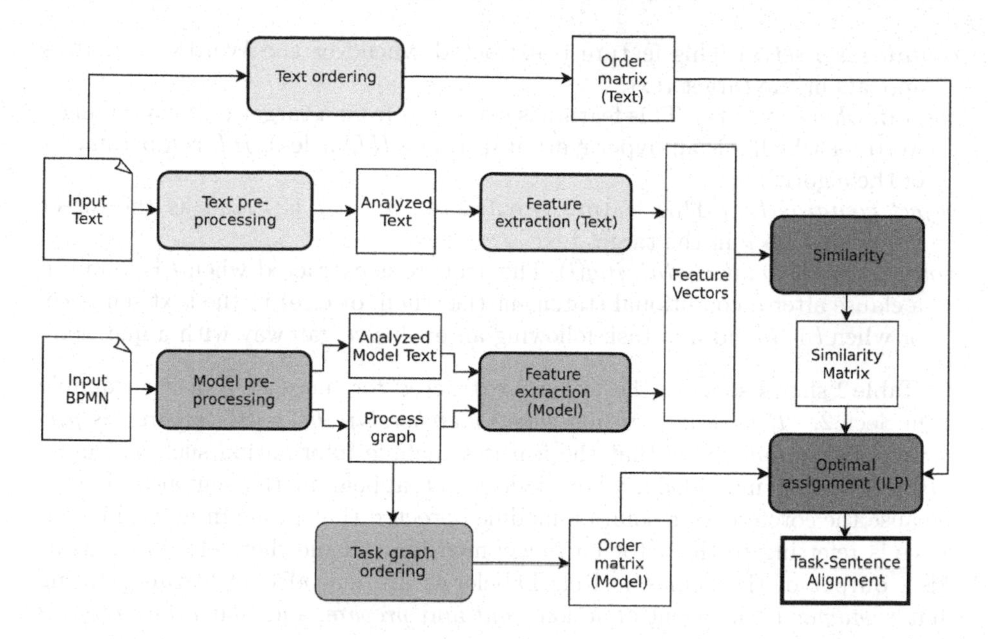

Fig. 2. Diagram illustrating the approach taken.

All the information gathered is then used in the feature extraction phase, explained in the next section.

5.3 Feature Extraction

Up to this point, the model and text are represented using different structures and handled separately. At this step they are both converted into an identical representation of feature vectors by the means of a feature extraction step. The purpose of this transformation is to enable the comparison by deriving a canonical representation. The motivation of using feature vectors is to aim for an *open* description of the text in both representations, i.e., to consider features as assignments to linguistic characteristics extracted from the text. We have considered the following linguistic characteristics in our approach (unless stated otherwise, *target text* in descriptions below refers to either a sentence in the textual description or to the label of a model task):

$contains\_lemma(l, pos)$ This feature is extracted from the target text if it contains a word with the lemma l and part-of-speech pos.

$contains\_action(a)$ This is extracted from a target text where the action a (typically a verb) is found.

$agent\_contains(l, v)$ This feature encodes who is performing the text or task action. It is extracted for text sentences whenever l is found as the agent of verb v, or for model tasks containing verb v and belonging to a swimlane/pool containing l.

contains_synset(s) This feature is extracted whenever the WordNet synset s appears in the target text.

contains_hypernym(s) This feature is extracted from a target text containing a word for which s is an hypernym[3] at distance HL or less. HL is a parameter of the algorithm.

object_contains(l, v) This feature is extracted when l is found as the direct object of verb v in the target text.

follows_conditional_containing(l) This feature is extracted when l is found in a clause after a conditional statement (i.e. then, or else) in the text sentence, or when l is found in a task following an exclusive gateway with a question.

Table 2 shows some of the features extracted for sentence 3 in the example from Sect. 2, *"If he wants an individual membership, he must prepare his personal information"*. Note that the features include information such as lemma *customer* being mentioned, when it does not appear in the sentence. This is because the coreference resolution module detected that pronoun *he* in this sentence is referring to the actor *customer* mentioned somewhere else in the text. Also, output of the Semantic Role Labeler is also encoded in features stating that *customer* is the agent of action *want* and *prepare*, and that *information* is the object of *prepare*.

Table 2. Set of features (some omitted for brevity) for example sentence 3.

contains_lemma(customer, noun)	contains_lemma(want, verb)
contains_lemma(individual, adj.)	contains_action(want)
contains_action(prepare)	contains_synset(09984659-n::client)
contains_hypernym(10741590-n::user)	agent_contains(customer, wants)
agent_contains(customer, prepare)	object_contains(prepare, information)

Clearly, because the features are instantiated by words, this generates an open space of potentially infinite dimensions. For instance, the feature *contains_action* is instantiated twice for the sentence *The crane catched a fish and flew away*: *contains_action*$(catch)$ and *contains_action*(fly). In practice, this is handled by using a sparse representation of vectors.

The set of features proposed encodes high-level semantic information such as: who is the agent of the action, what is the action, or under what conditions is the task executed. That context is sometimes crucial in detecting whether a task is describing an action, referring to it or just using similar terms. The model and the text should generate similar feature vectors whenever the similarity between a sentence and a task is high, and vice-versa. This means the chosen features must represent properties that can be found both in the BPMN model and the textual description.

[3] A word w_1 is a *hypernym* of w_2 iff w_1 describes a superclass of w_2 (e.g. *mammal* is a hypernym of *cat*, and *document* is a hypernym of *letter*). Hypernymy is obtained from WordNet.

5.4 Similarity Metrics

After the feature vector transformation defined in Sect. 5.3 it suffices to compare similarities between feature vectors in order to compute the similarity between a task and a sentence. In order to adjust the relevance of a feature f, we associate a scalar weight w_f to it as the product of two values: a constant value w_f^c that is particular for each feature class (e.g.: *contains_lemma*), and a variable value w_f^v whose magnitude depends on certain conditions. The set of constant weights of each feature class is a parameter of the algorithm. As an example, the particular weight of a feature such as *contains_lemma*(*customer*, *noun*) can be defined as the product of a constant factor for all instances of *contains_lemma* and the *tf-idf*[4] score of this lemma in the sentence.

Three similarity metrics are available as parameters: The *Cosine similarity* and the weighted versions of the *Jaccard index* and the *Overlapping index*. We have evaluated all three metrics and have chosen the last one as the default for our tool, since it gives more intuitive numerical values and the performance between all three does not differ significantly:

Weighted overlapping index This metric expands the Overlapping index by considering weighted elements in the set, such as in our case:

$$WeightedOverlapping(A, B) = \frac{\sum_{f \in A \cap B} w_f}{\sum_{g \in smallest(A,B)} w_g}$$

This metric returns a bounded value between 0 and 1.

5.5 Text and Model Ordering

When only considering the similarity metrics defined in the previous section, a task and a sentence might be very similar but may appear at very different parts of the corresponding representations [8]. For example, the action described by the sentence might occur in the last part of the text, while the task could be amongst the first tasks to execute in the process model. This means the chronological order of the events must be taken into account when trying to determine whether a task and a sentence refer to the same action.

Consequently, we seek to find the partial order relation $\preceq$ between the elements of both representations, text and model, such that $e \preceq e'$ means: "Element e happens before, or at the same time as e'". This allows us to define the strict order relation $\rightsquigarrow$ as

$$e \rightsquigarrow e' \iff e \preceq e' \wedge e' \npreceq e$$

In the process model, the computation of the strict ordering relation goes beyond the mere structure of the model, and instead should be computed from

[4] The *tf-idf* of a token t is the product of *tf* := (Number of appearances of t in its sentence/Number of tokens in that sentence) and *idf* := log_e(Total number of sentences/Sentences containing t).

the underlying behavior. Fortunately, there are efficient techniques to determine the strict order relation [19,20] of a process model. In this paper, the relation $\rightsquigarrow$ corresponds to that same relation in the *behavioral profile* of the model as explained in [19].

Using the example in Sect. 2, a full *behavioral profile* would be extracted containing relations such as $G \rightsquigarrow I$ (happens before), $B + C$ (exclusive) or $H||L$ (parallel).

For the case of the text, it has been shown that the ambiguities present in textual descriptions make it impossible to determine the order of the tasks in them with total certainty [21]. This makes it hard to precisely extract the order unless techniques for extracting temporal relations are applied [22,23]. In our case, we have chosen to simplify the problem assuming a sequential order of the events depicted in the text. This assumption fails whenever the text deliberately reports events in reverse order such as in: "Task A is performed. But before A, Task B must have been executed.". In practice we hardly found such reverse ordering constructions in the texts describing process models.

5.6 Optimal Alignment Computation

This final step aims to find the optimal alignment between sentences in the textual description and tasks in the model. That information is then used in order to compute the global similarity between the model and the text as a numeric score. The information found in the optimal alignment can also aid in finding the actual inconsistencies between both representations as seen in [8]: (i) Tasks describing actions not appearing in the text, (ii) Sentences describing actions which are not in the model, and (iii) Different orderings of tasks.

For a formal definition of the problem, let the task set be T, the sentence set be S and $sim(s, t)$ be the computed similarity between $s \in S$ and $t \in T$[5] (cf Sect. 5.4). We assume for all pairs of elements both in S and T the order relation $\rightsquigarrow$ has been computed.

We define an alignment as a partial function $f_A : T \twoheadrightarrow S$ of tasks to sentences such that $f_A(t) = s$, meaning that task t is describing the same actions as sentence s. In a fashion similar to that of [8], we define the optimal alignment f_A^* to be the alignment fulfilling the following properties:

Partial assignment The domain of f_A^*, denoted by $Dom(f_A^*)$ is a subset of the whole set of tasks, i.e. all $t \in T'$, for $T' \subseteq T$.

Order consistency Let $s = f_A^*(t)$ and $s' = f_A^*(t')$ for some pair of different tasks (t, t'). Then, the following restriction must hold: $t \rightsquigarrow t' \implies s \preceq s'$

Optimality The value of $\sum_{t \in Dom(f_A^*)} sim(t, f_A^*(t))$ is the maximum value such that the two other properties hold.

[5] In this case, $sim(s, t)$ corresponds to $WeightedOverlapping(v_s, v_t)$ where v_s and v_t are the feature vectors of s and t respectively.

In order to obtain a solution, the aforementioned properties can be encoded in the following ILP:

$$\textbf{maximize:} \sum_{s\in S}\sum_{t\in T} a_{t,s} \cdot sim(t,s)$$

subject to:

$$\forall t \in T: \qquad \sum_{s\in S} a_{t,s} = 1$$

$$\forall (s,s') \in S \times S, (t,t') \in T \times T, t \rightsquigarrow t' \wedge s' \rightsquigarrow s : a_{t,s} + a_{t',s'} \leq 1$$

variables:

$$\forall s \in S, t \in T: \qquad a_{t,s} \in \{0,1\}$$

The variables $a_{t,s}$ can be interpreted as: “Task t is assigned to sentence s”, i.e.: $a_{s,t} \iff s = f_A^*(t)$. The first family of constraints limits the number of sentences per task to exactly one[6]; this contradicts the requirement for function f_A^* to be partial, since a solution to the ILP model will has domain T. In practice, however, a threshold is used on the value $sim(t,s)$, and hence, assignments between tasks and sentences below this threshold are discarded. Finally, the second family of constraints encodes the *Order consistency* property by discarding the cases in which the order restriction would be violated.

Theorem 1. *The ILP model for aligning textual descriptions and process models is feasible and computes an optimal alignment f_A^* for a similarity metric sim.*

6 Experiments and Tool Support

The techniques of this paper have been implemented and are available as a web application[7]. The tool uses FreeLing for linguistic analysis, and Gurobi [24] as ILP solver. As similarity metric, we used the *weighted overlapping index*. Below we provide the two main experiments performed, devoted to analyze the positioning of the tool with respect to the state-of-the-art tool for the same task, (Sect. 6.1) and to test the tool capabilities in handling large instances (Sect. 6.2). The experiments for both tools have been performed on the same machine.

[6] Note that these equations can also be encoded using the *Special Ordered Sets* (*SOS*) constraint $\forall t : a_{t,1}, \cdots, a_{t,|S|}$, which denotes exactly the same constraint, and yields better performance in the ILP solvers that implement it.

[7] The web application is available at: http://xorrai.cs.upc.edu:8080/bpmninterface/. The tool we present in this paper corresponds to the *BPMN vs Text* tab.

6.1 Comparison with the Technique from [9]

To validate the quality of the results provided by our tool, we compare them with the ones generated by the approach in [9], on a gold standard from [13] that was later extended by the authors of [9]. We also expanded the gold standard with the last group of models, taken from [13]. The models in this benchmark were manually analyzed in [9,13] to obtain the correct assignment between tasks and sentences, so that the quality of a tool can be assessed.

Table 3 reports the results. For each model, we provide the number of tasks and sentences. Moreover, for each approach we report the accuracy (ratio of tasks correctly assigned to its matching sentence) and the execution time (average time per task) for each tool. To obtain a global perspective of the results, we provide a micro-average (total computation time over total number of tasks in all models), a macro-average (total computation time over number of models) and a median. The hughe differences between both methods are caused by a small subset of models that are more difficult to solve than the rest. Although our approach produces slightly better accuracies than [9], the difference is not significant. However, our approach can obtain the same accuracy in the alignment with a remarkable reduction of computation time.

Table 3. Accuracy and solving time of our proposal and the one in [9].

Model	$\|T\|$	$\|S\|$	[9] approach		Our proposal	
			Acc.	$^{ms}/_{task}$	Acc.	$^{ms}/_{task}$
Model1-2	8	6	100.0%	98	100.0%	29
Model1-4	7	11	100.0%	256	100.0%	45
Model10-1	4	3	75.0%	94	75.0%	27
Model10-10	10	8	70.0%	92	80.0%	26
Model10-11	9	7	77.8%	53	66.7%	23
Model10-12	5	4	80.0%	14	80.0%	23
Model10-13	4	3	100.0%	15	100.0%	25
Model10-14	10	5	50.0%	595	60.0%	29
Model10-3	12	11	91.7%	807	75.0%	28
Model10-4	11	9	90.9%	1,221	90.9%	28
Model10-5	4	4	100.0%	338	100.0%	24
Model10-6	4	3	75.0%	89	75.0%	20
Model10-7	8	7	100.0%	555	100.0%	19
Model10-8	5	7	80.0%	374	60.0%	27
Model10-9	8	5	100.0%	388	75.0%	23
Model2-1	26	38	76.9%	7,532	76.9%	134
Model2-2	19	30	63.2%	7,706	73.7%	84
Model3-1	6	7	100.0%	97	83.3%	28
Model3-2	6	4	100.0%	72	100.0%	20
Model3-3	4	5	100.0%	228	100.0%	29
Model3-4	2	4	50.0%	153	50.0%	56
Model3-5	11	9	81.8%	214	72.7%	31
Model3-6	6	8	83.3%	515	83.3%	28
Model4-1	18	40	33.3%	30,757	55.6%	173
Model5-1	2	6	0.0%	341	0.0%	73
Model5-2	5	5	60.0%	572	80.0%	30
Model5-3	9	10	55.6%	1,015	55.6%	34
Model6-2	4	5	75.0%	255	75.0%	33
Model6-3	5	9	80.0%	985	80.0%	1,880
Model6-4	9	14	66.7%	1,204	44.4%	47
Model7-1	4	7	100.0%	442	100.0%	30
Model8-1	5	3	100.0%	167	80.0%	18
Model8-2	5	6	40.0%	461	60.0%	26
Model8-3	5	5	100.0%	445	80.0%	26
Model9-1	7	8	71.4%	151	85.7%	33
Model9-3	6	4	100.0%	83	66.7%	25
Model9-4	7	5	28.6%	89	71.4%	26
Model9-5	8	7	62.5%	579	62.5%	24
Model9-6	8	13	37.5%	1,275	25.0%	45
BicycleManuf	9	12	100.0%	772	66.7%	41
ClaimsCreation	6	5	83.3%	467	100.0%	30
HotelService	12	11	91.7%	196	83.3%	33
Dispatch-of-g	7	7	71.4%	709	100.0%	35
Hospital	14	14	28.6%	25,109	71.4%	35
Hotel	12	11	83.3%	198	83.3%	30
Self-service	18	13	83.3%	1,002	88.9%	38
Underwriter	7	11	85.7%	274	100.0%	43
Zoo	15	12	46.7%	214	73.3%	31
Micro average			**73.7%**	**3,517**	**76.3%**	**76**
Macro average			**75.6%**	**1,860**	**76.4%**	**79**
Median			**80.0%**	**357.5**	**80.0%**	**29.5**

6.2 Experiments on Large Instances

In the previous experiment validated the quality of the results provided by our technique. In this second experiment we focus on the time performance, using models of increasing size. This will allow to extrapolate the capabilities of our approach for larger instances. For the sake of comparison, we also include the execution times for the current implementation of the tool described in [9].

Due to the small number of available model–text pairs, and to reduced range of model sizes in existing data, we opted for generating a synthetic dataset of model-text pairs. The model generation consists of two steps: first we use the PGL2 tool [25] to generate the structure of a BPMN model. The second step consists of enriching the generated model by replacing model labels with randomly generated task descriptions. Once a process model is generated, a text is also generated with a random number of sentences $|S| = |T| \pm k$, where $|T|$ is the number of tasks in the model, and k was set to three in the experiments. Both the text sentences and the task descriptions in the model are generated with a simple word–bigram Markov model built using [26], trained with all the textual descriptions from the benchmark in Sect. 6.1. The generated synthetic benchmark has 400 model–text pairs ranging from 1 to 115 tasks.

Figure 3 shows the execution time of both tools for all model sizes[8]. The plots show that our approach has an asymptotic behavior with a complexity much lower than the methods in [9]. Remarkably, there is a correlation between the variance in the execution time and the input size: from size 50 upwards in the plot of the right of Fig. 3, one can see that the execution time for models of similar size varies significantly. This suggests that other factors, apart from the model size, influence the execution time.

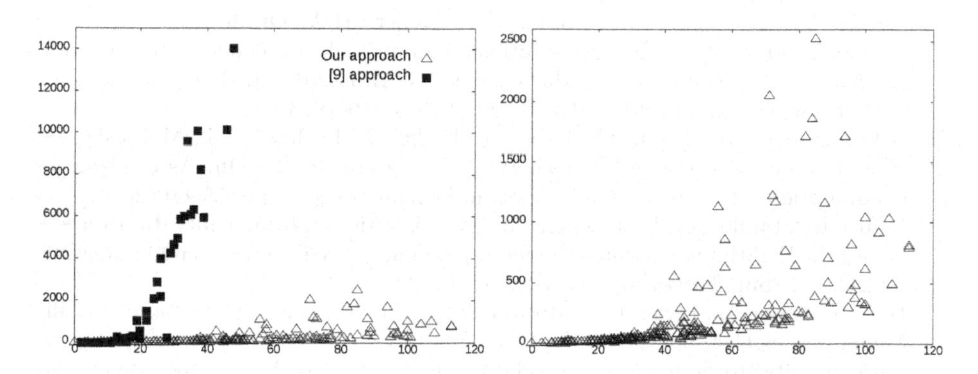

Fig. 3. Left: Execution times (in seconds) for [9] and our approach. Right: Zoom-in for the execution times of our approach.

[8] We could not include all the executions for the approach from [9] since instances bigger than 46 tasks hit the imposed 4 h time limit.

7 Conclusions and Future Work

In this paper we have proposed a novel approach for aligning textual descriptions and graphical models of processes. By applying a full linguistic analysis that results in an extensive set of features, and casting the problem as a mathematical optimization, we were able to align instances of unprecedented size. Moreover, in terms of quality the technique performs similar to the state of the art approach.

As a future work, we plan to expand the capabilities of the tool in different dimensions. First, we plan to incorporate the analysis of temporal relations in the text so that the control flow is better described. Second, a full exploration of the parameters of the technique (e.g., the weights for the similarity metric) will be done to boost the quality of the results. Finally, we plan to evaluate the tool in more realistic scenarios.

Acknowledgements. We would like to thank Han van der Aa and Henrik Leopold for their help and support to this work, and for sharing their software and part of the data used in the experiments of the paper. This work is funded by the Spanish Ministry for Economy and Competitiveness (MINECO), the European Union (FEDER funds) under grants COMMAS and Graph-Med (ref. TIN2013-46181-C2-1-R, TIN2016-77820-C3-3-R).

References

1. Leopold, H., Mendling, J., Polyvyanyy, A.: Supporting process model validation through natural language generation. IEEE Trans. Softw. Eng. **40**(8), 818–840 (2014)
2. Dumas, M., Rosa, M.L., Mendling, J., Reijers, H.A.: Fundamentals of Business Process Management. Springer, Heidelberg (2013)
3. van der Aa, H., Leopold, H., Mannhardt, F., Reijers, H.A.: On the fragmentation of process information: challenges, solutions, and outlook. In: Gaaloul, K., Schmidt, R., Nurcan, S., Guerreiro, S., Ma, Q. (eds.) CAISE 2015. LNBIP, vol. 214, pp. 3–18. Springer, Cham (2015). doi:10.1007/978-3-319-19237-6_1
4. Manning, C.D., Surdeanu, M., Bauer, J., Finkel, J., Bethard, S.J., McClosky, D.: The stanford CoreNLP natural language processing toolkit. In: Association for Computational Linguistics (ACL) System Demonstrations, pp. 55–60 (2014)
5. Padró, L., Stanilovsky, E.: Freeling 3.0: towards wider multilinguality. In: Proceedings of the Eighth International Conference on Language Resources and Evaluation, LREC, Istanbul, Turkey, pp. 2473–2479, May 2012
6. Bird, S., Loper, E., Ewan, K.: Natural Language Processing with Python. O'Reilly Media Inc., Sebastopol (2009)
7. Apache Software Foundation: Apache OpenNLP (2010). http://opennlp.apache.org/
8. van der Aa, H., Leopold, H., Reijers, H.A.: Detecting inconsistencies between process models and textual descriptions. In: Motahari-Nezhad, H.R., Recker, J., Weidlich, M. (eds.) BPM 2015. LNCS, vol. 9253, pp. 90–105. Springer, Cham (2015). doi:10.1007/978-3-319-23063-4_6
9. van der Aa, H., Leopold, H., Reijers, H.A.: Comparing textual descriptions to process models - the automatic detection of inconsistencies. Inf. Syst. **64**, 447–460 (2016)

10. Hevner, A.R., March, S.T., Park, J., Ram, S.: Design science in information systems research. MIS Q. **28**(1), 75–105 (2004)
11. Meziane, F., Athanasakis, N., Ananiadou, S.: Generating natural language specifications from UML class diagrams. Requir. Eng. **13**(1), 1–18 (2008)
12. Bajwa, I.S., Choudhary, M.A.: From natural language software specifications to UML class models. In: Zhang, R., Zhang, J., Zhang, Z., Filipe, J., Cordeiro, J. (eds.) ICEIS 2011. LNBIP, vol. 102, pp. 224–237. Springer, Heidelberg (2012). doi:10.1007/978-3-642-29958-2_15
13. Friedrich, F., Mendling, J., Puhlmann, F.: Process model generation from natural language text. In: Mouratidis, H., Rolland, C. (eds.) CAiSE 2011. LNCS, vol. 6741, pp. 482–496. Springer, Heidelberg (2011). doi:10.1007/978-3-642-21640-4_36
14. Rahm, E., Bernstein, P.A.: A survey of approaches to automatic schema matching. VLDB J. **10**(4), 334–350 (2001)
15. Cayoglu, U., et al.: Report: the process model matching contest 2013. In: Lohmann, N., Song, M., Wohed, P. (eds.) BPM 2013. LNBIP, vol. 171, pp. 442–463. Springer, Cham (2014). doi:10.1007/978-3-319-06257-0_35
16. de A.R. Gonçalves, J.C., Santoro, F.M., Baião, F.A.: Business process mining from group stories. In: Proceedings of the 13th International Conference on Computers Supported Cooperative Work in Design, CSCWD, Santiago, Chile, pp. 161–166, April 2009
17. Sinha, A., Paradkar, A.M.: Use cases to process specifications in business process modeling notation. In: IEEE International Conference on Web Services, ICWS, Miami, Florida, pp. 473–480, July 2010
18. Fellbaum, C.: WordNet. An Electronic Lexical Database. Language, Speech, and Communication. MIT Press, Cambridge (1998)
19. Weidlich, M.: Behavioural profiles: a relational approach to behaviour consistency. Ph.D. thesis, University of Potsdam (2011)
20. Polyvyanyy, A., Weidlich, M., Conforti, R., Rosa, M., ter Hofstede, A.H.M.: The 4C spectrum of fundamental behavioral relations for concurrent systems. In: Ciardo, G., Kindler, E. (eds.) PETRI NETS 2014. LNCS, vol. 8489, pp. 210–232. Springer, Cham (2014). doi:10.1007/978-3-319-07734-5_12
21. van der Aa, H., Leopold, H., Reijers, H.A.: Dealing with behavioral ambiguity in textual process descriptions. In: La Rosa, M., Loos, P., Pastor, O. (eds.) BPM 2016. LNCS, vol. 9850, pp. 271–288. Springer, Cham (2016). doi:10.1007/978-3-319-45348-4_16
22. Mirza, P.: Extracting temporal and causal relations between events. Ph.D. thesis, International Doctorate School in Information and Communication Technologies, University of Trento, Italy (2016)
23. UzZaman, N., Llorens, H., Derczynski, L., Allen, J., Verhagen, M., Pustejovsky, J.: SemEval-2013 Task 1: TEMPEVAL-3: evaluating time expressions, events, and temporal relations. In: Second Joint Conference on Lexical and Computational Semantics (*SEM), vol. 2: Proceedings of the Seventh International Workshop on Semantic Evaluation (SemEval 2013), Atlanta, Georgia, USA, pp. 1–9. Association for Computational Linguistics, June 2013
24. Gurobi Optimization Inc: Gurobi optimizer reference manual (2016). https://www.gurobi.com/documentation/6.5/refman.pdf
25. Burattin, A.: PLG2: multiperspective process randomization with online and offline simulations. In: Online Proceedings of the BPM Demo Track 2016, Rio de Janeiro, Brasil, September 2016
26. Schwartz, H.R.: Markov sentence generator (2010). https://github.com/hrs/markov-sentence-generator

Use Cases for Understanding Business Process Models

Banu Aysolmaz(✉) and Hajo A. Reijers

Business Informatics Group, Vrije Universiteit Amsterdam,
Amsterdam, The Netherlands
{b.e.aysolmaz,h.a.reijers}@vu.nl

Abstract. Process models are used by people for many different purposes. Depending on that purpose, users may look into process models in different ways. However, the current stream of research into process model comprehension does not explicitly consider the type of information that a user is seeking for. By failing to do so, attempts to improve the readability of process models may be lopsided at best. To overcome this situation, we propose a list of 17 so-called process model comprehension use cases. These capture the different types of information-seeking behavior of the users. We validated the list through interview and focus group studies, which included 24 participants from 8 organizations. Based on our findings, we present implications for researchers to re-investigate the comprehension topic. The use cases may also be beneficial for the development of modeling tools and process modelers to better support the user needs.

Keywords: Process model comprehension · Use case · Process perspective

1 Introduction

Conceptual modeling is an established means to perform systems analysis in information systems research [8]. Conceptual models are employed to fulfill a variety of purposes, most importantly to understand the information system under investigation, and facilitate the communication between different types of stakeholders [34]. A process model is a specific type of conceptual model listed among the most frequently used conceptual modeling types [8]. Process models represent business activities, events, and control flow relations that constitute a business process [21]. Process models may also incorporate aspects such as the data that is being processed, the organizational resources that are involved in their execution, and the information systems that are supporting the processes under consideration [26].

A precondition to use process models is that they are properly understood by the people who use them [21]. Streams of research have focused on the identification of factors that influence how users look into and understand process models

E. Dubois and K. Pohl (Eds.): CAiSE 2017, LNCS 10253, pp. 428–442, 2017.
DOI: 10.1007/978-3-319-59536-8_27

[3,11,21,25,27]. However, those studies generally do not take into account that the information that is being sought in a process model may differ depending on the user or the occasion. To illustrate this, let us consider the study on the use of abstract labels in process models (i.e. "*A*", "*B*") [21]. The authors show that the use of abstract labels may improve the understanding of a model by its users. However, this improvement manifests itself if a user looks at a process model to understand its *behavioral dimension*, i.e. the ways activities are being sequenced. Our point is that this specific *information-seeking goal* of the user is only one of the many different aims that people may have when consulting a process model. Clearly, abstract labels will not help to understand any aspects of the activities themselves, i.e. grasp its *functional dimension*.

We observe that existing research on process model comprehension does not explicitly consider the information-seeking objectives of the model user. This means that it is unclear how universally valid the factors are that have been identified as influential on process model comprehension so far. In addition, we may be missing what matters for other types of information-seeking than what has been investigated to date. Against this background, this paper aims to establish a basis for better understanding what individuals look for when using process models. The various information-seeking objectives are shaped in the form of so-called Business Process Model Comprehension (BPMC) use cases. The use cases are focused on the individual task of making sense of process models, in contrast to, for example, the purposes organizations have for them. The use cases are meant to be generic in the sense that they are independent of the specific notation used, the purpose for which the process model is developed, the business domain that the captured process is situated in, and so on.

We evaluate the relevance and completeness of the proposed use cases through a series of interviews and a focus group session. Overall, these involved 24 participants from 8 organizations. We establish how the different use cases are perceived with respect to their relevance and prevalence, also taking into account the various process roles a user may have. We further examine how easy or difficult it is to carry out the use cases when relying on state-of-the-art technology. Building on these findings, we identify implications for researchers into process model comprehension, for process modelers, and for developers of process modeling tools.

The remainder of this paper is organized as follows. In Sect. 2 we elaborate on the related work, which lead us to defining the use cases. In Sect. 3, we describe how we constructed the BPMC use case list, and introduce the design of our validation approach and the protocol used. In Sect. 4, we describe the implementation of the validation approach, and present the results in three parts: an overall evaluation, an evaluation based on process roles, and an evaluation considering modeling tools. In Sect. 5 we discuss the implications of our work for research and practice before concluding the paper in Sect. 6.

2 Related Work

The primary purpose of process models is to improve communication between stakeholders [28]. To ensure that this communication unfolds smoothly, it is necessary that a process model is correctly understood by its users [25]. Recker et al. define *process model comprehension* as "the ability of a user to retain domain information from the elements in a process model" [25]. Domain information to be retained from process models fall into four categories: *functional* (the activities performed), *behavioral* (sequencing and conditions between the activities), *organizational* (roles and systems that perform the activities), and *informational* (data and artifacts produced or manipulated) perspectives [7].

In the BPM field, factors influencing model comprehension are along three axes: content, content representation, and user characteristics [25]. The factors in the content and content presentation categories are, for example, modeling notations [24], symbol visualizations [11,13], labeling style [21], lay-outing [20], modeling direction [14], and complexity [10]. In the user characteristics category the factors mostly studied are: domain experience, process modeling knowledge, and process modeling experience [11,21,24,27]. In addition, deeper personal factors have been examined, such as cognitive style (spatial vs. verbal) [12], cognitive abstraction ability, and learning style [25]. Some personal factors depend on the context in which the user uses the process model. Among such factors are the intrinsic and extrinsic learning motivation, expectations, and strategy [25,29].

In contrast to the focus of *process model comprehension* on the retrieval of domain information, the studies mentioned do not explicitly define the type of information to be retained as a factor of comprehension. In most cases, the information-seeking behavior assumed by the user is not even mentioned. The BPM community mostly measures the comprehension of process models for cases where the user looks into the model to obtain information on the behavioral perspective [18]. Some studies explicate this fact by indicating that the comprehension questions asked are on control-flow aspects, e.g. [13]. Others take it for granted by not explicitly specifying the type of information to be retained, e.g. [21]. However, other perspectives are as important to fulfill the various purposes of using process models [1,16]. For example, project managers view roles to plan and monitor the project, while auditors investigate the activities and related deliverables to evaluate compliance [6].

In addition to the type of information sought, the number of process models used to retrieve such information is another dimension of process model use. The distinction between the examination of a single process vs. a set of processes is recognized by various studies on process model modularity [28,33]. Once again, the type of information to be retained from those process models are not explicitly reflected upon in these studies. At this stage, contradictory results seems to have emerged on multi-model comprehension (e.g. [28] vs. [33]). When considered more closely, one of the studies actually covers comprehension questions on only the behavioral perspective of the process models [28], while the other includes questions on the organizational and informational perspectives as well [33]. A reason for the incompatible results obtained in these experiments may be the difference in information-seeking behavior of the users, which is a further motivation for the presented work.

In summary, the type of task that a user performs has an impact on how the model is comprehended. In the BPM field, the effect of task differences are emphasized in terms of purpose, such as improvement and execution [12]. The term "*process use*" came into use that relates process model use to information-seeking [22]. However, current comprehension studies do not explicitly define how the users look into process models in order to get information on different process perspectives. Our motivation is to support the BPM community to explicitly characterize the various ways process models are read and consider the type of information sought as a factor in their own research endeavors. The set of use cases that may be used for this will be presented next.

3 Research Method

In this section, we first explain how we construct the use cases and present the list of BPMC use cases. We then introduce the design of the interviews and the focus group study we performed to validate the use case list, and lastly present the protocol devised for these studies.

3.1 Construction of the Use Cases

We start out with this section by defining the concept of a BPMC use case as "*a case where a users displays a certain type of information-seeking behavior to comprehend a process model or a set of process models*". Note that with this definition, we focus on the level of *understanding* a process model, in contrast to the superficial *reading* task that it pre-supposes. Specifically this means for our work, in accordance to the views of Von Foerster [15], that understanding a process model encompasses the notions of *intent* behind and *context* of the elements in a process model beyond the mere identification of their presence. In addition, we adopt the concept of information-seeking behavior as defined by Wilson: "*the purposive seeking of information as a consequence of a need to satisfy some goal*" [35]. The definition of a BPMC use case resembles the concept of *repeated process model use* as introduced by Nolte et al. [22], which explains how users employ process models to obtain information from these for the objective they wish to accomplish.

There are different perspectives that can be taken when organizing use cases in the context of understanding process models. Notably, use cases can be tied to *organizational* goals, such as process improvement, redesign, automation, and compliance checking [5,16]. Depending on the exact organizational goal, different insights should be retrievable from a process model. This underlines how relevant it is for both practice and industry to be aware of the purpose of a particular process model. However, regardless of the specific goal to inspect a process model, a person must make sense of its separate elements and their relations to build up a mental model of that process. This *individual* perspective, which is tied to the micro-structures within a process model, is where the focus of our use cases is. Clearly, there is a relation between the organizational use of a process model

Table 1. List of BPMC use cases

No	Name	Perspective	No. of Processes
1	Get an overview of the whole process	All	Single
2	Understand every aspect of a process in detail	All	Single
3	Understand a part of the process in detail	All	Single
4	Discover alternative ways of how a process can be carried out	Behavioral	Single
5	Understand how the process is carried out under specific circumstances	Behavioral	Single
6	Look up activities in a process	Functional	Single
7	Look up organizational units/roles in a process	Organizational	Single
8	Look up IT systems in a process	Organizational	Single
9	Look up how data is processed in a process	Informational	Single
10	Look up how parts of a process are related to each other	All	Single
11	Look up activities in a set of processes	Functional	Multiple
12	Look up organizational units/roles in a set of processes	Organizational	Multiple
13	Look up IT systems in a set of processes	Organizational	Multiple
14	Look up how data is processed in a set of processes	Informational	Multiple
15	Discover relations between multiple processes	All	Multiple
16	Understand how processes follow up on each other	Behavioral	Multiple
17	Understand the relation between main processes and subprocesses	Behavioral	Multiple

and this individual, sense-making task. Process models need to be understood by individuals on a micro-level to carry out problem-solving tasks on a higher, organizational level. Our motivation to focus on this individual, micro-level of the process model to generate use cases is that these will be relevant for a broad range of organizational purposes, exactly because they are so fundamental in nature.

Based on our view on BPMC use cases, we identified the set of BPMC use cases listed in Table 1. The use cases are organized along two dimensions, which align with our analysis of the literature (Sect. 2): (1) the perspective they are focused on (i.e. behavioral, functional, informational, organizational, and all), and (2) the number of processes examined during the information-seeking action. We identified three aspects for a use case: (1) the "*importance*" to assess the value of a use case [2,31]; (2) the "*prevalence*" to understand how often the use case is encountered; and (3) the "*difficulty*" of carrying out the use case based on the modeling tool used.

3.2 Design of the Interviews and Focus Group Study

We used interviews and focus group study to validate the relevance and completeness of the proposed BPMC use case list. Interviewing is the most prominent qualitative data collection technique [23]. It enables researchers to generate rich data from the individuals' experiential lives, and "*reach beyond the superficial layers of their experience*" [30]. We decided to use interviews to collect in-depth data on how professionals perceive the list of use cases in the context of their work. Focus group research, also known as group interview, is seen as a one-to-many version of interviews as a data collection technique [23]. It has an additional benefit of bringing varied opinions together in an interactive environment [32]. We planned to perform a focus group session to complement the data collected through interviews with opinions generated in an interactive setting.

We wanted to examine if a use case is relevant for people using process models in their business settings. Furthermore, we wanted to examine if the BPMC use case list is complete. Process model users with different roles may be displaying diverse information-seeking behaviors on process models. We aimed to capture this diversity by revealing opinions of professionals having different process roles. We used the following four most common process roles in the BPM field: *Process Analyst, Process Architect, Process Consultant, and Process Owner* [19]. Our main consideration for selecting participants for the interviews and the focus group session was to have all these process roles represented in the study. To take into account cultural variety, we aimed to select participating organizations from diverse sectors and geographical locations.

3.3 Interview and Focus Group Protocol

The protocol we planned to conduct an interview session was as follows. We started an interview by introducing the study and asking the participant to fill out a background survey. Then, for each use case, we presented the use case and followed the folllowing steps. We first asked the participant to score the importance and prevalence of the use case, together with the difficulty of the use case based on the process modeling tool used. For this purpose, the participant used a survey on which these three aspects were scored on a 5-point likert scale. We then asked the participant to elaborate on her scores, and provide examples from her work. Upon the completion of these steps for all use cases, we asked the participant to evaluate the completeness of the list, and provide recommendations for changes. Lastly, we asked the participant to provide improvement ideas for tool features to better support the process model use. The focus group protocol only differed from the interview protocol by allowing discussions among the participants.

We planned to validate the relevance of each use case by the importance and prevalence scores of the participants. If a participant would score the lowest (1 on the 5-point likert scale) for both the importance and the prevalence, it would mean that the use case is irrelevant for that participant. If a use case would be irrelevant for most of the participants, then we would conclude that it is an irrelevant use case. We also planned to evaluate the completeness of the use case list based on the comments of the participants. If the participants would not find the list complete and provide examples of additional use cases, we would conclude that the list is incomplete and update it accordingly. To verify our protocol, we performed two test interviews. The feedback from the test interviews supported that the protocol was clear and led to relevant discussions.

4 Data Analysis and Results

In this section, we first explain how we performed the interviews and the focus group study. Then, we present the analysis results in three sections: (1) an overall evaluation of the perceived importance and prevalence of the use cases,

Table 2. Overview of the participant organizations for the interviews (Organizations No. 1–7) and the focus group study (Organization No. 8)

Org. No.	Sector	Location	Process roles			
			Analyst	Architect	Consultant	Owner
1	Chemicals	NL		X	X	X
2	Banking	NL	X	X		X
3	Financial services	NL	X		X	X
4	Medical supplies	NL	X		X	
5	Public transportation	NL		X	X	
6	Process automation	AU			X	
7	Consultancy	AU	X		X	X
8	Consultancy	NL			X (7)	

(2) evaluation based on process roles, and (3) evaluation of the perceived difficulty of the use cases considering modeling tools.

4.1 Implementation of Interviews and Focus Group Study

In conformance with our selection criterion for the interviews and the focus group study participants, we selected 17 professionals from seven organizations for the interviews, and seven professionals from one organization for the focus group study. An overview of the participating organizations and the performed interviews/focus group sessions can be seen in Table 2. Seven organizations selected for the interviews operated in different sectors. Five of them are located in the Netherlands (NL), while two are located in Australia (AU). The participants of the interviews from each organization performed different process roles. The participants of the focus group session were the employees of the same consultancy company working with different clients from telecommunication and banking sectors. Overall, we reached a diverse set of participants who work with process models regularly, the median of the number of models read in the last year being 70. Each interview took around one hour, and the focus group session took 1.5 hours.

After the interviews and the focus group session, we transcribed and coded the recordings. First, we analyzed the first two interviews, and identified an initial set of codes and related categories. These two interviews were chosen due to their rich content, and the potential to include a high number of codes. All remaining interview and focus group transcripts were traversed and coded based on the initial category list. Whenever a new code was identified, previous transcripts were re-checked to see if this code was applicable.

We present the result of the survey data analysis in box plots in Figs. 1 and 3. The median scores are indicated by the horizontal lines in the boxes, and the boxes represent the lower to upper quartile of all data. Figure 1 displays the perceived importance and prevalence of the use cases, and Fig. 3 depicts the perceived difficulty of the use cases based on the tools used. The values for

Cronbach's alpha confirm the reliability of our instrumentation: it ranges from 0.8 for importance and prevalence, to 0.81 for difficulty. In the sections below, we present the findings from our interviews and focus group analysis together with the survey results.

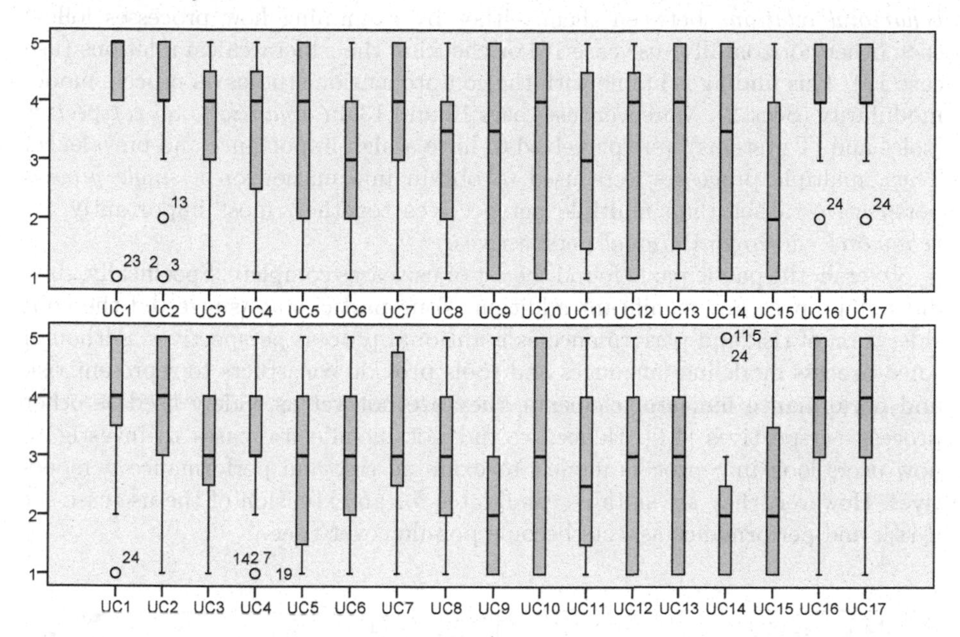

Fig. 1. Perceived importance (top) and prevalence (bottom) of the use cases (5: very important, and very frequent)

4.2 Overall Evaluation

As can be seen in Fig. 1, all of the use cases were perceived to have a high importancc (scorcs ovcr 4), while also being considered as moderately prevalent (scores over 3) by at least one participant. Only use case 15, discovering the relations between multiple processes, was perceived to have both a low importance and low prevalence (median scores of 2). Two use cases on seeking information on a *single* process model were perceived to be of high importance by most of the participants: understanding an individual process as a whole with a high-level perspective (use case 1), and with its complete details including the tasks, flow, roles, data, and IT systems (use case 2). Thus, use cases integrating *multiple perspectives* for a *single process* were important for all process roles.

Two bar charts comparing the perceived importance and prevalence of the use cases grouped by process perspectives can be seen in Fig. 2. The figure indicates that most process model users perceive the *behavioral perspective* to be highly important and prevalent, which is in line with the literature. However, while existing research focuses mostly on the behavioral perspective (Sect. 2), our results show that there are other process perspectives which are similarly important and prevalent for process model comprehension: the *functional* and *organizational* perspectives, as well as *multiple perspectives* combined (see Figs. 1 and 2).

Multiple processes were used by most of the participants to discover the *behavioral relations* between them, either by examining how processes follow each other horizontally (use case 16) or checking their hierarchical relations (use case 17). This finding is in line with the comprehension studies on process model modularity (Sect. 2). Moreover, use cases 12 and 13 on *organizational perspective* (roles and IT systems) were perceived to have a high importance and prevalence. Thus, multiple processes were used to obtain information on a *single process* perspective rather than multiple perspectives together, most importantly for *behavioral* and *organizational* perspectives.

Overall, the participants found the set of use cases complete. Specifically, they did not propose any significant addition. Four participants suggested the consideration of risk and performance as additional process perspectives. Although some process modeling languages and tools provide constructs to represent risk and performance indicator elements, they are not yet as widely used as other process perspectives [4,9]. Hence, we did not include use cases to investigate how users look into process models to examine risk and performance perspectives. However, they are suitable candidates for an extension of the use case set if risk and performance aspects become popular over time.

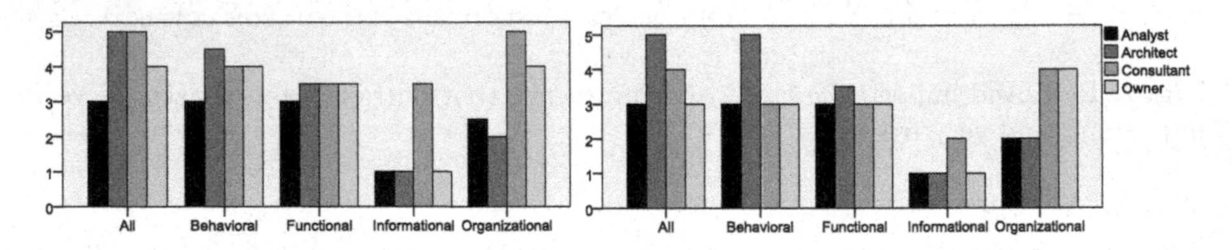

Fig. 2. Perceived importance (left) and prevalence (right) median scores for process perspectives

4.3 Process Role Based Evaluation

There is a high variability in the scores of the participants as can be observed in the box plots in Fig. 1. This variability, however, decreases if the scores are grouped per process role. This highlights the importance of the role of the model user for understanding the information she is seeking. Table 3 shows the median scores for the perceived importance and prevalence per process role, with a color-coded scale collapsed to three levels to better see the patterns in the Likert scale data [17]. Median scores lower than 3 are colored with light gray indicating low importance and prevalence, while the darkest gray is used for scores higher than 3 showing both high importance and prevalence.

Table 3 and Fig. 2 highlight the differences in process model use per process role. The *process analysts* mostly used an individual process, and looked at it from a general perspective (use cases 1 and 3). The specific information they wanted to get from a single process was about *activities* and *roles* (use cases 6 and 7). The *process owners* also favored the use cases on a single process, and mostly investigated a single process with a general perspective (use cases 1, 2, and 3). For them, the most important process perspective was the *organizational* perspective (use cases 7, 8, and 13). They analyzed the roles to "*complete things with the lowest amount of hand-overs possible*" (Process Owner 3).

The *process architects* were significantly more interested in the use cases on understanding *multiple process perspectives* and discovering relations among elements of a single or multiple processes than the other process roles (use cases 1, 2, 10, and 15). While many participants struggled to make sense of use case 15, discovering relations between multiple processes, a process architect stated that: "*this use case explains the value I generate in my job*". The *process consultant* group perceived the highest number of use cases to be of high importance. For some use cases, they emphasized that they are important even though not used very much. For example, process consultants 1, 3, and 8 stated that use cases 2 and 3 come into the scene only "*for impact analysis in process improvement initiatives*", and "*to solve specific technical issues*".

Two use cases were perceived by most participants to have a low prevalence: use cases 9 and 14. Both are about the *informational perspective*. The process consultants stated that the informational perspective is highly important, but because of the lack of sufficient data elements in the process models created by their organizations they would not be able to apply these use cases properly. However, this was seen as a "*missed opportunity*" (Process Consultants 1, 5, and 7), and a cause of integration problems between systems (Process Consultants 7, 8, and 10).

4.4 Evaluation Considering Modeling Tools

The scores for the perceived difficulty of carrying out the use cases with tools are depicted in Fig. 3. We categorized the tools used by the participants as *modeling tools* that natively implement process modeling functionalities (e.g. Aris, Adonis), and generic *drawing tools* that can be used for any type of modeling (e.g. Visio, Powerpoint).

For each use case involving multiple processes, apart from the last two, the specific information being sought was difficult to establish with a *drawing tool* (scores lower than 3). This can be expected, since drawing tools have hardly any features for process model analysis. What comes as a surprise is that the participants were content with their drawing tools for almost all use cases on a single process, and two use cases on multiple processes (use case 16 and 17). The participants preferred such tools for their simplicity and flexibility. Practical features such as email support motivated some organizations to move from Aris to Visio, and onwards to Powerpoint (Process Owner 2). The perceived difficulty scores for *modeling tools* display a high variation. Although such tools were

Table 3. Median use case scores for importance (Imp.) and prevalence (Prev.) per process roles, color-coded to three levels

	Analysts		Architects		Consultants		Owners	
UC	Imp.	Prev.	Imp.	Prev.	Imp.	Prev.	Imp.	Prev.
UC1	5	5	5	5	5	4	4	3
UC2	1	1	4	5	4	4	4	3.5
UC3	4	4	3	3	3.5	3	4.5	3
UC4	1	2	5	4	4	3	4	3
UC5	1	1	4	4	4	3	3	3
UC6	4	4	3	3	2	2.5	3.5	3
UC7	4	3	2	2	5	4	4	3
UC8	3	2	4	4	3.5	3	4	4
UC9	1	1	1	1	4	2	2	2.5
UC10	1	1	5	4	4	4	2	1.5
UC11	1	1	4	4	3.5	2.5	2.5	2
UC12	1	1	2	2	4	3	3	3
UC13	1	1	1	1	4.5	3.5	4.5	4
UC14	1	1	1	1	4	2	2.5	1.5
UC15	1	1	5	5	2.5	2	1	1
UC16	3	3	5	5	4.5	4	3.5	4
UC17	3	3	4	5	5	4	3.5	3

found to possess the functionality to perform most of the use cases, they were considered to be too complex. The participants viewed modeling tools as "*not so user friendly*" and "*odious pieces of software*".

Although, in general, participants were content with their tools, their statements pointed out the need for better features. For example, for use cases 4 and 5, many participants (i.e. Process Architects 1, 2, Analyst 1, and Consultants 3, 4) mentioned the need to distinguish the happy path from alternative paths. Process Analyst 1 specified the need to use "*colored activities or small icons*" to better see the roles. The findings together with the ideas for new features point out to the need for developing tools that are simple to use and do not have a steep learning curve for different user types.

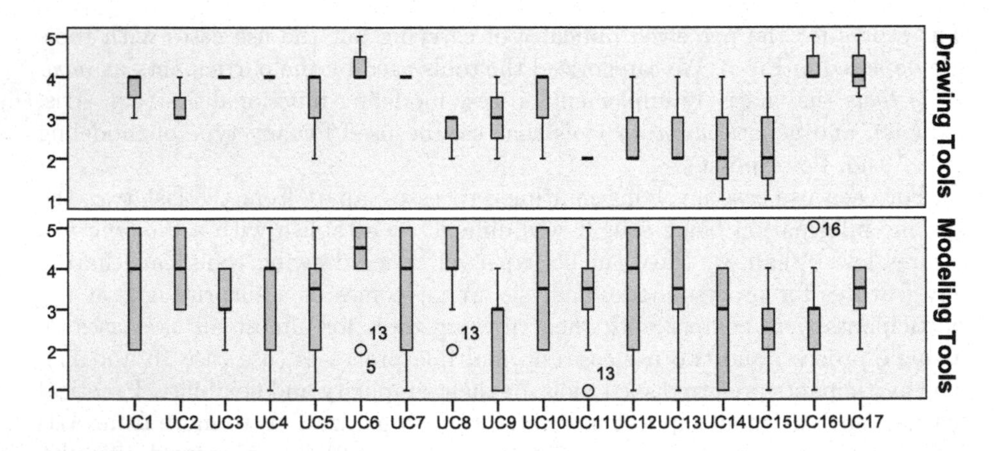

Fig. 3. Perceived difficulty of the use cases for tool types (5: very easy)

Based on our findings, in the next section we discuss the implications of our work for researchers, process model tool developers, and process modelers.

5 Discussion

The evaluation of the BPMC use case list provides numerous implications for researchers, tool developers, and modelers in the BPM field. Our results support the importance of the *behavioral perspective* of process models in the literature, while pointing out that there are other process perspectives which are similarly important and prevalent for process model comprehension (Fig. 2). In addition, our findings highlight the salient differences between the *information-seeking behaviors of process roles* (Table 3). In light of these implications, we list the following guidelines for process model comprehension researchers to follow while designing and performing process model comprehension research:

(1) Make an explicit choice of the use cases to work on,
(2) Consider process perspectives other than the behavioral perspective, most importantly *functional*, *organizational*, and an integration of *multiple perspectives*, and
(3) Consider that process roles have different information needs, and accordingly, that they employ diverse use cases.

Our evaluation of the difficulty perception for carrying out the use cases provides implications for process modeling tool developers. The high variation of scores with respect to perceived difficulty, specifically when tools specialized on process modeling are used, indicates that tool features cannot be utilized by the users properly (Fig. 3). The prevalent use of the drawing tools support this implication. Based on these, we suggest the following guidelines for process modeling tool developers to follow while developing new process modeling tool features:

(1) Focus on developing tools that are easy to use for different user types, and
(2) Check the use cases to see if the planned features match with the needs of the target users.

Lastly, the diversity of the use cases favored by process roles implies for process modelers that it is essential to understand the needs of users and plan modeling efforts accordingly. Based on this implication, we list the following guidelines for process modelers to follow while developing process models:

(1) Consider the purposes of process models not only at the organizational level, but also at the personal level to discover which of the use cases are important, and
(2) Spend the modeling efforts to cover process information essential for the users.

Some comments of the participants pointed to a number of opportunities to facilitate the information-seeking behavior of process model users by providing visualization techniques. These findings may provide directions to researchers for evaluating the impact of visualization techniques on process model comprehension, and to process modeling tool developers for adding new features. We derived the following suggestions on visualization techniques from the transcripts:

- control-flow based animation,
- visualizations to examine alternative paths,
- navigation among multiple processes,
- abstraction of information in combination with visualizations,
- automated creation of different process views, and
- visualizations for specific process perspectives (e.g. roles or systems).

A limitation of our work is formed by the number of the participants and the participating organizations. By using interviews and focus group study as the validation methodology, we collected in-depth qualitative data from a smaller group (for example, in comparison to surveys). The in-depth data enabled us to reach a deep understanding of the experiences of the professionals, and support the survey results with qualitative results. We designed our research to include participants of different process roles, and participating organizations from different sectors and locations. In this way we aimed to reveal different views on process model use.

6 Conclusions

Our motivation for this study was to capture the different types of information-seeking behavior that can be pursued by users of process models. The analysis of the related literature reveals that the type of information to be retained is not explicitly taken into consideration in process model comprehension research. However, the comprehension of the users may change based on how they use process models. Based on this observation, we constructed a list of BPMC use cases which categorizes the information-seeking behavior of the process model users in terms of process perspectives, and the number of process models under consideration. We performed interviews and focus group study to validate the relevancy and completeness of the use cases. We worked with 24 participants from 8 different organizations. The participants were process analysts, process architects, process consultants, and process owners. Results from the study indicate that users seek information on the organizational and functional perspectives as much as on the behavioral perspective. The combined use of these perspectives is similarly important, which is a completely new insight with respect to current literature. The perception of importance and prevalence of the use cases varies among process roles. Based on these indications, we provide directions to include process perspectives in further process model comprehension research. Additionally, we present a list of guidelines for process model tool developers and process modelers. In future work, the use of performance and risk information in process models is also worth to be investigated further.

Acknowledgement. This work has been supported by the European Union's Horizon 2020 research and innovation programme under the Marie Skłodowska-Curie grant agreement No 660646. We thank Ingmar Haasdijk for his support in performing the interviews.

References

1. van der Aalst, W.M.P.: Business process management: a comprehensive survey. ISRN Softw. Eng. **2013**, 1–37 (2013)
2. Ailenei, I., Rozinat, A., Eckert, A., Aalst, W.M.P.: Definition and validation of process mining use cases. In: Daniel, F., Barkaoui, K., Dustdar, S. (eds.) BPM 2011. LNBIP, vol. 99, pp. 75–86. Springer, Heidelberg (2012). doi:10.1007/978-3-642-28108-2_7
3. Aranda, J., Ernst, N., Horkoff, J., Easterbrook, S.: A framework for empirical evaluation of model comprehensibility. In: International Workshop on Modeling in Software Engineering (MISE 2007 ICSE Workshop 2007), pp. 7–7. IEEE, May 2007
4. Aysolmaz, B., Demirörs, O.: Unified process modeling with UPROM tool. In: Nurcan, S., Pimenidis, E. (eds.) CAiSE Forum 2014. LNBIP, vol. 204, pp. 250–266. Springer, Cham (2015). doi:10.1007/978-3-319-19270-3_16
5. Bandara, W., Gable, G.G., Rosemann, M.: Factors and measures of business process modelling: model building through a multiple case study. Eur. J. Inf. Syst. **14**(4), 347–360 (2005)
6. Browning, T.R.: On the alignment of the purposes and views of process models in project management. J. Oper. Manag. **28**(4), 316–332 (2010)
7. Curtis, B., Kellner, M.I., Over, J.: Process modeling. Commun. ACM **35**(9), 75–90 (1992)
8. Davies, I., Green, P., Rosemann, M., Indulska, M., Gallo, S.: How do practitioners use conceptual modeling in practice? Data Knowl. Eng. **58**(3), 358–380 (2006)
9. Davis, R., Brabander, E.: ARIS Design Platform Getting Started with BPM. Springer, London (2007)
10. Figl, K., Laue, R.: Influence factors for local comprehensibility of process models. Int. J. Hum Comput Stud. **82**, 96–110 (2015)
11. Figl, K., Mendling, J., Strembeck, M.: The influence of notational deficiencies on process model comprehension. J. Assoc. Inf. Syst. **14**(6), 312–338 (2013)
12. Figl, K., Recker, J.: Exploring cognitive style and task-specific preferences for process representations. Requir. Eng. **21**(1), 63–85 (2016)
13. Figl, K., Recker, J., Mendling, J.: A study on the effects of routing symbol design on process model comprehension. Decis. Support Syst. **54**(2), 1104–1118 (2013)
14. Figl, K., Strembeck, M.: On the importance of flow direction in business process models. In: Proceedings of 9th International Conference on Software Engineering and Applications, pp. 132–136 (2014)
15. van Foerster, H.: Understanding Understanding Essays on Cybernetics and Cognition. Springer Science+Business Media, New York (2003)
16. Giaglis, G.: A taxonomy of business process modeling and information systems modeling techniques. Int. J. Flex. Manuf. Syst. **13**(2), 209–228 (2001)
17. Grimbeek, P., Bryer, F., Beamish, W., D'Netto, M.: Use of data collapsing strategies to identify latent variables in CHP questionnaire data. In: Proceedings of 3rd Annual International Conference on Cognition, Language, and Special Education, Griffith University (2005)

18. Laue, R., Gadatsch, A.: Measuring the understandability of business process models - are we asking the right questions? In: zur Muehlen, M., Su, J. (eds.) BPM 2010. LNBIP, vol. 66, pp. 37–48. Springer, Heidelberg (2011). doi:10.1007/978-3-642-20511-8_4
19. Lohmann, P., Zur Muehlen, M.: Business process management skills and roles: an investigation of the demand and supply side of BPM professionals. In: Motahari-Nezhad, H.R., Recker, J., Weidlich, M. (eds.) BPM 2015. LNCS, vol. 9253, pp. 317–332. Springer, Cham (2015). doi:10.1007/978-3-319-23063-4_22
20. Mendling, J., Reijers, H.A., Cardoso, J.: What makes process models understandable? In: Alonso, G., Dadam, P., Rosemann, M. (eds.) BPM 2007. LNCS, vol. 4714, pp. 48–63. Springer, Heidelberg (2007). doi:10.1007/978-3-540-75183-0_4
21. Mendling, J., Strembeck, M., Recker, J.: Factors of process model comprehension-Findings from a series of experiments. Decis. Support Syst. **53**(1), 195–206 (2012)
22. Nolte, A., Bernhard, E., Recker, J., Pittke, F., Mendling, J.: Repeated use of process models: the impact of artifact, technological, and individual factors. Decis. Support Syst. **88**, 98–111 (2016)
23. Recker, J.: Scientific Research in Information Systems: A Beginner's Guide. Springer, Heidelberg (2013)
24. Recker, J., Dreiling, A.: The effects of content presentation format and user characteristics on novice developers' understanding of process models. Commun. Assoc. Inf. Syst. **28**(1), 65–84 (2011)
25. Recker, J., Reijers, H.A., van de Wouw, S.G.: Process model comprehension: the effects of cognitive abilities, learning style, and strategy. Commun. Assoc. Inf. Syst. **34**(9), 199–222 (2014)
26. Recker, J., Rosemann, M., Indulska, M., Green, P.: Business process modeling: a comparative analysis. J. Assoc. Inf. Syst. **10**(4), 333–363 (2009)
27. Reijers, H.A., Mendling, J.: A study into the factors that influence the understandability of business process models. IEEE Trans. Syst. Man Cybern. Part A Syst. Hum. **41**(3), 449–462 (2011)
28. Reijers, H.A., Mendling, J., Dijkman, R.M.: Human and automatic modularizations of process models to enhance their comprehension. Inf. Syst. **36**(5), 881–897 (2011)
29. Reijers, H.A., Recker, J., van de Wouw, S.G.: An integrative framework of the factors affecting process model understanding: a learning perspective. In: AMCIS 2010 Proceedings, pp. 1–10 (2010)
30. Schultze, U., Avital, M.: Designing interviews to generate rich data for information systems research. Inf. Organ. **21**(1), 1–16 (2011)
31. Smirnov, S., Reijers, H.A., Weske, M., Nugteren, T.: Business process model abstraction: a definition, catalog, and survey. Distrib. Parallel Databases **30**(1), 63–99 (2012)
32. Sobreperez, P.: Using plenary focus groups in information systems research: More than a collection of interviews. Electron. J. Bus. Res. Methods **6**(2), 181–188 (2008)
33. Turetken, O., Rompen, T., Vanderfeesten, I., Dikici, A., Moll, J.: The effect of modularity representation and presentation medium on the understandability of business process models in BPMN. In: La Rosa, M., Loos, P., Pastor, O. (eds.) BPM 2016. LNCS, vol. 9850, pp. 289–307. Springer, Cham (2016). doi:10.1007/978-3-319-45348-4_17
34. Wand, Y., Weber, R.: Research commentary: information systems and conceptual modeling–a research agenda. Inf. Syst. Res. **13**(4), 363–376 (2002)
35. Wilson, T.D.: Human information behavior. Inform. Sci. **3**(2), 49–55 (2000)

Business Process Adaptation

Predictive Business Process Monitoring Considering Reliability Estimates

Andreas Metzger(✉) and Felix Föcker

paluno – The Ruhr Institute for Software Technology,
University of Duisburg-Essen, Essen, Germany
{andreas.metzger,felix.foecker}@paluno.uni-due.de

Abstract. Predictive business process monitoring aims at predicting potential problems during process execution so that these problems can be proactively managed and mitigated. Compared to aggregate prediction accuracy indicators (e.g., precision or recall), prediction reliability estimates provide additional information about the prediction error for an individual business process. Intuitively, it appears appealing to consider reliability estimates when deciding on whether to adapt a running process instance or not. However, we lack empirical evidence to support this intuition, as research on predictive business process monitoring focused on aggregate prediction accuracy. We experimentally analyze the effect of considering prediction reliability estimates for proactive business process adaptation. We use ensemble prediction techniques, which we apply to an industry data set from the transport and logistics domain. In our experiments, proactive business process adaptation in general had a positive effect on cost in 52.5% of the situations. In 82.9% of these situations, considering reliability estimates increased the positive effect, leading to cost savings of up to 54%, with 14% savings on average.

Keywords: Business process monitoring · Proactive adaptation · Prediction · Empirical evaluation

1 Introduction

Predictive business process monitoring aims at anticipating potential process performance violations during the execution of a business process instance [15]. To this end, predictive business process monitoring predicts how an ongoing process instance will unfold up to its completion [18]. If a violation is predicted, a process instance may be proactively adapted to prevent the occurrence of violations [23]. As an example, if a delay in delivery time is predicted for an ongoing freight transport process, faster means of transport or alternative transport routes may be scheduled before the delay actually occurs.

A key requirement for the applicability of any predictive business process monitoring technique is that the technique delivers accurate predictions. Informally, prediction accuracy characterizes the ability of a prediction technique to

E. Dubois and K. Pohl (Eds.): CAiSE 2017, LNCS 10253, pp. 445–460, 2017.
DOI: 10.1007/978-3-319-59536-8_28

forecast as many true violations as possible, while – at the same time – generating as few false alarms as possible [23]. Prediction accuracy is important to avoid the execution of unnecessary process adaptations, as well as not to miss required process adaptations [20].

Research focused on improving a prediction technique's *aggregate* accuracy [1,2,5–7,11,13,16,19,22,25]. Aggregate accuracy takes into account the results of a *set* of predictions. Examples for aggregate accuracy metrics are precision, recall or mean average prediction error. Compared with aggregate accuracy metrics, prediction *reliability estimates* provide additional information about the error of an *individual* prediction for a given business process instance [4]. As an example, an aggregate accuracy of 75% means that, for a given prediction, there will be a 75% chance that the prediction is correct. In contrast, the reliability estimate of one prediction may be 60% while for another prediction it may be 90%. Reliability estimates thus facilitate distinguishing between more and less reliable predictions on a case by case basis. Reliability estimates can help decide whether to trust an individual prediction [12] and consequently whether to perform a proactive adaptation of the given process instance. In our freight transport example above, a process manager may only trust predictions with a reliability higher than 80%. Only then, the process manager would proactively schedule faster – and therefore also more expensive – means of transport.

Intuitively, considering reliability estimates sounds appealing, as reliability estimates offer more information to the process manager for decision making. However, we lack empirical evidence to support this intuition, as research on predictive business process monitoring focused on aggregate prediction accuracy. As an example, the process manager may be more conservative and act only if a prediction is reliable, which in turn should reduce the number of unnecessary process adaptations. Yet, it may also be that a process manager becomes too conservative and rejects relevant predictions deemed not reliable enough.

We experimentally analyze the effect of considering reliability estimates during predictive business process monitoring. We use an ensemble of artificial neural network prediction models, which we apply to an industry data set from the transport and logistics domain. Each prediction model aims at predicting whether a transport process instance may violate its delivery deadline. We consider reliability estimates for proactive process adaptation and analyze their effect from two complementary points of view. First, we analyze their effect on the rate of process performance violations (in our freight example, the rate of processes completed with delays). Second, we analyze their effect on costs.

After introducing relevant background and discussing related work in Sect. 2, we describe our experimental design in Sect. 3. In Sect. 4 we present and discuss our experimental results. Section 5 concludes with an outlook on future work.

2 Background and Related Work

2.1 Prediction Reliability

Background. Reliability estimates provide more information about the individual prediction error than aggregate accuracy metrics [4]. Reliability estimates can be computed in different ways. On the one hand, reliability estimates can be derived from information provided by individual prediction techniques. An example is decision tree learning (e.g., see [18]), which indicates the number of training examples correctly classified ("class support") and the percentage of training examples correctly classified ("class probability") for each prediction.

On the other hand, reliability estimates can be computed using ensemble prediction, as illustrated in Fig. 1. Ensemble prediction is a meta-prediction technique where the predictions of m prediction models are combined [21]. The main aim of ensemble prediction is to increase aggregate prediction accuracy. However, ensemble prediction also allows computing reliability estimates (e.g., see [3,4]). In our experiments, we use ensemble prediction to compute reliability estimates for *binary* predictions[1]. This means each prediction result T_i, $i = 1, \ldots, m$, is either of class "violation" or "non-violation". Formally, we compute reliability estimates as: $max_{i=1,\ldots,m}(\frac{|i:T_i=\text{"violation"}|}{m}, \frac{|i:T_i=\text{"non-violation"}|}{m})$.

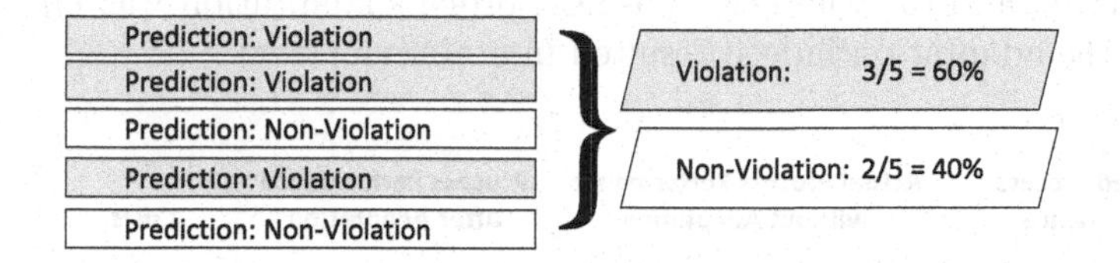

Fig. 1. Reliability estimates computed using ensemble prediction

Related Work. Research on predictive business process monitoring focused on improving aggregate prediction accuracy [1,2,5–7,11,13,16,19,22,25]. Only recently, reliability estimates have been considered in the context of predictive business process monitoring.

Maggi et al. [18] use decision tree learning for predictive business process monitoring. Reliability estimates are computed from class probabilities and class support. In their experiments, they report on the impact of considering reliability estimates on aggregate prediction accuracy. They observe that using reliability estimates may improve aggregate accuracy. They also measure the loss of predictions, i.e., the number of predictions that are not considered because they are below the threshold. They observe that the loss of predictions is usually not very high (around 20%). However, they provide no further analysis of their observations and the possible implications for considering reliability estimates.

Di Francescomarino et al. [12] present a general predictive business process monitoring framework, which can be tailored to fit a given data set. They use decision trees and random forests for prediction. Reliability estimates are computed from class probabilities and class support. If prediction reliability is above a certain threshold, the prediction is considered. In their experiments, they measure "failure rate" among other metrics to assess the performance of different framework instances. "Failure rate" is defined as the percentage of process

[1] Numeric predictions are part of our future work.

instances for which no reliable prediction could be given. They observe that "failure rate" may vary widely for the different framework instances. Yet, they provide no further analysis on the variables that may have an effect on "failure rate".

2.2 Costs

Background. Proactive process adaptation entails asymmetric costs. On the one hand, one may face penalties in case of violations; e.g., due to contractual arrangements (e.g., SLAs) or due to loss of customers. On the other hand, adapting the running business processes may incur costs; e.g., due to executing roll-back actions or due to scheduling alternative process activities.

Figure 2 shows a cost model that incorporates these two aforementioned cost drivers (based in parts on [19,20]). In this model, costs depend on (1) the actual process performance if no adaptation was taken, (2) whether the prediction was accurate, and (3) whether a business process adaptation was *effective*, i.e., whether the adaptation indeed resulted in a non-violation.

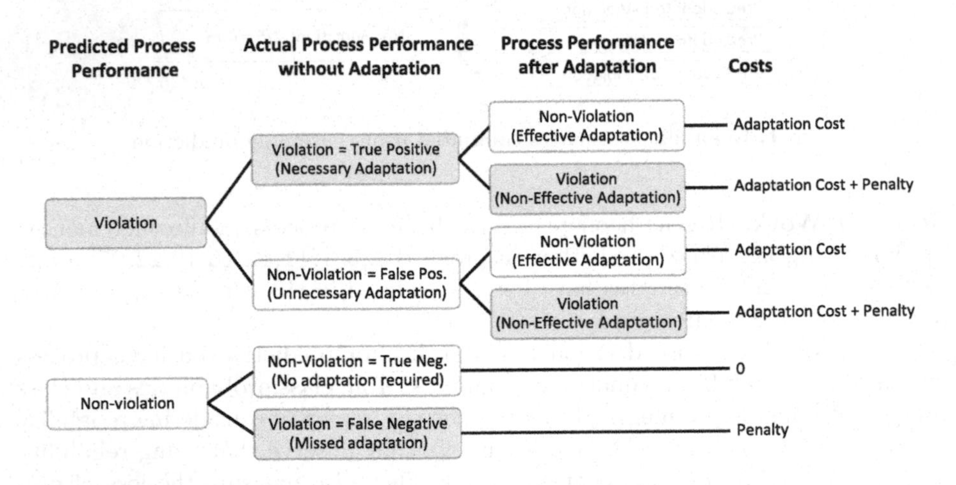

Fig. 2. Asymmetric costs of proactive business process adaptation

We use the cost in model Fig. 2 as basis for our experiments. We have purposefully chosen it to be simple, in order to concisely analyze and present our experimental results. Of course, costs may be more complex in reality. On the one hand, different shapes of penalties may exist [17]; e.g., penalties may be higher if the actual delays in a transport process are longer. On the other hand, adaptation costs may differ depending on the extent of changes needed for a specific business process instance; e.g., scheduling air transport as an alternative means of transport would typically be more expensive than truck transport.

Related Work. Different ways of factoring in costs during predictive business process monitoring and proactive process adaptation have been presented in the literature. On the one hand, costs may be considered by the prediction technique itself. A prominent class of approaches is cost-sensitive learning [10]. Cost-sensitive learning attempts to minimize costs due to prediction errors, rather than optimizing aggregate prediction accuracy. Cost-sensitive learning incorporates asymmetric costs into the learning of prediction models [26,27]. However, existing cost-sensitive learning techniques do not consider reliability estimates.

On the other hand, costs may be considered when deciding on proactive process adaptations. Cost-based adaptation attempts to minimize the overall costs of process execution and adaptation. Leitner et al. [17] were among the first to argue that the costs of adaptation should be considered when deciding on the adaptation of service-oriented workflows. They formalized an optimization problem taking into account costs of violations and costs of applying adaptations. Their experimental results indicate that cost reductions of up to 56% may be achieved. However, these cost-aware proactive adaptation techniques do not consider prediction reliability. In addition, they rest on the assumption that process adaptations are always effective (i.e., lead to non-violations), which may not give an accurate view of reality. In our experiments, we factor in both reliability estimates and the effectiveness of adaptations.

3 Experiment Design

As motivated in Sect. 1, we aim to analyze the effect of considering reliability estimates during predictive business process monitoring and proactive process adaptation. In this section, we describe the design of our experiments to answer the following two research questions:

RQ1: What effect does considering reliability estimates have on the *rate of non-violations*?
RQ2: What effect does considering reliability estimates have on *costs*?

Below, we define the experimental variables, introduce the industry data set, and describe how we implemented the prediction techniques used.

3.1 Experimental Variables

In our experiment, we consider the following dependent variables:

- *Non-violation rate:* We use the non-violation rate to answer **RQ1**. Given the number of process instances that completed with non-violations, l, and the number of all process instances, n, the non-violation rate is l/n.
- *Costs:* We use costs to answer **RQ2**. For each process instance, we compute its individual costs according to the cost model from Sect. 2.2. The total costs are the sum of the individual costs of all process instances.

We consider the following independent variables:

- *Reliability threshold* $\theta \in [0.5, 1]$. If the reliability estimate[2] for an individual process instance is higher than θ, we assume that a process manager would consider this a reliable prediction. As a result, the process manager would perform a proactive process adaptation if the prediction indicates a violation.
- *Adaptation effectiveness* $\alpha \in (0, 1]$. If an adaptation helps achieve a non-violation (cf. Fig. 2), we consider such an adaptation effective. We use α to represent the fact that not all adaptations might be effective. More concretely, α represents the probability that an adaptation is effective; e.g., $\alpha = 1$ means that all adaptations are effective. We do not consider $\alpha = 0$ as this means that no adaptation is effective.
- *Relative adaptation costs* $\lambda \in [0, 1]$. Based on our cost model from Sect. 2.2, λ expresses the costs of a business process adaptation, c_a, as a fraction of the penalty for process violation, c_p, i.e., $c_a = \lambda \cdot c_p$. Choosing $\lambda > 1$ would not make sense, as this leads to higher costs than if no adaptation is performed.

3.2 Industry Data Set

The data set[3] we use in our experiments stems from operational data of an international freight forwarding company. The data set covers five months of business operations and includes event logs of 3,942 business process instances, comprising a total of 56,082 activities. The processes and event data comply with IATA's Cargo 2000 standard[4]. Figure 3 shows the BPMN model of the business processes covered by the data set.

Up to three shipments from suppliers are consolidated and in turn shipped to customers to benefit from better freight rates or increased cargo security. The business processes are structured into incoming and outgoing transport legs, which jointly aim at ensuring that freight is delivered to customers on time. Each transport leg involves the execution of transport and logistics activities, which are labeled using the acronyms of the Cargo 2000 standard. A transport leg may involve multiple flight segments (e.g., if cargo is transferred to other flights or airlines at stopover airports), in which case, "RCF" loops back to "DEP". The number of segments per leg may range from one to four.

3.3 Implementation of Ensemble Prediction

We focus on predicting violations of business process performance metrics. Specifically, we aim at predicting, during process execution, whether a transport process instance may violate its delivery deadline. Thereby, process managers are warned about possible delays as early as possible (e.g., see [9]) so they can proactively adapt the running process instance.

[2] According to how we compute reliability estimates (see Sect. 3.3), the smallest reliability value that is possible is $\theta = 0.5$.
[3] Available from http://www.s-cube-network.eu/c2k.
[4] Cargo 2000 (now Cargo iQ: http://cargoiq.org/) is an initiative of IATA.

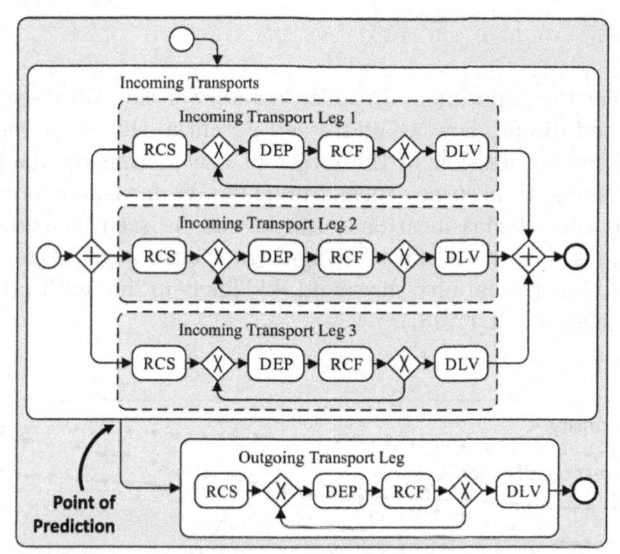

Fig. 3. Structure of Cargo 2000 transport and logistics process

Predictions may be performed at any point in time during process execution. For our experiment, we haven chosen to perform the predictions immediately after the synchronization point of the incoming transport processes as indicated in Fig. 3. Our earlier work has shown reasonably good prediction accuracy of more than 70% for this point in process execution, while still leaving time to execute actions required to respond to violations or mitigate their effects [19].

As prediction model, we use artificial neural networks (ANNs [14]), which have shown good results in our earlier work [19]. We use the implementation of ANNs (with their standard parameters) of the WEKA open source machine learning toolkit. As attributes for the ANN model, we use the expected and actual times for all process activities until the point of prediction (i.e., all activities of the incoming transports in Fig. 3), and the actual violation or non-violation of the delivery time of the completed process instance.

To automatically train the ensembles of ANNs and to compute the reliability estimates according to Sect. 2.1, we developed a Java tool that interfaces with WEKA. We use *bagging* (bootstrap aggregating) as a concrete ensemble prediction technique. Bagging generates m new training data sets by sampling from the whole training data set uniformly and with replacement. For each of the m new training data sets an individual prediction model is trained. Bagging is a generally recommended and used ensemble prediction technique for ANNs [8].

4 Results

Here, we present the experimental results[5] to answer the two research questions posed above, and discuss how we addressed potential threats to validity.

To give a first impression of the effect of considering reliability estimates, Fig. 4 shows aggregate accuracy measurements. We measured precision, recall, specificity and correct classification rate. As can be seen, considering reliability estimates has a positive effect on aggregate accuracy. Aggregate accuracy improves with higher reliability threshold θ. This is in line with previous empirical evidence (e.g., see [4,12,18]).

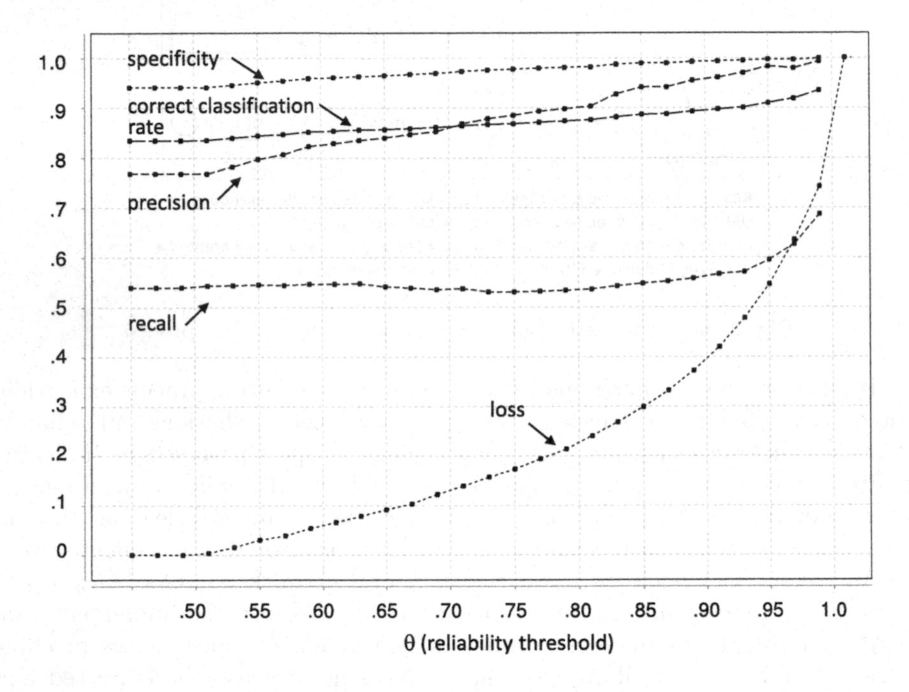

Fig. 4. Aggregate accuracy indicators and loss

In addition, Fig. 4 shows the loss of predictions, i.e., the rate of predictions that have a reliability estimate below the threshold θ. As can be seen, the loss of predictions increases with higher θ, and relatively more predictions are lost the higher θ gets. As we speculated in the introduction, this loss of predictions may imply that required process adaptations could be missed, as the process manager may be too conservative and reject relevant predictions with low reliability. In turn, the number of violation situations in which the process manager does not act may increase. We further explore this in the following sections.

[5] The raw data of our experiments is available from http://www.s-cube-network.eu/reliability/.

4.1 Results for RQ1 (Non-violation Rates)

RQ1 is concerned with the effect of reliability estimates on non-violation rates. Figure 5 shows the non-violation rates depending on the reliability threshold (θ) and the probability that adaptations are effective (α).

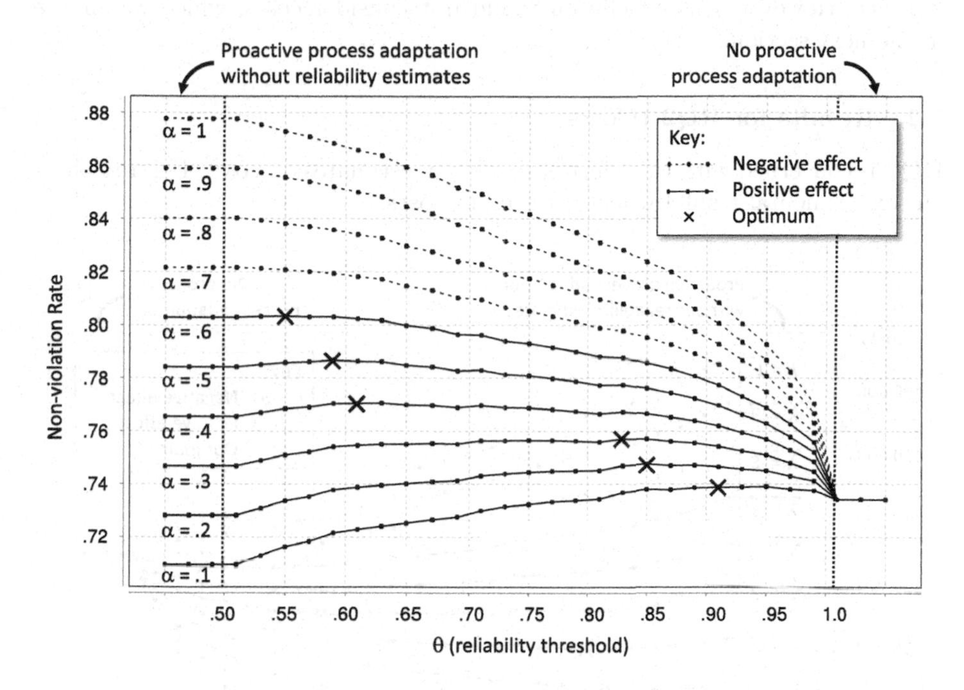

Fig. 5. Non-violation rates for varying adaptation effectiveness (α)

A positive effect means that non-violation rates are (1) higher than the non-violation rates if no proactive process adaption is performed (= value on the right hand side of the figure), and (2) higher than the non-violation rates when process adaptations are performed without reliability estimates (= values on the left hand side of the figure). This leads to two cases as indicated in Fig. 5:

- For $\alpha \geq .7$ (dashed lines), considering reliability estimates has a negative effect on non-violation rates and thus non-violation rates decrease. The reason is that with a higher loss of predictions (cf. Fig. 4), the number of missed adaptations increases. Yet, this is not compensated by fewer unnecessary adaptations. Due to the large α, each adaptation will lead to a non-violating situation with high probability. Thus performing too many adaptations seems to be better than performing too few.
- Reliability estimates can have a positive effect and lead to higher non-violation rates if $\alpha < .7$ (solid lines). For a given α, optimal non-violation rates are marked by "×" in Fig. 5.

In conclusion, our experimental results suggest the following answer to **RQ1**: *Considering reliability estimates can have a positive effect on non-violation rates if the probability of effective process adaptations is low.*

Conversely, this would imply that considering reliability estimates when the probability of effective process adaptations is high might not make sense in practice. However, this conclusion would not consider costs, which we analyze in the next section.

4.2 Results for RQ2 (Costs)

RQ2 is concerned with the effect of reliability estimates on costs. Figure 6 shows our experimental results when factoring in costs.

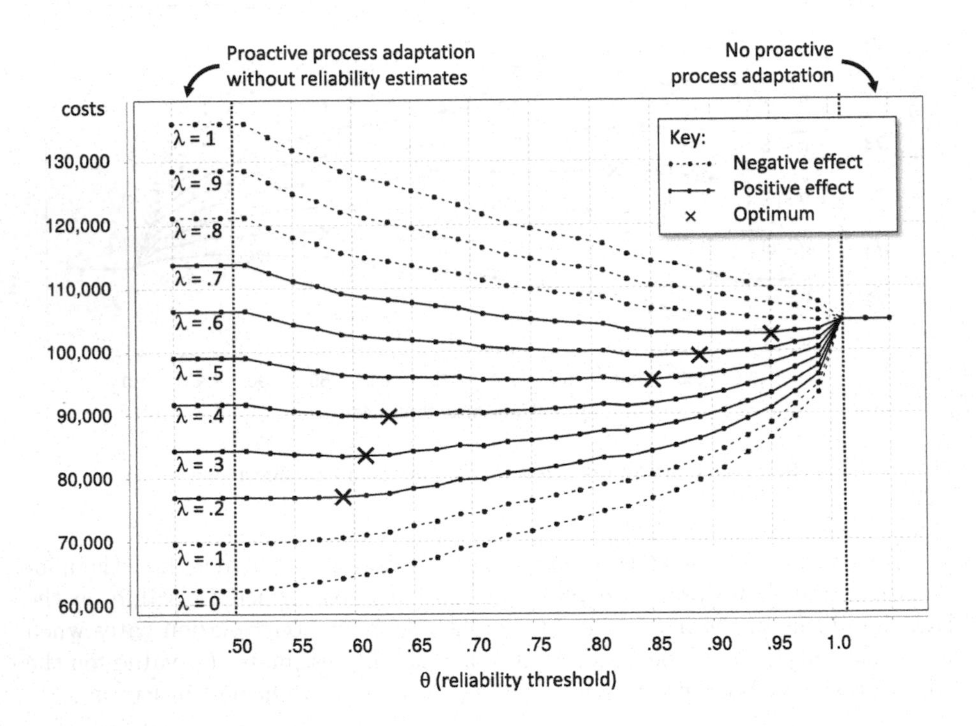

Fig. 6. Costs for $\alpha = .8$

We factor in costs according to the cost model from Sect. 2.2. Without loss of generality, penalty costs are set to 100. Adaptation costs are computed as fraction (λ) of penalty costs. We have chosen $\alpha = 0.8$, which is a relatively high probability of effective process adaptations. According to RQ1, considering reliability estimates for such α should have a negative effect.

A positive effect on costs means that costs are (1) lower than the costs if no proactive process adaption is performed (value on the right hand side of the figure), and (2) lower than the costs when process adaptations are performed without reliability estimates (values on the left hand side of the figure). This leads to three cases, as indicated in Fig. 6:

- For $\lambda \geq .8$ (dashed lines), proactive adaptation – independently of whether considering reliability estimates or not – leads to costs that are higher than not performing any proactive process adaptation. The reason is that the avoided penalties do not compensate the prohibitively high adaptation costs.
- For $\lambda < .2$ (dashed lines), considering reliability estimates during proactive process adaptation leads to higher costs than not considering reliability estimates. The reason is that due to the loss of predictions, the rate of missed adaptations may go up. As adaptation costs are low, investing in proactive adaptation – even if some are unnecessary – pays off to prevent penalties. It should be noted though, that even if one considered reliability estimates, costs would remain lower than if not performing any proactive adaptation.
- Reliability estimates have a positive effect for $.2 \leq \lambda \leq .7$ (solid lines). In these situations, there is an optimal choice of θ that leads to the lowest costs.

Above, α was fixed. To provide the complete picture, Fig. 7 depicts a matrix considering the complete ranges of α, λ and θ (cf. Sect. 3.1), thereby aggregating 5,000 experimental data points.

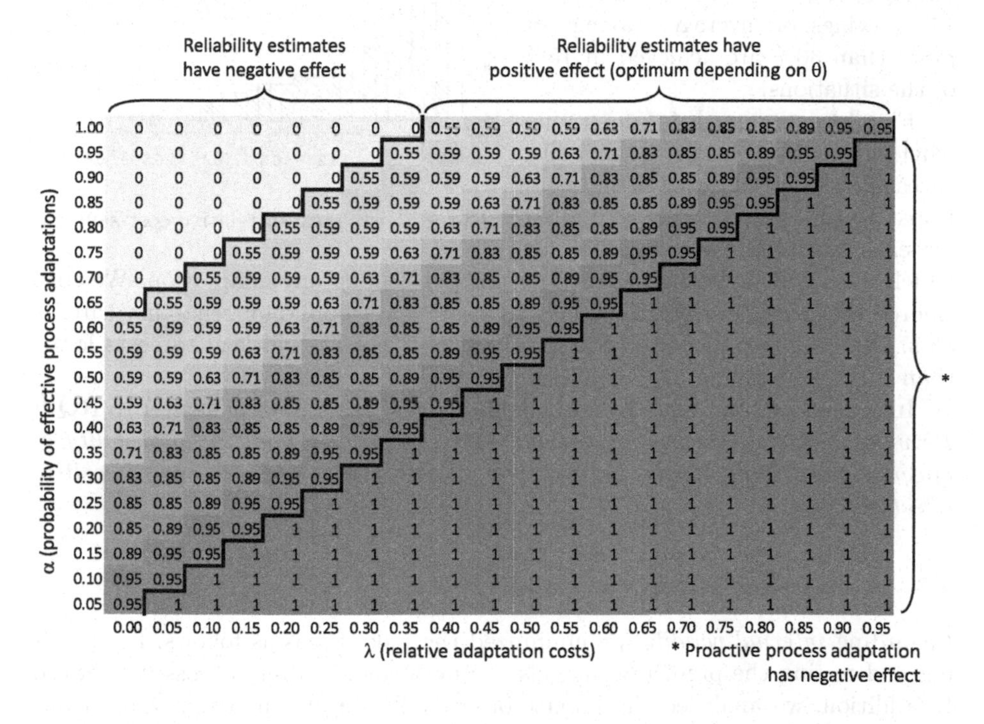

Fig. 7. Threshold θ that leads to minimal costs, depending on α and λ

For each combination of α and λ, the matrix shows the value of θ that leads to the lowest costs (these are the points marked with "×" in Fig. 6). If not considering reliability estimates performed best, this is indicated by $\theta = 0$. If no proactive adaptation performed best, this is indicated by $\theta = 1$. Again, we can differentiate three cases:

- Proactive process adaptation in general does not have a positive effect on costs if $\lambda \geq \alpha$. This is the case in 47.5% of all situations.
- Considering reliability estimates does not have a positive effect on costs if λ is small and α is large (9% of all situations). Again, even if one considered reliability estimates, costs would remain lower than if not performing any proactive adaptation.
- In the remaining 43.5% of all situations, considering reliability estimates can have a positive effect. Again, the minimal costs depend on the choice of θ.

To quantify the size of the effect on costs, we have measured the relative cost savings that may be achieved in each of the situations in which considering reliability estimates has a positive effect. Results are shown in Fig. 8. Savings range from 2% to 54%, with 14% savings on average. Savings of more than 30% are achieved in 15% of the situations.

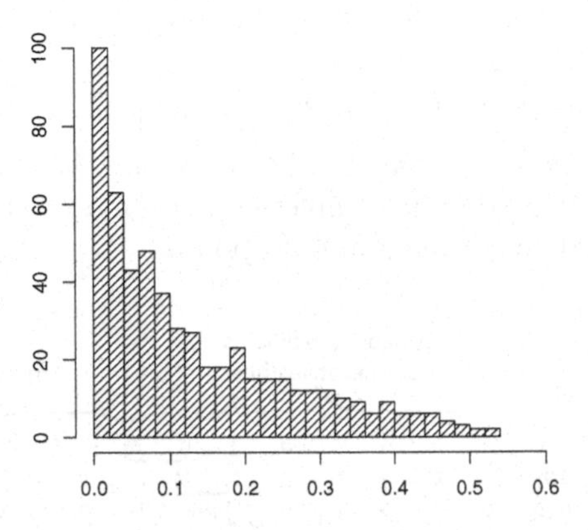

Fig. 8. Histogram of relative cost savings

Finally, we aimed to determine whether we can choose a reliability threshold that would work in all situations. To this end, we have computed for each situation the minimal θ for which costs will be below the costs of not performing any adaptation. We considered the largest of these minimal θ as a safe lower bound for reliability thresholds. Our results indicate that a threshold of $\theta > 80\%$ will lead to costs lower than if not performing any adaptation.

In conclusion, our experimental results suggest the following answer to **RQ2**: *Provided that the relative adaptation costs are smaller than the probability of effective process adaptations, considering reliability estimates can have a positive effect on costs.*

4.3 Addressing Threats to Validity

Regarding *internal validity*, we minimized the risk of bias as follows. For training and testing the prediction models, we performed a 10-fold cross-validation. In addition, we analyzed the impact of the following main parameters of our ensemble prediction technique: (1) *Computing reliability estimates*: In addition to computing reliability estimates as defined in Sect. 2.1, we used weighted reliability, which factors in the probability delivered by individual ANN predictions. Differences in results were marginal. (2) *Bootstrap size*: Bootstrap (see Sect. 3.3) refers to the size of the newly generated training data sets. We used 80%, 66%, and 50% as bootstrap sizes. There was not a clear trend that larger bootstrap sizes would perform better than smaller ones and different bootstrap sizes did not impact the general shape of the experimental results. (3) *Ensemble size*: We varied ensemble size from 2 to 100. The size of the ensemble did not lead to different principal findings. However, as expected, larger ensembles generally delivered better aggregate accuracy. More importantly, larger ensembles delivered more fine-grained reliability estimates.

Regarding *external validity*, our experimental results are based on a relatively large industry data set. We have specifically chosen different reliability thresholds (θ), different probabilities of effective process adaptations (α), and different adaptation costs (λ) to cover different possible situations that may be faced in practice. The process model covers many relevant workflow patterns [24]: sequence; exclusive choice and simple merge; cycles; parallel split and synchronization. Still, our data set is from a single application domain which thus may limit generalizability. As mentioned in Sect. 2.2, our cost model was purposefully chosen to be simple. Even though this cost model helped analyzing and understanding the effects of the independent variables in our experiment, it may have been too simple.

In view of *construct validity*, we took great care to ensure we measure the right things. In particular, we assessed the impact of considering reliability estimates from different, complementary angles: aggregate accuracy, loss, non-violation rates, and costs.

5 Conclusions and Perspectives

Our experimental evidence suggest that considering reliability estimates during predictive business process monitoring can have a positive effect on costs. With respect to the independent variables of our experiment, the effect mainly depends on the effectiveness of proactive process adaptations and the relative costs of these process adaptations, while the concrete reliability threshold has a secondary effect. In our experiments, proactive process adaptation in general had a positive effect on costs in 52.5% of the situations. In 82.9% of these situations, considering reliability estimates increased the positive effect, with cost savings ranging from 2% to 54%, and 14% on average. We also determined that even if one considered reliability estimates in the remaining 17.1% of situations, costs would remain lower than if not performing any proactive adaptation. Finally, our results suggest 80% is a safe lower bound for choosing reliability thresholds.

Our results also clearly indicate that considering reliability estimates does not lead to a positive effect in all situations. How to determine these situations up front remains an open question. This paper was a first step towards answering this question. We plan to gather further empirical data by replicating our experiments in other application domains, such as energy and e-commerce.

Further, we aim at using more complex cost models. These cost models will consider different shapes of penalties and different costs of adaptations, both of which depend on the extent of deviations from expected business performance metrics. We will therefore perform numeric predictions, instead of the binary predictions used in this paper, to quantify the extent of deviations. This will be complemented by case studies with industry to capture the perspective of users.

Acknowledgments. We thank Zoltán Ádám Mann for his constructive comments on earlier versions of the paper. Research leading to these results has received funding from the EFRE co-financed operational program NRW.Ziel2 under grant agreement 005-1010-0012 (LoFIP – Cockpits for Operational Management of Transport Processes) and from the European Unions Horizon 2020 research and innovation programme under grant agreement No. 731932 (TransformingTransport).

References

1. van der Aalst, W.M.P., Schonenberg, M.H., Song, M.: Time prediction based on process mining. Inf. Syst. **36**(2), 450–475 (2011)
2. Bevacqua, A., Carnuccio, M., Folino, F., Guarascio, M., Pontieri, L.: A data-adaptive trace abstraction approach to the prediction of business process performances. In: Hammoudi, S., Maciaszek, L.A., Cordeiro, J., Dietz, J.L.G. (eds.) 15th International Conference on Enterprise Information Systems (ICEIS 2013), Angers, France, pp. 56–65. SciTePress (2013)
3. Bosnic, Z., Kononenko, I.: Estimation of individual prediction reliability using the local sensitivity analysis. Appl. Intell. **29**(3), 187–203 (2008)
4. Bosnic, Z., Kononenko, I.: Automatic selection of reliability estimates for individual regression predictions. Knowl. Eng. Rev. **25**(1), 27–47 (2010)
5. Breuker, D., Delfmann, P., Matzner, M., Becker, J.: Designing and evaluating an interpretable predictive modeling technique for business processes. In: Fournier, F., Mendling, J. (eds.) BPM 2014. LNBIP, vol. 202, pp. 541–553. Springer, Cham (2015). doi:10.1007/978-3-319-15895-2_46
6. Cabanillas, C., Di Ciccio, C., Mendling, J., Baumgrass, A.: Predictive task monitoring for business processes. In: Sadiq, S., Soffer, P., Völzer, H. (eds.) BPM 2014. LNCS, vol. 8659, pp. 424–432. Springer, Cham (2014). doi:10.1007/978-3-319-10172-9_31
7. Castellanos, M., Salazar, N., Casati, F., Dayal, U., Shan, M.C.: Predictive business operations management. Int. J. Comput. Sci. Eng. **2**(5/6), 292–301 (2006)
8. Dietterich, T.G.: Ensemble methods in machine learning. In: Kittler, J., Roli, F. (eds.) MCS 2000. LNCS, vol. 1857, pp. 1–15. Springer, Heidelberg (2000). doi:10.1007/3-540-45014-9_1
9. Eder, J., Panagos, E., Rabinovich, M.: Workflow time management revisited. In: Bubenko, J., Krogstie, J., Pastor, O., Pernici, B., Rolland, C., Sølvberg, A. (eds.) Seminal Contributions to Information Systems Engineering: 25 Years of CAiSE, pp. 207–213. Springer, Heidelberg (2013). doi:10.1007/978-3-642-36926-1_16
10. Elkan, C.: The foundations of cost-sensitive learning. In: Nebel, B. (ed.) Proceedings 7th International Joint Conference on Artificial Intelligence, IJCAI 2001, Seattle, Washington, USA, 4–10 August 2001, pp. 973–978. Morgan Kaufmann (2001)
11. Feldmann, Z., Fournier, F., Franklin, R., Metzger, A.: Proactive event processing in action: a case study on the proactive management of transport processes. In: Chakravarthy, S., Urban, S., Pietzuch, P., Rundensteiner, E., Dietrich, S. (eds.) 7th International Conference on Distributed Event-Based Systems (DEBS 2013), Arlington, Texas, USA, pp. 97–106. ACM (2013)

12. Di Francescomarino, C., Dumas, M., Federici, M., Ghidini, C., Maggi, F.M., Rizzi, W.: Predictive business process monitoring framework with hyperparameter optimization. In: Nurcan, S., Soffer, P., Bajec, M., Eder, J. (eds.) CAiSE 2016. LNCS, vol. 9694, pp. 361–376. Springer, Cham (2016). doi:10.1007/978-3-319-39696-5_22
13. Grigori, D., Casati, F., Castellanos, M., Dayal, U., Sayal, M., Shan, M.C.: Business process intelligence. Comput. Ind. **53**(3), 321–343 (2004)
14. Haykin, S.: Neural Networks and Learning Machines: A Comprehensive Foundation, 3rd edn. Prentice Hall, Upper Saddle River (2008)
15. Jalonen, H., Lönnqvist, A.: Predictive business-fresh initiative or old wine in a new bottle. Manag. Decis. **47**(10), 1595–1609 (2009)
16. Kang, B., Kim, D., Kang, S.: Periodic performance prediction for real-time business process monitoring. Ind. Manag. Data Syst. **112**(1), 4–23 (2011)
17. Leitner, P., Hummer, W., Dustdar, S.: Cost-based optimization of service compositions. IEEE Trans. Serv. Comput. **6**(2), 239–251 (2013)
18. Maggi, F.M., Di Francescomarino, C., Dumas, M., Ghidini, C.: Predictive monitoring of business processes. In: Jarke, M., Mylopoulos, J., Quix, C., Rolland, C., Manolopoulos, Y., Mouratidis, H., Horkoff, J. (eds.) CAiSE 2014. LNCS, vol. 8484, pp. 457–472. Springer, Cham (2014). doi:10.1007/978-3-319-07881-6_31
19. Metzger, A., Leitner, P., Ivanović, D., Schmieders, E., Franklin, R., Carro, M., Dustdar, S., Pohl, K.: Comparing and combining predictive business process monitoring techniques. IEEE Trans. Syst. Man Cybern. Syst. **45**(2), 276–290 (2015)
20. Metzger, A., Sammodi, O., Pohl, K.: Accurate proactive adaptation of service-oriented systems. In: Cámara, J., de Lemos, R., Ghezzi, C., Lopes, A. (eds.) Assurances for Self-Adaptive Systems. LNCS, vol. 7740, pp. 240–265. Springer, Heidelberg (2013). doi:10.1007/978-3-642-36249-1_9
21. Polikar, R.: Ensemble based systems in decision making. IEEE Circuits Syst. Mag. **6**(3), 21–45 (2006)
22. Rogge-Solti, A., Weske, M.: Prediction of remaining service execution time using stochastic petri nets with arbitrary firing delays. In: Basu, S., Pautasso, C., Zhang, L., Fu, X. (eds.) ICSOC 2013. LNCS, vol. 8274, pp. 389–403. Springer, Heidelberg (2013). doi:10.1007/978-3-642-45005-1_27
23. Salfner, F., Lenk, M., Malek, M.: A survey of online failure prediction methods. ACM Comput. Surv. **42**(3), 10:1–10:42 (2010)
24. Skouradaki, M., Ferme, V., Pautasso, C., Leymann, F., van Hoorn, A.: Micro-benchmarking BPMN 2.0 workflow management systems with workflow patterns. In: Nurcan, S., Soffer, P., Bajec, M., Eder, J. (eds.) CAiSE 2016. LNCS, vol. 9694, pp. 67–82. Springer, Cham (2016). doi:10.1007/978-3-319-39696-5_5
25. Verenich, I., Dumas, M., La Rosa, M., Maggi, F.M., Di Francescomarino, C.: Complex symbolic sequence clustering and multiple classifiers for predictive process monitoring. In: Reichert, M., Reijers, H.A. (eds.) BPM 2015. LNBIP, vol. 256, pp. 218–229. Springer, Cham (2016). doi:10.1007/978-3-319-42887-1_18
26. Zadrozny, B., Elkan, C.: Learning and making decisions when costs and probabilities are both unknown. In: Lee, D., Schkolnick, M., Provost, F.J., Srikant, R. (eds.) Proceedings of the Seventh ACM SIGKDD International Conference on Knowledge Discovery and Data Mining, San Francisco, CA, USA, 26–29 August 2001, pp. 204–213. ACM (2001)
27. Zhao, H., Sinha, A.P., Bansal, G.: An extended tuning method for cost-sensitive regression and forecasting. Decis. Support Syst. **51**(3), 372–383 (2011)

Leveraging Game-Tree Search for Robust Process Enactment

Yingzhi Gou, Aditya Ghose(✉), and Hoa Khanh Dam

Decision Systems Lab, School of Computing and IT,
University of Wollongong, Wollongong, Australia
{yg452,aditya,hoa}@uow.edu.au

Abstract. A robust machinery for process enactment should ideally be able to anticipate and account for possible ways in which the execution environment might impede a process from achieving its desired effects or outcomes. At critical decision points in a process, it is useful for the enactment machinery to compute alternative flows by viewing the problem as an adversarial game pitting the process (or its enactment machinery) against the process execution environment. We show how both minimax search and Monte Carlo game tree search, coupled with a novel conception of an evaluation function, delivers useful results.

Keywords: Business process robustness · Business process flexibility · Game-tree search

1 Introduction

It is generally recognized that business processes need to be executed in a manner that is *robust* and *resilient* to changes in the operating environment within which these processes are executed. The challenge is not only to be *flexible* enough to deal with immediate *impediments* to process execution, but to also *anticipate* future states of affairs that might impede process execution (or the achievement of process goals). Impediments to the successful execution of a business process can appear in many forms. For instance, an outsourced search for past buying behaviour of a customer in a credit check process might return no results, or results for the wrong customer, thus preventing the successful execution of an instance of that process. An automated process for maintaining the ambient temperature inside a building might be impeded by a non-functioning air-conditioner, or by a faulty sensor that reports incorrect temperature readings. A clinical process might have to face obstacles caused by a patient who forgets (or deliberately ignores) to ingest a prescribed pill left at his/her bedside by a nurse.

Most of the examples above involve *functional impediments* (that prevent the achievement of functional process goals in a manner akin to the notion of obstacles [1]). *Non-functional impediments* can also occur, such as when the outsourced service for retrieving the past buying behaviour of a customer delays the

E. Dubois and K. Pohl (Eds.): CAiSE 2017, LNCS 10253, pp. 461–476, 2017.
DOI: 10.1007/978-3-319-59536-8_29

delivery of its results, thus preventing a process from meeting its non-functional requirements. The framework we develop in this paper is general enough to handle both kinds of impediments, but we mainly focus on functional impediments in the formalization and evaluation due to space restrictions.

Traditional conceptions of process designs that rely on task IDs to represent information about the *effects* of that task are not easily amenable to the kinds of analysis that would reveal whether a given state of affairs impedes the achievement of process goals. To perform this analysis, we would require an exhaustive enumeration of all possible states of the environment that might present obstacles to the successful execution of a process task - an often-impossible exercise. This analysis is significantly simpler (and can be performed at runtime) if processes are annotated with task post-conditions. For instance, a given state of the environment would impede the process if it negated any of the desired post-conditions at that point. A large body of reported work leverages semantic annotation of business process designs [2–10]. A number of proposals also address the problem of semantic annotation of web services in a similar fashion [11–14]. Our framework, therefore, leverages semantically annotated process models (i.e., process models where each task is annotated with post-conditions).

Our discussion above suggests that the relationship between a process and its operating environment can often be *adversarial.* The adversarial behaviour of the environment might be intentional (where entities within the environment might have an interest in preventing the successful execution of a process) or unintentional (where the natural behaviour of the environment throws up impediments). In either case, there is value in viewing the interaction between the process and the environment as an *adversarial game* pitting the process (which is, say, the maximizing player) against the environment (the minimizing player). The value of a game formulation stems from the following. In a manner akin to a traditional 2-player adversarial game, the process can reason about a sequence of moves it might make (tasks it might execute) that would help achieve process goals (winning states in a game formulation) in the face of counter-moves by the opposing player (impediments thrown up by the environment). The game is one of perfect information since the state of the game (in this case, the state of the process operating environment) is equally accessible to both players. The game involves turn-taking, with the process making a move, then the environment making a move and so on. While this does not necessarily exactly reflect what might happen in a real-world setting, it serves as an adequate abstraction. This game-tree search formulation of the problem relies on the process having access to some modicum of understanding of the behaviour of the environment (an *environment behaviour model*). In the simplest case, this might be a set of impediments (conditions in the operating environment) that might hold. To be maximally robust, the process might perform worst-case reasoning by assuming *extreme adversariality* of the environment, where the environment makes those conditions true that most impede the achievement of process goals. More sophisticated models of the behaviour of the environment (via state transition models or via the generation of impediments in a context-sensitive fashion) could also be used.

It is useful to consider the manner in which adversarial game-tree search might be incorporated into the process execution machinery. Game-tree search essentially involves *process re-consideration*, i.e., re-designing the normative process flow (i.e., the flow mandated by the process design). Given that our understanding of possible impediments occurring in the operating environment of the process is context-sensitive in general (in many settings, it is difficult to re-compute or predict these impediments at design time), it is useful to reconsider process designs during run-time. The granularity of reconsideration can be parametric. At the one extreme, we have *step-wise reconsideration*, where we re-visit what is to be done next after every step. More generally, we might adopt a policy of reconsidering after every k steps (or *k-step reconsideration*, the lower the k, the more reactive the process is). Process reconsideration can also be triggered by situations where the observed effects do not correspond to the expected effects (something referred to as *semantic non-conformance* in [15]). It is also useful to note that adversarial game-tree search can form the basis of *offline process design*, and the experimental results we present later in the paper may also be viewed as illustrating that use case. Process reconsideration can be used to decide the immediate next step, or the sequence of the following n steps (closely related to *k-step reconsideration*).

We offer two formulations of the *robust process design/execution problem*, first in terms of the well-known *minimax game tree search* algorithm (with α-β cutoffs), and second in terms of the *Monte Carlo tree search* algorithm. Our experimental evaluation suggests that this approach to achieving process robustness/resilience is practical. The experimental evaluation also offers a more nuanced understanding of the merits of minimax search with α-β cutoffs relative to Monte Carlo tree search. Ultimately, the intent is to compute a sequence of tasks (which might be at variance with the mandated process model) that is most likely to achieve process goals in the face of potential impediments. In the case of the clinical process example mentioned earlier in this section, a robust workaround would be to execute an additional task that involves a nurse monitoring the ingestion of the prescribed pill by the patient (similar workarounds can be imagined for the other example settings).

The rest of the paper is structured as follows. Section 2 describes the setting of semantically annotated process models as well as the normative and observed execution traces that the proposed framework leverages. Section 3 describes the formulation of the robust process enactment problem as adversarial game tree search. Section 4 provides a detailed experimental evaluation while Sect. 5 provides concluding remarks.

2 Processes Annotated with Post-conditions

In this section, we define the class of process models that our proposal relies on, specifically *semantically annotated process models*. We also define the notions of *normative* and *semantic execution trace* that we shall leverage in the heuristic evaluation required by game tree search (these latter notions were first defined in [15], and our exposition below summarizes those results). The definition of a semantically annotated process model refers to *effect scenarios*, which provide answers to the following question posed at design time: *given a process design and a designated point in that process design, what postconditions/effects would hold if the process were to execute up to that point?* We assume a setting where tasks are drawn from a *capability library* (that describes all of the tasks/capabilities that the enterprise is able to execute). We also assume that all tasks in the capability library are annotated with post-conditions that describe the context-independent effects of executing those tasks. To answer the question posed above, we need to *accumulate* these context-independent post-conditions to simulate the effects of process execution. Unlike a number of the process annotation approaches referred to in the introduction that accumulate task post-conditions by using the AI planning device of add-lists and delete-lists of effects, we use the *state update operator* approach from [5,8] (recall that a state update operator takes a state description and the effects of an action to generate one or more descriptions of the state that would accrue from executing this action in the input state). In our setting, the answer to the question posed above is non-deterministic in general, and is provided as a set of (mutually exclusive) *effect scenarios*. There are two reasons why we need these answers to be non-deterministic. First, in any process with XOR-branching, one might arrive at a given task via multiple paths, and the accumulated effects depend on the path taken. Since this analysis is done at design time, the specific path taken can only be determined at run-time (thus leading to non-determinism in the accumulated effects). Second, state update operators typically generate non-deterministic outcomes since the inconsistencies that commonly appear in state update can be resolved in multiple different ways. When the execution of a process leads to a state that is (possibly partially) characterized by an effect scenario, the execution of the next task in the model, or the occurrence of the next event, can lead to a very specific set of effect scenarios, determined by the *state update operator* being used. In effect, the process model determines a transition system, which determines how the partial state description contained in an effect scenario evolves as a consequence of the execution/occurrence of the next task (event) specified in the model. We assign each effect scenario appearing in a semantically annotated process model a unique ID (thus if the same partial description applies to a process at different points in its design, it would be assigned a distinct ID at each distinct point). We can thus refer to the *predecessors* (the effect scenarios that can lead to the current scenario via a single state update determined by the next task/event) and *successors* (the scenarios that can be obtained from the current scenario via a single state update determined by the next task/event) of each effect scenario with respect to the transition system implicitly defined by the process design.

Given these preliminaries, we define a **semantically annotated process model** $\mathcal{P}$ as a process model (such as a BPMN model) or a process graph (in the usual sense that the term is used in the literature - a formal definition is omitted to save space) in which each task or event is associated with a set of *effect scenarios.* Each effect scenario es is a 4-tuple $\langle ID, S, Pre, Succ\rangle$, where S is a set of sentences in the background language, ID is a unique ID for each effect scenario, Pre is a set of IDs of effect scenarios that can be valid *predecessors* in $\mathcal{P}$ of the current effect scenario, while $Succ$ is a set of IDs of effect scenarios that can be valid successors in $\mathcal{P}$ of the current effect scenario.

A semantically annotated process model is associated with a set of normative traces, each providing a semantic account of one possible way in which the process might be executed. Formally, a **normative trace** nt is a sequence $\langle \tau_1, es_1, \tau_2, \ldots es_{n-1}, \tau_n, es_n\rangle$, where

- Each of $\tau_1, \ldots, \tau_n$ is either an event or an activity in the process.
- $es_1 = \langle ID_1, S_1, \emptyset, Succ_1\rangle$ is the *initial effect scenario*, normally associated with the start event of the process;
- $es_n = \langle ID_n, S_n, Pre_n, \emptyset\rangle$ is the *final effect scenario*, normally associated with the end event of the process;
- $es_i \ldots, es_n$ are effect scenarios, and for each $es_i = \langle ID_i, S_i, Pre_i, Succ_i\rangle$, $i \in [2..n]$, it is always the case that $ID_{i-1} \in Pre_i$ and $ID_i \in Succ_{i-1}$.

We shall refer to the sequence $\langle \tau_1, \tau_2, \ldots, \tau_n\rangle$ as the *identity* of the trace nt. To simplify exposition, we will on occasion use es to refer to only the S in the 4-tuple denoting an effect scenario.

A **semantic execution trace** of a process $\mathcal{P}$ is a sequence $\langle \tau_1, o_1, \tau_2, o_2, \ldots, \tau_m, o_m\rangle$ where each τ_i is either a task or an event, and each o_i is a set of sentences in the background language that we shall refer to as an *observation* that describes (possibly incompletely) the state of the process context after each task or event. We shall refer to the sequence $\langle \tau_1, \tau_2, \ldots, \tau_m\rangle$ as the *identity* of the execution trace. Note that we do not require each τ_i to belong to the process design $\mathcal{P}$ to allow the possibility of actual executions being erroneous, or to represent on-the-fly re-designs.

3 The Robust Process Enactment Problem

We address the *robust process enactment problem*, defined as follows:
Given

- A semantically annotated process model $\mathcal{P}$,
- A capability library consisting of tasks with context-independent post-conditions $\mathcal{C}$ (in more sophisticated settings, we might view each element of $\mathcal{C}$ as having both a precondition *pre* and a postcondition *post*),
- An *environment behaviour model* $M : \mathcal{S} \rightarrow 2^{\mathcal{S}}$, where $\mathcal{S}$ is set of all possible states,
- A set of *goal conditions* (the achievement of any one of which would count as successful process execution) $\mathcal{G}$,
- The sequence of tasks $\langle \tau_1, \tau_2, \ldots, \tau_i\rangle$ that have been executed thus far,
- The current observed state o_i of the process operating environment, and
- A state update operator $\oplus$,

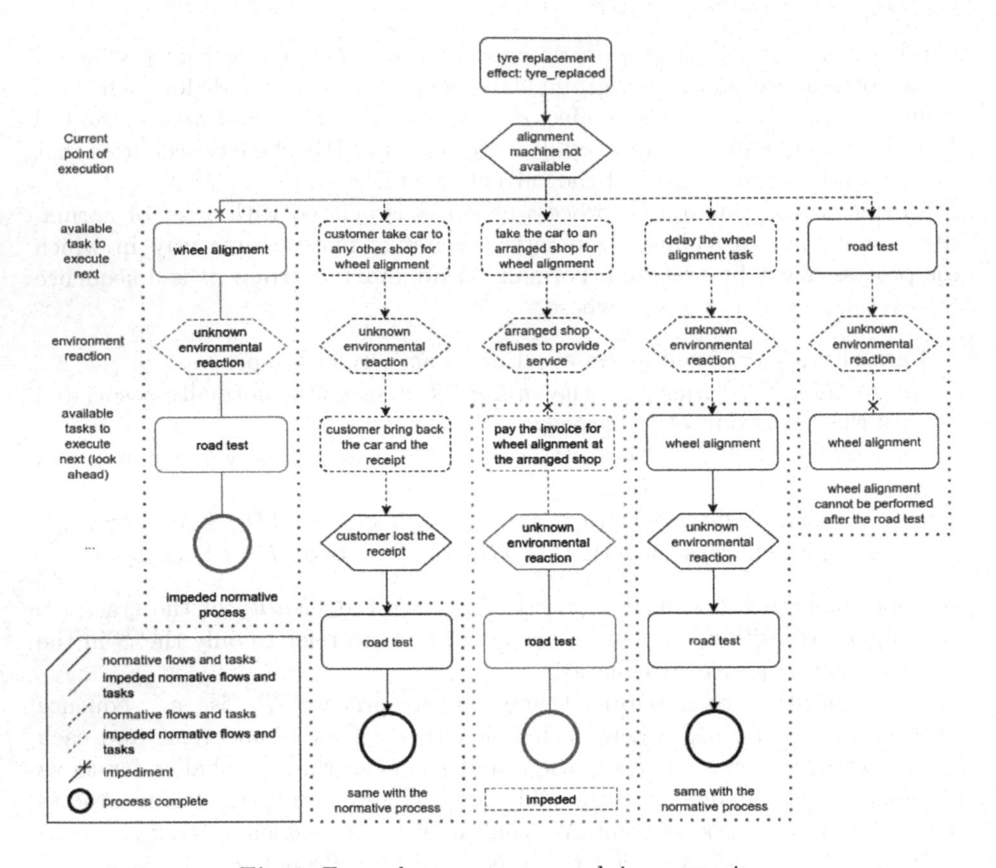

Fig. 1. Example: game tree search in car service

Determine:

- A sequence of tasks $\langle \tau_1, \tau_2, \ldots, \tau_i, \ldots, \tau_n \rangle$ where each $\tau_i \in \mathcal{C}$ that is *most likely* to achieve a goal-satisfying state (i.e., a state that makes at least one of the goal conditions true) under the assumption that the environment behaves in a *maximally adversarial* fashion.

Note that this formulation permits us to also consider other variations, such as:(1) determining what the next task should be, (2) determining what the next k tasks should be and (3) determining at the initial state what the complete sequence of tasks should be that would lead to a goal-satisfying state.

Consider for example a car servicing process in an auto repair/maintenance store that consists of a task that replaces the tyres of the car, then a wheel alignment task, followed by a road test. Suppose that the alignment machine in store is currently unavailable. As the result, the normative process task (i.e. wheel alignment) cannot be performed. The capability library of the store suggests some alternative tasks or task sequences can be executed to achieve the same process goal which may include (see Fig. 1).

(1) Ask the customer to take the car to another shop for wheel alignment and reimburse the customer against a receipt, then complete the remaining tasks in-store;
(2) The shop takes the car to a pre-arranged shop for wheel alignment, pays that shop, then completes the remaining tasks;
(3) Ask the customer to come back another day when the machine becomes available by delaying the currently impeded process;
(4) Rearrange the task sequence, i.e. skip the current task and complete the remaining tasks first, then do the wheel alignment later when the machine becomes available.

At first blush, all tasks/task sequences that resolve the current impediment seem to be equally feasible. However, if we look further into the future, the ramifications of some of the options above may cause problems for later tasks and impact quality of service requirements such as the overall customer satisfaction, service standards, etc. For example, if option (4) is taken and the road test is preformed before the wheel alignment, the test may be unsafe and the test result maybe inaccurate. In addition, after wheel alignment is performed, another road test may be required. Option (3) requires the customer schedule another time, which may lead to a dissatisfied customer. As the result, options (1) and (2) may be better options as they only delay the current process instance slightly during the time of the unavailable machine, and do not increase the possibility of any future impediments. They may however increase the cost, and in particular option (1) may reduce the customer satisfaction, as well as introduce some potential new impediments (worst case scenarios) such as the arranged shop refusing to provide wheel alignment service due to the large amount of requests that affect its normal operation, or the customer losing the receipt for reimbursement etc. Thus, the purpose of the game-tree search is to consider and evaluate all the feasible alternatives during process execution.

The general problem can be instantiated in a variety of ways. The assumption of maximally adversarial behaviour on the part of the environment is a form of worst-case reasoning. It entails that the environment will behave in a manner (consistent with the environment behaviour model) that most impedes process goal satisfaction. This does not necessarily mean that the environment is deliberately adversarial, but only that the worst-case behaviour of the environment has been taken into account in deciding what to do next during process enactment. We will say that a condition (made true by the environment) c **impedes** the achievement of a goal condition g if and only if $c \wedge g \models \perp$. In some cases, we might approximate the environment behaviour model via a set of conditions that the environment is capable of bringing about. In other cases, we might provide more sophisticated behaviour models in the form of state transition systems or sets of event-condition-action rules. The sequence of steps executed thus far might be empty if a procedure for solving this problem is invoked at the start of the execution of a process instance, or if the intent is to compute a maximally robust process design. The current state of the process operating environment is important as an independent input since the sequence of process steps executed might lead to a predicted state of affairs (via the accumulation of task post-conditions as discussed earlier) that might be at variance with the current state (this, in itself, can be a trigger for process reconsideration). When the intent is design-time analysis for computing robust process models, the current state might be left empty, or populated by the expected start state of the process (one could also reason by cases and compute multiple process models if a set of mutually exclusive start states need to be accounted for). The accumulation of task post-conditions involves the application of a state update operator. Several such operators have been proposed in the literature, two prominent ones being the Possible Worlds Approach (PWA) [16] and the Possible Models Approach [17].

Our proposal involves the use of game tree search to solve a 2-player adversarial game of perfect information in addressing the robust process enactment problem. The two players are the process and the environment. The game is one of perfect information since the state of the environment is equally accessible to both players. The simplest game tree search algorithm is *minimax search*, which involves a maximizing player (that seeks to maximize the payoff or utility) and a minimizing player (that seeks to minimize the payoff - all states of the game being assessed by the same utility/payoff function). The key data structure is a *game tree* where each node represents a state of the game and nodes at alternating levels represent states of the game that can be achieved via moves made by a given player. For a fully expanded game tree, the leaf nodes represent end-game states (these can be labelled with 1, -1 and 0 to represent a win, loss or draw for the maximizing player, or with values from a real-valued interval to represent degrees of winning etc. for the maximizing player). The minimax algorithm proceeds by propagating these values up the game tree, with a node corresponding to a state where the maximizing player makes a move being labelled with the maximum of the utility values of its child nodes (and the converse for nodes where the minimizing player makes a move). The intent is to obtain a payoff/utility value labelling all of the child nodes of the root of the tree (the state at which a move must be made by one of the players). Once these labels are obtained, the maximizing player selects that move that leads to the state with the highest utility (converse for the minimizing player). For most complex games (such as chess), the full tree is too large to enumerate, and search proceeds by cutting off the tree at a fixed (parametric) depth and treating the nodes at that depth as pseudo-leaf nodes. Since these nodes do not represent end-game states, they do not have exact payoff values associated with them. Instead, a *heuristic evaluation function* is used to estimate the "goodness" of a given node (an approximate indicator of the likelihood that a move leading to that node will eventually lead to a win for the maximizing player). Minimax search with α-β cutoffs involves bound propagation on payoff values to prune the search tree (we do not provide a more detailed exposition due to space constraints).

In our setting, each node represents a state of the process operating environment. The moves available to the *process* player correspond to tasks in the capability library while the moves available to the *environment* player correspond to the conditions (potential impediments) that can be made true by the environment as per the environment behavioural model. Both task post-conditions and impediments can be viewed as sentences in the underlying language. Given such a sentence e and a prior state s, the resulting state is denoted by $s \oplus e$ where $\oplus$ is the state update operator provided as input. State update operators generate possibly many non-deterministic outcomes in the general case (the Possible Worlds Approach, for instance, generates as a resulting state $s' \cup e$ for each maximal - with respect to set inclusion - subset of s that is consistent with e). The non-deterministic states associated with a given move represents a point of departure from standard minimax search (where a given move leads to a unique state). This can be handled easily by extending the worst-case reasoning approach that underpins minimax search. Thus, if a maximizing player contemplates a given move, it will pick the state with the lowest payoff amongst the possibly many states that can result from that move as the resulting state (converse for the minimizing player).

Designing a heuristic evaluation function that is able to estimate the likelihood of a given state leading to a "win" for the maximizing player is another challenge. The evaluation function we use in generating the experimental results presented in the next section is conceived with the following intuition in mind. Instead of assigning numeric values for each state, this function generates a preference ordering on a set of states (which can be used in much the same way as a set of numeric payoff values). A state s is preferred over another state s' if s is "closer" (in a sense to be made precise below) to either the nearest goal state or the nearest state in any normative execution trace with an *identity* (recall the definition at the end of Sect. 2) for which the sequence of tasks already executed serves as a prefix (and which has not been already traversed in the execution thus far). Given a set of sentences t and a background knowledge base KB, we use $Cn_{KB}(t)$ to denote the set of all logical consequences of $t \cup KB$. Let the union of the goal states and the states in the normative execution traces discussed above be referred to as the set of *desired states*. One plausible and intuitive means (but by no means the only one) of assessing the proximity of a state s to a desired state d (denoted by $f(s,d)$) is as follows:

$$f(s,d) = \frac{|Cn(s) \cap Cn(d)|}{|Cn(d)|} \tag{1}$$

This function obtains a higher value the closer the cardinality of the intersection of the set of consequences of s and d gets to the cardinality of d. In the experimental evaluation, we compute the number of clauses in a CNF representation of d that are entailed by s, as one computational realization of the expression above. Since we are able to work with ground theories (universally quantified rules in the KB are replaced by their ground instances - of which there is a relatively small number), we use the SAT4J SAT solver as our theorem prover.

Each step in the search process proceeds as follows. If the current (observed) state is o, and it is the *process* player's turn to make a move, then the set of feasible next states (that determine the next level of the game tree) is given by the set $o \oplus post$ for each *post* associated with available tasks in the capability library (in more sophisticated settings where we also have task pre-conditions, we determine whether $o \models pre$ before we conclude that a task is feasible to execute). If it is the *environment* player's turn to make a move, then the set of feasible next states is determined by $\bigcup M(s_i)$ for each s_i satisfying $o \models s_i$.

It is useful to consider the impact loops in a process in this context. It is fairly obvious that generating semantic annotations for process designs with loops is problematic (simply because we cannot predict at design time the number of times the process would loop). In the context of the robust process enactment problem, however, loops pose no problems. It is perfectly feasible for this framework to return a task sequence that includes multiple iterations of a task or task sequence, if that is the best strategy for dealing with potential obstacles (as a trivial example, we might end up needing to press a "temperature-up" button on a thermostat to achieve the desired temperature).

4 Evaluation

Let I being the set of *impediments* that the environment is capable of making true. For the purposes of experimental evaluation, we adopt a maximally adversarial model of the environment. We generate the set of impediments I by creating a distinct impediment from the negation of every clause in a conjunctive normal form (CNF) representation of a goal. Thus, given a set of goal states G_p (in CNF) of the process p, the set of impediments I_p is defined as:

$$I_p = \{\neg c | \forall c \in g, \forall g \in G_p\} \tag{2}$$

Minimax Tree Search: In this evaluation we use minimax tree search with α-β cutoffs. Due to the complexity of the search, we limit the depth of the game tree to 5. The heuristic evaluation function discussed in the previous section is applied to the pseudo-leaf nodes at this depth.

Monte Carlo Tree Search: We compare the performance of minimax search with α-β cutoffs against a popular Monte Carlo Tree Search(MCTS) algorithm, namely Upper Confidence Bounds for Trees (UCT) (the description of the algorithm can be found in [18]) with a random play-out simulation to evaluate a given state. Every time the process needs to select the next task to execute, the tree is sampled $5n$ times where n is the number of possible tasks available for the process to select. We then select a leaf node that is not a terminal state (i.e., a goal state), expand it and preform random play-out at all the newly expanded nodes. The random play-out is a simulated game play where each player randomly selects a move at every turn until the game reaches a terminal state or until the time runs out (we use a timeout of 3 s). The value 1 is returned when a goal state is reached in the random play-out. Alternatively, 0 is returned if a goal state cannot be reached in the given time (3 s).

Evaluation Data: Semantically annotated process models that generate sensible results are difficult to randomly generate. Two sets of hand-crafted semantically annotated process models are used in this evaluation. The first set of 8 processes are structurally and semantically simpler. Process1 is the simplest, with only 4 tasks in sequence, 1 or 2 assertions in the effects of each task and 3 rules in the background knowledge base. Process2 has the same number of tasks as Process1 but with one extra XOR branch and slightly more complex semantic annotations. Process3 is also a sequence of tasks, but with more complex semantic annotations. For the rest of the processes (Process4 to Process8), we progressively increase either the structural complexity (i.e. more tasks and/or more XOR branches), or increase the complexity of the semantic annotations. Process8 is a "real world" process created using information available at workflowpatterns.com.

The second set of processes have considerably greater structural and semantic complexity relative to the first set. The number of unique tasks (capabilities) in each process in this set varies from 10 to 100, with the number of XOR gates varying from 1 to 15. In terms of semantic complexity, we use between 20 to 50 propositional state variables to describe states of objects in the environment (which is expressive enough for most task effects/postconditions of interest). We assume that each task will impact between 1 to 5 state variables. We use between 20 to 50 rules in a background knowledge base that constrain the state changes.

Evaluation Setup: For every process, we first compute all the unique instances (i.e. sequence of tasks and events from beginning to the end of the process) and for each of these instances, we simulate the process execution by computing a normative trace (as defined earlier and in [15]). This is the base line simulation without any impediments, with each normative trace leading to a goal state (this is used to compute the success rate, i.e., the number of goal-satisfying instances divided by the number of distinct normative traces). Then we generate a sequence of impediments of length of $(n-1)$ where n is the number of tasks in the process instance, by randomly selecting impediments from I_p. We insert one impediment after every completed task (except when the goal is realized after a task, which is when we force the simulation to stop).

We run three kinds of simulations:

- *Standard Process (execution):* In this simulation, we use the exact sequence of tasks in the process instances (but with impediments inserted after every task) to see if, in a maximally adversarial environment, the process is still able to achieve its goal.
- *MCTS:* Here, the next task for the process to execute is selected using MCTS. Again, one impediment will appear after each task unless after the task, the goal is achieved, or, there are no more impediments.
- Minimax Tree Search The setup is the same with MCTS except the next task is selected using the minimax algorithm.

Evaluation Results: Figure 2 shows a summary of the evaluation on the simple process set, where each row is the summary of instances of a process in the simple process set except the first row, which is a summary of all process instances. The number of available tasks indicates how many distinct tasks populate the capability library, which translates to the number of tasks that are used to

	Number of Available Tasks	Total Process Instances	Success Count			Average Simulation Time (seconds)		Average Decision Time (seconds)	
			Standard Process	MCTS	Minimax	MCTS	Minimax	MCTS	Minimax
Over All	N/A	294	101	192	276	376.238	532.469	81.466	171.180
Process1	4	6	0	4	6	38.425	0.592	10.859	0.296
Process2	4	43	15	28	41	89.260	2.520	27.274	1.037
Process3	10	26	0	16	26	149.188	5.786	38.293	5.786
Process4	7	41	20	23	35	499.695	512.851	112.779	142.486
Process5	7	58	26	42	50	554.554	953.894	133.316	277.424
Process6	9	43	21	34	43	165.946	61.557	36.333	23.369
Process7	10	48	11	32	47	642.830	1454.933	116.251	529.812
Process8	9	29	8	13	28	414.598	256.789	76.512	60.750

Fig. 2. Summary of result—simple process set

construct the process model in the standard process simulation, and the number of "moves" for MCTS and minimax tree search to consider at each step (when it is the *process* players turn to make a move). The number of total process instances indicates the total number of process instances that have been simulated, where each instance uses the same sequence of impediments. The success counts record the number of times each method (standard process, MCTS, and minimax tree search) successfully achieves the goals of the process. The average simulation time measures the total time MCTS or minimax tree search takes to terminate in seconds (the termination means either the goal is realized or the two methods have used the same number of tasks compared to the standard process). The average decision time measures the average time taken by MCTS or minimax tree search to find the next best task to execute.

It is clear that the standard, predefined process is not reactive enough in this setting where the environment constantly acts against reaching a goal state. MCTS shows improvements in the overall success rate but minimax tree search is able to achieve the highest rate of success. The downside to using minimax search is the computational cost (average decision time).

For processes with simpler semantics (Process1, Process2, and Process3), minimax tree search makes a decision much faster compared to MCTS, and the time spent increases when there are more available tasks to evaluate for both methods. However, for processes that have complex semantics (larger number of rules in the knowledge base and larger sets of assertions in the postconditions of each task, as exemplified by Process4, Process5, Process6, and Process7), the time spent by minimax tree search increases dramatically, and minimax tree search takes longer than MCTS except for Process6. Process6 is a special case, possibly because the set of rules in the knowledge base create a simpler problem for the underlying reasoning machinery to solve. Overall, in all 294 process instances, it is clear that MCTS is more efficient for large complex processes. Minimax tree search achieves a higher success rate, but can take a very long time to decide on the next best move for large complex processes.

The next set of results involve the complex set of processes. The major issue in conducting this evaluation was that the minimax tree search took more memory than available (2 GB) in the experimental setup leading to the simulation be

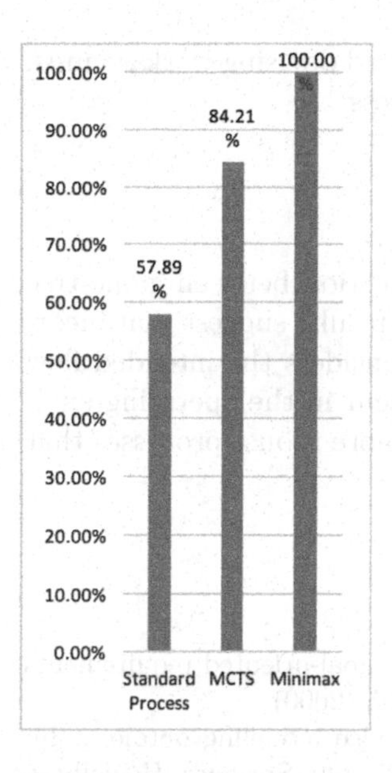

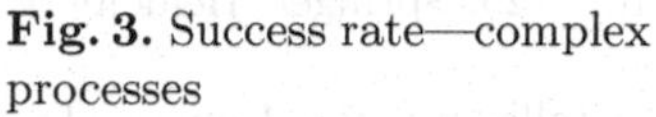

Fig. 3. Success rate—complex processes

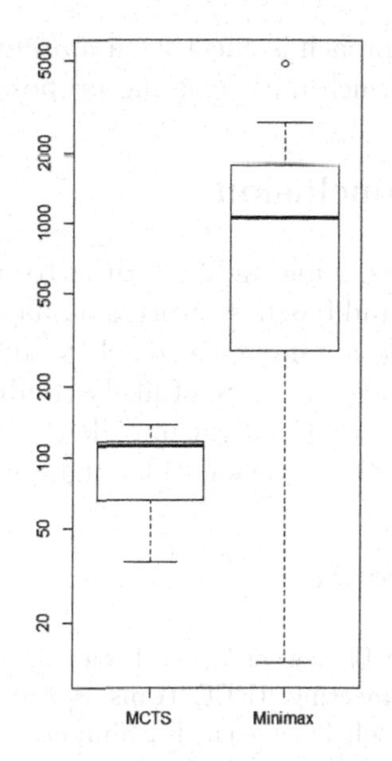

Fig. 4. Average decision time (seconds)—complex processes

terminated. Consequently, we are only able to complete a small number of simulations successfully given the time and space limitation with the unoptimized prototype used in the evaluation. Some of the issues we had with the more complex process models can be overcome by optimizing the game tree search as well as the actual implementation, which is beyond the scope of this paper. Figure 3 show the success rate of the 3 methods, and Fig. 4 illustrates the time taken by MCTS and minimax tree search to select the next task to execute, which shows that MCTS is able select tasks relatively quickly to achieve a more than 80% chance of success.

5 Related Work

Process flexibility has long been recognized as an issue in real world business process management [19–23]. Part of the existing literature on process flexibility addresses flexibility by design [24], including exception handling [22], or achieving minimal deviation from a design during execution [15]. Other parts of that literature addresses flexibility at runtime [25], by taking into account risk [26], by generating optimized enactment plans given multiple optimization objectives [27] and in contexts where processes are human-driven [28]. Agent technology has also been used to model flexible processes, as the agent architectures are designed to deal with a flexible environment [20]. Schuschel and Weske adapt planning algorithms developed in the agent community for process planning [29].

Our approach is effective in *anticipating* impediments and devising workarounds, issues which most existing proposals tend not to address.

6 Conclusion

This paper highlights a hitherto under-explored connection between game-tree search and business process management. Preliminary results suggest that incorporating a game-tree search based module which reconsiders the intended flow of a process in view of likely conditions that might occur in the operating environment which might impede the process can lead to more robust processes that achieve their goals despite these impediments.

References

1. Van Lamsweerde, A., Letier, E.: Handling obstacles in goal-oriented requirements engineering. IEEE Trans. Softw. Eng. **26**(10), 978–1005 (2000)
2. Fensel, D., Facca, F., Simperl, E., Toma, I.: Web service modeling ontology. In: Fensel, D., et al. (eds.) Semantic Web Services, pp. 107–129. Springer, Heidelberg (2011)
3. Fensel, D., Lausen, H., Polleres, A., Bruijn, J., Stollberg, M., Roman, D., Domingue, J.: Enabling Semantic Web Services: The Web Service Modeling Ontology. Springer, Heidelberg (2006)
4. Hepp, M., Leymann, F., Domingue, J., Wahler, A., Fensel, D.: Semantic business process management: a vision towards using semantic Web services for business process management. In: IEEE International Conference on e-Business Engineering (ICEBE 2005), pp. 535–540. IEEE (2005)
5. Hinge, K., Ghose, A., Koliadis, G.: Process SEER: a tool for semantic effect annotation of business process models. In: Proceedings of the 13th IEEE International EDOC Conference (EDOC-2009), IEEE Computer Society Process (2009)
6. Di Pietro, I., Pagliarecci, F., Spalazzi, L.: Model checking semantically annotated services. IEEE Trans. Softw. Eng. **38**, 592–608 (2012)
7. Smith, F., Proietti, M.: Rule-based behavioral reasoning on semantic business processes. In: ICAART, pp. 130–143. SciTePress (2013)
8. Weber, I., Hoffmann, J., Mendling, J.: Beyond soundness: on the verification of semantic business process models. Distrib. Parallel Databases **27**, 271–343 (2010)
9. Di Francescomarino, C., Ghidini, C., Rospocher, M., Serafini, L., Tonella, P.: Semantically-aided business process modeling. In: Bernstein, A., Karger, D.R., Heath, T., Feigenbaum, L., Maynard, D., Motta, E., Thirunarayan, K. (eds.) ISWC 2009. LNCS, vol. 5823, pp. 114–129. Springer, Heidelberg (2009). doi:10.1007/978-3-642-04930-9_8
10. Ghose, A., Koliadis, G.: Auditing business process compliance. In: Krämer, B.J., Lin, K.-J., Narasimhan, P. (eds.) ICSOC 2007. LNCS, vol. 4749, pp. 169–180. Springer, Heidelberg (2007). doi:10.1007/978-3-540-74974-5_14
11. Martin, D., et al.: Bringing semantics to web services: the OWL-S approach. In: Cardoso, J., Sheth, A. (eds.) SWSWPC 2004. LNCS, vol. 3387, pp. 26–42. Springer, Heidelberg (2005). doi:10.1007/978-3-540-30581-1_4

12. Meyer, H.: On the semantics of service compositions. In: Marchiori, M., Pan, J.Z., Marie, C.S. (eds.) RR 2007. LNCS, vol. 4524, pp. 31–42. Springer, Heidelberg (2007). doi:10.1007/978-3-540-72982-2_3
13. Montali, M., Pesic, M., van der Aalst, W.M.P., Chesani, F., Mello, P., Storari, S.: Declarative specification and verification of service choreographiess. ACM Trans. Web **4**, 1–62 (2010)
14. Smith, F., Missikoff, M., Proietti, M.: Ontology-based querying of composite services. In: Ardagna, C.A., Damiani, E., Maciaszek, L.A., Missikoff, M., Parkin, M. (eds.) Business System Management and Engineering. LNCS, vol. 7350, pp. 159–180. Springer, Heidelberg (2012). doi:10.1007/978-3-642-32439-0_10
15. Gou, Y., Ghose, A., Chang, C.-F., Dam, H.K., Miller, A.: Semantic monitoring and compensation in socio-technical processes. In: Indulska, M., Purao, S. (eds.) ER 2014. LNCS, vol. 8823, pp. 117–126. Springer, Cham (2014). doi:10.1007/978-3-319-12256-4_12
16. Ginsberg, M.L., Smith, D.E.: Reasoning about action I: a possible world approach. Artif. Intell. **35**(2), 165–195 (1988)
17. Winslett, M.: Reasoning about action using a possible models approach. Urbana **51**, 61801 (1988)
18. Browne, C.B., Powley, E., Whitehouse, D., Lucas, S.M., Cowling, P.I., Rohlfshagen, P., Tavener, S., Perez, D., Samothrakis, S., Colton, S.: A survey of Monte Carlo tree search methods. IEEE Trans. Comput. Intell. AI Games **4**(1), 1–43 (2012)
19. van der Aalst, W.M.P., Jablonski, S.: Dealing with workflow change: identification of issues and solutions. Comput. Syst. Sci. Eng. **15**(5), 267–276 (2000)
20. Buhler, P.A., Vidal, J.M.: Towards adaptive workflow enactment using multiagent systems. Inf. Technol. Manag. **6**(1), 61–87 (2005)
21. Heinl, P., Horn, S., Jablonski, S., Neeb, J., Stein, K., Teschke, M.: A comprehensive approach to flexibility in workflow management systems. In: Proceedings of the International Joint Conference on Work Activities Coordination and Collaboration (WACC 1999), pp. 79–88 (1999)
22. Klein, M., Dellarocas, C.: A knowledge-based approach to handling exceptions in workflow systems. Comput. Support. Coop. Work **9**, 399–412 (2000)
23. Reijers, H.A.: Workflow flexibility: the forlorn promise. In: Proceedings of the Workshop on Enabling Technologies: Infrastructure for Collaborative Enterprises, WETICE, pp. 271–272(2006)
24. Hermann, T., Hoffman, M., Loser, K.U., Moysich, K.: Semistructured models are surprisingly useful for user-centered design. In: Proceedings of COOP 2000 Designing Cooperative Systems, pp. 159–174 (2000)
25. Murguzur, A., De Carlos, X., Trujillo, S., Sagardui, G.: Context-aware staged configuration of process variants@runtime. In: Jarke, M., Mylopoulos, J., Quix, C., Rolland, C., Manolopoulos, Y., Mouratidis, H., Horkoff, J. (eds.) CAiSE 2014. LNCS, vol. 8484, pp. 241–255. Springer, Cham (2014). doi:10.1007/978-3-319-07881-6_17
26. Conforti, R., de Leoni, M., La Rosa, M., van der Aalst, W.M.P.: Supporting risk-informed decisions during business process execution. In: Salinesi, C., Norrie, M.C., Pastor, Ó. (eds.) CAiSE 2013. LNCS, vol. 7908, pp. 116–132. Springer, Heidelberg (2013). doi:10.1007/978-3-642-38709-8_8
27. Jiménez-Ramírez, A., Barba, I., Del Valle, C., Weber, B.: Generating multi-objective optimized business process enactment plans. In: Salinesi, C., Norrie, M.C., Pastor, Ó. (eds.) CAiSE 2013. LNCS, vol. 7908, pp. 99–115. Springer, Heidelberg (2013). doi:10.1007/978-3-642-38709-8_7

28. Baumann, M., Baumann, M.H., Schönig, S., Jablonski, S.: Enhancing feasibility of human-driven processes by transforming process models to process checklists. In: Bider, I., Gaaloul, K., Krogstie, J., Nurcan, S., Proper, H.A., Schmidt, R., Soffer, P. (eds.) BPMDS/EMMSAD -2014. LNBIP, vol. 175, pp. 124–138. Springer, Heidelberg (2014). doi:10.1007/978-3-662-43745-2_9
29. Schuschel, H., Weske, M.: Integrated workflow planning and coordination. In: Mařík, V., Retschitzegger, W., Štěpánková, O. (eds.) DEXA 2003. LNCS, vol. 2736, pp. 771–781. Springer, Heidelberg (2003). doi:10.1007/978-3-540-45227-0_75

Predictive Business Process Monitoring with LSTM Neural Networks

Niek Tax[1], Ilya Verenich[2,3](✉), Marcello La Rosa[2], and Marlon Dumas[3]

[1] Eindhoven University of Technology, Eindhoven, The Netherlands
n.tax@tue.nl
[2] Queensland University of Technology, Brisbane, Australia
{ilya.verenich,m.larosa}@qut.edu.au
[3] University of Tartu, Tartu, Estonia
marlon.dumas@ut.ee

Abstract. Predictive business process monitoring methods exploit logs of completed cases of a process in order to make predictions about running cases thereof. Existing methods in this space are tailor-made for specific prediction tasks. Moreover, their relative accuracy is highly sensitive to the dataset at hand, thus requiring users to engage in trial-and-error and tuning when applying them in a specific setting. This paper investigates Long Short-Term Memory (LSTM) neural networks as an approach to build consistently accurate models for a wide range of predictive process monitoring tasks. First, we show that LSTMs outperform existing techniques to predict the next event of a running case and its timestamp. Next, we show how to use models for predicting the next task in order to predict the full continuation of a running case. Finally, we apply the same approach to predict the remaining time, and show that this approach outperforms existing tailor-made methods.

1 Introduction

Predictive business process monitoring techniques are concerned with predicting the evolution of running cases of a business process based on models extracted from historical event logs. A range of such techniques have been proposed for a variety of prediction tasks: predicting the next activity [2], predicting the future path (continuation) of a running case [25], predicting the remaining cycle time [27], predicting deadline violations [22] and predicting the fulfillment of a property upon completion [20]. The predictions generated by these techniques have a range of applications. For example, predicting the next activity (and its timestamp) or predicting the sequence of future activities in a case provide valuable input for planning and resource allocation. Meanwhile, predictions of the remaining execution time can be used to prioritize process instances in order to fulfill service-level objectives (e.g. to minimize deadline violations).

Existing predictive process monitoring approaches are tailor-made for specific prediction tasks and not readily generalizable. Moreover, their relative accuracy varies significantly depending on the input dataset and the point in time when

E. Dubois and K. Pohl (Eds.): CAiSE 2017, LNCS 10253, pp. 477–492, 2017.
DOI: 10.1007/978-3-319-59536-8_30

the prediction is made. A technique may outperform another one for one log and a given prediction point (e.g. making prediction at the mid-point of each trace), but under-perform it for another log at the same prediction point, or for the same log at an earlier prediction point [12,22]. In some cases, multiple techniques need to be combined [22] or considerable tuning is required (e.g. using hyperparameter optimization) [11] in order to achieve more consistent accuracy.

Recurrent neural networks with Long Short-Term Memory (LSTM) architectures [14] have been shown to deliver consistently high accuracy in several sequence modeling application domains, e.g. natural language processing [23] and speech recognition [13]. Recently, Evermann et al. [9] applied LSTMs to predictive process monitoring, specifically to predict the next activity in a case.

Inspired by these results, this paper investigates the following questions: (i) can LSTMs be applied to a broad range of predictive process monitoring problems, and how? and (ii) do LSTMs achieve consistently high accuracy across a range of prediction tasks, event logs and prediction points? To address these questions, the paper puts forward LSTM architectures for predicting: (i) the next activity in a running case and its timestamp; (ii) the continuation of a case up to completion; and (iii) the remaining cycle time. The outlined LSTM architectures are empirically compared against tailor-made approaches with respect to their accuracy at different prediction points, using four real-life event logs.

The paper is structured as follows. Section 2 discusses related work. Section 3 introduces foundational concepts and notation. Section 4 describes a technique to predict the next activity in a case and its timestamp, and compares it against tailor-made baselines. Section 5 extends the previous technique to predict the continuation of a running case. Section 6 shows how this latter method can be used to predict the remaining time of a case, and compares it against tailor-made approaches. Section 7 concludes the paper and outlines future work directions.

2 Related Work

This section discusses existing approaches to predictive process monitoring for three prediction tasks: time-related predictions, predictions of the outcome of a case and predictions of the continuation of a case and/or characteristics thereof.

2.1 Prediction of Time-Related Properties

A range of research proposals have addressed the problem of predicting delays and deadline violations in business processes. Pika et al. [24] propose a technique for predicting deadline violations. Metzger et al. [21,22] present techniques for predicting "late show" events (i.e. delays between the expected and the actual time of arrival) in a freight transportation process. Senderovich et al. [28] apply queue mining techniques to predict delays in case executions.

Another body of work focuses on predicting the remaining cycle time of running cases. Van Dongen et al. predict the remaining time by using non-parametric regression models based on case variables [8]. van der Aalst et al. [1]

propose a remaining time prediction method by constructing a transition system from the event log using set, bag, or sequence abstractions. Rogge-Solti and Weske [27] use stochastic Petri nets to predict the remaining time of a process, taking into account elapsed time since the last observed event. Folino et al. [10] develop an ad-hoc clustering approach to predict remaining time and overtime faults. In this paper, we show that prediction of the remaining cycle time can be approached as a special case of prediction of a process continuation. Specifically, our approach is proven to generally provide better accuracy than [1,8].

2.2 Prediction of Case Outcome

The goal of approaches in this category is to predict cases that will end up in an undesirable state. Maggi et al. [20], propose a framework to predict the outcome of a case (normal vs. deviant) based on the sequence of activities executed in a given case and the values of data attributes of the last executed activity in a case. This latter framework constructs a classifier on-the-fly (e.g. a decision tree or random forest) based on historical cases that are similar to the (incomplete) trace of a running case. Other approaches construct a collection of classifiers offline. For example, [19] construct one classifier for every possible prediction point (e.g. predicting the outcome after the first event, the second one and so on). Meanwhile, [12] apply clustering techniques to group together similar prefixes of historical traces and then construct one classifier per cluster.

The above approaches require one to extract a feature vector from a prefix of an ongoing trace. De Leoni et al. [18] propose a framework that classifies possible approaches to extract such feature vectors.

In this paper, we do not address the problem of case outcome prediction, although the proposed architectures could be extended in this direction.

2.3 Prediction of Future Event(s)

Breuker et al. [3] use probabilistic finite automaton to tackle the next-activity prediction problem, while Evermann et al. [9] use LSTMs. Using the latter approach as a baseline, we propose an LSTM architecture that solves the next-activity prediction problem with higher accuracy than [3,9], and that can be generalized to other prediction problems.

Pravilovic et al. [26] propose an approach that predicts both the next activity and its attributes (e.g. the involved resource). In this paper we use LSTMs to tackle a similar problem: predicting the next activity and its timestamp.

Lakshmanan et al. [16] use Markov chains to estimate the probability of future execution of a given task in a running case. Meanwhile, Van der Spoel et al. [29] address the more ambitious problem of predicting the entire continuation of a case using a shortest path algorithm over a causality graph. Polato et al. [25] refine this approach by mining an annotated transition system from an event log and annotating its edges with transition probabilities. In this paper, we take this latter approach as a baseline and show how LSTMs can improve over it while providing higher generalizability.

3 Background

In this section we introduce concepts used in later sections of this paper.

3.1 Event Logs, Traces and Sequences

For a given set A, A^* denotes the set of all sequences over A and $\sigma = \langle a_1, a_2, \ldots, a_n \rangle$ a sequence of length n; $\langle\rangle$ is the empty sequence and $\sigma_1 \cdot \sigma_2$ is the concatenation of sequences σ_1 and σ_2. $hd^k(\sigma) = \langle a_1, a_2, \ldots, a_k \rangle$ is the prefix of length k $(0 < k < n)$ of sequence σ and $tl^k(\sigma) = \langle a_{k+1}, \ldots, a_n \rangle$ is its suffix. For example, for a sequence $\sigma_1 = \langle a, b, c, d, e \rangle$, $hd^2(\sigma_1) = \langle a, b \rangle$ and $tl^2(\sigma_1) = \langle c, d, e \rangle$.

Let $\mathcal{E}$ be the event universe, i.e., the set of all possible event identifiers, and $\mathcal{T}$ the time domain. We assume that events are characterized by various properties, e.g., an event has a timestamp, corresponds to an activity, is performed by a particular resource, etc. We do not impose a specific set of properties, however, given the focus of this paper we assume that two of these properties are the timestamp and the activity of an event, i.e., there is a function $\pi_\mathcal{T} \in \mathcal{E} \to \mathcal{T}$ that assigns timestamps to events, and a function $\pi_\mathcal{A} \in \mathcal{E} \to \mathcal{A}$ that assigns to each event an activity from a finite set of process activities $\mathcal{A}$.

An *event log* is a set of events, each linked to one trace and globally unique, i.e., the same event cannot occur twice in a log. A trace in a log represents the execution of one case.

Definition 1 (Trace, Event Log). *A* trace *is a finite non-empty sequence of events $\sigma \in \mathcal{E}^*$ such that each event appears only once and time is non-decreasing, i.e., for $1 \leq i < j \leq |\sigma| : \sigma(i) \neq \sigma(j)$ and $\pi_\mathcal{T}(\sigma(i)) \leq \pi_\mathcal{T}(\sigma(j))$. $\mathcal{C}$ is the set of all possible traces. An* event log *is a set of traces $L \subseteq \mathcal{C}$ such that each event appears at most once in the entire log.*

Given a trace and a property, we often need to compute a sequence consisting of the value of this property for each event in the trace. To this end, we lift the function f_p that maps an event to the value of its property p, in such a way that we can apply it to sequences of events (traces).

Definition 2 (Applying Functions to Sequences). *A function $f \in X \to Y$ can be lifted to sequences over X using the following recursive definition: (1) $f(\langle\rangle) = \langle\rangle$; (2) for any $\sigma \in X^*$ and $x \in X$: $f(\sigma \cdot \langle x \rangle) = f(\sigma) \cdot \langle f(x) \rangle$.*

Finally, $\pi_\mathcal{A}(\sigma)$ transforms a trace σ to a sequence of its activities. For example, for trace $\sigma = \langle e_1, e_2 \rangle$, with $\pi_\mathcal{A}(e_1) = a$ and $\pi_\mathcal{A}(e_2) = b$, $\pi_\mathcal{A}(\sigma) = \langle a, b \rangle$.

3.2 Neural Networks and Recurrent Neural Networks

A neural network consists of one layer of *inputs units*, one layer of outputs units, and multiple layers in-between which are referred to as *hidden units.* The outputs of the input units form the inputs of the units of the first *hidden layer* (i.e., the first layer of hidden units), and the outputs of the units of each hidden layer form the input for each subsequent hidden layer. The outputs of the last hidden layer form the input for the output layer. The output of each unit is a function over the weighted sum of its inputs. The weights of this weighted sum performed in each unit are learned through gradient-based optimization from training data that consists of example inputs and desired outputs for those example inputs. Recurrent Neural Networks (RNNs) are a special type of neural networks where the connections between neurons form a directed cycle.

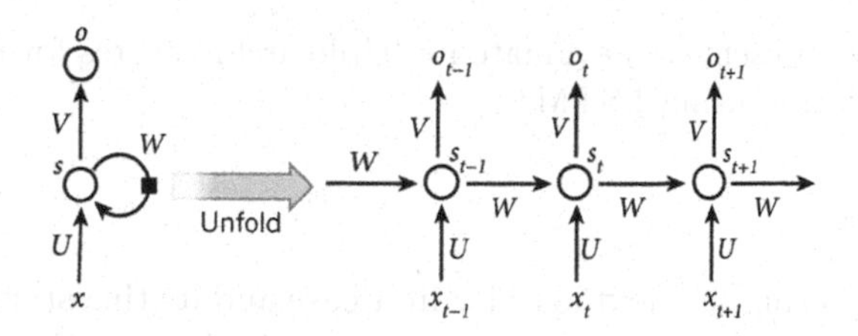

Fig. 1. A simple recurrent neural network (taken from [17]).

RNNs can be unfolded, as shown in Fig. 1. Each step in the unfolding is referred to as a time step, where x_t is the input at time step t. RNNs can take an arbitrary length sequence as input, by providing the RNN a feature representation of one element of the sequence at each time step. s_t is the hidden state at time step t and contains information extracted from all time steps up to t. The hidden state s is updated with information of the new input x_t after each time step: $s_t = f(Ux_t + Ws_{t-1})$, where U and W are vectors of weights over the new inputs and the hidden state respectively. Function f, known as the activation function, is usually either the hyperbolic tangent or the logistic function, often referred to as the sigmoid function: $sigmoid(x) = \frac{1}{1+exp(-x)}$. In neural network literature the sigmoid function is often represented with the letter σ, but we will fully write *sigmoid* to avoid confusion with traces. o_t is the output at step t.

3.3 Long Short-Term Memory for Sequence Modeling

A Long Short-Term Memory model (LSTM) [14] is a special Recurrent Neural Network architecture that has powerful modeling capabilities for long-term dependencies. The main distinction between a regular RNN and a LSTM is that the latter has a more complex memory cell C_t replacing s_t. Where the value of state s_t in a RNN is the result of a function over the weighted average over s_{t-1} and x_t, the LSTM state C_t is accessed, written, and cleared through controlling gates, respectively o_t, i_t, and f_t. Information on a new input will be accumulated to the memory cell if i_t is activated. Additionally, the past memory cell status C_{t-1} can be "forgotten" if f_t is activated. The information of C_t will be propagated to the output h_t based on the activation of output gate o_t. Combined, the LSTM model can be described with the following formulas:

$$f_t = sigmoid(W_f \cdot [h_{t-1}, x_t] + b_f) \qquad C_t = f_t * C_{t-1} + i_i * \tilde{C}_t$$
$$i_t = sigmoid(W_i \cdot [h_{t-1}, x_t] + b_i) \qquad o_t = sigmoid(W_o[h_{t-1}, x_t] + b_o)$$
$$\tilde{C}_t = tanh(W_c \cdot [h_{t-1}, x_t] + b_C) \qquad h_t = o_t * tanh(C_t)$$

In these formulas all W variables are weights and b variables are biases and both are learned during the training phase.

4 Next Activity and Timestamp Prediction

In this section we present and evaluate multiple architectures for next event and timestamp prediction using LSTMs.

4.1 Approach

We start by predicting the next activity in a case and its timestamp, by learning an activity prediction function f_a^1 and a time prediction function f_t^1. We aim at functions f_a^1 and f_t^1 such that $f_a^1(hd^k(\sigma)) = hd^1(tl^k(\pi_{\mathcal{A}}(\sigma)))$ and $f_t^1(hd^k(\sigma)) = hd^1(tl^k(\pi_{\mathcal{T}}(\sigma)))$ for any prefix length k. We transform each event $e \in hd^k(\sigma)$ into a feature vector and use these vectors as LSTM inputs $x_1, \ldots, x_k$. We build the feature vector as follows. We start with $|A|$ features that represent the type of activity of event e in a so called *one-hot encoding*. We take an arbitrary but consistent ordering over the set of activities A, and use $index \in A \rightarrow \{1, \ldots, |A|\}$ to indicate the position of an activity in it. The one-hot encoding assigns the value 1 to feature number $index(\pi_{\mathcal{A}}(e))$ and a value of 0 to the other features. We add three time-based features to the one-hot encoding feature vector. The first time-based feature of event $e = \sigma(i)$ is the time between the previous event in the trace and the current event, i.e., $fv_{t1}(e) = \begin{cases} 0 & \text{if } i = 1, \\ \pi_{\mathcal{T}}(e) - \pi_{\mathcal{T}}(\sigma(i-1)) & \text{otherwise.} \end{cases}$. This feature allows the LSTM to learn dependencies between the time differences at different points (indexes) in the process. Many activities can only be performed during office hours, therefore we add a time feature fv_{t2} that contains the time within the day (since midnight) and fv_{t3} that contains the time within the week (since midnight on Sunday). fv_{t2} and fv_{t3} are added to learn the LSTM such that if the last event observed occurred at the end of the working day or at the end of the working week, the time until the next event is expected to be longer.

At learning time, we set the target output o_a^k of time step k to the one-hot encoding of the activity of the event one time step later. However, it can be the case that the case ends at time k, in which case there is no new event to predict. Therefore we add an extra element to the output one-hot-encoding vector, which has value 1 when the case ends after k. We set a second target output o_t^k equal to the fv_{t1} feature of the next time step, i.e. the target is the time difference between the next and the current event. However, knowing the timestamp of the current event, we can calculate the timestamp of the following event. We optimize the weights of the neural network with the Adam learning algorithm [15] such that the cross entropy between the ground truth one-hot encoding of the next event and the predicted one-hot encoding of the next event as well as the mean absolute error (MAE) between the ground truth time until the next event and the predicted time until the next event are minimized.

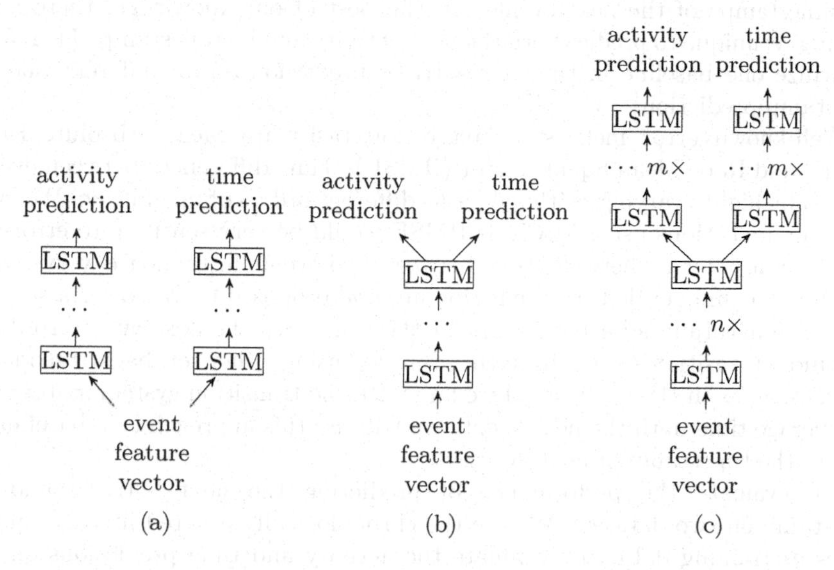

Fig. 2. Neural network architectures with single-task layers *(a)*, with shared multi-tasks layer *(b)*, and with $n + m$ layers of which n are shared *(c)*.

Modeling the next activity prediction function f_a^1 and time prediction function f_t^1 with LSTMs can be done using several architectures. Firstly, we can train two separate models, one for f_a^1 and one for f_t^1, both using the same input features at each time step, as represented in Fig. 2(a). Secondly, f_a^1 and f_t^1 can be learned jointly in a single LSTM model that generates two outputs, in a multi-task learning setting [4] (Fig. 2(b)). The usage of LSTMs in a multi-task learning setting has shown to improve performance on all individual tasks when jointly learning multiple natural language processing tasks, including part-of-speech tagging, named entity recognition, and sentence classification [6]. A hybrid option between the architecture of Figs. 2(a) and (b) is an architecture of a number of shared LSTM layers for both tasks, followed by a number of layers that specialize in either prediction of the next activity or prediction of the time until the next event, as shown in Fig. 2(c).

It should be noted that activity prediction function f_a^1 outputs the probability distribution of various possible continuations of the partial trace. For evaluation purposes, we will only use the most likely continuation.

We implemented the technique as a set of Python scripts using the recurrent neural network library `Keras` [5]. The experiments were performed on a single NVidia Tesla k80 GPU, on which the experiments took between 15 and 90 s per training iteration depending on the neural network architecture. The execution time to make a prediction is in the order of milliseconds.

4.2 Experimental Setup

In this section we describe and motivate the metrics, datasets, and baseline methods used for evaluation of the predictions of the next activities and of the timestamps of the next events. To the best of our knowledge, there is no existing technique to predict both the next activity and its timestamp. Therefore, we utilize one baseline method for activity prediction and a different one for timestamp prediction.

Well-known error metrics for regression tasks are Mean Absolute Error (MAE) and Root Mean Square Error (RMSE). Time differences between events tend to be highly varying, with values at different orders of magnitude. We evaluate the predictions using MAE, as RMSE would be very sensitive to errors on outlier data points, where the time between two events in the log is very large.

The remaining cycle time prediction method proposed by van der Aalst et al. [1] can be naturally adjusted to predict the time until the next event. To do so we build a transition system from the event log using either set, bag, or sequence abstraction, as in [1], but instead we annotate the transition system states with the average time until the next event. We will use this approach as a baseline to predict the timestamp of next event.

We evaluate the performance of predicting the next activity and its timestamp on two datasets. We use the chronologically ordered first 2/3 of the traces as training data, and evaluate the activity and time predictions on the remaining 1/3 of the traces. We evaluate the next activity and the timestamp prediction on all prefixes $hd^k(\sigma)$ of all trace σ in the set of test traces for $2 \leq k < |\sigma|$. We do not make any predictions for the trace prefix of size one, since for those prefixes there is insufficient data available to base the prediction upon.

Helpdesk Dataset. This log contains events from a ticketing management process of the help desk of an Italian software company[1]. The process consists of 9 activities, and all cases start with the insertion of a new ticket into the ticketing management system. Each case ends when the issue is resolved and the ticket is closed. This log contains around 3,804 cases and 13,710 events.

BPI'12 Subprocess W Dataset. This event log originates from the Business Process Intelligence Challenge (BPI'12)[2] and contains data from the application procedure for financial products at a large financial institution. This process consists of three subprocesses: one that tracks the state of the application, one that tracks the states of work items associated with the application, and a third one that tracks the state of the offer. In the context of predicting the coming events and their timestamps we are not interested in events that are performed automatically. Thus, we narrow down our evaluation to the work items subprocess, which contains events that are manually executed. Further, we filter the log to retain only events of type *complete*. Two existing techniques [3,9] for the next activity prediction, described in Sect. 2, have been evaluated on this event log with identical preprocessing, enabling comparison.

---

[1] doi:10.17632/39bp3vv62t.1.

[2] doi:10.4121/uuid:3926db30-f712-4394-aebc-75976070e91f.

Table 1. Experimental results for the Helpdesk and BPI'12 W logs.

Layers	Shared	N/l	Helpdesk					BPI'12 W				
			MAE in days				Accuracy	MAE in days				Accuracy
			Prefix 2	4	6	All		Prefix 2	10	20	All	
LSTM												
4	4	100	3.64	2.79	2.22	3.82	0.7076	1.75	1.49	1.02	1.61	0.7466
4	3	100	3.63	2.78	2.21	3.83	0.7075	1.74	1.47	1.01	1.59	0.7479
4	2	100	3.59	2.82	2.27	3.81	0.7114	1.72	**1.45**	1.00	1.57	0.7497
4	1	100	3.58	2.77	2.24	3.77	0.7074	1.70	1.46	1.01	1.59	0.7522
4	0	100	3.78	2.98	2.41	3.95	0.7072	1.74	1.47	1.05	1.61	0.7515
3	3	100	3.58	2.69	2.22	3.77	0.7116	**1.69**	1.47	1.02	1.58	0.7507
3	2	100	3.59	2.69	2.21	3.80	0.7118	**1.69**	1.47	1.01	1.57	0.7512
3	1	100	3.55	2.78	2.38	3.76	**0.7123**	1.72	1.47	1.04	1.59	0.7525
3	0	100	3.62	2.71	2.23	3.82	0.6924	1.81	1.51	1.07	1.66	0.7506
2	2	100	3.61	2.64	**2.11**	3.81	0.7117	1.72	1.46	1.02	1.58	0.7556
2	1	100	3.57	**2.61**	**2.11**	3.77	0.7119	**1.69**	**1.45**	1.01	**1.56**	**0.7600**
2	0	100	3.66	2.89	2.13	3.86	0.6985	1.74	1.46	0.99	1.60	0.7537
1	1	100	**3.54**	2.71	3.16	**3.75**	0.7072	1.71	1.47	**0.98**	1.57	0.7486
1	0	100	3.55	2.91	2.45	3.87	0.7110	1.72	1.46	1.05	1.59	0.7431
3	1	75	3.73	2.81	2.23	3.89	0.7118	1.73	1.49	1.07	1.62	0.7503
3	1	150	3.78	2.92	2.43	3.97	0.6918	1.81	1.52	1.14	1.71	0.7491
2	1	75	3.73	2.79	2.32	3.90	0.7045	1.72	1.47	1.03	1.59	0.7544
2	1	150	3.62	2.73	2.23	3.83	0.6982	1.74	1.49	1.08	1.65	0.7511
1	1	75	3.74	2.87	2.35	3.87	0.6925	1.75	1.50	1.07	1.64	0.7452
1	1	150	3.73	2.79	2.32	3.92	0.7103	1.72	1.48	1.02	1.60	0.7489
RNN												
3	1	100	4.21	3.25	3.13	4.04	0.6581					
2	1	100	4.12	3.23	3.05	3.98	0.6624					
1	1	100	4.14	3.28	3.12	4.02	0.6597					
Time prediction baselines												
Set abstraction [1]			6.15	4.25	4.07	5.83	-	2.71	1.64	1.02	1.97	-
Bag abstraction [1]			6.17	4.11	3.26	5.74	-	2.89	1.71	1.07	1.92	-
Sequence abstraction [1]			6.17	3.53	2.98	5.67	-	2.89	1.69	1.07	1.91	-
Activity prediction baselines												
Evermann et al. [9]			-	-	-	-	-	-	-	-	-	0.623
Breuker et al. [3]			-	-	-	-	-	-	-	-	-	0.719

4.3 Results

Table 1 shows the performance of various LSTM architectures on the helpdesk and the BPI'12 W subprocess logs in terms of MAE on predicted time, and accuracy of predicting the next event. The specific prefix sizes are chosen such that they represent *short*, *medium*, and *long* traces for each log. Thus, as the BPI'12 W log contains longer traces, the prefix sizes evaluated are higher for this log. In the table, *all* reports the average performance on all prefixes, not just the three prefix sizes reported in the three preceding columns. The number of shared layers represents the number of layers that contribute to both time and activity prediction. Rows where the numbers of shared layers are 0 correspond to the architecture of Fig. 2(a), where the prediction of time and activities is performed with separate models. When the number of shared layers is equal to the number of layers, the neural network contains no specialized layers, corresponding to the architecture of Fig. 2(b). Table 1 also shows the results of predicting the time until the end of the next event using the adjusted method from van der Aalst et al. [1] for comparison. All LSTM architectures outperform the baseline approach on all prefixes as well as averaged over all prefixes on both datasets. Further, it can be observed that the performance gain between the best LSTM model and the best baseline model is much larger for the short prefix than for the long prefix. The best performance obtained on next activity prediction over all prefixes was a classification accuracy of 71% on the helpdesk log. On the BPI'12 W log the best accuracy is 76%, which is higher than the 71.9% accuracy on this log reported by Breuker et al. [3] and the 62.3% accuracy reported by Evermann et al. [9]. In fact, the results obtained with LSTM are consistently higher than both approaches. Even though Evermann et al. [9] also rely on LSTM in their approach, there are several differences which are likely to cause the performance gap. First of all, [9] uses a technique called *embedding* [23] to create feature descriptions of events instead of the features described above. Embeddings automatically transform each activity into a "useful" large dimensional continuous feature vector. This approach has shown to work really well in the field of natural language processing, where the number of distinct words that can be predicted is very large, but for process mining event logs, where the number of distinct activities in an event log is often in the order of hundreds or much less, no useful feature vector can be learned automatically. Second, [9] uses a two-layer architecture with 500 neurons per layer, and does not explore other variants. We found performance to decrease when increasing the number of neurons from 100 to 150, which makes it likely that the performance of a 500 neuron model will decrease due to overfitting. A third and last explanation for the performance difference is the use of multi-task learning, which as we showed, slightly improves prediction performance on the next activity.

Even though the performance differences between our three LSTM architectures are small for both logs, we observe that most best performances (indicated in bold) of the LSTM model in terms of time prediction and next activity prediction are either obtained with the completely shared architecture of Fig. 2(b) or with the hybrid architecture of Fig. 2(c). We experimented with decreasing the number of neurons per layer to 75 and increasing it to 150 for architectures with one shared layer, but found that this results in decreasing performance in both tasks. It is likely that 75 neurons resulted in underfitting models, while 150 neurons resulted in overfitting models. We also experimented with traditional RNNs on one layer architectures, and found that they perform significantly worse than LSTMs on both time and activity prediction.

5 Suffix Prediction

Using functions f_a^1 and f_t^1 repeatedly allows us to make longer-term predictions that predict further ahead than a single time step. We use $f_a^\perp$ and $f_t^\perp$ to refer to activity and time until next event prediction functions that predict the whole continuation of a running case, and aim at those functions to be such that $f_a^\perp(hd^k(\sigma)) = tl^k(\pi_{\mathcal{A}}(\sigma))$ and $f_t^\perp(hd^k(\sigma)) = tl^k(\pi_{\mathcal{T}}(\sigma))$

5.1 Approach

The suffix can be predicted by iteratively predicting the next activity and the time until the next event, until the next activity prediction function f_a^1 predicts the end of case, which we represent with $\perp$. More formally, we calculate the complete suffix of activities as follows:

$$f_a^\perp(\sigma) = \begin{cases} \sigma & \text{if } f_a^1(\sigma) = \perp \\ f_a^\perp(\sigma \cdot e), \text{with } e \in \mathcal{E}, \pi_{\mathcal{A}}(e) = f_a^1(\sigma) \wedge & \\ \quad \pi_{\mathcal{T}}(e) = (f_t^1(\sigma) + \pi_{\mathcal{T}}(\sigma(|\sigma|))) & \text{otherwise} \end{cases}$$

and we calculate the suffix of times until the next events as follows:

$$f_t^\perp(\sigma) = \begin{cases} \sigma, & \text{if } f_t^1(\sigma) = \perp \\ f_t^\perp(\sigma \cdot e), \text{with } e \in \mathcal{E}, \pi_{\mathcal{A}}(e) = f_a^1(\sigma) \wedge & \\ \quad \pi_{\mathcal{T}}(e) = (f_t^1(\sigma) + \pi_{\mathcal{T}}(\sigma(|\sigma|))) & \text{otherwise} \end{cases}$$

5.2 Experimental Setup

For a given trace prefix $hd^k(\sigma)$ we evaluate the performance of $f_a^\perp$ by calculating the distance between the predicted continuation $f_a^\perp(hd^k(\sigma))$ and the actual continuation $\pi_{\mathcal{A}}(tl^k(\sigma))$. Many sequence distance metrics exist, with Levenshtein distance being one of the most well-known ones. Levenshtein distance is defined as the minimum number of insertion, deletion, and substitution operations needed to transform one sequence into the other.

Levenshtein distance is not suitable when the business process includes parallel branches. Indeed, when $\langle a, b\rangle$ are the next predicted events, and $\langle b, a\rangle$ are the actual next events, we consider this to be only a minor error, since it is often not relevant in which order two parallel activities are executed. However, Levenshtein distance would assign a cost of 2 to this prediction, as transforming the predicted sequence into the ground truth sequence would require one deletion and one insertion operation. An evaluation measure that better reflects the prediction quality of is the Damerau-Levenstein distance [7], which adds a swapping operation to the set of operations used by Levenshtein distance. Damerau-Levenshtein distance would assign a cost of 1 to transform $\langle a, b\rangle$ into $\langle b, a\rangle$. To obtain comparable results for traces of variable length, we normalize the Damerau-Levenshtein distance by the maximum of the length of the ground truth suffix and the length of the predicted suffix and subtract the normalized Damerau-Levenshtein distance from 1 to obtain Damerau-Levenshtein Similarity (DLS).

To the best of our knowledge, the most recent method to predict an arbitrary number of events ahead is the one by Polato et al. [25]. The authors first extract a transition system from the log and then learn a machine learning model for each transition system state to predict the next activity. They evaluate on predictions of a fixed number of events ahead, while we are interested in the continuation of the case until its end. We redid the experiments with their ProM plugin to obtain the performance on the predicted full case continuation.

For the LSTM experiments, we use a two-layer architecture with one shared layer and 100 neurons per layer, which showed good performance in terms of next activity prediction and predicting the time until the next event in the previous experiment (Table 1). In addition to the two previously introduced logs, we evaluate prediction of the suffix on an additional dataset, described below, which becomes feasible now that we have fixed the LSTM architecture.

Environmental Permit Dataset. This is a log of an environmental permitting process at a Dutch municipality.[3] Each case refers to one permit application. The log contains 937 cases and 38,944 events of 381 event types. Almost every case follows a unique path, making the suffix prediction more challenging.

5.3 Results

Table 2 summarizes the results of suffix prediction for each log. As can be seen, the LSTM outperforms the baseline [25] on all logs. Even though it improves over the baseline, the performance on the BPI'12 W log is low given that the log only contains 6 activities. After inspection we found that this log contains many sequences of two or more events in a row of the same activity, where occurrences of 8 or more identical events in a row are not uncommon. We found that LSTMs have problems dealing with this log characteristic, causing it to predict overly long sequences of the same activity, resulting in predicted suffixes that are much longer than the ground truth suffixes. Hence, we also evaluated suffix prediction on a modified version of the BPI'12 W log where we removed repeated occurrences of the same event, keeping only the first occurrence. However, we can only notice a mild improvement over the unmodified log.

Table 2. Suffix prediction results in terms of Damerau-Levenshtein Similarity.

Method	Helpdesk	BPI'12 W	BPI'12 W (no duplicates)	Environmental permit
Polato [25]	0.2516	0.0458	0.0336	0.0260
LSTM	0.7669	0.3533	0.3937	0.1522

[3] doi:10.4121/uuid:26aba40d-8b2d-435b-b5af-6d4bfbd7a270.

6 Remaining Cycle Time Prediction

Time prediction function $f_t^{\perp}$ predicts the timestamps of all events in a running case that are still to come. Since the last predicted timestamp in a prediction generated by $f_t^{\perp}$ is the timestamp of the end of the case, it is easy to see that $f_t^{\perp}$ can be used for predicting the remaining cycle time of the running case. For a given unfinished case σ, $\hat{\sigma}_t = f_t^{\perp}(\sigma)$ contains the predicted timestamps of the next events, and $\hat{\sigma}_t(|\hat{\sigma}_t|)$ contains the predicted end time of σ, therefore the estimated remaining cycle time can be obtained through $\hat{\sigma}_t(|\hat{\sigma}_t|) - \pi(\sigma(|\sigma|))$.

6.1 Experimental Setup

We use the same architecture as for the suffix prediction experiments. We predict and evaluate the remaining time after each passed event, starting from prefix size 2. We use the remaining cycle time prediction methods of van der Aalst et al. [1] and van Dongen et al. [8] as baseline methods.

6.2 Results

Figure 3 shows the mean absolute error for each prefix size, for the four logs (Helpdesk, BPI'12 W, BPI'12 W with no duplicates and Environmental Permit). It can be seen that LSTM consistently outperforms the baselines for the Helpdesk log. An exception is the BPI'12 W log, where LSTM performs worse than the baselines on short prefixes. This is caused by the problem that LSTMs have in

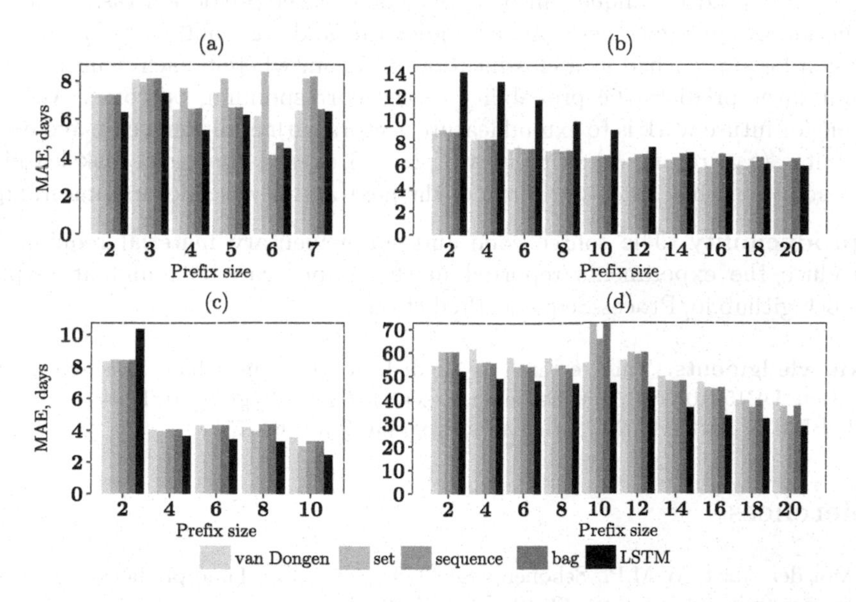

Fig. 3. MAE values using prefixes of different lengths for *helpdesk* (a), *BPI'12 W* (b), *BPI'12 W (no duplicates)* (c) and *environmental permit* (d) datasets.

predicting the next event when the log has many repeated events, as described in Sect. 5. This problem causes the LSTM to predict suffixes that are too long compared to the ground truth, and, thereby, also overestimating the remaining cycle time. We see that the LSTM does outperform the baseline on the modified version of the BPI'12 W log where we only kept the first occurrence of each repeated event in a sequence. Note that we do not remove the last event of the case, even if it is a repeated event, as that would change the ground truth remaining cycle time for the prefix.

7 Conclusion and Future Work

The foremost contribution of this paper is a technique to predict the next activity of a running case and its timestamp using LSTM neural networks. We showed that this technique outperforms existing baselines on real-life data sets. Additionally, we found that predicting the next activity and its timestamp via a single model (multi-task learning) yields a higher accuracy than predicting them using separate models. We then showed that this basic technique can be generalized to address two other predictive process monitoring problems: predicting the entire continuation of a running case and predicting the remaining cycle time. We empirically showed that the generalized LSTM-based technique outperforms tailor-made approaches to these problems. We also identified a limitation of LSTM models when dealing with traces with multiple occurrences of the same activity, in which case the model predicts overly long sequences of the same event. Addressing this latter limitation is a direction for future work.

The proposed technique can be extended to other prediction tasks, such as prediction of aggregate performance indicators and case outcomes. The latter task can be approached as a classification problem, wherein each neuron of the output layer predicts the probability of the corresponding outcome. Another avenue for future work is to extend feature vectors with additional case and event attributes (e.g. resources). Finally, we plan to extend the multi-task learning approach to predict other attributes of the next activity besides its timestamp.

Reproducibility. The source code and supplementary material required to reproduce the experiments reported in this paper can be found at http://verenich.github.io/ProcessSequencePrediction.

Acknowledgments. This research is funded by the Australian Research Council (grant DP150103356), the Estonian Research Council (grant IUT20-55) and the RISE_BPM project (H2020 Marie Curie Program, grant 645751).

References

1. van der Aalst, W.M.P., Schonenberg, M.H., Song, M.: Time prediction based on process mining. Inf. Syst. **36**(2), 450–475 (2011)

2. Becker, J., Breuker, D., Delfmann, P., Matzner, M.: Designing and implementing a framework for event-based predictive modelling of business processes. In: Proceedings of the 6th International Workshop on Enterprise Modelling and Information Systems Architectures, pp. 71–84. Springer, Heidelberg (2014)
3. Breuker, D., Matzner, M., Delfmann, P., Becker, J.: Comprehensible predictive models for business processes. MIS Q. **40**(4), 1009–1034 (2016)
4. Caruana, R.: Multitask learning. Mach. Learn. **28**(1), 41–75 (1997)
5. Chollet, F.: Keras (2015). https://github.com/fchollet/keras
6. Collobert, R., Weston, J.: A unified architecture for natural language processing: deep neural networks with multitask learning. In: ICML, pp. 160–167. ACM (2008)
7. Damerau, F.J.: A technique for computer detection and correction of spelling errors. Commun. ACM **7**(3), 171–176 (1964)
8. van Dongen, B.F., Crooy, R.A., van der Aalst, W.M.P.: Cycle time prediction: when will this case finally be finished? In: Meersman, R., Tari, Z. (eds.) OTM 2008. LNCS, vol. 5331, pp. 319–336. Springer, Heidelberg (2008). doi:10.1007/978-3-540-88871-0_22
9. Evermann, J., Rehse, J.R., Fettke, P.: A deep learning approach for predicting process behaviour at runtime. In: Proceedings of the 1st International Workshop on Runtime Analysis of Process-Aware Information Systems. Springer, Rio de Janeiro (2016)
10. Folino, F., Guarascio, M., Pontieri, L.: Discovering context-aware models for predicting business process performances. In: CoopIS, pp. 287–304 (2012)
11. Francescomarino, C.D., Dumas, M., Federici, M., Ghidini, C., Maggi, F.M., Rizzi, W.: Predictive business process monitoring framework with hyperparameter optimization. In: Nurcan, S., Soffer, P., Bajec, M., Eder, J. (eds.) CAiSE 2016. LNCS, vol. 9694, pp. 361–376. Springer, Cham (2016). doi:10.1007/978-3-319-39696-5_22
12. Francescomarino, C.D., Dumas, M., Maggi, F.M., Teinemaa, I.: Clustering-based predictive process monitoring. CoRR (2015). http://arxiv.org/abs/1506.01428. to appear in Transactions on Services Computing
13. Graves, A., Mohamed, A.R., Hinton, G.: Speech recognition with deep recurrent neural networks. In: IEEE International Conference on Acoustics, Speech and Signal Processing, pp. 6645–6649. IEEE (2013)
14. Hochreiter, S., Schmidhuber, J.: Long short-term memory. Neural Comput. **9**(8), 1735–1780 (1997)
15. Kingma, D., Ba, J.: ADAM: a method for stochastic optimization. In: Proceedings of the 3rd International Conference for Learning Representations (2015)
16. Lakshmanan, G.T., Shamsi, D., Doganata, Y.N., Unuvar, M., Khalaf, R.: A markov prediction model for data-driven semi-structured business processes. Knowl. Inf. Syst. **42**(1), 97–126 (2015)
17. LeCun, Y., Bengio, Y., Hinton, G.: Deep learning. Nature **521**(7553), 436–444 (2015)
18. de Leoni, M., van der Aalst, W.M.P., Dees, M.: A general process mining framework for correlating, predicting and clustering dynamic behavior based on event logs. Inf. Syst. **56**, 235–257 (2016)
19. Leontjeva, A., Conforti, R., Francescomarino, C.D., Dumas, M., Maggi, F.M.: Complex symbolic sequence encodings for predictive monitoring of business processes. In: Motahari-Nezhad, H.R., Recker, J., Weidlich, M. (eds.) BPM 2015. LNCS, vol. 9253, pp. 297–313. Springer, Cham (2015). doi:10.1007/978-3-319-23063-4_21

20. Maggi, F.M., Francescomarino, C.D., Dumas, M., Ghidini, C.: Predictive monitoring of business processes. In: Jarke, M., Mylopoulos, J., Quix, C., Rolland, C., Manolopoulos, Y., Mouratidis, H., Horkoff, J. (eds.) CAiSE 2014. LNCS, vol. 8484, pp. 457–472. Springer, Cham (2014). doi:10.1007/978-3-319-07881-6_31
21. Metzger, A., Franklin, R., Engel, Y.: Predictive monitoring of heterogeneous service-oriented business networks: the transport and logistics case. In: 2012 Annual SRII Global Conference, pp. 313–322. IEEE (2012)
22. Metzger, A., Leitner, P., Ivanovic, D., Schmieders, E., Franklin, R., Carro, M., Dustdar, S., Pohl, K.: Comparing and combining predictive business process monitoring techniques. IEEE Trans. Syst. Man Cybern.: Syst. **45**(2), 276–290 (2015)
23. Mikolov, T., Sutskever, I., Chen, K., Corrado, G.S., Dean, J.: Distributed representations of words and phrases and their compositionality. In: Advances in Neural Information Processing Systems, pp. 3111–3119 (2013)
24. Pika, A., van der Aalst, W.M.P., Fidge, C.J., ter Hofstede, A.H.M., Wynn, M.T.: Predicting deadline transgressions using event logs. In: Rosa, M., Soffer, P. (eds.) BPM 2012. LNBIP, vol. 132, pp. 211–216. Springer, Heidelberg (2013). doi:10.1007/978-3-642-36285-9_22
25. Polato, M., Sperduti, A., Burattin, A., de Leoni, M.: Time and activity sequence prediction of business process instances. arXiv preprint (2016). arXiv:1602.07566
26. Pravilovic, S., Appice, A., Malerba, D.: Process mining to forecast the future of running cases. In: Appice, A., Ceci, M., Loglisci, C., Manco, G., Masciari, E., Ras, Z.W. (eds.) NFMCP 2013. LNCS, vol. 8399, pp. 67–81. Springer, Cham (2014). doi:10.1007/978-3-319-08407-7_5
27. Rogge-Solti, A., Weske, M.: Prediction of remaining service execution time using stochastic petri nets with arbitrary firing delays. In: Basu, S., Pautasso, C., Zhang, L., Fu, X. (eds.) ICSOC 2013. LNCS, vol. 8274, pp. 389–403. Springer, Heidelberg (2013). doi:10.1007/978-3-642-45005-1_27
28. Senderovich, A., Weidlich, M., Gal, A., Mandelbaum, A.: Queue mining - predicting delays in service processes. In: CAiSE, pp. 42–57 (2014)
29. van der Spoel, S., van Keulen, M., Amrit, C.: Process Prediction in Noisy Data Sets: A Case Study in a Dutch Hospital. In: Cudre-Mauroux, P., Ceravolo, P., Gašević, D. (eds.) SIMPDA 2012. LNBIP, vol. 162, pp. 60–83. Springer, Heidelberg (2013). doi:10.1007/978-3-642-40919-6_4

Data Mining

Searching Linked Data with a Twist of Serendipity

Jeronimo S.A. Eichler[1(✉)], Marco A. Casanova[1], Antonio L. Furtado[1], Lívia Ruback[1], Luiz André P. Paes Leme[2], Giseli Rabello Lopes[3], Bernardo Pereira Nunes[1,6], Alessandra Raffaetà[4], and Chiara Renso[5]

[1] Department of Informatics, Pontifical Catholic University of Rio de Janeiro, Rio de Janeiro, RJ, Brazil
{jeichler, casanova, furtado, lrodrigues, bnunes}@inf.puc-rio.br
[2] Fluminense Federal University, Niterói, RJ, Brazil
lapaesleme@ic.uff.br
[3] Federal University of Rio de Janeiro, Rio de Janeiro, RJ, Brazil
giseli@dcc.ufrj.br
[4] Università Ca' Foscari, Venice, Italy
raffaeta@unive.it
[5] ISTI/CNR, Pisa, Italy
chiara.renso@isti.cnr.it
[6] Federal University of the State of Rio de Janeiro, Rio de Janeiro, RJ, Brazil

Abstract. Serendipity is defined as the discovery of a thing when one is not searching for it. In other words, serendipity means the discovery of information that provides valuable insights by unveiling previously unknown knowledge. This paper focuses on the problem of Linked Data serendipitous search. It first discusses how to capture a set of serendipity patterns in the context of Linked Data. Then, the paper introduces a Linked Data serendipitous search application, called the Serendipity Over Linked Data Search tool – SOL-Tool. Finally, the paper describes experiments with the tool to illustrate the serendipity effect using DBpedia. The experimental results present a promissory score of 90% of unexpectedness for real-world scenarios in the music domain.

Keywords: Serendipity · Linked data · Information retrieval

1 Introduction

Serendipity is defined as "the art of making an unsought finding" [18]. The term was coined by Horace Walpole, based on the tale of *The Three Princes of Serendip*, wherein the mentioned princes made several discoveries of things they were not looking for by accident and sagacity. In the literature, the term serendipity is used to describe a breakthrough discovery caused by chance encounters [3]. As described in [3], there are two key aspects of serendipity: the accidental nature and the surprise of finding something unexpected, the *chance*; the breakthrough or discovery made by drawing an unexpected

E. Dubois and K. Pohl (Eds.): CAiSE 2017, LNCS 10253, pp. 495–510, 2017.
DOI: 10.1007/978-3-319-59536-8_31

connection, the *sagacity*. That is, serendipity promotes the encounter of unexpected information to provide valuable insights by unveiling previously unknown knowledge.

Serendipity can be used in the context of the Web of Data to explore, filter and extract relevant information from different datasets. As argued in [17], serendipity provides a holistic and ecological approach to information acquisition in information systems by complementing querying and browsing interactions.

Specifically, this paper addresses the problem of *Linked Data serendipitous search*, briefly defined as a search process over Linked Data with the following characteristics. The input to the search process is a query Q over a Linked Data dataset D. The process returns a result list for Q, as usual, plus triples related to the results of Q by some serendipity pattern. The process gradually exhibits the result list – including the triples found by serendipity – and allows the user to perhaps change the focus of his search to one of the triples found by serendipity.

Despite its potential, to design an application that incorporates serendipity is a challenging task. Iaquinta et al. [8] argue that to conceptualize, analyze and implement serendipity turns out to be a difficult task due to its subjective nature. To overcome this issue, we present four patterns that formalize how to capture serendipitous events in the Linked Data scenario: *analogy*, *surprising observation, inversion* and *disturbance*. These patterns are taken from Van Andel's list of seventeen serendipity patterns [18], each one representing a different form in which serendipity can occur. We discarded some of the patterns in Van Andel's list since they are not amenable to formalization in the context of Linked Data search.

We propose a query modification process to present three main strategies to capture the selected serendipity patterns. To capture the analogy and the surprising observation patterns, the process explores the results of the user's query to invoke secondary queries with the recently acquired information. To capture the disturbance pattern, the process adopts strategies to change the order of the result list to expose items that the user would normally neglect. Finally, to capture the inversion pattern, the process analyzes the query to formulate alternative queries.

To summarize, the main contributions of this paper are threefold: (1) a discussion on how to capture a set of serendipity patterns in the context of Linked Data search; (2) the introduction of a Linked Data search tool, called *Serendipity Over Linked Data Search Tool - SOL*; and (3) the description of experiments with the search tool.

The remainder of the paper is structured as follows. Section 2 provides an overview of the state-of-the-art in the field. Section 3 discusses the notion of serendipity and examines serendipity patterns. Section 4 illustrates how to capture four serendipity patterns in the context of Linked Data search. Section 5 details the architecture of the search tool and its main components. Section 6 describes experiments with the search tool. Finally, Sect. 7 draws some conclusions.

2 Related Work

In [1] a notion of item regions is defined in order to introduce serendipity in a movie recommender system. Basically, in this work, movies and users are grouped into regions based on attribute similarity whereas collaborative filtering is used to identify regions that are underexposed to the users. Therefore, this approach is able to suggest movies that are strongly related to the user's interest but which are not popular in his community.

In [16] the category representation of DBpedia is used to suggest lateral topics to a given subject. This approach relies on a shortest path distance algorithm to compute the proximity of the categories used in the graph exploration.

Similarly to [1], AURALIST [19] combines item-based collaborative filtering with a clustering algorithm to produce serendipitous music recommendations. To introduce serendipity among its results, AURALIST considers two approaches. First, it computes the artist's diversity by considering in how many users' communities he is popular, reasoning that an unheard artist may be considered in suggestions for that community. Second, AURALIST adopts a similar approach to that of the Intra-List Similarity [20] with cosine similarity to compute the similarity between items in a cluster of related artists.

In [2] a recommender system is presented. It aims at improving user's satisfaction by combining unexpectedness with utility. To achieve this goal, the system calculates unexpectedness as the distance between an unvisited item and the set of all items visited by the user. Utility is understood as the overall rate of an item.

In the scenario of Web search, Bordino et al. [4] create a recommender system that induces serendipity by suggesting search queries that are relevant to the content of a page. The system extracts entities representing the content of a page and then builds a graph containing entities and queries. Finally, it adapts the PageRank algorithm to this graph to associate entities with relevant query suggestions.

A different approach is taken by FEEGLI [15], that augments search results with information extracted from Facebook 'like' activity from the user. Results that match the user interests are highlighted with a different color.

Our proposal, the SOL-Tool, combines some characteristics of these works. Similarly to our approach with analogy, Stankovic et al. [16] rely on the category representation of DBpedia to present unexpected suggestions. Although our approach uses the category structure of DBpedia, it does not depend on any specific category while [16] uses a set of categories as a starting point for the proximity computation.

Our serendipitous component (Sect. 4.2) augments the search results similarly to FEEGLI. While FEEGLI highlights only the information that matches the 'like' activity, the SOL-Tool search engine provides new information related to search results and also provides some explanation of the connection by using the RDF syntax.

3 Serendipity

In an extensive study of serendipity, Van Andel [18] lists seventeen serendipity patterns, each one representing a different form in which serendipity can occur. In this section, we present the patterns that we found to be best amenable to be captured in the context of Linked Data search.

The *analogy pattern* is characterized by seeking similarity between objects from the same or totally distinct domains [18]. Basically, it consists of extracting relevant characteristics of an object in order to apply this knowledge to identify another object.

A widely popular example of analogy is the insight of Archimedes to measure a crown's volume after stepping into a bathtub.

The *surprising observation pattern* is characterized by surprise caused by an unexpected event. It indicates a trail that can lead to new information about a known entity and represents the fact that some entities can have different facets (or views) covering different domains. A subpattern of surprising observation is the *repetition of surprising observation*. As the name implies, it involves the recurrence of the previous pattern and serves as a strong indication of the relevance of the respective observation. To illustrate the repetition of the surprising observation pattern, Van Andel [18] cites the discovery of AIDS as an epidemic after registering a high number of cases.

The *inversion* pattern depicts the unexpected aspect of serendipity, i.e., it changes the expectation of the experiment, guiding the solution towards a completely new direction. It establishes a breakthrough discovery where the insight is the opposite to the previous intent.

The *disturbance* pattern is characterized by a change of perception caused by an occurrence that affects the regular activity of a person. The *disturbance pattern* is fired by a chaotic event that introduces other variables into the problem. For example, Van Andel [18] narrates the creation of Radio-astronomy that originated from the noise observed in transatlantic telephone calls, with a periodicity of 23 h and 56 min.

4 Capturing Selected Serendipitous Patterns in the Context of Linked Data Search

This section discusses how to capture the serendipitous patterns of Sect. 3 in the context of Linked Data search. It also provides a case study scenario with the purpose of illustrating the use of the serendipity patterns. The scenario is based on the DBpedia dataset and focuses on the music domain. In this scenario, serendipity search can increase the user satisfaction by providing interesting and non-obvious artists or songs. The section starts with a very brief review of RDF.

4.1 Basic Concepts

We start by recalling a few concepts related to the *Resource Description Framework* (RDF) data model [5] and the SPARQL query language [7].

A *Uniform Resource Identifier* (URI) represents an *entity* of the real world. A literal is a string representing a (datatype) value. An RDF *term* is a URI or a literal. An RDF triple is a triple *(s,p,o)*, where *s* and *p* are URIs and *o* is either a URI or a literal; a triple *(s,p,o)* states that its *subject s* has *property p* whose value is *object o*. We disregard the so-called *blank nodes* in this paper, which could always be replaced by Skolem URIs [5]. A dataset *D* is a set of RDF triples. We say that an *entity* of *D* is a URI that occurs as a subject or object of a triple in *D*.

Entities are typically assigned to *classes*, which may in turn be organized as a *class hierarchy*. This is captured in RDF with the help of the predefined terms *rdf:type*, *rdfs:Class* and *rdfs:subclassOf*, where the first term belongs to the RDF vocabulary and the last two terms to the RDF Schema vocabulary. The term *owl:Thing* of the OWL vocabulary denotes the universe, i.e., the set of all things.

We also take into consideration the annotation property *rdfs:seeAlso* and the OWL property *owl:sameAs*. *rdfs:seeAlso* is used to indicate an entity that might provide additional information about the subject entity whereas the *owl:sameAs* property is used to indicate that two URI references refer to the same thing i.e. they represent the same real-world object.

We use the SPARQL query language [7] to access a dataset. A SPARQL query has a target clause that specifies how the results of the query are constructed. The query language supports two basic query types. The target clause of a *select query* Q specifies a list of variables; each solution mapping of Q therefore induces a tuple of variable bindings, called a *result* of Q. The target clause of a *construct query* Q in turn specifies a set of triple patterns; each solution mapping of Q in this case induces a set of RDF triples, also called a *result* of Q. In either case, the evaluation of a query Q may produce several results, induced by several distinct solution mappings, which we assume to be ordered in a *result list*.

4.2 Serendipitous Search

To perform a serendipitous search, we apply a query modification process that enables the application to transform a submitted query. This allows the application to act before or after the query is actually executed. Therefore, the application can adopt different strategies at different phases of execution.

As already pointed out in the introduction, we resort to three main strategies to capture the selected serendipity patterns with the query modification process. In order to capture the analogy and the surprising observation patterns, the process uses the results of the user's query to invoke secondary queries with the recently acquired information to augment the results list with serendipitous content. To capture the inversion pattern, the process analyzes the query to formulate alternative queries. Finally, to capture the disturbance pattern, the process follows strategies to change the order of the result list.

The serendipitous search problem is formally defined as follows.

Given a query Q, a *serendipitous processing* of Q will add new triples to each result of Q. More precisely, let $D_1,\ldots,D_m$ be a set of datasets, called the *query environment*, and Q be a query over D_k, with $k \in [1,m]$. A *serendipitous result list* of Q over $D_1,\ldots,$ D_m is a list of pairs of sets $((T_1,S_1),\ldots,(T_n,S_n))$ such that, for each $i \in [1,n]$, T_i is a result of Q over D_k, called the *regular component* of (T_i,S_i), and S_i is a set of triples, called the *serendipitous component* of (T_i,S_i), computed from the datasets in the query environment.

We note that the triples in a serendipitous component S_i may use terms in the vocabulary and refer to entities outside the query environment. Indeed, in Sects. 4.3 and 4.4, we will formalize the analogy and the surprising observation patterns as new queries that return triples which are serendipitously related to the original result of Q. Such triples will form the second set in each pair of sets in the result list.

Consider that a user is searching for English rock guitarists using DBpedia. To address his goal the user may use the category English rock guitarists to formulate the query. The regular component of the result list includes entities that match the solution mapping of the query, such as, "Mick Jagger", "George Harrison", "John Lennon". The serendipitous component contains a set of triples that serendipitously connect new entities to those in the result list. For example, the serendipitous component may return a set of triples linking "John Lennon" to "Roy Harper" or "Ringo Starr" through the analogy property *soltool:analogousTo*, created for SOL-Tool.

The following sections discuss the strategies to capture each serendipity pattern. To simplify the discussion, all examples consider a query, referred to as *UQ1*, about English rock guitarists:

UQ1 Entities from English rock guitarist category

```
SELECT distinct ?entity WHERE{
  ?entity dct:subject
       <http://dbpedia.org/resource/Category:English_rock_guitarists>.
  }
```

Note that this query uses the *English rock guitarists* category of DBpedia and the *dct:subject* property from Dublin Core vocabulary, used to assign entities to categories.

Furthermore, we stress that a serendipitous result is an ordered list of pairs of sets. Hence, we may devise a presentation process that gradually exhibits the pairs of sets returned – including those found by serendipity – and that allows the user to browse through the partial result list and perhaps change the focus of the search to one of the entities in a serendipitous component. In Sect. 4.6, we will formalize the disturbance pattern as strategies to modify the order of the sets of triples in the result list.

4.3 Capturing the Analogy Pattern

To capture analogy, we first introduce a new property, *analogousTo*, to be expressed by triples of the form (*s,analogousTo,o*), which intuitively indicate that entities *s* and *o* are analogous.

More precisely, let Q be a query submitted to a dataset D_k and T_i be a result of Q for D_k. If e is an entity that occurs in T_i, then the search process might look for or compute a triple of the form (*e,analogousTo,o*) in D_k and include the triple in the serendipitous component corresponding to T_i.

We propose to compute *analogousTo* using a family of similarity functions adopting the same strategy used to compute the *sameAs* property, except that the properties to be compared would be chosen according to some set of criteria that better capture analogy, rather than the *sameAs* property.

One approach is to define a *query context* that reflects the interests of a group of users. For example, consider the entities "John Lennon" and "Roy Harper", both belonging to the *English rock guitarists* category and both of which were influenced by the American novelist and poet "Jack Kerouac", a pioneer of the Beat Generation; that is, "John Lennon" and "Roy Harper" are both linked to "Jack Kerouac" through the *dbo: influenced* property of the DBpedia property ontology. For this point of view,

"John Lennon" and "Roy Harper" are understood to be *analogous*, in that, as noted, they belong to the same category and are connected to the same entity with respect to the *dbo: influenced* property. For this scenario, the search process must fill in the Analogy Query Template 1, *AQT1*, with information acquired from the user's query. To do so, the search process executes a valid SPARQL query by replacing the [*result-uri*] field with the results of the *UQ1*query:

AQT1 Using influenced property to find analogous entities

```
CONSTRUCT {[result-uri] soltool:analogousTo ?analogousEntity} WHERE {
  ?auxInfluence dbo:influenced ?analogousEntity;
              dbo:influenced [result-uri].
  [result-uri] dct:subject ?auxCategory.
  ?analogousEntity dct:subject ?auxCategory.
  FILTER (?analogousEntity != [result-uri] ) }
```

We also propose a different query context to take advantage of DBpedia category hierarchy. For example, we might move up in the category hierarchy from *English rock guitarists* to *English guitarists* and then down to *English bass guitarists*, a narrower category. Thus, we would conclude that an entity of *English rock guitarists* is analogous to an entity of *English bass guitarists* with respect to the *English guitarists* category. Similarly to *AQT1*, the search process must fill in the Analogy Query Template 2, *AQT2*, with information acquired from the user's query in order to capture this pattern. One characteristic of this template is that the subquery selects, among the categories of the *UQ1* results, that with the lowest number of entities linked to it in order to find a more specific category subset. To achieve this goal, *AQT2* uses the *skos: broader* property from SKOS ontology, a standard vocabulary for organization systems:

AQT2 Using category hierarchy to find analogous entities

```
CONSTRUCT {[result-uri] soltool:analogousTo ?analogousEntity} WHERE {
   ?analogousEntity dct:subject ?category.
   ?auxCategory skos:broader ?superCategory.
   ?category skos:broader ?superCategory.
   {
        SELECT ?auxCategory (count(?categoryClient))
        WHERE {
                [result-uri] dct:subject ?auxCategory.
                ?categoryClient dct:subject ?auxCategory.
        }
        GROUP BY ?auxCategory
        ORDER BY (count(?categoryClient))
        LIMIT 1
   }
   FILTER (?analogousEntity != [result-uri] )
}  LIMIT 2
```

A variation of *AQT2* is the Analogy Query Template 3, *AQT3*, that randomly selects categories of the [*result-uri*] field:

AQT3 Using category hierarchy to find analogous entities

```
CONSTRUCT {[result-uri] soltool:analogousTo ?analogousEntity} WHERE {
   ?analogousEntity dct:subject ?category.
   ?auxCategory skos:broader ?superCategory.
   ?category skos:broader ?superCategory.
   {
         SELECT ?auxCategory
         WHERE {
               [result-uri] dct:subject ?auxCategory.
         }
         LIMIT 1 OFFSET RAND()
   }
   FILTER (?analogousEntity != [result-uri] )
} LIMIT 2
```

Note that *AQT1* relies on a vocabulary specific to the arts domain, the *dbo:influenced* property, while *AQT2* and *AQT3* use only Linked Data standard vocabularies and, therefore, they can be adopted for several domains.

Finally, we observe that this approach uses the familiar notion of similarity functions and, therefore, it may take advantage of tools, such as Limes [13] and Silk [9] to offline precompute *analogousTo* triples, and add these triples to a dataset.

4.4 Capturing the Surprising Observation Pattern

To capture the surprising observation pattern, we suggest to reinterpret the *rdfs:seeAlso* property in such a way that a triple of the form *(s,rdfs:seeAlso,o)* would intuitively indicate that any user interested in entity *s* might also be interested in entity *o*. Indeed, the *rdfs:seeAlso* property is commonly used as a wildcard to relate contents with loose connections.

In DBpedia, for example, there is a *rdfs:seeAlso* property linking "George Harrison" to "Apple Records". This link may be motivated by an analysis of the connection between "George Harrison" and "The Beatles" and the connection between "The Beatles" and the "Apple Records". For this scenario, the search process must fill in the Surprising Observation Query Template 1, *SOQT1*, with information from the *UQ1* results:

SOQT1 Using seeAlso property to find surprising observation

```
CONSTRUCT {[result-uri] rdfs:seeAlso ?surprise} WHERE {
   [result-uri] rdfs:seeAlso ?surprise. }
```

Another surprising observation is the inclusion of other members of the same band of a given musical artist. This can be captured with the *associatedBand* property, as described in the Surprising Observation Query Template 2, *SOQT2*:

SOQT2 Using associatedBand *property to find surprising observation*

```
CONSTRUCT {[result-uri] rdfs:seeAlso ?surprise} WHERE {
  [result-uri] dbo:associatedBand ?band.
  ?surprise dbo:associatedBand ?band.
}
```

Computing the *rdfs:seeAlso* property is a difficult issue though. A simple solution would be to define *(s,rdfs:seeAlso,o)* as *(s,owl:sameAs,o)*, provided that entity *s* is defined in the dataset the query refers to and that *o* is an entity defined in another dataset listed in the query environment, but coming from a different domain. For example, consider the case of a dataset D_k about the music domain, which contains information, such as musical artists, their albums and their songs. Suppose that Q is a query submitted to D_k and T_i is a result of Q over D_k. If e is a singer that occurs in T_i, then the search process might look for a triple of the form *(e,owl:sameAs,o)* in D_k, where o is an entity defined in D_j, with $j \neq k$, and include *(e,owl:sameAs,o)* in the serendipitous component corresponding to T_i. If D_j is a dataset about actors, the user may be told that singer e is also an actor, like "David Bowie" or "Jared Leto".

According to this strategy, using the query *UQ1*, the surprising observation pattern suggests the "David Bowie" entity of New York Times dataset for users who searches for "David Bowie" in DBpedia, if the New York Times dataset belongs to the query environment. The Surprising Observation Query Template 3, *SOQT3*, depicts the template to capture this occurrence:

SOQT3 Using sameAs property to find surprising observation

```
CONSTRUCT {[result-uri] rdfs:seeAlso ?surprise} WHERE {
  [result-uri] owl:sameAs ?surprise. }
```

4.5 Capturing the Inversion Pattern

As anticipated in the introduction, we suggest to adopt a completely different strategy to capture the inversion pattern. Very briefly, the suggested strategy allows the user to stop consuming the result list obtained for a query *Q*, and restart the search process with a new query *Q'* based on some entity observed in the serendipitous component of a result of *Q*. That is, the user would retarget his search based on some entity the search process may have passed in a serendipitous component. This pattern may be quite useful when the user does not find enough information with his query but does not know what else to search for.

The inversion pattern relies on the category representation of DBpedia to present alternative queries to the user. To do so, the search process executes the user query and retrieves the three most popular categories of the results i.e. the categories that most appear in the results. With this information, the search process builds an alternative query allowing the user to restart the search process with a different perspective.

To reproduce this behavior, the search process must proceed in two steps. First, it uses the Category Frequency Query Template 1, *CFQT1*, to get the three categories with more entities linked to it. The search process fills the template with two information from the user's query string: the output variable of the query string represented by the [*var*] field and the query string itself represented by the [*user-query*] field:

CFQT1 Extracting the most used categories from the subquery

```
SELECT  (COUNT(?s) AS ?counter) ?category WHERE {
   ?s  dct:subject ?category.
   FILTER ( ?s = [var])
   {
       [user-query]
   }}
 }
```

Second, the search process fills in the Inversion Query Template 1, *IQT1*, with information acquired from the *CFQT1* by replacing the [*categories-list*] term with results of the previous query.

IQT1 Building alternative query

```
SELECT ?entity ?catAux WHERE {
   ?entity dct:subject ?catAux.
   FILTER (?catAux IN ([categories-list]) )
} LIMIT 100
```

For example, assume the search process receives *UQ1*. First, the search process uses *CFQT1*, to discover that the three most frequent categories of *UQ1* are: *English rock guitarists*, *Living people* and *English male singers*. Then, it completes the *IQT1* template with the acquired information as depicted in the example below.

Example of alternative query to UQ1

```
SELECT ?entity ?catAux WHERE {
   ?entity dct:subject ?catAux.
  FILTER (?catAux IN
       (<http://dbpedia.org/resource/Category:English_rock_guitarists>,
         <http://dbpedia.org/resource/Category:Living_people>,
         <http://dbpedia.org/resource/Category:English_male_singers>))}
```

4.6 Capturing the Disturbance Pattern

We also suggest to adopt a strategy based on the result list to capture the disturbance pattern. This strategy perturbs the order of the result list obtained for a query *Q* by randomly bringing results further down the result list to near the top of the list. The user who issued query *Q* would therefore be exposed to results that he would normally neglect, and consequently his perception of the query result list would be changed.

This strategy stems from two motivations. First, if query *Q* returns a result list ordered by any ranking criterion *X*, then the disturbance pattern has the ability to smooth the impact of *X*. Second, if no ordering criterion is provided, the dataset endpoint may use its own ordering, in other words, the query will highlight results using a criterion that is not clear for the application or the user.

For example, consider that a user modifies the *UQ1* so that the results are ordered alphabetically. The disturbance pattern switches the position of "Adrian Portas" and "Würzel", both English rock guitarists.

5 SOL-Tool the Serendipity Over Linked Data Search Tool

The *Serendipity Over Linked Data Search Tool* – SOL-Tool was developed in Java with the Jena framework[1], a well-stabilized framework for Linked Data query processing and data manipulation, and Java Concurrent API[2] to parallelize the task of invoking remote datasets.

5.1 Architecture

The SOL-Tool modular architecture is organized in way that allows the search process to: (1) isolate the logic task of displaying the results from the rest of the search process; (2) permit not only users but also other applications to consume the search process of the tool; (3) take actions before, during and after the execution of the user's query; (4) attach additional information to every item of a query result; (5) address remote datasets independently; (6) enable the different query strategies for different scenarios; and (7) parallelize the query execution. Figure 1 depicts the SOL-Tool architecture.

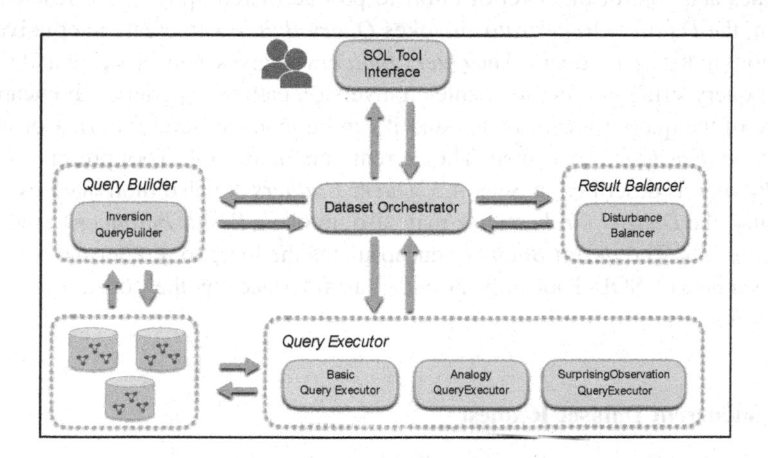

Fig. 1. The SOL-Tool architecture

To handle (1) and (2), the SOL-Tool *Interface* merely acts as the interface of the search engine with the user or other application receiving a SPARQL query and returning its results. This enables future versions of the SOL-Tool search engine to be instantiated as a Web service for other applications. Then, the *SOL-Tool Interface* starts the *Dataset Orchestrators* with a catalogue of datasets.

Motivated by (3), (4) and (5), the *Dataset Orchestrator* is responsible for interacting with a single dataset and managing the acquired data. The *Dataset Orchestrator* first uses the *Basic Query Executor* to process the user's query and retrieves its results.

---

[1] https://jena.apache.org/.

[2] https://docs.oracle.com/javase/8/docs/api/?java/util/concurrent/package-summary.html.

The *Basic Query Executor* is just a basic type of *Query Executor* that receives a SPARQL query, processes it and returns its results.

For every result of the user's query, the *Dataset Orchestrator* invokes *Query Executors* to process secondary queries and locate content that is serendipitously related to the respective result. The *Dataset Orchestrator* then delegates the task of querying its dataset to the *Query Executor*.

Motivated by (5) and (6), the *Query Executor* defines how to query the dataset. It encapsulates the logic of the query executed, in other words, it describes the serendipity patterns in terms of a SPARQL query that can be submitted to the dataset. To adapt the search process to different scenarios and behaviors, the SOL-Tool provides different *Query Executors* as described in Sects. 4.3 and 4.4, and it also provides an interface to easily build new ones. Secondary tasks of the *Query Executor* include parsing the results and handling eventual network exceptions.

It is worth noting that the *Dataset Orchestrator* encompasses the strategy of the search process while the *Query Executor* retains its logic. Thus, a *Dataset Orchestrator* acts as a façade for encapsulating several *Query Executors* to address the same dataset with different approaches. This design allows the application to adopt different approaches and control the level of effort to produce serendipity in the results.

Then, the *Dataset Orchestrator* invokes *Query Builders* to create alternative query suggestions to the user's query. The *Query Builders* receives a query string and returns a different query string in order to enable an inversion pattern experience. It encapsulates the logic of the query transformation and it can be invoked before, during or after the *Basic Query Executor* is executed. The current version of SOL-Tool presents only one *Query Builder* as described in Sect. 4.5. *Query Builders* are also motivated by (5).

Finally, the *Dataset Orchestrator* may also invoke a *Result Balancer* to reorder the obtained results. The *Result Balancer* encapsulates the logic to reorder the results. The current version of SOL-Tool only provides an interface for the construction of new *Result Balancers*.

5.2 Concurrent Dataset Request

As most of the effort spent by the application relies on invoking remote dataset endpoints, a critical factor since early implementations is the impact of latency in overall performance, i.e., the time that the application waits for remote servers to respond. To address this problem, the application resorts to the Java concurrent API to invoke SPARQL requests concurrently.

To reproduce this behavior, every *Query Executor* must implement a *call* method that is responsible for executing the SPARQL request and returning the query results. Therefore, the *Dataset Orchestrator* invokes the *Query Executors* asynchronously and aggregates the results that come from the remote dataset endpoint. The *Dataset Orchestrator* incorporates a MapReduce strategy [10] to combine the results related to an entity from many *Query Executors*. For example, assume that the user query returns an entity *e*. The *Dataset Orchestrator* will invoke *Query Executors* to find content that is serendipitously related to *e*. All data content found are grouped together using the URI from *e*.

With this configuration, the SOL-Tool application executes a basic search in less than 6% of the time of the single thread version. For comparison, *UQ1* was executed 10 times using the single thread and the multi-thread version of SOL-Tool. The average time of the single thread is 144 s, while the average time of the multi-thread (with a pool of 50 threads) is 7.4 s.

6 Experiments

From the recommender systems literature, a common approach to evaluate quality is to measure the accuracy of the results. However, as argued in [12], other metrics should be considered since very accurate results may lead the user to a bubble where he is only exposed to similar and obvious information. To overcome this problem we adopt unexpectedness to measure the serendipity of the results.

In [12] the unexpectedness of the results is evaluated by comparing the acquired results to a more primitive baseline system. However, as Kaminskas and Bridge [11] point out, this approach has several drawbacks: for example, the evaluation is sensitive to the baseline system. They then propose a different approach for measuring unexpectedness based on the dissimilarity of content labels. It uses the complement of the Jaccard similarity to compute the distance between two items. Therefore, the unexpectedness of an item is computed as the minimum distance of this item to previously seen items.

The experiment in this section uses the content-based metric [11] to evaluate the level of unexpectedness of the serendipitous component of the SOL-Tool, compared to its regular component. In order to select the item labels properly, the experiment adopts the Type Query Template, *TQT1*, that extracts the types associated with a given [*entity*] entity.

TQT1 Extracting the type of an entity

```
SELECT distinct ?type WHERE{
   [entity] rdf:type ?type.}
```

Duc to the size of DBpedia, we adopted the same strategy as [14] and limited the scope of the evaluation by restricting the user's query to retrieve entities of the type *MusicalArtist* and *Band* from DBpedia ontology, which have 50,978 and 33,613 entities, respectively. The User Query 2, *UQ2*, selects entities of the type *MusicalArtist*.

UQ2 Entities from MusicalArtist type

```
SELECT distinct ?subject WHERE{
   ?subject rdf:type <http://dbpedia.org/ontology/MusicalArtist>. }
```

The User Query 3, *UQ3*, selects entities of the type *Band* and is defined similarly to *UQ2*.

Table 1 depicts the average unexpectedness of the serendipity component of *UQ2* and *UQ3* with SOL-Tool and SOL-Tool-1, a variation of SOL-Tool that limits the number of results to one entity per Query Executor. This customization is possible due to the parameterization of the limit value of the Query Executor templates.

The overall result of Table 1 indicates that the SOL-Tool performs well when proving unexpected results for the selected inputs. This outcome illustrates the fact that the application adopts different strategies to present serendipitous content.

A concern of the metric [11] is the influence of very dissimilar items on unexpectedness computation. This issue is partially addressed by the SOL-Tool application because each serendipity pattern explores how entities are related. For example, consider the entity that represents the "Juli" band retrieved by executing *UQ3*. The execution of *TQT1* extracts 32 type labels of the "Juli" entity and 320 type labels of the entities encountered with the serendipitous search of *UQ3*, but from those 320 labels, there are 27 type labels that also belong to "Juli". The unexpected score of this item is 0.93, in spite of finding 85% of "Juli" type labels.

An additional interesting information of Table 1 is the loss of unexpectedness when limiting the number of results per Query Executor. The configuration of these parameters may be used to leverage the tradeoff between the quality of results and the effort spent in the search. This matter represents an interesting topic for future study.

Table 1. Experimental results.

Query	Unexpectedness average	Query	Unexpectedness average
UQ2	0.90	*UQ2* with limited Query Executors	0.80
UQ3	0.88	*UQ3* with limited Query Executors	0.81

7 Conclusions and Future Works

In this paper, we addressed Linked Data serendipitous search, with three main contributions. First, we proposed three main strategies to capture selected serendipity patterns in the context of Linked Data search. Second, we briefly described the architecture of a Linked Data serendipitous search application, SOL-Tool, which supports extensions to customize different steps of the search process. Third, we described experiments with the tool to illustrate the serendipity effect, using DBpedia.

The implementation of the SOL tool is ongoing work. In parallel, we are designing experiments to measure the user degree of satisfaction and the quality of the serendipitous results, which proved to be a challenging goal. This qualitative evaluation enables the analysis of what strategies are more useful for the users.

A prime objective of the SOL-Tool architecture is to aid the user, as much as possible, to achieve his goals when responding to queries. One way to enhance serendipity is to employ query modification to encompass *latent goals* [6], which are not explicitly addressed in the current query. New queries may be directed to stress whatever is eventually found related to other recent queries. For (a real) example, apparently, there is nothing in common between such disparate domains as "guitarists" and "salads". And yet, a user visiting Quebec, who first asks about "Quebec" and "guitarists", and later, when planning for dinner, asks about "restaurants" and "salads", may be told – in unexpected detail – that one restaurant features "good salads, nice live guitarist". Thus, the serendipitous component can be made more responsive to the user's interests and goals, either merely involved in a multiple-query session as in the above example, or registered among the objectives of a daily agenda, or more elaborately deduced from some user profile representation.

Another future work we intend to conduct is the development of a keyword-based search application that uses the SOL-Tool search engine to locate Linked Data serendipitous content, which will abstract the complexity of writing SPARQL queries.

References

1. Abbassi, Z., Amer-Yahia, S., Lakshmanan, L.V., Vassilvitskii, S., Yu, C.: Getting recommender systems to think outside the box. In: Proceedings of 3rd ACM Conference on Recommender Systems, pp. 285–288 (2009)
2. Adamopoulos, P., Tuzhilin, A.: On unexpectedness in recommender systems: or how to expect the unexpected. In: Workshop on Novelty and Diversity in Recommender Systems, at the 5th ACM International Conference on Recommender Systems, pp. 11–18 (2011)
3. André, P., Teevan, J., Dumais, S.T.: Discovery is never by chance: designing for (un) serendipity. In: Proceedings of 7th ACM Conference on Creativity and Cognition, pp. 305–314 (2009)
4. Bordino, I., De Francisci Morales, G., Weber, I., Bonchi, F.: From machu_picchu to rafting the urubamba river: anticipating information needs via the entity-query graph. In: Proceedings of the 6th ACM International Conference on WSDM, pp. 275–284 (2013)
5. Cyganiak, R., Wood, D., Lanthaler, M.: RDF 1.1 Concepts and Abstract Syntax. W3C Recommendation 25/02/2014. http://www.w3.org/TR/rdf11-concepts/)
6. De Bruijn, O., Spence, R.: A new framework for theory-based interaction design applied to serendipitous information retrieval. ACM TOCHI **15**(1), 1–38 (2008)
7. Harris, S., Seaborne, A.: SPARQL1.1Query Language W3C Recommendation (2013)
8. Iaquinta, L., De Gemmis, M., Lops, P., Semeraro, G., Filannino, M., Molino, P.: Introducing serendipity in a content-based recommender system. In: Proceedings of 8th IEEE International Conference on Hybrid Intelligent Systems – HIS 2008, pp. 168–173 (2008)
9. Isele, R., Jentzsch, A., Bizer, C.: Silk server-adding missing links while consuming linked data. In: Proceedings of 1st International Conference on Consuming Linked Data, pp. 85–96 (2010)
10. Leskovec, J., Rajaraman, A., Ullman, J.D.: Mining of Massive Datasets. Cambridge University Press, Cambridge (2014)
11. Kaminskas, M., Bridge, D.: Measuring surprise in recommender systems. In: Proceedings the Workshop on Recommender Systems Evaluation (2014)
12. Murakami, T., Mori, K., Orihara, R.: Metrics for evaluating the serendipity of recommendation lists. In: Satoh, K., Inokuchi, A., Nagao, K., Kawamura, T. (eds.) JSAI 2007. LNCS (LNAI), vol. 4914, pp. 40–46. Springer, Heidelberg (2008). doi:10.1007/978-3-540-78197-4_5
13. Ngomo, A.C.N., Auer, S.: Limes-a time-efficient approach for large-scale link discovery on the web of data. In: Proceedings of International Conference on Artificial Intelligence, pp. 2312–2317 (2011)

14. Passant, A.: dbrec — music recommendations using DBpedia. In: Patel-Schneider, P.F., Pan, Y., Hitzler, P., Mika, P., Zhang, L., Pan, J.Z., Horrocks, I., Glimm, B. (eds.) ISWC 2010. LNCS, vol. 6497, pp. 209–224. Springer, Heidelberg (2010). doi:10.1007/978-3-642-17749-1_14
15. Rahman, A., Wilson, M.L.: Exploring opportunities to facilitate serendipity in search. In: Proceedings of 38th International ACM SIGIR Conference on Research and Development in Information Retrieval, pp. 939–942 (2015)
16. Stankovic, M., Breitfuss, W., Laublet, P.: Linked-data based suggestion of relevant topics. In: Proceedings of 7th International Conference on Semantic Systems, pp. 49–55 (2011)
17. Toms, E.G.: Serendipitous information retrieval. In: Proceedings of DELOS Workshop: Information Seeking, Searching and Querying in Digital Libraries, pp. 17–20 (2000)
18. Van Andel, P.: Anatomy of the unsought finding. Serendipity: origin, history, domains, traditions, appearances, patterns and programmability. Br. J. Philos. Sci. **45**(2), 631–648 (1994)
19. Zhang, Y.C., Séaghdha, D.Ó., Quercia, D., Jambor, T.: Auralist: introducing serendipity into music recommendation. In: Proceedings of 5th ACM International Conference on Web Search and Data Mining, pp. 13–22 (2012)
20. Ziegler, C.N., McNee, S.M., Konstan, J.A., Lausen, G.: Improving recommendation lists through topic diversification. In: Proceedings of 14th International Conference on WWW, pp. 22–32 (2005)

Extraction of Embedded Queries via Static Analysis of Host Code

Petros Manousis[1(✉)], Apostolos Zarras[1], Panos Vassiliadis[1], and George Papastefanatos[2]

[1] Department of Computer Science and Engineering, University of Ioannina (Hellas), Ioannina, Greece
{pmanousi,zarras,pvassil}@cs.uoi.gr
[2] ATHENA Research and Innovation Center, IMIS, Athens, Greece
gpapas@imis.athena-innovation.gr

Abstract. Correctly identifying the embedded queries within the source code of an information system is a significant aid to developers and administrators, as it can facilitate the visualization of a map of the information system, the identification of areas affected by schema evolution, code migration, and the planning of the joint maintenance of code and data. In this paper, we provide a solution to the problem of identifying the location and semantics of embedded queries with a generic, language-independent method that identifies the embedded queries of a data-intensive ecosystem, regardless of the programming style and the host language, and represents them in a universal, also language-independent manner that facilitates the aforementioned maintenance, evolution and migration tasks with minimal user effort and significant effectiveness.

Keywords: Reverse engineering of database queries · Query extraction · Embedded queries

1 Introduction

To operate properly, data-intensive applications rely on *embedded queries*, that are programmatically constructed (typically, in progressive, incremental fashion) to facilitate the retrieval of data from the underlying databases. *Identifying the location and semantics of these queries and making them available to developers is very important.* In a most common scenario, database schema migration, refactoring and evolution require the appropriate visualization and inspection of data-related code, spread across multiple modules and files, for evaluating the impact of the schema change to the overall software ecosystem. As another example, when an administrator wants to modify a part of the database, it is imperative that the developers of the surrounding applications are informed on the change and have the means to identify the parts of the code that are going to be affected by that change [1,2].

E. Dubois and K. Pohl (Eds.): CAiSE 2017, LNCS 10253, pp. 511–526, 2017.
DOI: 10.1007/978-3-319-59536-8_32

```
1 $result = db_query('SELECT source, alias FROM {url_alias} WHERE source in
      (:system) AND language = :language_none ORDER BY pid asc;', $args);
```

```
1 function _profile_get_fields($category,$register=FALSE) {
2  $query = db_select('profile_field');
3  if ($register) {
4   $query->condition('register',1);
5  }
6  else {
7   $query->condition('category',db_like($category),'LIKE');
8  }
9  while (!user_access('administer users')) {
10  $query->condition('visibility',PROFILE_HIDDEN,'<>');
11 }
12 return $query->fields('profile_field')->orderBy('category','ASC')
13    ->orderBy('weight','ASC')->execute();
14 }
```

Fig. 1. Embedded queries of Drupal-7.39; string (top) and object based (bottom) (Color figure online)

Yet, obtaining these queries is an extremely painful process. An embedded query is, typically, progressively constructed via a sequence of source code statements that modify the query internals according to user choices. In the past, the most popular way to perform this task was via *string-based* embedded queries (Fig. 1 top). String-based queries were authored in SQL and parts of the query clauses were added or modified according to the context via if statements.

However, programming practice has departed from the traditional string-based construction of embedded queries and, *developers now employ certain reusable host language facilities (e.g., a specific API provided by the host language), to programmatically construct and execute the respective queries.* We call this way of query construction *object-based* as queries are formed as objects of the host language that are further manipulated by functions of an API that is responsible for the integration with the database. See Fig. 1 for the construction of such a query; the query is represented by an object, under the variable $query and further modified by the host PHP code via calls to the methods of a database-related API.

The state of the art methods and tools on query extraction do not support a general, easily understood and language-independent method for the identification of embedded queries, especially when it comes to object-based ones (see Sect. 6). The current methods and tools work only in specific environments (e.g., Java, or C#) via translating the object-based queries to string-based ones, or examine only the queries that are most likely to be generated by the execution flow of the source code [1,3].

To address these shortcomings, in this paper, we propose a principled, customizable language-independent *method that is able to (a) identify the embed-*

ded queries of a data-intensive ecosystem, regardless of the programming style and the host language, as well as by finding all their variations due to branching statements, and at the same time, (b) represent them in a universal, language-independent manner that can later facilitate migration or reconstruction, with (c) minimal user effort and significant effectiveness.

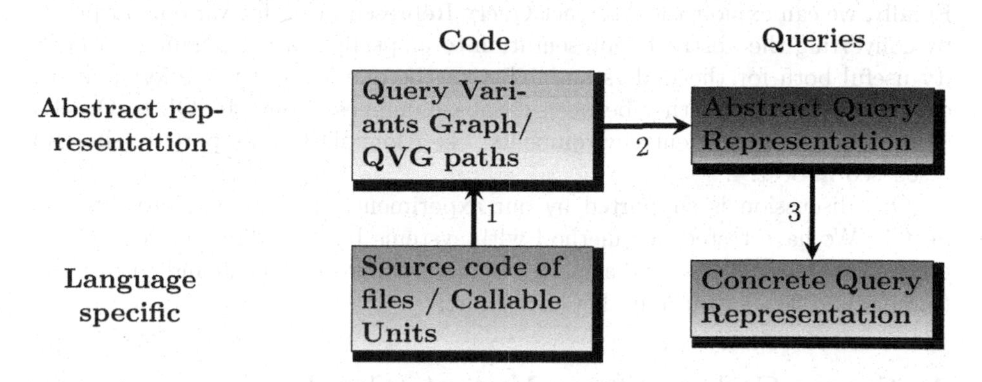

Fig. 2. The steps of our method

Our method consists of four parts, depicted in Fig. 2. As discussed in Sect. 2, we start with source code files as input. Initially, we decompose the input files to their structural parts (functions/methods) and we keep only these parts of the code that host queries. For simplicity reasons, in this paper we focus on SPJ string-based queries and data-retrieval object-based operations. Still, our approach is also applicable to a wider class of queries as well as DML operations. In the context of our language-independent approach, we uniformly will hereafter refer to functions/methods/procedures/routines as *Callable Units.* In general, a Callable Unit is: "a sequence of program instructions that perform a specific task, packaged as a unit"[1]. For those Callable Units we create an abstract representation of their code that we call *Query Variants Graph (QVG).* A QVG is a tree-like graph representation of a Callable Unit that uses the database. Due to the existence of branch and loop statements in the code, our next task is to traverse the Query Variants Graph and find every possible variation of a query that could occur at runtime. The result is a set of *QVG paths*, i.e., path traversals from the root of the QVG till one of its leafs. Observe that our representation abstracts the syntax details of the host language, thus it is language-independent, depending only on premises like Callable Units, and branch and loop statements that are practically universal. Our next step is the extraction of queries from the QVG paths and their representation into a generic, language-independent model. To represent queries in our model, we introduce an extensible pallet of *Abstract Data Manipulation Operators* with fundamental data transformation

[1] https://en.wikipedia.org/wiki/Subroutine.

and filtering operators. This facilitates a universal representation of queries, independently of the source language (thus the need for extensibility). So, in Sect. 3 we present how queries are represented as combinations of these operators, via a model of representation which we call *Abstract Query Representation* (AQR). An AQR is a directed acyclic graph with nodes that describe the database-related parts of the code and its purpose is to formally represent the queries. Finally, we can exploit the Abstract Query Representation for various purposes, by converting the abstract representation to a specific, target language, a facility useful both for the understandability of the queries and for different kinds of migrations – e.g., either between database engines (from MySQL to Oracle) or to completely different environments, like MongoDB. This part is (shortly) discussed in Sect. 4.

Our discussion is supported by our experimental assessment, presented in Sect. 5. We have tested our method with systems built in different source languages (PHP and C++) and achieve very high numbers of recall and correctness (larger than 80%) with quite low user effort.

2 Source Code to Query Variants Graph

In this section, we address the problem of identifying all the variants of the queries that exist in the source code of a given information system. To do so, we initially abstract the input of this step, which is the source code of the information system, to a Query Variants Graph that removes the language-specific control statements such as branch and loop statements of the host language. Next, we generate every possible query variant via traversing the QVG paths. Thus, the result of this step is a set of QVG paths for every query-related Callable Unit of the information system.

2.1 QVG Construction

Starting from a set of files that constitute the source code of an information system, our first step is to identify the query-related files and skip everything else. Then, we decompose these files to their Callable Units and we perform a second layer filtering keeping only the query-related Callable Units, such as those of Fig. 1 which query two relational tables.

Extraction of Callable Units. The first intermediate step towards abstracting the source code in language-independent format is the extraction of Callable Units. We initially check whether a file contains any database-related code statement either checking for query-related statements through string-based pattern matching or for query-related object initializations. If there is no such statement, we skip the file. Otherwise, we split it to its Callable Units. Similarly, we omit Callable Units without embedded queries in them. Thus, we end up working only with query-embedding Callable Units, significantly reducing the amount of work and resources needed to be invested in the subsequent steps.

The Price to Pay. To extract the appropriate information from the source files, we need to perform simple extractions from the source code. This requires (a) *physical level information* like the location of the source code and the parts of it that are to be ignored (e.g., binary files), (b) *query-related information* denoting the terms signifying a query, and, (c) *language-specific information.*

Concerning the query-related information, as already mentioned, we discern between two categories of hosting. In the first case, where queries are handled as strings, we need to know the API functions that use that string, so as to perform slicing in order to find the query strings (in our example of Fig. 1 the function contains the complete query string). In the second case, where queries are handled as objects and their definition is manipulated via a dedicated API for query construction, we need to know the API functions that construct an object-based query.

The way we do this is by splitting the original project to Callable Units on the basis of a formally specified grammar that requires the user to enter *once per language*: (i) how the comments start and end (both single-line and multiple-line comments), (ii) how the string values are described in the host language (eg. in C++ this is done by using the character: '"'), (iii) if there are characters that "escape" the string value markers (e.g., in C++ the character: '\'), (iv) finally how to treat the branch and loop statements of the host language. In this grammar, we treat nearly all loop statements similarly to branch statements. Remember that we are doing *static* analysis to dig out the query semantics. As loops are typically populating filters with values produced at runtime, we only need to handle the contents of the loop once, to identify the used expression along with the usage of an artificial set-valued pseudo-constant without practically misrepresenting the query's semantics.

Query Variants Graphs. Having explained the input and the method for the extraction of Callable Units, we now move on to describe the abstract representation of the code.

A Query Variants Graph is a graph with nodes the blocks of the source code, without branch and loop statements. The edges correspond to the control flow of the code (aka they "consume" the branch and loop statements). A formal definition of the Query Variants Graph is described in Definition 1.

Definition 1. ***Query Variants Graph*** - *a directed rooted graph $QVG(V, E, r)$, where V is the set of nodes of the graph corresponding to elements of a Callable Unit, E, the set of directed edges connecting elements of the Callable Unit together, and r belongs to V is the root node, with the following properties:*

1. *The root of the graph corresponds to the entire Callable Unit CU.*
2. *Sibling nodes have the following properties:*
   - *they share the same code both among them and also with their parent, both before and after the branching/looping statement of their parent*
   - *each sibling replaces the branching/looping block (including the branch/loop statement) of their parent with exactly one alternative execution block*
   - *for every alternative branching/looping block there is exactly one sibling node.*

```
1  function _profile_get_fields($category,$register=FALSE) {
2   $query = db_select('profile_field');
3   if ($register) {
4    $query->condition('register',1);
5   }
6   else {
7    $query->condition('category',db_like($category),'LIKE');
8   }
9   while (!user_access('administer users')) {
10   $query->condition('visibility',PROFILE_HIDDEN,'<>');
11  }
12  return $query->fields('profile_field')->orderBy('category','ASC')
13    ->orderBy('weight','ASC')->execute();
14 }
```


(a) The example of Fig. 1 bottom, annotated with (a)sequential blocks (with horizontal labels) and (b) Loop and branch blocks (with vertical labels).

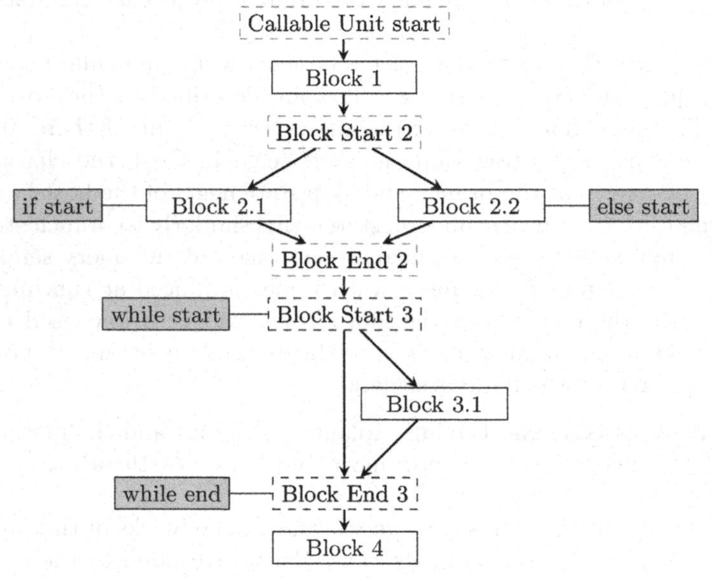

(b) Query Variants Graph of modified reference example.

Fig. 3. The example of Fig. 1 in two representations: (a) text and (b) graph.

Algorithm 1 serves the creation of the Query Variants Graph tree. A Callable Unit is decomposed to its blocks, starting with the first branch or loop block. The code of that block is split to its components and each one of them becomes a "sibling" node of the QVG. After that, the remaining code is checked again for branch/loop blocks, and, of course, the "siblings" are checked for branch/loop blocks too.

```
   Input: A Callable Unit (CU)
   Output: The root node for the Query Variants Graph of CU Callable Unit's
           source code (along with the rest of the tree that is constructed).
 1 Block = new node;
 2 Block = CreateGraph(CU, Block);
   Procedure CreateGraph(CU, Parent)
 1     Block = new node;
 2     branches = code of the first branch/loop block;
 3     if branches ≠ ∅ then
 4         if branches ≠ contain final alternative then
 5             branches += empty branch statement;
           end
 6         BlockStart = new node;
 7         preceding = code before the start of first branch block;
 8         if preceding ≠ ∅ then
 9             Block = preceding;
10             link BlockStart to Block;
11             link Block to Parent;
           end
12         else
13             link BlockStart to Parent;
           end
14         BlockEnd = new node;
15         foreach sibling ∈ branches do
16             link BlockEnd to CreateGraph(sibling, BlockStart);
17             remove examined code;
           end
18         return CreateGraph(M, BlockEnd);      ▷ Code after 1st branch
       end
19     else
20         Block = all CU code;                  ▷ Block without branch/loop
21         link Block to Parent;
22         return Block;
       end
```

Algorithm 1. Creation of Query Variants Graph

2.2 QVG Path Identification

In this subsection, we address the problem of identifying the different variants of a query that may occur during the execution of the code. This is done via a DFS-like algorithmic approach, where we traverse every Query Variants Graph path, regardless of whether the path contains query-related code or not. Algorithm 2 formally describes how we identify the variants of a query.

We perform a top-down traversal of the graph and we keep all code statements encountered from the root to each visited node, in a variable, called QP in our algorithm.

```
Input: A Callable Unit (CU)
Output: The database-related QVG paths of a Callable Unit (queryVariants).
Variables: queryVariants = ∅, codeUpToNow = ∅;
1 TraversePaths(CU.Block, codeUpToNow, queryVariants);
Procedure TraversePaths(v, codeUpToNow, queryVariants)
1   QP = codeUpToNow + statements of v;
2   if v has no children then
3       if QP ≠ ∅ then
4           queryVariants+ = QP;
        end
    end
5   else
6       forall w : children of v do
7           TraversePaths(w, QP, queryVariants);
        end
    end
```

Algorithm 2. Creation of QVG paths for a Callable Unit *CU*

Initially, we start from the root node of the QVG(*CU.Block*), with an empty list of query variants (named *queryVariants*) and an empty string statement (named *codeUpToNow*). For each node that we visit, we append in *QP* the code statements of the visited node. Then, we check if the visited node has any children nodes. If the node has no children nodes and *QP* is not empty, then we have finished with a traversal and we add the contents of *QP* to the *queryVariants* list. The contents of *QP* are the code statements from the *CU.Block* node up to a "leaf" node of QVG. If the node we visited has children nodes, then for each one of them we recursively call the *TraversePaths* procedure, giving as starting node the child node that we want to visit, as "up to now" string statements the *QP* variable and as list, the *queryVariants* list of paths.

The difference of *TraversePaths* procedure to the well known DFS algorithm is that we do not mark the nodes we visit. This is because we may encounter a node in more than one traversals, coming from different ancestor nodes. Thus, the information that is kept in a node (the contents of *QP* that are the code statements that we encountered till the node we have reached) differs on each traversal, and marking it as visited would produce wrong results. Observe the Query Variants Graph of Fig. 3b: the bottom *Block 4* node is used in four different traversals, marking it as visited after the first traversal would result in ignoring its statements in the remaining three traversals.

Coming back to our reference example, we can see that the Query Variants Graph of Fig. 3b provides four different traversals. The *Block 1* and *4* nodes are used in all traversal. The first traversal uses the *Block 2.1* node and does not use the *3.1* node. The second traversal differs to the previous one only in one place: instead of *2.1* node, this traversal uses the *2.2* node. The other two traversals of Query Variants Graph of the *_profile_get_fields* Callable Unit use the *3.1* node that was previously excluded from the traversals.

3 From QVG Paths to Abstract Query Representations

In this section, we introduce a universal way to represent the query variants that we obtained from the QVG traversals. Moreover, since this is an abstract query representation, it should be able to describe any database query, despite of how it was created (object-based or string-based queries).

To represent queries, we use an extensible pallet of Abstract Data Manipulation Operators (*ADMO*) that represent the different parts of a query. Our operators cover the relational algebra, therefore we are able to represent queries embedded in relational database management systems. The operators are given in Table 1. The Abstract Data Manipulation Operator pallet is extensible; new operators can be added to cover cases of non relational databases.

Table 1. Abstract Data Manipulation Operator with a description of the part of a query that they represent

Source	Describes a provider of information in a query (e.g., a table in SQL)
Projector	Describes an output attribute (e.g., the SELECT attributes in SQL)
Comparator	Describes a filter that the output of the query should fulfil (e.g., the conditions of the WHERE clause in SQL)
Grouper	Used for summarizing of the output (used for grouping the incoming data in groups, each group identified by a unique combination of grouper values, e.g., the attributes of the GROUP BY clause in SQL)
Ordering	Used for sorting of the output (e.g., the attributes of the ORDER BY clause in SQL)
Limiter	Used for restricting the size of the output (e.g., the TOP/LIMIT clauses of an SQL query)
Aggregator	Used for applying an aggregate function to a input attributes (e.g., the MIN, MAX, COUNT, SUM, AVG functions in SQL)

Definition 2. ***Abstract Query Representation (AQR)*** - *An abstract query representation* $AGR = (V, E)$ *is a directed acyclic graph whose nodes,* V*, are Abstract Data Manipulation Operators that describe a part of the query. An edge* $e \in E$ *from a node* v_i *to a node* v_j *specifies that the execution of the statement represented by* v_i *precedes the execution of the statement represented by* v_j*. The set of nodes* $V = Start \cup Nodes \cup End$*, is a union that comprises the following nodes:*

- *A node Start that specifies the beginning of a query variant q.*
- *A set of nodes Nodes that represent Abstract Data Manipulation Operators which serve for generating the different parts of the query variant q. Each one of the nodes is an Abstract Data Manipulation Operator (ADMO) as described in Table 1.*
- *A node End that serves for concluding the generation of q.*

Input: A QVG path of a Callable Unit (P), a mapping (M) of the API functions to ADMOs
Output: The Abstract Query Representation of P.
1 Add Start node for AQR;
2 **foreach** $QVGNode\ N \in P.nodes$ **do**
3     $functionsOfNode$ = split contents of N to its functions;
4   **foreach** $F \in functionsOfNode$ **do**
5         $FAMDOs = M(F)$; ▷ Find the ADMO nodes for function F
6   **foreach** $fadmo \in FAMDOs$ **do**
7   Set function's F parameters to $fadmo$'s ADMO parameters;
8   Add $fadmo$ to AQR;
          end
      end
  end
9 Add End node for Abstract Query Representation;

Algorithm 3. Transforming a QVG path to its AQR representations

Algorithm 3 formally describes the AQR construction from QVG paths. For the string-based constructed queries, the mapping of the SQL parts to the AQR nodes is a straightforward procedure. Using as reference the example of Fig. 1 we tokenize the first parameter of *db_query* function (which is our input) to the parts that are between the capitalized words with *blue* color. Then, we add Projector operators for each of the values that follow the SELECT keyword as a parameter to each node. We add a Source operator for the value that follows the FROM keyword, with its parameter (*url_alias* in our example). We add comparator operators (with their parameters) for the values that follow the WHERE & AND keywrods. Finally, we add an orderding operator (with its parameters) for the value that follows the ORDER BY keyword. Table 1 describes all possible keyword - ADMO combinations for the SQL queries.

Observe that since a string-based query might be modified in the source code, we may need to perform slicing (forward slicing, as mentioned in [4]) to find out whether our query was modified or not (in our example it is not happening). In our approach, we perform slicing only on the code of the Callable Unit that we examine. Inter slicing techniques that use dependency graphs to identify the parts of the queries that are constructed in other Callable Units (e.g., see [5]) have not proved to be necessary in our experiments; of course, they are a clear extension for future work.

In the case of object-based constructed queries, we need some additional input in order to construct the AQR out of the variants we obtained from Algorithm 2. We initially retrieve the contents of the variants and we decompose the statements of those variants to the API functions of the project we examine, as we need to map the functions of the project's API to the Abstract Data Manipulation Operators of Table 1. This is work performed exactly once, and it is project-related (since each project has it's own API). In Sect. 5 we discuss the developer's effort for this task. In Fig. 4 we see the creation of an AQR that comes from the first traversal of the *_profile_get_fields* Callable Unit. The project's API functions are translated to Abstract Data Manipulation Operators.

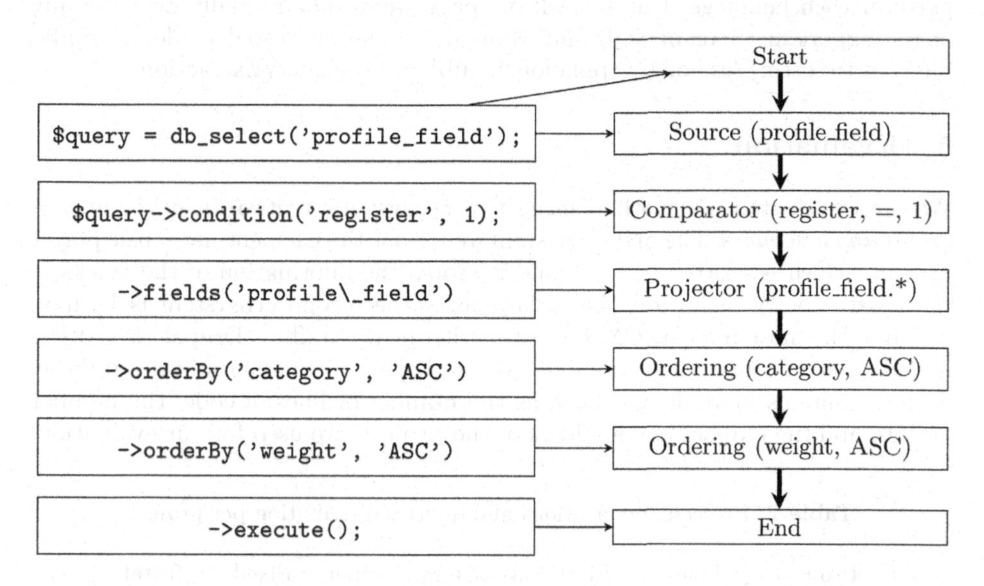

Fig. 4. Abstract query representation of the third QVG path of object-based query of Fig. 1. On the left we have the source code that constracts the query and on the right we have the AQR nodes with their parameters.

The AQR representation allows us to compare queries on the similarity of their structure. That is useful because we might obtain query variants (in one of the Callable Units that we examine) with identical structure (albeit, possibly with different values). This is due to branch/loop blocks in the source code of a Callable Unit that are unrelated to the query-object, and since we consider all query variants as valid for our research, we need to identify the same ones here. Therefore, we can use the Abstract Query Representation, and see if there are any AQRs with the exact same operators, carrying the exact same ADMO parameters. Since we need only one of those queries, we eliminate the AQR duplicates. This is a rather simple task, since a simple walk over the Abstract Data Manipulation Operators of the Abstract Query Representation can provide us the information needed for the comparison.

4 From AQRs to Concrete Query Representations

The Abstract Query Representation would be of small use, if we could not translate the AQRs to concrete queries for a specific query environment, so, the next step of our method is to be able to transform the model representation of AQR to a text-based representation of a concrete query environment. The query environments on which we have up to now performed this model-to-text transformation are SQL and MongoDB.

To export the Abstract Query Representation to a concrete language we need to gather the nodes of the AQR in groups and use those groups for the output parts of each language. Due to lack of space we do not formally describe any of the export methods of SQL and MongoDB. The interested reader is kindly referred to: http://cs.uoi.gr/~pmanousi/publications/queryExtraction/.

5 Evaluation

We have evaluated our method using two ecosystems written in *different programming languages*. The first ecosystem we used is the Clementine[2] music player project, which is written in C++ and it stores the information of the tracks of the music library of its users in a database. The second ecosystem is Drupal, which is the most popular CMS on sites with heavy traffic[3]. Drupal[4] is written in PHP and it stores the contents of the web pages it manages in a database. Table 2 contains more details, such as the number of lines of code, the number of files, and the number of subfolders of the projects we used for our evaluation.

Table 2. Projects' descriptions and queries distribution per project

Project	Lines of code	Files	Sub-folders	Variant queries	Fixed queries	Total
Clementine	210053	3072	159	10	14	24
Drupal	325421	1096	137	10	84	94

Effectiveness. We need to verify the extent to which our method retrieves and correctly reconstructs queries from the application scripts of the ecosystem. The performance measures for this kind of assessment are recall and correctness. *Recall* is defined as the fraction of the retrieved queries of each file over the actually existing ones. *Correctness* is defined as the fraction of the correctly reconstructed queries over the retrieved ones. A correct reconstruction of a query involves (a) retrieving all its structural parts and (b) assembling them correctly, in order to result in a correct and complete query. Table 2 depicts the distribution of queries that were either single path (fixed) queries or produced due to branch and loop statements of the host language (variant queries).

Recall. To assess recall, we need to *manually* verify the percentage of queries that our method extracts with respect to the queries that actually exist in the code. Due to the vastness of the task, we have sampled the 10% of the database-related files. This is a standard practice in the software engineer community whenever the size of a project is too large for full manual inspection. We manually inspected the code of the evaluated files and we were unable to find any

[2] https://www.clementine-player.org/.
[3] See http://w3techs.com/technologies/market/content_management.
[4] http://ftp.drupal.org/files/projects/drupal-7.39.tar.gz.

other query, besides the ones that our tool reported. In the functions that were repeating a query in one or more places in their source code, we reported only one occurrence of the query, since there was no variation. If a query changes, then we report the "new" query (the modified one) as well. Our manual inspection was further supported by automated searches in the source code. For Clementine, we decided to focus on a single table of the database. Then, we can search for all occurrences of the table's name. For Drupal, we took advantage of the fact that there are specific functions for querying the database, as prescribed by its manual (both for string-based and for object-based queries): https://api.drupal.org/api/drupal/includes!database!database.inc/function/).

Correctness. Regarding the correctness of our method, we examined the sample files on whether the queries that were translated to SQL query environment were correct or not. The correctness for the Drupal project is 95.6% and for the Clementine project is 79.1%. To explain what we considered as a correct query we created the following taxonomy of query classes:

1. *Fixed structure*: This class has the queries that can be translated to one of our concrete query environments and run without issues.
   (a) *All parts fixed*: queries that have no variable at all
   (b) *Variable values in "filtering"*: queries that contain a variable that gets its value at execution time but does not intervene with the query structure. In most cases this is a variable that is the second part of a comparison. In our reference example of Fig. 1, Line 7 contains the $*category* variable which can be replaced by a value, producing a valid query.
2. *Variable structure*: in this class we have variables that alter the query structure. This means that the data providers are unknown to us, so in order to produce a valid query we needed to know in advance the values of the parameters that were given to the calls of those Callable Units.

Table 3. Breakdown of generated queries per query class.

	Query class	Drupal-7.39	Clementine 1.2.3
Valid:	*All* parts fixed	28/94 (*29.7%*)	5/24 (*20.8%*)
Valid:	Variable *values*	61/94 (*64.9%*)	14/24 (*58.3%*)
	Overall	89/94 (**95.6%**)	19/24 (**79.1%**)
Invalid:	Variable *structure*	05/94 (*04.4%*)	05/24 (*20.9%*)

Table 3 contains the number of queries that belong to each classification for each one of our case studies, which consequently provide the precision measurement for our method. Observe that the internal breakdown for the different categories (rows in the table) is quite different for the two cases. However, *we do achieve 100% correctness and recall for the two first categories.* For the last category, we fail to produce an abstract representation due to the fact, that many times the variable structure refers to a variable table in the FROM clause that is assigned at runtime. A flexible handling of such occurrences (with variable tables involved) is part of future work.

Table 4. User effort (number of functions to translate/lines of code)

Project	API func./LOC	Host lang. (func./LOC)	Method fixed input
Clementine (C++)	4/59	9/341	11
Drupal (PHP)	11/251	9/347	11

User Effort. As previously stated at Sect. 3, there is a preprocessing step that is needed in order to translate the projects API database-related functions to Abstract Data Manipulation Operators. In Table 4 we describe the user's effort for the two projects that we examined. The effort is measured in the number of functions that needed translation from the project's API, and in the lines of code that were written for the translation of those API functions to Abstract Data Manipulation Operator.

6 Related Work

The state of the art on query extraction includes some interesting techniques that facilitate various engineering tasks like error checking, fault diagnosis, query testing prior execution, and change impact analysis.

Specifically, Christensen et al. [3] propose an approach that identifies type and syntax errors in Java source code, due to queries are constructed through string concatenation. To this end, the authors perform static source code analysis, based on flow graphs and finite state automata. Gould et al. [6,7] use slicing to identify the SQL related parts in Java source code. Then, all the variations of a query are formed and tested for type (using the DB schema description) and syntax errors. In a similar vein, Annamaa et al. [8] propose a method for testing database queries before their actual execution. The method identifies SQL queries embedded into Java source code, via searching for a given set of related functions. van den Brink et al. [9] use control and data-flow analysis to assess the quality of SQL queries, embedded in PL/SQL, COBOL and Visual Basic source code, while Ngo and Tan [10] rely on symbolic execution to extract database interaction points from PHP applications. Maule et al. [1] employ query extraction to identify the impact of relational database schema changes upon object-oriented applications. The proposed method targets C# applications and is based on data-flow analysis, performed via a k-CFA algorithm. Finally, Cleve et al. [11] propose a concept location technique that starts from a given SQL query and finds the specific source code location where the query is formed. This effort targets Java source code that uses JDBC or Hibernate.

Overall, although the existence of all these methods verifies the importance of the problem, the state of the art has dealt with query extraction (a) in a language-dependent way and (b) as the means, but not the main focus of research. Differently from the state of the art approaches, *we propose a general-purpose query extraction method that clearly separates technology-specific from technology-independent aspects*. Our method extracts *all* the variants of the queries that can be generated at runtime and *produces query representations in more than one target query languages*.

7 Conclusion and Future Work

We have presented a method that identifies the embedded queries within a database-related software project, independently of host language and programming style. Our method constructs every variation of a query that can be produced due to branch and loop statements of the source code's host language during runtime, and represents the queries in a generic, language-independent way that facilitates the exporting of these queries to more than one concrete query environments. As next steps, we intend to improve the effectiveness of our method, by capturing more flexible query construction patterns. We also consider to extend the number of host languages (besides PHP and C++) for our method's usability.

References

1. Maule, A., Emmerich, W., Rosenblum, D.S.: Impact analysis of database schema changes. In: Proceedings of the 30th International Conference on Software Engineering (ICSE), pp. 451–460 (2008)
2. Manousis, P., Vassiliadis, P., Papastefanatos, G.: Automating the adaptation of evolving data-intensive ecosystems. In: Ng, W., Storey, V.C., Trujillo, J.C. (eds.) ER 2013. LNCS, vol. 8217, pp. 182–196. Springer, Heidelberg (2013). doi:10.1007/978-3-642-41924-9_17
3. Christensen, A.S., Møller, A., Schwartzbach, M.I.: Precise analysis of string expressions. In: Cousot, R. (ed.) SAS 2003. LNCS, vol. 2694, pp. 1–18. Springer, Heidelberg (2003). doi:10.1007/3-540-44898-5_1
4. Gallagher, K., Binkley, D.: Program slicing. In: Frontiers of Software Maintenance, FoSM 2008, pp. 58–67. IEEE (2008)
5. Cleve, A., Henrard, J., Hainaut, J.: Data reverse engineering using system dependency graphs. In: Proceedings of the 13th Working Conference on Reverse Engineering (WCRE), pp. 157–166 (2006)
6. Gould, C., Su, Z., Devanbu, P.T.: Static checking of dynamically generated queries in database applications. In: Proceedings of the 26th International Conference on Software Engineering (ICSE), pp. 645–654 (2004)

7. Wassermann, G., Gould, C., Su, Z., Devanbu, P.T.: Static checking of dynamically generated queries in database applications. ACM Trans. Softw. Eng. Methodol. **16**(4), 14 (2007)
8. Annamaa, A., Breslav, A., Kabanov, J., Vene, V.: An interactive tool for analyzing embedded SQL queries. In: Ueda, K. (ed.) APLAS 2010. LNCS, vol. 6461, pp. 131–138. Springer, Heidelberg (2010). doi:10.1007/978-3-642-17164-2_10
9. van den Brink, H., van der Leek, R., Visser, J.: Quality assessment for embedded SQL. In: Proceedings of the 7th IEEE International Conference on Source Code Analysis and Manipulation (SCAM), pp. 163–170 (2007)
10. Ngo, M.N., Tan, H.B.K.: Applying static analysis for automated extraction of database interactions in web applications. Inf. Softw. Technol. **50**(3), 160–175 (2008)
11. Nagy, C., Meurice, L., Cleve, A.: Where was this SQL query executed? A static concept location approach. In: 22nd IEEE International Conference on Software Analysis, Evolution, and Reengineering (SANER), pp. 580–584 (2015)

Table Identification and Reconstruction in Spreadsheets

Elvis Koci[1,2(✉)], Maik Thiele[1], Oscar Romero[2], and Wolfgang Lehner[1]

[1] Database Technology Group, Department of Computer Science, Technische Universität Dresden, Dresden, Germany
{elvis.koci,maik.thiele,wolfgang.lehner}@tu-dresden.de
[2] Departament d'Enginyeria de Serveis i Sistemes d'Informació (ESSI), Universitat Politècnica de Catalunya-BarcelonaTech, Barcelona, Spain
{ekoci,oromero}@essi.upc.edu

Abstract. Spreadsheets are one of the most successful content generation tools, used in almost every enterprise to perform data transformation, visualization, and analysis. The high degree of freedom provided by these tools results in very complex sheets, intermingling the actual data with formatting, formulas, layout artifacts, and textual metadata. To unlock the wealth of data contained in spreadsheets, a human analyst will often have to understand and transform the data manually. To overcome this cumbersome process, we propose a framework that is able to automatically infer the structure and extract the data from these documents in a canonical form. In this paper, we describe our heuristics-based method for discovering tables in spreadsheets, given that each cell is classified as either header, attribute, metadata, data, or derived. Experimental results on a real-world dataset of 439 worksheets (858 tables) show that our approach is feasible and effectively identifies tables within partially structured spreadsheets.

Keywords: Speadsheet · Document · Tabular · Grid · Table · Layout · Recognition · Identification

1 Introduction

Spreadmarts, i.e. reporting or analysis systems running on desktop software, are used in more than 90% of all organizations [7]. 41% of these are built with Excel [7] which can be found on most office computers and, hence, do not incur any additional costs. Besides the low costs there are plenty of other reasons for using Excel as a data analysis tool, such as the high degree of autonomy, the fast information provisioning process compared to data warehouses, and the user desire to protect interests. While spreadmart solutions have their raison d'être, they come with the risk that information stored in them is getting lost since they are not part of the enterprise-wide administration. The problem of visibility is partly tackled by new information management principles such as *data lakes* [11,12] but the core problem still remains: how to extract and harvest

E. Dubois and K. Pohl (Eds.): CAiSE 2017, LNCS 10253, pp. 527–541, 2017.
DOI: 10.1007/978-3-319-59536-8_33

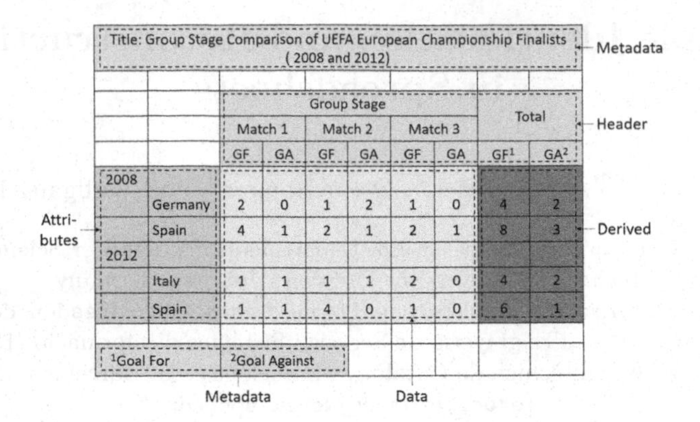

Fig. 1. Cell classification label [10]

the rich information found in spreadsheet formats enabling their reuse and thus fostering the understanding of data maintained in these files.

Our aim is to overcome this challenge by focusing our efforts on approaches for table identification and layout inference in spreadsheets. In a previous paper [10], we have proposed a machine learning approach for layout inference. We focused on the level of individual cells, considering a large number of features not covered by related work. From these, 43 were chosen for the final evaluation. The results show very high accuracy with all the defined classes (labels for the cells), and an overall 97% F1 measure.

Figure 1 provides examples for each of the cell labels. *Header* and *Data* are the basic building blocks of a table. In addition to this, we are using the notion of *Attributes*, i.e. specific data fields on the left of the table structured in a hierarchical way. *Derived* cells hold aggregations of data cells. Finally, *Metadata* cells provide additional information about the table as a whole (e.g., the title) or its parts (e.g., the unit of numeric values in a column). Additional information on these labels and the overall project can also be found on our website[1].

In this paper, we build upon these notions developing novel techniques to identify and reconstruct tables. Our approach takes as input the results from the cell classification task. Cells are then grouped to form regions (clusters) based on their label and location. These regions become the input for our heuristics framework, called TIRS (Table Identification and Reconstruction in Spreadsheets), which outputs tables and their layout. In the following sections we describe in detail each individual step of this process.

The subsequent parts of the paper are organized as follows: In Sect. 2, we define the concepts used throughout the proposed approach. The steps and heuristics for the table identification process are described in Sect. 3. In Sect. 4, we present the results of our evaluation. Finally, we review related work on table identification in Sect. 5, and conclude this paper with a short summary in Sect. 6.

[1] https://wwwdb.inf.tu-dresden.de/research-projects/deexcelarator.

2 Preliminaries

In the following sections, we define the concepts that are used in our heuristical framework, TIRS, and we discuss the pre-processing phase of our approach.

2.1 Cell Clusters

We decided to group cells based on the label they were assigned during the classification process and their location. We believe that these larger structures will help us streamline the table identification process. It is much simpler and intuitive to work on collections of cells rather than on individual cells. Furthermore, we have to handle a much smaller number of elements, thus decreasing the complexity of the overall process.

In the following paragraphs we provide formal definitions of the concepts used throughout the creation of the cell clusters. We start with the definition of the structure used to represent a sheet, which is referred to as worksheet in the Microsoft Excel environment.

Definition 1 (Worksheet Matrix). *A worksheet is represented by an m-by-n matrix of cells, denoted as $\mathcal{W}$. We refer to a cell in the matrix as $\mathcal{W}_{i,j}$.*

In this paper, we look at worksheets whose cells were previously classified by our method [10]. We assign a label to each non-empty cell.

Definition 2 (Classified Cell). *Is a cell in a worksheet, s.t.* $\texttt{Empty}(\mathcal{W}_{i,j}) \neq 1$ *and* $\texttt{Label}(\mathcal{W}_{i,j}) = \ell$. *Here, function* `Empty` *returns 1 for empty cells (i.e., without value), 0 otherwise. Function* `Label` *returns the label assigned to a classified cell, where* $\ell \in Labels, Labels = \{Data, Header, Attribute, Metadata, Derived\}$.

As we stated in the beginning of this section, our goal is to cluster cells. We initiate this process at the row level by grouping together consecutive cells of the same label. We refer to these mini row clusters as *Label Intervals*.

Definition 3 (Label Interval ($\mathcal{LI}$)). *A label interval is a submatrix of $\mathcal{W}$, denoted as $\mathcal{W}[i; j, j']$. For every cell $\mathcal{W}_{i,j''}$ in $\mathcal{LI}$, where $j \leq j'' \leq j'$, the* $\texttt{Label}(\mathcal{W}_{i,j''}) = \ell$. *To ensure maximal intervals, we enforce that* $\texttt{Label}(\mathcal{W}_{i,j-1}) \neq \ell$ *and* $\texttt{Label}(\mathcal{W}_{i,j'+1}) \neq \ell$.

We proceed further by grouping cells to even larger clusters, which we call *Label Regions*($\mathcal{LR}$*s*). Intuitively, $\mathcal{LR}s$ can be seen as an attempt to bring together $\mathcal{LI}s$ of the same label[2] from consecutive rows of $\mathcal{W}$. This is not straightforward, since the start column, end column, and order (size) can vary among these $\mathcal{LI}s$. Therefore, we target those $\mathcal{LI}s$ that are at least partially stacked vertically.

Definition 4 (Stacked $\mathcal{LI}s$). *Let I be the collection of all $\mathcal{LI}s$ in $\mathcal{W}$, then I_k and $I_{k'}$ are stacked iff there exists at least a pair $(\mathcal{W}_{i,j}, \mathcal{W}_{i+1,j})$ of cells s.t $\mathcal{W}_{i,j}$ in I_k, $\mathcal{W}_{i+1,j}$ in $I_{k'}$.*

[2] More specifically, all cells from these intervals have the same label.

We aim at constructing maximal $\mathcal{LR}s$, by merging all intervals of the same label that are vertically stacked.

Definition 5 (Label Region($\mathcal{LR}$)). *A label region is a $p \times q$ matrix of cells, where $1 \leq p \leq m$ and $1 \leq q \leq n$. In the trivial case a $\mathcal{LR}$ is made of a single $\mathcal{LI}$ (i.e., $\mathcal{LR}$ and $\mathcal{LI}$ are the same matrix). Otherwise, let r and $r+1$ be the indices of any two consecutive rows in $\mathcal{LR}$, where $1 \leq r < r+1 \leq p$. Then, there exists a pair of same-label stacked intervals (I_k,$I_{k'}$) that respectively correspond to stacked sub-matrices in row r and $r+1$ of $\mathcal{LR}$. An interval $I_{t''}$* **is not** *part of $\mathcal{LR}$ iff it has a different label or it has the same label but is not stacked with any of intervals in $\mathcal{LR}$.*

Note that a $\mathcal{LR}$ is not a submatrix of $\mathcal{W}$. They share $\mathcal{LI}s$, but the remaining parts of the $\mathcal{LR}$ might be different. We use empty cells to fill the gaps from the clustered $\mathcal{LI}s$, when necessary. In this way we ensure equally sized columns and equally sized rows for $\mathcal{LR}$ matrices.

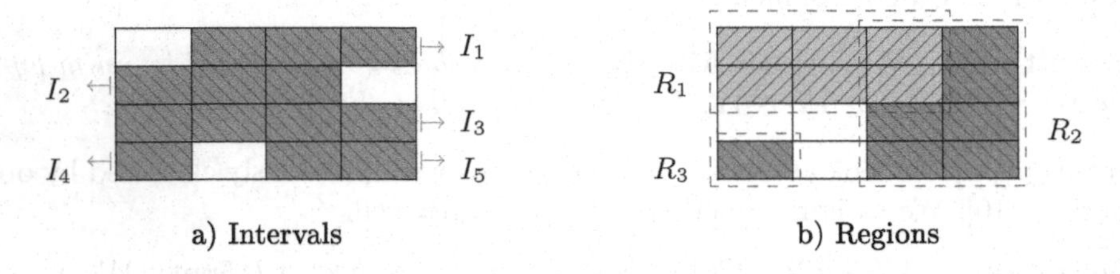

Fig. 2. Cell clustering

Example. In Fig. 2, we provide two examples that illustrate how we cluster classified cells. Blue (backward-sloping lines) cells are of the same label λ_1, and green (forward-sloping lines) cells of the same label λ_2. The ones that are blank represent empty cells or cells that were assigned a different label than λ_1 and λ_2. In Fig. 2(a) cells are clustered into five label intervals. The label intervals I_4 and I_5, although in the same row, are separated because there is a cell of a different label between them. All intervals in Fig. 2(a) can be clustered into one label region. Contrary, in Fig. 2(b) there are three label regions, two blue (R_2 and R_3) and one green (R_1). We note that R_1 and R_2 "overlap". In the following sections we discuss how we treat these cases. For now we can say that this "overlap" hints some kind of relation between these regions. Also, the case of R_3 is particular, since it is a single cell region. Such cases can happen when it is not possible to cluster the cells both row-wise and column-wise.

2.2 Rectangular Abstractions

Although cell matrices are suitable structures for maintaining the $\mathcal{LR}s$, it is rather challenging to define heuristics on top of them. Therefore, we decided to go for a more abstract representation, namely the rectangle. An $\mathcal{LR}$ can be seen as a rectangular structure that bounds cells of the same label. In the literature this is called the minimum bounding rectangle (MBR) for a set of objects, and is commonly used for tasks of spatial nature [4,13].

In our case, MBRs exist in the space defined by the original worksheet. The top-left corner of the worksheet becomes the origin (0, 0). As shown in Fig. 3, the x-axis extends column-wise, while the y-axis extends row-wise. The edges of the MBRs are either parallel or perpendicular with these axes.

In this coordinate system, cells are rectangles, having unit width and unit height. As such, a cell $\mathcal{W}_{i,j}$ is represented by the coordinates[3]: $x_{min} = j - 1$, $x_{max} = j$, $y_{min} = i - 1$, and $y_{max} = i$.

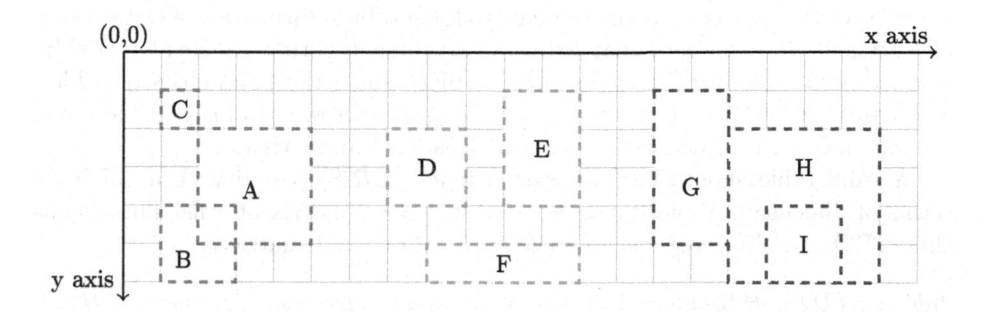

Fig. 3. Spatial relations between rectangles in a worksheet

We can determine the MBR coordinates for a $\mathcal{LR}$ from the indices of the cells it bounds. Specifically, we focus on the top-left and bottom-right cells in the $\mathcal{LR}$.

2.3 Spatial Arrangements

Here, we provide some of the notions used to describe spatial relations between the rectangles ($\mathcal{LR}s$). Our aim is to explain them intuitively using the examples in Fig. 3. Similar notions have been defined more formally in [13].

We start with the concepts that describe the relative location of rectangles. We use the notions *on the left of* and *on the right of* to describe relations like D to E and E to D, respectively. Likewise, F is *under* E, and the other way around E is *above* F. We can make these relations even more specialized. For example, F it is *not strictly under* E, since F is wider. However, D is *strictly on the left of* E, since its projection to the y-axis is within (covered by) E's y-axis projection. We are also interested in intersecting rectangles, and we have distinguished several of such cases: Two rectangles might *overlap*, such as A and B. They could *meet at a vertex*, like C and A. Rectangles G and H *meet at* or partially *share an edge*. Finally, rectangle I is *inside* rectangle H.

[3] Note, MBRs rely on a reference coordinate system, while $\mathcal{LR}s$ rely on the spreadsheet notation (i.e., column and row numbers).

3 Table Identification

TIRS consists of a series of heuristics that are based on the concepts presented in the previous sections. In addition to covering various table layouts, we had to minimize the effects of incorrect classifications and empty cells (i.e., missing values). Furthermore, we opted for heuristics that work on worksheets having multiple tables, stacked horizontally and/or vertically.

3.1 Tables in TIRS

Data, Header, and Attribute regions play the most important role in our analysis, since for us they are the base ingredients to form tables. Intuitively, a Data region ($\mathcal{LRD}$) acts like the core that brings everything together. A Header ($\mathcal{LRH}$) and Attribute region ($\mathcal{LRA}$) can help us distinguish the boundaries of tables. Therefore, we refer to them as "fences", a term borrowed from [1]. Fences can be horizontal (only Headers) or vertical (Headers[4] and Attributes).

A valid table should have at least a fence ($\mathcal{LRF}$) paired with a $\mathcal{LRD}$. In terms of dimension, tables must be at least a 2×2 matrix of cells. This means that $\mathcal{LRD}$ and $\mathcal{LRF}$ regions are at least 1×2 or 2×1 matrices.

$$table := \{Data, HHeaders, VHeaders, Attributes, Derived, Metadata, Other\}$$

Tables extracted by TIRS can be stored as collections of $\mathcal{LR}s$. More specifically, as shown above, a table has seven distinct sets of $\mathcal{LR}s$. For most of the cases we organize the regions forming the table by their label. We specialize Headers to vertical and horizontal. While the set "Other" contains regions for which we can not tell the layout function despite of their label. We provide more details on the latter in the following sections.

Finally, we utilize the MBR concept for tables, in addition to label regions. A table MBR is the minimum bounding rectangle for the $\mathcal{LR}s$ that compose it.

3.2 Pairing Fences with Data Regions

As mentioned in the previous section, TIRS needs to pair $\mathcal{LRD}s$ with $\mathcal{LRF}s$ to form tables. Valid pairs comply with the following three conditions.

C1. The $\mathcal{LRF}$ is on the top or on the left of the $\mathcal{LRD}$ although not necessarily adjacent to it.

C2. For a $\mathcal{LRF}$, the selected $\mathcal{LRD}$ is the closest[5]. Specifically, for a horizontal fence we measure the distance from the top edge of the Data region. Respectively, we work with the left edge for vertical fences.

---

[4] Vertical Headers occur infrequently in our annotated dataset for "pivoted" tables.

[5] We quantify this using the smallest Euclidean distance between two MBRs.

C3. The pair of MBRs representing correspondingly the $\mathcal{LRD}$ and the $\mathcal{LRF}$ are projected in one of the axes, depending on the fence orientation. The length of the segment shared by both projections represents the overlap. We transform the overlap into a ratio by dividing it with the largest projection.

$$\frac{Overlap(xProjection(\mathcal{LRD}), xProjection(\mathcal{LRF}))}{Max(xProjection(\mathcal{LRD}), xProjection(\mathcal{LRF}))} > \theta \quad (1)$$

Equation 1 shows how to calculate this for the x-axis (relevant to horizontal fences). The threshold θ was determined empirically and set to 0.5.

3.3 Heuristics Framework

The TIRS framework is composed of eight heuristic steps (activities). The initial Data-Fence pairs are created in the first five steps. While, the subsequent activities aim at completing the table construction by incorporating the remaining unpaired regions. In the following paragraphs we present each step and illustrate their relevance with examples from Fig. 4.
We should note that the examples in Fig. 4 hide the complexity of tables in our real-world dataset. For instance, fences might contain hierarchical structures, spanning in multiple rows and columns. Furthermore, misclassifications and empty cells can occur in arbitrary locations, and implicate various label regions (not only fences).

S1. In the first step, we attempt to create one-to-one pairs of Fence-Data, based on the three conditions listed in Sect. 3.2. Figure 4(a) and (d) provide examples of such tables.
S2. Mainly due to misclassifications multiple fence regions can be found that satisfy C1 and C2, but fail to comply with C3. An example is shown in Fig. 4(b). In such cases, we treat the individual regions as one composite fence, omitting the in-between "barriers". Equations 2 and 3 respectively show how to calculate the overlap ratio and projection-length to the x-axis for a composite fence ($\mathcal{CF}$), containing N sub regions. We handle these calculations similarly for y-axis projections. Having the results from the equations, we proceed to check if C3 is satisfied.

$$cmp\_overlp = \sum_{i=1}^{N} Overlap(xProjection(\mathcal{LRD}), xProjection(\mathcal{CF}_i)) \quad (2)$$

$$cmp\_length = \sum_{i=1}^{N} xProjection(\mathcal{CF}_i) \quad (3)$$

S3. There can be a fence (simple or composite) that satisfies C3, but it is located inside the Data region far from the top edge or left edge. This might happen due to incorrect classification in worksheets that contain conjoined tables (i.e., not separated by empty columns or rows). We provide an example in

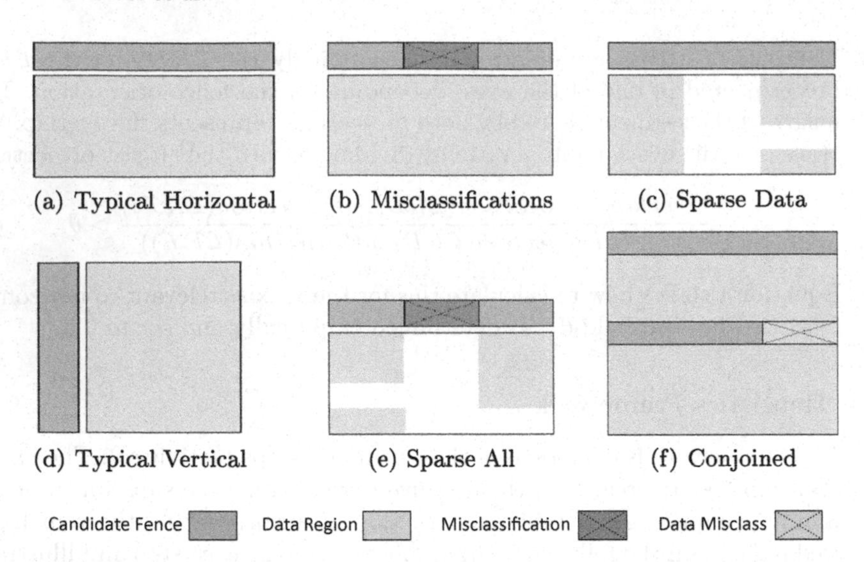

Fig. 4. Table types: cases b, c, e, and f also occur for tables with vertical fences

Fig. 4(f). When such a fence is identified, we separate the Data region into two parts. When the fence is horizontal, we pair it with the lower part, otherwise with the right part.

S4. There are cases where "small" Data regions are under or on the right of a "bigger" fence (e.g. the table in Fig. 4(c)). For these cases, the fence is treated as first-class citizen. Data regions that comply to condition C1 and are closer to this fence, than other ones, are grouped together. Again, we use similar formulas to Eqs. 2 and 3 to calculate the overlap and the projection-length of composite Data regions.

S5. At this step, we take a much more aggressive approach, in order to form tables with the remaining unpaired regions. We start by grouping fences. When working horizontally, we merge fences whose y-axis projections overlap. Likewise, we look for overlaps on the x-axis for vertical fences. Afterwards, we proceed in the same way as in step S4. Figure 4(e) illustrates a table that can be the output of this step.

S6. Here, we attempt to incorporate unpaired regions located in-between existing tables (i.e., constructed during S1–S5). In addition to the Data and fences, we also consider Metadata and Derived regions. For a pair of tables stacked horizontally, we assign the unpaired regions to the top table. When working with vertically stacked tables, we favor the left one. Obviously this and the following step, make sense when there are more than one extracted tables.

S7. We proceed by merging tables whose MBRs overlap. This will correct inconsistencies that might have happened during the previous steps. For example, a Data region is partially under a fence from another table.

S8. Finally, we assign the remaining unpaired regions, of all labels, to the nearest existing table.

Algorithm 1. Table creation in TIRS

```
   Input: Set of LRDs (D), set of LRHs (H), set of LRAs (A)
   Output: Set of extracted tables from the worksheet (T)
1  begin
2      T ← ∅;
3      UF ← ∅, UD ← D ;                        // UF: unpaired LRFs,UD: unpaired LRDs
4      O ← {Horizontal, Vertical};
5      foreach o in O do
6          if o == Horizontal then UF ← H else UF ← UF ∪ A;
7          foreach d in UD do
8              f ← GetNext(UF), newtbl ← false;
9              while f ≠ null and newtbl == false do
10                 if IsValidPair({d},{f},o) then                // S1: line 10-12
11                     (T, UF, UF) ← Construct({d},{f}, UD, UF, T, o);
12                     newtbl = true;
13                 else if IsDataBreaker(d,f) then               // S3: line 13-16
14                     (d1, d2) ← BreakInTwoParts(d,f);
15                     (T, UF, UF) ← Construct({d2},{f}, UD, UF, T, o);
16                     d ← d1;
17                 f ← GetNext(UF);
18             if newtbl == false then                           // S2: line 18-20
19                 CF ← GetCompositeFence(d, UF, o);
20                 if IsValidPair({d}, CF, o) then
21                     (T, UF, UF) ← Construct({d}, CF, UD, UF, T, o)
22     UH ← UF ∩ H, UA ← UF ∩ A;             // Extract unpaired Headers & Attributes
23     foreach o in O do
24         if o == Horizontal then UF ← UH else UF ← UF ∪ UA;
25         foreach f in UF do                                    // S4: line 23-25
26             CD ← GetCompositeData({f}, o, UD);
27             if IsValidPair(CD,{f},o) then
28                 (T, UD, UF) ← Construct(CD,{f}, UD, UF, T, o);
29         foreach MF in MergeByOrientation(UF,o) do             // S5: line 26-28
30             CD ← GetCompositeData(MF, o, UD);
31             if IsValidPair(CD, MF, o) then
32                 (T, UF, UF) ← Construct(CD, MF, UD, UF, T, o)
33     return T;
34 Function Construct(SD,SF,UD,UF,T,o):   // SD: Selected LRDs, SF: Selected LRFs
35     table ← CreateTable(SD,SF,o);
36     TT ← T, TUD ← UD, TUF ← UF;            // Temporary variables in this function
37     (TUD, TUF) ← FilterOutPaired(table, TUD, TUF);
38     ConT ← HandleTableBreakers(table, TUF, o);       // Trivial case ConT = {table}
39     foreach t in ConT do
40         foreach u in {TUD ∪ TUF} do
41             if IsInside(table,u) or IsOverlap(table,u) then AddOtherRegion(table,u) ;
42         (TUD, TUF) ← FilterOutPaired(table, TUD, TUF);
43         TT ← TT ∪ {t};
44     return (TT, TUD, TUF);
```

Algorithm 1 provides a high level view from the execution of table creation steps (S1–S5). For each individual step S1 to S5, we first process horizontal and then vertical fences. Our empirical analysis showed the former are by far more common, thus we prioritize them. Additionally, we give priority to Headers over Attributes. It is fair to claim that Headers represent more "secure" fences, since less misclassification involve this label compared to Attributes [10]. Another details is that of S4 and S5 being executed only after all the types of fences are processed by steps S1–S3.

Furthermore, to avoid any inconsistencies, after the table creation we execute a series of operations. We incorporate regions that partially overlap or fall inside (complete overlap) the table (line 34–35). We exclude the paired regions from the next iterations (line 31 and 36). Also, we call function *HandleTableBreakers*, which basically is a batch execution of step S3.

Finally, at line 35 we use function *AddOtherRegion*. At this point of the algorithm we can not tell what the role of the fully or partially overlapping region is, since we already have paired the main components of the table. Therefore, we keep such regions at a special set called “Other”.

4 Experimental Evaluation

In the following subsections, we discuss the evaluation of our proposed approach. Firstly, we present the dataset that was used for our experiment. Afterwards, we define how we measure the success of our method, and present the results of our evaluation.

4.1 Dataset of Annotated Tables

For our experiments we have considered spreadsheets from three different sources. EUSES [8] is one of the oldest and most frequently used copora. It has 4,498 unique spreadsheets, which are gathered through Google searches using keywords such as “financial” and “inventory”. The ENRON corpus [9] contains over 15,000 spreadsheets, extracted from the Enron email archive. This corpus is of a particular interest, since it provides access to real-world business spreadsheets used in industry. The third corpus is FUSE [3] that contains 249,376 unique spreadsheets, extracted from Common Crawl[6].

From these three corpora, we randomly selected and annotated 216 spreadsheet documents. This translates into 465 individual worksheets. The annotations were performed by experts from our group, using a tool we developed in our previous work [10]. Each non-empty cell was assigned one of the five predefined labels (see Fig. 1). Additionally, we recorded tables as ranges of cells (storing the address of the top-left and bottom-right cells). Thus, for each annotated cell we can tell the table it belongs to.

For the evaluation of TIRS, we used 858 annotated tables. Out of this, 541 come from FUSE, 222 from ENRON, and 95 from EUSES. We should note that we omitted from our analysis 26 worksheets (40 “tables”). These worksheets contain only Data, and no fences. During the annotation phase we marked these Data as valid tables. However, later we decided to exclude them, since they do not comply anymore to our table definition (see Sect. 3.1).

4.2 Evaluation Objectives and Metrics

An extracted table T_e is considered a match to an annotated table T_a when they share at least 80% of their cells, considering only the Data, Header, and

[6] http://commoncrawl.org/.

Attribute regions (as mentioned in Sect. 3, these regions form the base of tables). To perform the comparison, we represent both T_e and T_a as rectangles. For a pair T_e and T_a we evaluate the spatial match using the formula below, where $\gamma = 0.8$.

$$match(T_e, T_a) = \frac{overlap(area(T_e), area(T_a))}{max(area(T_e), area(T_a))} \geq \gamma \tag{4}$$

We should note the reasons behind the omission of Derived and Metadata regions. Firstly, as can be seen from our table definition, they are not a must for its existence. Secondly, Metadata and Derived are not necessarily always related to a single table. During the annotation phase, we encountered Metadata that provide information relevant to multiple tables in the worksheet. Also, in our dataset a small number of Derived regions contain aggregations coming from several tables. Such regions, related to multiple tables, emerge "orphan" from our annotation phase, since we avoid assigning a table to them. Clearly, there is the need for more sophisticated ways to handle Metadata and Derived, but for the moment we exclude them from our analysis.

4.3 Evaluation Results

We present our evaluation per corpus, per number of misclassifications in the worksheet, and finally per table arrangements. The latter is related to the way tables are stacked in the worksheet.

We use precision and recall [14] to evaluate how good our approach is at identifying spreadsheet tables. In our context, precision measures the percentage of extracted tables (T_e), i.e., that match an annotated table (T_a). While, recall measures the percentage of T_a that were matched by our method.

Additionally, we compare the number of T_e with the number of T_a in the worksheet. The ratio where these numbers are equal is recorded by the "Equal" metric. The "Not Equal" metric records the cases these numbers differ (i.e., we extracted more or fewer tables than the actual number of tables in the worksheet).

As seen in Fig. 5(a), our approach performs considerably well for FUSE tables, but poorly for ENRON tables. During an empirical examination, we noted that tables from ENRON tend to have a more complex structure, when compared to the other two corpora. We believe this to be the main reason for low scores in this corpus. This claim is further enforced by the results of the cell classification evaluation [10], where ENRON worksheets exhibit more misclassifications.

For EUSES, considering also Fig. 5(b), we are able to match well the actual number of tables in worksheets, but in terms of precision and recall we do not achieve that high scores. It seems that for a number of cases the extracted tables do not overlap significantly (≥80%) with the annotated tables in the worksheet.

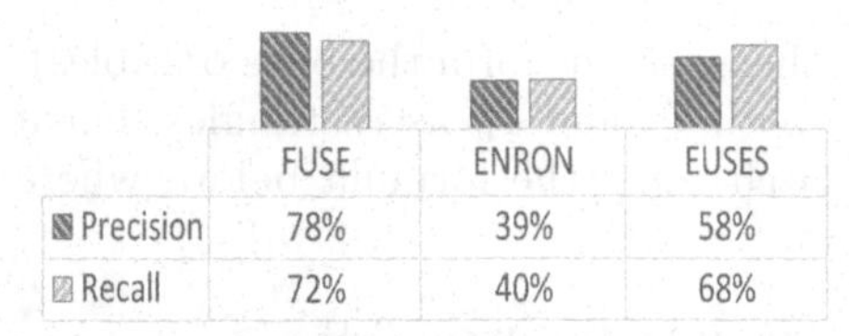

	FUSE	ENRON	EUSES
Precision	78%	39%	58%
Recall	72%	40%	68%

(a) Precision and Recall

	FUSE	ENRON	EUSES
Equal	82%	52%	85%
Not Equal	18%	48%	15%

(b) Matching Number of Tables

Fig. 5. Results per corpus

	None	Few(1-3)	Bunch(4-7)	Many(8-∞
Precision	82%	56%	60%	53%
Recall	82%	53%	53%	57%

(a) Precision and Recall

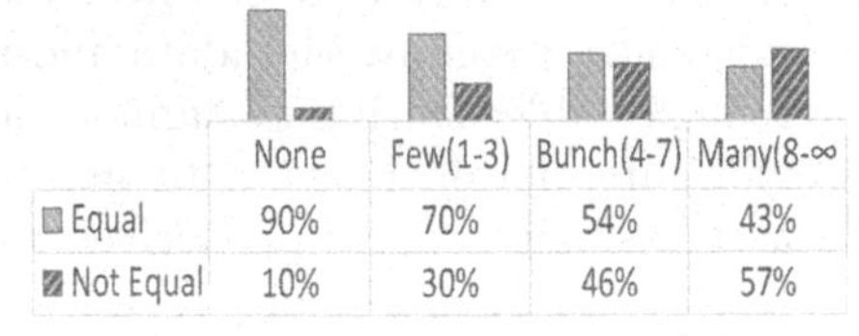

	None	Few(1-3)	Bunch(4-7)	Many(8-∞
Equal	90%	70%	54%	43%
Not Equal	10%	30%	46%	57%

(b) Matching the Number of Tables

Fig. 6. Results per number of misclassifications

Figure 6 shows that our method performs well when there are no misclassifications. In contrast to what we expected, precision and recall do not follow a decreasing trend as we move to worksheets with more incorrect classifications. This is not the case for the *equal* and the *not equal* metrics.

We believe that in the case of precision and recall factors other than the number of incorrect classifications have strong influence. The graphs presented in Fig. 7 seem to support this claim.

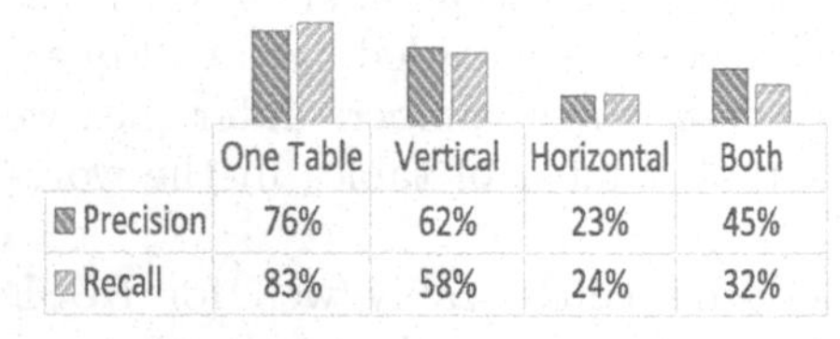

	One Table	Vertical	Horizontal	Both
Precision	76%	62%	23%	45%
Recall	83%	58%	24%	32%

(a) Precision and Recall

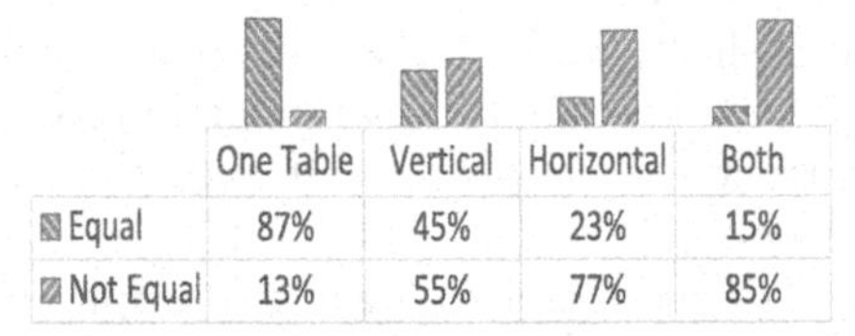

	One Table	Vertical	Horizontal	Both
Equal	87%	45%	23%	15%
Not Equal	13%	55%	77%	85%

(b) Matching the Number of Tables

Fig. 7. Results per table arrangements

We observe that our method performs well for worksheets that contain one table, as shown in Fig. 7. We can also say, that precision and recall are tolerable for tables stacked vertically (row-wise). However, for horizontal alignments (column-wise) our scores are quite low. Probably, this impacts the performance for worksheets that contain both horizontal and vertical alignments of tables.

We believe the fact that we give more priority to horizontal fences, as mentioned mentioned at the end of Sect. 3.3, can explain the results in Fig. 7. Clearly, we have biased TIRS towards tables stacked vertically. This is for a good reason, since they appear more frequently.

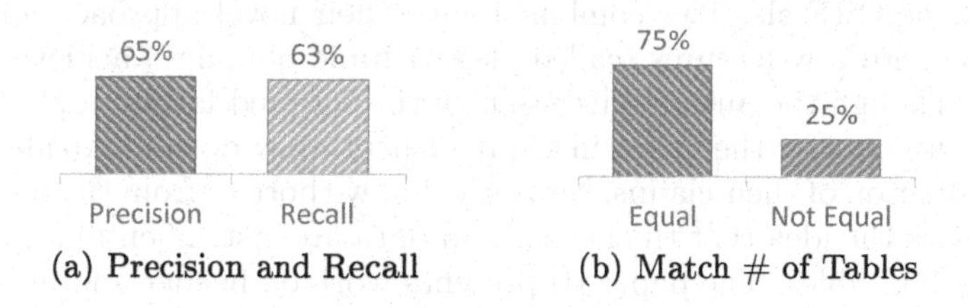

(a) **Precision and Recall** (b) **Match # of Tables**

Fig. 8. Overall results

In Fig. 8 we provide the overall results from our evaluation. In general, it is difficult to assess the performance of our approach, since to the best of our knowledge there is no similar work to directly compare these results with (see also Sect. 5). On the one hand, the precision and recall measures, provided in Fig. 8(a), are lower than expected. On the other hand, the results presented in Fig. 8(b) are satisfactory.

Closing the evaluation remarks, we point out that cells wrongly classified as Data and Header play a considerable role in the performance of TIRS. As we previously mentioned in this section, we exclude Metadata and Derived from our evaluation, and only consider the other three remaining labels. However, misclassifications might introduce Data and Header where there should have been Derived and Metadata cells. The classification results, presented in our previous paper [10], show that 98.7% of the misclassified Derived were labeled Data. For incorrectly classified Metadata, 43% were mistakenly marked as Data and 44% as Header. Such misclassifications often increase the size of T_e, and make it difficult to identify a match (true positive). In other words, T_e and T_a might share all the cells of the true table base (i.e., the annotated Fence and Data regions), but few incorrectly classified cells in T_e effectively reduce the ratio of their overlap (see Eq. 4).

5 Related Work

In this section, we review some of the related work on table identification and layout inference in spreadsheets. At [5] the authors present their work on what they call data frame spreadsheets (i.e., containing attributes or metadata regions on the top/left and a block of numeric values). Using linear-chain, conditional random field (CRF), they perform a sequential classification of rows in the worksheet, in order to infer its layout. Their next immediate focus is extracting the hierarchies found on the top (Header) and left (Attribute) regions. They proceed with the extraction of the data in the form of relational tuples, based on the information they inferred about the structure of data frame. In contrast to us, the authors do not distinguish the individual tables in the worksheet, but rather assume only data-frame like spreadsheets. At [2], the authors present their work on schema extraction for Web tabular data, including spreadsheets. They extensively evaluated various methods for table layout inference, all operating at the row level. The CRF classifier combined with their novel approach for encoding cell features into row features (called "logarithmic binning") achieves the highest scores. Though the authors discuss how the inferred layout could be used to extract the schema for the tables in a spreadsheet, they do not provide an experimental evaluation of their claims. Nevertheless, we borrow from them and enforce with our work the idea that the header and data are instrumental for identifying and processing tables. The paper [1] presents work on header and unit inference for spreadsheets. Unlike us, the authors take a software engineering perspective. They utilize the inferred table structure to identify unit errors in spreadsheets. The authors have defined a set of heuristics based spatial-analysis algorithms, and a framework that allows them to combine the results from these algorithms. Unlike in our work, their spatial use cell features (e.g., content type and formula referencing), rather a pre-assigned labels from a classification task. Additionally, they have evaluated their approach in two datasets, containing 10 and 12 spreadsheets, respectively. They report few errors regarding the header inference, which is one of their main targets. However, the authors do not discuss how their framework performs on the table level. At [6], the authors present DeExcelerator, a framework which takes as input partially structured documents, including spreadsheets, and automatically transforms them into first normal form relations. For spreadsheets, their approach works based on a set of simple rules and heuristics that resulted from a manual study on real-world examples. Their framework operates on different granularity levels (i.e., row, column, and cell), considering the content, formating, and location of the cell/s. They evaluated the performance of their system on a sample of 50 spreadsheets extracted from data.gov, using human judges (10 database students). In contrast, we performed our evaluation in a much larger dataset covering a broader spectrum of spreadsheets.

6 Conclusions and Future Work

In this paper we presented TIRS, a heuristics based framework for table identification in spreadsheet. Unlike related work, we utilized the location and the labels assigned to the cells from a classification method we developed in a previous work. We introduced the concept of label regions and their representation as minimum bounding rectangles. The latter is a vital tool for defining a rich set of heuristics, such as the ones used in TIRS. For our evaluation, we used a large dataset of tables, covering various domains and formats. The results show that we achieve satisfactory performance in the sample of worksheets from FUSE and in worksheets that contain one table. The lowest scores come from ENRON worksheets and worksheets that contain horizontally stacked tables.

We see two possible actions to improve our approach in the future. Firstly, we can come up with more specialized heuristics, taking into account also the domain of the spreadsheets. Here, in addition to the labels, we could utilize various cell features in a similar fashion as in related work. Secondly, we can enrich TIRS with more sophisticated techniques, coming from fields such as machine learning and statistics.

Acknowledgments. This research has been funded by the European Commission through the Erasmus Mundus Joint Doctorate "Information Technologies for Business Intelligence - Doctoral College" (IT4BI-DC).

References

1. Abraham, R., Erwig, M.: Header and unit inference for spreadsheets through spatial analyses. In: VL/HCC 2004, pp. 165–172. IEEE (2004)
2. Adelfio, M.D., Samet, H.: Schema extraction for tabular data on the web. VLDB **6**(6), 421–432 (2013)
3. Barik, T., Lubick, K., Smith, J., Slankas, J., Murphy-Hill, E.: FUSE: a reproducible, extendable, internet-scale corpus of spreadsheets. In: MSR 2015 (2015)
4. Caldwell, D.R.: Unlocking the mysteries of the bounding box (2005)
5. Chen, Z., Cafarella, M.: Automatic web spreadsheet data extraction. In: SSW 2013, p. 1. ACM (2013)
6. Eberius, J., Werner, C., Thiele, M., Braunschweig, K., Dannecker, L., Lehner, W.: DeExcelerator: a framework for extracting relational data from partially structured documents. In: CIKM 2013, pp. 2477–2480. ACM (2013)
7. Eckerson, W.W., Sherman, R.P.: Strategies for managing spreadmarts. Bus. Intell. J. **13**(1), 23–24 (2008)
8. Fisher, M., Rothermel, G.: The EUSES spreadsheet corpus: a shared resource for supporting experimentation with spreadsheet dependability mechanisms. In: SIGSOFT 2005, vol. 30, pp. 1–5. ACM (2005)
9. Hermans, F., Murphy-Hill, E.: Enron's spreadsheets and related emails: a dataset and analysis. In: Proceedings of ICSE 2015. IEEE (2015)
10. Koci, E., Thiele, M., Romero, O., Lehner, W.: A machine learning approach for layout inference in spreadsheets. In: KDIR (2016)
11. Mohanty, H., Bhuyan, P., Chenthati, D.: Big Data: A Primer. Springer India, New Delhi (2015)
12. O'Leary, D.E.: Embedding ai and crowdsourcing in the big data lake. IEEE Intelligent Systems **29**(5), 70–73 (2014)
13. Papadias, D., Theodoridis, Y.: Spatial relations, minimum bounding rectangles, and spatial data structures. International Journal of Geographical Information Science **11**(2), 111–138 (1997)
14. Ting, K.M.: Precision and recall. In: Encyclopedia of machine learning, pp. 781–781. Springer (2011)

Process Discovery

Data-Driven Process Discovery - Revealing Conditional Infrequent Behavior from Event Logs

Felix Mannhardt[1(✉)], Massimiliano de Leoni[1],
Hajo A. Reijers[1,2], and Wil M.P. van der Aalst[1]

[1] Eindhoven University of Technology, Eindhoven, The Netherlands
{f.mannhardt,m.d.leoni,h.a.reijers,w.m.p.v.d.aalst}@tue.nl
[2] Vrije Universiteit Amsterdam, Amsterdam, The Netherlands

Abstract. Process discovery methods automatically infer process models from event logs. Often, event logs contain so-called noise, e.g., infrequent outliers or recording errors, which obscure the main behavior of the process. Existing methods filter this noise based on the frequency of event labels: infrequent paths and activities are excluded. However, infrequent behavior may reveal important insights into the process. Thus, not all infrequent behavior should be considered as noise. This paper proposes the Data-aware Heuristic Miner (DHM), a process discovery method that uses the data attributes to distinguish infrequent paths from random noise by using classification techniques. Data- and control-flow of the process are discovered together. We show that the DHM is, to some degree, robust against random noise and reveals data-driven decisions, which are filtered by other discovery methods. The DHM has been successfully tested on several real-life event logs, two of which we present in this paper.

Keywords: Process mining · Process discovery · Event logs · Noise · Rules

1 Introduction

Process models are used by organizations to document, specify, and analyze their processes [1]. A process model describes the expected behavior of a process in terms of its activities (i.e., units of work) and their ordering. Most contemporary processes are supported by information systems. Often, those systems record information about the execution of processes in databases. With the abundance of such data, there is a growing interest in *process discovery* [2], i.e., revealing the actual execution of processes from events. Process discovery methods automatically infer process models from *event logs*.

One important challenge for process discovery methods is to handle event logs with *noise* [2,3]. In practice, event logs often contain noise, e.g., out-of-order events, exceptional behavior, or recording errors [4]. Including all such infrequent events in the process discovery often leads to unusable, complex models. Therefore, *noise filtering methods* that distinguish noise from the regular behavior of the process may be useful.

Some of the early techniques for process discovery assumed noise-free event logs (e.g., the Alpha algorithm [5] and the region based approaches [6]). These techniques are of limited use in real-life settings. Most of the more recent and more sophisticated

E. Dubois and K. Pohl (Eds.): CAiSE 2017, LNCS 10253, pp. 545–560, 2017.
DOI: 10.1007/978-3-319-59536-8_34

process discovery methods support noise filtering [3]. Existing noise-filtering methods are based on frequencies [7–10], machine-learning techniques [11,12], genetic algorithms [13], or probabilistic models [14,15]. All of those methods focus on the *control-flow perspective* (i.e., the event labels) when filtering noise. Dedicated noise filtering methods [16,17] are also based on frequencies.

However, processes are often governed by rules. Decision are taken on the basis of available data, available resources, and the process context. Some paths may be executed infrequently because the corresponding conditions are rarely fulfilled. *Existing methods based solely on the control-flow perspective would disregard such infrequent behavior as noise.* However, some infrequent behavior may be characterized by very deterministic rules, and, thus, be of great interest to process analysts (e.g., in the context of risks and fraud). For example, shortcuts in a process might only be taken by a specific resource, undesired behavior might be subject to conditions, and infrequently actions might be legitimate only for special types of cases. These kind of events should not be set aside as *noise*. Methods exist to discover such decision rules [18–20] but all rely on a previously discovered process model of the process. Hence, existing methods do not leverage the full potential of the *data perspective*. Data- and control-flow need to be discovered together. Recent work on declarative process discovery [21] considers the data perspective. However, similar to association rule mining, sets of rules rather than full process models are returned.

In this work, we propose the Data-aware Heuristic Miner (DHM), which takes the data perspective into account when discovering the control flow of a process. The DHM uses classification techniques to reveal data dependencies between activities, and uses these data dependencies to *distinguish noise from infrequent conditional behavior*. It returns process models that yield a better insight into the data perspective of processes by revealing hidden data dependencies while filtering random noise. The evaluation on real-life cases shows that the DHM reveals additional insights *not* returned by state-of-the-art process discovery methods. We confirmed the discovered conditions with a domain expert for one of the real-life event logs. The experiment on the synthetic data shows that the DHM is resilient to a certain degree of randomly injected noise, which is not characterized by data conditions. It rediscovers the original model, whereas earlier techniques either show too much, or too little behavior. The *contribution of this paper* is a process discovery method that is able to *distill important information from infrequent behavior* instead of dismissing it as noise.

The remainder of this paper is structured as follows. We start by introducing the problem with an example in Sect. 2. Then, required preliminaries are introduced in Sect. 3. Section 4 presents our novel process discovery method. We evaluate our method using both synthetic and real-life data in Sect. 5. Finally, Sect. 6 concludes the paper.

2 Problem Description

Figure 1 shows a simplified process from the health care domain. We use this example in the paper to motivate the relevance of the data perspective for noise filtering. When patients arrive at the hospital they are assigned a triage priority, registered and assigned to a responsible nurse. Only in exceptional cases, patients are assigned the *white* triage priority. Those patients typically, leave the emergency ward directly after registration since their injuries do not require the attendance of a doctor Ⓐ. All other patients are admitted to the emergency ward. While patients are in the emergency ward a nurse periodically checks their condition. In parallel to this, for the group of patients under consideration, an X-ray is taken and a doctor visits the patient. There are two different work practices regarding these two activities. Normally, the doctor visits the patients after which the X-Ray is taken. One particular nurse (Alice) re-sequences these activities in the reversed order to improve the process: first the X-ray is taken and, only thereafter, the doctor visits the patient Ⓑ. As this work practice is only followed by one nurse, it is observed less frequently. Afterwards, the doctor visits the patient one more time and decides on the type of dismissal. Then, the patient is prepared for a possible transfer. For patients with the *out* dismissal type an ambulance needs to be organized Ⓒ. This process contains three examples of infrequent, data-dependent behavior: Ⓐ a data-dependent path, Ⓑ data-dependent re-sequencing, and Ⓒ a data-dependent activity. The goal of our work is to rediscover such behavior, while ignoring random noise.

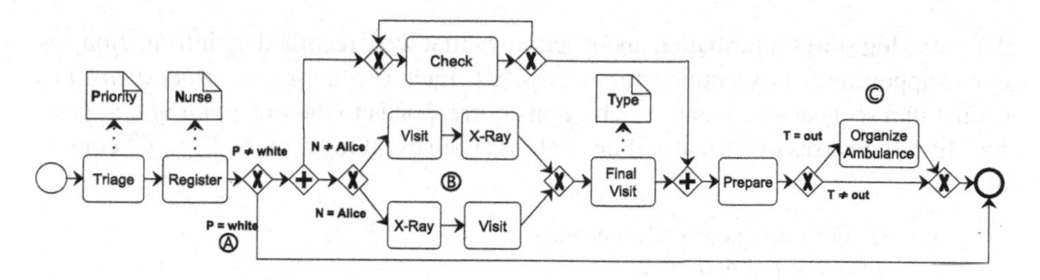

Fig. 1. A simplified process in BPMN notation from the emergency ward of a hospital, which is used as motivating example throughout this paper.

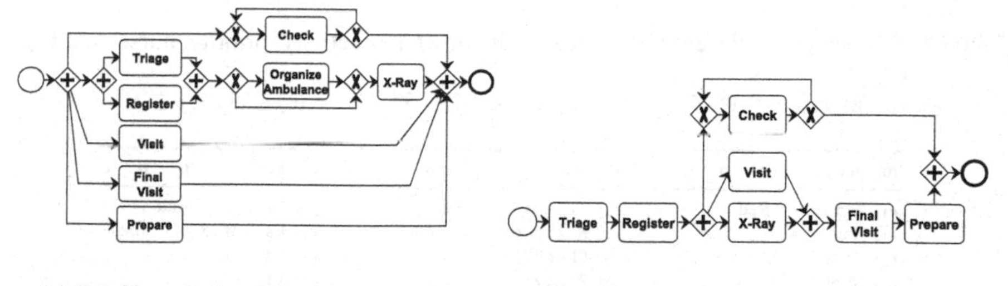

(a) IM filters little of the injected noise and fails to reveal behavior Ⓐ and Ⓑ.

(b) HM filters the injected noise well, but fails to show behavior Ⓐ, Ⓑ and Ⓒ.

Fig. 2. Models discovered by IM and HM on an event log generated from the example process.

Assume an event log of the process in Fig. 1 obtained from the information systems of the hospital. As motivated in the introduction, it is likely that this event log contains noise. We applied both the Heuristic Miner (HM) [8] and the Inductive Miner (IM) [9] as representatives of discovery methods supporting noise filtering on such an event log with a controlled degree of noise[1]. Figure 2 shows the resulting process models in BPMN notation. Clearly, both methods are unaware of the data perspective. Therefore, they fail to distinguish between random noise and the infrequent data-dependent behavior Ⓐ, Ⓑ, and Ⓒ. It might be possible to tweak the parameters of the algorithms such that more behavior is revealed (e.g., through grid search). Still, finding the correct parameter setting that does not include unrelated noise requires deep knowledge about the underlying process. Therefore, this is often not feasible. Moreover, it is not possible to reveal the infrequent data-dependent behavior by using decision mining techniques. Those techniques can only reveal decision rules for paths that are reflected in the process model, thus low-frequent but deterministic behavior remains undetected.

In the remainder of this paper, we describe the DHM, which extends the ideas of the HM with the use of classification techniques to reveal data dependencies. Our method, indeed, rediscovers the behavior of the process as shown in Fig. 1.

3 Preliminaries

An **event log** stores information about activities that were recorded by information systems supporting the execution of a process [2]. Each execution of a *process instance* results in a sequence of events. Each events corresponds to the *execution of one activity*. Given universes of attributes A and values U, an event log $L = (E, \Sigma, \#, \mathscr{L})$ consists of:

- E a finite set of unique event identifiers;
- $\Sigma \subseteq U$ a finite set of activities;
- $\# : E \to (A \not\to U)$ obtains the attribute values recorded for an event;
- $\mathscr{L} \subseteq E^*$ the set of traces over E. A trace $\sigma \in \mathscr{L}$ records the sequence of events for one process instance. Each event occurs only in a single trace.

Table 1. Three traces of the example process with attributes **act**ivity, **p**riority, **n**urse, and **t**ype.

(a) Trace $\sigma_1 \in \mathscr{L}$

id	act	p	n	t
e_{11}	Triage	Red		
e_{12}	Register		Joe	
e_{13}	Check			
e_{14}	Check			
e_{15}	Check			
e_{16}	Visit			
e_{17}	X-Ray			
e_{18}	F. Visit			ICU
e_{19}	Prepare			

(b) Trace $\sigma_2 \in \mathscr{L}$

id	act	p	n	t
e_{21}	Triage	Red		
e_{22}	Register		Alice	
e_{23}	Check			
e_{24}	X-Ray			
e_{25}	Visit			
e_{26}	Check			
e_{27}	F. Visit			out
e_{28}	Prepare			
e_{29}	Org. Amb.			

(c) Trace $\sigma_3 \in \mathscr{L}$

id	act	p	n	t
e_{31}	Triage	Red		
e_{32}	Register		Joe	
e_{33}	Check			
e_{34}	Visit			
e_{35}	X-Ray			
e_{36}	Check			
e_{37}	Check			
e_{38}	F. Visit			NC
e_{39}	Prepare			

Given an event $e \in E$, we write $\#_a(e) \in U$ to obtain the value $u \in U$ recorded for attribute $a \in A$. We require events to record at least the activity attribute: $\#_{act}(e) \in \Sigma$

[1] Here, in 5% of the cases one additional event was randomly executed out of the original order.

is the *name of the activity* that caused the event. Given a trace $\langle e_1,\ldots,e_n\rangle \in \mathscr{L}$, we define $val : E \to (A \not\to U)$ to collect the *latest attribute values* recorded before an event occurred, i.e., $val(e_i) = val(e_{i-1}) \oplus \#(e_{i-1})$ with special case $val(e_1) = f_\varnothing$.[2] We denote the *predecessor event* in the trace by ${}^\bullet(e_i) = e_{i-1}$ with special case ${}^\bullet(e_1) = \perp$. Finally, in the remainder of this paper, we assume that a particular event log $L = (E,\Sigma,\#,\mathscr{L})$ exists to avoid unnecessary notation.

Example 1. Table 1 shows three traces $\sigma_1,\sigma_2,\sigma_3 \in \mathscr{L}$ based on the process shown in Fig. 1. Each event has a unique identifier. We can identify the activity of event e_{11} as $\#_{act}(e_{11}) = Triage$. Moreover, event e_{11} writes the attribute value $\#_{Priority}(e_{11}) = \text{Red}$. We obtain the latest attribute values recorded before e_{18} occurred as $val(e_{18}) = f$, with $f(Priority) = \text{Red}$ and $f(Nurse) = \text{Joe}$.

Our method uses **Causal nets (C-nets)** to represent the discovered process model [8, 22]. A C-net is a tuple $(\Sigma, s_i, s_o, D, I, O)$ where:

- Σ is a finite set of activities;
- $s_i \in \Sigma$ is the unique start activity;
- $s_o \in \Sigma$ is the unique end activity;
- $D \subseteq \Sigma \times \Sigma$ is the dependency relation;
- $B = \{X \subseteq \mathscr{P}(\Sigma) \mid X = \{\varnothing\} \vee \varnothing \notin X\}$ are possible bindings;[3]
- $I \in \Sigma \to B$ is the set of input bindings per activity;
- $O \in \Sigma \to B$ is the set of output bindings per activity,

such that the dependency relations match the input and output bindings, i.e., $D = \{(s_1,s_2) \in \Sigma\times\Sigma \mid s_1 \in \bigcup_{\beta\in I(s_2)} \beta \wedge s_2 \in \bigcup_{\beta\in O(s_1)} \beta\}$. We require C-nets to have a unique start and end activity, i.e., $\{s_i\} = \{s \in \Sigma \mid I(s) = \{\varnothing\}\}$ $\{s_o\} = \{s \in \Sigma \mid O(s) = \{\varnothing\}\}$. The input and output binding functions of a C-net define its language. We describe the C-net semantics by example, the full semantics are described in [22].

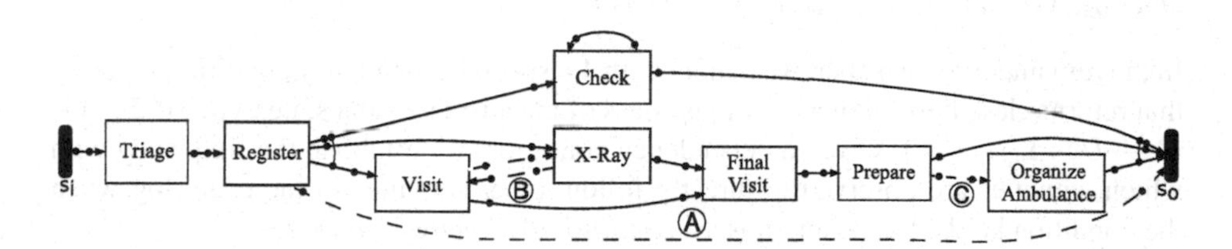

Fig. 3. A causal net (C-net) of the example process. Activities are depicted with boxes, the dependency relations as edges, and the binding functions as black dots on the edges. The unique start and end activities are shown as black boxes. The dotted edges are explained in Sect. 5.

Example 2. Figure 3 shows how the example from Fig. 1 can be modeled as C-net. Activities are depicted with boxes and dependency relations as edges. There are unique start and end activities: s_i and s_o. Output and input bindings are depicted by black dots

[2] $f \oplus g$ denotes the overriding union of f and g, and $f_\varnothing : \varnothing \to U$ is the empty function.
[3] $\mathscr{P}(\Sigma)$ denotes the powerset of set Σ.

on the edges in Fig. 3. Bindings indicate which combinations of activities can precede or follow a given activity. Connected dots show activities belonging to the same binding. We abbreviate activity names by using the first letter. For example, after activity s_i, activities T and R follow in a sequence, i.e., $O(s_i) = \{\{T\}\}$, $I(T) = \{\{s_i\}\}$ and $O(T) = \{\{R\}\}, I(R) = \{\{T\}\}$. Then, there are multiple alternative choices. Three output bindings are defined for R: $O(R) = \{\{s_o\}, \{C,X\}, \{C,V\}\}$. Each set of activities represents a possible choice of following activities (XOR gateway). Either only s_o, or both C and X, or both C and V need to happen. Activities in the same set can be executed in parallel (AND gateway).

4 Data-Driven Process Discovery

The DHM builds on the insight that infrequent but data-dependent process behavior is of great interest to process analysts and, thus, should not be disregarded as noise. We extend the ideas of the HM [8] with a measure for *conditional dependency*.

4.1 Data-Aware Dependency Measure

To discover data-dependent behavior in the event log, we make use of classification techniques (e.g., decision trees). More specifically, we rely on binary classifiers predicting directly-follows relations based on attribute values recorded in the event log. We denote these classifiers as *dependency conditions*.

Definition 1 (Dependency conditions). *Given universes of attributes A, values U, and activities $\Sigma \subseteq U$, we define the dependency conditions $C \in (\Sigma \times \Sigma) \to ((A \not\rightarrow U) \to \{0,1\})$. A* dependency condition *$C_{a,b}(x) = (C(a,b))(x)$ is a binary classifier that predicts whether an event of activity a is directly followed by an event of activity b for the attribute values $x \in (A \not\rightarrow U)$, i.e., $C_{a,b}(x) = 1$ when* **b** *is predicted to directly follow* **a** *and $C_{a,b}(x) = 0$ when a* different *activity is predicted.*

In the remainder of the paper, we denote with **1** a special dependency condition function that returns classifiers predicting 1 regardless of the attribute values, i.e., $\forall a,b \in \Sigma, \forall x \in (A \not\rightarrow U) : \mathbf{1}_{a,b}(x) = 1$. Given a dependency condition, we establish the frequency with which activities are observed to directly follow other activities in the event log when the condition holds. We denote this as: *conditional directly follows*.

Definition 2 (Conditional directly follows relation). *Given activities $a,b \in \Sigma$ and dependency conditions C, we write $a >^{C,L} b$ if and only if an execution of activity a with the latest attribute values x is* directly followed *by an execution of activity b under dependency condition $C_{a,b}(x)$. We denote the frequency of a conditional directly follows relation $a >^{C,L} b$ in the event log as:*

$$|a >^{C,L} b| = |\{e \in E \mid \#_{act}({}^{\bullet}(e)) = a \wedge {}^{\bullet}(e) \neq \perp \wedge \#_{act}(e) = b \\ \wedge C_{a,b}(val(e)) = 1\}|.$$

Now, we define a data-aware variant of the dependency measure proposed by the HM.

Definition 3 (Conditional dependency measure). *Given activities $a, b \in \Sigma$ and dependency conditions C. We define $a \Rightarrow^{C,L} b : \Sigma \times \Sigma \rightarrow [-1,1]$ as the strength of the causal dependency from a to b under condition $C_{a,b}$ in the event log:*

$$a \Rightarrow^{C,L} b = \begin{cases} \frac{|a >^{C,L} b| - |b >^{C,L} a|}{|a >^{C,L} b| + |b >^{C,L} a| + 1} & for\ a \neq b, \\ \frac{|a >^{C,L} a|}{|a >^{C,L} a| + 1} & otherwise. \end{cases}$$

The intuition behind the data-aware variant of these measures is that a relation (a,b) should be included in the dependency relations of the discovered causal net when it is clearly characterized by a certain dependency condition $C_{a,b}$.

Example 3. Consider an event log L with 50 traces like σ_1, 50 traces like σ_2 and 50 traces like σ_3 as shown in Table 1. We determine the conditional dependency measure $X \Rightarrow^{C,L} V$ from activity X-Ray (X) to activity Visit (V). We assume that condition $C_{X,V}(v)$ returns 1 only if attribute *Nurse* values takes on the value Alice. Then, we obtain the number of times X is directly followed by V under condition $C_{X,V}$ as $|X >^{C,L} V| = 50$, and the number of times V is directly followed by X under conditions C as $|V >^{C,L} X| = 0$. Therefore, the conditional dependency measure under conditions C is $X \Rightarrow^{C,L} V = \frac{50-0}{50+0+1} \approx 0.98$. This indicates a strong dependency relation from activity X to activity V under condition $C_{X,V}$. By contrast, if we consider the unconditional dependency measure $X \Rightarrow^{1,L} V$, then we obtain $\frac{50-100}{50+100+1} \approx -0.33$. Thus, when disregarding the data perspective, both activities appear to be executed in parallel.

4.2 Discovering Data Conditions

We described the *conditional directly-follows relation* and the *conditional dependency measure*. We use the latter measure to determine which relations should be included in the C-net. Both concepts rely on discovered *dependency conditions*. Here, we describe how to train a classifier that can be used as dependency condition. We build a set of training instances for every combination of activities $(a,b) \in \Sigma \times \Sigma$.

In the remainder, $\mathbb{B}(X)$ denotes the set of all multi-sets over a set X. We use $X = [a^2, b]$ as a short-hand notation to denote the multi-set $X = [a,a,b]$, and $\uplus$ to denote the sum of two multi-sets, i.e., $X \uplus [b,c] = [a^2, b^2, c]$.

Definition 4 (Training Instances). *Given a source activity $a \in \Sigma$, a candidate activity $b \in \Sigma$, and a dependency threshold $\theta_{dep} \in [0,1]$. Let $a^\bullet \subseteq \Sigma$ be the set of activities s that directly follow a in the event log with an unconditional dependency measure above the threshold θ_{dep}, i.e., $a^\bullet = \{s \in \Sigma \mid a \Rightarrow^{1,L} s \geq \theta_{dep}\}$. We collect those events $X_{L,a,b} \subseteq E$ that directly follow an execution of* **a** *in the event log, and refer to activities in* $\mathbf{a}^\bullet$*, or to the candidate activity* **b**, *i.e., $X_{L,a,b} = \{e \in E \mid {}^\bullet(e) = a \land \#_{act}(e) \in a^\bullet \cup \{b\}\}$. Function $T_{L,\theta_{dep}} \in (\Sigma \times \Sigma) \rightarrow \mathbb{B}((A \not\rightarrow U) \times \{1,0\})$ returns the multi-set of training instances:*

$$T_{L,\theta_{dep}}(a,b) = \biguplus_{e \in X_{L,a,b}} [(val(e), cl(e))] \text{ with } cl(e) = \begin{cases} 1, & for\ \#_{act}(e) = b \\ 0, & for\ \#_{act}(e) \neq b \end{cases}$$

Conceptually, our method is independent of the used classification algorithm. Concretely, we employ decision trees (C4.5) [23] as an efficient method that result in human interpretable conditions. We build the dependency conditions C by assembling a set of training instances $T_{L,\theta_{dep}}(a,b)$ and training a decision tree for each possible relation $(a,b) \in \Sigma \times \Sigma$. Only good dependency conditions with discriminative power are used later on. We use a score $q(C_{a,b}) \in [0,1]$ to determine the quality of a particular condition $C_{a,b}$. There are many possible performance measures for binary classification algorithm that can be used together with our method. None of the measures is universally accepted, the correct choice depends on the concrete application area.

We opted for Cohen's kappa (κ) [24], which indicates whether the prediction was better than a prediction by chance (i.e., for $\kappa > 0$). Kappa favors a good prediction performance on the minority class, which is a desirable property in our setting. Moreover, it has been recommended for nonparametric binary classifiers, such as C4.5, on data with imbalanced class priors [25]. However, we do *not* claim κ to be the best measure and, thus, foresee other measures to be plugged-in depending on the application area.

Example 4. Consider the dependency threshold $\theta_{dep} = 0.9$ and an event log containing 150 traces, where 50 traces record the same values as σ_1, 50 traces the same values as σ_2 and 50 traces the same values as σ_3. We train a classifier for the dependency condition $C_{X,V}$, i.e., the dependency relation from X-Ray (X) to Visit (V) using the training instances $T_{L,\theta_{dep}}(X,V)$. The training instances are $T_{L,\theta_{dep}}(X,V) = [(v_1,\text{Final Visit})^{50},(v_2,\text{Visit})^{50}]$ with attribute value functions $v_1(P) = \text{Red}$, $v_1(N) = \text{Joe}$ and $v_2(P) = \text{Red}$, $v_2(N) = \text{Alice}$. Please note that there is no instance with the activity Check (C) since the unconditional dependency measure $X \Rightarrow^{1,L} C$ is below the threshold of 0.9. Therefore, the instances based on trace σ_3 are not included as we already know that activity C is in parallel to X. We train a C4.5 decision tree and obtain the dependency condition $C_{X,V}$ with $C_{X,V}(v_2) = 1$ and $C_{X,V}(v_1) = 0$.

4.3 Data-Driven Discovery of Causal Nets

We describe the DHM method that builds C-nets based on *conditional dependencies*. The DHM supports four user-specified thresholds that can be used to tune the noise filtering capabilities to specific needs of the user. All thresholds range between 0 and 1:

- θ_{obs}, the observation threshold, which controls the relative frequency of relations;
- θ_{dep}, the dependency threshold, which controls the strength of causal dependencies;
- θ_{bin}, the binding threshold, which controls the number of bindings;
- θ_{con}, the condition threshold, which controls the quality of data-dependencies.

We discover a C-net $(\Sigma, s_i, s_o, D, I, O)$ from event log $L = (E, \Sigma, \#, \mathscr{L})$ and thresholds $\theta_{obs}, \theta_{dep}, \theta_{bin}, \theta_{con}$ in the following steps.

1. We want to ensure that the resulting C-net has a **unique start and end activity**. Therefore, we add artificial start and end events to all traces, i.e., $\forall_{\sigma \in \mathscr{L}}(\sigma = (e_i, e_1, \ldots, e_n, e_o) \wedge \#_{act}(e_i) = s_i \wedge \#_{act}(e_o) = s_o)$ and $\Sigma = \Sigma \cup \{s_i, s_o\}$.

2. We build the set of standard **dependency relations** as follows:

$$D = \{(a,b) \in \Sigma \times \Sigma \mid a \Rightarrow^{1,L} b \geq \theta_{dep} \wedge \frac{|a >^{1,L} b|}{|\mathscr{L}|} \geq \theta_{obs}\}.$$

3. We **discover the dependency conditions** C by training classifiers for each pair $(a,b) \in \Sigma \times \Sigma$ using the training instances $T_{L,\theta_{dep}}(a,b)$.
4. We add the **conditional dependency relations** to D. We use θ_{con} instead of θ_{obs} to obtain infrequent, high-quality data conditions:

$$D = D \cup \{(a,b) \in \Sigma \times \Sigma \mid q(C_{a,b}) \geq \theta_{con} \wedge a \Rightarrow^{C,L} b \geq \theta_{dep}\}.$$

5. Some activities $s \in \Sigma$ might not have a predecessor or successor in the directed graph induced by D. Intuitively, each task in a process should have a cause (predecessor) and an effect (successor) [8], all tasks in **the C-net should be connected**. Therefore, we propose two alternative heuristics to enforce this:
   - *all-task-connected heuristic* proposed by the HM [8], or
   - the *accepted-task-connected heuristic*, a new heuristic.

   Here, we describe the new *accepted-task-connected heuristic*. We repeatedly connect only those activities that are already part of the dependency graph using their best neighboring activities until all activities have a cause and an effect. Then, set $\overline{D}$ of relations necessary to connect all activities accepted so far is:

$$\overline{D} = \{(a,b) \in \Sigma \times \Sigma \mid (\nexists x\, (a,x) \in D \wedge \forall y\, (a \Rightarrow^{1,L} b) \geq (a \Rightarrow^{1,L} y)) \\ \vee (\nexists x\, (x,b) \in D \wedge \forall y\, (a \Rightarrow^{1,L} b) \geq (y \Rightarrow^{1,L} b)\}.$$

   We extend the dependency relations with the new relations, i.e., $D = D \cup \overline{D}$. There might be new, unconnected activities in D. Therefore, we *repeat adding the best neighboring activities* until set $\overline{D}$ is empty.
6. We discover the **input and output binding functions** of the C-net. For the output binding function $O(a)$ of an activity $a \in \Sigma$, we need to determine which executions of $b \in \Sigma$ (with $(a,b) \in D$) were caused by an execution of activity **a**. We use the heuristic proposed by the HM [8] and repeat it for completeness. The heuristic considers activity **b** to be caused by activity **a** only if it is the nearest activity that *may have caused* **b**. Any other activity **s** executed in between **a** and **b** should not be a possible cause of **b**, i.e., $(s,b) \notin D$. Given a trace $\sigma = \langle e_1, \ldots, e_i, \ldots, e_n \rangle \in \mathscr{L}$, the set of activities $\overline{O}(e_i) \subseteq \Sigma$ that were caused by an event e_i is:

$$\overline{O}(e_i) = \{b \in \Sigma \mid \#_{act}(e_i) = a \\ \wedge \exists_{i<j \leq n}\, \#_{act}(e_j) = b \wedge (a,b) \in D \\ \wedge \forall_{i<k<j}\, (\#_{act}(e_k), b) \notin D\}.$$

   We determine the frequency $|o|_{L,a} \in \mathbb{N}$ of an output binding $o \subseteq \Sigma$ for activity $a \in \Sigma$ in the event log L as:

$$|o|_{L,a} = \left|\{e \in E \mid \#_{act}(e) = a \wedge \overline{O}(e) = o\}\right|.$$

Then, we build the complete multi-set of output bindings with the most frequent bindings. Those bindings that fulfill the user-specified binding threshold θ_{bin}:

$$O(a) = \{o \subseteq \Sigma \mid \frac{|o|_{L,a}}{max_{\overline{o} \subseteq \Sigma}(|\overline{o}|_{L,a})} \geq \theta_{bin}\}.$$

The input binding function I is obtained by reversing the same approach.

Within the scope of this paper, we do not elaborate on the other heuristics of the HM [8], such as long-distance, length-two loops, and the relative-to-best. Those heuristics and improvements to the HM described by the Fodina miner [26] can be used together with the DHM. The choice which heuristics to apply highly depends on the process at hand. For example, the *all-task-connected heuristic* results in a process model with all observed activities regardless of the chosen observation frequency threshold θ_{obs}. Even activities that are only observed once are added. This might not be desirable as very infrequent activities might be considered as noise. Therefore, we introduced the new accepted-task-connected heuristic.

5 Evaluation

We implemented the DHM in the open-source framework ProM[4]. The package *Data-AwareCNetMiner* provides a *highly interactive tool*, which allows to quickly discover C-nets for different parameter settings and to explore the discovered data dependencies. C-nets can be converted to Petri nets or BPMN models. Therefore, existing tools can be used on the results. We applied our method to both synthetic and real-life event logs.

5.1 Synthetic - Handling Noise

Event Log and Methods. We generated an event log with 100,000 traces and approximately 900,000 events by simulating the process model shown in Fig. 3. There are three data attributes: Priority (P), Nurse (N), and Type (T). We adjust the frequency distributions of these attributes such that paths A, B, and C in model Fig. 3 are recorded infrequently. Specifically, only 1.4% of the traces record $P = white$, 19.1% of the traces record $N = Alice$, and 4.3% of the traces record $T = out$. We compared three methods: our proposed method (DHM), the heuristic miner with frequency filtering (HMF), and the heuristic miner without frequency filtering (HMA). All three methods, used thresholds $\theta_{obs} = 0.06$ (0.0 for HMA), $\theta_{dep} = 0.9$, $\theta_{bin} = 0.1$, $\theta_{con} = 0.5$ together with the *accepted-task-connected heuristic*. We used C4.5 as classifier and estimated its performance using 10 times 10-fold cross validation.

Experimental Design. The experiment should evaluate the noise filtering capabilities of our method. Therefore, we injected noise into the event log by randomly adding *one additional event* to an increasing number of traces.[5] Then, we compared the discovered dependency relations with those of the reference model (Fig. 3) in terms of graph

[4] The package *DataAwareCNetMiner* can be downloaded from http://promtools.org.

[5] The synthetic event logs can be downloaded from http://dx.doi.org/10.4121/uuid:32cad43f-8bb9-46af-8333-48aae2bea037.

edit distance (GED) [27]. We did not use fitness, precision, or behavioral comparison measures as those would not be applicable in this setting. Fitness and precision do not measure the performance wrt. the reference model (gold standard). Moreover, when the discovered models are not sound (e.g., having a deadlock), the behavior may be undefined even when the model is close to the original. Behavioral measures would also fail to distinguish the difference between the data-dependent re-sequencing of activities (pattern Ⓒ in Fig. 3) and simple parallelism. For example, both in Fig. 3 and in Fig. 2(b) activities `Visit` and `X-Ray` are behaviorally in parallel.

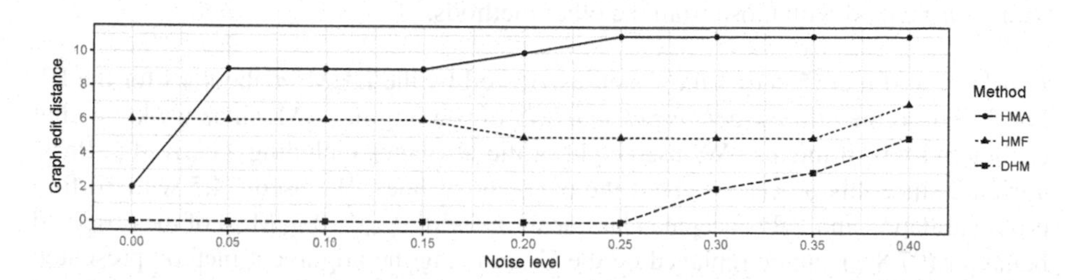

Fig. 4. Graph edit distances between the dependency relations discovered by the compared methods and the reference dependency relations for varying amounts of injected noise.

Results. All models could be discovered in about 3 s using 2 GB of memory. Our method was able to rediscover the conditional relations Ⓐ, Ⓑ and Ⓒ, i.e., the red edges in Fig. 3. The original rules $P = white$ and $T = out$ were discovered for relations Ⓐ and Ⓑ. For path Ⓒ, two rules were discovered: $N = Alice$ for the edge from X-Ray to Visit and $N \neq Alice$ for the edge from Visit to X-Ray. Our method discovered the data-dependent re-sequencing of activities Visit to X-Ray, whereas the standard HM (cf. BPMN model in Fig. 2(b)) considered both activities as parallel. Figure 4 shows the result of the GED measurement for noise levels ranging from 0% to 40%. Our method (DHM) handles the added noise well until 25% of the traces were modified. The HM with frequency-based noise filtering (method HMF) is also unaffected by the injected noise. However, it fails to discover the reference model even without noise, as shown in Fig. 2(b). The GED of the method HMF improves after injecting noise in 20% of the traces because the frequency of relation Ⓒ increases by chance. When lowering the observation frequency threshold (method HMA), the injected noise quickly affects the discovery and undesirable dependencies appear. We did not include the IM in Fig. 4, as it returns models with a different structure. However, the models returned by the IM are already undesirable for an event log with 5% noise, c.f., Fig. 2(a).

5.2 Real-Life - Revealing Data Dependencies

We used two real-life event logs to show that our method can reveal infrequent behavior in a practical setting. Using the DHM important conditional dependencies can be found where existing methods abstract away such dependencies.

Data and Methods. The *Road Fines* (RF) event log was recorded by an information system that handles road-traffic fines by an Italian local police force [28,29]. This event log contains about 150,000 cases, 500,000 events, and 9 data attributes. The *Hospital Billing* (HB) event log was obtained from the ERP system of a hospital. It contains 100,000 cases with 550,000 events and 38 data attributes related to the billing of medical services. We applied the proposed method (DHM), the HM with the same frequency filter settings (HMF) and the Inductive Miner (IM) to both event logs. Without a reference model and knowledge about expected noise levels, we could not compare the discovered models to a gold standard. Therefore, we compare the novel insights obtained by using our method with those from the other methods.

Road Fines. Figure 5 shows the C-net discovered by the DHM in about 4 s for the RF log. We used the *all-task-connected heuristic* of the original HM, since we know that each activity is of interest. We used eight of the attributes including a derived `isPaid` attribute since this process is about the payment of fines. We used C4.5 with 10-fold cross validation and only accepted classifications with $\theta_{con} \geq 0.5$. Most of the observed behavior (97.8%) can be replayed on the C-net using the alignment method presented in [22]. Our method reveals three additional relations (red edges), which are numbered in Fig. 5. Table 2 lists the conditional data-dependency measure, the frequency, as well as quality and used attributes of the obtained dependency condition for each relation. The first two relations target activity *Add Penalty* and both have a very good quality score. The decision rule for relation ① mainly depends on the value of the `dismissal` attribute. Cases with values `G` do not receive a penalty, whereas cases with value `NIL` receive a penalty depending on the fine amount, the number of points, and the article. According to [29] this is to be expected as those cases are dismissed by the judge. Relation ② is mainly based on the attribute `isPaid`. Unpaid fines that have with a small `amount` of less than 35 EUR receive a penalty. Relation ③ was discovered for cases with a `dismissal` value of # or G. It is to be expected that the process finishes for cases with this code, since those cases are dismissed by the prefecture. Interestingly, this relation also occurs for cases with a `dismissal` value of NIL and high postal expenses. This should not happen, since those fines still need to be paid [29]. The DHM revealed three data dependencies that give more insights into the recorded behavior without obstructing the process model with infrequent noise. In the model obtained by IM none of the three relations are directly visible. Therefore, current decision mining techniques would not be able to discover the conditions.

Hospital Billing. Figure 6 shows the C-net discovered by the DHM in about 3 s for the HB event log. The discovered model fits 97% of the observed behavior. We used the new *accepted-task-connected heuristic* since not all of the 21 activities may be of interest. We discovered the model using C4.5 on a subset of 13 attributes. Here, the quality threshold is set to $\theta_{con} \geq 0.6$ and the quality is, again, determined by 10-fold cross validation. Compared to the model returned by the HMF, our method revealed six additional dependencies. Again, we numbered these relations in Fig. 6, and list some key statistics in Table 3. For the purpose of this evaluation, we discussed the discovered conditional dependencies with a domain expert from the hospital who works in this process. Relation ① is based on a special `closeCode` that is used when nothing can be billed and,

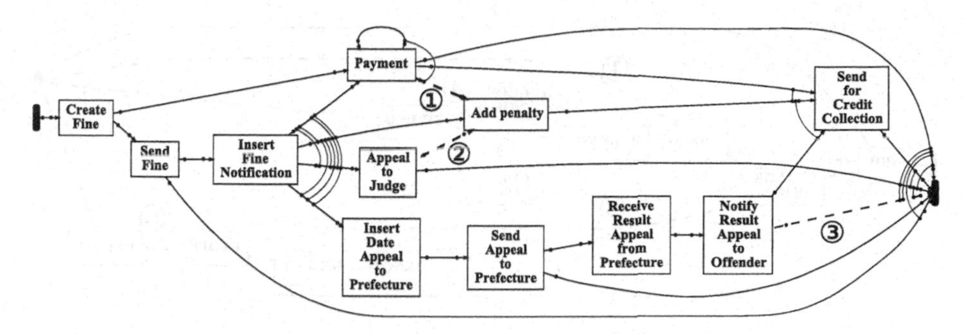

Fig. 5. Process model discovered for the RF log. The numbered edges were added by our method.

Table 2. Dependency conditions discovered for the RF log.

Nr	Source	Target	Count	Quality	Dependency	Used Attributes
1	Appeal to judge	Add penalty	279	0.86	0.93	amount, dismissal, points, article
2	Payment	Add penalty	3,629	0.89	1	amount, isPaid
3	Not. Res. Appeal to Off	End	83	0.56	0.98	dismissal, expense

hence, the process ends. Relation ② occurs mostly for two specific `caseType` values. According to the domain expert both case types correspond to exceptional cases: one is used for intensive care and the other for cases for which codes cannot be obtained (*Code Nok*). Relation ③ is, again, related to a specific `caseType`. This type is used for intensive-care activities as well and, often, does not require a code to be obtained. Relation ④ is also mainly related to the `caseType` and to some degree to the medical `specialty`. Both relation ⑤ and relation ⑥ are conditional to the attribute `closed`, which indicates whether the invoice is closed or not. Clearly, deleted cases should not be in the closed status, whereas reopened cases with a change in diagnosis can be eventually closed in the future. The process model discovered by the DHM provides a balanced view on the interesting infrequent paths of the billing process together with the more frequent, regular behavior. Moreover, additional insight is provided by revealing the conditions with which infrequent paths occur. Again, the model returned by the IM did not include any of the six paths.

Limitations. We acknowledge that there are some limitations to our method. First, we only consider conditional directly-follows dependencies. Like most process mining approaches, our method requires sufficiently large event logs. Small event logs might, by chance, not contain all directly-follows relations. Moreover, more complex patterns of conditional infrequent behavior, e.g., longer sequences or sub-processes, cannot be discovered. Second, there is a risk that the returned C-nets are unsound [22] since our method is based on the HM. However, recent research shows that it is possible to structure the discovered model afterwards [30]. Third, as all data-driven method the DHM

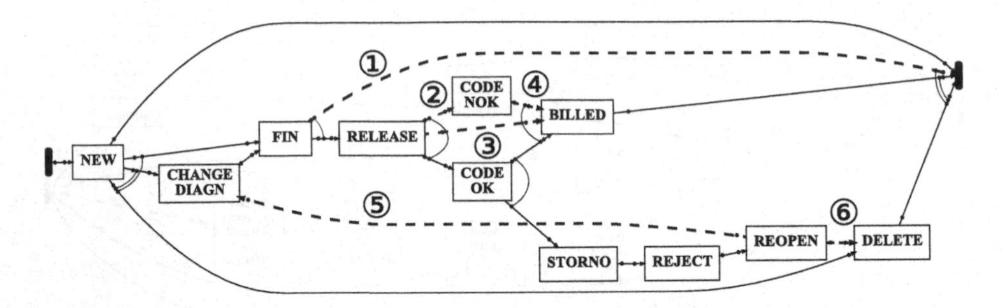

Fig. 6. Process model discovered for the HB. The numbered edges are added by our method.

Table 3. Dependency conditions discovered for the HB log.

Nr	Source	Target	Count	Quality	Dependency	Used attributes
1	Fin	End	3,619	0.98	1	closeCode
2	Release	Code Nok	1,674	0.62	0.99	caseType
3	Release	Billed	468	0.93	0.98	caseType
4	Code Nok	Billed	1,481	0.84	0.99	caseType, specialty
5	Reopen	Delete	1,128	0.83	0.81	closed
6	Reopen	Change Diagn	212	0.97	0.99	closed

relies on data attributes and infrequent process paths being recorded. Last, we used only two real-life event logs in the evaluation. Therefore, only limited claims on the general applicability of the method can be made. We have also tested the DHM on other event logs. However, very few event logs with data attribute are publicly available.

6 Conclusion

We presented the Data-aware Heuristic Miner (DHM), a *process discovery* method that *reveals conditional infrequent behavior* from event logs. The DHM distinguishes undesired noise from infrequent behavior that can be characterized by conditions over the data attributes of the event log. This is the *first approach that uses both event labels and data attributes when discovering the control-flow*. Dependency conditions are discovered using classification techniques, and, then, embedded in a complete process discovery algorithm built upon the Heuristic Miner. The returned process models are annotated with information on the discovered rules. We applied the DHM to a synthetic and two real-life events logs of considerable size and complexity. We showed that the DHM can efficiently handle large event logs and is robust against typical levels of random noise. The evaluation on two real-life cases shows that the DHM provides insights that could be easily missed when relying on state-of-the-art, frequency-based techniques. In our future work, we would like to extend the idea from directly-follows relations to more complex patterns of conditional behavior (e.g., long-term dependencies).

The DHM successfully reveals data dependencies based on directly-follows relations, but dependencies that cannot be captured by directly-follows relations might be missed.

References

1. Davies, I., Green, P., Rosemann, M., Indulska, M., Gallo, S.: How do practitioners use conceptual modeling in practice? Data Knowl. Eng. **58**(3), 358–380 (2006)
2. van der Aalst, W.M.P.: Process Mining - Data Science in Action, 2nd edn. Springer, Heidelberg (2016)
3. Weerdt, J.D., Backer, M.D., Vanthienen, J., Baesens, B.: A multi-dimensional quality assessment of state-of-the-art process discovery algorithms using real-life event logs. Inf. Syst. **37**(7), 654–676 (2012)
4. Suriadi, S., Andrews, R., ter Hofstede, A., Wynn, M.: Event log imperfection patterns for process mining: towards a systematic approach to cleaning event logs. Inf. Syst. **64**, 132–150 (2017)
5. van der Aalst, W.M.P., Weijters, T., Maruster, L.: Workflow mining: discovering process models from event logs. IEEE Trans. Knowl. Data Eng. **16**(9), 1128–1142 (2004)
6. Carmona, J., Cortadella, J., Kishinevsky, M.: A region-based algorithm for discovering petri nets from event logs. In: Dumas, M., Reichert, M., Shan, M.-C. (eds.) BPM 2008. LNCS, vol. 5240, pp. 358–373. Springer, Heidelberg (2008). doi:10.1007/978-3-540-85758-7_26
7. Günther, C.W., van der Aalst, W.M.P.: Fuzzy mining – adaptive process simplification based on multi-perspective metrics. In: Alonso, G., Dadam, P., Rosemann, M. (eds.) BPM 2007. LNCS, vol. 4714, pp. 328–343. Springer, Heidelberg (2007). doi:10.1007/978-3-540-75183-0_24
8. Weijters, A., Ribeiro, J.: Flexible heuristics miner (FHM). In: CIDM, pp. 310–317. IEEE (2011)
9. Leemans, S.J.J., Fahland, D., van der Aalst, W.M.P.: Discovering block-structured process models from event logs containing infrequent behaviour. In: Lohmann, N., Song, M., Wohed, P. (eds.) BPM 2013. LNBIP, vol. 171, pp. 66–78. Springer, Cham (2014). doi:10.1007/978-3-319-06257-0_6
10. Liesaputra, V., Yongchareon, S., Chaisiri, S.: Efficient process model discovery using maximal pattern mining. In: Motahari-Nezhad, H.R., Recker, J., Weidlich, M. (eds.) BPM 2015. LNCS, vol. 9253, pp. 441–456. Springer, Cham (2015). doi:10.1007/978-3-319-23063-4_29
11. Goedertier, S., Martens, D., Vanthienen, J., Baesens, B.: Robust process discovery with artificial negative events. J. Mach. Learn. Res. **10**, 1305–1340 (2009)
12. Ponce-de-León, H., Carmona, J., vanden Broucke, S.K.L.M.: Incorporating negative information in process discovery. In: Motahari-Nezhad, H.R., Recker, J., Weidlich, M. (eds.) BPM 2015. LNCS, vol. 9253, pp. 126–143. Springer, Cham (2015). doi:10.1007/978-3-319-23063-4_8
13. Buijs, J., van Dongen, B.F., van der Aalst, W.M.P.: A genetic algorithm for discovering process trees. In: IEEE Congress on Evolutionary Computation, pp. 1–8. IEEE (2012)
14. Rembert, A.J., Omokpo, A., Mazzoleni, P., Goodwin, R.T.: Process discovery using prior knowledge. In: Basu, S., Pautasso, C., Zhang, L., Fu, X. (eds.) ICSOC 2013. LNCS, vol. 8274, pp. 328–342. Springer, Heidelberg (2013). doi:10.1007/978-3-642-45005-1_23
15. Bellodi, E., Riguzzi, F., Lamma, E.: Statistical relational learning for workflow mining. Intell. Data Anal. **20**(3), 515–541 (2016)
16. Ghionna, L., Greco, G., Guzzo, A., Pontieri, L.: Outlier detection techniques for process mining applications. In: An, A., Matwin, S., Raś, Z.W., Ślęzak, D. (eds.) ISMIS 2008. LNCS, vol. 4994, pp. 150–159. Springer, Heidelberg (2008). doi:10.1007/978-3-540-68123-6_17

17. Conforti, R., Rosa, M.L., ter Hofstede, A.H.M.: Filtering out infrequent behavior from business process event logs. IEEE Trans. Knowl. Data Eng. **29**(2), 300–314 (2017)
18. Rozinat, A., Mans, R.S., Song, M., van der Aalst, W.M.P.: Discovering simulation models. Inf. Syst. **34**(3), 305–327 (2009)
19. de Leoni, M., van der Aalst, W.M.P.: Data-aware process mining: discovering decisions in processes using alignments. In: SAC 2013, pp. 1454–1461. ACM (2013)
20. Bazhenova, E., Buelow, S., Weske, M.: Discovering decision models from event logs. In: Abramowicz, W., Alt, R., Franczyk, B. (eds.) BIS 2016. LNBIP, vol. 255, pp. 237–251. Springer, Cham (2016). doi:10.1007/978-3-319-39426-8_19
21. Schönig, S., Ciccio, C., Maggi, F.M., Mendling, J.: Discovery of multi-perspective declarative process models. In: Sheng, Q.Z., Stroulia, E., Tata, S., Bhiri, S. (eds.) ICSOC 2016. LNCS, vol. 9936, pp. 87–103. Springer, Cham (2016). doi:10.1007/978-3-319-46295-0_6
22. van der Aalst, W., Adriansyah, A., van Dongen, B.: Causal nets: a modeling language tailored towards process discovery. In: Katoen, J.-P., König, B. (eds.) CONCUR 2011. LNCS, vol. 6901, pp. 28–42. Springer, Heidelberg (2011). doi:10.1007/978-3-642-23217-6_3
23. Quinlan, J.R.: C4.5: Programs for Machine Learning. Morgan Kaufmann, Burlington (1993)
24. Cohen, J.: A coefficient of agreement for nominal scales. Educ. Psychol. Measur. **20**(1), 37–46 (1960)
25. Ben-David, A.: About the relationship between ROC curves and Cohen's kappa. Eng. Appl. Artif. Intell. **21**(6), 874–882 (2008)
26. vanden Broucke, S.: Advances in process mining: artificial negative events and othertechniques. Ph.D. thesis, KU Leuven (2014)
27. Dijkman, R., Dumas, M., García-Bañuelos, L.: Graph matching algorithms for business process model similarity search. In: Dayal, U., Eder, J., Koehler, J., Reijers, H.A. (eds.) BPM 2009. LNCS, vol. 5701, pp. 48–63. Springer, Heidelberg (2009). doi:10.1007/978-3-642-03848-8_5
28. de Leoni, M., Mannhardt, F.: Road traffic fine management process (2015). doi:10.4121/uuid:270fd440-1057-4fb9-89a9-b699b47990f5
29. Mannhardt, F., de Leoni, M., Reijers, H.A., van der Aalst, W.M.P.: Balanced multi-perspective checking of process conformance. Computing **98**(4), 407–437 (2016)
30. Augusto, A., Conforti, R., Dumas, M., Rosa, M., Bruno, G.: Automated discovery of structured process models: discover structured vs. discover and structure. In: Comyn-Wattiau, I., Tanaka, K., Song, I.-Y., Yamamoto, S., Saeki, M. (eds.) ER 2016. LNCS, vol. 9974, pp. 313–329. Springer, Cham (2016). doi:10.1007/978-3-319-46397-1_25

An Approach for Incorporating Expert Knowledge in Trace Clustering

Pieter De Koninck(✉), Klaas Nelissen, Bart Baesens, Seppe vanden Broucke, Monique Snoeck, and Jochen De Weerdt

Faculty of Economics and Business, Research Center for Management Informatics, KU Leuven, Naamsestraat 69, 3000 Leuven, Belgium
pieter.dekoninck@kuleuven.be

Abstract. Trace clustering techniques are a set of approaches for partitioning traces or process instances into similar groups. Typically, this partitioning is based on certain patterns or similarity between the traces, or done by discovering a process model for each cluster of traces. In general, however, it is likely that clustering solutions obtained by these approaches will be hard to understand or difficult to validate given an expert's domain knowledge. Therefore, we propose a novel semi-supervised trace clustering technique based on expert knowledge. Our approach is validated using a case in tablet reading behaviour, but widely applicable in other contexts. In an experimental evaluation, the technique is shown to provide a beneficial trade-off between performance and understandability.

Keywords: Trace clustering · Process mining · Domain knowledge · Semi-supervised learning

1 Introduction

Process mining is a research field at the crossroads of data mining and business process management. Its main reason of existence stems from the vast amount of data that is generated in modern information systems, and the desire of organizations to extract meaningful insights from this data. Generally speaking, three subdomains exist within process mining: process discovery, a set of techniques concerned with the elicitation of process models from event data; conformance checking, a set of techniques that aim to quantify the conformance between a certain process model and a certain event log; and process enhancement, approaches that aim to extend existing or discovered process models by using other data attributes such as resource or timing information [18].

Trace clustering, or the partitioning of traces of behaviour in an event log into separate clusters, is mainly related to the *process discovery* sub-domain of process mining. Process discovery techniques aim to discover a process model from an event log. However, when this event log consists of real-life behaviour, it is likely to contain highly varied and complex behavioural structures. This leads

E. Dubois and K. Pohl (Eds.): CAiSE 2017, LNCS 10253, pp. 561–576, 2017.
DOI: 10.1007/978-3-319-59536-8_35

to a lower quality of the process models which can be discovered. Therefore, it is desirable to first split the event log into several different clusters of traces, and then discover a process model for each trace cluster separately. By doing so, the goal is to achieve a higher quality of the process models.

From an application-oriented point of view, trace clustering techniques have proven to be a valuable asset in multiple contexts, with applications ranging from incident management to health care [10,11]. Nonetheless, trace clustering, like traditional clustering, is hindered by its unsupervised nature: it is often hard to validate a clustering solution, even for domain experts. This problem has been recognized in [7], in which an approach is proposed to increase understandability of trace clustering solutions by extracting short and accurate explanations as to why a certain trace is included in a certain cluster.

Although explaining cluster solutions to domain experts is a valid approach for enhancing the understandability of trace clustering solutions, it remains a post-processing step. A potentially better approach for improving trace clustering solutions is to directly take an expert's opinion into account while performing the clustering. This is the core contribution of this paper: an approach for incorporating expert knowledge into a trace clustering is proposed. In a real-life case study, based on behaviour of newspaper readers, our approach is shown to lead to clustering solutions that are more in line with the expert's expectations, without substantially diminishing the quality of the clustering solution.

In light of this objective, the rest of this paper is structured as follows: in Sect. 2, the field of trace clustering is described and potential approaches for the incorporation of expert knowledge are investigated. Furthermore, Sect. 3.1 describes our proposed approach. In Sect. 4, the motivating case study is outlined, illustrating a specific situation in which expert knowledge is used to enhance the justifiability of trace clustering solutions. Subsequently, the contribution of our novel approach is evaluated in Sect. 5. Finally, a conclusion and outlook towards future work is provided in Sect. 6.

2 Potential Approaches for Incorporating Expert Knowledge

In this section, a short overview of trace clustering is provided. Then, we conceptually discuss how expert knowledge can be represented and how it can be incorporated in a trace clustering approach. The three distinct categories delineated here are: expert-driven initialization, constraint clustering, and complete expert clustering. Finally, we describe how our approach fits into the methodology of [12].

2.1 Existing Approaches for Traditional Trace Clustering

Typically, the starting point of a trace clustering exercise is an event log, which is a set of traces. Each trace is a registered series of events (instantiations of activities), possibly along with extra information on the event, such as the resource that executed the event or time information. A trace clustering is then a partitioning of an event log into different clusters such that each trace is assigned to a single cluster.

A wide variety of trace clustering techniques exist. Broadly speaking, there are three main categories of trace clustering techniques: those based on direct instance-level similarity, those based on the mapping of traces onto a vector space model, and those based on process model quality. With regards to direct instance-level similarity, i.e. the direct quantification of the similarity between two traces, an adapted Levenshtein distance could be computed as in [3]. An alternative set of approaches are those where the behaviour present in each trace is mapped onto a vector space of features [4]. The third category regards process model quality as an important goal for trace clustering. An approach based on the active incorporation of the process model quality of process models discovered from each cluster has been described in [10].

2.2 Incorporating Expert Knowledge: Expert-Driven Initialization

A first potential approach is based on expert-driven initialization. It is conceptually related to semi-supervised learning [2], in the sense that the user is expected to manually assign a small subset of traces to a cluster, after which an automatic clustering algorithm extends the clusters to the entire dataset. The approach is especially useful for centroid-based algorithms like *k-means*, which often rely on a random initialization of seeds in order to commence the clustering. By setting these seeds based on the domain knowledge of an expert instead of randomly, the confidence of an expert in the solution should increase, and with it the justifiability of the solution.

With regards to the three types of trace clustering described in Sect. 2.1, it is clear that including expert-driven knowledge directly in the similarity between traces is not attainable. If the underlying technique used to cluster the traces is seed-based, such as k-means, then the expert-driven pre-defined clusters could be chosen as seeds. The same observation holds for clustering traces which have been mapped onto a vector space model, if this vector space representation is clustered in a seed-based way. If a hierarchical technique is preferred for clustering the vector space representation, the incorporation is less straightforward. Finally, a process model-driven trace clustering technique that is based on initialization does not exist yet.

2.3 Incorporating Expert Knowledge: Constrained Clustering

A second potential approach is the use of constraints. Rather than provide a starting subset of clustered traces, the expert provides a set of constraints to which the clustering solution is expected to conform (either strictly or at a penalty). Typical examples of expert constraints are must-link constraints, which indicate that two elements must be included in the same cluster, and cannot-link constraints, indicating that two elements should not be clustered together [20].

In the specific application of constrained clustering to traces, a general must-link constraint that applies to all algorithms is related to process instances and distinct process instances: trace clustering techniques that construct clusters based on process instances should ensure that all process instances pertaining to the same distinct process instance, are included in the same cluster.

2.4 Incorporating Expert Knowledge: Complete Expert Solution

A final possible input type of expert knowledge can be a complete clustering solution based on the expert's expectations. If the expert's expectations can be captured using an automatic clustering technique, the availability of such a complete solution is not far-fetched. In other cases, the opinion of a human expert could be based on features of the traces which are not incorporated into a trace clustering solution. In such a case, a clustering obtained with the use of these features could be a useful starting point for a clustering exercise. Two different approaches can be conceived to deal with this complete expert clustering. On the one hand, one could apply a trace clustering technique on the event log from scratch to obtain a regular trace clustering solution. Then, the solution of the expert and the regular trace clustering solution can be combined to create a *consensus clustering*. The idea is to quantify how often two elements are clustered together in different solutions, and then construct a final partitioning based on this quantification. Consensus clustering has been used in a multiple-view trace clustering technique [1]. Nonetheless, consensus clustering is mainly useful for combining a higher number of different solutions. If there are only two solutions to combine, creating a consensus may prove difficult. On the other hand, in a case where a single complete expert clustering is available, a different strategy could be to take this complete clustering as a starting point: re-cluster the traces which are grouped together by the expert, but whose grouping hinders the performance the clustering on other objectives, such as process model quality.

2.5 Organizational Aspects

According to PM^2, a process mining methodology, 4 types of roles are typically involved in a process mining project: business owners, business experts, system experts and process analysts. Ideally, the expert knowledge comes from a business expert who knows the business aspect and executions of the processes [12]. The expectations of the experts are to be captured in the Extraction stage, when process knowledge is transferred from the business expert to the process analyst, who will be performing the process discovery and trace clustering.

The approach presented in the next section of this paper is based on incorporating expert knowledge starting from a complete expert solution. This is done by re-clustering the event log based in a process model-driven approach. Initialization- and constraint-based approaches remain open for future research.

3 Incorporating Expert Knowledge in Trace Clustering

3.1 Proposed Approach

In this section, a novel trace clustering algorithm is described, specifically designed to be driven by expert knowledge[1]. Corresponding to Sect. 2.4 a trace clustering technique that starts from a complete expert solution is described. The technique is based on the multi-objective approach described in [6].

In general, the technique consists of three phases:

Phase 1. An initialization phase, during which the clusters are initialized.
Phase 2. A trace assignment phase, during which traces are assigned to the cluster which leads to the best results, if that best result is sufficiently good.
Phase 3. A resolution phase, during which traces that where not assigned in the previous phase, are either included in an additional separate cluster, or in the best possible existing cluster.

Algorithm 1. Expert-Driven Trace Clustering: **Phase 1**

Input: FixedPercentage := the percentage of distinct process instances per cluster that should not be changed
Phase 1: Initialization
1: **function** INITIALIZE(event log L, discovery technique PD, metric m, cluster value threshold cvt, trace value threshold tvt)
2: Determine the number of clusters nb from the event log
3: Create clusters CS equal to this number of clusters
4: For each trace with a label, include it in its cluster and remove it from the log
5: **for** $c \in CS$ **do** % for each cluster
6: $initNumbDPIinCluster := |c|$
7: **while** $|c| > FixedPercentage * initNumbDPIinCluster$ **do**
8: $t :=$ least frequent dpi in c
9: $PM := PD(c \cup t)$ % Mine a process model which includes the current trace t
10: $tmv := getMetricValue(m, PM, t))$% Get result of metric on just this trace
11: $cmv := getMetricValue(m, , PM, CS[c] \cup t))$% Get result of metric on entire cluster
12: **if** $(tmv >= tvt) \wedge (cmv >= cvt)$ **then**
13: **break** % Break from while: quality is sufficient, metrics are over threshold
14: **else**% Metrics are below threshold
15: $c := c \setminus t$ % Remove trace from cluster
16: $L := L \cup t$ % Add trace to log of traces to assign later
17: **end if**
18: **end while**
19: **end for**
20: return$((CS, L))$ % Return initialized clusters and remaining traces
21: **end function**

Phase 1: Initialization. The first phase is an initialization phase, which is described in Algorithm 1. The algorithm is structured as follows: first, a set of clusters is built by extracting the number of different clusters in the pre-clustered event log. Then, each distinct process instance (*dpi*) is added to its respective cluster. Next, traces are removed from each cluster to increase the process model

[1] The algorithm has been implemented as a plugin for ProM 6, and is available on http://processmining.be/expertdriventraceclustering/.

Algorithm 2. Expert-Driven Trace Clustering: **Phase 2** and **3**

Input: L := grouped and ordered event log, completely pre-clustered, cvt := cluster value threshold, tvt:= trace value threshold; $SeparateBoolean$:= true if unassignable traces should be grouped in a separate cluster;
Input: Configuration: PD:= a process discovery technique, m:= a process quality metric
Output: CS := A set of clusters

```
1: (CS, L) := Initialize(L, PD, m, cvt, tvt) % Do Phase 1

        Phase 2: Trace assignment
2: U := {} % List of unassignable traces
3: for t ∈ L do % Loop over the distinct traces which were not assigned to a cluster in Phase 1
4:     bestCluster := −1 % Temporary value for assignment
5:     bestCMV := −1; bestTMV := −1; % Temporary values for optimization
6:     for c := (0 → |CS| − 1) do % Inspect each possible cluster
7:         PM := PD(CS[c] ∪ t) % Mine a process model including current trace t
8:         tmv := getMetricValue(m, PM, t))% Get result of metric on just this trace
9:         cmv := getMetricValue(m, PM, CS[c] ∪ t))% Get result of metric on entire cluster
10:        if (tmv >= tvt) ∧ (cmv >= cvt) then % Check thresholds
11:            if cmv > bestCMV ∨ (cmv = bestCMV ∧ tmv > bestTMV) then
12:                bestCMV := cmv; bestTMV := tmv; bestCluster := c
13:            end if
14:        end if
15:    end for
16:    if bestCluster >= 0 then% If the trace t could be assigned to a cluster
17:        CS[bestCluster]:= CS[bestCluster] ∪ t % Add trace to cluster
18:        L:= L \ t % Remove trace from log
19:    else% If the trace t could not be assigned to a cluster
20:        U:= U ∪ t % Add trace to unassignable
21:        L:= L \ t % Remove trace from log
22:    end if
23: end for

        Phase 3: Unassignable resolution
24: if SeparateBoolean then
25:     CS[n_b + 1] := U % Add remaining traces to a new cluster
26: else
27:     Add each trace to the cluster in CS using the same procedure as in phase 2, without checking
    the thresholds anymore. Furthermore, the trace and cluster metric values are now calculated
    without rediscovering a process model each time.
28: end if
29: return CS
```

quality of each cluster. Nonetheless, a certain percentage of dpi per cluster can be fixed: dpi's will not be removed when there are less traces left in the cluster than a *FixedPercentage* given by the user. For each of the clusters, traces are removed in order from least frequent dpi to most frequent dpi. Dpi frequency, or distinct process frequency, is the frequency with which a certain process instance (trace) is present in the event log. For each trace, starting with the least frequent, a process model PM is mined and the trace is removed if the *trace metric value* and *cluster metric value* are not above the declared thresholds. The *trace metric value* is the result of the metric computed on the mined process model using only the trace that is under scrutiny. The *cluster metric value* is obtained by calculating this result using all traces in the cluster, including the trace to be added. Two options are possible: if both values are above the threshold, the cluster is of sufficient quality, and no traces are removed from the cluster any more. If this is not the case, the trace is removed and added to the traces that will be assigned to a cluster in a later phase.

Phase 2: Trace Assignment. The second phase is detailed in Algorithm 2, and described here. After the initialization, the set of remaining traces to be clustered will be assigned to the cluster they fit best with. This is done by mining a process model, and calculating the *trace metric value* and *cluster metric value* for each cluster. Four situations are possible: (1) the *cluster metric value* is the highest one, in which case the cluster is denoted as the current best; (2) the *cluster metric value* is only equal to the current highest value but the *trace metric value* is higher than the current best, in which case the cluster is also denoted as the current best; (3) the values are above the threshold but lower than the current best found in one of the other clusters, in which case the trace will not be added to the cluster which is currently being tested; or (4) these values are below the provided thresholds, and again the trace will not be added to the cluster which is currently being tested.

After determining the best cluster, the distinct process instance is added to the best possible cluster. If no best possible cluster exists (because the metric values were below the threshold for each of the clusters), the distinct process instance is added to the set of unassignable traces.

Phase 3: Unassignable Resolution. In the third phase, any remaining traces which were not assignable to a cluster in Phase 2 will be assigned to a cluster. They are either added to a separate cluster (if *SeparateBoolean* is true), or they are added to the best possible existing cluster. This assignment is done from most frequent distinct process instance to least frequent process instances, following the same procedure as in Phase 2, with the exception that the thresholds are no longer checked.

3.2 Configuration

In this subsection, a small discussion is provided on how the algorithm could be configured. While the choice of the two thresholds, the fixed percentage for the initialization, and the choice whether or not to separate the not-assignable traces are important decisions, these are case-specific decisions. The algorithm allows these to be set by the user: higher thresholds combined with the separation of traces that do not exceed these thresholds will likely lead to small but highly qualitative clusters and one large surplus-cluster, which may be desirable in some cases but not in all.

In terms of the metric chosen as input for the clustering, this depends on the expectation of the underlying process models. A wide array of accuracy and simplicity metrics for discovered process models have been described in the literature (e.g. [9]). In general, a weighted metric such as the robust F-score proposed in [8] might be appropriate, since it provides a balance between fitness and precision.

A similar argument holds for the process discovery technique one could use. A wide array of techniques exist, and our approach can be combined with most of them. Observe that the chosen technique should be able to discover processes with a decent performance, since a high number of processes needs to be discovered in certain steps of our algorithm. In [10], the preference goes to Heuristics Miner [21]. Other possibilities are Inductive Miner [15] and Fodina [19].

4 Motivating Case Study: Reading Behaviour in Tablet Newspapers

4.1 Case Description

We performed experiments with people who read a digital newspaper using a tablet app. We set up two types of experiments: qualitative, in which 30 people were interviewed about their typical newspaper reading behaviour by an experienced independent marketer; and quantitative experiments, in which 209 paying subscribers of the newspaper allowed us to track every device interaction with the app during one month of habitual news reading.

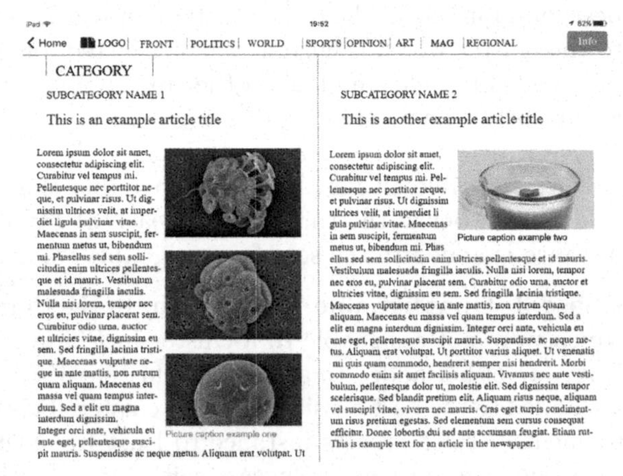

Fig. 1. Anonymized screenshot of one newspaper page in the app.

The app's name cannot be mentioned due to confidentiality reasons, but it exists already for several years and has more than 10,000 monthly active users. The newspaper brand is one of the most popular in a Western-European country.

As can be seen in Fig. 1, the app is not just a replica of a regular newspaper in print, but is optimized for tablet and mobile use. Reading through the newspaper with this app can be considered a process and investigated with process mining techniques. The user starts on page one, and can swipe horizontally, going from page to page, choosing on which articles to spend more time, and the process ends when the user decides to quit reading. In this tablet-optimized version of the newspaper, a couple of additional features also allow users to jump between pages, thereby skipping content to e.g. immediately go to the start of a new news category like Sports, Opinions, and so on.

An experienced marketer from an independent marketing bureau did interviews with 30 people in total. Each interview had a duration of two hours. The marketer had experience working with the same app and newspaper brand for other market studies, and was considered to be a domain expert by the journalists and editors of the newspaper. The end result of these interviews was a presentation of a set of typical reader profiles, with a textual explanation about what kind of reading behaviour characterized each reader profile.

This set of reader profiles can be considered to be expert-driven clusters. Note that this expert-driven clustering is not based on actual data of the reading process of these users, but on the self-reported reading behaviour of the interviewed users. Using users' self-reported behaviour is typically how companies do user segmentation if they want to get insight into the different types of users that use their app, especially if there is no data available about how their product is actually used.

We worked together with Twipe[2], the company which developed the app, to modify the app so every user interaction could be logged. A selection of paying subscribers of the newspaper was e-mailed with an invitation to fill in a recruitment survey. The recruitment survey assessed eligibility for participation in the experiment. It consisted of socio-demographic questions and questions concerning the users' typical reading behaviour. Based on the answers to this survey, a sample of candidate participants could be drawn that was representative for the newspaper's population of subscribers. All of the candidate participants were acquainted with the app and used it regularly (at least weekly, often more frequently). This set of candidate participants received a personal invitation to download the modified version of the app they normally used for reading the newspaper, and to use that version during one month. Eventually, we collected useful data for 209 experiment participants, and ended up with 2900 useful reading sessions.

4.2 Application of Data-Driven Clustering

Recall from the previous section that the domain expert created textual descriptions of cluster profiles. The variables used to describe these profiles are used for data-driven clustering approaches, to come up with a full expert solution. These variables contain information such as the reading moment, length of a session, how focused a reader is, how thoroughly the paper is read, etc. For the clustering, three distinct approaches were taken: (1) A traditional *k-means* was performed using these variables. (2) Given the textual description of cluster profiles by the expert, representative observations are defined for each cluster. Then, these representative observations are used as centroids in a *single nearest neighbour* approach. Each trace is included in the cluster of the centroid it is closest to in terms of normalized values on the variables. (3) The third approach consists of starting from these same centroids, and using those centroids as initial seeds in a seeded version of the *k-means* algorithm.

4.3 Transforming Case to Enable Trace Clustering

In order to create insight into the reading process followed by the users, the low-level interaction data as described in Sect. 4.1 needs to be mapped onto intuitive high-level activities. Four groups of activities were defined: (1) activities that lead to the start of a reading session, either by starting the application or reopening

[2] www.twipemobile.com.

it from the background of the tablet; (2) activities concerning a user spending time reading an article; (3) activities concerning a user inspecting an image; and (4) activities concerning a user shutting down her session.

In terms of granularity of the reading activity, two aspects were considered for inclusion: the time spent on the article, and the newspaper category the article belonged to. After descriptive analysis of the data, the following transformation was applied. With regards to reading times, a typical user reading in the newspaper's language will read about 240 words per minute [5]. A reading activity is defined as a *read-page*-event if the user spent enough time on the article to read at least half of the text. Similarly, a *scan-page*-event is defined to have occurred if a reader has taken the time to read a quarter of the text, and a *skip-page*-event if the reader only took the time to read the title of the article. Additionally, the newspaper also consists of 8 different categories. Extending the read, scan and skip events with these categories leads to a total number of 24 different reading events. Next to text categories, the *inspect-image*-event was also divided into categories, creating 8 distinct image-events. Overall, this brings the number of activities to 34 (1 *launch*-event, 24 page-reading events, 8 image-related events and 1 *quit*-event). Self-loops between activities were disregarded. Finally, observe that the created event log contains a wide variety of behaviour: of 2900 reading sessions, there are 2794 distinct process instances. For an exemplary excerpt, see Table 1.

Table 1. Example event log of the tablet reading process

Session	Time	Activity type	User
1	16-06-2015 08:02	Launch	John Doe
1	16-06-2015 08:03	Read-page-front	John Doe
1	16-06-2015 08:03	Read-page-politics	John Doe
1	16-06-2015 08:04	Scan-page-politics	John Doe
1	16-06-2015 08:04	Inspect-image-sport	John Doe
1	...	...	...
1	16-06-2015 08:24	Quit	John Doe
2	16-06-2015 08:32	Launch	Jane Doe
2	...	...	...

5 Experimental Evaluation

In this section, we will apply a number of data-driven clustering approaches, existing trace clustering techniques, and our expert-driven trace clustering technique, on the newspaper reading data. The obtained clustering solutions are then compared in terms of process model quality.

5.1 Setup

Techniques. All techniques are listed in Table 2, with an indication of whether they are data-driven techniques, trace clustering techniques, or expert-driven techniques. Five pure trace clustering techniques are incorporated for comparison: *ActFreq* and *ActMRA* [10], two process-quality based techniques, *GED* [3], a direct instance-similarity technique, and two vector-space model-based methods, *MRA* [4] and *3-gram* [17]. Three data-driven clustering techniques are included, one of which requires no expert knowledge (*k-means*), and two that do (*k-seeded* and 1*nn*). Finally, ActSemSup_{exp} is the general name for our proposed expert-driven trace clustering technique, where *exp* is the technique that is used to obtain the expert knowledge: *k-seeded* or 1*nn*. All settings are tested with 4,5 and 6 clusters, in line with the expectations of the domain expert.

Table 2. Clustering techniques compared in the experimental evaluation

Shorthand	Technique	Implementation (plugin/package)	Data clustering	Trace clustering	Expert driven
k-means	Traditional k-means	Stats (R)	✓		
k-seeded	Seeded k-means	Stats (R)	✓		✓
1nn	Single nearest neighbour	Class (R)	✓		✓
ActFreq	Frequency-based ActiTraC	ActiTraC (ProM 6)		✓	
ActMRA	Distance-based ActiTraC	ActiTraC (ProM 6)		✓	
MRA	AHC - Maximal Repeat Alphabet	GuideTreeMiner (ProM 6)		✓	
GED	AHC - Generic Edit Distance	GuideTreeMiner (ProM 6)		✓	
3-gram	AHC - 3-grams	GuideTreeMiner (ProM 6)		✓	
$ActSemSup_{k-seeded}$	Semi-supervised ActiTraC Expert input from *k-seeded*	Own plugin (ProM 6)		✓	✓
$ActSemSup_{1nn}$	Semi-supervised ActiTraC Expert input from *1nn*	Own plugin (ProM 6)		✓	✓

AHC: Agglomerative Hierarchical Clustering

Configuration of $ActSemiSup_{exp}$: *FixedPercentage* := 0.75, *PD* := Fodina, *m* := F1-Score, *cvt* := 0.27, *tvt* := 0.27, *SeparateBoolean* := False

Metrics. To evaluate the quality of the clustering solutions, a process model is mined for each cluster, using the Fodina technique [19]. The accuracy of each process model discovered per cluster is then measured using the F1-score as proposed by [8], where p is a precision metric and r is a recall metric:

$$F1_B = 2 * \frac{p_B * r_B}{p_B + r_B}$$

In this paper, the recall metric we have chosen is behavioural recall r_b [14], and the precision metric we use is etc^{p} [16]. Finally, a weighted average F-score metric for the entire clustering solution is then calculated as follows, similar to the approach in [10], where k is the number of clusters in C and n_i the number of traces in cluster i:

$$F1_C^{WA} = \frac{\sum_{i=1}^{k} n_i F1_i}{\sum_{i=1}^{k} n_i}$$

Furthermore, we can calculate the relative improvement of our semi-supervised technique with expert knowledge ($ActSemiSup_{exp}$) opposed to the best pure trace clustering technique (TC) as follows:

$$RI(ActSemiSup_{exp}, TC) = \frac{F1^{WA}_{ActSemiSup_{exp}}}{F1^{WA}_{TC}}$$

Three situations might arise: (1) $RI > 1$: in that case, the expert-driven technique creates a solution which is able to combine higher ease-of-interpretation with better results in terms of process model quality; (2) $RI = 1$: the expert-driven technique leads to higher ease-of-interpretation from an expert's point of view without reducing model quality; and (3) $RI < 1$: there is a trade-off present between clustering solutions which are justifiable for an expert and the optimal solution in terms of process model quality.

One final metric we propose to compare how similar two clustering solutions are, is the Normalized Mutual Information [13]. With it, we can illustrate how similar the solution found by our semi-supervised approach is to the complete expert clustering it used as input. This value is a decent proxy for how easy-to-interpret the solution is given the expert knowledge used to create the input clustering. It is defined as follows: let k_a be the number of clusters in clustering a, k_b the number of clusters in clustering b, n the total number of traces, n^a_i the number of elements in cluster i in clustering a, n^b_j, the number of elements in cluster j in clustering b, and n^{ab}_{ij} the number of elements present in both cluster i in clustering a and cluster j in clustering b. The NMI is then defined as:

$$NMI(a,b) = -2\frac{\sum_{i=1}^{k_a}\sum_{j=1}^{k_b} n^{ab}_{ij} log(\frac{n^{ab}_{ij} n}{n^a_i n^b_j})}{\sum_{i=1}^{k_a} n^a_i log(\frac{n^a_i}{n}) + \sum_{j=1}^{k_b} n^b_j log(\frac{n^b_j}{n})}$$

5.2 Results

The results in terms of F1-score are presented in Fig. 2. A couple of observations can be made from this figure. First, since the F1-score is a metric scaled between 0 and 1, it is clear that the overall results are rather low. Nonetheless, all clustering solutions have a weighted average behavioural recall between 0.88 and 0.92. The reason for the low F1-scores lies in the precision: due to the high variability of behaviour (many distinct process instances) in the event log, all clustering solutions perform rather low in terms of etc^p.

Secondly, observe that all clustered solutions outperform the non-clustered event log (1 cluster). This is mainly due to the precision of the clusters, which increases if a higher number of clusters is used. This observation is supported by the ordering of the results across different numbers of clusters: all other things being equal, the F1-score at 6 clusters is always the highest, except for the *ActMRA* and *MRA* solutions.

Furthermore, it is noticeable that *ActMRA* (at a cluster number of 4 and 5), and *ActFreq* (at a cluster number of 6) attain the highest quality of the existing

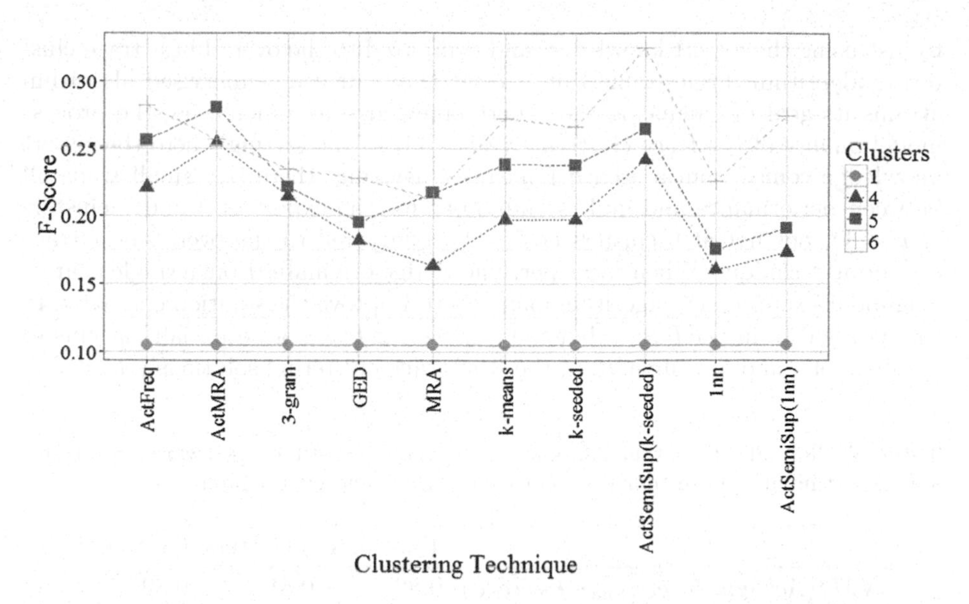

Fig. 2. Weighted average F1-score results for different clustering techniques and number of clusters

data-driven and trace clustering techniques. Observe as well that the data-driven clustering techniques *k-means* and *k-seeded* perform quite well in terms of process model quality, on par with dedicated trace clustering techniques, especially at higher cluster numbers.

Table 3. Relative improvement of the semi-supervised clustering solutions compared to just using the expert knowledge and compared to the overall best trace clustering algorithm

	4 clusters	5 clusters	6 clusters
$RI(ActSemiSup_{k\text{-}seeded}, k\text{-}seeded)$	1.22	1.11	1.21
$RI(ActSemiSup_{k\text{-}seeded}$, best trace cl.)	0.94	0.94	1.14
$RI(ActSemiSup_{1nn}, 1nn)$	1.08	1.09	1.22
$RI(ActSemiSup_{1nn}$, best trace cl.)	0.68	0.68	0.97
Best clustering is *ActMRA* at 4 and 5 clusters and *ActFreq* at 6			

The most important remark concerns the quality attained by the semi-supervised algorithm. Both when using the results of the *k-seeded* algorithm as expert knowledge, as well as when using the results of the *1nn* clustering as expert knowledge, the F1-score improves. To illustrate this, Table 3 contains the results of the relative improvement of the semi-supervised algorithm compared to just using the expert knowledge, and compared to the overall best trace clustering algorithm. From Table 3, it is clear that our semi-supervised algorithm attains its goal of enhancing the expert knowledge and increasing the process model quality of the trace clustering ($RI > 1$). In the setting where the expert knowledge comes from a seeded k-means clustering, there is a small trade-off between performance and understandability for the expert at 4 and 5 clusters ($RI < 1$), but not at 6 clusters ($RI > 1$), compared to the overall best trace clustering technique. When the expert knowledge originates from a single nearest neighbour-exercise, our algorithm manages to improve the solution compared to the data clustering ($RI > 1$), but there is a clear trade-off, especially at cluster numbers of 4 and 5, compared to the best trace clustering solutions ($RI < 1$).

Table 4. Normalized mutual information between semi-supervised clustering result and expert input, and regular trace clustering result and expert input

	4 clusters	5 clusters	6 clusters
$NMI(ActSemiSup_{k\text{-}seeded}, k\text{-}seeded)$	0.82	0.81	0.80
$NMI(ActSemiSup_{1nn}, 1nn)$	0.67	0.71	0.76
$NMI(ActMRA, k\text{-}seeded)$	0.07	0.08	0.08
$NMI(ActMRA, 1nn)$	0.02	0.04	0.07

Finally, Table 4 contains values for the Normalized Mutual Information, capturing the similarity between the input of the semi-supervised trace clustering solutions and their solutions. For comparison, the NMI of the *ActMRA*-technique with both inputs is provided as well. It is clear that the semi-supervised solutions are much more in line with the expectations of the expert input, as illustrated by their high NMI-values.

6 Conclusion

In a situation where an expert has a preconceived notion of what a clustering should look like, it is unlikely that a trace clustering algorithm will lead to clusters which are in line with his or her expectations. Motivated by a case in tablet reading behaviour, this paper proposes an *expert-driven trace clustering* technique that balances improvement in terms of trace clustering quality with the challenge of making clusters more interpretable for the expert. In an experimental evaluation, we have shown how our algorithm creates more interpretable solutions which are simultaneously better in terms of trace clustering quality then purely using an expert-driven data clustering, and in some cases even produce higher quality than dedicated trace clustering techniques.

Several different avenues for future work exist: (1) phase 1 of our approach could be adapted for non-complete expert input; (2) an evaluation could then be performed regarding how much expert knowledge is needed to achieve high quality clustering results; (3) our algorithm could be extended with a window-based assignment strategy, to increase performance and make the direct incorporation of other data possible; (4) the case study could be extended using the self-reported clustering of the readers; and (5) our approach could be validated in other use cases.

References

1. Appice, A., Malerba, D.: A co-training strategy for multiple view clustering in process mining. IEEE Trans. Serv. Comput. **PP**(99), 1 (2015)
2. Basu, S., Banerjee, A., Mooney, R.: Semi-supervised clustering by seeding. In: Proceedings of 19th International Conference on Machine Learning (ICML-2002), pp. 27–34 (2002)
3. Bose, R.P.J.C., van der Aalst, W.M.P.: Context aware trace clustering: towards improving process mining results. In: SDM, pp. 401–412 (2009)
4. Bose, R.P.J.C., van der Aalst, W.M.P.: Trace clustering based on conserved patterns: towards achieving better process models. In: Rinderle-Ma, S., Sadiq, S., Leymann, F. (eds.) BPM 2009. LNBIP, vol. 43, pp. 170–181. Springer, Heidelberg (2010). doi:10.1007/978-3-642-12186-9_16
5. Buzan, T., Spek, P.: Snellezen. Tirion (2009)
6. De Koninck, P., De Weerdt, J.: Multi-objective trace clustering: finding more balanced solutions. In: Business Process Management Workshops 2016 (2016, accepted)
7. De Koninck, P., De Weerdt, J., vanden Broucke, S.K.L.M.: Explaining clusterings of process instances. Data Mining Knowl. Discov. **31**(3), 1–35 (2016)
8. De Weerdt, J., De Backer, M., Vanthienen, J., Baesens, B.: A robust f-measure for evaluating discovered process models. In: 2011 IEEE Symposium on Computational Intelligence and Data Mining (CIDM), pp. 148–155. IEEE (2011)
9. De Weerdt, J., De Backer, M., Vanthienen, J., Baesens, B.: A multi-dimensional quality assessment of state-of-the-art process discovery algorithms using real-life event logs. Inf. Syst. **37**(7), 654–676 (2012)
10. De Weerdt, J., Vanden Broucke, S., Vanthienen, J., Baesens, B.: Active trace clustering for improved process discovery. IEEE Trans. Knowl. Data Eng. **25**(12), 2708–2720 (2013)
11. Delias, P., Doumpos, M., Grigoroudis, E., Manolitzas, P., Matsatsinis, N.: Supporting healthcare management decisions via robust clustering of event logs. Knowl.-Based Syst. **84**, 203–213 (2015)
12. van Eck, M.L., Lu, X., Leemans, S.J.J., van der Aalst, W.M.P.: PM^2: a process mining project methodology. In: Zdravkovic, J., Kirikova, M., Johannesson, P. (eds.) CAiSE 2015. LNCS, vol. 9097, pp. 297–313. Springer, Cham (2015). doi:10.1007/978-3-319-19069-3_19
13. Fred, A., Lourenço, A.: Cluster ensemble methods: from single clusterings to combined solutions. In: Okun, O., Valentini, G. (eds.) Supervised and Unsupervised Ensemble Methods and their Applications, pp. 3–30. Springer, Heidelberg (2008)
14. Goedertier, S., Martens, D., Vanthienen, J., Baesens, B.: Robust process discovery with artificial negative events. J. Mach. Learn. Res. **10**, 1305–1340 (2009)

15. Leemans, S.J.J., Fahland, D., van der Aalst, W.M.P.: Discovering block-structured process models from event logs - a constructive approach. In: Colom, J.-M., Desel, J. (eds.) PETRI NETS 2013. LNCS, vol. 7927, pp. 311–329. Springer, Heidelberg (2013). doi:10.1007/978-3-642-38697-8_17
16. Muñoz-Gama, J., Carmona, J.: A fresh look at precision in process conformance. In: Hull, R., Mendling, J., Tai, S. (eds.) BPM 2010. LNCS, vol. 6336, pp. 211–226. Springer, Heidelberg (2010). doi:10.1007/978-3-642-15618-2_16
17. Song, M., Günther, C.W., van der Aalst, W.M.P.: Trace clustering in process mining. In: Ardagna, D., Mecella, M., Yang, J. (eds.) BPM 2008. LNBIP, vol. 17, pp. 109–120. Springer, Heidelberg (2009). doi:10.1007/978-3-642-00328-8_11
18. Van der Aalst, W., Adriansyah, A., Van Dongen, B.: Replaying history on process models for conformance checking and performance analysis. Wiley Interdiscip. Rev. Data Min. Knowl. Discov. **2**(2), 182–192 (2012)
19. Vanden Broucke, S.K.L.M.: Artificial negative events and other techniques. Ph.D. thesis, KU Leuven (2014)
20. Wagstaff, K., Cardie, C., Rogers, S., Schrödl, S., et al.: Constrained k-means clustering with background knowledge. In: ICML, vol. 1, pp. 577–584 (2001)
21. Weijters, A., van Der Aalst, W.M., De Medeiros, A.A.: Process mining with the heuristics miner-algorithm. Technische Universiteit Eindhoven, Technical report WP 166, pp. 1–34 (2006)

Mining Business Process Stages from Event Logs

Hoang Nguyen[1(✉)], Marlon Dumas[2], Arthur H.M. ter Hofstede[1], Marcello La Rosa[1], and Fabrizio Maria Maggi[2]

[1] Queensland University of Technology, Brisbane, Australia
huanghuy.nguyen@hdr.qut.edu.au, {a.terhofstede,m.larosa}@qut.edu.au
[2] University of Tartu, Tartu, Estonia
{marlon.dumas,f.m.maggi}@ut.ee

Abstract. Process mining is a family of techniques to analyze business processes based on event logs recorded by their supporting information systems. Two recurrent bottlenecks of existing process mining techniques when confronted with real-life event logs are scalability and interpretability of the outputs. A common approach to tackle these limitations is to decompose the process under analysis into a set of stages, such that each stage can be mined separately. However, existing techniques for automated discovery of stages from event logs produce decompositions that are very different from those that domain experts would produce manually. This paper proposes a technique that, given an event log, discovers a stage decomposition that maximizes a measure of modularity borrowed from the field of social network analysis. An empirical evaluation on real-life event logs shows that the produced decompositions more closely approximate manual decompositions than existing techniques.

Keywords: Process mining · Decomposition · Clustering · Modularity · Multistage

1 Introduction

Process mining offers numerous opportunities to extract insights about business process performance and conformance from event logs recorded by enterprise information systems [1]. Among other things, process mining techniques allow analysts to discover process models from event logs for as-is analysis, to check the conformance of recorded process executions against normative process models, or to visualize process performance indicators. Process mining techniques however suffer from scalability issues when applied to large event logs, both in terms of computational requirements and in terms of interpretability of the produced outputs. For example, process models discovered from large event logs are often spaghetti-like and provide limited insights [1].

A common approach to tackle this limitation is to decompose the process into stages, such that each stage can be mined separately. This idea has been successfully applied in the context of automated process discovery [2] and performance mining [3]. The question is then how to identify a suitable set of stages and how to

E. Dubois and K. Pohl (Eds.): CAiSE 2017, LNCS 10253, pp. 577–594, 2017.
DOI: 10.1007/978-3-319-59536-8_36

map the events in the log into stages. For simpler processes, the stage decomposition can be manually identified, but for complex processes, automated support for stage identification is required. Accordingly, several automated approaches to stage decomposition have been proposed [4–6]. However, these approaches have not been designed with the goal of approximating manual decompositions, and as we show in this paper, the decompositions they produce turn out to be far apart from the corresponding manual decompositions.

This paper puts forward an automated technique to split an event log into stages, in a way that mimics manual stage decompositions. The proposed technique is designed based on two key observations: (i) that stages are intuitively fragments of the process in-between two milestone events; and (ii) that the stage decomposition is modular, meaning that there is a high number of direct dependencies inside each stage (high cohesion), and a low number of dependencies across stages (low coupling) – an observation that has also been applied in the context of process model decomposition [7] and more broadly in the fields of systems design and programming in general. For example, a loan origination process at a bank has multiple stages such as the application is assessed (accepted/rejected milestone), offered (offer letter sent milestone), negotiated (agreement signed milestone), and settled (agreement executed milestone). There may be many back-and-forth or jumps inside a stage, but relatively little across these stages.

The proposed technique starts by constructing a graph of direct control-flow dependencies from the event log. Candidate milestones are then identified by using techniques for computing graph cuts. A subset of these potential cut points is finally selected in a way that maximizes the modularity of the resulting stage decomposition according to a modularity measure borrowed from the field of social network analysis. The technique has been evaluated using real-life logs in terms of its ability to approximate manual decompositions using a well-accepted measure for the assessment of cluster quality.

The rest of the paper is structured as follows. Section 2 discusses related work. Section 3 presents the proposed technique and Sect. 4 describes its empirical evaluation. Finally, Sect. 5 summarizes the contributions and outlines future work directions.

2 Related Work

The problem of automated decomposition of event logs into stages has been approached from multiple perspectives. For example, Carmona et al. [4] extract a transition system from an event log and apply a graph cut algorithm over this transition system to identify stages. A formal divide and conquer framework has been defined and formalized in [5], which has led to several instantiations and applications in case studies [2,6,8]. The key idea of this framework is to cluster activities in event logs by first constructing an activity causal graph from the logs and then searching for regions of heavy connected edges (edges with high weights) as activity clusters. A recent work of local process model discovery [9] also seeks to cluster activities into subsets in order to speed up its performance as well as to increase the quality of the detected models. It uses three heuristics based on Markov clustering, log entropy and maximal relative information gain.

The above decompositions have been applied to automated process discovery. Other decomposition techniques have been proposed in the context of performance mining. For example, the Performance Analysis with Simple Precedence Diagram plug-in ProM [10] uses a medoid-based approach to find activity clusters. Given a similarity measure between activities, this technique identifies possible medoids and a membership function to determine to which medoid an activity should be assigned. A similar approach has been proposed in the context of queue mining from event logs [11].

None of the above techniques has been designed and evaluated in the view of producing stage decompositions that approximate manual ones. In the experiments reported later, we assess the performance of [10] and [5,6,8] with respect to manual decompositions, and compare it to the approach proposed in this paper.

Other related work deals with the problem of identifying sub-processes in an event log [12,13]. The output of these techniques is a log of the top-level process and a set of logs of sub-processes thereof. This output is not a stage decomposition. In a stage decomposition, every activity label in the log must be assigned to exactly one stage, i.e. the stages must form a partition of the set of activity labels, whereas the techniques described in [12,13] do not ensure that every activity label belongs to only one sub-process. In fact, these techniques do not guarantee that any sub-process will be found at all.

3 Stage Decomposition Technique

The proposed technique for extracting stages from an event log proceeds in two steps. In the first step, we construct a weighted graph from the event log capturing the direct-follows relation between activities in the process. In the second step, we split the nodes in the graph (i.e. the activities) into stages with the aim of maximizing a modularity measure. Below we introduce each of these two steps in detail.

3.1 From Event Log to Flow Graph

Table 1 shows an example event log of a loan origination process. An event log consists of a set of *cases*, where a case is a uniquely identified execution of a process. For example, the loan application identified by c_2 is a case. Each case consists of a sequence of *events*. An event is the most granular element of a log and is characterized by a set of attributes such as *timestamp* (the moment when the event occurred), *activity label* (the name of the action taken in the event), and *event types* relating to the activity lifecycle, such as "schedule", "start", and "complete".

Definition 1 (Event Logs). *An event log EL is a tuple (E, ET, A, C, time, act, type, case), where E is a set of events,* $ET = \{start, complete\}$ *is a set of*

Table 1. Example event log.

Case ID	Event ID	Event type	Timestamp	Activity label
c_1	e_1	Start	05.10 09:00:00	Update application
	e_2	Complete	05.10 10:00:00	Update application
c_2	e_3	Start	06.10 09:00:00	Update application
	e_4	Complete	06.10 10:00:00	Update application
	e_5	Start	08.10 09:00:00	Check application
	e_6	Complete	08.10 10:00:00	Check application
	e_7	Start	09.10 08:30:00	Check application
	e_8	Complete	09.10 09:00:00	Check application
c_3	e_9	Start	08.10 09:00:00	Update application
	e_{10}	Complete	08.10 10:00:00	Update application
	e_{11}	Start	09.10 09:00:00	Check application
	e_{12}	Complete	09.10 09:15:00	Check application
	e_{13}	Start	11.10 09:00:00	Follow-up offer
	e_{14}	Complete	11.10 10:00:00	Follow-up offer

event types, A is a set of activity labels, C is a set of cases, time: $E \rightarrow \mathbb{R}_0^+$ is a function that assigns a timestamp to an event, act: $E \rightarrow A$ is a function that assigns an activity label to an event, type: $E \rightarrow ET$ is a function that assigns an event type to an event, and case: $E \rightarrow C$ relates an event to a case. We write $e \lesssim_E e'$ iff $time(e) \leq time(e')$. In this paper, we only use "complete" events, denoted as E^c, where $E^c = \{e \in E | type(e) = complete\}$.

A *process graph* is a directed graph in which *nodes* represent activities and *edges* represent direct-follows relations between activities. For example, if activity b occurs after activity a in a case, the graph contains a node a, a node b and a directed edge from a to b. In addition, edges carry *weights* representing the frequency of the direct-follows relation between two related activities in the log.

Definition 2 (Process Graph). *A process graph of an event log EL=(E, ET, A, C, time, act, type, case) is a graph $G_{EL} = (V_{EL}, F_{EL}, W_{EL})$, where:*

- *V_{EL} is a set of nodes, each representing an activity, i.e. $V_{EL} = A$.*
- *F_{EL} is a set of directed edges, each representing the direct-follows relation between two activities based on "complete" events. Activity a_2 directly follows activity a_1 if there is a case in which the "complete" event e_2 of a_2 follows the "complete" event e_1 of a_1 without any other "complete" events in-between, i.e. e_1 is in a direct "complete" sequence with e_2. Event e_1 is in a direct "complete" sequence with e_2, denoted $e_1 \longrightarrow e_2$, iff $e_1 \in E^c \wedge e_2 \in E^c \wedge e_1 \neq e_2 \wedge case(e_1) = case(e_2) \wedge e_1 \lesssim_E e_2 \wedge \nexists e_3 \in E^c[e_3 \neq e_1 \wedge e_3 \neq e_2 \wedge case(e_3) = case(e_1) \wedge e_1 \lesssim_E e_3 \wedge e_3 \lesssim_E e_2]$. Thus, $F_{EL} = \{(a_1, a_2) \in V_{EL} \times V_{EL} | \exists e_1, e_2 \in E^c[act(e_1) = a_1 \wedge act(e_2) = a_2 \wedge e_1 \longrightarrow e_2]\}$.*

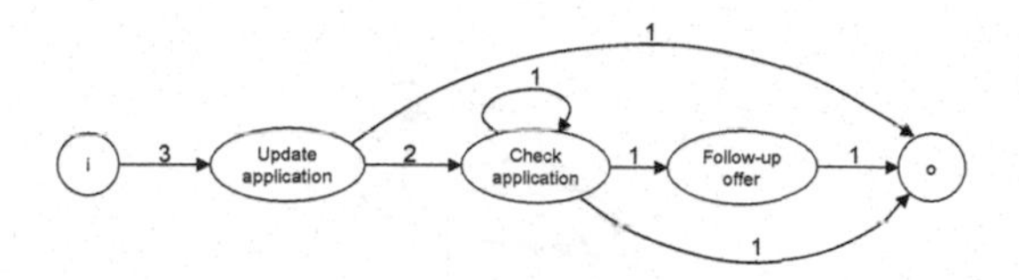

Fig. 1. Flow graph created from the event log in Table 1.

- W_{EL} *is a function that assigns a weight to an edge,* W_{EL}: $F_{EL} \rightarrow \mathbb{N}_0^+$. *The weight of an edge connecting node* a_1 *to node* a_2*, denoted* $W_{EL}(a_1, a_2)$*, is the frequency of the direct-follows relation between* a_1 *and* a_2 *in the log, i.e.* $W_{EL}(a_1, a_2) = |\{(e_1, e_2) \in E^c \times E^c | act(e_1) = a_1 \wedge act(e_2) = a_2 \wedge e_1 \longrightarrow e_2\}|$.

The process graph constructed above has a set of start nodes called *firstacts* containing the first activities of all cases, and a set of end nodes called *lastacts* containing the last activities of all cases, i.e. $firstacts(V_{EL}) = \{a \in V_{EL} | \exists e \in E^c\colon [act(e) = a \wedge \nexists e' \in E^c | e' \longrightarrow e]\}$, and $lastacts(V_{EL}) = \{a \in V_{EL} | \exists e \in E^c\colon [act(e) = a \wedge \nexists e' \in E^c | e \longrightarrow e']\}$.

From a process graph, we can derive a corresponding *flow graph*, which has only one source node i and one sink node o.

Definition 3 (Flow Graph). *The flow graph of a process graph* $G_{EL} = (V_{EL}, F_{EL}, W_{EL})$ *is a graph* $FL(G_{EL}) = (V_{EL}^{FL_G}, F_{EL}^{FL_G}, W_{EL}^{FL_G})$*, where:*

- $V_{EL}^{FL_G} = V_{EL} \cup \{i, o\}, \{i, o\} \cap V_{EL} = \varnothing$.
- $F_{EL}^{FL_G} = F_{EL} \cup \{(i, x) | x \in firstacts(V_{EL})\} \cup \{(x, o) | x \in lastacts(V_{EL})\}$
- $W_{EL}^{FL_G}(a_1, a_2) = \begin{cases} W_{EL}(a_1, a_2) & \text{if } a_1 \neq i \wedge a_2 \neq o \\ |\{e \in E^c | act(e) = a_2 \wedge [\nexists e' \in E^c | e' \longrightarrow e]\}| & \text{if } a_1 = i \\ |\{e \in E^c | act(e) = a_1 \wedge [\nexists e' \in E^c | e \longrightarrow e']\}| & \text{if } a_2 = o \end{cases}$

Figure 1 illustrates a flow graph constructed from the example log in Table 1, while Fig. 2 shows a flow graph created from a simulated log.

3.2 Stage Decomposition and Quality Measure

We assume that a process stage exhibits a *quasi-SESE* (single entry single exit) fragment on a flow graph. A quasi-SESE fragment is a MEME (multi-entry multi-exit) fragment, which has one entry point with high inflow and one exit point with high outflow (see Fig. 2), where inflow (outflow) is the total weight of the incoming (outgoing) edges. The entry and exit points are *transition nodes* between stages. We aim at developing a technique to extract a list of stages from a flow graph called a *stage decomposition*, where stages are sets of nodes.

In order to measure the quality of stage decompositions, we use *modularity* [14], which was proposed for detecting community structures in social networks. A community structure is characterized by a high density of edges within a community and a low number of edges connecting different communities. The

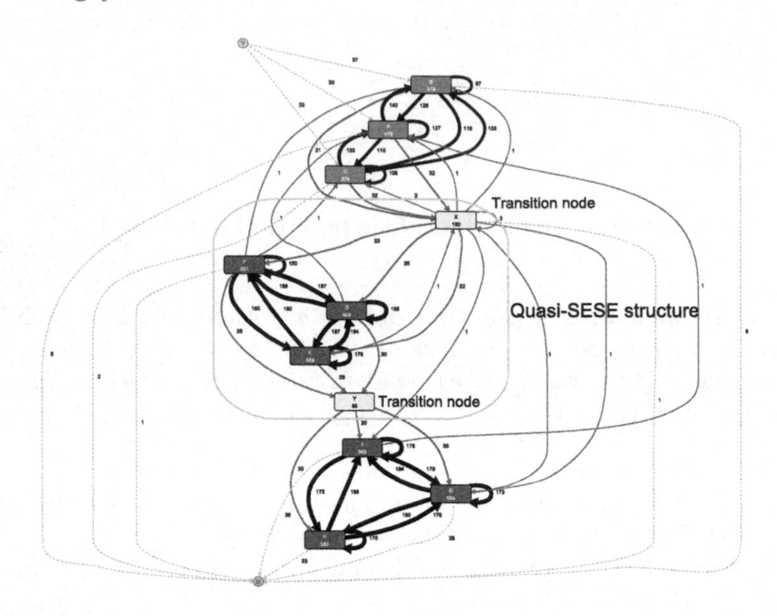

Fig. 2. Example quasi-SESE fragments.

higher the modularity is, the more a network exhibits a community structure. In this paper, we use a variant of modularity for weighted and directed graphs which are the characteristics of the flow graphs defined above.

Let S be a stage decomposition extracted from a flow graph based on an event log EL, and $S_i \in S$, where $i = 1 \ldots |S|$, be a stage. Let $W_{EL}^{FL_G}(S_i, S_j)$ be the total weight of edges connecting S_i to S_j (excluding self-loops), $W_{EL}^{FL_G}(S_i, S_j) = \sum_{a_1 \in S_i, a_2 \in S_j, a_1 \neq a_2} W_{EL}^{FL_G}(a_1, a_2)$. Let W^T be the total weight of all edges in the graph excluding self-loops, $W^T = \sum_{a_1, a_2 \in V_{EL}^{FL_G}, a_1 \neq a_2} W_{EL}^{FL_G}(a_1, a_2)$. The modularity of a stage decomposition is computed based on a *modular graph* which is the flow graph with a special treatment for transition nodes (see Fig. 3). Every transition node in the stage decomposition is split into two child nodes, one as an end node of one stage and the other as a start node of the next stage. The edges connected to the transition node are connected to the child nodes accordingly. The child nodes are also connected between each other through a new edge with weight equal to zero. In this way, the weight of edges in the modular graph remains the same as in the original graph. The modular graph is used for computing modularity because it can well reflect the quality of stage decomposition.

Let $W_{EL}^{FL'_G}(S_i, S_j)$ be the total weight of edges connecting S_i to S_j in the modular graph. The modularity of a stage decomposition S is computed as follows.

$$Q = \sum_{i=1}^{|S|} (E_i - A_i^2) \quad (1)$$

where $E_i = \frac{W_{EL}^{FL'_G}(S_i,S_i)}{W^T}$ is the fraction of edges that connect nodes within stage S_i and $A_i = \frac{\sum_{j=1}^{|S|} W_{EL}^{FL'_G}(S_j,S_i)}{W^T}$ is the fraction of edges that connect to stage S_i, including those within stage S_i and those from other stages.

Stage decomposition may become overly fragmented as a fragment could in principle be composed of only two strongly connected activities. Therefore, we introduce *minimum stage size* indicating the smallest number of activities in any given stage as a user parameter for stage decomposition. Through this, one can decide on what level of granularity they may want to look at stages.

3.3 Stage Decomposition Algorithm

Given an event log, we seek to find a stage decomposition that can maximize modularity. To this end, we propose a technique that starts from the flow graph constructed from the log, and recursively decomposes it into sets of nodes using the notion of min-cut as calculated by Ford-Fulkerson's algorithm. Note that the min-cut here is the one found in the graph after a node has been removed. The set of edges in that min-cut is called a *cut-set* associated with the removed node, and the total weight of edges in the cut-set is called *cut-value*. Together, a node and its cut-set form a border between two graph fragments. The lower the cut-value is, the more the related fragments will resemble quasi-SESE fragments. Therefore, if we find a set of nodes with low cut-values, we can take multiple graph cuts on those nodes and their cut-sets to obtain a stage decomposition that can approximate the maximum modularity.

Transition nodes intuitively have lower cut-values than the min-cut found by Ford-Fulkerson's algorithm in the original flow graph (called *source-min-cut*). Thus, we can use the source-min-cut as a threshold when selecting a candidate list of cut-points, i.e. nodes with cut-values smaller than that of the source-min-cut will be selected. Further, in a flow graph, the source-min-cut can be computed in constant time as it is equal to the set of outgoing edges of the source node of the graph or the set of incoming edges of the sink node.

Once we have a candidate list, the key question is how to find a subset of nodes to form a stage decomposition that can maximize modularity. One way is to generate all possible subsets from the list, create stage decompositions based on all subsets, and select the one that has the highest modularity. However, this approach may suffer from combinatorial problems if the number of candidate nodes is large. For example, if we assume that the flow graph has 60 nodes and the candidate list has 30 nodes, the total number of subsets would be $\binom{30}{1} + \binom{30}{2} + ... + \binom{30}{30} = 1{,}050{,}777{,}736$. We thus propose two algorithms (Algorithms 1 and 2) to find a stage decomposition that can approximate the maximum modularity. The inputs to the algorithms are an event log and a minimum stage size.

Algorithm 1 is a greedy algorithm. The main idea (Lines 9–22) is to search in the candidate list for a cut-point that can result in a stage decomposition with two stages and of highest modularity. Then it removes the node from the candidate list (Line 20) and searches in the list again for another cut-point that can create a new decomposition with three stages and of highest modularity, i.e. higher than the former decomposition and the highest among all decompositions with three stages, and so on until it cannot either find a stage decomposition of higher modularity or all new decompositions have a stage of smaller size than the minimum stage size. Note that stage decomposition is recursive meaning a stage in the current decomposition will be decomposed into two sub-stages based on a selected cut-point (Line 14). Modularity is computed according to Eq. 1 based on the modular graph as described above (Line 15).

Algorithm 2 has the same structure as Algorithm 1, but uses the lowest cut-value as a heuristic. Firstly, it sorts the candidate list in ascending order of cut-values, then it sequentially picks every node from the list to create recursive stage decompositions until the modularity is not increased or all new decompositions have a stage of smaller size than the minimum threshold.

The worst-case time complexity of functions used in the algorithms can be computed as follows. The *create_flow_graph* function is $O(V + F)$, where $V = V_{EL}^{FL_G}$ and $F = F_{EL}^{FL_G}$. The *node_min_cut* function removes a node from the graph and uses Ford-Fulkerson's algorithm to find a min-cut; it is $O(Fw)$, where w is the maximum weight of edges in the flow graph [15]. The *source_min_cut* function is $O(1)$ since it only computes the total weight of edges originating from the source node. The *find_cut_stage* function searches a stage that contains the current node in the current stage decomposition; it is $O(V)$. The *cut_graph* function (Algorithm 3) is $O(V + F)$, which performs a depth-first search to find disconnected components in the graph [15]. The *copy_sd* function is $O(V)$ (replace a stage with two sub-stages). The *modularity* function is $O(V + F)$, which involves copying the original graph to a new one with a special treatment for cut-points ($O(V + F)$) and computing the modularity based on Eq. 1 ($O(F)$). The *get_activity_labels* function is $O(V)$ (extract activity labels from nodes). The *sort* function (Algorithm 2) is $O(V \log V)$. Based on these observations, the complexity of Algorithm 1 is $O(V^2(V + F)))$, and Algorithm 2 is $O(V(V + F))$.

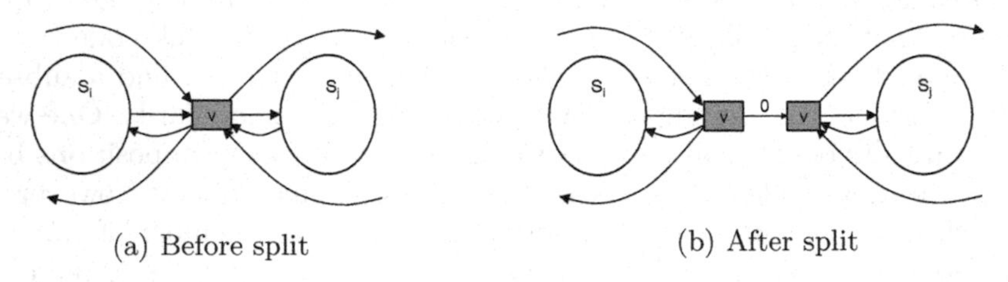

(a) Before split (b) After split

Fig. 3. Treatment for transition nodes in computing modularity.

4 Evaluation

We call our technique *Staged Process Miner* (SPM) and implemented it as a ProM plug-in as well as a stand-alone Java tool[1]. We evaluated the technique

[1] Available from http://apromore.org/platform/tools.

Algorithm 1. Highest Modularity Stage Decomposition

```
   Input: EL: an event log
          minStateSize: minimum number of activities in a stage
   Output: A sequence of stages, each is a set of activity labels
 1 G = create_flow_graph(EL)
 2 CandidateNodes := {}
 3 forall v in V_EL^FLG \ {i, o} do
 4     <v.mincut, v.cutset>:= node_min_cut(G, v)
 5     if v.mincut < source_min_cut(G) then
 6         CandidateNodes := CandidateNodes ∪ {v}
 7 CurrentBestSD := [V_EL^FLG \ {i, o}]
 8 NewBestSD := CurrentBestSD
 9 while CandidateNodes ≠ {} do
10     forall v in CandidateNodes do
11         CutStage := find_cut_stage(CurrentBestSD, v)
12         <PreStage, SucStage>:= cut_graph(G, v, CutStage)
13         if |PreStage| ≥ minStateSize and |SucStage| ≥ minStateSize then
14             NewSD := copy_sd(CurrentBestSD, CutStage, PreStage, SucStage)
15             if modularity(NewSD, G) > modularity(NewBestSD, G) then
16                 NewBestSD := NewSD
17                 BestCutPoint := v
18     if NewBestSD ≠ CurrentBestSD then
19         CurrentBestSD := NewBestSD
20         CandidateNodes := CandidateNodes \ {BestCutPoint}
21     else
22         break // stop when modularity is not increased
23 return get_activity_labels(CurrentBestSD)
```

Algorithm 2. Lowest Cut-value Stage Decomposition

```
   Input: EL: an event log
          minStageSize: minimum number of activities in a stage
   Output: A sequence of stages, each is a set of activity labels
   // Line 1-7 is the same as Algorithm 1
 8 Candidates_sorted := sort(CandidateNodes, min_cut, asc)
 9 while Candidates_sorted ≠ [] do
10     v := head(Candidates_sorted)
11     CutStage := find_cut_stage(CurrentBestSD, v)
12     <PreStage, SucStage>:= cut_graph(G, v, CutStage)
13     if |PreStage| ≥ minStateSize and |SucStage| ≥ minStateSize then
14         NewSD := copy_sd(CurrentBestSD, CutStage, PreStage, SucStage)
15         if modularity(NewSD, G) > modularity(CurrentBestSD, G) then
16             CurrentBestSD := NewSD
17         else
18             break // stop when modularity is not increased
19     Candidates_sorted := tail(Candidates_sorted)
20 return get_activity_labels(CurrentBestSD)
```

through a range of real-life logs and against two baselines. The input to the technique is an event log and the minimum stage size; the output is an ordered set of activity sets, where each activity set represents a stage. The ProM plug-in also offers a visualization of the stage decomposition as *staged process maps*, where boxes represent stages and list all activities that belong to a given stage,

Algorithm 3. *cut_graph*

```
Input: G: a flow graph
       v: a node
       CutStage: a node set containing v
Output: a pair of subsets of CutStage
1 G_aftercut := remove_edges(remove_node(G, v), v.cutset)                    // Graph cut
2 G_source := source_graph(G_aftercut)              // The subgraph containing the source
3 PreStage := (CutStage ∩ V_G_source) ∪ {v}
4 SucStage := CutStage \ PreStage
5 return <PreStage, SucStage>
```

and arcs between stages report the frequency of handover from one stage to the other (the thicker the arc, the higher the frequency) – see Fig. 5 for an example.

The purpose of this research is to determine if it is possible to algorithmically produce stage decompositions of event logs that mimic decompositions produced manually by domain experts. Accordingly, we define the quality of a stage decomposition in terms of its similarity relative to a manually produced ground truth, the evaluation aims at addressing the following top-level question:

Q1. How does the quality of the stage decomposition produced by our technique compare to that of existing baselines?

The decomposition produced by our technique depends on the selected minimum stage size. Accordingly, we also address the following ancillary question:

Q2. How does the quality of the decomposition produced by our technique vary depending on the minimum stage size?

4.1 Datasets

We used seven publicly available, real-life event logs. These include two logs from the Business Process Intelligence (BPI) Challenge 2012 and 2013, and five logs from the BPI Challenge 2015. Table 2 reports descriptive statistics on the size of these datasets.

BPI12[2] is a loan origination process in a Dutch bank. Its stages are: (i) pre-assess application completeness, (ii) assess eligibility, (iii) offer & negotiate loan packages with customers, iv) validate & approve. As a ground truth, these stages are marked in the log by milestone events occurring at the end of each stage, such as A_PREACCEPTED (stage i) and A_ACCEPTED (stage ii), where "A" stands for Application. We preprocessed this log by replacing a group of milestone events occurring usually simultaneously at the end of a stage with one representative milestone event only.

BPI13[3] is an IT incident handling process at Volvo Belgium. A stage in this process reflects the IT helpdesk level (team) where an IT incident ticket is processed. The IT department has three levels from 1 to 3. The ground truth of stages thus is the helpdesk level of the resource who initiates an event. This log

[2] doi:10.4121/uuid:3926db30-f712-4394-aebc-75976070e91f.

[3] doi:10.4121/uuid:500573e6-accc-4b0c-9576-aa5468b10cee.

is preprocessed by selecting only complete cases, i.e. cases that have completed all stages.

BPI15[4] is a set of five logs from five Dutch municipalities relating to a building permit application process. This process has many stages, such as: (i) application receipt, (ii) completeness check of the application, (iii) investigation leading to a resolution (e.g. accept, reject, ask for more info), (iv) communication of the resolution, (v) public review, (vi) decision finalization, and (vii) objection and complaint filing. The ground truth of stages in this process is encoded in the action_code field which has a generic format 01_HOOFD_xyy, where x indicates the stage number and yy indicates the activity code within the stage. This log is preprocessed by selecting only events of the main process (i.e. events with HOOFD code), and then selecting cases that have completed stage 1 to stage 4, which show strong quasi-SESE fragments.

Table 2. Statistics on the datasets used in the evaluation.

Dataset	Business process	Number of cases	Number of events	Event classes
BPI12	Loan origination	13,087	127,290	19
BPI13	IT incident handling	175	1,996	27
BPI15-1	Building permit application	834	11,451	61
BPI15-2		618	8,979	52
BPI15-3		1,013	13,929	60
BPI15-4		792	10,710	50
BPI15-5		951	13,682	56

4.2 Baselines

We used two baseline techniques in our evaluation: the *Divide and Conquer framework* (DC) and the *Performance Analysis with Simple Precedence Diagram* (SPD) presented in Sect. 2. They are both available in ProM.

DC consists of a set of ProM plug-ins run in sequence: Discover Matrix, Create Graph, Create Clusters and Modify Clusters. These plug-ins require one to configure many parameters, notably the number of clusters and the target cluster size. This tool-chain is designed to be used in an interactive manner where users can see how their selected parameters affect the decomposition through visualizations. Since clusters must be disjoint in a stage decomposition, we select parameters for this tool-chain in such a way to only generate disjoint clusters.

SPD takes as input an event log and a number of clusters to be produced. The output is a diagram called *Simple Precedence Diagram* where nodes are clusters of activities. The plug-in uses medoid-based fuzzy clustering. In order to obtain disjoint clusters, we adapted the membership function such that given an activity it only returns one medoid with the highest membership value.

[4] doi:10.4121/uuid:31a308ef-c844-48da-948c-305d167a0ec1.

4.3 Accuracy Index

To assess the accuracy of a stage decomposition against the ground truth, we experimented with three well-known external indexes of clustering quality: *Rand*, *Fowlkes–Mallows* and *Jaccard* [16]. These indexes are used to evaluate the similarity of two clusterings. The higher the index is, the more similar the two clusterings are. In our tests, the Rand Index was very high even for less similar clusterings while Jaccard was often low even for very similar clusterings. Fowlkes–Mallows provided more reasonable results between those returned by the other two indexes. Thus, we decided to report the results using the Fowlkes–Mallows index only, given that Rand and Jaccard also showed consistent results across all datasets and techniques.

The formula for Fowlkes–Mallows is provided below, where n_{11} is the number of activities that are in the same stage in both decompositions, and $n_{10}(n_{01})$ is the number of activities that are in the same stage in the first (second) decomposition but in different stages in the second (first) decomposition.

$$\text{Fowlkes–Mallows} = \frac{n_{11}}{\sqrt{(n_{11} + n_{10})(n_{11} + n_{01})}} \tag{2}$$

4.4 Results

We present the evaluation results in light of the two questions defined above.

Q1. How does the quality of the stage decomposition produced by our technique compare to that of existing baselines?

We run DC, SPD and SPM with different parameter settings and chose for each technique the configuration that achieves the highest accuracy in terms of the Fowlkes–Mallows index. The best configuration for each technique is reported in Table 3. Further values used for DC are: Modify Clusters Miner = "Incremental using Best Score (Overlapping Only)"; Cohesion/Coupling/Balance/Overlap Weight = 100/100/0/100, while all other parameters we used default values, e.g. Discovery Matrix Classifier = Activity.

Table 4 shows the Fowlkes–Mallows index for the three techniques, for each log. SPM, in either of its two variants (highest modularity and lowest cut-value) consistently outperformed the two baseline techniques across all datasets, with slightly higher results achieved by the highest modularity algorithm. These results attest the appropriateness of the modularity measure for stage decomposition, with lowest cut-value being a good approximation of the ground truth. In addition, our heuristics-based techniques with highest modularity and lowest cut-value can approximate the optimal selection of cut-points when comparing with the exhaustive technique for BPI12 and BPI13 logs. For BPI15-x logs, the exhaustive technique does not finish after running for several hours due to the large number of combinations of cut-points. For example, BPI15-1 has 61 activities and 30 candidate cut-points and, for minStageSize = 4, the total number of combinations of cut-points is 614,429,471 ($\binom{30}{1} + \binom{30}{2} + ... + \binom{30}{15}$).

Table 3. Parameters configuration for the evaluated techniques.

Dataset	DC			SPD	SPM
	No. of clusters	Target cluster size	Weight threshold	No. of clusters	Minimum stage size
BPI12	4	5	0.943	4	3
BPI13	3	5	0.834	3	5
BPI15-1	4	12	0.432	4	4
BPI15-2	4	12	0.425	4	4
BPI15-3	4	12	0.527	4	4
BPI15-4	4	12	0.597	4	5
BPI15-5	4	12	0.507	4	5

Table 4. Fowlkes–Mallows index for the evaluated techniques.

Dataset	Stages	DC	SPD	SPM		
				Highest modularity	Lowest cut-value	Exhaustive
BPI12	4	0.30	0.49	**1.0**	0.92	1.0
BPI13	3	0.36	0.73	**0.78**	**0.78**	0.78
BPI15-1	4	0.40	0.54	0.90	**0.92**	Timed-out
BPI15-2	4	0.40	0.52	**0.92**	0.76	Timed-out
BPI15-3	4	0.42	0.50	**0.86**	**0.86**	Timed-out
BPI15-4	4	0.45	0.57	**0.72**	**0.72**	Timed-out
BPI15-5	4	0.46	0.49	**0.83**	**0.83**	Timed-out

As an example, Fig. 4 shows the decomposition identified by our technique (highest modularity) and by the two baselines, for the BPI2015-2 log, on top of the direct-follows graph of the event log. Here activities have been color-coded (or marked in shaded areas) based on the clusters they belong to. We can observe that in both the baselines, stage boundaries are not sharply defined, with many activities being mixed between stages.

The low accuracy of the two baselines is due to the underlying clustering approach used. DC searches for clusters starting from heavy edges (edges with high weights) and growing the cluster to other connected edges with weight over a threshold. This is the reason why it can detect some regions that cover an actual stage, but fails to determine exactly where to stop clustering. SPD searches for clusters based on medoids, i.e. a central node in a direct-follows graph that is close to all other nodes in a cluster, where closeness is measured by the frequency of the direct-follows relation between activities. SPD thus tends to produce a large cluster covering several actual stages because stages are usually

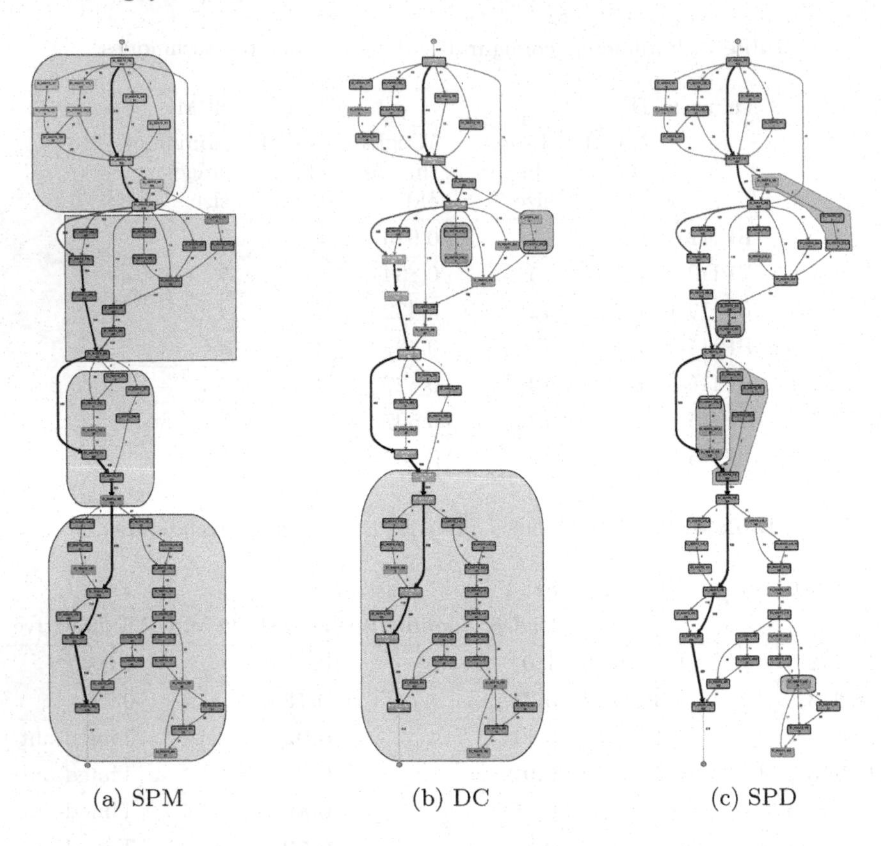

(a) SPM (b) DC (c) SPD

Fig. 4. Stage decomposition for the BPI15-2 log. Shaded areas are activity clusters. Activities not in any shaded areas belong to one big cluster.

strongly connected via transition nodes. In general, both baseline techniques are unable to detect stage boundaries.

In addition, only our technique can retrieve stages in the correct order, while ordering is not part of the results provided by the two baseline techniques. We can see this, for example, in Figs. 5 and 6, which show the stage decomposition for the BPI12 and BPI13 logs provided by our ProM plug-in.

To complement our comparison with baselines, we also experimented with three clustering techniques proposed in local process model discovery [9]. They are based on well-established heuristics used in data mining, such as Markov clustering, log entropy, and maximal relative information gain. However, the results obtained are very different from the ground truth, with Fowlkes–Mallows Index always being below 0.5.

In terms of runtime performance, both our technique and the two baselines perform within reasonable bounds, in the order of seconds (see Table 5). However, the exhaustive technique could not finish for BPI15-x logs after running for several hours.

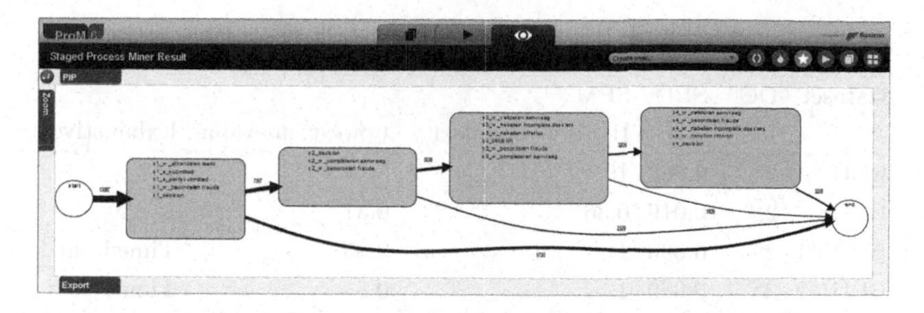

Fig. 5. Stage decomposition produced by SPM for the BPI12 log.

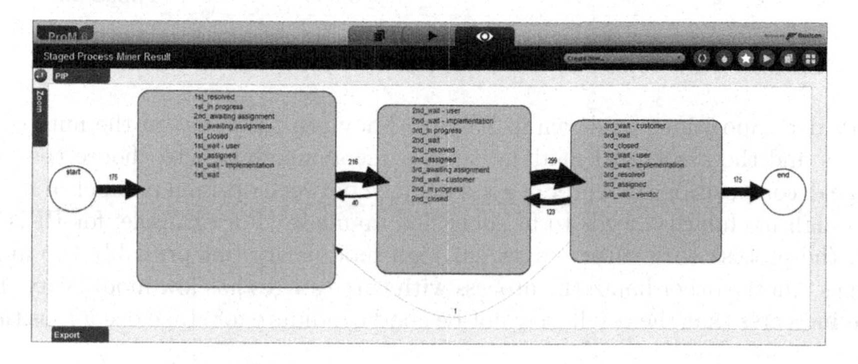

Fig. 6. Stage decomposition produced by SPM for the BPI13 log.

Q2. How does the quality of the decomposition produced by our technique vary depending on the minimum stage size?

To answer this question, we run our technique with the highest modularity algorithm using different values of minimum stage size (minSS), from 2 to half of the total number of activities in an event log. Table 6 provides the characteristics of different stage decompositions, each for a minSS value. It shows that the modularity is higher when minSS is small and peaks when minSS is equal to 2. This is because, when minSS is small, the technique is allowed to decompose the graph into stages as much as possible to increase modularity. For example, for minSS = 2, the best stage decomposition for BPI15-1 log has 7 stages, in which two stages have size 2 (i.e. two activities), one has size 3, one has size 5, one has size 11, one has size 14, and one has size 24.

Notably, in Table 6, for each dataset, one resulting decomposition is very close to the ground truth, such as minSS = 3 for BPI12 (FM = 1.0), minSS = 9 for BPI13 (FM = 0.85), minSS = 4 for BPI15-1 (FM = 0.90), minSS = 4 for BPI15-2 (FM = 0.92), and minSS = 4 for BPI15-3 (FM = 0.86). This suggests how to use our technique for stage-based analysis. Users may decide not to fix the minimum stage size, run the technique for different sizes (as we did in this second experiment) and choose the stage decomposition that best suits their needs. For example, for BPI15-1 log, they can vary the minSS parameter to view different

Table 5. Run-time performance (in seconds)

Dataset	DC[a]	SPD	SPM		
			Highest modularity	Lowest cut-value	Exhaustive
BPI12	2	0.563	10	5	158
BPI13	2	0.019	0.36	0.31	1
BPI15-1	2	0.096	1	0.85	Timed-out
BPI15-2	2	0.069	1	0.85	Timed-out
BPI15-3	2	0.070	1	0.87	Timed-out
BPI15-4	2	0.050	1	0.64	Timed-out
BPI15-5	2	0.072	1	0.73	Timed-out

[a]Estimated due to manual use of plugins

stage decompositions as shown in Table 6. They can then rely on the number of stages and the associated modularity as a recommendation to choose the best stage decomposition. However, a good balance between optimal number of stages and high modularity needs to be identified manually. For example, for BPI15-1 log, the process with seven stages has high modularity but probably too many stages. On the other hand, the process with three stages has low modularity that also indicates that the result may not be good candidate for stage decomposition.

5 Conclusion

Given a business process event log, the technique presented in this paper partitions the activity labels in the log into stages delimited by milestones. The idea is to construct a direct-follows graph from the log, to identify a set of candidate milestones via a minimum cut algorithm, and to heuristically select a subset of these milestones. The paper considered two greedy heuristics: one that selects at each step the milestone with the lowest cut-value, and another that selects milestones that maximize modularity, using a modularity measure originally designed for social networks.

The technique has been implemented as a plug-in in the ProM framework, which splits an event log into stages and generates a staged process map. Experimental results on seven real-life event logs show that: (i) both heuristics significantly outperform previously proposed event log decomposition techniques in terms of the concordance of the produced decompositions relative to manual decompositions; and (ii) the stage decompositions generated by maximizing modularity outperform those based on cut-value. The latter result confirms previous empirical observations in the field of process model decomposition [7], while demonstrating the applicability of a modularity measure for social networks in this setting.

The proposed technique has a range of applications in the field of process mining. For example, stage decompositions can be used to scale up automated process discovery techniques [5,6] or to produce decomposed metrics and visual-

Table 6. Highest Modularity SPM with different minimum stage sizes (MinSS = Minimum Stage Size, Mod = Modularity, FM = Fowlkes–Mallows).

MinSS	BPI12			BPI13			BPI15-1			BPI15-2			BPI15-3		
	Stages	Mod	FM	Stages	Mod	FM	Stages	Mod	FM	Stages	Mod	FM	Stages	Mod	FM
2	6	0.70	0.75	6	0.67	0.56	7	0.80	0.82	7	0.79	0.82	7	0.82	0.76
3	4	0.59	**1.00**	4	0.61	0.72	5	0.77	0.83	5	0.77	0.84	6	0.80	0.75
4	4	0.57	0.81	4	0.61	0.72	4	0.73	**0.90**	4	0.72	**0.92**	4	0.73	**0.86**
5	3	0.55	0.82	3	0.58	0.78	4	0.73	0.90	4	0.72	0.92	4	0.73	0.86
6	3	0.44	0.70	3	0.58	0.78	4	0.73	0.90	4	0.72	0.92	4	0.73	0.86
7	2	0.40	0.67	3	0.58	0.78	4	0.73	0.90	4	0.72	0.92	4	0.73	0.86
8	2	0.40	0.67	3	0.58	0.78	5	0.69	0.61	4	0.68	0.72	4	0.73	0.86
9	2	0.34	0.54	3	0.52	**0.85**	5	0.69	0.61	4	0.68	0.72	4	0.73	0.86
10				2	0.38	0.65	4	0.68	0.73	4	0.68	0.72	4	0.73	0.86
11				2	0.38	0.65	4	0.68	0.73	4	0.68	0.72	4	0.68	0.67
12				2	0.38	0.65	4	0.68	0.73	3	0.58	0.66	4	0.68	0.67
13				2	0.38	0.65	3	0.68	0.73	3	0.58	0.66	3	0.57	0.65
14							3	0.57	0.66	3	0.58	0.62	3	0.57	0.65
15							3	0.57	0.66	3	0.58	0.62	3	0.57	0.65
16							3	0.56	0.63	2	0.49	0.74	3	0.57	0.65
17							3	0.56	0.63	2	0.49	0.74	3	0.56	0.62
18							2	0.49	0.74	2	0.49	0.74	2	0.49	0.69
19							2	0.49	0.74	2	0.49	0.74	2	0.49	0.69
20							2	0.49	0.74	2	0.49	0.74	2	0.49	0.69
21							2	0.49	0.74	2	0.49	0.74	2	0.49	0.69
22							2	0.49	0.74	2	0.49	0.74	2	0.49	0.69
23							2	0.49	0.74	2	0.49	0.74	2	0.49	0.69
24							2	0.49	0.74	2	0.48	0.73	2	0.49	0.69
25							2	0.49	0.74	2	0.48	0.73	2	0.49	0.69
26							2	0.49	0.74				2	0.48	0.68
27							2	0.49	0.74				2	0.48	0.68
28							2	0.48	0.73				2	0.48	0.68
29							2	0.48	0.73						

izations for performance analysis [3]. Investigating these applications is an avenue for future work.

Beyond the field of process mining, the proposed technique could find application in the realm of customer journey analysis, by allowing analysts to identify stages from customer session logs. With suitable extensions, the technique could also be used to compute abstracted views of large event sequences for interactive visual data mining.

Acknowledgments. This research is funded by the Australian Research Council (grant DP150103356) and the Estonian Research Council (grant IUT20-55).

References

1. van der Aalst, W.M.: Process mining: discovering and improving spaghetti and lasagna processes. In: Proceedings of CIDM. IEEE (2011)
2. Hompes, B.F.A., Verbeek, H.M.W., Aalst, W.M.P.: Finding suitable activity clusters for decomposed process discovery. In: Ceravolo, P., Russo, B., Accorsi, R. (eds.) SIMPDA 2014. LNBIP, vol. 237, pp. 32–57. Springer, Cham (2015). doi:10.1007/978-3-319-27243-6_2
3. Nguyen, H., Dumas, M., Hofstede, A.H.M., Rosa, M., Maggi, F.M.: Business process performance mining with staged process flows. In: Nurcan, S., Soffer, P., Bajec, M., Eder, J. (eds.) CAiSE 2016. LNCS, vol. 9694, pp. 167–185. Springer, Cham (2016). doi:10.1007/978-3-319-39696-5_11
4. Carmona, J., Cortadella, J., Kishinevsky, M.: Divide-and-conquer strategies for process mining. In: Dayal, U., Eder, J., Koehler, J., Reijers, H.A. (eds.) BPM 2009. LNCS, vol. 5701, pp. 327–343. Springer, Heidelberg (2009). doi:10.1007/978-3-642-03848-8_22
5. Van Der Aalst, W.M.: A general divide and conquer approach for process mining. In: Proceedings of FedCSIS, pp. 1–10. IEEE (2013)
6. Verbeek, H., van der Aalst, W.M., Munoz-Gama, J.: Divide and conquer. Technical report, BPM Center Report Series (2016)
7. Reijers, H.A., Mendling, J., Dijkman, R.M.: Human and automatic modularizations of process models to enhance their comprehension. Inf. Syst. **36**(5), 881–897 (2011)
8. Verbeek, H.M.W., Aalst, W.M.P.: Decomposed process mining: the ILP case. In: Fournier, F., Mendling, J. (eds.) BPM 2014. LNBIP, vol. 202, pp. 264–276. Springer, Cham (2015). doi:10.1007/978-3-319-15895-2_23
9. Tax, N., Sidorova, N., van der Aalst, W.M., Haakma, R.: Heuristic approaches for generating local process models through log projections. In: Proceedings of CIDM (2016)
10. Dongen, B.F., Adriansyah, A.: Process mining: fuzzy clustering and performance visualization. In: Rinderle-Ma, S., Sadiq, S., Leymann, F. (eds.) BPM 2009. LNBIP, vol. 43, pp. 158–169. Springer, Heidelberg (2010). doi:10.1007/978-3-642-12186-9_15
11. de Smet, L., van der Aalst, W., Verbeek, H.: Queue mining: combining process mining and queueing analysis to understand bottlenecks, to predict delays, and to suggest process improvements. Master thesis, Eindhoven University of Technology (2014)
12. Li, J., Bose, R.P.J.C., Aalst, W.M.P.: Mining context-dependent and interactive business process maps using execution patterns. In: Muehlen, M., Su, J. (eds.) BPM 2010. LNBIP, vol. 66, pp. 109–121. Springer, Heidelberg (2011). doi:10.1007/978-3-642-20511-8_10
13. Conforti, R., Dumas, M., García-Bañuelos, L., La Rosa, M.: BPMN miner: automated discovery of BPMN process models with hierarchical structure. Inf. Syst. **56**, 284–303 (2016)
14. Newman, M.E., Girvan, M.: Finding and evaluating community structure in networks. Phys. Rev. E **69**(2), 026113 (2004)
15. Cormen, T.H., Leiserson, C.E., Rivest, R.L., Stein, C.: Introduction to Algorithms. MIT Press, Cambridge (2009)
16. Halkidi, M., Batistakis, Y., Vazirgiannis, M.: On clustering validation techniques. J. Intell. Inf. Syst. **17**(2–3), 107–145 (2001)

Business Process Modeling Notation

Visual Modeling of Instance-Spanning Constraints in Process-Aware Information Systems

Manuel Gall(✉) and Stefanie Rinderle-Ma

Faculty of Computer Science, University of Vienna, Vienna, Austria
{manuel.gall,stefanie.rinderle-ma}@univie.ac.at

Abstract. Instance-Spanning Constraints (ISCs) have raised attention just recently although they are omnipresent in practice to define conditions across multiple instances or processes, e.g., bundling of cargo. It would be crucial to convey ISC information on, e.g., shared instance resources to users. However, no approach for visualizing ISCs has been presented yet. To overcome this gap we analysed literature and derived visualization requirements for constraints on multiple instances of the same or different processes. The proposed language ISC_Viz is based on BPMN-Q and incorporates existing visual notations to reduce the cognitive load on the user. The applicability of ISC_Viz is shown along 114 ISC modeling examples. Moreover, a questionnaire-based study with 42 participants is conducted in order to assess the usability of ISC_Viz.

Keywords: Constraint visualization · Instance-Spanning Constraints · Compliance · Process-aware information systems

1 Introduction

In many cases, business process instances are not executed in an isolated fashion, but share, for example, resources. Restrictions and properties on these interconnections can be expressed based on so called Instance-Spanning Constraints (ISC) [3]. More precisely, ISCs can span multiple instances, but also multiple processes. An example for an ISC spanning multiple instances of the same process is synchronization at a critical resource (e.g., wait until resource is fully loaded). Imposing an order between treatments for a patient in two medical processes is an example for a process-spanning ISC. As shown by a recent study [14], ISC examples can be found for almost any domain. Although ISCs might refer to design time aspects of business processes, the lion's share of ISC examples becomes effective during runtime [3].

Thus a comprehensive ISC support for business processes is indispensable. This includes formalisms to specify ISC and associated verification techniques in order to check for ISC violations. However, as stated in [9] checking constraints by only providing some kind of *violation: yes/no* answer is in general not sufficient. In turn, it is crucial to adequately include users in the constraint checking process

E. Dubois and K. Pohl (Eds.): CAiSE 2017, LNCS 10253, pp. 597–611, 2017.
DOI: 10.1007/978-3-319-59536-8_37

as often the users are required to handle constraint violations. In order to be able to deal with constraints and their violations it is necessary that users can understand constraints.

Thus visual modeling languages for constraints in business processes are required. For constraints that do not span any instances or processes, i.e., so called intra-instance constraints (IIC), some proposals for visual modeling languages exist, for example, BPMN-Q [2] and extended Compliance Rule Graphs (eCRG) [7]. These languages, however, were not designed having ISC in mind. Hence, overall, there is no language that supports the visual modeling of constraints spanning multiple instances or processes. However, this would be very important since ISC might be even harder to understand than IIC due to the additional information on the spanning part of the constraints.

Thus this work aims at developing a visual modeling language for ISC. In detail the goals are to

- define requirements for an ISC modeling language.
- elaborate and implement a visual modeling language for ISC.
- show the applicability and usability of the suggested language.

In order to reach these goals, the work at hand follows the design science research methodology (cf. [18]). At first, requirements are derived from existing work on constraints in general and ISC specifically. Existing proposals for visual constraint modeling languages in the business process domain are evaluated along the requirements. As a result an existing language is chosen as fundament for elaborating the visual ISC modeling language ISC_Viz, i.e., the resulting artifacts are a collection of requirements, an assessment of existing languages, and ISC_Viz. ISC_Viz is then evaluated in two ways. Its applicability is shown by modeling the representative ISC for each of the categories introduced in [3] and modeling the complete ISC example data set of 114 real-world ISC presented in [14]. The usability of the language is evaluated based on a user study. Stakeholders of the proposed solution can be process and constraint designers, auditors, as well as process participants.

The paper is structured as follows. Section 2 derives requirements for a visual ISC modeling language and Sect. 3 evaluates existing constraint modeling languages along these requirements. In Sect. 4, a visual modeling language for ISC is proposed. Section 5 presents the evaluation. In Sect. 6 related approaches are discussed and Sect. 7 closes with a summary.

2 Requirements

To create a visual language that fits the needs of ISC we derive requirements from existing work. *Ly et al.* [9] introduces a framework for Compliance Monitoring Functionalities (CMF). This framework consists of three groups of requirements, i.e., modeling requirements, execution requirements and user requirements. In the following, we focus on CMF modeling requirements as input for deriving requirements on modeling instance spanning constraints (ISC). The modeling requirements consist of three functionalities referring to time, data, and resources. These three functionalities can be mapped to requirements for modeling ISC.

1. *Time* enables the specification of temporal constraints, e.g., for a specific moment in time and period of time.
2. *Data* can be restricted to one instance or shared between multiple instances of different processes. We differentiate between two data types. *Process data* consists of input and output data which is read or written when a task is executed. *Execution data* is created by executing instances and can be seen as meta data, i.e., how many instances of a certain process are currently running.
3. *Resources* can be restricted i.e. one resource can be accessed by a maximum of five instances simultaneously.

These requirements are refined within the IUPC [11] framework and the CRISP project [3]. The IUPC framework helps to identify process constraints based on several criteria. These criteria are used to define our ISC requirements.

4. *Behavior:* describes in which order tasks are executed. A compliance rule engine might, for example, enforce that a certain task has to be executed before another.
5. *Structural Pattern:* defines the connection between constraint and process. A structural pattern consists of one or multiple tasks.
6. *Trigger:* defines when the constraint is checked. A constraint can be checked based on time and structural pattern. Time can be a specific point in time or a recurring check every day at a certain time. Structural pattern is triggered before or after a task is executed and might involve data and or resources.
7. *Interoperability:* describes that one constraint might span multiple of these requirements, e.g., a booking process has to be executed within a certain time and depends on a specific resource. The proposed visualization shall be able to comprehend different constraint types within one visualization without additional semantics.
8. *Spanning Processes:* ISC can span single or multiple processes [3]. A constraint only referring to one process has to span multiple instances in order to be considered an ISC.
9. *Spanning Instances:* Typically, ISC impose constraints on multiple instances. A constraint that refers to instances in a separate way, i.e., does not span any instances, is referred to as intra-instance constraint (IIC). Taking a design time perspective, ISC can also span multiple processes, but no instances.
10. *Action* refers to the behavioral part of the IUPC framework e.g. synchronization between process instances. Such a synchronization needs two actions *wait* to stop all involved instances before or after a certain activity and *start* to start execution of the synchronous activities.

These 10 requirements build the foundation for evaluating and selecting a visual modeling language. The selected language is then extended to support ISC.

3 Analyzing Visual Constraint Modeling Languages

Our goal is to propose a visual modeling language for ISC that can be used for IIC. For this reason we take a look at current visual constraint modeling languages in the area of business processes and evaluate them along the ISC requirements set out in Sect. 2. The following sections contain a brief description of each language and show a visual model of an IIC for illustrative purposes. As representative IIC we are using an example from a study on constraint visualization, i.e., *"c5: The testing has to be followed by an approval and the integration. Additionally, no changes shall take place between the approval and the integration."* [10]. Assume that this IIC is enacted on the BPMN model depicted in Fig. 1.

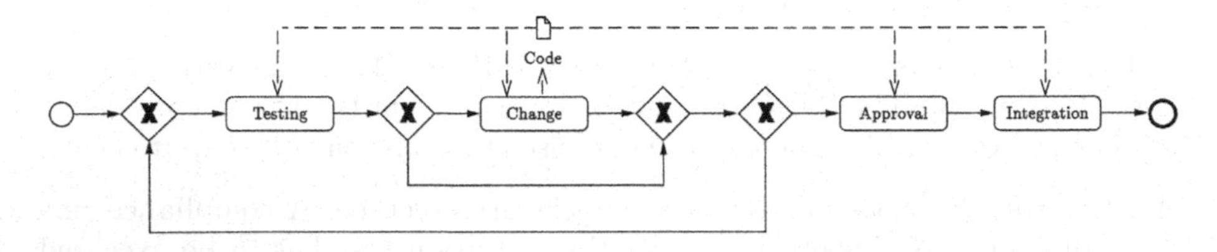

Fig. 1. Code testing example c5 from [10] modeled with BPMN.

To the best of our knowledge, BPMN-Q [2] and eCRG [7] are the only visual modeling languages for constraints in the business process context. Hence both languages are selected as candidates for extension towards modeling ISC and evaluated along the harvested requirements in the following.

3.1 BPMN-Q

BPMN-Q [2] extends BPMN to enable visual query modeling based on a set of processes. However, BPMN-Q can be easily adjusted for compliance checking and hence constitutes a candidate language for visual ISC modeling. One of the strengths of BPMN-Q is that it does not introduce a completely new visual notation as it is based on BPMN. There are a few additional language elements to be learned. In the initial version of BPMN-Q *Awad* focus on control flow. In [2] the approach is extended towards visual modeling of data and resources [1]. Currently the notion of time constraints is not integrated with BPMN-Q. However BPMN allows for modeling time-related information such as point in time and time spans. Overall, this covers the modeling requirements for ISC modeling. Finally, BPMN-Q can be mapped onto past linear time logic (PLTL).

Figure 2 visualizes the constraint *c5* with BPMN-Q syntax.

3.2 Extended Compliance Rules Graphs – eCRG

Compliance Rule Graphs (CRG) [10] initially focused on visually modeling control flow related constraints. The approach was extended (eCRG) [8] to enable

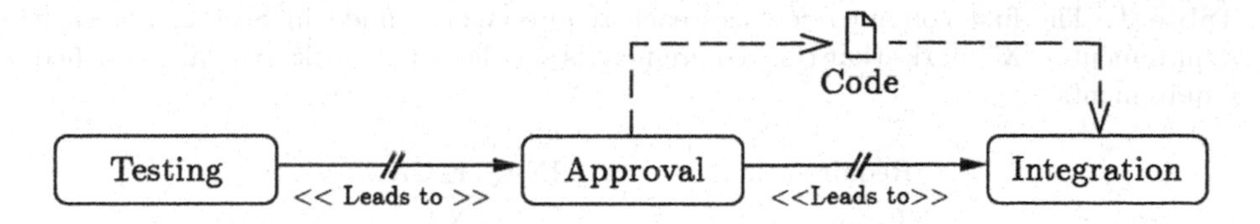

Fig. 2. Code testing example *c5* modeled with BPMN-Q

modeling of time, data, and resource constraints. Time constraints can be modeled in eCRGs in different ways, e.g., by modeling a particular point in time or so called time distance. The latter allows for modeling time constraints for single and multiple tasks. eCRG does not enable the modeling of *execution data.* Figure 3 visualizes constraint *c5* in eCRG syntax.

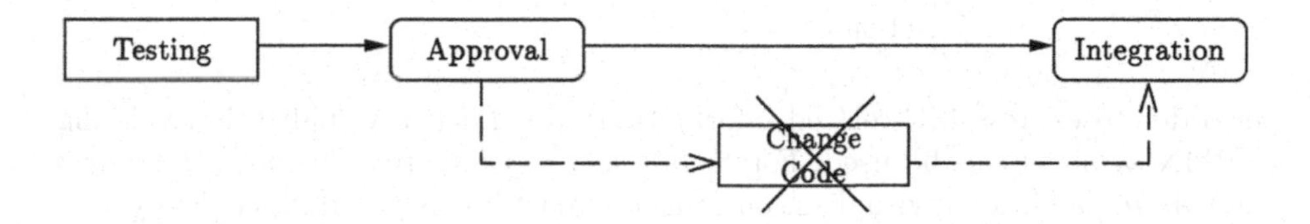

Fig. 3. Code testing example *c5* modeled with E-CRG

3.3 Requirements Analysis

As shown in Table 1 BPMN-Q and eCRG fulfill some of the requirements. Both deal with time and data constraints in a different way, but do not allow for modeling the full capabilities that are required for ISC such as execution data. None of the languages enables the modeling of "spanning information" at process and instance level. Moreover, it is not possible to model that certain actions are to be enforced.

By using the existing BPMN visualization for time the shortcoming of BPMN-Q compared to eCRG is minimal. An advantage of BPMN-Q might be that the underlying process modeling notation BPMN is known to a broader audience. As information on the underlying process models plays a vital role for ISC (even more than for IIC), we finally opted for BPMN-Q as the fundament for developing ISC_Viz. In particular, this requires to propose an extension covering time/data/trigger/action visualization and the instance spanning part of constraints.

4 ISC_Viz

The requirements analysis revealed that BPMN-Q needs extensions with respect to *Trigger*, *Spanning Processes*, *Spanning Instances*, and *Action* (cf. Table 1)

Table 1. The first column references each requirement defined in Sect. 2. For each requirement a "X" marks that this requirement is satisfied, a ~ marks partially satisfied requirements.

Requirements	BPMN-Q	E-CRG
Time	~	X
Data	~	~
Resources	~	~
Behavior	X	X
Structural pattern	X	X
Trigger	~	~
Interoperability	X	X
Spanning processes		
Spanning instances		
Action		

in order to express ISC-related information. For *Trigger* visualization existing BPMN symbols can be used. For *Spanning Processes and Spanning Instances* and *Action* additional visualization concepts must be proposed. Specifically, this means to enrich a graph with additional information. In order to not reinvent the wheel, experience from visualization approaches in the business process domain are considered, i.e., the work on visualizing differences between business process in [4]. In this work, nine visualization possibilities, e.g., shapes, color, and symbols, were analyzed in order to suggest a generic visualization that can be applied to a wide range of process model types.

4.1 Visualizing Spanning Processes and Spanning Instances

As the goal is to extend BPMN-Q with information on *Spanning Processes* and *Spanning Instances* we need a visual style that can be incorporated into the language. For example, adding new shapes for process and instance spanning information does not seem to be sufficient due do the number of new shapes that is necessary for expressing, for example, spanning data elements, time elements, and task dependencies.

We [4] emphasize that colors and symbols are suitable to visualize differences between multiple processes. Color is a visual element that is currently not used within BPMN-Q. By using color to express information on *Spanning Processes* and *Spanning Instances* two additional visual elements are introduced. The "standard" black version for IIC remains the same and two new versions using different colors are introduced for ISC, i.e., *Green* visualizes *Spanning Instances*, while *Blue* visualizes *Spanning Processes.*

4.2 Visualizing Actions

Besides color *we* [4] recommend the usage of symbols to show differences between graphs. For visualizing actions such symbols offer various advantages over color.

An advantage is that different types of actions can be expressed as various symbols are available. Colors are technically not limited, but the cognitive perception is restricted with respect to distinguishing colors. Another advantage of using symbols is extensibility. So far a set of actions for one subject has been described such as start and wait actions connected with an activity. However, further actions are conceivable. In this case these new actions can be visualized using additional symbols. The set of symbols suggested in this paper is known from user interfaces like execution engines and media player controls. Figure 4 depicts the symbols suggested in this work for the action part described in current literature [11,15].

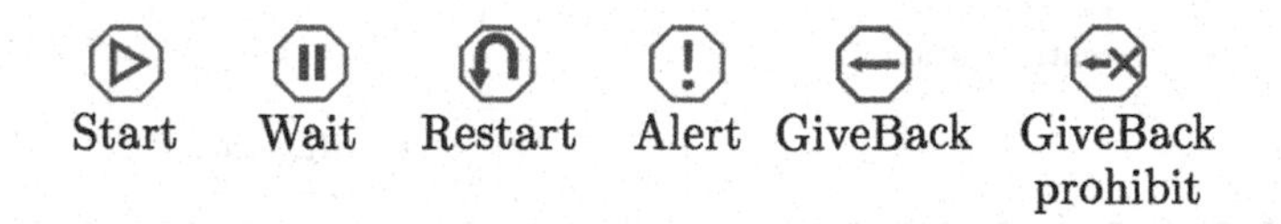

Fig. 4. Selected actions and associated symbols (Color figure online)

4.3 Visualizing Trigger

For trigger visualization symbols from BPMN are used. For constraints involving data and resources we use *conditional.Conditional trigger* describes the integration of external business rules which is suitable for compliance rules. Data and resources checked within the trigger are visualized with arrows leading to the trigger. Time constraints are visualized with the BPMN *Timer*. The *timer trigger* allows for expressing points in time, time spans, and timeouts. In order to differentiate between intra-instance and instance-spanning we use a different color for ISC triggers.

4.4 Complete Visualization

Overall, the proposal is to visualize the spanning part of a constraint with color, the more complex actions with symbols, and the trigger with BPMN symbols.

Illustrating the extensions to BPMN-Q Fig. 5 shows a process model and the ISC *"Wait until centrifuge is filled."* [14]. At first, some explanation is given on the meaning of the colors. Then the general structure of the language is described.

- Green activity shows that this constraint spans multiple instances.
- Purple shows a trigger with a data constraint "execution data". Centrifugation is only done when the centrifuge is full. Information if the centrifuge is full can be derived from other instances. When there are 5 mixtures waiting for centrifugation (execution data) and the centrifuge allows for 6 mixtures then all 6 instances resume work after the 6th mixture is put into the centrifuge.

- Red are the actions as they perform critical tasks and influence the process execution. In this example all instances are stopped before centrifugation until the centrifuge is full. When the centrifuge is full all instances resume their work.

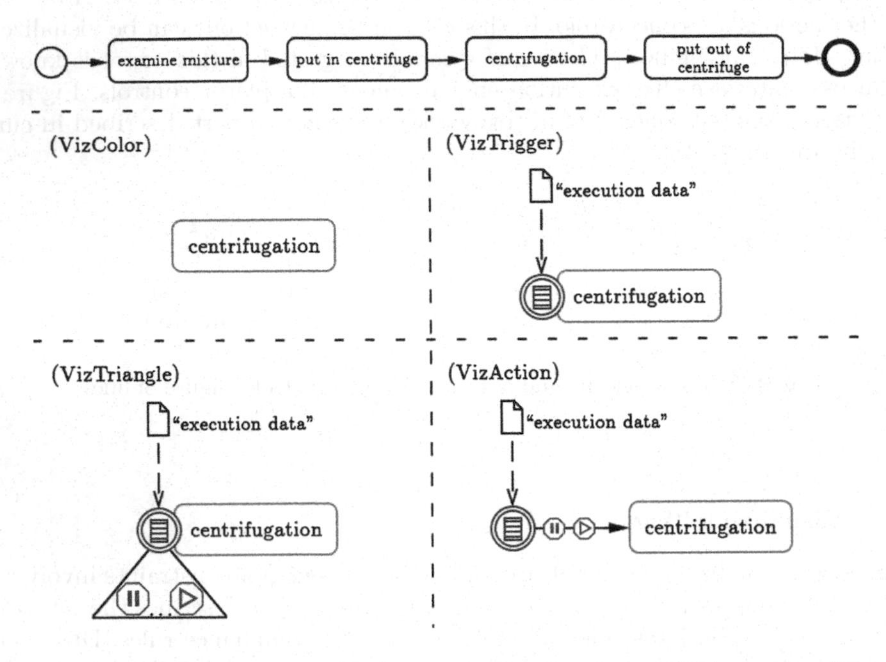

Fig. 5. Top: shows a process model for a centrifugation process. Bottom: visualizes an ISC with trigger and actions. (Color figure online)

As can be seen from Fig. 5 the constraint is modeled in four ways as it is not yet answered how many details shall be shown to the user. These four types are referenced by the following evaluation as follows.

- *VizColor*: visualizes the spanning part of the constraint.
- *VizTrigger*: is based on *VizColor* and adds the *trigger* visualization.
- *VizTriangle*: is based on *VizTrigger* with additional *action* visualization. To show the actions within a triangle is a way to keep the constraint vertically small when multiple activities with diverse trigger and actions are involved.
- *VizAction*: describes the same information as *VizTriangle*, but with a different visualization of the *action* part. Here, the actions are modeled and visualized in a more process-oriented way and thus connected by edges.

5 Evaluation

We evaluate the ISC_Viz proposal in two ways. First a questionnaire is addressing visual detail and understanding of modeled constraints. Secondly, the applicability is illustrated by modeling examples for each category introduced by *Fdhila et al.* [3].

5.1 Questionnaire

The questionnaire was designed aiming at two goals. The first goal was to identify which of the proposed visualizations is preferred by the participants. Second goal was to identify how certain BPMN-Q language extensions such as actions and trigger are understood by the participants.

Method. The initial draft of the questionnaire was designed based on the guidelines by *Porst* [13]. Structured with an introduction, questions targeting the visualization and gathering empirical data. The introduction briefly explained ISC and provided an example process consisting of three constraints where each one was visualized with all four types presented in Sect. 4.4. First question of the questionnaire was about visual preference. Based on three example constraints participants had to mark their preferred type. Further questions from this section refer to, for example, assignment of attributes (spanning, trigger, actions) for a given constraint, based on a visualization selecting an appropriate textual description, ranking of visualizations, animation, and color validation. The questionnaire concludes with demographic questions about age, employment, and gender.

This draft was refined with a 2-stage pretest. In the first stage the questions were discussed with a group of peers familiar with ISC. Goal of this stage was to validate the understanding and goal behind each question. Outcome of this stage was a refinement of question and answer wording. The second stage consisted of a test where three participants from the target audience performed the questionnaire. These three participants were allowed and encouraged to ask questions, but those questions were just noted and not answered. Based on this stage the introduction was changed as participants were confused what the difference between trigger and action is.

As ISC visualization is a new and arising research topic there does not exist a large group of experts for participating in the questionnaire. Therefore the target audience was set to participants familiar with process modeling visualizations as this is one of the foundations our visualization builds upon. On a scale from 1 (expert) to 7 (never worked with process models) the participants rated themselves with a mean (2.90) and median (3). In total 42 computer science students from three master courses participated in the questionnaire. The majority of participants (59.52%) were men, (30.95%) women, (7.14%) with no answer and (2.39%) other. The questionnaire and respective answers are available from[1].

Results. The questionnaire was printed and while all questions besides the demographic questions are mandatory it is up to the participant if the question is answered. From the set of 42 participants two missed to answer a question. The answers of these two participants were retained within the dataset. For affected evaluations we will outline that answers are missing.

---

[1] http://gruppe.wst.univie.ac.at/projects/crisp/index.php?t=visualization.

The goal is to measure how well the ISC_Viz proposal is understood with focus on the extensions, i.e., *Spanning Processes*, *Spanning Instances*, *Trigger*, and *Action*. In order to evaluate the understanding the participants had to categorise six visual ISC examples. For each example the participants had to check a range of constraint properties, for example, *Spanning* or *Not Spanning*. These properties are reflected on the X-Axis of Fig. 6. On the Y-Axis the accumulated mean number from the 6 example processes and according percentages are shown. High values on the Y-Axis show a high accordance with our proposed ISC_Viz language. When a visualization shows a property and a participant marked it then this counts as one participant. When a visualization shows a property and a participant has not marked this property then this does not count. Contrary to this when no property is shown and a participant marked one this does not count and when the participant did not mark the property it counts. For example, Fig. 5 *VizAction* is given we expect a participant to mark the following properties *Spanning*, *Data Constraint*, *Action Wait* and *Trigger Before*. This leads us to a result where we can see that symbols for action (*Action_Give_back*, *Action Restart*, *Action Wait*) are in accordance by a mean of 35.5 (84.52%) participants. *Trigger After* shows a mean of 33.83 (80.56%) participants in accordance and seems to be understood very well while *Trigger Before* seemed to be confusing with 28.83 (68.65%) accordance. *Time Constraints* themselves seem to be clear 38.33 (91.27%) to the participants while data constraints show an accordance of 25 (59.52%). This is a surprising result as the data constraint is not changed in visual representation compared to BPMN.

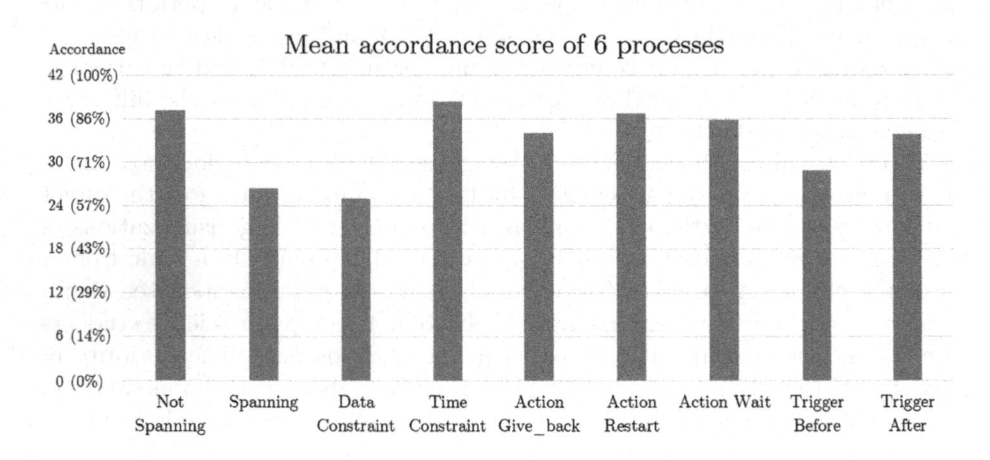

Fig. 6. Results of questionnaire: understanding of ISC_Viz.

As their first task the participants had to select their preferred type based on a short textual description of a constraint. The descriptions increased in difficulty. The first example was a simple constraint spanning instances, the second and third example constraint span processes. First and second descriptions used the same type of data element (execution data) while the third used a specific data element. Table 2 shows the distribution over 41 participants. Each participant was allowed to select one type per description. *VizColor* was chosen in 6.5% of the cases. *VizTriangle* sums up to 23.58% and is evenly distributed among the examples. *VizTrigger* sums up to 33.33% and favours the simple examples while *VizAction* clearly favours the complex example3 with a total of 36.59%.

Table 2. For each example column the distribution is shown across all 4 types.

Type	Example 1	Example 2	Example 3	Sum	Percentage
VizColor	5	2	1	8	6.50%
VizTrigger	16	18	7	41	33.33%
VizTriangle	10	8	11	29	23.58%
VizAction	10	13	22	45	36.59%

While the classification above was shown at the beginning of the questionnaire the following ranking was conducted after working through various ISC examples. The task was to rank the types beginning from 1 (best) to 4. Table 3 summarizes these results. Analysis with the Friedman test show an order preference with $\chi^2(3) = 59.69, p < .0001$, with *VizAction* being best ranked mean (1.64) followed by *VizTrigger* (1.95), *VizTriangle* (2.79) and concluding with *VizColor* (3.62). However an analysis with Wilcoxon signed-rank test shows no significant difference between *VizAction* and *VizTrigger* ($Z = -1.27, p = .102$). When comparing the second and third example based on Friedman test with Wilcoxon test a significant difference is observed ($Z = -3.02, p = .0.00126$).

Further into the questionnaire the participants had to answer if expand functions are preferred. Extending *VizTrigger* to *VizTriangle* is preferred by 47.61% and *VizTrigger* to *VizAction* is preferred by 66.67%.

Table 3. Each column represents the ranking achieved by the type. Low ranking represents preferred visualization.

Rank	*VizColor*	*VizTrigger*	*VizTriangle*	*VizAction*
1	1	15	4	22
2	4	14	11	13
3	5	13	17	7
4	32	0	10	0
Sum	152	82	117	69
Mean	3.62	1.95	2.79	1.64

The visualization part of the questionnaire concluded with a question what a green activity expresses. From 42 participants 35 (83.33%) answered instance spanning, 6 (14.29%) marked process spanning, and 1 (2.38%) did not answer the question. This shows that the participants understood that the spanning part of the constraint is expressed by color.

In summary these results suggest that either *VizAction* or *VizTrigger* are suited for visualizing constraints. Based on the fact that *VizAction* ranks better in both cases, the first more intuitive rating and the second ranking we suggest the usage of *VizAction* for visual modeling of ISC.

For creating a modeling tool for ISC_VIZ we suggest the usage of expand and collapse interaction between *VizTrigger* and *VizAction.*

As another result, the name for the *trigger before* and *trigger after* are changed to *conditional before* and *conditional after* to be more precise and to have a clear distinction to the *timer* trigger.

Table 4. For each category by *Fdhila et al.* [3] we picked one example from *Rinderle-Ma et al.* [14] which will be modeled with ISC_Viz

Context	Requirements	Rule
Multiple	Multiple	"A user is not allowed to execute more than 100 tasks (of any workflow) in a day"
Multiple	Single	"Maximal KWP-2000 Connections The number of connections to KWP2000 should not exceed 10"
Single	Multiple	"There should not exist more than one instance of W such that the input parameters (say loan customer) is the same and the loan amount sums up to $100K during a period of one month"
Single	Single	"Wait until centrifuge is filled"

5.2 Example Based Evaluation

Based on the results from the questionnaire the following examples are visualized with *VizAction.* Our examples are picked from a meta study on run-time ISC [14]. Each example fits one category of the classification introduced by [3]. The classification is divided into a category for design-time and four categories for run-time. Figure 7 shows how these categories differentiate from each other. Context expresses the spanning part of constraints. A constraint is considered *single* spanning when the constraint spans only processes or instances and *multi* spanning when it spans both. Modeling requirements are for example time, data and resources. Modeling requirements are considered *single* when a constraint uses none or one modeling requirement. Constraints that involve more then one modeling requirement are expressed as *multi.* For our evaluation we pick one example from the meta study per category and model these constraints with our ISC_Viz language. To give a comprehensive view all constraints from Table 4 are visualized within Fig. 7.

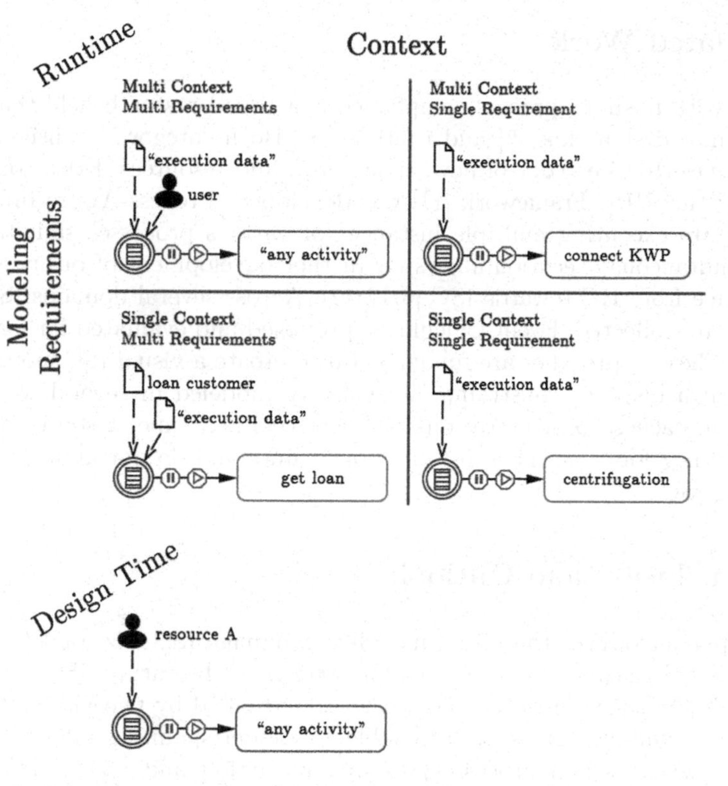

Fig. 7. Each of the categories from [3] is represented with one example plus one design time example.

As *we* [14] do not provide any design time ISC, in addition, the following example constraint is introduced:

A resource is shared among processes but cannot be accessed at the same time by multiple instances.

For a better understanding of possible violations of the design time ISC, assume the following two situations reflected in the associated process models. *Process one uses the resource every day at 8 pm for 30 min. Process two needs to use the resource every Monday at 8 pm for two hours.* With these two textual descriptions it is clear to see that a violation will happen every Monday when two processes try to access the resource at the same time.

Figure 7 depicts the ISC_Viz models for all five ISC examples. It can be seen that ISC_Viz enables the modeling of ISC representatives for all categories. In addition to the examples provided in Table 4 all 114 ISC from the meta study [14] are modeled with ISC_Viz. The models can be found here[2].

[2] http://gruppe.wst.univie.ac.at/projects/crisp/index.php?t=visualization.

6 Related Work

Dealing with business process compliance is a broad research field that can be divided into design time [5] and runtime [9]. Both categories consider various perspectives [16], i.e., control flow, time, data, and resources. For a comprehensive view the iUPC Framework [11] was developed. Process-Aware Information Systems are executing multiple instances of various processes simultaneously. This simultaneous execution allows for further development of business process compliance from IIC towards ISC [6,12,17]. Across several domains ISC examples [14] are collected. Event Calculus is proposed and evaluated for formalizing ISC [3]. These approaches are fundamental to create a visual ISC modeling language. Intra instance constraints are visually modeled in several ways [2,10]. These approaches consider various perspectives, i.e., time, resource and data. However they focus on intra-instance constraints and do not allow for visually modeling ISC.

7 Conclusion and Outlook

This paper introduces the visual modeling language ISC_Viz for IIC and ISC. Specifically the latter has not been addressed in the literature. ISC_Viz is based on BPMN-Q for the intra-instance part and extended by two visual styles, i.e., colors and symbols. These styles enable to model spanning information (i.e., between instances and processes) as well as action and trigger information. ISC_Viz was evaluated with respect to its applicability and usability. More precisely, 114 real-world ISC examples were modeled using ISC_Viz. Moreover, the approach was evaluated with 42 participants. The latter showed that ISC_Viz can be understood with little training. This proposal builds the basis for future research on visualization of ISC, for example, the visualization of compliance violations.

Acknowledgment. This work has been funded by the Vienna Science and Technology Fund (WWTF) through project ICT15-072.

References

1. Awad, A., Weidlich, M., Weske, M.: Specification, verification and explanation of violation for data aware compliance rules. In: Baresi, L., Chi, C.-H., Suzuki, J. (eds.) ICSOC/ServiceWave -2009. LNCS, vol. 5900, pp. 500–515. Springer, Heidelberg (2009). doi:10.1007/978-3-642-10383-4_37
2. Awad, A.: BPMN-Q: a language to query business processes. In: Proceedings of EMISA 2007, pp. 115–128 (2007)
3. Fdhila, W., Gall, M., Rinderle-Ma, S., Mangler, J., Indiono, C.: Classification and formalization of instance-spanning constraints in process-driven applications. In: La Rosa, M., Loos, P., Pastor, O. (eds.) BPM 2016. LNCS, vol. 9850, pp. 348–364. Springer, Cham (2016). doi:10.1007/978-3-319-45348-4_20

4. Gall, M., Wallner, G., Kriglstein, S., Rinderle-Ma, S.: A study of different visualizations for visualizing differences in process models. In: Jeusfeld, M.A., Karlapalem, K. (eds.) ER 2015. LNCS, vol. 9382, pp. 99–108. Springer, Cham (2015). doi:10.1007/978-3-319-25747-1_10
5. Ghose, A., Koliadis, G.: Auditing business process compliance. In: Krämer, B.J., Lin, K.-J., Narasimhan, P. (eds.) ICSOC 2007. LNCS, vol. 4749, pp. 169–180. Springer, Heidelberg (2007). doi:10.1007/978-3-540-74974-5_14
6. Heinlein, C.: Workflow and process synchronization with interaction expressions and graphs. In: International Conference on Data Engineering, pp. 243–252 (2001)
7. Knuplesch, D., Reichert, M., Kumar, A.: Visually monitoring multiple perspectives of business process compliance. In: Motahari-Nezhad, H.R., Recker, J., Weidlich, M. (eds.) BPM 2015. LNCS, vol. 9253, pp. 263–279. Springer, Cham (2015). doi:10.1007/978-3-319-23063-4_19
8. Knuplesch, D., Reichert, M., Ly, L.T., Kumar, A., Rinderle-Ma, S.: On the formal semantics of the extended compliance rule graph. Technical report UIB-2013 - 05, Ulm University, Ulm, April 2013
9. Ly, L.T., Maggi, F.M., Montali, M., Rinderle-Ma, S., van der Aalst, W.M.P.: Compliance monitoring in business processes: functionalities, application, and tool-support. Inf. Syst. **54**, 209–234 (2015)
10. Ly, L.T., Rinderle-Ma, S., Dadam, P.: Design and verification of instantiable compliance rule graphs in process-aware information systems. In: Pernici, B. (ed.) CAiSE 2010. LNCS, vol. 6051, pp. 9–23. Springer, Heidelberg (2010). doi:10.1007/978-3-642-13094-6_3
11. Mangler, J., Rinderle-Ma, S.: IUPC: identification and unification of process constraints. CoRR abs/1104.3609 (2011). http://arxiv.org/abs/1104.3609
12. Pflug, J., Rinderle-Ma, S.: Dynamic instance queuing in process-aware information systems. In: Symposium on Applied Computing, pp. 1426–1433 (2013)
13. Porst, R.: Fragebogen. Ein Arbeitsbuch. VS Verlag für Sozialwissenschaften, Wiesbaden (2008)
14. Rinderle-Ma, S., Gall, M., Fdhila, W., Mangler, J., Indiono, C.: Collecting examples for instance-spanning constraints. Technical report abs/1603.01523, CoRR (2016)
15. Rinderle-Ma, S., Mangler, J.: Integration of process constraints from heterogeneous sources in process-aware information systems. In: International Workshop on Enterprise Modelling and Information Systems Architectures, pp. 51–64 (2011)
16. Sadiq, S., Governatori, G., Namiri, K.: Modeling control objectives for business process compliance. In: Alonso, G., Dadam, P., Rosemann, M. (eds.) BPM 2007. LNCS, vol. 4714, pp. 149–164. Springer, Heidelberg (2007). doi:10.1007/978-3-540-75183-0_12
17. Warner, J., Atluri, V.: Inter-instance authorization constraints for secure workflow management. In: Symposium on Access Control Models and Technologies, pp. 190–199 (2006)
18. Wieringa, R.: Design Science Methodology for Information Systems and Software Engineering. Springer, Heidelberg (2015)

Linking Data and BPMN Processes to Achieve Executable Models

Giuseppe De Giacomo[1], Xavier Oriol[2], Montserrat Estañol[2,3], and Ernest Teniente[2(✉)]

[1] Sapienza Università di Roma, Rome, Italy
degiacomo@dis.uniroma1.it
[2] Universitat Politècnica de Catalunya, Barcelona, Spain
{xoriol,estanyol,teniente}@essi.upc.edu
[3] SIRIS Lab, Research Division of SIRIS Academic, Barcelona, Spain

Abstract. We describe a formally well founded approach to link data and processes conceptually, based on adopting UML class diagrams to represent data, and BPMN to represent the process. The UML class diagram together with a set of additional process variables, called Artifact, form the information model of the process. All activities of the BPMN process refer to such an information model by means of OCL operation contracts. We show that the resulting semantics while abstract is fully executable. We also provide an implementation of the executor.

Keywords: BPMN · UML · Data-aware processes · Artifact-centric processes

1 Introduction

The two main assets of any organization are (*i*) information, i.e., data, which are the things that the organization knows about, and (*ii*) processes, which are collections of activities that describe how work is performed within an organization.

Obviously there is the need for representing and making explicit and precise the contents of these two assets. This has led to conceptual models for data, such as UML class diagrams [1], and conceptual models for processes, such as BPMN [2,3]. Unfortunately these conceptual models are only rarely formally related [4,5]. In fact, they are typically developed by different teams, the data management team and the process management team, respectively, which use their own models and methodologies. This leads to the development of two independent and unrelated designs and formalizations, one concerned with data and one with processes, while the interaction between the two is neglected [6,7].

Moreover, when we arrive to tools for process simulation, monitoring and execution, the two aspects need to come together, and indeed all tools, such as Bizagi Studio or Signavio, provide a typically proprietary way to realize the connection. However such a connection is essentially done *programmatically*, by

E. Dubois and K. Pohl (Eds.): CAiSE 2017, LNCS 10253, pp. 612–628, 2017.
DOI: 10.1007/978-3-319-59536-8_38

defining an internal data model and associating it to the BPMN constructs in the process through suitable *business rules* expressed as actual code (e.g., written in JAVA) to detail what happens to the data and how data are exchanged with the users and other processes. Unfortunately, this way of connecting data and processes becomes elicited programmatically, but not conceptually.

Recent research is bringing forward the necessity of considering both data and processes as first-class citizens in process and service design [7–9]. In particular, the so called artifact-centric approaches, which advocate a sort of middle ground between a conceptual formalization of dynamic systems and their actual implementation, are promising to be quite effective in practice [6,10,11].

In this paper, inspired by artifact-centric approaches, we consider the case in which the data of the domain of interest of a given process are conceptually represented using a UML class diagram, while the process itself is described in BPMN. We adopt UML and BPMN as they are the standard and the most common formalisms for conceptual representation of data in software engineering and processes in BPM, respectively. In this way, we do not propose yet-another-formalism, but combine standard ones in a new integrated way to link data and processes. Other languages might be chosen as well as long as they have an unambiguous semantics, e.g. ORM/ER-diagrams for defining the data, or UML activity diagrams, as used for instance in [12], to define the process.

The key idea underlying our proposal is that, in order to link both formalisms, we propose also: (1) the notion of Artifact, which acts as a collection of process variables to be associated with a process instance, and (2) the specification of how the process activities refer and update the variables of the Artifact, or the domain data. Both concepts can be formally specified through standard languages that suitable accommodate our UML and BPMN diagrams. Indeed, the Artifact can be represented as a new class of the UML class diagram with its convenient attributes and associations to the rest of UML classes, and the process activities can be specified through OCL operation contracts. Again, other languages might be chosen to establish the link, but the crucial point here is to choose a language whose expressiveness is, essentially, first-order logics (i.e., relational algebra), as it happens with the OCL expressions mostly used [13].

In this way, the executability of the overall framework can rely on relational SQL technology, since the data to insert/delete/return by each activity can be characterized through a relational-algebra query, and thus, an SQL statement. In particular, the UML class diagram is encoded as a relational database, the BPMN diagram as a Petri net, and the OCL contracts as logic rules that derive which SQL statements must be applied to the database when an activity is executed. As a proof of concept, we have developed a prototype, written in Java, which allows loading at compile time all the models in our framework and then execute their operations at run time in a relational database.

2 Preliminaries

UML Class Diagrams and Their Instances. A *UML class diagram* [1] is formed by a hierarchy of *classes*, n-ary *associations* among such classes (where some of them might be reified, i.e., *association classes*), and *attributes* inside these *classes*. In addition, a UML schema might be annotated with *minimum/maximum* multiplicity constraints over its association-ends/attributes, and hierarchy constraints (i.e., disjoint/complete constraints). In this paper, we use the notation $C \sqsubseteq C'$ to refer that C is a subclass of C'. We adopt a *conceptual perspective* (as opposed to a *software perspective*) of UML class diagrams, as typical of the analysis phase of the development process [14].

Moreover, for convenience, we assume that the UML class diagram contains only those features that can be mapped into SQL tables with primary/foreign key constraints. For example we express in the diagram optional/mandatory (min multiplicity 0 or 1), single/multivalued properties (max multiplicity 1 or *), but not, e.g., min/max multiplicity 3. All other expressions are assumed to be written and treated as OCL constraints (see below). A *UML class diagram instance* is a set of objects and relationships among such objects. Each object is classified as an *instance* of one or more UML classes, and each relationship as an *instance* of one UML association. We assume that, whenever an object o is classified as an instance of C, and $C \sqsubseteq C'$, then, o is also classified as an instance of C'. Note that this process of *completing* the classifications of an object can be automatically computed through a chase over the UML class hierarchy. This automatic mechanism is called *ISA closure*.

OCL. OCL [15] is a textual language for defining queries over a UML schema, whose result depends on the contents of its UML instance. In particular, OCL boolean expressions are widely used to define: (1) textual integrity constraints that should be satisfied by UML instances of the schema, (2) operation contracts pre/postconditions, that is, expressions that should be satisfied by the UML instances of some schema before/after executing some operation, and (3) queries specifying the return value of some operation. OCL expressions are usually tied to a particular context UML class. For instance, the OCL operation contract of a certain operation is tied to the class in which the operation is defined. In this situation, the OCL expression *self*, refers to the object in which the operation is invoked (in a similar way to the Java keyword *this*). Similarly, an OCL constraint tied to some class C uses *self* to refer to any instance of C.

The core idea underlying OCL is the notion of *navigation*. Given an OCL expression referring to an object, such as *self*, we can navigate to *objects/values* related to such object through some association/attribute using the name of the association-end/attribute we want to traverse. For instance, the OCL expression *self.album* tied to some context class *Artist* returns the albums related to the particular artist referred by *self*. A navigation can also be defined starting from an OCL expression referring to a collection of objects. For instance, the OCL expression *Artist.allInstances()* refers to the set of all *Artist* objects, thus, *Artist.allInstances().album* returns all the albums that can be obtained from all the artists. Moreover, due to this capability of navigating from collections, OCL permits chaining one navigation after another. For instance, *self.album.track* refers to all the tracks of all the albums of a particular *Artist self*. Given these navigations, OCL offers several OCL operators to obtain basic type values (such as boolean, or integer values), or other collections from them. For instance, *self.album.track->forAll(o|o.duration >0)* returns true iff all the durations of all the tracks *o* of some artist *self* are greater than 0.

We assume in this paper that all OCL expressions are written in the first-order fragment of OCL [13], that is the fragment of OCL that can be seen as fully declarative and encodable into relational algebra. Essentially, this excludes OCL operations involving *iterate*, *closure*, basic data type operations (such as String *concat*), and *OrderedSet* and *Bag* data types.

BPMN. BPMN (*Business Process Model and Notation*) [3] is a widely used and well-known ISO and OMG standard language for modeling business processes. It provides a graphical and intuitive notation which can be easily understood by business people, analysts and developers. In a nutshell, the language uses nodes to represent the activities or tasks of the process, whose execution order is determined by a set of directed edges. Different gateway nodes are available to control the flow, to allow for parallel or alternative execution paths, for instance. Moreover, using BPMN it is also possible to represent the interaction between different parties involved in the process, the message flow between them or the objects involved in the process, just to mention a few examples. The diagram has token semantics. As the different activities take place, the token (or tokens) flows through the diagram allowing the execution of the following activities. Due to this, it is possible to formalize a subset of the language into a Petri net [16]. This results in precise execution semantics for the BPMN diagram.

3 Linking Data and BPMN Models

We illustrate our proposal for linking process and data by means of the following example. As we are going to see, the main advantage of our proposal is that, in addition to the benefits of an artifact-centric approach which lets us represent both the structural (i.e., the data) and the dynamic (i.e., the activities or tasks) dimensions of the process, our models provide enough information to achieve their automatic executability.

Example. We aim at realizing a process to create playlists from tracks of musical albums. In particular, the process should deal with the following data and process flow:

- **Data:** Each album has a title, a date of first release and exactly one associated artist. An artist has a name and is either a physical person or a group. Each artist has one album at least. Albums contain one or more tracks. Each track has a number, a name and a duration and belongs to exactly one album. Some albums are special editions and, in that case, may contain bonus tracks. Playlists have a name and contain a nonempty set of tracks (for simplicity the order is not of interest).

- **Process flow:** Iteratively, the process asks the user for the name of an artist and continues with two parallel branches. The first calculates and returns to the user the set of tracks that are part of a special edition recorded by the artist; then, it asks the user to select a subset of these tracks and builds a playlist with them. In the second, the process obtains the set of playlists containing a track by the selected artist. At the end of the two branches, the set of tracks in the new playlist is returned to the user. After this, the user decides whether he/she wishes to continue adding playlists to the system or end the process.

In our proposal, we express the data requirements as a UML class diagram (see Fig. 1), while the process flow is expressed in the BPMN (as shown in Fig. 2). Notice that, as usual in BPMN, we have adopted *message events* for simple activities that only catch data from the user, or throw data to the user. These include `ArtistSelected`, `TracksPLnameSelected`, `PlaylistSent`, and `Continue`.

Now, our goal is to link the process events with the data. To do so, we need to ensure that the UML class diagram contemplates all the data modified/accessed in every atomic activity, decision, and message received or sent in the BPMN. Since, typically, the execution of a process needs to store some extra information in *process variables* (e.g., we need to remember the artist selected by the user at the beginning of the process since it is used in later BPMN events), we have to extend the class diagram to capture them. In particular, we consider a new class we call *Artifact* containing such *process variables*. To differentiate this class from the rest, we label it with the stereotype *Artifact*.

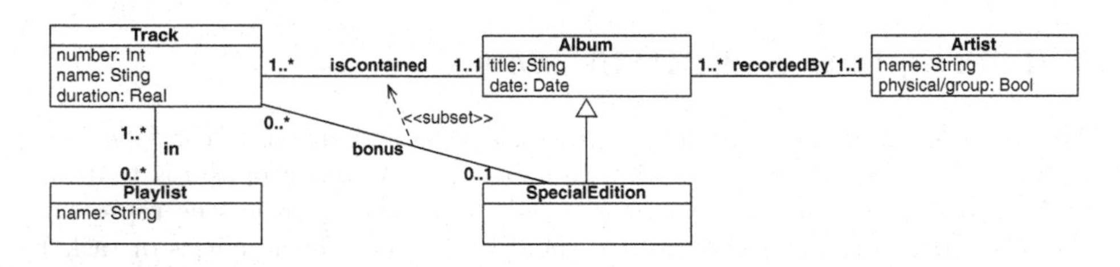

Fig. 1. Class diagram for our playlist example

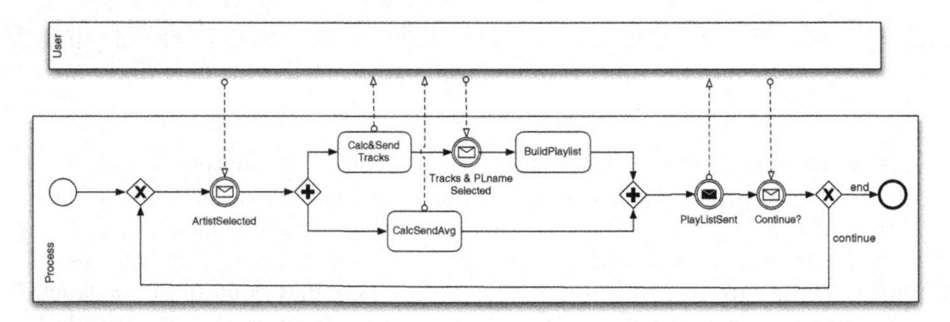

Fig. 2. BPMN diagram representing a process for creating playlists.

For instance, Fig. 3 shows the Artifact for our ongoing example. This artifact is able to store the artist selected in the beginning of the process (through an association to *Artist*), the name of the playlist to create (through the attribute *plname*), the tracks to add in this new playlist (association to *Track*), the created playlist itself (association to *Playlist*), and whether the user selects to end the process or continue (attribute *end*).

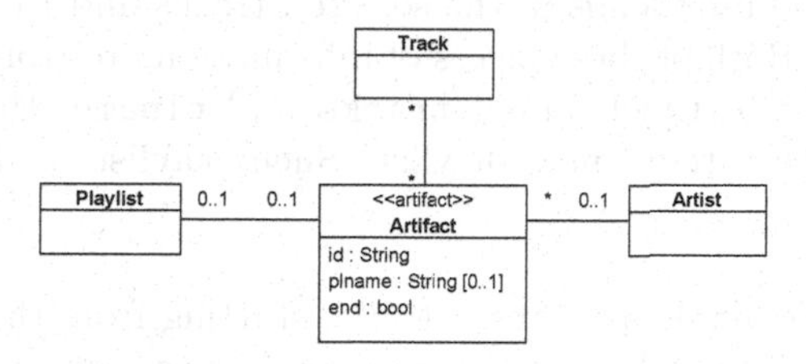

Fig. 3. Class diagram with the representation of the artifact

Representing the process variables as an *Artifact* class associated to the rest of elements in the class diagram provides the advantages of the object oriented paradigm. That is, we can specify modifications over the process data by specifying creations, deletions, and updates of objects/relations of that artifact. Note that, in this way:

- We avoid errors in the execution of the model, as we ensure that the artifact is linked to a specific instance of a class and not to an id of an instance which may not exist, due to the fact that the id is wrong.
- We simplify the definition of the operation contracts by manipulating objects (i.e. instances of classes) instead of identifiers.

Then, the idea is that, when a new process instance starts, a new *Artifact* object is created to store all these process variables. Observe that this behavior is similar to the use case controller in [17], as one class holds the required information for the execution of several related operations or tasks.

The UML class diagram and its instantiation, including the artifact, can be thought of as the *information model* of the process. Note that this instantiation can be seen (and in fact, stored) as a relational database (i.e., a first-order model).

Now, for any time instant, we define the *state* of the process as: (a) The instantiation of the UML class diagram including the artifact; (b) The positions of the tokens in the BPMN diagrams. Using this notion of state, we can describe precisely the process in terms of *state evolution.* For instance, our previous process can be described precisely as follows:

1. At the beginning of an iteration a message with the selected artist as payload comes in; such artist is stored in the Artifact through the corresponding association.

2. Then, concurrently the process follows two branches.
   - First branch:
     (a) The `CalcSendTracks` activity calculates all tracks that are part of some special edition recorded by the artist in `artist` and sends them to the user; the tracks resulting from the calculation are *not* stored in the Artifact, as they are not further used in the process, but are instead directly sent to the user.
     (b) Then, the user sends in the selected tracks and the name of the new playlist. Both of these pieces of information are stored in the Artifact.
     (c) Using the Artifact stored `tracks` and `plname`, the `BuildPlayList` activity creates a new playlist. Such playlist is then stored in the Artifact.
   - Second branch:
     (a) The `CalcSendPlaylists` activity, starting from the Artifact's stored artist, collects all its tracks, computes the set of playlists that already exist which contain tracks by the selected artist and sends it to the user. Notice that, since this result is not used anymore in the process, it is *not* stored in the Artifact.
3. After these two branches complete their computations and join, a message with the newly created playlist is sent to the user.
4. Finally the `Continue?` activity gets the info of whether the user wants to continue or not, and stores it in the Artifact boolean variable `end`. Then, depending on this information, the XOR-gateway ends the process or performs another iteration.

This description of the state evolution can be made completely executable by (1) specifying the previous activities and start/end/message event through a formal language; and (2) adopting the Petri Net semantics for BPMN control flow.

Thus, for this purpose, we specify each activity in the BPMN diagram through an OCL operation contract. Each OCL operation will have a precondition, stating the conditions that must be true *before* the task can take place, and a postcondition, indicating the resulting state of the system *after* the operation's execution. Some of the tasks will only return information to the user without making any changes (we will call them queries): these tasks will include the keyword `result` as part of the postcondition. OCL operation contracts need to refer to the instances of `Artifact` to get rid explicitly of the information manipulated by the process.

In Table 1 we show the OCL operation contracts for the BPMN diagram in Fig. 2. Note that we have also specified a contract for the start and end event in this diagram. The former (`Initialize`) is in charge of instantiating the artifact that will keep the information for the execution of the current process. The latter (`End`) is in charge of deleting the artifact and its relationships. Except for the task `Initialize`, which is a class operation, the rest of the tasks are instance operations invoked over the artifact being manipulated by the process (the one created by `Initialize`).

Table 1. OCL contracts for the events and activities of the BPMN diagram

Start Event	`context artifact::Initialize()`
	`post: Artifact.allInstances()->exists(af | af.oclIsNew() and af.end=false and result=af)`
	`Initialize` creates a new artifact with its end attribute set to false.

Artist Selected	`context artifact::ArtistSelected(artist:Artist)`
	`post: self.artist=artist`
	`ArtistSelected` assigns the artist given as input to the process's artifact.

Calc Send Tracks	`context artifact::CalcAndSendTracks(): Set(Track)`
	`post: result = Track.allInstances()->select(t | t.album.artist = self.artist and t.album.oclIsTypeOf(SpecialEdition))`
	`CalcSendTracks` obtains all the tracks and selects those belonging to an album whose artist is equal to the artist linked to the artifact and which are part of an special edition. It returns this list as a result.

Tracks Plname Selected	`context artifact::TracksPlnameSelected(trackL:Set(Track), plName:String)`
	`post: self.track=trackL and self.plname=plName`
	`TracksPlnameSelected` assigns the set of tracks provided as input to the artifact, and stores the playlist name given as input in the corresponding attribute of the artifact.

Build Playlist	`context artifact::BuildPlaylist()`
	`post: Playlist.allInstances()->exists(pl | pl.oclIsNew() and pl.name=self.plname and pl.track->includesAll(self.track))`
	`BuildPlaylist` creates a new instance of Playlist (`oclIsNew`). Its name is the name stored in the artifact and its tracks will correspond to the tracks linked to the artifact.

Calc Send Playlists	`context artifact::CalcSendPlaylists(): Set(Playlist)`
	`post: result = self.artist.album.track.playlist->asSet()`
	`CalcSendPlaylists` obtains the playlists that already exist which contain tracks by the selected artist and sends this information to the user.

Playlist Sent	`context artifact::PlaylistSent(): Playlist`
	`post: result = self.playlist`
	`PlaylistSent` returns the playlist that has been created (the one assigned to the artifact) as a result.

Continue	`context artifact::Continue(e:bool)`
	`post: self.end=e`
	`Continue` updates the value of attribute `end` in the artifact with the given input.

End Event	`context artifact::End()`
	`post: Artifact.allInstances()->excludes(self)`
	`End` deletes the artifact linked to this instance of the process and all the relationships it takes part in.

4 Achieving Executable Business Process Models

To make this framework executable, we encode the UML class diagram as a relational database manageable through SQL, the BPMN diagram as a Petri net, and the OCL contracts as logic rules that derive which SQL statements must be applied to the database when the corresponding activity is executed. In this way, we get the executability of the framework benefiting from standard relational database technology.

From the Class Diagram to a Database Schema. We encode the UML class diagram into a relational database following well-known techniques of database design [18]. Note that in this step we also store the Artifact (i.e., the process variables) in the database since the Artifact appears in the UML schema.

From the BPMN Diagram to a Petri Net. The BPMN diagram can be formalized into a Petri net by following [16]. This proposal focuses on formalizing the control-flow (i.e. the execution order of the tasks and events) of BPMN models, which is exactly what we need in this case. Roughly, each task will map to a transition with one input and one output place. Gateway nodes will, in the general case, correspond to a combination of places and silent transitions, to represent the routing behaviour of the gateway. This translation to a Petri Net is needed to make sure formally that the order of execution of the processes is exactly the one defined by the BPMN.

Petri nets also require an initial marking, which represents the initial state of the BPMN model. In general, this means placing a single token in the place that corresponds to the start node of the BPMN model. By following the token semantics of the resulting Petri net, it is possible to know exactly which tasks or events are ready to take place.

The Petri net we obtain in our example is shown in Fig. 4. Each task corresponds to a labelled transition, which has one input and one output place. Each gateway node maps to a set of places and transitions. For instance, the XOR merge gateway placed before the task `ArtistSelected` corresponds to the transitions and places inside the dotted rectangle in Fig. 4. The initial marking consists in putting a token in the most left-side place (the one with no input arcs).

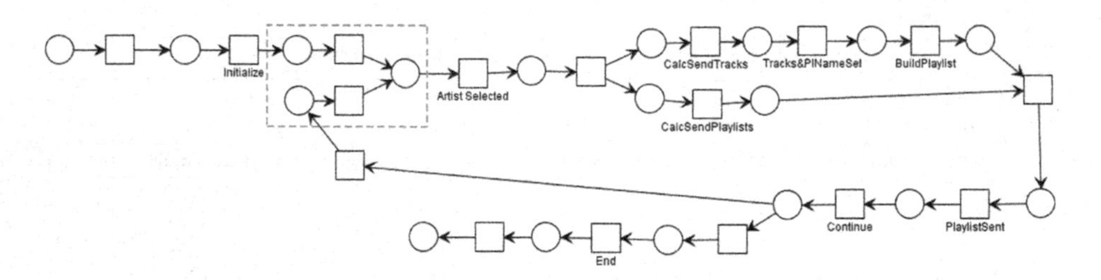

Fig. 4. Petri net resulting from the transition of the BPMN. The dotted rectangle shows the transitions and places corresponding to the translation of the XOR merge gateway placed before `ArtistSelected`.

From the OCL Operation Contracts to Logic Derivation Rules. Each OCL operation contract is encoded into a set of logic rules which, intuitively, derive the SQL insertions/deletions/updates that we must perform on the SQL database when applying the operation. In this way, we move from the declarative OCL specifications to an imperative formalism that can be executed.

The logic rules we obtain from each operation have the following form:

$$ins\_P(\overline{x}) :- opName(a), arg0\_opName(\overline{x_0}), ..., argN\_opName(\overline{x_n}), pre(\overline{x_{pre}}), query(\overline{x_q})$$
$$del\_P(\overline{x}) :- opName(a), arg0\_opName(\overline{x_0}), ..., argN\_opName(\overline{x_n}), pre(\overline{x_{pre}}), query(\overline{x_q})$$
$$result(\overline{x}) :- opName(a), arg0\_opName(\overline{x_0}), ..., argN\_opName(\overline{x_n}), pre(\overline{x_{pre}}), query(\overline{x_q})$$

The head of each rule determines the kind of SQL statement to apply (insertion, deletion, or query), while the body specifies for which values. That is, intuitively, a rule of the first form states that when a user invokes operation *opName* to artifact a with the n arguments specified in *arg0_opName*, ..., *argN_opName*, then some facts $P(\overline{x})$ must be inserted in the database if the precondition encoded by $pre(\overline{x_{pre}})$ is satisfied.

The variables $\overline{x}$ are instantiated using the arguments given by the user $\overline{x_0}$, ..., $\overline{x_n}$, or even the result of a first-order query $query(\overline{x_q})$ that retrieves values from the current database state (or process data stored in the artifact a). If the query returns a set of tuples, or one argument itself is a set of tuples, the rule derives as many insertions as elements in the set.

Similarly, rules of the second and third form state deletions of facts and specify the tuples to return to the user as result. Attribute modifications are encoded by using the well-known strategy of combining a deletion and an insertion rule for the same fact.

The translation from OCL contracts to this logic formalism is an extension of the one in [19]. In particular, the extension we propose in this paper is intended to: (1) allow using the query $query(\overline{x_q})$ to instantiate the variables used in the insertions/deletions to apply, (2) deal with *OCL Set* typed arguments, and (3) retrieving results for the user.

Given an OCL contract, its translation into logics consists in two steps. The first one parses the OCL postcondition to identify the different rules we need to create (i.e., it identifies the heads of the different rules to build). The second is in charge of creating the bodies of these rules, which is done by parsing the operation name, arguments, and the pre/postcondition to identify how to instantiate the variables from the rule head.

Identifying the Head. We analyze the OCL postcondition to determine which kind of *updates* are performed by the operation. Essentially, such updates are: object creation/deletion, object specialization/generalization, relationship insertion/deletion, attribute insertion/deletion/modification, and queries. Each of these updates will lead to one or several derivation rules. For instance, an object creation of class C, where C is a subclass of C', leads to a derivation rule of the form $ins\_C(o)$, together with another derivation rule of the form $ins\_C'(o)$. Intuitively, the set of derivation rules generated for each object insertion/deletion performs the *ISA closure* as stated in the Preliminaries.

In Table 2 we show how we identify such updates and the derivation rules they originate. This table is an extension of the translating rules defined in [19] to sets and data extracted from the database. Intuitively, we traverse the OCL postcondition to find the OCL patterns stated in the left column of the table and, for each match, we create a new derivation rule as stated in the right column. In this table, we use o and u to refer to OCL object expressions of type C, and a and b to refer to OCL value expressions (such as constants). Moreover, we use *role* to refer to property call navigations through associations R, *attr* to property call navigations to attributes A, and *query* to refer to an OCL query expression. Finally, we assume that $\bar{t}$ is a tuple of n variables, where n is the arity of the *TupleType* returned by the OCL query, or 1 if the OCL query returns an object/value.

Table 2. OCL patterns to derivation rules

OCL pattern	Update kind	Derivation rules to create
o.oclIsNew()	Object creation	ins_C(o) ins_C'(o), for each C $\sqsubseteq$ C'
C.allInstances()->excludes(o)	Object deletion	del_C(o) del_C'(o) for each C' $\sqsubseteq$ C del_C"(o) for each C $\sqsubseteq$ C"
o.oclIsKindOf(C')	Object specialization	ins_C'(o) ins_C"(o) for each C' $\sqsubseteq$ C" $\sqsubseteq$ C
not o.oclIsKindOf(C')	Object generalization	del_C'(o) del_C"(o) for each C" $\sqsubseteq$ C'
o.role->includes(u) o.role->includesAll(u)	Relationship insertion	ins_R(o, u)
o.role->excludes(u) o.role->excludesAll(u)	Relationship deletion	del_R(o, u)
o.oclINew() and o.attr = a	Attribute insertion	ins_A(o, a)
o.attr = null	Attribute deletion	del_A(o, a)
o.attr = b	Attribute update	ins_A(o, b) del_A(o, a)
result = query	Query	result($\bar{t}$)

Deriving the Body. Once we know the kind of updates each operation applies, we have to determine the values for which they should be applied. This is achieved by means of the expression in the body of the rule, which consists of two different parts: one which is common to all derivation rules of each operation specifying the operation name, arguments and precondition; and a specific part for each derivation stating the specific queries (i.e., a conjunctions of literals referring to the database state) used to instantiate the variables in the rule. We explain each part in the following.

- *Common part of the body.* The common part of the body consists of one literal representing the operation we are translating *opName(a)*, whose unique variable represents the artifact in which we are applying the operation, the arguments $arg0\_opName(\overline{X_0})$, ... , $argN\_opName(\overline{X_n})$ representing the values given by the user to perform such operation, and one logic query $pre(\overline{X_{pre}})$ encoding the precondition of the operation. Such logic query is obtained by translating the OCL precondition into logics according to the proposal in [20].
- *Specific part of the body.* The queries in this part are obtained through the logic translation of the *o*, *u* object expressions, *a*, *b* value expressions and the *query* expression appearing in Table 2, which is only performed if the expressions do not explicitly refer to operation arguments (since they have been encoded already previous step). We also use [20] to perform this encoding. Essentially, this consists in translating each OCL navigation as a sequence of logic atoms representing the different associations it traverses to. For instance, *t.album.artist* is translated into $track(T, Al) \wedge recordedBy(Al, Ar)$. The idea of the translation is that, each logic variable used in the navigations represents a different UML object, and thus, can be further used to state conditions over such object. For instance, *specialEdition(Al)* states that the UML object represented by the variable *Al* is a specialEdition.

As an example, the OCL contracts of the operations *BuildPlaylist* and *CalcSendTracks* are translated as the rules set shown in Listings 1.1, and 1.2. Note that the variables in the head of the rules are instantiated using queries in the body of the rules.

Listing 1.1. Logic encoding for task *BuildPlaylist*

```
ins_Playlist(Pl) :- buildplaylist(A), artifactPlname(A,Pl)
ins_TrackIn(Tr, Al, Pl) :- buildplaylist(A), artifactPlname(A,Pl),
    artifactTrack(A,Tr,Al)
ins_ArtifactPlaylist(A,Pl) :- buildplaylist(A), artifactPlname(A,Pl)
```

Listing 1.2. Logic encoding for task *CalcSendTracks*

```
result_CalcSendTracks(T,Al) :- calcSendTracks(A), track(T,Al), recordedBy(Al,
    Ar), artifactArtist(A,Ar), specialEdition(Al)
```

5 Executing the Framework

The proposed framework allows us to automatically and unambiguously execute processes defined according to our specification models. We have built a Java library for this purpose[1]. This library permits loading in compilation time the underlying semantic models of the framework and executing its operations at runtime. That is:

[1] A prototype of this library together the necessary code/models to execute the BPM used in this paper can be found at http://www.essi.upc.edu/~xoriol/opexec/.

- *Given (at compilation time)*: (1) a SQL database connection encoding a UML schema, (2) a set of derivation rules defining the semantics of the operations, (3) a map from the logic predicates to the SQL tables/columns.
- *Given (at runtime)*: (4) an operation name, (5) the values for their arguments.
- *Executes (at runtime)*: (6) the updates specified in the derivation rules of the operation in the database, and (7) returns to the user the information specified in the *result* part of the operation.

The current version of the Java library does not check yet whether the operations executed by the user match the order imposed by the Petri nets. However, we understand that this critical (and necessary) functionality may be achieved by integrating any Petri Net simulator in our library and this is why we have left implementation of this part for future work. In contrast, the tool works in any relational database management system and it is able to check whether the executed operations cause the violation of some integrity constraint (such as the min/max multiplicity constraints of the UML class diagram, other UML class diagram annotations such as *subset*), by means of the implementation of the incremental integrity checking approach in [21].

Operation Executor Library Architecture. The architecture of our library is shown in Fig. 5. Briefly, a user loads (at compilation time) the previous models in the *Controller* component, which stores them. When the user wants to start executing the process, he/she invokes the controller to instantiate a new *ProcessExecutor*. This class executes all the operation invocations of such process instance. Thus, each instance of this class has its own (unique) artifact ID, which is used to store, in the database, all the process data related to such process instance. When a user invokes an operation to the *ProcessExecutor*, the *ProcessExecutor* creates an *OperationExecutorThread*, in which we store the

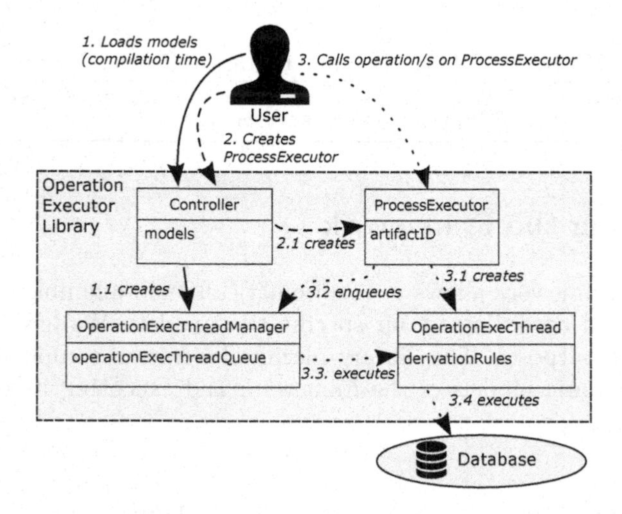

Fig. 5. OperationExecutor Java library architecture

derivation rules related to such operation. Then, the *ProcessExecutor* adds it to the *OperationExecutionThreadManager*. This component is in charge of executing the operation as soon as it can be executed. When the *OperationExecutionThread* is executed, it performs the following steps:

1. It instantiates the updates (insertions/deletions) that it must apply according to the derivation rules and the database state.
2. It checks that these updates do not cause any constraint violation according to the incrementally checking method defined in [21].
3. If no violation is found, the updates are translated as SQL insert/delete/update statements and executed, and the query to retrieve the result of the operation execution is performed (if the operation returns some result).
4. Otherwise, an exception is thrown.

6 Related Work

In the following, we first discuss related frameworks for linking data and process models, and then, discuss several of their formalizations to achieve their executability.

In terms of the framework for modeling data and business processes, many of the existing works [9–11] use languages grounded on logic, which are formal and unambiguous but more difficult to understand than BPMN and UML. There are other approaches which use graphical representations which are more intuitive and appealing to business analysts and developers, such as [12,22,23]. [23] is based on the Guard-Stage-Milestone approach, which represents the evolution of each relevant object in a lifecycle following a more declarative approach than ours. [22] uses *artifact union graphs*, which are similar to Petri nets, to represent the process. [12] is the most similar approach to ours and relies on various UML diagrams (different to the ones we consider) and OCL contracts to represent the data and the process. However, none of these works deal with process executability; most of them focus on studying the correctness of the model.

Regarding process executability, BPEL (or WS-BPEL) allows to specify executable business processes using an XML format which makes it difficult to read. Although there is a mapping between BPMN 2.0 and BPEL it is incomplete and suffers from several issues [24]. The work of [25] uses XML nets, a Petri-net-based process modelling approach which is meant to be executable. It uses a graphical language, which maps to a DTD (XML Document Type Definition) to represent the data required by the process, and the data manipulations are graphically shown in the XML net. In contrast to our approach, this solution is technology-based, as the specification of the models is based on XML, and details of how to achieve executability are not explained.

YAWL [26] is a workflow graphical language whose semantics are formally defined and based on Petri nets, with its corresponding execution engine. The language offers both a control-flow and data-flow perspective of the process, where data is defined following an XML format. Intuitively, the tasks are then annotated with their inputs and outputs, but they do not allow defining what changes are made by each of them. Therefore, the execution engine only detects missing information and it is not able to fully execute the operation.

In [27] an hybrid model using a data-oriented declarative specification and a control-flow-oriented imperative specification of a business process are defined. Using this approach it is possible to obtain automatically an imperative model that is executable in a standard Business Process Management System. However, data is defined as a set of unstructured variables and the pre and postconditions merely state conditions over the data, instead of indicating exactly what is done by the different tasks.

Earlier, similar attempts to ours are [28,29]. Both approaches focus on defining a conceptual model which can then be automatically translated to achieve execution. However, the purpose of [28] is different to ours: their main goal is to be able to validate the model through execution, while ours is to achieve executability by using the current *de facto* standard languages for data and process representation. Similarly, the approach in [29] - which translates the models into Pascal - is outdated by current, object-oriented programming languages.

In addition, it is worth noting that most of these proposals do not use standard formalisms for conceptual representation, as we do.

7 Conclusions

We have proposed a framework to link data and business processes, which can be to be executed automatically. It uses the BPMN language to represent the processes, the UML class diagram for the data, and OCL operation contracts to define what do the tasks in the process. Using these languages, we are not proposing any yet-another-formalism but using a standard one in a new integrated way to link data and processes.

We have shown the feasibility of our approach by creating a Java library which, given a model, is able to execute the tasks and update the information base accordingly. Before applying the changes, the tool performs an incremental checking of integrity constraints to determine if there are any violations. If this is the case, it will throw an exception. Otherwise, it applies the changes to the underlying database that stores the data. All of this is performed without requiring user intervention.

With the approach we present here, we blur the distinction between specification and implementation, since the specification itself is executable.

Acknowledgments. This work has been partially supported by the Ministerio de Economia y Competitividad (project TIN2014-52938-C2-2-R), by the Generalitat de Catalunya (through 2014 SGR 1534), and by the Sapienza project "Immersive Cognitive Environments".

References

1. OMG: Unified Modeling Language (UML) superstructure, version 2.0. (2005). http://www.uml.org/

2. Weske, M.: Business Process Management: Concepts, Languages, Architectures. Springer, Heidelberg (2007)
3. Dumas, M., Rosa, M.L., Mendling, J., Reijers, H.: Fundamentals of Business Process Management. Springer, Heidelberg (2013)
4. Reichert, M.: Process and data: two sides of the same coin? In: Meersman, R., Panetto, H., Dillon, T., Rinderle-Ma, S., Dadam, P., Zhou, X., Pearson, S., Ferscha, A., Bergamaschi, S., Cruz, I.F. (eds.) OTM 2012. LNCS, vol. 7565, pp. 2–19. Springer, Heidelberg (2012). doi:10.1007/978-3-642-33606-5_2
5. van der Aalst, W.M.P.: A decade of business process management conferences: personal reflections on a developing discipline. In: Proceedings of BPM 2012 (2012)
6. Cohn, D., Hull, R.: Business artifacts: a data-centric approach to modeling business operations and processes. IEEE-BDE **32**(3), 3–9 (2009)
7. Bhattacharya, K., Caswell, N.S., Kumaran, S., Nigam, A., Wu, F.Y.: Artifact-centered operational modeling: lessons from customer engagements. IBM J. **46**(4), 703–721 (2007)
8. Hull, R.: Artifact-centric business process models: brief survey of research results and challenges. In: OTM Confederated International Conference (2008)
9. Deutsch, A., Hull, R., Patrizi, F., Vianu, V.: Automatic verification of data-centric business processes. In: Proceedings of ICDT, pp. 252–267(2009)
10. Bagheri Hariri, B., Calvanese, D., De Giacomo, G., Deutsch, A., Montali, M.: Verification of relational data-centric dynamic systems with external services. In: Proceedings of PODS, pp. 163–174 (2013)
11. Belardinelli, F., Lomuscio, A., Patrizi, F.: Verification of agent-based artifact systems. J. Artif. Intell. Res. **51**, 333–376 (2014)
12. Estañol, M., Sancho, M.-R., Teniente, E.: Verification and validation of UML artifact-centric business process models. In: Zdravkovic, J., Kirikova, M., Johannesson, P. (eds.) CAiSE 2015. LNCS, vol. 9097, pp. 434–449. Springer, Cham (2015). doi:10.1007/978-3-319-19069-3_27
13. Franconi, E., Mosca, A., Oriol, X., Rull, G., Teniente, E.: Logic foundations of the OCL modelling language. In: Proceedings of Logics in Artificial Intelligence - 14th European Conference, JELIA 2014, Funchal, Madeira, Portugal, 24–26 September 2014, pp. 657–664 (2014)
14. Fowler, M., Scott, K.: UML Distilled - Applying the Standard Object Modeling Laguage. Addison-Wesley, Boston (1997)
15. OMG: Object Constraint Language (UML), version 2.4. Object Management Group (OMG) (2014). http://www.omg.org/spec/OCL/
16. Dijkman, R.M., Dumas, M., Ouyang, C.: Semantics and analysis of business process models in BPMN. Inf. Softw. Technol. **50**(12), 1281–1294 (2008)
17. Larman, C.: Applying UML and Patterns, 2nd edn. Prentice Hall, Upper Saddle River (2002)
18. Teorey, T., Lightstone, S., Nadeau, T.: Database Modeling and Design, 4th edn. Morgan Kaufmann, San Francisco (2006)
19. Queralt, A., Teniente, E.: Reasoning on UML conceptual schemas with operations. In: Eck, P., Gordijn, J., Wieringa, R. (eds.) CAiSE 2009. LNCS, vol. 5565, pp. 47–62. Springer, Heidelberg (2009). doi:10.1007/978-3-642-02144-2_9
20. Queralt, A., Teniente, E.: Verification and validation of UML conceptual schemas with OCL constraints. ACM Trans. Softw. Eng. Methodol. **21**(2), 13 (2012)
21. Oriol, X., Teniente, E.: Incremental checking of OCL constraints with aggregates through SQL. In: 34th International Conference on Conceptual Modeling, ER 2015, pp. 199–213 (2015)

22. Borrego, D., Gasca, R.M., López, M.T.G.: Automating correctness verification of artifact-centric business process models. Inf. Softw. Technol. **62**, 187–197 (2015)
23. Damaggio, E., Hull, R., Vaculín, R.: On the equivalence of incremental and fixpoint semantics for business artifacts with Guard-Stage-Milestone lifecycles. Inf. Syst. **38**(4), 561–584 (2013)
24. Fabra, J., de Castro, V., Álvarez, P., Marcos, E.: Automatic execution of business process models: exploiting the benefits of model-driven engineering approaches. J. Syst. Softw. **85**(3), 607–625 (2012)
25. Lenz, K., Oberweis, A.: Modeling interorganizational workflows with XML nets. In: HICSS-34. IEEE Computer Society (2001)
26. Foundation, T.Y.: YAWL - User Manual. Version 4.1. (2016). http://www.yawlfoundation.org/pages/support/manuals.html
27. Parody, L., López, M.T.G., Gasca, R.M.: Hybrid business process modeling for the optimization of outcome data. Inf. Softw. Technol. **70**, 140–154 (2016)
28. Lindland, O.I., Krogstie, J.: Validating conceptual models by transformational prototyping. In: Rolland, C., Bodart, F., Cauvet, C. (eds.) CAiSE 1993. LNCS, vol. 685, pp. 165–183. Springer, Heidelberg (1993). doi:10.1007/3-540-56777-1_9
29. Mylopoulos, J., Borgida, A., Greenspan, S.J., Wong, H.K.T.: Information system design at the conceptual level - the taxis project. IEEE Database Eng. Bull. **7**(4), 4–9 (1984)

Discovery of Fuzzy DMN Decision Models from Event Logs

Ekaterina Bazhenova[1(✉)], Stephan Haarmann[1], Sven Ihde[1], Andreas Solti[2], and Mathias Weske[1]

[1] Hasso Plattner Institute at the University of Potsdam, Potsdam, Germany
{ekaterina.bazhenova,mathias.weske}@hpi.de,
{sven.ihde,stephan.haarmann}@student.hpi.de
[2] Vienna University of Economics and Business, Vienna, Austria
solti@ai.wu.ac.at

Abstract. Successful business process management is highly dependent on effective decision making. The recent Decision Model and Notation (DMN) standard prescribes decisions to be documented and executed complementary to processes. However, the decision logic is often implicitly contained in event logs, and "as-is" decision knowledge needs to be retrieved. Commonly, decision logic is represented by rules based on Boolean algebra. The formal nature of such decisions is often hard for interpretation and utilization in practice, because imprecision is intrinsic to real-life decisions. Operations research considers fuzzy logic, based on fuzzy algebra, as a tool dealing with partial knowledge. In this paper, we explore the possibility of incorporating fuzziness into DMN decision models. Further, we propose a methodology for discovering fuzzy DMN decision models from event logs. The evaluation of our approach on a use case from the banking domain shows high comprehensibility and accuracy of the output decision model.

Keywords: Fuzzy logic · Decision models · Decision mining · DMN · Event logs

1 Introduction

Decisions play an important role in enterprise's business processes. This has become a premise for an increased interest of academia and industry towards different aspects of integrated process and decision management. Recently, the Decision Model and Notation (DMN) was released [17], which prescribes modeling decisions complementary to processes. The combined usage of the DMN standard and Business Process Model and Notation (BPMN) [16] is recommended in order to encapsulate process and decision logic, and to increase reuse of decisions in processes.

Decision logic is normally represented by *crisp* decision rules based on Boolean algebra. This imposes certain limitations on its application, as imprecision is often involved in real-life decisions. Operations research considers *fuzzy*

E. Dubois and K. Pohl (Eds.): CAiSE 2017, LNCS 10253, pp. 629–647, 2017.
DOI: 10.1007/978-3-319-59536-8_39

logic, based on fuzzy algebra, as a tool dealing with partial input knowledge [6,22]. Fuzzy rules represent strings encoding the semantic meaning of a certain probability behind a value range, e.g., "If loan duration is long, then risk is very high". Since the meaning can be derived directly from the representation, it is generally considered that fuzzy rules are more comprehensible compared to crisp rules [12]. Moreover, using literals across rules increases decision flexibility, as it allows a consistent adaptation of all rules by adjusting only the underlying mappings. In this paper, we incorporate fuzziness into DMN decision models by utilizing fuzzy decision tables, and introduce fuzzy hit policies.

Further, to assist enterprises with efficient decision management, knowledge about "as-is" decision making needs to be retrieved. This can be done by analysing process event logs and discovering decision rules from them. Existing approaches to decision discovery consider only either mining of independent fuzzy rule sets [12], or crisp decision models [5,9,18]. In order to provide useful insights into the discovery of fuzzy DMN decision models from event logs, we propose a methodology which consists of five steps: (1) Identification of fuzzy subsets and corresponding membership functions corresponding to the data attributes from the event log; (2) Discovery of process decisions and dependencies between them; (3) Application of fuzzy learners for fuzzy rules discovery; (4) Construction of fuzzy decision tables based on discovered rules; (5) Identification of fuzzy hit policy for decision tables. In order to test the validity of the proposed approach, we implement it and conduct validation experiments on a simulated event log for the use case of loan assessment in banks. The evaluation results show good interpretability and accuracy of the output fuzzy DMN decision model.

The remainder of this work is structured as follows. Section 2 introduces the motivation for deriving fuzzy DMN models on an example, followed by related work. Section 3 presents our formal framework. Section 4 introduces the methodology for mining fuzzy decision models, which is followed by Evaluation and Conclusion sections.

2 Background

In this section, we motivate the need for our approach and describe related work.

2.1 Motivating Example

We consider a business process of credit-risk assessment (Fig. 1a). This use case is inspired by a real data set from a major Benelux financial company, also used in [3].

The process starts with the registration of the user's claim details such as *duration, amount*, and *premium* in the bank information system. There are two decisions involved in this process, which according to our interviews with a partner bank are performed by loan experts in about 20% of cases. At p_1 the type of application check is chosen, and at p_3 the claim is evaluated for approval which

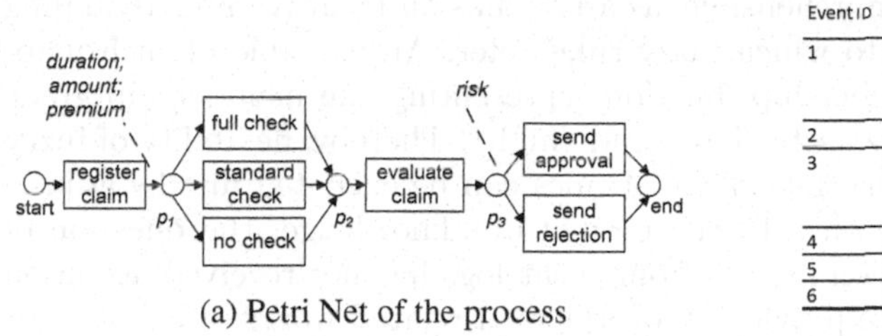

(a) Petri Net of the process

Event ID	Trace ID	Activity	Attributes
1	1	register claim	duration=14 [mths] amount=9700 [EUR] premium=FALSE
2	1	full check	-
3	2	register claim	duration=28 [mths] amount=2000 [EUR] premium=TRUE
4	2	no check	-
5	1	evaluate claim	risk=high
6	1	send rejection	-

(b) Process event log

Fig. 1. Example business process of credit-risk assessment

happens alongside with assigning *risk* to the claim. An example execution log is given in Fig. 1b.

The problem is that this process model does not explicitly contain the decision rules, so the decisions done by experts are only implicitly contained in the event log. There exist many works using statistical means for discovery of decision rules [21], but direct application of them can lead to the unjust treatment of an individual applicant, e.g., judging creditability just by the applicant's nationality [7]. Thus, for companies it is important to have interpretive models explaining how a certain decision is made. To achieve this, we propose to derive DMN decision models, explaining and representing explicitly process decisions, from event logs. An example of a DMN model consisting of a decision requirements diagram (DRD) and decision logic layers is shown in Fig. 2.

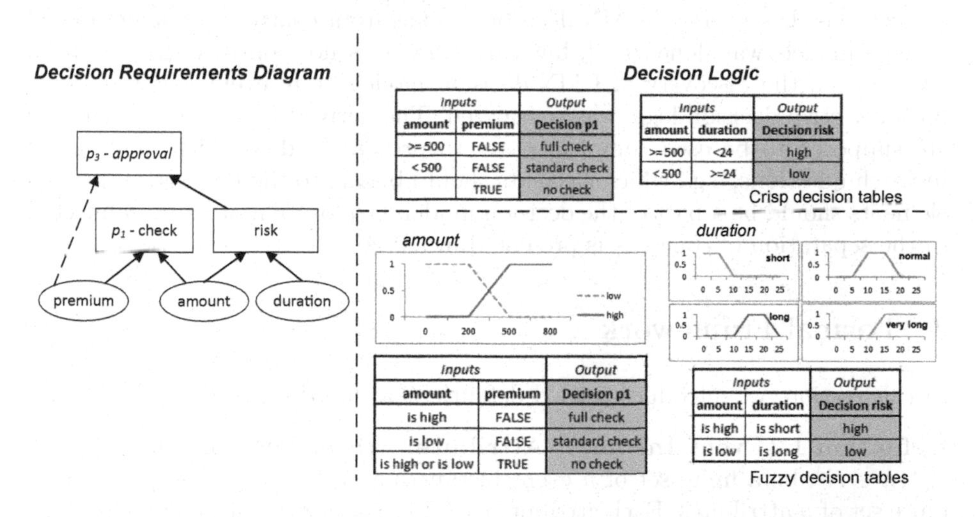

Fig. 2. DMN decision requirements diagram and two types of decision logic

The decision logic corresponding to the DRD can be designed in the form of either crisp, or fuzzy decision tables, as shown in the figure. Fuzzy rules are considered to be more comprehensible, as a user has an intuitive understanding of the linguistic concepts to which fuzzy rules refer. An example of such mapping is a trapezoidal membership function representing the membership grade of attribute *amount* in fuzzy sets "low", and "high". Thereby, flexibility of fuzzy decision models is higher as the change of rules can be executed just by adjusting the membership functions. To the best of our knowledge, the question of deriving fuzzy DMN decision models from event logs has not received attention yet. In the next section, we provide an overview of related works.

2.2 Related Work

The presented problem was addressed in the literature from different perspectives. The first category of related work deals with mining of independent fuzzy rule sets. In [8,11,15], a concept of fuzzy rule bases and techniques to design them are introduced. Fuzzy rules learning as introduced in works [12,13] can be applied for solving our problem, but process context and metrics were not taken into account. Fuzzy mining of rules represent a more general case of mining crisp rule bases from data [3,21]. The incorporation of fuzziness within the concept of decision tables was done in [19], but this work only accounts for the design of decision tables, and no knowledge discovery is applied.

With respect to process context, one of the first works in this direction was done in [18] for discovery of control flow decisions in processes from event logs. Mining of complex decision logic for process branching conditions with the help of decision tree learning was done in [9], and in [14]. These two works do not mine dependencies between process decisions, and they also do not consider fuzziness in decisions. Discovery of DMN decision models from control-flow structures of process models was done in [4], but this work does not consider the execution level. In [5], the discovery of DMN decision models from event logs was done, but only crisp decision logic was considered. The derived DMN decision models are supposed to be used complementary to process models which raises novel research questions, e.g., which elements should belong to the process, and which elements should be a part of the decision model. Exploration of issues connected to the separation of concerns is presented in [10,20].

3 Formal Framework

In this section, we introduce needed definitions as follows.

Definition 1 (Event Instance, Attribute, Trace, Log). Let $E = \{e_1, ..., e_n\}, n \in \mathbb{N}^+$ be a finite set of n event instances and $A = \{a_1, ..., a_v\}, v \in \mathbb{N}^+$ a finite set of v attributes. Each attribute $a \in A$ is associated with a domain $D(a)$, which represents a set of either numeric, or nominal values. Each event instance $e \in E$ has tuples $(a, d(a))$, $a \in A$, $d(a) \in D(a)$ assigned to it. A trace is a finite sequence of event instances $e \in E$, such that each event instance appears in it once. An event log L is a multi-set of traces over E. $\diamond$

Figure 1b shows an example event log where event instances are labeled by names of executed activities associated with values of data attributes attached to them.

Definition 2 (Decision Requirements Diagram). A *decision requirements diagram DRD* is a tuple (D_{dm}, ID, IR) consisting of a finite non-empty set of decision nodes D_{dm}, a finite set of input data nodes ID, and a finite non-empty set of directed edges IR representing the information requirements such as $IR \subseteq D_{dm} \cup ID \times D_{dm}$, and $(D_{dm} \cup ID, IR)$ is a directed acyclic graph. ◇

A decision may additionally reference the decision logic level where its output is determined through an undirected association. One of the most widely used representation for decision logic is a decision table, which we utilize for the rest of the paper. Figure 2 demonstrates an example DRD and corresponding decision tables.

Facilitation of fuzzy logic implies that the crisp values of data attributes from the event log are to be perceived as a matter of truth value ranging between completely true and completely false. In order to facilitate handling of decision rules in a fuzzy manner, below we introduce a set of necessary definitions. Given is an event log L, and a corresponding set of v attributes of the event instances $A = \{a_1, \ldots, a_v\}, v \in \mathbb{N}^+$.

Definition 3 (Fuzzy Subset, Membership Function). A domain set $D(a)$ for an attribute $a \in A$ has K^a *fuzzy subsets* characterized by tuples $FS_i^a = \{(d, l_i^a, \mu_{l_i}^a) | d \in D(a)\}$, if for each $i \in [1; K^a]$ there exist:

- linguistic terms l_i^a labelling fuzzy subsets FS_i^a;
- *membership functions* $\mu_{l_i}^a : D(a) \longrightarrow [0, 1]$ which represent the grade of membership of attribute values from $D(a)$ in a fuzzy subset FS_i^a by mapping each value $d \in D(a)$ to a real number in the interval $[0, 1]$. ◇

We identify a fuzzy set with its membership function. An example of a membership function is presented with the help of a graph in Fig. 2 for the attribute *amount*. In this case, $K^{amount} = 2$, and the domain set $D(amount)$ has two fuzzy subsets FS_1^{amount} and FS_2^{amount} characterized correspondingly by membership functions μ_{low}^{amount} and μ_{high}^{amount}. This example is illustrated with the help of *trapezoidal membership function*, as one of the most widely used types of membership functions. However, the approach proposed in our paper is general and can be used for the other types of membership functions, e.g., triangular-shaped, Gaussian curve, etc. [6].

Fuzzy logic of decision models can be expressed through fuzzy decision rules and fuzzy decision tables. Fuzzy decision tables consist of fuzzy rules which represent "if-then" mapping between a subset of event log attributes associated with corresponding linguistic terms, and an output process variable associated with a set of labels.

Definition 4 (Elemental Fuzzy Decision Rule, Fuzzy Decision Table). An *elemental fuzzy decision rule (FDR)* is a mapping: defn

$$R_j : a_1 \ is \ l_{x_1}^{a_1}, \ldots, a_w \ is \ l_{x_w}^{a_w} \longrightarrow c_{j,z}, \quad (1)$$

where the attributes $\{a_1, \ldots, a_w\} \subseteq A$ are inputs, $l^{a_1}_{x_1}, \ldots, l^{a_w}_{x_w}$ are linguistic terms labeling fuzzy subsets associated with the inputs, and $c_{j,z}$ is the $z-th$ label of a process variable serving as a rule output, such that $z \in \mathbb{N}^+$, $1 \leq w \leq v, |A| = v, 1 \leq x_1 \leq K^{a_1}, \ldots, 1 \leq x_w \leq K^{a_w}$. A *fuzzy decision table (FDT)* is a set of fuzzy decision rules $\bigcup R_j$, $j \in \mathbb{N}^+$. ◇

Below are examples of elemental fuzzy decision rules (see also FDT in Fig. 2):

$$amount\ is\ high,\ premium\ is\ FALSE \longrightarrow p_1 = full\ check \quad (2)$$

$$amount\ is\ low,\ duration\ is\ long \longrightarrow risk = low \quad (3)$$

The definition of elemental fuzzy rule sets can be extended to *conjunctive normal form of fuzzy rules (CNF)*, where each attribute $a_i, 1 \leq i \leq v$ can be associated with a set of $p \in \mathbb{N}^+$ several linguistic terms $\{l^{a_i}_{x_i,1}, \ldots, l^{a_i}_{x_i,p}\}$ which are joined by a disjunctive operator. Fuzzy rule bases in CNF form are also called Mamdani rules [6]. An example of CNF fuzzy rule is following (see also FDT in Fig. 2):

$$amount\ is\ high\ or\ low,\ premium\ is\ TRUE \longrightarrow p_1 = no\ check \quad (4)$$

Mapping a runtime input for a set of fuzzy rules to an output is called *inference*. There exist multiple inference techniques, and the method that is most closely matching the real-world problem should be chosen [6]. We address this question further in the paper.

4 Methodology

DMN decision model consists of a DRD representing decisions and its dependencies, and of a decision logic layer expressed by sets of rules. Fuzziness is not relevant for DRDs, as they store names of decisions and dependencies between them (see Fig. 2). In contrast, decision rules might incorporate fuzziness. Such a view does not violate the DMN standard, so we adopt it and use the term Fuzzy DMN (FDMN) for such kind of decision models. This section consists of five subsections representing consequent steps in our methodology of mining FDMN from event logs, see Fig. 3:

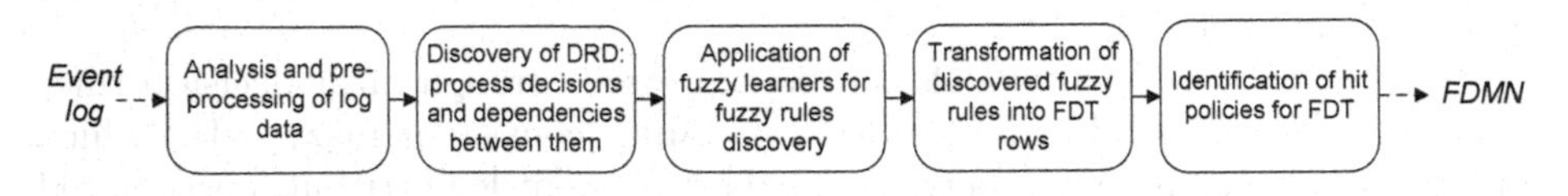

Fig. 3. Our approach for discovering Fuzzy DMN (FDMN) models from event logs

4.1 Analysis and Preprocessing of Log Data

Given is a an event log L, and a corresponding set of attributes of the event instances $A = \{a_1, \ldots, a_v\}, v \in \mathbb{N}^+$. Firstly, we preprocess log data in such a way that fuzzy learning of rules can be applied on it. For that, for each attribute there should exist membership functions that describe them in linguistic terms, e.g., that the value of an attribute is "low" or "high". Specifically, we need to find $\mu^a_{l_i} : D(a) \longrightarrow [0, 1]$ for each attribute $a \in A$ from the event log, which we propose to do by the procedure ConstructMF from Algorithm 1. In the procedure, we iterate over all attributes from the event log. If the attribute domain is nominal by itself, the membership function is constructed as a characteristic function (Lines 4–7). Otherwise, if the attribute domain is numerical, an expert should set the number K^a of fuzzy subsets for this domain, that are to be generated, and assign corresponding linguistic terms. For our use case (see Fig. 2), the expert would set $K^a = 2$ for attribute *amount*, and assign two linguistic terms: *low* and *high*.

Algorithm 1. Preprocessing of Data Attributes from Event Log

```
 1: procedure ConstructMF(eventLog L, attributes A)
 2:     for all a ∈ A do
 3:         if D(a) is a set of nominal values then
 4:             if d(a) = l then
 5:                 μ^a_l = 1
 6:             else
 7:                 μ^a_l = 0
 8:         else
 9:             K^a ← a number of fuzzy subsets                     ▷ Expert input
10:             for all i ∈ [1; K^a] do
11:                 l^a_i ← assign a linguistic term   ▷ Expert input, e.g., "low", "high"
12:                 μ^a_l =BuildNumAttributesMF()      ▷ Either expert input or FCM
```

Function BuildNumAttributesMF can be realized using two approaches. The first approach involves experts which express their opinions on how well attributes a∈A can be associated with fuzzy subsets FS^a_i, $i \in [1; K^a]$. The details of construction of membership functions based on expert opinions are out of scope of this current paper, as they can be found in [23]. The expert approach can be recommended when there is not enough input data allowing to derive the membership function automatically. As the input event log in our case is supposed to be large, we propose to utilize the second approach – the *Fuzzy C-Means (FCM)* algorithm described in [8], as it allows to automatically derive membership functions for data attributes from event logs. Applicable to our case, the FCM-algorithm is able to calculate the degree of membership $\mu^a_{l_i}$ of data attribute value a from the event log in each of i clusters, such that $1 \leq i \leq K^a$. FCM requires the number of clusters as an input, which is equal to the number of fuzzy subsets obtained from an expert in Line 9. Example membership functions for our use case are visualized in Fig. 2 for variables *amount* and *duration* with respective values.

4.2 Discovery of DRD

Discovery of DRDs from event logs represents a classification problem over crisp data. We distinguish between two types of process decisions: (1) *control flow decisions* represented in process models by split gateways (e.g., decision from Eq. 2), and (2) *data decisions* reflecting dependencies between values of data attributes in the event log (e.g., decision from Eq. 3). We use the C4.5 classifier for learning both types of decisions taking event log attributes and transition labels as features, because it generally delivers a computationally inexpensive classification based on few comprehensible business rules, with a small need for customization [21]. For finding dependencies between decisions, we utilize the same classifier, taking the event log attributes and found decision outcomes as features. Each mined decision is added to the set of decision nodes D_{dm} of the output DRD. Each attribute influencing these decisions which is not a decision by itself is added to the set of input data nodes ID of the output DRD. All dependencies are added to the set of information requirements IR of the output DRD.

The output of this step is a DRD (see Fig. 2 for an example) consisting of a set of $PDN \in \mathbb{N}^+$ decisions $\{(A_1, C_1), ..., (A_{PDN}, C_{PDN})\}$, where PDN stands for process decisions number. Herewith, $A_{pdn} = \{a_1, ..., a_g\} \subseteq A$, $1 \leq g \leq v, pdn \in [1, ..., PDN]$, are attributes influencing these decisions. A more detailed description of mining DRDs from event logs can be found in our previous work [5].

4.3 Application of Fuzzy Learners for Fuzzy Rules Discovery

After discovering process decisions (A_{pdn}, C_{pdn}), $1 \leq pdn \leq PDN$ from the event log, we aim at discovering of fuzzy rules corresponding to these decisions. Thus, we iterate over the set of PDN decisions and solve for each of them the classification problem presented in Fig. 4. Here the training data is comprised in the event log subset $L_{pdn} \subseteq L : A_{pdn} \subseteq A$ containing only values of attributes that are influencing the given process decision.

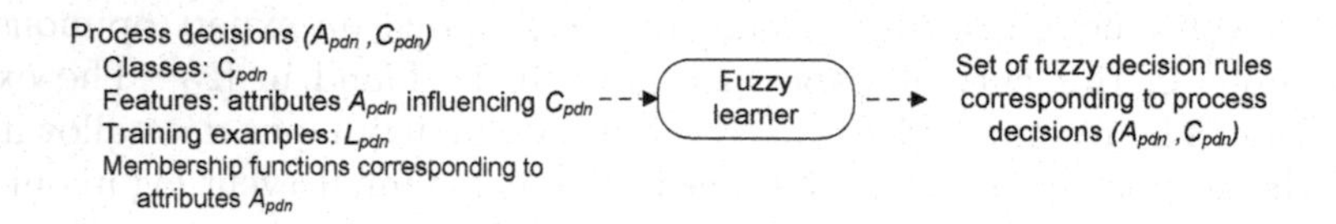

Fig. 4. Classification problem of discovering fuzzy decision rules from event logs

As our goal is to output the explanatory models describing decisions made in the past and recorded in the event log, we take into account that the fuzzy learners should provide good *accuracy* and *interpretability* of results. To explore the appropriateness of known fuzzy classification algorithms in achieving our goals, we did experiments on applying the genetic [12] and NEFCLASS [15] algorithms, both of which are well-known fuzzy classifiers that infer fuzzy classification rules. Below we provide short descriptions of algorithms taking into account modifications needed for solving our problem of deriving fuzzy rule sets from event logs.

Genetic Algorithm (GA). Genetic algorithm (GA) is successfully applied for solving fuzzy classification tasks [8,11,12]. Also, GA suits us because it is applicable for training sets with large dimensions, which is typical for event logs. The heuristic character of GA does not guarantee optimality of solution, but it provides approximate solutions close to optimal, which is appropriate for business environments. Below we consider the adaptation of GA applicable to our problem.

GA0. For utilizing GA, we firstly need to represent our problem in a genetic form. For that, we view fuzzy decision rules (FDR) discovered from event logs as so called chromosomes. Given is a process decision (A_{pdn}, C_{pdn}) where $A_{pdn} = \{a_1, ..., a_g\} \subseteq A$, $1 \leq g \leq v$ is a set of influencing attributes from the corresponding event log subset L_{pdn}.

Definition 5 (Chromosome). A *chromosome* corresponding to the event log subset L_{pdn} is a string G_t, $t \in \mathbb{N}^+$, which is a concatenation of two bit strings S_t and B_t, where:

- $S_t = \{s_1, ..., s_v\}$ is a string of bits $s_i, 1 \leq i \leq g$ indicating the presence of an attribute $a \in A_{pdn}$ in a rule antecedent of the chromosome;
- $B_t = \{b_1, ..., b_u\}$ is a string of bits b_k denoting the presence of a linguistic term l_i^a labeling fuzzy subsets $FS_i^a, i \in [1;K^a]$ in the rule antecedent of the chromosome, where $u, k \in [1; \sum_{j=1}^{g} K^{a_j}]$. ◇

Fuzzy rules are composed of a chromosome serving as the rule antecedent, and of a consequent that is chosen according to the majority class of the training instances covered by the rule antecedent. Example fuzzy rules are presented in Fig. 5a.

	s^{amount}	$s^{duration}$	$s^{premium}$	l_{low}^{amount}	l_{high}^{amount}	$l_{short}^{duration}$	$l_{long}^{duration}$	$l^{premium}$	p1
Rule from Eq.2	1	0	1	0	1	0	0	0	full check
Rule from Eq.4	1	0	1	1	1	0	0	1	no check

(a) Example chromosomes with corresponding consequents for rules from Equations 2, 4

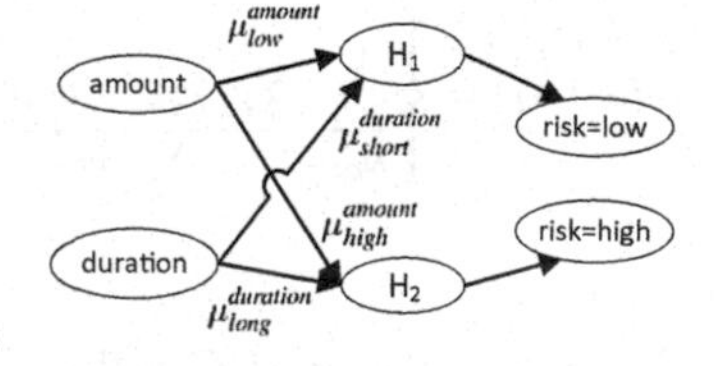

(b) Example perceptron

Fig. 5. Example representation of rules for the GA and NF classifiers

GA1. At this step of GA, in each iteration $t \in \mathbb{N}^+$ a chromosome consisting of a fuzzy rule G_t is randomly generated. Next, the rule error $E(G_t)$ is computed by checking its degree of matching between the rule antecedent of instances from the event log subset L_{pdn} and the generated rule antecedent:

$$E(G_t) = \frac{\sum_{a|c_a \neq c_t} w_a \mu^a_{G_t}}{\sum_a w_a \mu^a_{G_t}}, \tag{5}$$

We utilize a boosting approach from [12] which modifies iterative fuzzy rule learning in an incremental fashion. The idea is to repeatedly train a weak classifier on various training data distributions, which shows a considerable improvement in accuracy of the results. The weights of event instances $e_k, 1 \leq k \leq n$ from the current distribution that are correctly classified by the rule G_t are reduced by a factor reflecting the error rate of the generated rule: $w_k(t+1) = w_k[(1-E(R_t))/E(G_t)]^{\mu^a_{R_t}}$. Misclassified or uncovered examples keep their original weights. Thereby, boosting increases the relative weight of those examples which are "hard to learn". We calculate the chromosome consequent c_t as an output of the boosting classifier considering the vote of the rule G_t, weighted by logarithmic accuracy, on event instances from the event log L_{pdn} by t-norm (cf. [12]):

$$c_t = \underset{c_m}{\text{argmax}} \sum_{G_t|c_t=c_m} \log \frac{1-E(G_t)}{E(G_t)} \min_{j=1}^{w(t)} \mu^a_{l_j} \tag{6}$$

GA2. For building next generation of chromosomes, the rules that have a good fitness are kept. We calculate fitness function as a product of normalized values of such functions as class coverage CC, rule coverage RC, and rule consistency RCS:

$$f(G_t) = \overline{CC(G_t)} \times \overline{RC(G_t)} \times \overline{RCS(G_t)} \tag{7}$$

The class coverage CC is defined as the ratio of the number of training instances covered by the rule G_t to the overall number of training instances carrying the same class label c_i: $CC(G_t) = \sum_{a|c_a=c_t} w_a \mu^a_{G_t} / \sum_{a|c_a=c_t} w_a$.

$$RC(G_t) = \begin{cases} 1, & n > k_{cov}; \\ \frac{1}{k_{cov}} \frac{\sum_{a|c_a=c_t} w_a \mu^a_{G_t}}{\sum_a w_a}, & o/w. \end{cases} \quad RCS(G_t) = \begin{cases} 0, & n_c^+ \times \varepsilon < n_c^-; \\ \frac{n_c^+ - \frac{n_c^-}{\varepsilon}}{n_c^+}, & o/w. \end{cases} \tag{8}$$

The rule coverage RC reflects the fraction of instances covered by the rule k_{cov}, irrespective of the class label. If $M \in \mathbb{N}^+$ is a number of classes having the same number of instances in the event log, a reasonable choice for fraction of covered instances is $k_{cov} = 1/M$, as no rule can cover more than such fraction of instances without covering other (false) instances. For example, the number of classes for decision p_1 (see Fig. 2) is equal to 3, therefore, k_{cov} is chosen as 0.33. The rule consistency RCS demands that a rule covers a large number of correctly classified weighted instances $n_c^+ = \sum_{a|c_a=c_t} w_a \mu^a_{G_t}$, and a small number of incorrectly classified weighted instances $n_c^- = \sum_{a|c_a \neq c_t} w_a \mu_{G_t}^a$. Herewith, parameter $\varepsilon \in [0;1]$ determines the maximal tolerance for the error made by an individual rule (see Eq. 8). Specific for our use case, as it contains not so many decision classes, we choose $\varepsilon = 0.2$. If classes from the log have unevenly distributed number of instances, it is advisable to choose smaller values of ε.

GA3. The GA algorithm iterates $t = t+1$ and repeats steps *GA1, GA2* until a given condition is fulfilled. The termination conditions can be chosen by a process analyst, depending on the requirements stemming from the business environment. For example, the algorithm can stop if a prespecified minimal rule coverage is reached. Also, if the number of rules, that are *not* added to the rule set, reaches a prespecified threshold, the algorithm can be stopped in order to avoid obtaining only redundant or low-performing rules. We discuss in the evaluation section on the example of our use case the possibility of combining termination criteria related both to properties of rule sets, and resulting fuzzy decision tables into which the discovered rules are transformed later.

Neurofuzzy Algorithm NEFCLASS (NF). Neural networks are also broadly applied to solve fuzzy classification problems, and the NEFCLASS algorithm (NF) is one of the most widely used [12]. NF is also known for producing simple and comprehensible fuzzy rules [15], which is appropriate for the business environment.

NF0. For using NF, we firstly need to represent our problem in a neuro-fuzzy terminology. In such a way, we view the system assisting with mining fuzzy decision rules as a *3-layer fuzzy perceptron*, or simply *perceptron*. Again, given is a process decision (A_{pdn}, C_{pdn}) where $A_{pdn} = \{a_1, ..., a_g\} \subseteq A$, $1 \leq g \leq v$ is a set of influencing attributes from the corresponding event log subset L_{pdn}. An example perceptron is visualized in Fig. 5b.

Definition 6 (Perceptron). A *perceptron* is a network representation of fuzzy classification problem in the form of a neural network $\Pi = (U, \Omega, \Upsilon)$, where

- $U = U_1 \cup U_2 \cup U_3$ is a set consisting of a set $U_1 = \{a_1, ..., a_g\}$ of attributes influencing the process decision (input neurons), a set $U_2 = \{H_1, ..., H_r\}, r \in \mathbb{N}^+$ of fuzzy rules (hidden neurons), and a set $U_3 = \{c_1, ..., c_z\}, z \in \mathbb{N}^+$ of the process decision classes (output neurons);
- $\Omega(a, h) = \mu_h^a$ is a fuzzy weight defined as the membership grade of the value of input neuron $a \in U_1$ in a fuzzy subset provided by the hidden rule unit $h \in U_2$;
- Υ is a mapping that assigns activation functions as follows: $\Upsilon_h = \min_{a \in U_1} \Omega(a, h)$ if $u \in U_1 \cup U_2$, and $\Upsilon_c = \dfrac{\sum_{h \in U_2} \Omega(H, c) \Upsilon_h}{\sum_{h \in U_2} \Omega(H, c)}$ if $u \in U_3$.

◇

NF1. At each step of the algorithm, an event instance from the event log subset L_{pdn} is chosen consequently. Based on this instance, a rule H_t :

a_1 is $l^{a_1}_{x_1}, \ldots, a_{pdn}$ is $l^{a_{pdn}}_{x_{pdn}} \longrightarrow c_{t,z}$ is generated, where A_{pdn} is a subset of influencing attributes, and $c_{t,z}$ is the label of the $z{-}th$ class of the rule $H_t, t \in \mathbb{N}^+$, of the process decision (A_{pdn}, C_{pdn}) with the values corresponding to the records in the event log. Further, initialization of the perceptron should be done by creating g nodes in input layer $U_1 = \{a_1, ..., a_{pdn}\}$ corresponding to each attribute in the generated rule. Each input neuron $a \in U_1$ is characterized by K^a fuzzy sets FS^a_i, $i \in [1; K^a]$. Thus, at the iteration t, for each input neuron $a_j \in U_1$ the membership function is found such that $\mu^a_{l_j}(a) = max_{i \in \{1,...,K^a\}}\{\mu^a_i(a_j)\}$. If the hidden layer U_2 of the perceptron does not have a hidden rule node $h \in H$ such that $\Upsilon(a_1, h) = \mu^{a_1}_{l_1}, ..., \Upsilon(a_g, h) = \mu^{a_g}_{l_g}$, then such node is created. Hereby, the class $c_{t,z}$ is assigned as the consequent of the rule.

NF2. When adding the generated rules to the outcome rule base, only the rules that have good fitness are kept. For tuning the perceptron weights, we apply the rule H_t on each instance $e_w = (A^w, c^w), w \in \mathbb{N}^*$ from the event log L_{pdn} with the overlapping antecedent and compare the factual class assigned from the event log c^w, and class predicted by the perceptron. We identify the rule fitness as the ratio of the number of the correctly classified instances by the rule $TP(H_t)$ to the sum of number of the correctly and incorrectly classified instances $FP(H_T)$ in the event log subset L_{pdn}:

$$f(H_t) = \frac{TP(H_T)}{TP(H_T) + FP(H_T)} \tag{9}$$

For example, in our further implementation we only keep rules with fitness $f(H_t) \geq 0.1$.

NF3. The algorithm iterates $t = t{+}1$ and repeats steps *NF1, NF2* until a given condition happens. Again, different termination conditions can be chosen with respect to the business environment. As a new rule is generated for each event instance, the algorithm can be stopped when complete event log is processed. As this might produce a large amount of rules, the number of first rules to be generated can be prespecified. More complex termination criteria for the NF classifier can be found, e.g., in [12].

4.4 Transformation of Discovered Fuzzy Rules into FDT Rows

The outcome of application of fuzzy learners described at the previous step are fuzzy rule sets corresponding to each process decision (A_{pdn}, C_{pdn}), $1 \leq pdn \leq PDN$, where PDN is the number of discovered process decisions, and $A_{pdn} = \{a_1, ..., a_g\} \subseteq A$, $1 \leq g \leq v$ are attributes influencing them. For each of the process decisions (A_{pdn}, C_{pdn}), a corresponding set of frn fuzzy rules is discovered: $R_{pdn} = \{R_1, ..., R_{frn}\}, frn \in \mathbb{N}^+$. Next, the discovered fuzzy rule sets need to be transformed into fuzzy decision tables (FDTs), which are to be used further during process execution. Therefore, the FDT *interpretability* is of the highest importance. However, direct application of discovered fuzzy rule sets might provide low FDT interpretability because of duplications and overlapping of rules and attributes. Below we describe these issues in more detail and propose the ways to overcome them. Some of the steps are similar to the stages of manual designing of fuzzy decision tables described in [19].

Step 1: Removal of duplications. Duplicated rules will lead to FDT with duplicated rows, so the first step is to remove all duplicate rules from the base.

Step 2: Splitting CNF Rules. Some fuzzy rule learners, as the genetic one, might generate the rule bases consisting of fuzzy rules represented by CNF. As the CNF rules can represent very complex structures, to improve the linguistic interpretability, we propose to replace them by a set of equivalent elemental rules. In particular, each discovered rule $R_y^{pdn} \subseteq R^{pdn}, 1 \leq y \leq frn$ can be represented in the following form: $R_y^{pdn} = (\bigcup_{j,i}(a_j, \mu_{l_i}^{a_j}(a_j), \mu_{l_i}^{a_j}), c_{y,z}), 1 \leq j \leq g, 1 \leq i \leq K^{a_j}$. Then, the corresponding set of elemental rules RS_y^{pdn} can be identified as the Cartesian product of (1) all possible subsets of the rule antecedent containing all attributes of the rule in a couple with the single value of the corresponding fuzzy subset; and (2) the value of the rule class:

$$RS_y^{pdn} = \bigcup_{j,i}(a_j, \mu_{l_i}^{a_j}(a_j)) \times c_{y,z} \tag{10}$$

For example, let the following rule R be given in natural language:

R: *amount is high or low, duration is short or long* $\longrightarrow$ *risk* = *high*

Then the corresponding set of simple rules is $RS = \bigcup_i R_i, 1 \leq i \leq 4$,

R_1 : *amount is high, duration is short* $\longrightarrow$ *risk* = *high*
R_2 : *amount is low, duration is short* $\longrightarrow$ *risk* = *high*
R_3 : *amount is high, duration is long* $\longrightarrow$ *risk* = *high*
R_4 : *amount is low, duration is long* $\longrightarrow$ *risk* = *high*

Step 3: Mapping simple rules to FDT rows. Further, each elemental rule RS_y^{pdn}, $1 \leq y \leq frn$ is mapped to a corresponding row in a FDT which represents a union of all the fuzzy elemental rules $\bigcup_y RS_y{}^{pdn}$. If a rule has no linguistic literal for an attribute, the corresponding cell is left blank, meaning that this attribute has no influence on the outcome.

Step 4: FDT optimization. There can be rules represented by multiple rows, which differ only in the irrelevant attributes' values. If we find such rules, we aggregate them into one row by removing these attributes, because they do not impact the outcome. For example, see Fig. 6 where the contracted FDT is derived from the expanded FDT by combining logically adjacent rows that leads to the same action configuration.

4.5 Identification of Hit Policies for Generated FDT

Each discovered fuzzy rule, for which its antecedent matches the runtime input, contributes to an output through the compositional rule called *inference*. In

Inputs			Output
amount	duration	premium	risk
low	shortf	alse	low
low	shortt	rue	low

Inputs			Output
amount	duration	premium	risk
low	short	-	low

Fig. 6. Example of rule reduction in a FDT

DMN, inference is described by hit policies which specify how the table output is obtained, if there are multiple rule matches for a given set of inputs. A *single hit policy* returns the output of one rule; a *multiple hit policy* returns the output of multiple rules, or an aggregation of rules. The activation of a hit policy corresponds to the phase of process execution. During instantiation of processes, the process activity that invokes a corresponding decision model supplies the decision-making system with input data which can be crisp or fuzzy. Below we propose a hit policy formula for FDT.

Given is a process decision (A_{pdn}, C_{pdn}), $1 \leq pdn \leq PDN$, where PDN is a number of discovered process decisions, and $A_{pdn} = \{a_1, ..., a_g\} \subseteq A$, $1 \leq g \leq v$ are attributes influencing them. For the process decision (A_{pdn}, C_{pdn}), a corresponding FDT consisting of a set of discovered fuzzy decision rules $R^{pdn} = \bigcup_j R_j, j \in \mathbb{N}^*$ is processed according to the procedures from the previous section. Let an event instance e occur further during the process execution.

Then, the activation $\mathcal{A}$ for a rule $R_j, j \in \mathbb{N}^*$ describes the probability of a value from the class C_{pdn} to be correct for the given instance e. For calculating the activation rule value, we propose to utilize an adapted "min-max" operator, one of the most widely used composition operators suitable for Mamdani rule bases [22]:

$$M(R_j, e) = \min_k [\bigcup_{k \in [1;g]} \max_i \; (\bigcup_{i \in [1; K^{a_k}]} \mu_{l_i}^{a_k}) \;], \tag{11}$$

where $1 \leq k \leq g : a_k \in e,\ a_k \in A_{pdn}$, so only attributes of an event instance which influence the process decision are evaluated. Let a loan application process be executed with the instance data $amount = 200[EUR]$, $duration = 30[mths]$, $premium = TRUE$, and imagine that the activation rule from Eq. 3 needs to be calculated. Here $k = 2$, and, consulting the membership functions, we establish that $\mu_{low}^{amount} = 1$, $\mu_{high}^{amount} = 0$, and $\mu_{short}^{duration} = 0.6$, $\mu_{long}^{duration} = 0.4$. Then, $\mathcal{A}(R, e) = \min\ [\bigcup \max(\{1;0\},\{0.6;0.4\})] = 0.6$. Analogously, activation values for all the rules in a set $R^{pdn} = \bigcup_j R_j, j \in \mathbb{N}^*$ are evaluated, and the rule maximizing the value of the activation rule is chosen.

In order to further improve the accuracy of FDT hit policies, we propose to additionally weight the discovered rules by their error rate on instances from the event log. Then, even if several different rules are evaluated to the same value by the "min-max" operator, the rule which best corresponds to decisions recorded in the event log is hit:

$$\mathcal{A}(R_j, e) = W(R_j, L_{pdn}) * M(R_j, e) \tag{12}$$

Here, the weight variable $W(R_j, L_{pdn})$ characterizes how good the rule classifies the instances from the event log subset L_{pdn} corresponding to the process decision (A_{pdn}, C_{pdn}). The calculation of the weight value depends on the applied fuzzy learner. For GA, this value is equal to the logarithmic accuracy of the rule $\log(1 - E(R_j))/E(R_j)$ from Eq. 5. For the NF, this value is equal to the rule fitness $f(R_j) = TP(R_j)/(TP(R_j) + FP(R_j))$ from Eq. 9. Assigning the weights to rules in such a way can also contribute to satisfying the condition of *exclusivity* of decision rules in FDT, if that is required by user. Then, the rows are sorted by their weights, and while iterating over the rows, a rule is removed if it overlaps with the previous one. The low quality rows can also be removed, if some threshold is established.

With respect to the DMN standard, all the DMN hit policies can be applied to FDMN. Fuzzy activation rules are not foreseen though. However, the standard recommends to implement custom post processing steps in combination with the *Collect Hit* policy, which can be used considering the activation function from Eq. 12.

5 Evaluation

In order to validate the presented methodology, we developed an open-source prototype of it[1]. Our experiments consisted of applying the methodology from Fig. 3 on a test log, and evaluating the interpretability and accuracy of the output FDMN.

Test Setting. For the test data, we considered the loan assessment process from Fig. 1a. Estimating the distributions of parameters from a real credit-risk data set [3], we simulated an event log consisting of 1000 process instances with the help of the simulation software CPN Tools [1]. The generated log contained two numeric attributes *duration* and *amount*, and two nominal attributes *premium* and *risk*. Corresponding membership functions were derived using Matlab [2], as it has an implementation of FCM. The resulted membership functions for *amount* and *duration* can be seen in Fig. 2. With the help of the DMN Analysis plug-in designed by us in our previous work [5], three process decisions were discovered: (1) control flow decision p_1 with influencing attributes *amount* and *premium*; (2) control flow decision p_3 with the influencing attribute *risk*; and (3) data decision *risk* with influencing attributes *duration* and *amount*. Next, we applied both GA and NF classifiers for discovering FDTs. For fuzzy rules obtained by the GA classifier, the maximal rule error was set to 0.2, the minimal coverage was set to 0.42, and the minimal fitness was set to 0.1. The minimal fitness for NF was also set to 0.1. We ran the GA classifier until the number of low-performing rules, that were not added to the output rule sets corresponding to process decisions, reached a threshold of 50000 rules. The NF classifier was running until the complete event log was processed. Both algorithms also stopped if the output decision table was *complete*, which means that for all combinations of input

[1] https://bpt.hpi.uni-potsdam.de/Public/MiningFuzzyDMN.

values there was a rule that covered it. The average run time for discovering FDT per process decision was 44.2 s for the GA classifier, and 1.8 s the for the NF classifier.

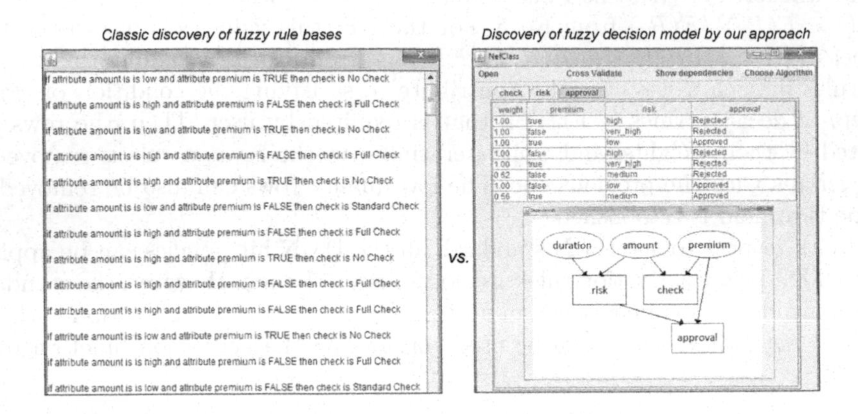

Fig. 7. Screenshots of the results from our prototype

Interpretability of the Output FDMN. A screenshot of the FDMN, which our application outputs for the input log, is presented on the right side of Fig. 7. Corresponding to each decision in the DRD are the FDTs, which are obtained by the NF classifier, and post-processed according to our methodology. In the left side of the picture one can see the direct application of "state-of-the-art" NF classification for process decision *check*, which yields a large fuzzy rule base that is difficult for humans to interpret. In contrast, FDMN derived by our methodology (on the right side of Fig. 7) consists of compact FDTs incorporating rule weights and fuzzy hit policies, and it shows dependencies between decisions. It has to be noted that the interpretability of the output FDMN highly depends on the fuzzy algorithm applied for learning the model. According to our observations, NF often leads to a smaller amount of rules than GA.

Accuracy of the Output FDMN. To evaluate the accuracy of the output FDMN, we used 10-fold cross validation over the test log [21]. Here, the accuracy is equal to the average number of event instances that are correctly classified by the rules in FDTs divided by the total number of all instances. Further, we created incorrect log entries by randomly selecting from 0% to 10% of the event log instances, and randomly replacing their class labels with distinct class labels. The resulted accuracy of the classifiers with respect to the introduced noise is presented in Fig. 8.

Both classifiers achieved high accuracy for the event log without noise. Further, it can be seen, that NF shows a good stability, as it preserves a very good accuracy of ca. 90.21% in the presence of 10% input data noise. GA shows less stability as its accuracy reduces to ca. 82.10% in the presence of 10% input data noise. Setting the algorithms parameters can be used to adjust the desired user's

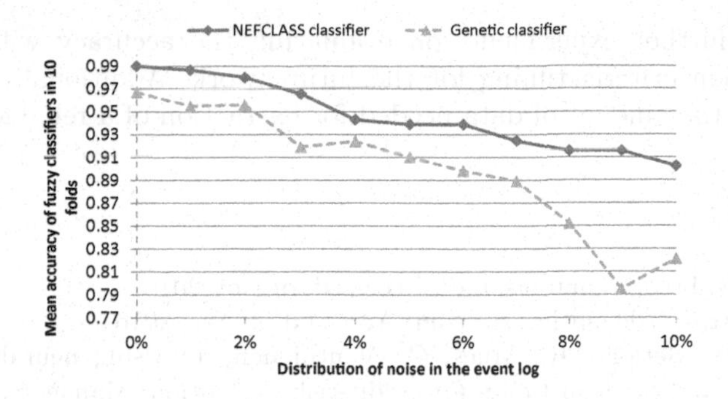

Fig. 8. Mean FDMN accuracy in 10 folds with respect to introduced noise in the log

output. For example, if a smaller amount of rules for better human interpretability is needed, the threshold has to be higher than 0.1 used in our case, although the accuracy might decrease. Further experiments on evaluating the accuracy with regards to tuning of termination criteria are planned for future work.

6 Conclusion

Recently, many efforts were made to standardize process decisions with respect to the separation of process and decision concerns [10,20]. Although the DMN standard is developed for this purpose, currently it is not well suited for managing fuzzy decisions. For example, the hit policies proposed by the standard can not handle overlapping fuzzy rules. Usage of FDMN models that consist of crisp DRDs referencing fuzzy decision tables, as proposed by us, is not yet foreseen by the standard, but is compliant with it.

To assist companies with automated construction of FDMN models, we introduced a methodology for mining them from event logs. Hereby, we explored application of the genetic and NEFCLASS classifiers for learning fuzzy rules in the process context. Further, we proposed a formula for the fuzzy activation rule as a FDT hit policy. Evaluation demonstrates that the interpretability of the mined FDMN is better than that of mined sets of fuzzy rule bases. Also, the accuracy of the output FDMN is high, so it can serve as an explanatory model based on historical data. Further, the derived FDMN can be automated and executed complementary to the process model.

With regards to the methodology limitations, for some steps of it, the domain knowledge is required. For example, an analyst has to describe the fuzzy subsets for the attributes from the event log. Also, it is recommended that an expert tunes the parameters of the fuzzy classifiers, such as termination criteria, or rules fitness threshold, depending on requirements of the business environment. FDMN mining, like other classification problems, often leads to the necessity to find a compromise between interpretability and accuracy of the output model.

We plan further experiments on evaluating the accuracy with regards to the termination criteria tuning for the future work. Additionally, we plan an evaluation of the amount of data needed for extraction of a reliable set of rules.

References

1. CPN Tools. http://cpntools.org/. Accessed 29 Nov 2016
2. Matlab. https://de.mathworks.com. Accessed 29 Nov 2016
3. Baesens, B., Setiono, R., Mues, C., Vanthienen, J.: Using neural network rule extraction and decision tables for credit-risk evaluation. Manag. Sci. **49**(3), 312–329 (2003)
4. Batoulis, K., Meyer, A., Bazhenova, E., Decker, G., Weske, M.: Extracting decision logic from process models. In: Zdravkovic, J., Kirikova, M., Johannesson, P. (eds.) CAiSE 2015. LNCS, vol. 9097, pp. 349–366. Springer, Cham (2015). doi:10.1007/978-3-319-19069-3_22
5. Bazhenova, E., Buelow, S., Weske, M.: Discovering decision models from event logs. In: Abramowicz, W., Alt, R., Franczyk, B. (eds.) BIS 2016. LNBIP, vol. 255, pp. 237–251. Springer, Cham (2016). doi:10.1007/978-3-319-39426-8_19
6. Bede, B.: Mathematics of Fuzzy Sets and Fuzzy Logic. Studies in Fuzziness and Soft Computing, vol. 295. Springer, Heidelberg (2013)
7. Capon, N.: Credit scoring systems: a critical analysis. J. Mark. **46**(2), 82–91 (1982)
8. Chiu, S.L.: Fuzzy model identification based on cluster estimation. J. Intell. Fuzzy Syst. **2**(3), 267–278 (1994)
9. Leoni, M., Dumas, M., García-Bañuelos, L.: Discovering branching conditions from business process execution logs. In: Cortellessa, V., Varró, D. (eds.) FASE 2013. LNCS, vol. 7793, pp. 114–129. Springer, Heidelberg (2013). doi:10.1007/978-3-642-37057-1_9
10. Debevoise, T., Taylor, J.: The MicroGuide to Process Modeling and Decision in BPMN/DMN. CreateSpace Independent Publishing Platform (2014)
11. Gonzalez, A., Perez, R.: Completeness and consistency conditions for learning fuzzy rules. Fuzzy Sets Syst. **96**(1), 37–51 (1998)
12. Hoffmann, F., Baesens, B., Mues, C., Van Gestel, T., Vanthienen, J.: Inferring descriptive and approximate fuzzy rules for credit scoring using evolutionary algorithms. Eur. J. Oper. Res. **177**(1), 540–555 (2007)
13. Hubbard, E.M., Diester, I., Cantlon, J.F., Ansari, D., van Opstal, F., Troiani, V.: The evolution of numerical cognition: from number neurons to linguistic quantifiers. J. Neurosci. **28**(46), 11819–11824 (2009)
14. Mannhardt, F., de Leoni, M., Reijers, H.A., van der Aalst, W.M.P.: Decision mining revisited - discovering overlapping rules. In: Nurcan, S., Soffer, P., Bajec, M., Eder, J. (eds.) CAiSE 2016. LNCS, vol. 9694, pp. 377–392. Springer, Cham (2016). doi:10.1007/978-3-319-39696-5_23
15. Nauck, D.: Fuzzy data analysis with NEFCLASS. Int. J. Approximate Reasoning **32**(2), 103–130 (2003)
16. OMG. Business Process Model and Notation (BPMN), v.2.0.2 (2013)
17. OMG. Decision Model And Notation (DMN), v.1.1 (2016)
18. Rozinat, A., van der Aalst, W.M.P.: Decision mining in ProM. In: Dustdar, S., Fiadeiro, J.L., Sheth, A.P. (eds.) BPM 2006. LNCS, vol. 4102, pp. 420–425. Springer, Heidelberg (2006). doi:10.1007/11841760_33

19. Vanthienen, J., Wets, G., Chen, G.: Incorporating fuzziness in the classical decision table formalism. Int. J. Intell. Syst. **11**(11), 879–891 (1996)
20. Von Halle, B., Goldberg, L., Model, T.D.: A Business Logic Framework Linking Business and Technology. Taylor and Francis Group, Abingdon (2010)
21. Witten, I.H., Frank, E.: Data Mining: Practical Machine Learning Tools and Techniques, 2nd edn. Morgan Kaufmann Publishers Inc., San Francisco (2005)
22. Zadeh, L.A.: Fuzzy sets. Inf. Control **8**(3), 338–353 (1965)
23. Zimmermann, H.J.: Fuzzy Set Theory and Its Applications, 3rd edn. Kluwer Academic Publishers, Norwell (1996)

Author Index